Star Trek FAQ 2.0

Series Editor: Robert Rodriguez

Star Trek FAQ 2.0

Everything Left to Know About Next Generation, the Movies, and Beyond

Mark Clark

APPLAUSE
THEATRE & CINEMA BOOKS
An Imprint of Hal Leonard Corporation

Published in 2013 by Applause Theatre & Cinema Books
An Imprint of Hal Leonard Corporation
7777 West Bluemound Road
Milwaukee, WI 53213
Trade Book Division Editorial Offices
33 Plymouth St., Montclair, NJ 07042

The FAQ series was conceived by Robert Rodriguez and developed with Stuart Shea.
Printed in the United States of America

Book design by Snow Creative Services

Library of Congress Cataloging-in-Publication Data

Clark, Mark, 1966–
   Star trek FAQ 2.0 : everything left to know about the next generation, the movies, and beyond / Mark Clark.
      pages cm
   Includes bibliographical references and index.
   ISBN 978-1-55783-793-6 (pbk. : alk. paper)
1. Star Trek television programs—Miscellanea. 2. Star Trek films—Miscellanea.
I. Title.
   PN1992.8.S74C53 2013
   791.45'75—dc23
                                                                2013011545

www.applausebooks.com

For Vivianne and Thomas, my personal Next Generation

Contents

Foreword   ix

Acknowledgments   xiii

Introduction: The Best of Both Worlds   xv

1   Return to Tomorrow: *Star Trek: The Motion Picture* (1979)   1

2   Chain of Command: Roddenberry's Successors   9

3   Where Is Thy Sting? *The Wrath of Khan* and the Death of Spock (1982)   18

4   A Leonard Nimoy Film: *Star Trek III: The Search for Spock* (1984)   27

5   Breakthrough: *Star Trek IV: The Voyage Home* (1986)   36

6   The Offspring: Creating *The Next Generation*   45

7   Rightful Heirs: The Pre-*Trek* Careers of the *Next Generation* Cast   54

8   Identity Crisis: *The Next Generation*, Season One (1987–88)   63

9   The Captain's Chair: *Next Generation* Directors   81

10   The Masterpiece Society: Sets, Costumes, Makeup, Special Effects and Music   88

11   Too Short a Season: *The Next Generation*, Season Two (1988–89)   97

12   And the Children Shall Lead: Roddenberry's Successors, Part II   113

13   Shatner's Folly: The *Final Frontier* Debacle (1989)   121

14   The Bonding: *The Next Generation*, Season Three (1989–90)   129

15   Heroes: Guest Stars and Secondary Cast Members, Part One   146

16   Villains: Guest Stars and Secondary Cast Members, Part Two   156

17   New Ground: *The Next Generation*, Season Four (1990–91)   166

18   Friends and Family: Guest Stars and Secondary Cast Members, Part Three   184

19   The Trek Not Taken: *The Academy Years*   195

20   The Big Goodbye: *Star Trek VI: The Undiscovered Country* (1991)   200

21   Resistance Is Futile: *The Next Generation*, Season Five (1991–92)   210

22   New Life and New Civilizations: The Next Generation of *Star Trek* Aliens   227

23   Prime Directives: Social Commentary and Recurring Themes on *The Next Generation*   237

24   Peak Performance: *The Next Generation*, Season Six (1992–93)   246

25   Mess Call: The Food and Beverages of *Star Trek*   262

26   "Make It So": The Quotable *Next Generation*   268

27   All Good Things: *The Next Generation*, Season Seven (1993–94)   280

28 The Next Phase: *Star Trek Generations* (1994)   296
29 I Borg: *Star Trek: First Contact* (1996)   304
30 Descent: *Star Trek: Insurrection* (1998)   312
31 Journey's End: *Star Trek Nemesis* (2002)   320
32 Starship Mine: Patrick Stewart's Finest Moments   327
33 A Fistful of Datas: Brent Spiner's Finest Moments   335
34 Heart of Glory: The Emergence of Michael Dorn   342
35 The High Ground: Shining Moments for Jonathan Frakes,
    LeVar Burton, Marina Sirtis, Gates McFadden, Wil Wheaton,
    and Denise Crosby   349
36 Thine Own Self: The Post-*Trek* Careers of the *Next Generation* Cast   359
37 When the Bough Breaks: The Decline and Fall of the
    Star Trek Empire   368
38 Do It Yourself: *New Voyages* and Other Fan-Made Treks   378
39 Starfleet Commendations Revisited: Awards Won (and Lost)
    1980–2010   385
40 *Star Trek* Lives! The Continuing Voyages   393

Bibliography   401
Index   405

Foreword

I was a latecomer. I don't really know why. Probably it's because when Star Trek debuted, I was all of ten years old. I don't know about your house, but in mine, I had no say in what we watched during prime time. Furthermore, my parents had absolutely zero interest in science fiction of any sort. The Twilight Zone, Outer Limits, and their ilk remained unsampled in the David household for the duration of their television existence.

No, for me my introduction to *Star Trek* did not come until after the show was off the air from its original run. I remember quite distinctly when it happened: I was in junior high, going through book offerings in the latest Scholastic catalog. For some reason—and I have no idea why to this day—the cover to *Star Trek 3* leapt out at me. Let me clarify that this was not the movie of the same name, but rather the third book produced by James Blish. It consisted entirely of novelizations of assorted episodes. I was unaware of that; I just assumed them to be original stories. Ultimately it didn't matter. It was intriguing enough to me to warrant spending however much was required to obtain the paperback back in those days: fifty cents, whatever.

I became entranced with what I read. It was my introduction to the triumvirate of Kirk, McCoy, and Spock. I read the book several times and then quickly searched out books one and two in the local bookstore (which I pretty much single-handedly kept in business since I was apparently the only person in Verona, New Jersey, who ever actually read anything).

Eventually I caught up with the program as it entered syndication. I remember clearly my first episode: "Is There in Truth No Beauty?," the one with the Medusan ambassador who drives Spock temporarily insane. I happened to tune into it right during the part where Spock is going crazy. Even though I had the short stories as the foundation for my comprehension, I was still unclear what was going on. And so I was turned off from *Star Trek* upon my first viewing. Several years later, my parents acquired a color television for the first time. I put it on and what was on the air? "Is There in Truth No Beauty?" The exact same moment of Spock being driven nuts.

Yet somehow, once we had a color set, I felt compelled to actually try and catch up with the series. I did so and eventually fell in love with it all over again, including discovering the episodes that James Blish had novelized.

Some years later, an article in *TV Guide* revealed the existence of the very first *Star Trek* convention that had been held some weeks earlier. The article was a revelation. By that point I was well into my teens. The notion that there were other people out there who were as obsessed with *Star Trek* as I was was something of a revelation. The following year I was actually in attendance, going in the company of a guy named Steve Kitty who was actually staying there for it. And you have to understand that having my overly protective parents signing off on my going to New York at that age was really a pretty major deal for me.

But it would turn out to be merely the first of the major impacts that *Star Trek* would have in my life.

I met my first wife at a *Star Trek* convention, and even though the marriage ended in divorce, I have three lovely daughters who literally owe their lives to Gene Roddenberry.

Not only that, but as my career continued, my path constantly crossed those of the actors whose work I had admired during the original *Star Trek*. I wound up cowriting a comic book story with George Takei, which started a friendship and series of collaborations that ended up with me being invited to his wedding (with Nichelle Nichols hanging on my shoulder at the reception because she had injured her foot).

When James Doohan ran into problems writing his autobiography, I was hired by Simon & Schuster to fly out to Washington and spend a week interviewing him so that I could then cowrite it with him.

I wound up serving as the point man for a flying security wedge of people pressed into the job of getting Leonard Nimoy out of a convention, and I presented both Nimoy and later Shatner with an achievement award (the Julie award) at Dragon*Con. And that doesn't even count the various associations I've made with cast members of *Star Trek: The Next Generation*.

So this might leave you with the question of what *Star Trek* means to me as an individual. I mean, it has had a major effect on my life. Between all the *Star Trek* novels I've written, conventions I've gone to, and friends I've made as a result, it should—indeed, must—have some great, deeper meaning to me. Certainly I have spent many years pondering the many levels of meaning from the different programs, movies, books, and fan productions.

I've read so many essays about *Star Trek*, including the one that David Gerrold wrote to the book that preceded this one (a volume that I strongly suggest you read if you have not already. Personally I think Mark Clark has outdone himself with this volume. His history is unassailable and his opinions about different aspects of *Star Trek* are absolutely invaluable).

So with all that to draw upon, what deep and profound *Star Trek* meanings have I come up with? After many years of thought, here's what I've got:

It was a TV show. No different from other TV shows. Better than some—hell, better than many—and inferior to others.

I mean, I could write a dissertation on the differences between original and *Next Gen*. How TOS represented America before the lessons of Vietnam, when we could go into any situation and overwhelm it through logic or, when that failed, simply beating the crap out of it. Whereas *Next Gen* was clearly a post-Vietnam series, in which situations were discussed ad infinitum and more often than not, the solution came not through personality or dynamics but some manner of clever technobabble.

I could write about the Kirk/McCoy/Spock relationship and how it managed to encapsulate everything that was good about *Star Trek*. On the one hand, we had McCoy, arguing from the heart. On the other, Spock arguing from the mind. And in between them, James T. Kirk, the everyman who had to balance both sides and come up with the resolution to whatever he was facing. It's a purity of emotion that no other *Star Trek* program has ever managed to emulate.

But what would be the point? You might have contrary opinions, and I'm hardly in a position to discuss it with each and every one of you. So instead, I would suggest that you dive straight into Mark's book and see his various opinions as disseminated throughout the entire history of *Star Trek*. And then you can go argue with him.

As for *Star Trek*, at this point we are eagerly awaiting the debut of *Star Trek into Darkness*. Through the efforts of modern moviemakers, a new generation of fans is falling under the spell of the original crew, albeit there are many different faces to be seen playing the familiar characters. In a way, I almost envy these fans. I'm sure that many of them have never seen the original cast and have no interest in the original program. To them, Capt. Kirk is Chris Pine and Spock is Zachary Quinto. That's fine I suppose. Every generation should be able to have its own interpretations. Still, my hope is that books like this one will spur people's interest enough to go back and immerse themselves in the series that I enjoyed. The series that started it all. Even if it was just a television show.

Peter David
Long Island, April 2013

Peter David is an award-winning author of novels, comic books, and teleplays, including dozens of highly regarded *Star Trek* novels such as *Imzadi, I, Q* (cowritten with John de Lancie), and the breakthrough *New Frontier* series, the first *Trek* novels to focus on characters not originating with the various television series. He also coauthored actor James Doohan's memoir, *Beam Me Up, Scotty*. The prolific David has written for several live-action and animated television series including *Babylon Five*, and has worked on many comic books, including various *Star Trek* titles and an acclaimed, twelve-year run writing *The Incredible Hulk*.

Acknowledgments

I deeply appreciate the assistance of all those who supported me during my two-year mission to write the *Star Trek FAQ* books, especially:

Bryan Senn, a treasured friend and the best proofreader in the galaxy.

The Reverend Julie Fisher, whose astute suggestions improved both books.

Preston Hewis of East Bank Images, who photographed most of the memorabilia pictured in this book.

Marybeth Keating, my editor and champion at Applause Books.

Jaime Nelson of Applause Books publicity and marketing, for her tireless efforts to ensure readers take notice.

The Applause Books art department, for designing such beautiful paperbacks.

Rob Rodriguez, FAQ Series originator and overseer, for his continued enthusiasm.

Ron and Margaret Borst, Kip Colegrove, David Harnack, David Hogan, Mark Miller, Lynn Naron, Ted Okuda, and Cricket Park, for their friendship and support.

Everyone who bought a copy of *Star Trek FAQ*, especially those who returned for this sequel. I thank you, my family thanks you, and my creditors thank you. And I hope you enjoy this book as much as the original.

The cast, crew, and writers of the *Star Trek* movies and *Star Trek: The Next Generation*. If legends can be underappreciated, you are.

And, finally, to my wife Vanessa, for everything.

May you all live long and prosper.

Introduction

The Best of Both Worlds

"His fiction is inspired by vast views of a universe better conceived and better executed than the one we live in. Consequently, his stories are highly imaginative. Supposedly based upon science, they portray an evolution of mankind onward and upward into a social order that is only a dream."

Astonishingly, those words were *not* written about Gene Roddenberry. Although they seem to echo criticisms frequently lobbed at the man nicknamed "the Great Bird of the Galaxy," they derive from the 1940 edition of *Prose and Poetry of England*, a high school textbook originally copyrighted in 1934. The object of the editors' derision is author H. G. Wells, who they dismiss as a literary lightweight. "In spite of Mr. Wells' contemporary popularity, his works will not interest the future," they write. "His science is too unscientific, his fiction too unreal." Time and again over the past forty-plus years, *Star Trek* has been written off in much the same manner, but like the works of Wells, it continues to captivate its audience.

As I write this, *Star Trek* finds itself in the midst of a third major comeback. The once-thriving franchise disappeared from movie screens after *Star Trek Nemesis* misfired in 2002 and from television following the cancellation of *Star Trek: Enterprise* in 2005. The audience for *Star Trek* novels and comic books also dwindled, and the franchise slipped into limbo until director J. J. Abrams revived it with the blockbuster reboot *Star Trek* in 2009. Abrams's sequel is due to reach movie theaters about the same time as this book, but it will take a few more films, or a new TV show, for *Star Trek* to fully recapture the glory of its heyday from the late 1980s and early 1990s. Even if that never happens, however, *Star Trek* will survive—in reruns, on home video, and in the hearts and minds of generations of fans all over the world. Its guiding optimism and its eagerness to take risks both in form and in content, imprinted in the DNA of the franchise by Roddenberry, remain sources of fascination and inspiration for generations of fans.

One *Trek* Mind

As the title indicates, *Star Trek FAQ 2.0* is the companion volume to *Star Trek FAQ: Everything Left to Know About the First Voyages of Starship Enterprise*, released in 2012 by Applause Books. If you haven't read that one, don't worry. You can enjoy this book even if you skipped the first volume. *Star Trek FAQ* recounted the creation of the original *Star Trek*, its untimely cancellation, and its unprecedented, near-miraculous resurrection in the 1970s. *Star Trek FAQ 2.0* picks up the story from there, beginning with the near-death experience that was *Star Trek: The Motion Picture* (1979) and continuing through the franchise's second amazing revival, fueled by a blockbuster trilogy of feature films and the wildly successful *Star Trek: The Next Generation* series.

As a film historian, I address *Star Trek* as a unified franchise, with a shared history and a single (albeit at times fragmented) fan base. That's how Paramount Pictures executives thought of *Star Trek*. And for more than twenty years, the movies and various television series interacted with one another in sometimes surprising ways, creating synergies that helped *Star Trek* soar to the pinnacle of its popularity and mainstream acceptance in the early 1990s, but later exacerbating the decline of the franchise when Nielsen ratings and box-office receipts slumped in the early 2000s. Looking at the franchise holistically, I believe, reveals fresh insights into the backstage dynamics of both the movies and the television programs and provides new perspectives on why audiences embraced some products and rejected others. This approach also sets *Star Trek FAQ 2.0* apart from most *Star Trek* histories, which typically treat the original program, the movies, *The Next Generation*, and the various spin-off series all as distinct entities.

In fact, *Star Trek FAQ 2.0* is not only dissimilar from most other *Star Trek* books, but also unlike the original *Star Trek FAQ* in many respects. Since many readers of this book will have read the first one, I feel compelled to explain some of the more striking differences between the two volumes.

Star Trek FAQ: The Next Generation

Star Trek FAQ 2.0 is my fourth book. I have learned over the years that if you approach a project of this type with curiosity and an open mind, you often wind up with a work that is somewhat different than the one you originally envisioned. As it is researched and written, a book chooses its own personality and shapes itself as themes and story lines emerge. Some are more willful than others, but I've never had a book go its own way quite as much as this one.

Originally, I planned to make *Star Trek FAQ 2.0* a virtual clone of *Star Trek FAQ*, mirroring the structure and approach of the well-received original. But I should have known that no book largely about *Star Trek: The Next Generation* would settle for being a simple copy of a previous work. Instead, I wound up with a book that is in many respects the polar opposite of the first one. Although both books share a common mission, they express themselves very differently. Like the first volume, *Star Trek FAQ 2.0* was created to condense the sprawling jumble of information written about *Star Trek* (for books, magazines, websites, and television programs) into a convenient, coherent, and convivial resource. Both were created primarily for fans who loved one or more of the many *Trek* shows and movies but who may not think of themselves as "Trekkers"; for those curious about the history of the franchise but intimidated by the labyrinthine jumble of *Trek* material available in bookstores, libraries, and on the Internet. However, I believe that die-hard fans who have already read extensively on the subject will find much of interest here, too, in part because of the book's fresh, unified approach to the subject.

The pivotal difference between *Star Trek FAQ 2.0* and the first book is its scope. The original *Star Trek FAQ* concerned itself primarily with the classic *Trek* program, which ran for just 79 episodes. This book provides detailed coverage of the first eleven *Star Trek* feature films and all 176 episodes of *Star Trek: The Next Generation*, along with a cursory overview of the other three *Trek* spin-off series (*Deep Space Nine, Voyager,* and *Enterprise*). Working with a similar page count as the first volume, I was forced to abandon some intriguing but nonessential topics, including chapters dealing with *Star Trek* novels, comic books and video games, and the classic program's winding journey through various home video formats. (Some of this material may become available at HalLeonard.com or my Star Trek FAQ Books page on Facebook.) While a few quirky topics are covered, for the most part *2.0* is a more straitlaced, level-headed work compared to the impulsive, devil-may-care original. Or, to put it another way, while *Star Trek FAQ* was more Kirk-ish, *Star Trek FAQ 2.0* is more Picard-like. One is not necessarily superior to the other, just different.

Perhaps the most obvious contrast between the original *Star Trek FAQ* and this follow-up is that although I avoided an episode-by-episode breakdown of the classic series in the previous book, I include such a survey of *The Next Generation* in *2.0.* After wracking my brain for months, I simply could not devise a more elegant way to cover this much longer series in anything approaching a comprehensive manner. It also seemed appropriate to offer season-by-season, show-by-show examination of what was (from a ratings perspective, anyway) the most successful of all *Star Trek* series. In these capsule entries, I have tried to reduce plot synopsis to a bare minimum and to provide illuminating anecdotes from the episode's production history whenever possible. From these brief write-ups and the longer introductory passages to each chapter, I believe readers will glean something of the extraordinary effort and imagination that writers, directors, technicians, artisans, and actors poured into each episode—even the bad ones. And, yes, these entries also include my critical evaluation of each installment. I call 'em like I see 'em. Your mileage may vary. *Star Trek FAQ 2.0* also features similarly structured chapters devoted to each of the eleven *Star Trek* movies.

The menu also includes chapters devoted to the other key contributors, both behind and in front of the camera, during the rise and fall and rise of the franchise from 1979 through 2009. Another noticeable change is that while the first book was divided into behind-the-scenes and on-the-screen sections, this content is mixed throughout *2.0,* again in the interest of a more rounded approach to the material. Finally, the various chapters of the original *Star Trek FAQ* were crafted to be readable in any order. While that remains true of

Star Trek FAQ 2.0, this volume was constructed with greater narrative continuity and rewards front-to-back consumption. This change enabled me to minimize repetition between chapters. Hopefully, those of you who enjoyed the first book will also like this one, despite (or even because of) these changes.

It has been a joy to make this voyage. Thanks for joining me.

Mark Clark, Mentor on the Lake, Ohio, 2013

Return to Tomorrow

Star Trek: The Motion Picture (1979)

For nearly a decade, fans lobbied for the return of *Star Trek*. Since the show's cancellation in the spring of 1969, Trekkers incessantly bombarded NBC Television and Paramount Pictures with letters and cards requesting—no, *demanding*—the return of their beloved program. These die-hard devotees accomplished the previously unthinkable, turning a poorly rated, prematurely cancelled TV show into a cultural touchstone and, perhaps more relevantly, a multimillion-dollar revenue engine through their loyal viewership of the series' syndicated reruns and their insatiable appetite for *Trek*-themed books, toys, clothing and collectibles. The franchise's short-lived metamorphosis into a Saturday morning cartoon in 1973–74 did little to quell the clamor for new live-action adventures.

As early as 1972, Paramount began to ponder the possible resurrection of *Star Trek*, as either a television show or a feature film. But executives dithered and vacillated. They were reluctant to take any steps that might erode the value of the series' extremely profitable syndicated repeats, yet remained eager to milk as much cash as possible from the *Trek* phenomenon, which was assumed to be a passing fad. A five-year string of false starts and scuttled projects ensued, as Paramount tried to develop a low-budget *Star Trek* theatrical feature and later a new television series, without success. (For more on this exasperating era in *Trek* history, see Chapter 41 of the original *Star Trek FAQ*.)

Finally, in March 1978, under intense pressure to respond to 20th Century-Fox's game-changing blockbuster *Star Wars* with a similarly exploitable sci-fi product, Paramount officially announced the forthcoming *Star Trek: The Motion Picture*. At an enormous publicity event with reporters from all over the world, the studio unveiled plans for a $15 million sci-fi epic produced by Gene Roddenberry and directed by Oscar winner Robert Wise (who in 1951 had made *The Day the Earth Stood Still*), which would reunite the entire cast of the TV series and introduce new characters.

Fans were jubilant, and their expectations, stoked by grandiloquent studio publicity, soared. Most believed that, on the wide canvas of the big screen, with an ample budget, a generous shooting schedule, and state-of-the-art visual effects, *The Motion Picture* would represent the franchise's crowning achievement, a product superior in every respect to the TV series that had spawned it. This was precisely what Paramount *wanted* fans to believe. One television

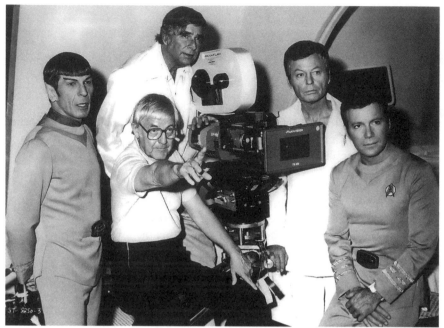

In this publicity photo, Gene Roddenberry looks over director Robert Wise's shoulder. He did the same thing throughout production of *Star Trek: The Motion Picture*. Also pictured are stars Leonard Nimoy (left), DeForest Kelley, and William Shatner (right).

ad addressed the series' cultural impact and the palpable fervor for *Star Trek*'s revival overtly. Sonorous narrator Orson Welles called the TV show "a common experience remembered around the world" and promised, "Now Paramount Pictures brings the memory to life." The film's theatrical trailer promised that *The Motion Picture* would "startle your senses" and "challenge your intellect." Naturally, Roddenberry and Wise wanted to deliver a product that lived up to the hype. Unfortunately, an array of problems quickly beset the production, compromising the movie's ability to meet fans' and filmmakers' lofty aspirations and Paramount's overinflated ballyhoo.

Script Wars

From the outset, the greatest difficulty facing *The Motion Picture* was its screenplay—or lack thereof. Beginning in 1975, series creator Roddenberry and a host of other writers had developed more than half a dozen concepts, ranging from one-page story ideas to complete scripts, most of which had been rejected for one reason or another. The most recent iteration, titled "In Thy Image," had been written by Harold Livingston to serve as the pilot episode of the abandoned *Star Trek: Phase II* television show. The story originated with a thumbnail idea ("Robot's Return") created for Roddenberry's failed *Genesis II* series, which was expanded into a thirty-two-page treatment by noted science fiction author Alan Dean Foster.

The scenario was highly reminiscent of the classic episode "The Changeling," penned by John Meredith Lucas, integrating key elements from a rejected screenplay written by Roddenberry in 1975 titled *The God Thing*. The *Enterprise*, led by Admiral James T. Kirk and Captain Willard Decker (son of Commodore Decker from the classic episode "The Doomsday Machine"), races to intercept a giant, fantastically powerful object of unknown origin. The object, known as V'ger, destroys a Klingon Bird of Prey and a Federation space station, and appears unstoppable. To communicate with the humans, V'ger takes over the body of a beautiful female alien Starfleet officer, Lieutenant Ilia. Eventually, it's revealed that "V'ger" is a centuries-old Earth space probe that had gained both sentience and fantastic powers during its travels through the galaxy. Now it's returning to Earth to link with its creator and share all it has learned during its long voyage, but it considers organic life inferior.

Livingston took umbrage when Roddenberry heavily rewrote his teleplay and then signed it "by Gene Roddenberry and Harold Livingston." (Ultimately, only Livingston would receive screenplay credit.) After lodging fruitless protests with Paramount executive Jeffrey Katzenberg, Livingston walked away from the project. For a while the script existed in two competing forms—Livingston's unadulterated version and Roddenberry's rewrite. Director Robert Collins, who had been chosen to helm the pilot episode of *Phase II*, tried to blend both into a single product, but he was let go and replaced by Wise when *Star Trek* moved from television to the big screen. Then the screenplay was handed off to writer Dennis Clark, but he, too, clashed with Roddenberry. After three months of bickering, and with the script still inadequate, Clark was released from the picture. The biggest problem with the screenplay was that no one could devise a satisfactory ending to the story.

So, in the spring of 1978, Katzenberg lured Livingston back into the fold. The studio hoped that the screenwriter could quickly resolve the remaining story issues before shooting began in June. However, this would have required him to establish some sort of working rapport with Roddenberry, and, as Livingston told William Shatner for his book *Star Trek Movie Memories*, "I couldn't stand the son of a bitch." The feeling was mutual, and the two men launched a war of revisions, with Roddenberry rewriting Livingston, Livingston revising Roddenberry's changes, Roddenberry reworking Livingston's revision of his initial rewrite, and on and on, ad infinitum, ad nauseam. This conflict continued throughout production. Filming began without a completed script, and revised pages arrived on the set daily. In their book *The Making of Star Trek: The Motion Picture*, Roddenberry and his assistant Susan Sackett describe the ensuing chaos: "At one point, each day's scenes were being rewritten several times a day, and it became necessary to note on the pages the hour of the day when these pages had been rushed to the stage so the actors could learn their most recent lines and Bob Wise would know what he was shooting."

Vision Quest

The lack of a finalized script created a conceptual vacuum, which cast and crew members with competing visions attempted to fill. *The Motion Picture* was Robert Wise's film. Everyone held the director in the highest esteem, and he made all the big-picture decisions. But Wise knew almost nothing about *Star Trek* (he had only watched the show once or twice before signing on), and often deferred to Roddenberry on the fine-grain details. This enabled Roddenberry to exert considerable influence. Wise remained open to input from other sources, too, including Livingston and actors Leonard Nimoy and Shatner, among others. Soon everyone was chiming in with ideas about everything, often leaving with ruffled feathers when their suggestions were shot down. While the free flow of ideas is seldom a bad thing, all these competing voices and bruised egos introduced additional confusion and stress into the troubled production, which was already running severely behind schedule and over budget. Principal photography finally wrapped months late, on January 26, 1979. Everyone breathed a sigh of relief—until they got a look at the special effects footage that had been created for the picture.

Not-So-Special Effects

Back in August 1966, with the network premiere of *Star Trek* just weeks away, Roddenberry discovered that the Howard Anderson Company, the firm contracted to produce the show's special visual effects, would be unable to meet its obligations. He scrambled to hire three additional visual effects companies in order to obtain acceptable footage in the quantity and with the speed necessary for the series to meet its merciless production deadlines.

In early 1979, Roddenberry must have experienced an eerie sense of déjà vu.

He and Wise were appalled when they reviewed the visual effects footage created, at great expense, by Robert Abel & Associates. They deemed it unusable, which meant the shots would have to be redone—at even greater expense. Special effects were obviously a make-or-break element of *The Motion Picture*, which (following the rival sci-fi smashes *Star Wars*, *Close Encounters of the Third Kind*, and *Superman: The Movie*) had emerged as Paramount's highest production priority. So, to ensure the film would have the requisite wow factor, the studio engaged A-list talent for this critical do-over: Douglas Trumbull, who created the visual effects for Stanley Kubrick's landmark *2001: A Space Odyssey* (1968) and for *Close Encounters* (1977), and John Dykstra, who had worked on *Star Wars* (1977).

The work was costly and time-consuming, pushing the project's already bloated budget even higher and forcing the movie to be edited in a last-minute frenzy. Due to overruns in all departments, *Star Trek: The Motion Picture*, originally budgeted at $15 million, wound up costing a colossal $46 million, the second-most-expensive Hollywood film up to that point. The only movie with higher costs was *Superman: The Movie* (1978), but that production included principal photography for two releases, both the original and *Superman II* (1980).

Adjusting for inflation, *The Motion Picture* cost over $160 million in today's dollars. *Star Wars*, comparatively, had cost $11 million, or about $42 million in inflation-adjusted figures. The budget impact of *The Motion Picture*'s visual effects fiasco was staggering, but from a creative standpoint, the pressure it placed on the film's editing process proved to be just as costly.

Blind (Release) Date

Originally, *Star Wars* had been assigned a Christmas 1976 release date. But the film's original edit, by John Jympson, was a stodgy, slow-moving disaster. So the release was pushed back five months, allowing director George Lucas and three editors to prune and reshape the movie, shortening sequences and employing quick cuts, speedy "wipes," and other techniques to accelerate the pace and inject energy. The result was the billion-dollar blockbuster the rest of Hollywood has been chasing ever since. *Close Encounters*, originally slated to be issued in summer of 1977, was delayed until November due to similar difficulties. The result was another smash. But apparently Paramount Pictures learned nothing from these examples.

All Roddenberry's and Wise's difficulties with *The Motion Picture* were exacerbated by Paramount's intransigence regarding the film's release date. The studio's teaser trailer had promised that the *Star Trek* movie was "coming this Christmas," and executives would brook no slippage from the film's announced nationwide release on December 7, 1979. Legions of fans had the date circled on their calendars, and many planned to queue up in homemade Starfleet uniforms. A gala premiere was scheduled for December 6 in Washington, D.C.

Visual effects sequences were still being shot at the point in the production cycle when most films were being test screened. Unlike all of Wise's other movies, there was no time for the standard "sneak preview" to gauge audience reaction, or to fix any problems that may have been identified. Because the effects footage was so late in arriving, Wise and editor Todd Ramsay had virtually no opportunity to edit these sequences. As a result, many of them (notably Captain Kirk's inspection of the space-docked, retrofitted *USS Enterprise*) dragged on far too long. Instead, Wise and Ramsay worked frantically, splicing in the effects shots until the last possible moment. Their goal was merely to assemble the film in time so prints could be struck and shipped to theaters. The print that Wise personally carried from L.A. to D.C. for the premiere was still wet.

Wise later admitted that he was never happy with the theatrical release version of *The Motion Picture*, which he considered unfinished. Fans lobbied for the film to be reedited and reissued in a "special edition," like the one granted *Close Encounters* in 1980. That didn't happen, but a new cut of *The Motion Picture*, including twelve minutes' worth of sequences shortened or deleted from the theatrical version, was created for the picture's initial television broadcast in February 1983. Finally, in 2001, Paramount released to DVD and home video a Director's Edition of the film overseen by Wise, with tighter editing and new, computer-generated visual effects.

Reception

Paramount's previews had pledged that *Star Trek: The Motion Picture* would "startle your senses" and "challenge your intellect," but it should have warned that it would also test your patience. After decades of anticipation and months of publicity build-up, the movie delivered something few expected: boredom. Over the years, the film has gained derisive nicknames like *The Slow Motion Picture* and *The Emotionless Picture.* In his autobiography, *Beam Me Up, Scotty,* actor James Doohan admits that he fell asleep during the movie's world premiere.

While a handful of critics—notably the unnamed *Variety* reviewer—praised *The Motion Picture,* most eviscerated it, including influential reviewers at the *Washington Post, New York Times, Chicago Tribune, Time,* and *Newsweek.* Many had sneered at *Star Trek* and its fans all along, and took this opportunity to try to finally bury the franchise. Critics and casual viewers alike derided the film's slow pace, lack of human drama, and overreliance on visual effects. Many of *Star Trek*'s intensely loyal core fans reacted with confusion and dismay. Although some Trekkers genuinely enjoyed the film, most felt let down. However, fearing that the failure of *The Motion Picture* would mean the death of *Star Trek,* many remained reluctant to express their disappointment openly. Some went to see *The Motion Picture* multiple times in hopes of finally "getting" the movie.

The film's box-office receipts tell the story. It earned a near-record gross of $12 million during its first weekend and a then-record $17 million in its first week, but receipts quickly declined. *The Motion Picture* had none of the staying power of *Star Wars,* which in some markets remained in first-run theaters for more than a year. Eventually, *Star Trek*'s worldwide gross would total $139 million—an impressive figure, but less than Paramount expected and nothing like the results for *Star Wars,* which earned $461 million in the U.S. alone. Perhaps even worse, while *Star Wars* toys and collectibles continued to fly off the shelves, retailers couldn't give away *Star Trek: The Motion Picture* action figures, T-shirts, and other tie-ins. Tellingly, however, classic *Trek* merchandise continued to move.

The Motion Picture earned three Oscar nominations (Best Art Direction, Best Visual Effects, and Best Original Score), but this provided little consolation. In his memoir *Warped Factors,* Walter Koenig admits, "I never thought there would be another *Star Trek* movie after this one."

Assessing *The Motion Picture*

The Motion Picture isn't the worst *Star Trek* film. That dubious distinction belongs to William Shatner's addle-brained *Star Trek V: The Final Frontier.* But in many respects, the first *Trek* movie is the least rewarding. It's a demanding, even grueling, viewing experience—despite its languid pace, viewers must pay rapt attention to understand what's going on—yet it returns comparatively little in terms of visceral thrills, emotional impact, or intellectual illumination.

Although he didn't receive story or screenplay credit, *The Motion Picture* stemmed from an idea by Roddenberry and repeats many of the failings that doomed *Star Trek*'s rejected original pilot, "The Cage." It's static, with too little action and a tendency to bog down in pseudo-metaphysical folderol. Its characters are poorly defined, especially the new ones—Ilia, the bald Deltan played by model Persis Khambatta, and Captain Decker, played by Stephen Collins. The familiar supporting characters are given little to do. Even Spock is poorly utilized. The character wasn't included in Livingston's original teleplay, since Nimoy had declined to appear in *Phase II*. Once the project moved to the big screen and Nimoy signed on, Spock was shoehorned into the story. He doesn't join his old crewmates until the film is half over, and even then—after trying to purge his remaining human emotions while studying on Vulcan—he seems little like the Spock fans knew and loved on TV. The sterile, retrofitted *Enterprise*, full of gleaming silver walls and officers in neutral-colored uniforms, harkens back to the bland, militaristic look of "The Cage," rather than the color-splashed starship seen on later *Trek* episodes. And the mood of the piece remains somber and humorless. For instance, Shatner, Nimoy, and DeForest Kelley ad-libbed a humorous epilogue, which Wise rejected as "inappropriate," even though the jokey wrap-up on the bridge was one of the series' most frequently used and charming devices.

Many of these flaws are foundational and stem from the selection of the V'ger scenario among other competing story

TV Guide ad for a television broadcast of *The Motion Picture*. The television version included scenes trimmed from the theatrical release and, with commercials, ran three hours. This in an era without DVRs (or fast-forward buttons).

concepts. The faceless V'ger is more an idea than a character. It is a problem to be solved, not a villain to be reckoned with, and the film suffers badly from this lack of a dynamic adversary. As a result, even the later Director's Edition represents only a marginal improvement over the bewildering original. In retrospect, it's difficult to fathom what anyone saw in this scenario in the first place, especially when other, more action-oriented stories were available.

Ultimately, *The Motion Picture* is too familiar and too alien at the same time, and in all the wrong ways. The plot, which should have been fresh and exciting, seems stale and lifeless. Most fans immediately made the connection with "The Changeling" and saw the film's big "surprise"—that V'ger is actually a twentieth-century NASA Voyager space probe—coming a light year away. Meanwhile, the cherished characters and settings, which fans yearned to reconnect with, are missing or needlessly altered. Spock has the wrong personality, and what good are Starfleet uniforms that don't come in blue, gold, and red? As mentioned, the movie has a tendency to bog down in overlong visual effects sequences. While the effects themselves are extremely impressive, they don't look like *Star Trek* visuals. The lingering shots of the space-docked *Enterprise*, for instance, plays more like the icy, antiseptic space station sequence from *2001* than like anything originating from the *Trek* canon, before or since. Although every member of the cast had moments of brilliance on the TV show, none of them distinguish themselves here. Collins gives the film's best performance, even though the hastily improvised finale relies on an extremely contrived and highly unlikely last-minute change of heart by Captain Decker. Khambatta is simply terrible. The only truly outstanding contribution to *The Motion Picture* comes from composer Jerry Goldsmith, whose Oscar-nominated score is thrilling. His "*Star Trek* Fanfare" would serve as the title theme for *Star Trek: The Next Generation*, and would be revived in many subsequent *Trek* movies.

Given these dispiriting results, it's no wonder Koenig, like many fans, feared that *The Motion Picture* spelled doom for *Star Trek*. But of course, the franchise survived. The only casualty was Roddenberry's perch as the Great Bird of the Galaxy.

2

Chain of Command

Roddenberry's Successors

S*tar Trek: The Motion Picture* careened wildly over budget, underperformed at the box office, earned scathing reviews and left even the most avid Trekkers puzzled and disheartened. The movie turned a profit, mostly due to the massive pent-up demand for new *Trek* product, but fell far short of Paramount Pictures' lofty, *Star Wars*-like ambitions. Someone had to pay for this disappointment, and Gene Roddenberry was stuck with the tab.

As the producer of the film, Roddenberry had supplied the thumbnail story idea that grew into the ill-conceived screenplay for *The Motion Picture*. As the so-called Great Bird of the Galaxy, he had exerted a guiding influence over the project, especially since director Robert Wise often deferred to him on the specifics of the *Star Trek* milieu. Roddenberry had always insisted that he alone was the ultimate arbiter of what was and wasn't *Trek*. Now his autocratic methods boomeranged on him, helping make him the lone fall guy for the movie's many failings. Although Roddenberry remained culpable, there was plenty of blame to go around.

Fingers could have been pointed at the Howard Anderson Company, whose failure to deliver satisfactory visual effects proved catastrophic for both the film's budget and its postproduction schedule. Coscreenwriter David Livingston was as much at fault for the weak script as Roddenberry. Then there was Wise, whose unfamiliarity with *Star Trek* remained sorely visible in every frame of the completed film. Even though *The Motion Picture* was, after all, *his* movie, the affable and respected Wise received a pass. Executives, including Michael Eisner and Jeffrey Katzenberg, shared responsibility, too. They had approved Roddenberry's V'ger scenario as the basis for the film and forced a product Wise considered unfinished into theaters through their intransigence regarding its release date. But Paramount's power brokers couldn't—or wouldn't—fire themselves. They couldn't fire Roddenberry, either, since through his Norway Corporation, established to create the TV series, he owned a half-interest in *Star Trek*. But Paramount could clip Roddenberry's wings.

Despite its many problems, *The Motion Picture* had turned a profit of about $90 million (once production and marketing costs were removed from its $139 million box-office tally). This was enough to suggest that the *Trek* franchise might be sustainable if it were placed under new management. So Paramount brass retained Roddenberry at a hefty salary but removed him from control of the franchise. Roddenberry accepted the meaningless title of "Executive Consultant," perhaps at first not realizing how marginalized he would become. But beginning with *Star Trek II: The Wrath of Khan*, the Great Bird no longer ruled the roost.

Harve Bennett

Roddenberry's unlikely successor as commander in chief of *Star Trek* was producer Harve Bennett. No one was more surprised by this turn of events than Bennett himself.

Born Harve Bennett Fischman on August 17, 1930, in Chicago, Bennett was intelligent and experienced. His first exposure to show business was as a contestant on the Quiz Kids radio show as a child in the 1940s. He graduated from UCLA's theater program in 1953 and worked briefly as a columnist for the Chicago *Sun-Times*. After serving two years in the U.S. Army, he began his career in television as a production assistant at CBS. Bennett then jumped to ABC, where he eventually rose to the post of Vice President of Programming. For ABC he was involved in the development of hit series, including *Batman*,

Producer Harve Bennett (center) replaced Gene Roddenberry in *Star Trek*'s proverbial captain's chair beginning with *The Wrath of Khan*. With (left to right) DeForest Kelley, George Takei, John Vargas, Nichelle Nichols, Walter Koenig, James Doohan, William Shatner, and Leonard Nimoy.

The Fugitive, Bewitched, and the pioneering nighttime soap opera *Peyton Place.* In 1965, Bennett was the executive attached to the Roddenberry-produced pilot *The Long Hunt of April Savage,* which starred Robert ("Gary Seven") Lansing. Bennett okayed making the pilot but ultimately passed on the series.

He left ABC in the late 1960s and entered production, realizing he would rather create shows than book them. He enjoyed early success with *The Mod Squad,* a hip, racially integrated police drama that ran on ABC from 1968 through 1973, which Bennett cocreated with producer Aaron Spelling. In the 1970s, Bennett joined Universal Pictures Television, where he produced several highly rated series and miniseries, including *The Six Million Dollar Man* (1974–78) and *The Bionic Woman* (1976–78). Late in the decade, following the cancellation of *The Six Million Dollar Man,* Bennett left Universal and partnered with producer Harris Katleman to form Bennett-Katleman Productions, which oversaw production of TV movies and miniseries for Columbia Pictures Television. In late 1980, he parted company with Katleman and joined Paramount Pictures, where he won an Emmy for the 1982 telefilm *A Woman Called Golda,* a biopic about Israeli Prime Minister Golda Meier, starring (in her final role) screen legend Ingrid Bergman and featuring Leonard Nimoy. But, as it turned out, *Golda* would be the less significant of Bennett's two 1982 features.

Bennett had been at Paramount for only a few weeks when he was summoned into a meeting with Barry Diller and Michael Eisner, then the top-ranking executives in the company, and Charles Bluhdorn, the famously plainspoken owner of Gulf + Western, a corporate conglomerate that had purchased Paramount in 1966. Bennett had no idea what the meeting was about. Then Bluhdorn asked Bennett for the producer's opinion of *Star Trek: The Motion Picture.* Realizing it was unwise to mince words with the no-nonsense magnate, Bennett replied frankly he thought *The Motion Picture* was boring and described how his restless children kept asking to run to the snack bar throughout the film.

Then, as Bennett has recounted in numerous interviews, Bluhdorn asked Bennett if he thought he could make a better *Star Trek* movie. Bennett said that yes, he could.

"Could you make it for less than forty-five fucking million dollars?" Bluhdorn asked, glaring at Diller and Eisner. Unbeknownst to the producer, Diller and Eisner had chosen Bennett for the assignment based on his track record for bringing in projects on time and on budget.

"Where I come from, I could make five or six movies for that," Bennett replied.

"Do it," Bluhdorn ordered.

Bennett was thrilled. He had longed to make the jump from television to feature film production, but such opportunities rarely present themselves. Now he had been handed the keys to a multimillion-dollar movie franchise. There was just one problem: Bennett knew almost as little about *Star Trek* as Wise had known before he signed on to direct *The Motion Picture.* Unlike Wise, however,

Bennett set out to steep himself in the idiom, promptly screening all seventy-nine episodes of the series. It was his idea to make the second *Trek* film a direct sequel to the classic adventure "Space Seed," and to bring back the villainous Khan Noonien Singh, played by Ricardo Montalban. Serving as executive producer, Bennett developed an early treatment with screenwriter Jack Sowards, then brought in Nicholas Meyer to complete the screenplay and direct the film, and Robert Sallin to serve as producer.

When he asked what role Roddenberry would play in the project, Bennett was told that he should listen to suggestions from *Star Trek*'s creator but should not feel beholden to Roddenberry's advice. None of this sat well with Roddenberry, who resented being reduced to a figurehead. "Gene cast me immediately as an interloper," Bennett told Roddenberry biographer Joel Engel. "There wasn't a single issue . . . that was not resisted in memo by Gene." Roddenberry bad-mouthed Bennett at every opportunity and tried to monkey wrench *Star Trek II: The Wrath of Khan*. (More on that in the next chapter.)

Despite—or even, ironically, in part because of—Roddenberry's meddling, the second *Trek* movie was a smash. This secured Bennett's place in the franchise's power structure and pushed Roddenberry permanently to the wings, at least with regard to the feature films. For the next decade Bennett, assisted by Meyer, Leonard Nimoy, and others, controlled the *Trek* movie series. In addition to his duties as producer, Bennett wrote *Star Trek III: The Search for Spock*, cowrote *Star Trek IV: The Voyage Home* with Meyer, and helped develop the story for *Star Trek V: The Final Frontier*. Bennett also enjoyed an on-screen cameo in *The Final Frontier* as a Starfleet admiral, but his relationships with the studio and with William Shatner were damaged during the production of this misfire. Bennett's association with the franchise ended with a dispute over what direction the series should take following *Star Trek V* (see Chapter 19, "The Trek Not Taken").

After leaving *Star Trek*, Bennett continued writing and producing, primarily for television. His final completed project was the syndicated sci-fi series *Time Trax* (1993–95). He is now semiretired. In an audio commentary on *The Search for Spock* DVD, Leonard Nimoy says that Bennett "took *Star Trek*, which was a beached whale after *Star Trek I*, and put it back in the water and made it float with *Star Trek II*, and got us going again when it was in danger of floundering and dying."

Nicholas Meyer

Although he had hit on an exciting concept for *Star Trek II*, neither Bennett nor writing partner Jack Sowards could produce a workable screenplay. After four drafts the script remained unsatisfactory. That's where Nicholas Meyer came in.

Meyer, born Christmas Eve, 1945, in Manhattan, had been a movie buff since childhood, and had made a feature-length 8 mm home movie adaptation of Jules Verne's *Around the World in 80 Days* as a teenager. After graduating from the University of Iowa film program in 1964, he took a lowly position in Paramount Pictures' publicity office in New York. He first visited a Hollywood movie set as the publicist for Arthur Hiller's tearjerker *Love Story* (1970), an experience Meyer translated into a behind-the-scenes paperback titled *The Love Story Story* (1971). While hardly an astonishing literary debut, the profits from this book gave Meyer the wherewithal to relocate to Los Angeles and launch his screenwriting career. He toiled in anonymity in the story department at Warner Brothers for two years until a 1972 Writers Guild strike forced him to pursue other endeavors, starting with a novel titled *The Seven-Per-Cent Solution*, in which Sherlock Holmes joins forces with Sigmund Freud. The book changed publishers three times due to difficulties with the estate of Sir Arthur Conan Doyle, but became one of the best-selling novels of 1974 once it finally reached bookstores.

Meyer's Vietnam-themed detective novel *Target Practice*, written after *The Seven-Per-Cent Solution* but unencumbered by legal wrangling, was published earlier the same year. It didn't sell as well but earned glowing reviews and was nominated for an Edgar Award. Meanwhile, ABC produced Meyer's offbeat teleplay *Judge Dee and the Monastery Murders*, about a killing in a seventh-century Taoist monastery, as a Movie of the Week. Response was so positive that a sequel was commissioned and written, but later cancelled. In all, it was a breakout year for Meyer, whose only pre-1974 screen credit had been the campy sci-fi-comedy *Invasion of the Bee Girls* (1973), a script that had been heavily rewritten (and dumbed down) without his involvement.

The writer's profile continued to rise over the next few years. In 1975, CBS produced his teleplay *The Night That Panicked America*, about the furor surrounding Orson Welles's 1938 *War of the Worlds* radio broadcast. The following year, Meyer penned the screenplay for director Herbert Ross's big-screen adaptation of *The Seven-Per-Cent Solution*, earning an Oscar nomination for his work, and published a second best-selling Holmes pastiche, *The West End Horror*, in which the detective crosses paths with luminaries including Oscar Wilde and Bram Stoker. Meyer cowrote the adventure novel *Black Orchid* (1978) with Barry Kaplan. Then he cowrote and directed *Time After Time* (1979), a charming romantic sci-fi thriller in which H. G. Wells (Malcolm McDowell) travels from the Victorian era to the future (circa 1979) in pursuit of Jack the Ripper (David Warner) and falls in love with a twentieth-century woman (Mary Steenburgen). The film earned enthusiastic reviews and was a modest box-office success. In 1981, Meyer published another novel, the semiautobiographical *Confessions of a Homing Pigeon*, but was frustrated in his efforts to find a studio willing to purchase his screenplay *Conjuring*, based on Robinson Davies's allegorical novel *Fifth Business*, about a rural Canadian schoolteacher. With his screen career at an impasse, his friend Karen Moore, an executive at Paramount, suggested Meyer contact Bennett, who needed help with the script for the new *Star Trek* movie.

Like Bennett, Meyer knew very little about *Star Trek*, but he trusted Moore's advice. Meyer and Bennett clicked immediately, and Meyer became excited about the project when he gleaned parallels between *Trek* and author C. S. Forester's Horatio Hornblower novels. (Meyer did not yet know that the Hornblower books had been one of Roddenberry's primary inspirations for *Star Trek*.) He eagerly agreed to direct the picture. Faced with a time crunch (again, Paramount had locked the production into an immovable release date), Meyer performed a feverish rewrite—combining the best elements from all four existing scripts into a single, coherent narrative—in a mere twelve days. Because he was not yet officially under contract at this point, Meyer received no writing credit and no pay for these efforts, but without them *Star Trek II*, like its predecessor, would have lurched into production without a completed screenplay or might have been cancelled altogether.

The Wrath of Khan (1982) was not an easy production, but the resulting picture pleased both critics and ticket buyers. Trekkers were ecstatic. So were Paramount executives, who tried to involve Meyer in every subsequent *Trek* film featuring the original cast. The studio wanted him to write and direct *Star Trek III: The Search for Spock* (1984), but Meyer declined because he didn't want to be involved with Spock's resurrection, which he felt cheapened the previous film. Nevertheless, Meyer returned to coauthor the screenplay for *Star Trek IV: The Voyage Home* (1986). Paramount asked him to write *Star Trek V: The Final Frontier* (1989), but Meyer declined because he thought (correctly) that the basic premise was flawed. Yet he returned to cowrite and direct *Star Trek VI: The Undiscovered Country* (1991). The long-standing consensus among fans is that the even-numbered *Trek* films are superior to the odd-numbered ones. If so, it's because *Treks II*, *IV* and *VI* were elevated by Meyer's keen wit and impeccable story sense.

In between *Trek* projects, Meyer kept himself busy with numerous other movies and books, the most notable being *The Day After* (1983), a hard-hitting ABC telefilm about the aftermath of a nuclear war. Nearly thirty-nine million viewers tuned in for its initial broadcast, making *The Day After* the most-watched made-for-TV movie in history. It also earned seventeen Emmy nominations. Meyer served as an uncredited script doctor on Adrian Lyne's thriller *Fatal Attraction* (1987). But most of his higher-profile efforts flopped, including the Tom Hanks-John Candy Peace Corps comedy *Volunteers* (1985) and the Gene Hackman-Mikhail Baryshnikov spy thriller *Company Business* (1991). Since *Star Trek VI*, Meyer's works have included screenplays for *Sommersby* (1993), with Richard Gere and Jodie Foster; *The Informant* (1997), with Timothy Dalton; and *The Human Stain* (2003), with Anthony Hopkins and Nicole Kidman; among other projects for the big and small screens. He published a third Holmes novel, *The Canary Trainer* (1993), as well as an autobiography titled *The View from the Bridge* (2009). Meyer has struggled to recapture his early commercial success but remains active; as of this writing (in the fall of 2012), he had two projects lined up for 2013. His screenplay *Taliesin*, a story involving architect Frank Lloyd Wright, was in preproduction, and he was announced as the director of *A Half of Two Lives*, based on a book by Alison Waley.

Leonard Nimoy

Actor Leonard Nimoy and Roddenberry had fought a series of bitter skirmishes over the years. The actor went toe-to-toe with Roddenberry and Desilu management after the first season of the original program, demanding a higher salary and other considerations. He clashed with the Great Bird over royalties from the Dot Records album *Mr. Spock's Music from Outer Space* and from other merchandise bearing Nimoy's (Spock's) likeness. In the 1970s, Nimoy filed a Screen Actors Guild complaint against Roddenberry for showing the *Star Trek* blooper reel at speaking engagements without permission of, or providing compensation for, the show's cast. The list of grievances goes on and on, but one of the core issues separating the two men was that both were jealously protective of Spock. Each considered himself the character's creator, yet the two sometimes disagreed about what the Vulcan should say or do in a given situation. With Roddenberry's ouster, Nimoy now had the last word.

As the film series progressed, Nimoy exerted increasing control over the franchise, emerging—along with Bennett and Meyer—as the third creative cornerstone of the *Trek* feature films. He used his star power as leverage to gain the director's chair for *The Search for Spock* and *The Voyage Home*. He collaborated with Bennett to develop the story for *The Voyage Home* and with Meyer on the story for *The Undiscovered Country*. He also served as executive producer on

Writer-director Nicholas Meyer consults with Leonard Nimoy regarding a scene from *The Wrath of Khan*. Meyer had a hand in all of the "good, even-numbered" *Star Trek* movies.

Undiscovered Country following Bennett's departure. After the *Wrath of Khan*, the only original-cast *Trek* movie in which Nimoy did not play a key creative role was Shatner's misbegotten *Final Frontier*. He was even offered the chance to develop a new *Star Trek* television series but turned it down. (For details, see Chapter 6, "The Offspring.")

Other Power Brokers

Others who wielded greater creative control than Roddenberry over the *Star Trek* films included:

Robert Sallin—Bennett brought in his college buddy Robert Sallin to produce *Star Trek II: The Wrath of Khan*, but their friendship deteriorated over the course of the production. Sallin also clashed with Nicholas Meyer, who in his autobiography reports that Sallin tried to have the director fired shortly after production began. *The Wrath of Khan* remains Sallin's only movie as a producer. Sallin was born in Oakland, Pennsylvania, in the 1930s and became involved with show business as a child. By age fourteen he was appearing on World War II–era patriotic radio broadcasts in the Pittsburgh area (as part of the Junior American Red Cross of the Air) and occasionally appearing on national *U.S. Steel Hour* radio dramas, which were sometimes broadcast from Pittsburgh. His family moved to Los Angeles when he was sixteen years old, and he graduated from UCLA's film program in 1953. Although he made occasional forays into mainstream production—such as directing the telefilm *The Picasso Summer* (1969), starring Albert Finney and based on a Ray Bradbury story—Sallin's primary business was Kaleidoscope Productions, a company he founded that made television commercials. After *Star Trek*, Sallin helmed a handful of television episodes and directed second-unit material for director Richard Donner's *Assassins* (1995), starring Sylvester Stallone and Antonio Banderas, but worked primarily in commercials and other ventures. He is currently employed as a freelance creative and management consultant. His clients have included Turner Broadcasting, the University of California-Santa Barbara, and the Los Angeles Police Department.

William Shatner—Jealous of Nimoy's growing influence over the franchise, Shatner invoked the "favored nations clause" in his contract, which essentially granted him equal right to every reward shown Nimoy, up to and including directing a film. The ensuing fiasco (see Chapter 13, "Shatner's Folly") had grim consequences for the franchise and for Shatner's nascent directorial career.

Gary Nardino—Nardino, born August 26, 1935, in Garfield, New Jersey, served as executive producer on *Star Trek III: The Search for Spock*. A former talent agent, Nardino became president of Paramount Pictures Television in 1977, where he oversaw the development of hit comedies such as *Cheers, Taxi, Mork & Mindy,* and *Family Ties*, as well as miniseries and TV movies, including Bennett's *A Woman Called Golda*. In 1988, he left Paramount to assume control of embattled Orion

Pictures. He was working as an executive at Warner Brothers Television in 1998 when he suffered a fatal stroke at age sixty-two.

Ralph Winter—Winter, born April 24, 1952, in Glendale, California, was another Paramount Pictures Television veteran who had worked on *Happy Days*, *Laverne & Shirley*, and *Mork & Mindy*. His feature film career began with *The Wrath of Khan*, where he served as a postproduction supervisor. With *The Search for Spock*, Winter was elevated to the post of Associate Producer. He went on to Executive Produce *Star Trek IV: The Voyage Home* and *Star Trek V: The Final Frontier*, and to coproduce *Star Trek VI: The Undiscovered Country* with Steven-Charles Jaffe. It was the beginning of an ongoing, highly profitable career in motion picture production. His highest-profile post-*Trek* credits include six movies based on Marvel Comics characters (the first four X-Men features and both Fantastic Four films) and Tim Burton's 2001 *Planet of the Apes* remake.

Steven-Charles Jaffe—Steven-Charles Jaffe was a friend of Nicholas Meyer who served as coproducer and second-unit director on *The Undiscovered Country*. He is the son of Herb Jaffe, who produced Meyer's *Time After Time*. The younger Jaffe worked with his father and as an associate producer and second-unit director on *Time After Time*. He also shot second-unit footage for Meyer's *The Day After*. Steven-Charles Jaffe's filmography is full of dark, quirky features, such as the cannibalism-themed comedy *Motel Hell* (1980), the white-trash vampire flick *Near Dark* (1987), the underrated *The Fly II* (1989), and the cyberpunk thriller *Strange Days* (1995), all of which he produced. Jaffe also worked as executive producer on the Oscar-nominated *Ghost* (1990).

3

Where Is Thy Sting?

The Wrath of Khan and the Death of Spock (1982)

S *tar Trek* had flirted with extinction throughout its existence. It seemed doomed in 1965, following the failure of its original pilot, "The Cage," but NBC granted the show a reprieve by ordering an unprecedented second pilot. The series could have ended after its first or second season, but write-in campaigns by ardent fans helped keep it on the air. Even following its apparent demise in 1969, when NBC cancelled the show, *Star Trek* refused to stay dead. It endured in syndicated reruns, as a Saturday morning cartoon show, and with novels and comic books.

The demoralizing, underperforming *Star Trek: The Motion Picture* (1979) dealt a serious blow to the franchise. Two years later, as Paramount warily entered preproduction on a second movie, *Trek*'s survival once again hung in the balance. Another critical and commercial disappointment would almost certainly have consigned the franchise to oblivion. For *Star Trek* to endure, executive producer Harve Bennett and director Nicholas Meyer, both newcomers, needed to deliver a high-quality product capable of satisfying a disgruntled fan base while also crossing over to attract general audiences. And they had to do it on a budget of just over $11 million ($34 million less than *The Motion Picture*). Few were optimistic about their chances.

Luring Nimoy and Soothing Shatner

Leonard Nimoy was one of those who believed the franchise had reached a dead end. Following the miserable experience of making *The Motion Picture*, not to mention the film's punishing reviews, Nimoy decided he was finished with *Star Trek*. So Bennett's first task was to convince the actor to return to the fold. The producer came up with a novel inducement: the opportunity to play Spock's death scene. This piqued the actor's interest. "Certainly this will be the last of the *Star Trek* movies," the actor reasoned, as he explained in a documentary included on the *Star Trek II: The Wrath of Khan* DVD. "If they make this one, I can't see them making any more. And maybe it would be an interesting final curtain for the Spock character to go out in a blaze of glory."

Bennett's original concept was to kill Spock early in the film, delivering a jolt similar to the one director Alfred Hitchcock achieved by murdering Janet Leigh's character twenty minutes into *Psycho* (1960). He also planned to make the second *Trek* movie a sequel to the classic episode "Space Seed," with Captain Kirk battling a revenge-crazed Khan Noonien Singh (Ricardo Montalban). Bennett's vision was to combine a rip-snorting action-adventure yarn with a thoughtful subplot in which Kirk (and the rest of the crew) grappled with the inevitable realities of aging and death. Nimoy liked this approach and signed on to appear in the movie.

Unfortunately, Bennett and writing partner Jack Sowards struggled to assemble a satisfactory script out of these elements. After four tries they farmed the screenplay out to Samuel Peeples (who had penned the second *Star Trek* pilot, "Where No Man Has Gone Before"), but the script Peeples delivered veered away from the original concept and eliminated Khan entirely. Finally, under intense deadline pressure, Nicholas Meyer stepped in. He agreed to direct the film and hastily assembled a screenplay that combined the best elements from Bennett and Sowards's first four drafts, ignoring the Peeples version. Meyer also inserted more humor into the dialogue. Bennett was elated with the result, but additional screenplay problems lay ahead.

When William Shatner read Meyer's script, he balked. Always protective of Kirk's heroic, virile persona (not to mention his own image), Shatner expressed concern over scenes in which Kirk donned eyeglasses and brooded about his fiftieth birthday. In his book *Star Trek Movie Memories*, Shatner admits that "I had to be dragged in, kicking and screaming" to the project. In addition to Shatner, DeForest Kelley and George Takei initially had misgivings about the Bennett-Sowards-Meyer screenplay as well, disappointed that McCoy and (especially) Sulu were relegated to the periphery of the story. Meyer made some minor modifications to the screenplay and smoothed the cast's ruffled feathers. But still greater revisions were forthcoming.

The Caged Bird

Cast members' qualms with the script were mild compared to the apoplectic reaction of Gene Roddenberry. The Great Bird had pitched his own concept for the film—a time-travel story in which the *Enterprise* journeys back to 1963 and tries to stop the assassination of President John F. Kennedy. Bennett politely refused this idea, primarily because the ending would be an anticlimax (history couldn't be changed, so the mission was destined to fail). Still nursing a bruised ego from this rejection, Roddenberry read through *Star Trek II* and erupted in outrage. He complained that the scenario was too violent, too militaristic, and "not *Star Trek*." He objected to virtually everything in the script. Most of all, however, Roddenberry abhorred the idea of killing Spock. NBC had attempted to eliminate the character from the show after "The Cage," but Roddenberry had stood his ground: There could be no *Star Trek* without Spock, he insisted. Roddenberry remained convinced that Spock's death would destroy the franchise. And, according to Bennett and Meyer, he tried to stop it from happening.

Even though the whole *Star Trek II* creative process was supposed to be shrouded in secrecy, Paramount was soon buried in an avalanche of letters from fans irate over Spock's impending demise. Nimoy also began receiving venomous hate mail. According to one account, Roddenberry's secretary, Susan Sackett, spilled the beans at a *Trek* convention in England. But Bennett and Meyer both blame Roddenberry for the leak. "He was furious," Bennett told an interviewer from the Trek Nation website. "Gene let the fanzines know that [we] were going to kill Spock and thousands of letters came in." Ironically, however, Roddenberry's efforts to derail *The Wrath of Khan* provided the impetus for changes that ensured its success.

Bennett faced a quandary. The leak had nullified the *Psycho*-style shock impact of Spock's death, but Nimoy had agreed to appear in the film primarily to play the death scene. To resolve this conundrum, Bennett again turned to Meyer. The director made a pair of brilliant revisions to the screenplay. First, the "Kobayashi Maru" training sequence, in which Starfleet cadets fight a simulated battle with the Klingons aboard a replica of the *Enterprise*, was moved from the middle of the story to the beginning. Spock would play dead as part of the simulation, allaying (it was hoped) fans' concerns over rumors of the character's demise. Meyer even included a joke to further defuse the scuttlebutt. "Aren't you dead?" Kirk asks Spock after the training session. Second, Spock's actual death was moved to the climax, where it has far greater emotional impact. These were pivotal changes. In its final form, *The Wrath of Khan* packs an emotional wallop it would not otherwise have delivered. Many fans entered the film worried about Spock's rumored death, were reassured by the opening scene, and forgot the rumors as the engrossing story progressed, only to be surprised (and moved) after all by Spock's heroic self-sacrifice.

Second Thoughts

In its final form, *Star Trek II: The Wrath of Khan* opens with Lieutenant Saavik (Kirstie Alley) leading the *Enterprise* bridge crew in a hopeless rescue mission. Spock and the other bridge officers are "killed" as part of a training simulation at Starfleet Academy, where Admiral Kirk is now stationed. Spock is training cadets, including his young half-Vulcan, half-Romulan protégé, Saavik. Meanwhile, Captain Terrell (Paul Winfield) and first officer Pavel Chekov (Walter Koenig) of the USS *Reliant* are searching for a lifeless planet to test an experimental terra-forming device known as Project Genesis. They stumble upon and are captured by Khan and the remnants of his genetically engineered, superhuman colony. Shortly after being exiled to an uninhabited world by Kirk (at the end of "Space Seed"), an astronomical disaster rendered the planet nearly uninhabitable and killed most of Khan's party, including his wife. Bent on revenge, Khan uses an alien parasite to gain mental control of Terrell and Chekov, takes control of the *Reliant*, and sets out to capture the Genesis device, which could also be used as a planet-destroying weapon. The *Enterprise*, crewed by Academy cadets, along with Kirk, Spock, McCoy, Sulu, and Uhura, is diverted from a routine training mission to investigate a cryptic message from research station Regula I, where Genesis was developed. The mission reunites Kirk with an old flame, Dr. Carol Marcus (Bibi Besch). Viewers also learn that Dr. Marcus bore him a son, David (Merritt Butrick), but denied him access to the child. Kirk and Khan fight a pair of skirmishes in space. Both ships are badly damaged in the first battle, and Spock sacrifices his life to avert the *Enterprise*'s destruction at the conclusion of the second encounter.

As shooting progressed, Bennett and Meyer realized they were on to something. The dailies were promising, the cast was happy, and Paramount executives were encouraged. In fact, the project was going so swimmingly that Bennett and Nimoy began to have second thoughts about Spock's death. If the movie was a hit and the series continued, both wanted flexibility to revive Spock. When it came time to shoot the emotional death scene, Bennett asked if Nimoy could improvise some bit of business that could serve as a "hinge" for future stories. Nimoy's solution was elegant: Before making the ultimate sacrifice, Spock mind-melds with the unconscious McCoy and whispers a single word: "Remember!" No one knew yet what this meant, but it opened numerous possibilities.

Meyer and editor William Dornish assembled an early cut of the film, which generated great enthusiasm from all the insiders who saw it. But how would fans and casual viewers respond? The next step was a test screening. Even though many of the effects shots from Industrial Light & Magic were not complete (the audience saw filmed storyboards in place of this footage), *Star Trek II* played to a select audience in the Paramount Theater on the studio lot. It went over beautifully—until the end, which left audiences in stunned, teary-eyed silence.

In this early version, the film concluded with Spock's funeral and Kirk's heartrending eulogy for his lost friend. ("Of all the souls I have encountered in my travels, his was the most . . . human.") There was no ambiguity regarding the Vulcan's fate. He was not is-he-or-isn't-he dead, not until-the-next-movie dead but, as the Coroner of Munchkin Land might declare, "really most sincerely dead." The audience's shell-shocked reaction did not bode well for the commercial prospects of the film, which otherwise looked to be a smash. Already, Bennett and Nimoy had hedged their bets with the "remember" business. Now they felt it was necessary to be overt about the possible resurrection of the character. Meyer objected vehemently, arguing that hinting at Spock's revival would make the Vulcan's death seem like a manipulative ploy. He suggested that Nimoy should read the famous *Star Trek* voice-over ("Space, the final frontier . . .") prior to the end credits rolling, an idea that was duly implemented. But Bennett wanted to go further. Against the furious protests of Meyer, who did not have final cut authority, Bennett shot some pickup footage to revise the ending of the picture, including Kirk's lines about "returning to this place." He also commissioned the concluding visual effects sequence, revealing Spock's coffin on the Genesis planet.

The revised *Wrath* was retested, and this time the audience responded with a rapturous ovation. Bennett believed that the new ending restored the sense of hope that is the eternal hallmark of the franchise. "I felt like all of us had done something right and noble," Bennett said in a documentary included on the *Wrath of Khan* DVD. "I know it sounds corny, but I walked out the theater that night saying 'Yeah, that's the way it should be.'"

This *TV Guide* ad for a network broadcast of *Star Trek II: The Wrath of Khan* billed the film as a clash between "two mortal enemies." But the film's tight budget and Montalban's *Fantasy Island* schedule prevented Kirk and Khan from meeting face to face.

What's in a Name?

To reach this point, Bennett and Meyer had cleared numerous obstacles.

Roddenberry continued to harangue Bennett over various aspects of the production. He objected to the redesigned, faux naval uniforms created by costume designer Robert Fletcher and to production designer Joe Jennings's re-dressed sets, which transformed the sleek, pristine *Enterprise* of *The Motion Picture* into a busier, more functional-looking ship. Bennett politely thanked Roddenberry for his input but implemented none of his suggested changes.

The picture's tight budget forced some creative compromises. Due to cost constraints and limitations on Montalban's availability (the actor had to return to his hit TV show *Fantasy Island*), a planned mano a mano slugfest between Kirk and Khan was scrapped. As a result, the two adversaries never meet face-to-face in *The Wrath of Khan*, which was a major disappointment to Shatner. Also, while ILM created marvelous visual effects for the picture, financial concerns forced Bennett to recycle a great deal of effects footage from *The Motion Picture*, especially during *Khan*'s first act.

Even the film's title was a source of conflict. Meyer had subtitled the picture *The Undiscovered Country*, a Shakespearean reference to death derived from the famous "to be or not to be" monologue in *Hamlet*. Paramount's marketing department wanted something more exploitable, so executives rechristened the film *Star Trek II: The Vengeance of Khan*. But that moniker raised the ire of 20th Century-Fox, because executives there considered it too similar to the already announced title of George Lucas's upcoming *Star Wars* film, *The Revenge of the Jedi*. To avoid possible litigation by Fox, Paramount removed *Vengeance* from the title of *Star Trek II* and replaced it with *Wrath*. The studio came to rue this decision when theater owners complained that moviegoers didn't know what "wrath" meant and when, at the last minute, Lucas retitled his film *The* Return *of the Jedi*. Nine years later, Paramount agreed to let Meyer use *The Undiscovered Country* in the title of *Star Trek VI*.

Reception

By any name, however, *Star Trek II* was a triumph.

The Wrath of Khan, released June 4, 1982, grossed nearly $79 million in the U.S. alone, becoming the sixth-biggest box-office attraction of the year in America. Counting international receipts, the film grossed $96.8 million—that's over $232 million in inflation-adjusted terms. Paramount earned untold millions more in ancillary revenue through the sale of action figures, T-shirts, and other tie-ins, which (in contrast with the first film) sold briskly, and with the sale of the movie's television broadcast rights.

Fans were jubilant, and even the critics were impressed. Janet Maslin of the *New York Times* said it all in the first line of her review: "Now, this is more like it!" Many critics who lambasted *The Motion Picture* turned an about-face and praised *The Wrath of Khan*. A few reviewers, notably Arnold Moss of the *Washington Post*, seemed to agree with Meyer about the film's revised ending. Moss complained that Spock's death seemed like a gimmick, "an unnecessary twist, which the filmmakers are obviously well-prepared to fudge in case the public demands another sequel." Which, of course, the public did.

The Wrath of Khan failed to earn any Academy Award nominations. However, at the 1982 Saturn Awards (bestowed annually since 1972 to honor achievement in science fiction, fantasy, and horror in film and television), *The Wrath of Khan* was nominated in eight categories and won two awards, Best Director for Meyer and Best Actor for Shatner. The movie was also nominated for a Hugo at the 1983 WorldCon but lost to director Ridley Scott's *Blade Runner.*

Assessing *The Wrath of Khan*

The Wrath of Khan offers everything its predecessor promised but failed to deliver. It's a thrilling, fast-paced sci-fi adventure rich in both sustained suspense and character exploration. The story wades into meaningful thematic currents on the way to a powerful emotional payoff. Not only is *Khan* a worthy successor to the television series, but in some respects it represents an improvement on the classic program. Not only is the movie far superior in all technical aspects (sets, costumes, special effects), as almost any feature film would be, but it's also better scripted, directed, and performed than the vast majority of the seventy-nine original episodes.

Although piecing it together was a painful process, the film's dramatic structure is masterful, with early scenes (especially those involving Khan) providing the initial thrust and events steadily gaining momentum as the story progresses. The dialogue is crisp and often witty, supplying both amusing bons mot (such as McCoy asking Kirk, as young Saavik steers the *Enterprise* out of space dock, "Would you like a tranquilizer?"), a Spock-McCoy verbal joust, and some eminently quotable ethical observations (including Spock's assertion that "The needs of many outweigh the needs of the few, or the one"). Best of all, where the classic series often settled for heavy-handed moralizing (and *The Motion Picture* came off as ponderous and self-important), *The Wrath of Khan* almost effortlessly addresses weighty, timeless concerns, such as aging and death. It also provides the franchise's definitive statement about the self-destructive folly of seeking revenge, a theme also present in a handful of classic episodes.

Meyer's direction is a model of narrative precision and clarity. While not renowned for his visual style, he includes several deep-focus compositions that greatly enhance the unfolding drama, particularly during Spock's funeral, as the black torpedo-coffin slowly glides toward the camera, flanked on either side by mourning crewmates.

Meyer also excelled at eliciting impressive, naturalistic performances from his cast. Shatner is outstanding as the aging Kirk, who must not only overcome a powerful adversary but make peace with his estranged son and cope with the loss of his closest friend. Shatner's performance wasn't achieved easily—in Meyer's autobiography, the director cops to shooting several takes of key scenes so that Shatner would become tired or bored, toning down the actor's tendency to overemote. Yet the resulting portrayal ranks among the least affected and most touching in Shatner's extensive filmography. Ricardo Montalban matches Shatner with a superb performance as Khan, playing a slightly more deranged version of the character than the one from "Space Seed."

Were it not for the scintillating performances of Shatner and Montalban, Nimoy would steal the film as the resolute Vulcan, whose death scene is

Kirstie Alley (front) left a favorable impression as the half-Vulcan, half-Romulan Saavik in *The Wrath of Khan*. Merritt Butrick, playing Kirk's son, David, was less effective.

everything the actor hoped for. Koenig, often underutilized on the series, shines in his unusually meaty role. The well-chosen supporting players also perform commendably. Alley, "introduced" here (five years prior to her *Cheers* stardom), seems competent and likeable as Saavik. Besch, a veteran television actress who later appeared in Meyer's *The Day After* (1983), appears credible both as a brilliant scientist and as Kirk's ex. The only weak link is Merritt Butrick in his underwritten role as Kirk's son. Fortunately, Butrick's screen time is limited.

The picture also benefits from a rousing score by James Horner, a young composer "discovered" by Meyer, who proved to be a capable replacement for Jerry Goldsmith. The movie isn't perfect (its biggest flaw may be that it wastes the characters of Uhura and Sulu), yet most fans and critics hail *Star Trek II: The Wrath of Khan* as the best *Star Trek* feature film. While this is true, that assessment sells the picture short. Taking a wider view, *Khan* stands among the most exhilarating science fiction adventure movies of the 1980s, alongside *The Empire Strikes Back* (1980), *The Road Warrior* (1981), *Blade Runner* (1982), *The Return of the Jedi* (1983), *The Terminator* (1984), *Aliens* (1986), and *Predator* (1987). For Bennett, it was also a tough act to follow.

4

A Leonard Nimoy Film

Star Trek III: The Search for Spock (1984)

Star Trek II: The Wrath of Khan had been in theaters for less than a week when Paramount Pictures CEO Michael Eisner phoned producer Harve Bennett with a simple message: Start planning *Star Trek III*.

That was the good news. The bad news was that, although the conclusion of the second *Star Trek* movie not-so-subtly hinted at the return of Spock and the continuation of the series, none of the cast members were under contract to appear in a third film. Entering preproduction for *Khan*, many insiders expected the second film to be the last, so no future provisions had been made. This left Bennett to recruit the *Enterprise* crew for another voyage. Most of them quickly re-upped, but not Leonard Nimoy.

Theoretically, the conclusion of *Star Trek II*—with Spock's body left on the Genesis Planet—left open numerous possibilities, including leaving the Vulcan dead or casting a younger actor to replace Nimoy as a regenerated Spock. But pursuing any of those options would have sparked a fan revolt. Trekkers wanted the real Spock (Nimoy) reunited with his comrades from the starship *Enterprise*. Bennett knew this, the studio knew it, and so did Nimoy.

Coup de Spock

Nimoy's willingness to work with Bennett to create a "hinge" for the next film (improvising the "remember" mind meld with McCoy just prior to Spock's death), combined with Bennett's insistence on adding new footage to create a more hopeful, upbeat ending to *The Wrath of Khan*, had placed the actor in a commanding position in negotiations with the studio. He could have demanded an astronomical salary, a hefty chunk of the profits, or other concessions, but Nimoy wanted just one thing from the third *Trek* film—the chance to direct.

Nicholas Meyer, who had helmed *Khan*, declined to participate in *Star Trek III*. He was still miffed at Bennett about the altered finale of *Star Trek II* and opposed the idea of reviving Spock. This created a vacancy in the director's chair. While he knew *Star Trek* inside out, Nimoy hardly possessed an extensive directorial résumé. By 1982, he had helmed two television episodes (including an installment of *Rod Serling's Night Gallery*) and *Vincent*, a telefilm adapted from his one-man play about Vincent van Gogh. Prior to *Star Trek III*, he would also direct an episode of William Shatner's police drama, *T. J. Hooker*. No one else with such meager credentials would have been considered to supervise a complex, multimillion-dollar production like *The Search for Spock*. But Nimoy remained adamant that he would appear in the film only if he could also direct it. (Meyer encouraged Nimoy to take this hard-line approach.) Paramount executives had to choose between two risky options: Either hand *Star Trek III* over to an unproven director or move forward without the franchise's most popular star.

The studio sent Nimoy mixed messages about their decision. At first Paramount's Gary Nardino, who would serve as executive producer for the third film, and studio chief Michael Eisner expressed enthusiasm for the idea of Nimoy directing. Nimoy left meetings with both men confident that a deal would soon be in place. Then, as the actor-director has recounted in many interviews, weeks dragged by while Nimoy heard nothing. No word from the studio to him, his agent, or his attorney. Silence. Finally, an increasingly impatient and agitated Nimoy, against the advice of his agent, broke down and phoned Eisner directly. Nimoy was shocked to learn that Eisner had decided against hiring him to direct the film because the CEO had heard that the actor hated Spock, hated *Star Trek*, and had it written into his contract for *Star Trek II* that Spock must die. Nimoy, flabbergasted, insisted none of those things were true and encouraged Eisner to check his contract for *Star Trek II* for confirmation. Eisner, relieved, assured Nimoy that that wouldn't be necessary. Nimoy was soon in receipt of a contract to direct and star in *Star Trek III*, which he speedily signed. The actor claims he has no idea about the source of Eisner's misinformation. However, these sorts of rumors about Nimoy had been circulating since the late 1970s, following the publication of the actor's misleadingly named memoir *I Am Not Spock* (1976).

Gaining Eisner's approval was only the first hurdle Nimoy had to leap as he moved from star to director. He was surprised to learn that some of his cast mates also had reservations. "They were uneasy because of the shift in dynamic, and they wondered, 'Why is Leonard being given this job?'" Nimoy wrote in his 1993 memoir, *I Am Spock*. "'Is this an ego trip, a lark, or is he really serious about this job?'" Fortunately, Nimoy eventually won over the cast with his openness, competence, and attention to detail. Although on *The Next Generation* and later TV series, cast members often directed episodes, no *Trek* actor had directed a *Star Trek* project prior to *The Search for Spock*.

Return to Genesis

With the contract drama concluded, Bennett and Nimoy began meeting to plot the story, which Bennett initially titled *Star Trek III: Return to Genesis*. The tentpole story points were self-evident: The movie had to explain what that "remember" business between Spock and McCoy was all about, had to depict Kirk and friends returning to Genesis planet to retrieve Spock's body, and had to conclude with the Vulcan somehow resurrected. Bennett and Nimoy agreed that the story needed a strong antagonist, and Nimoy suggested using the series' most popular villains, the Klingons (seen briefly at the beginning of *The Motion Picture* and unheard from since). Nimoy also told Bennett that he wanted the story to be "operatic"—full of high drama and big, emotional moments. Nimoy liked Bennett's suggestion that the Klingons' quest for the Genesis device could serve as a parallel with the nuclear arms race. Bennett, who received sole credit for the screenplay, reports that the script came together easily. He wrote the last scene first, backed into the rest of the narrative, and the pieces simply fell into place. It was a refreshing change from the agonizing process of writing the first two *Star Trek* films.

The story picks up where the previous film left off, as the battle-damaged *Enterprise* limps home, with Kirk, still mourning the loss of Spock and McCoy, behaving erratically for reasons unknown. Instead of the hero's welcome the young crew expects, Starfleet Command receives the returnees coolly and reveals

Front and back of a ticket to the San Francisco premiere of *The Search for Spock*. Note that, to preserve the "mystery" of the film's ending, Leonard Nimoy is listed as director but not as a member of the cast.

plans to decommission the twenty-year-old *Enterprise* in favor of new "trans-warp" vessels such as the *USS Excelsior*, a gleaming new craft parked alongside Kirk's ship in space dock. Then Spock's farther, Sarek, arrives and explains that his son likely shared his *katra* (essentially, his consciousness or soul) with another person prior to his death. Kirk realizes that McCoy has Spock's *katra* (passed through the "remember" mind meld), which accounts for the physician's strange behavior. Sarek explains that Kirk must bring Spock's body and McCoy to Vulcan, so a ritual can be performed to restore Spock. Unfortunately, Starfleet has quarantined the Genesis planet, so Kirk is forbidden from retrieving Spock's remains. Undaunted, he, Scotty, Sulu, and Chekov steal the *Enterprise* and risk their careers to travel to Genesis anyway. (This story element recalls the classic episode "The Menagerie," in which Spock hijacks the *Enterprise* and travels to the forbidden planet Talos IV for the benefit of Captain Pike.) Meanwhile, Lieutenant Saavik and Kirk's son, David, leading a scientific survey of the Genesis Planet, discover that the Genesis Effect has regenerated Spock, now a young child. However, the planet and the boy Vulcan are both aging rapidly and will soon die, due to a defect in the Genesis Process. Spock will survive only if he is removed from the planet. To further complicate matters, Klingon agents led by the ruthless Captain Kluge have learned of the Genesis device and grasp its potential as a weapon. They set out to Genesis to learn its secrets, setting up a confrontation with Kirk that will result in, among other ramifications, the death of Kirk's son and the destruction of the *Enterprise*. Ultimately, however, Spock is restored.

Roddenberry Strikes Again

The blockbuster success of *The Wrath of Khan* was a personal disaster for Gene Roddenberry, who had insisted that killing Spock would destroy the franchise. With a hit movie under his belt, Bennett was less inclined than ever to heed the advice of his famous "executive consultant." But that didn't stop Roddenberry from peppering the producer and Nimoy with memos excoriating the screenplay. In place of Bennett's scenario, the Great Bird pitched a slightly revised version of his JFK time-travel yarn, originally proposed for *Star Trek II*. He was passionately opposed to the destruction of the starship *Enterprise*, which he considered synonymous with *Trek* itself. Once again, Roddenberry allegedly tried to sabotage the proceedings by leaking Bennett's plans to destroy the *Enterprise*, a story element that, like Spock's death in *Wrath of Khan*, was supposed to remain secret. However, the ensuing fan write-in campaign was less vociferous this time and had no meaningful impact.

Part of Roddenberry's emotional reaction to the loss of the *Enterprise* was that he believed the iconic spacecraft would be replaced by the *Excelsior*. Roddenberry feared that Bennett was trying to remake the entire franchise in his own image, even down to Kirk's ship. Various accounts conflict regarding whether or not Bennett actually considered replacing the *Enterprise*, but a slightly modified version of the classic vessel, bearing the same name and the designation NCC-1701-A, would debut in the next film.

Bennett's biggest challenge wasn't static from Roddenberry, it was bringing in another sci-fi spectacular on a modest budget. Based on the strong performance of its predecessor, Paramount granted *Star Trek III* $18 million in production funds, a 50 percent increase over *Khan*'s $12 million cost. But most of the extra money went to Industrial Light & Magic, since the third film featured more extensive special effects footage than the second, including two space battles, the space dock sequence, and the climactic breakup of the Genesis planet, among other shots. Cast salaries also increased. Bennett and Nimoy were able to reuse sets, costumes, and props from the previous entries, saving some money, but the budget remained tight. The most significant budget-related sacrifice was that, aside from a single day of location shooting, the entire picture was filmed on Paramount soundstages. Originally, cinematographer Charles Correll hoped to shoot the picture in Hawaii. For the most part, Nimoy did an excellent job of disguising these limitations, but there was no hiding the cut-rate sets and costumes created for the climactic sequence on Vulcan.

Who's Who

Once Nimoy came on board, most aspects of *Star Trek III* came together more easily than with *Star Trek II*. The only area that presented greater problems was casting. Originally, Nimoy wanted actor James Edward Olmos to play the Klingon captain Kruge. But Paramount officials objected to casting the talented but then little-known actor (soon to gain fame on *Miami Vice* and later to star in the "reimagined" *Battlestar Galactica*) because Olmos was wiry and stood just 5-foot-9, hardly the imposing stature of a Klingon warrior. Nimoy stressed that he could make Olmos appear bigger through costuming and camera angles, but his arguments failed to convince the suits. Nimoy acquiesced, reluctant to throw his weight around on *The Search for Spock*, his first feature film. His second choice—Christopher Lloyd, best known for his loony portrayal of "Reverend" Jim Ignatowski on *Taxi*—also caused consternation, but the studio grudgingly agreed. At least Lloyd had the height for the part; he was 6-foot-1.

The next major casting issue was Lieutenant Saavik. Producers were unable to reach an agreement with Kirstie Alley to return as the half-Vulcan, half-Romulan character. So, reluctantly, Nimoy hired novice Robin Curtis for the role. Like Alley before her, Curtis received special "introducing" billing as Saavik. To portray legendary Vulcan leader T'Lar, Nimoy hired esteemed stage actress Dame Judith Anderson, but not without difficulty. Anderson at first declined the part but reconsidered after her grandson, a *Trek* fan, urged her to appear in the film. Merritt Butrick returned as Kirk's son, David Marcus, and Mark Lenard reprised his role as Spock's father, Sarek, from the classic episode "Journey to Babel." Notably, no effort was made to include Majel Barrett-Roddenberry as Christine Chapel. The character hadn't appeared in *Star Trek II*, either, perhaps to avoid further entanglements with her husband. In any case, Gene Roddenberry took his wife's absence from the cast as another personal affront.

With the cast assembled, production ran smoothly until very late in the schedule when a fire broke out on the Paramount soundstage where the Genesis planet scenes were being filmed. Cast and crew members, including William Shatner, pitched in to extinguish the blaze. Shatner, in his book *Star Trek Movie Memories* and elsewhere, explains that he worked enthusiastically to battle the fire because a ruined set would have threatened the shooting schedule, and if *Star Trek III* ran over schedule, it would have created a conflict with the start of shooting for Season Two of *T. J. Hooker*.

Truth in Advertising

During production, Bennett and Nimoy went to great lengths to keep two secrets, but in the end their efforts came to nothing.

The producer and director intended the destruction of the *Enterprise* to be a jaw-dropping surprise that would leave audiences stunned. This plan was compromised when the fan press learned about it. But it was completely undone by Paramount's publicity department, which included footage of the ship blowing apart in the movie's trailer and billed the film as "the final voyage

TV Guide Close-Up advancing the initial TV broadcast of *The Search for Spock*, on the Showtime Network. Paramount Pictures generated millions of additional revenue selling the television rights to the popular *Star Trek* movies.

of the starship *Enterprise*." Bennett and Nimoy were dismayed but powerless to alter the advertising campaign.

The duo also took extraordinary measures to protect the "secret" of Spock's return. Working copies of the script referred to the character as "Nacluv" (Vulcan spelled backwards), and daily call sheets listed Nimoy as "Frank Force." To further enhance the illusion that Spock might not appear in the movie, Nimoy's name was not included among the cast in the opening credits and not listed on the movie's poster or other promotional materials. But who were Bennett and Nimoy trying to kid? Rather than *Return to Genesis*, the studio had dubbed the film *The Search for Spock*. No moviegoer would walk into a movie called *The Search for Spock* without expecting Spock to be found. And while Nimoy's name wasn't listed among the film's cast, movie posters were dominated by a ghostly image of Spock's (Nimoy's) face.

Reception

Star Trek III: The Search for Spock, released June 1, 1984, was an immediate hit. The picture scored a stronger opening than *The Wrath of Khan*, grossing $2.4 million more than the previous film in its first week. *The Search for Spock* didn't have as much box-office endurance, however, pulling in a total of $76.5 million in the U.S. and $87 million worldwide, falling short of *Khan*'s $79 million domestic and $97 million worldwide earnings. In inflation-adjusted terms, *Star Trek III* grossed about 190 million bucks, another impressive haul. It was the ninth-biggest box-office attraction in the U.S. that year.

Nowadays, *The Search for Spock* is typically lumped in with the inferior odd-numbered entries in the series. However, most fans and critics praised the film upon its release. While it wasn't embraced as enthusiastically as *Khan*, it received the endorsement of most reviewers. Many critics singled out Nimoy's direction and the film's visual effects for praise. The Academy Awards overlooked *Star Trek III* as it had *Star Trek II*, but *The Search for Spock* earned six Saturn Award nominations. It was also nominated for a Hugo Award but lost to *The Return of the Jedi*. *The Search for Spock* featured the closing title ". . . And the Adventure continues . . . ." If nothing else, the picture left fans eager to see what would happen next. And it made enough money to ensure that the studio would green-light another installment, so fans could learn the answer.

Assessing *The Search for Spock*

The Search for Spock remains the most underrated entry in the *Star Trek* film series. Although it contains some disappointing passages, overall it's a solid, entertaining adventure that balances action and character development effectively and delivers a satisfying emotional payoff.

Many of the film's weaknesses are inherent in its position as the middle leg of an unplanned but emerging trilogy (the stories *of Star Trek*s *II, III* and *IV* link to form a single arc). *The Empire Strikes Back* aside, most middle thirds of trilogies are perfunctory entries that exist to resolve issues left open by the first picture and to set up events that play out in the third. *The Search for Spock* performs precisely these functions. And, like most Parts Two of Three, it is best judged within the framework of the larger story, which it serves well. Taken on its own merits, however, it has its distinct liabilities and assets.

Bennett's easily assembled screenplay may have come together *too* effortlessly. While it resolves all the lingering mysteries from *The Wrath of Khan*, it does so in predictable ways. There's nothing particularly thrilling or eye-opening about the story. The death of Kirk's son, David, registers little impact because audiences barely know the character, who again receives little screen time. Whatever emotional power the destruction of the *Enterprise* might have had was severely diminished by the film's advertising campaign. Perhaps the story's biggest drawback is that Spock is barely in it. (Nimoy has about three minutes of screen time.) But this was the toll to be paid for the previous film's famous finale. In general, the screenplay suffers from Nicholas Meyer's absence. The dialogue isn't as sharp, and some scenes fall flat. A sequence in which McCoy attempts to charter a ship to fly to the forbidden Genesis planet comes off as an embarrassingly poor imitation of the famous Mos Eisley cantina scene from *Star Wars*, in which Luke Skywalker and Ben Kenobi hire Han Solo to transport them to Alderaan. Also, while *The Search for Spock* delivers a toe-to-toe slugfest between Kirk and his adversary, something *Star Trek II* lacked, the fight itself plays like a leftover from the TV series. Plans for a more spectacular battle, fought among giant rocks shooting up from the surface of the dying planet, were scuttled when the hydraulic rocks failed to function properly. Finally, the picture contains too much stock footage from the previous film, beginning with a three-minute recap of Spock's demise and the conclusion of *The Wrath of Khan*. Spock's death scene is revisited three times in all, including a re-creation of it between the mind-melded Kirk and Sarek, with Sarek repeating Spock's dialogue. The film needed either the flashback prologue or this scene, but not both.

What it lacks in originality, however, Bennett's screenplay makes up for in construction. Its pace is quick, and one scene flows into the next with the kind of story logic that makes events seem inevitable. While his dialogue isn't as consistently crisp as Meyer's, Bennett's script contains some good lines, ranging from Kirk's opening log entry (in which he compares Spock's death to "an open wound") to Spock's touching, understated final words ("Jim. Your name is Jim."). Bennett also gives all the series regulars—including, this time, Uhura and Sulu—a moment to shine. Nimoy's direction is remarkably good for a rookie filmmaker, and his style proves very similar to Meyer's (straightforward, with little flash but a keen eye for composition and narrative clarity), bringing a sense of continuity to the series. Like Meyer, he also excels at working with actors and elicits mostly strong performances from the cast. Shatner follows up his fine work in *The Wrath of Khan* with another good outing, and Lloyd proves surprisingly effective as the merciless Kruge. Both Shatner and Lloyd deliver performances in the "operatic" register Nimoy wanted, but they are appropriate to the vehicle. DeForest Kelley tops them both with his multifaceted performance as the *katra*-carrying McCoy. Butrick, as David, seems more at ease here than in *Khan*. Anderson brings gravitas and dignity to her brief role as T'Lar, and James B. Sikking (from television's *Hill Street Blues*) delights in his small but amusing role as the smug commander of the USS *Excelsior*. Unfortunately, Curtis leaves much to be desired as Saavik, never displaying the command of the character Alley demonstrated in *Star Trek II*.

It adds up to a movie of far greater value than its lowly reputation as one of the "bad, odd-numbered ones" would indicate.

5

Breakthrough

Star Trek IV: The Voyage Home (1986)

Even though the third *Star Trek* feature netted slightly less for Paramount Pictures than the second, mostly due to its higher budget, there was never any question that the series would continue. At first, however, doubt surrounded whether or not the fourth installment would involve William Shatner, or any of the other original cast members.

That's because, entering contract negotiations for the film, Shatner demanded a sizable pay increase. Shatner and Leonard Nimoy's contracts contained a "favored nations clause," guaranteeing parity of pay and perks between the franchise's two stars. So if Shatner's pay increased, so did Nimoy's. Plus, agents for the other cast members typically negotiated fees that were, in effect, indexed to the salaries of Shatner and Nimoy. If the stars' pay went up 50 percent, the supporting players would demand a similar percentage increase (albeit of a much smaller salary number). The bottom line was that if Shatner's salary went up, everyone else's increased, too. This worried Paramount executives, who considered low production costs essential to the ongoing viability of the series. They questioned whether *Star Trek* could remain profitable with a higher payroll, especially since special effects costs continued to escalate. At the same time, the cast's advancing age was impossible to hide and had become a target for critics and stand-up comedians. James Doohan, Nichelle Nichols, and DeForest Kelley now little resembled the Scotty, Uhura, and McCoy from *Star Trek*'s never-ending reruns, and Shatner himself looked less and less like the James T. Kirk of the classic series.

In an attempt to solve both of the studio's problems at a stroke, producer Harve Bennett floated the idea of replacing the original crew. He suggested making a prequel set at Starfleet Academy, with younger performers stepping into the roles as youthful versions of Kirk, Spock, and the other characters. Although Bennett would later write a complete Starfleet Academy screenplay (see Chapter 19, "The Trek Not Taken"), his proposal was not developed at this time. The studio did, however, use the Academy concept as a negotiating ploy and convinced Shatner to sign on for a relatively reasonable $2 million. Overall cast salaries increased but were balanced out by a smaller-than-expected allowance for visual effects. In the end, Paramount budgeted *Star Trek IV* at $25 million—a moderate increase over the previous movie's $18 million cost.

Given his exemplary performance at the helm of *The Search for Spock*, Nimoy didn't have to twist arms to earn a second turn in the director's chair. In an interview included on the *Star Trek IV: The Voyage Home* DVD, Nimoy recounts that Paramount Chief Operating Officer Jeffrey Katzenberg encouraged him to make a *Star Trek* film that reflected his personal vision. "The training wheels are off," Katzenberg told Nimoy.

Murphy's Law

With the regular cast secured and a director on board, the next major task was developing a screenplay. Several story threads were left dangling at the conclusion of *Star Trek III*: Spock was back, but not quite himself; our heroes had been left without a starship; and Kirk and his crew were in deep guano after breaking seemingly every Starfleet regulation on the books. Nothing short of saving the world would get them off the hook this time. All these open issues needed to be resolved to clear the slate for future installments.

In their initial discussions, Bennett and Nimoy decided that the new film should involve time travel, like some of the classic series' most beloved episodes ("The City on the Edge of Forever," "Tomorrow Is Yesterday," etc.). Bennett proposed that the crew journey "back" to present-day Earth (circa 1986). This would not only control production costs but also enable the film to comment on current events. Nimoy suggested that, after two pictures filled with death and destruction, *Star Trek IV* should be lighter in tone, featuring less violence and more comedy, again like some of the classic series' most cherished episodes ("The Trouble with Tribbles," "A Piece of the Action," etc.). Then Nimoy hit on the ingenious idea of the ex-crew of the *Enterprise* venturing back in time to save humpback whales from extinction. The story elements were rapidly coalescing when an unexpected ingredient suddenly entered the mix—Eddie Murphy.

At the time, Murphy was emerging as a comedy superstar. The *Saturday Night Live* alum had made four films, all released by Paramount, beginning with *48 HRS.* in 1982. His most recent picture, *Beverly Hills Cop*, had been the highest-grossing film released in 1984, earning $235 million in America and $316 million worldwide. In all, his first four movies had collected a total of $371 million in the U.S. alone. After *Beverly Hills Cop*, Murphy had carte blanche at the studio. He was also a long-standing *Star Trek* fan. So when he expressed interest in appearing in the next *Star Trek* picture, Paramount executives seemed eager to accommodate him. The fact that Bennett and Nimoy already envisioned *The Voyage Home* as a comedy made the idea seem less far-fetched. The writing team of Steve Meerson and Peter Krikes was assigned to develop a screenplay based on the story outlined by Bennett and Nimoy, including a prominent role for Murphy.

Eventually, however, the Murphy-*Trek* crossover crumbled. When the trade papers reported that Murphy would appear in *Star Trek IV*, panicked fans began writing letters to Paramount, urging them to keep the comedian out of *Trek*. Trekkers, shaken by memories of comedian Richard Pryor's disastrous appearance in *Superman III* (1983), believed Murphy's presence would demean the franchise. Critic Leonard Maltin wrote that *Superman III* "trashed everything that Superman was about for the sake of cheap laughs and a co-starring role for Richard Pryor." Fans feared the same would happen to *Star Trek* if Murphy were involved. Studio chiefs were troubled by the vitriolic fan response and began to rethink the wisdom of placing both of its golden eggs in the same basket.

Meanwhile, Meerson and Krikes delivered a screenplay that disappointed both Bennett and Nimoy. In their script, Murphy would have played an eccentric college professor who believes in extraterrestrials and plays whale song in his classroom. This version would have included several notable deviations from the final film, including a sequence in which the Klingon Bird of Prey accidentally decloaks overhead during a Super Bowl halftime show and is mistaken for a special effect, and the revelation that Saavik is pregnant with Spock's child. (In the previous film, she mated with him on the Genesis Planet, while he was a regenerated and rapidly aging teenager undergoing his first *pon farr*.) In the end, Murphy withdrew from the project, skipping *Star Trek IV* to star in director Michael Ritchie's offbeat action-comedy *The Golden Child* (1986), in which Murphy's character sets out to free a young Tibetan boy with mystical superpowers. In subsequent interviews, Murphy expressed regret at appearing in *The Golden Child* instead of *The Voyage Home*.

Meyer to the Rescue (Again)

With Murphy's departure, Bennett and Nimoy found themselves with a rapidly approaching deadline and no usable script. So Dawn Steele, a Paramount executive and longtime friend of *Wrath of Khan* director Nicholas Meyer, called Meyer. Finally recovered from his sore feelings over Bennett's changes to *Star Trek II*, Meyer agreed to help. The two men divided the screenplay between them, with Bennett rewriting the sequences set in the future and Meyer reworking those set in the present day. Bennett and Meyer decided to combine three characters, including the one originally written for Murphy, into the new character of marine biologist Dr. Gillian Taylor (played by Catherine Hicks), who would also provide a romantic interest for Kirk. Since, coincidentally, this film, like Meyer's *Time After Time* (1979), was a time-travel story set in San Francisco, Meyer recycled some material cut from the earlier picture, including the famous sequence in which Kirk and Spock are annoyed by a punk rocker blasting music from a boom box.

In its final form, the story opens with Kirk, Spock, McCoy, Scotty, Chekov, and Uhura preparing to leave Vulcan and face Starfleet discipline for their actions in the previous film. Saavik remains on Vulcan. With the *Enterprise* blown to smithereens, Kirk and friends must travel home in their commandeered Klingon Bird of Prey. As they approach Earth, however, they discover that the planet is being destroyed by a massive, power-draining alien probe, which is transmitting indecipherable messages into the Earth's oceans. Spock and Uhura eventually determine that the alien probe is communicating in the song of humpback whales, a species hunted to extinction hundreds of years earlier. Kirk decides to take the ship back to the late twentieth century, capture a pair of humpbacks, and bring them forward in time to communicate with the aliens; otherwise, human civilization on Earth will be obliterated.

The trip into the past damages the rickety Bird of Prey. To accomplish their mission: Kirk and Spock must find a pair of humpbacks (luckily, two are on display at a nearby aquarium); McCoy and Scotty must find a way to synthesize "transparent aluminum," needed to convert the Bird of Prey's hold into a whale habitat; Sulu must gain access to a helicopter, needed to transport the aluminum; and Uhura and Chekov must siphon some photons from the nuclear reactor of an aircraft carrier in order to help repair the Bird of Prey's damaged dilithium crystals. Kirk and Spock make common cause with Dr. Taylor, a marine biologist from the aquarium, who fears for the safety of the whales, which are about to be returned to the sea at the height of whaling season. The only crew member to encounter serious difficulty is Chekov, who is injured while fleeing naval security. Kirk and McCoy, aided by Taylor, mount a rescue operation to save Chekov from the horrors of twentieth-century medicine. Eventually, the whales are beamed aboard and all the principles—even, in a twist, Taylor—journey to the twenty-third century so the humpbacks can respond to the alien probe. Earth is saved. In appreciation, Starfleet drops all charges against Kirk except

At the conclusion of *The Voyage Home*, our heroes get their first look at the gleaming new *Enterprise-A*. From left to right: Leonard Nimoy, George Takei, DeForest Kelly, Nichelle Nichols, James Doohan, and William Shatner.

one—disobeying a direct order. As "punishment" for this infraction, Kirk is busted from admiral back to captain and assigned to command a starship—the newly commissioned *Enterprise-A*.

This conclusion tied the dangling threads of the series' unplanned trilogy into a tidy bow. The script came together easily and rapidly, although Meyer and Bennett clashed again over the story's final act. Meyer vehemently opposed the idea of Dr. Taylor traveling into the future, even though *Time After Time* concluded with H. G. Wells's love interest, Amy Robbins (Mary Steenburgen), making a one-way trip into the past.

This time around, Bennett, Meyer, and Nimoy worked with relatively little interference from Gene Roddenberry. Although the Great Bird suggested an alternate time-travel story line—once again involving the assassination of John F. Kennedy—once that proposal was shot down, he made few waves. Ultimately, Meerson and Krikes proved more troublesome than Roddenberry. The screenwriters filed a dispute with the Writers Guild to earn screen credit on the film, even though Bennett insisted virtually nothing of their work remained in the final version. Meerson and Krikes won, and as a result, *The Voyage Home* bears a convoluted writing credit: "Story by Harve Bennett & Leonard Nimoy. Screenplay by Steve Meerson & Peter Krikes and Harve Bennett & Nicholas Meyer."

The cast enjoyed shooting *The Voyage Home* in part because, unlike most *Star Trek* pictures, it included a great deal of location work. From left to right: Walter Koenig, Leonard Nimoy, DeForest Kelley, William Shatner, Nichelle Nichols, and George Takei, filming on the streets of San Francisco.

Smooth Sailing (Mostly)

From all reports, *The Voyage Home* was the smoothest-running production of all the original-cast *Star Trek* features. Aside from the Murphy boondoggle, there were no problems casting guest actors. Shooting began on February 24, 1986, and wrapped ahead of schedule on May 5. To the delight of Paramount, Nimoy delivered the movie under budget by nearly a million dollars.

The cast enjoyed making the picture, not least because the story's contemporary setting allowed for extensive location work, something not possible on any previous *Trek* film. They also enjoyed the screenplay, which provided moments for each of the supporting characters to take center stage. Originally, the script included an additional highlight for Sulu, who would have met a young boy he recognizes as his distant ancestor. This scene had to be scrapped when the young actor froze before the cameras and was unable to perform. *The Voyage Home* also features the final appearance of Majel Barrett-Roddenberry as Christine Chapel. Now-Commander Chapel is briefly glimpsed amid the chaos at Starfleet headquarters during the movie's opening scenes. The present-day setting freed Paramount to incorporate some rare (for *Star Trek*) product placements. As a result, Captain Kirk drinks Michelob beer and Scotty uses an Apple computer.

Despite the relative ease of the production, the relationship between Bennett and Nimoy deteriorated throughout shooting, with the two men squaring off in a series of turf wars. At one point, Nimoy barred Bennett from the set. In retrospect, Nimoy believes the studio created these problems by sending mixed messages to the film's two creative forces, assuring both Bennett and Nimoy that each held ultimate authority. Tensions between the two men escalated further in postproduction, when Paramount, after viewing a rough cut of the film, asked Nimoy to subtitle the "dialogue" between the whales and the probe during the story's climax. Bennett was willing to acquiesce to studio pressure, but Nimoy, who feared any translation would render this vital sequence laughable, steadfastly refused. Meyer backed Nimoy. Eventually, the studio caved, and the film was issued without subtitles. Nimoy and Bennett agreed on at least one point: dedicating the film to the crew of the space shuttle *Challenger*, which exploded shortly after liftoff on January 28, 1986, while *Star Trek IV* was in preproduction. *The Voyage Home* opens with a touching title card written by Bennett, stating that the "courageous spirit" of the *Challenger* crew "will live to the 23rd century and beyond."

Reception

Released on November 26, 1986 (Thanksgiving weekend), *The Voyage Home* was a crossover smash that appealed to a much wider audience than *Star Trek*'s core fan base. *Star Trek IV* became the highest-grossing film of the series so far, raking in $109 million in America and $133 million total. It was the fifth-most-popular box-office attraction of the year in the U.S. Among other films, *The Voyage Home* outearned director James Cameron's *Aliens* ($86 million) in America, although *Aliens* outgrossed *Star Trek IV* overseas (making $183 million overall). *Star Trek* also outperformed Murphy's *The Golden Child*, which earned $80 million despite mixed reviews. *The Voyage Home* remained the franchise's top moneymaker until director J. J. Abrams's blockbuster reboot *Star Trek* in 2009.

The Voyage Home also received a warm critical reception, gathering enthusiastic notices from reviewers across the U.S., including the usually skeptical critics at the *New York Times*, *Washington Post*, and *Newsweek*. Trekkers loved the film, and the picture's broad appeal went a long way toward making *Star Trek* socially acceptable with general audiences. Many viewers who claimed not to like *Trek* enjoyed *The Voyage Home*. Even Oscar smiled on the film, which earned four Academy Award nominations (for its cinematography, music, sound, and sound effects), although it failed to bring home a statuette. The movie was also nominated for an award by the American Society of Cinematographers. At the Saturn Awards, *The Voyage Home* and *Aliens* were both nominated in eleven categories. *Star Trek* won the trophy for Best Costumes, but *Aliens* won everything else. At the 1987 WorldCon, *The Voyage Home* received a Hugo nomination as Best Dramatic Presentation but lost again to *Aliens*.

Assessing The Voyage Home

No *Star Trek* movie is more pure fun than *The Voyage Home*. It's bright, funny, upbeat, comedic science fiction, filled with charming character moments and laced with a cogent ecological message. There are very few SF films anything like it.

For *Star Trek* fans, the picture serves as a gratifying conclusion to the informal trilogy that began with *The Wrath of Khan* and continued with *The Search for Spock*. As indicated by its popularity among non-Trekkers, however, *Star Trek IV* also works brilliantly as a stand-alone feature. Very few third films in a trilogy can make this claim. *The Voyage Home* also stands apart from other entries in the *Star Trek* series—and most other sci-fi pictures in general—in its simplicity and lack of flash. For instance, while the film boasts outstanding visual effects, they are uncommonly subtle—nothing like the spectacular outer space shootouts from the previous two films. Perhaps the highest compliment that can be paid to the picture's special effects artists is that many moviegoers never realized that no actual whales were filmed during the creation of this movie. Instead, effects artists brought the animals to life using miniature models and animatronic replicas. Similarly, few viewers could have guessed that the oceangoing scenes were actually shot in a giant water tank in the Paramount parking lot. The movie's sound design is no less subtle or persuasive, particularly the much-debated "dialogue" between the whales and the probe.

The lack of visual panache enables viewers to concentrate on the story and the characters, both of which are finely wrought. The narrative structure is sound, with a credible dramatic threat undergirding the mostly comic events of the mission itself. With Meyer back in the fold, the dialogue sparkles, especially during the 1986 sequences. The film is almost overloaded with offhanded moments of fish-out-of-water hilarity, such as Spock asking Kirk, after the two have been refused entry on a bus, "What does it mean—'exact change?'" or Scotty trying to converse with an Apple desktop the same way he talks to the *Enterprise* computer. The supporting cast is seen to greater advantage here than in any other *Star Trek* feature, and no other original cast movie better highlights the dynamic relationship of the Kirk-Spock-McCoy trio, or the diverse but brilliantly meshed performance styles of Shatner, Nimoy, and Kelley. All these strengths are enhanced by Nimoy's seamless, story-first direction. His accomplishment here is especially impressive since, unlike the last film, he also had a great deal of screen time in this picture. The experience of directing and starring in the same film was so physically and mentally exhausting for Nimoy, who was forced to endure hours in the makeup chair each day in addition to his many other duties, that he never again directed a movie in which he appeared.

Star Trek IV: The Voyage Home is simply a delight. Its runaway success had a couple of major consequences.

First, it firmly established Nimoy as a bankable director. This status would be confirmed the following year when he helmed *Three Men and a Baby*, starring Tom Selleck, Ted Danson, and Steven Guttenberg. This Americanization of a 1985 French comedy (*Trois Hommes et un Couffin*) went on to become the top-grossing movie of 1987, earning a staggering $168 million in the U.S. alone. Nimoy remained an in-demand filmmaker until the box-office failure of his Gene Wilder

Critics Gene Siskel and Roger Ebert, like most reviewers, gave *Star Trek IV: The Voyage Home* two thumbs up.

comedy *Funny About Love* in 1990. His busy directorial career altered the course of events in the *Star Trek* franchise.

Second, the wide appeal of *The Voyage Home* strengthened the resolve of Paramount executives to move forward with an ambitious but risky venture they had been considering for some time: *Star Trek*'s return to television.

6

The Offspring

Creating *The Next Generation*

I n the early 1970s, when fans first began bombarding Paramount Pictures
with letters demanding the return of *Star Trek*, the studio nixed the idea
of reviving the series in part because it feared new episodes would erode
the value of the show's wildly profitable syndicated reruns. For Paramount, the
original program was a perpetual revenue machine, raking in millions of dollars
annually without a dime in production costs, and (thanks to the studio-friendly
contracts of the 1960s) with virtually no residual payments to the cast and crew.

Eventually, however, the market for *Star Trek* reruns began to cool. By the
time *Star Trek IV: The Voyage Home* reached theaters in 1986, the classic series had
been running in syndication for seventeen years, playing five nights a week in
many cities. There was a limit to how many times even the most devoted Trekkers
could watch the same seventy-nine episodes. Besides, while it wouldn't receive an
official home video release until 1989, many fans owned VCRs and had taped the
entire series. Also, the increasing technical sophistication and elaborate visual
effects of more recent science fiction films, including the *Star Trek* movies, made
the classic series seem quaint. For all these reasons, the show's ratings gradually
declined. Many stations switched *Star Trek* from nightly to weekly broadcasts.
Others dropped it altogether. Paramount realized that if it wanted to continue
to draw riches from its *Trek* gold mine, it would have to open a new vein.

Roddenberry Redux

With this in mind, in early 1986 Paramount Television boss Mel Harris began
to assemble the players who would orchestrate *Star Trek*'s return to the small
screen. Accounts differ regarding the earliest stages of this process. According
to some sources, including David Alexander's authorized biography of Gene
Roddenberry, Paramount approached the Great Bird and asked him to create
and oversee the new series. Roddenberry declined, worried that the new program would detract from the original, and concerned about the physical and
emotional wear and tear of returning to weekly production. So the studio
approached other producers. According to Edward Gross and Mark Altman's
book *Captains' Logs*, however, Paramount came to Roddenberry only *after*
Leonard Nimoy turned Harris down due to conflicts with his then-thriving directorial career and producers Sam and Greg Strangis delivered an unsatisfactory

Spock, I authorize shore leave for the crew here in Phoenix.

Yes, captain, it's a truly fascinating environment.

STAR TREK

WEEKNIGHTS AT 6. 15

KNXV-TV

In the mid-1980s many television stations, including KNXV-15 in Phoenix, still ran classic *Star Trek* episodes every Monday through Friday. But as ratings began to decline, the demand for fresh *Trek* product increased.

proposal. The Strangises' rejected outline operated on the same wavelength as Harve Bennett's Starfleet Academy concept and featured a crew of fresh-faced cadets. Roddenberry entered (or reentered) the picture in late September 1986, shortly after the Strangis treatment was discarded. Since he still owned a half-interest in the franchise, sooner or later the studio would have had to cut some sort of deal with Roddenberry to move forward with the new program.

If he initially balked at the prospect of a new *Star Trek*, the Great Bird was well motivated for a return to his old perch. The potential financial rewards were significant, of course. Perhaps as importantly to Roddenberry, the new series offered him a chance to make up for slights suffered at the hands of Paramount executives in recent years and to correct the "damage" (as he saw it) done to the franchise by the recent feature films, which he considered too militaristic and "not *Star Trek*." After spending the past six years as an "executive consultant" on the *Trek* movies, and wielding about as much directional control as a hood ornament, Roddenberry demanded complete creative authority over the new series. Reluctantly, Harris agreed. Then Roddenberry began to fashion a new show that would more fully reflect his vision of *Star Trek*—less bellicose and more uplifting in tone and spirit.

Another reason Roddenberry agreed to do the new series was because he wouldn't have to deal with headache-inducing network censors this time around; *The Next Generation* would be produced for first-run syndication. This wasn't the original plan. Harris had spent most of the summer of 1986 trying to find a network home for the program. The new *Trek* series represented a major investment for the studio, with production costs running about $1.2 million per episode ($2.4 million in inflation-adjusted terms). Network licensing fees would have helped defray some of those costs, but Paramount demanded that broadcasters commit to a full season, twenty-six installments, up front. NBC, CBS, and ABC passed, dubious of the potential ratings for a *Star Trek* series not including Kirk, Spock and McCoy. The fledgling Fox network gave the show serious consideration but would commit to buying only thirteen episodes, with a subsequent order of thirteen more installments dependent on the program's performance in the Nielsen ratings. Finally, in early August, Harris decided to proceed without a network partner. Paramount would market the new series directly to the hundreds of stations already airing *Star Trek* reruns, some of which had been clamoring for new *Trek* product for nearly two decades. And it offered those stations a sweetheart deal: They could have the series for free, but Paramount would control seven of the twelve minutes worth of commercial airtime included in every episode. The studio sold those seven minutes to national advertisers. Local stations made money by selling the remaining five minutes of airtime.

Future Perfect

To assist with the creation of the new *Star Trek*, Roddenberry called upon key collaborators from the old one, including coproducer Robert Justman, postproduction supervisor Edward Milkis, costume designer William Ware Theiss, and screenwriter David Gerrold (author of "The Trouble with Tribbles"). Roddenberry utilized many ideas derived from Gerrold's 1973 book *The World of Star Trek*, which pointed out several conceptual weaknesses in the classic series, such as the foolish practice of sending all the senior officers on dangerous away missions. Gerrold also suggested that the ship's officers should include a counselor to help crew members cope with the psychological rigors of a lengthy deep-space mission. Later, Roddenberry engaged former story editor Dorothy Fontana to write the series' pilot teleplay.

Roddenberry refused to accept a simple rehash of the original program. He wanted the new show to be as distinct as possible from its parent, while remaining recognizable as *Star Trek*. To balance these competing needs for distance and continuity, he decided the new series should be a sequel. However, it took a while to decide how much time should have elapsed between the classic series and the new one. At first, the plan was to set the new show in the twenty-fifth century, about 150 years later than Captain Kirk's adventures. Eventually, the setting was changed to the twenty-fourth century, about a hundred years post-Kirk. Several titles were considered, including *Star Trek: The New Adventure, Star Trek: Enterprise VII,* and *Star Trek: A New Beginning,* before the familiar *Star Trek: The Next Generation* was finally chosen. Paramount officially announced the new series on October 10, 1986, less than a month past the twentieth anniversary of the first series' premiere broadcast.

For Roddenberry, *Star Trek* had always served, first and foremost, as a vehicle for promoting his progressive philosophy, including his belief in the perfectibility of the human race. He believed that the *Trek* feature films had strayed from this mission and tried to put the franchise back on course with *The Next Generation*. Since the new series was set a century later than the original, he believed it should reflect the ongoing maturation of our species. Starfleet officers of the twenty-fourth century would be of even higher moral caliber than their twenty-third-century counterparts; therefore, Roddenberry forbade the depiction of interpersonal conflicts among the crew. Technology would be more sophisticated and more reliable, so he also banned plots based on mechanical malfunctions. And, since humans would have expanded farther into the galaxy, Roddenberry insisted that stories deal with different alien species than those featured in the classic program. This meant no Vulcans, Klingons, or Romulans, since these no longer qualified as "new life and new civilizations." All of these directives, which created difficulties for the show's writers, were eventually modified or abandoned, but they reflected Roddenberry's determination to steer the franchise back toward his utopian vision of the future.

Bringing the Vision into Focus

While Roddenberry, Justman, Gerrold, and producers Herb Wright and Robert Lewin bashed out the overall concept for the series, a carefully selected team of craftsmen and artisans, supervised by Milkis, began to design and build it.

Production designer Andrew Probert created both the exterior and interiors of the "Galaxy Class" *Enterprise-D* and other spacecraft during the show's first season. His *Enterprise* was larger yet sleeker than its twenty-third-century predecessor. Inside, the ship was far more spacious and so finely appointed that some wags complained the vessel resembled a spacefaring Ritz-Carlton. Probert was ably assisted by art director Herman Zimmerman and artists Rick Sternbach and Michael Okuda, who redesigned many props, including the updated phasers and tricorders. All three quickly became important contributors to the franchise and coordinated with the writing staff to assure consistency in the show's

LOYAL TO THE ORIGINAL CREW OF THE ENTERPRISE

Some fans of classic *Trek* felt betrayed by *The Next Generation*, since the series did not involve Kirk, Spock, and McCoy. This bumper sticker, produced in the late 1980s, says it all.

Treknobabble. Zimmerman went on to earn four Emmy nominations and to design the Deep Space Nine space station.

Costume designer Theiss, one of the key veterans of the classic series, ignored the naval-inspired maroon garments created for the feature films and developed a slick-looking update on his iconic gold, red, and blue uniforms from the original program. Although the traditional colors were retained, the departments signified by the colors changed, with red now indicating command and gold now designating operations and security. Blue continued to identify science and medical personnel. Theiss's most controversial creation for the new series was the "skant" uniform—a unisex, one-piece garment featuring a short skirt, worn by both male and female crewmembers. Deanna Troi appears in a skant in the pilot episode, "Encounter at Farpoint." The skant was seen occasionally, worn by background characters, in other Season One adventures but was abandoned in later years.

Roddenberry contracted with George Lucas's Industrial Light & Magic, which had supplied visuals for most of the *Trek* movies, to work on the series pilot and hired supervisors Dan Curry and Rob Legato to oversee the creation of the extensive special visual effects needed on a weekly basis thereafter. *The Next Generation* was rapidly taking shape. Meanwhile, Roddenberry and the writing team were busily imagining who would wear the costumes, occupy the sets, and handle the props that were being designed.

A New Crew

It was a given that the aging and expensive original cast would not be involved in the new series. From the outset, both Roddenberry and Paramount also wanted *The Next Generation* to feature a large ensemble. This stood in contrast to the original *Trek*, which, like most shows of its era, had been dominated by a few stars. *Next Gen* was designed to balance the story focus among a wider assortment of characters. There were both creative and practical reasons for this approach, which had been popularized by hit programs such as *The Waltons* (1972–81), *Hill Street Blues* (1981–87), and *Cheers* (1982–93). The ensemble format opened additional story possibilities for screenwriters and reassured producers, since the series could continue even if key cast members departed or died—as happened over the lifetime of all three of those programs.

In filling out the roster for the new crew, Roddenberry revisited his concepts for the aborted *Star Trek: Phase II* series, which had transformed into *Star Trek: The Motion Picture*. The *Next Gen* crew, like the one seen in *The Motion Picture*, would include an experienced captain (Julien Picard, replacing James T. Kirk), a dynamic young first officer (Commander William Ryker, stepping in for Willard Decker), and a sexy female alien (Betazoid Counselor Deanna Troi, in place of Deltan Lieutenant Ilia). In a thinly veiled attempt to revive Questor, the robotic protagonist from Roddenberry's failed 1970s pilot *The Questor Tapes*, Roddenberry added an android to the bridge crew—Lieutenant Commander

Data. The character was intended to function as an equivalent to Spock, capable of providing detached commentary on humanity's strengths and weaknesses from an alien perspective.

Roddenberry was deeply impressed by tougher-than-leather Private Vasquez (Jenette Goldstein) from *Aliens* (1986) and created a Latina security chief, Lieutenant Macha Hernandez, in her image. The Great Bird also decided to make the ship's chief surgeon a woman and named the character Beverly Crusher. In what proved to be a controversial move, Roddenberry and his team decided that twenty-fourth-century Starfleet vessels should also carry officers' children. This seemed to open promising potential stories about the challenges of growing up in outer space. To explore these narrative possibilities, the widowed Dr. Crusher was given a teenage daughter, Leslie Crusher.

To broaden the diversity epitomized by the *Enterprise* crew, Roddenberry created a handicapped bridge officer—the blind Lieutenant Geordi La Forge. At first, Geordi served as the ship's navigator, because Roddenberry did not envision the *Enterprise*'s chief engineer as an important character. (Roddenberry had tried to eliminate Scotty after *Star Trek*'s second pilot, "Where No Man Has Gone Before," because he considered the character superfluous. Because James Doohan was already under contract, Scotty was retained.) During *The Next Generation*'s debut season, various actors appeared as the ship's engineering chief. Roddenberry named Geordi in memory of quadriplegic Trekker George La Forge, a "superfan" whose devotion to the show was renowned in the *Trek* fan community. Roddenberry formed a personal friendship with La Forge, who passed away in 1975.

Finally, despite Roddenberry's initial aversion to all things Klingon, Justman suggested adding "a Klingon marine" to the bridge crew. Justman argued that the character's presence on the *Enterprise* and the depiction of the Federation and the Klingons as allies rather than enemies would provide a perfect illustration of the social advances made from the original show to *The Next Generation*. Roddenberry was skeptical at first and deliberated for weeks before finally giving his approval. Once the crew was complete, all that remained was to find the actors who would bring these characters to life.

A New Cast

As the casting phase began, Milkis departed and was replaced by young Paramount executive Rick Berman. Even though he knew little about *Star Trek* before joining the team, within a few seasons Berman would replace Roddenberry as the show's driving creative force. In December 1986, he, Roddenberry, Justman, and casting director Junie Lowry set out to identify eight talented but little-known performers who would comprise the show's core ensemble. Producers were looking for unknowns primarily because they couldn't afford to hire established stars, but also because it was feared that actors already identified with other characters would seem out of place in the

Star Trek universe. (These concerns were borne out decades later. When Scott Bakula was cast as Captain Jonathan Archer on *Enterprise*, many fans carped, "What's the guy from *Quantum Leap* doing on *Star Trek*?") Finding actors who suited the characters and also demonstrated chemistry as a unit was an arduous process for the producers and a nerve-wracking one for the performers, most of whom were called back for a grueling series of interviews and auditions. Several notable actors were in the running for the show's lead roles. And in some cases, the characters were reimagined to suit the talent hired.

The captain proved to be especially difficult to cast, in part because Roddenberry wanted to emphasize Picard's Gallic lineage (which supposedly included Jacques Cousteau) by hiring a French speaker for the role, or at least someone who could do a convincing French accent. Early on, Patrick Bauchau, a Belgian actor who had worked primarily in France, was considered a favorite to

A new crew for a new series, from left to right: Wil Wheaton as Wesley Crusher, LeVar Burton as Geordi La Forge, Marina Sirtis as Deanna Troi, Jonathan Frakes as William Riker, Patrick Stewart as Jean-Luc Picard, Gates McFadden as Beverly Crusher, Michael Dorn as Worf, Denise Crosby as Tasha Yar, and Brent Spiner as Data.

win the role. Later, veteran American television actor Stephen Macht emerged as a strong candidate. Others considered for the part included Roy Thinnes, who had starred in *The Invaders*, a sci-fi series produced by Quinn Martin in 1967–68, and Yaphet Kotto, best remembered as James Bond villain Mr. Big in *Live and Let Die* (1973) and as Parker in *Alien* (1979). But Roddenberry and Berman weren't sold on any of these options. Then, in early 1987, Justman saw Royal Shakespeare Company veteran Patrick Stewart perform at an acting workshop at UCLA and enthusiastically recommended the actor for the role. Despite Stewart's decidedly British accent (not what Roddenberry envisioned) and unmistakably bald head (hard to sell to Paramount executives), Justman believed Stewart projected the rare combination of commanding presence and inner warmth needed for the role. Berman agreed, but Roddenberry remained reluctant. "Gene did not like the idea of a bald English guy taking over and stepping into the shoes of William Shatner," Rick Berman said in a 2006 interview for the Archive of American Television. "He acknowledged what a wonderful actor Patrick was; he just wasn't his image of who the captain should be." But after auditioning more than fifty actors, Berman said, "nobody was even close to Patrick." So, in the absence of any better alternatives, Roddenberry caved and agreed to go with Stewart. "Once he decided Patrick was the character, he wrote the character for Patrick," Justman told author Larry Nemecek for his *Star Trek: The Next Generation Companion*. This explains why Captain Jean-Luc (formerly Julien) Picard sips Earl Grey instead of Bordeaux.

Selecting the *Enterprise*'s second-in-command was no easier task. Jonathan Frakes endured a half-dozen auditions before winning his role as Commander William Riker (note the new spelling). Frakes was then best known for his work in a pair of highly rated historical miniseries (*North and South*, 1985, and *North and South Book II*, 1986) and a recurring role on the nighttime soap *Falcon Crest* in 1985. Roddenberry identified Frakes as his choice for the part early on and met with the actor privately to coach him before his later auditions. To win the role, Frakes had to outperform a clutch of other candidates who were initially favored by Paramount. These included Vaughn Armstrong, who became a frequent guest star in various *Trek* series, often appearing under heavy makeup. He played a Klingon, a Romulan, a Borg, and two different Cardassians before winning the recurring role of Admiral Maxwell on *Star Trek: Enterprise*. Also considered as Number One was the dashing William O. Campbell, who landed the title role of the Season One episode "The Outrageous Okona," and the versatile Jeffrey Combs, who later won recurring roles on *Deep Space Nine*, where he appeared as both the Ferengi Brunt and the Vortan Weyoun, and on *Enterprise*, where he played the Andorian Shran.

British actress Marina Sirtis auditioned for the role of security chief Hernandez, and Denise Crosby tried out for the part of Counselor Troi. Roddenberry was impressed with both women but decided to flip their roles, hiring Sirtis as Troi and Crosby as the security chief, whose name and ethnicity were changed to suit the actress's blonde hair and blue eyes. Others considered as the *Enterprise* security chief included Rosalind Chao, who went on to play Miles O'Brien's wife, Keiko, on *The Next Generation* and *Deep Space Nine.*

Texan Brent Spiner earned his role as Data over a field of aspirants that also included Eric Menyuk, who later appeared on *Next Gen* as the mysterious extraterrestrial known only as the Traveler. Spiner was an experienced stage actor who had recently moved to Hollywood and had a recurring role on the sitcom *Night Court.* Fellow Texan Michael Dorn, who had extensive television experience (mostly in small roles), was hired to play the "Klingon marine" eventually named Worf. His competition included Avery Brooks, who later played Commander Benjamin Sisko—Worf's boss—on *Deep Space Nine.* Ohioan Gates McFadden, a versatile theatrical performer and puppeteer with training in mime and dance, auditioned for the series on a lark and won the part of Dr. Crusher. Others competing for the role included British actress Jenny Agutter, best remembered for her costarring roles in *Logan's Run* (1976) and *An American Werewolf in London* (1981).

At the time, the most recognizable name among *The Next Generation* cast was LeVar Burton, who, like Patrick Stewart, came highly recommended by Bob Justman. The two had worked together on a failed series pilot, *Emergency Room,* in 1983. Burton remained best known for his heartrending, Emmy-nominated portrayal of Kunta Kinte, a young African shipped to America and sold into slavery during the opening installment of the groundbreaking miniseries *Roots* (1977). He was also widely recognized as the host of the acclaimed PBS children's program *Reading Rainbow,* which began in 1983 and continued until 2006. However, apart from *Reading Rainbow,* Burton's career had slowed in the 1980s, enabling Roddenberry to acquire his services at an affordable rate. Other actors who auditioned for the role included Tim Russ, who later portrayed Vulcan security officer Tuvok on *Voyager,* and a young Wesley Snipes.

Apart from Burton, the highest-profile member of the cast in 1987 was fifteen-year-old Wil Wheaton, who had earned rave reviews for his performance in Rob Reiner's *Stand by Me* (1986), a dark coming-of-age picture based on a Stephen King novella. Despite a disastrous first audition, Wheaton was called back and soon won the role of Dr. Crusher's offspring. When Wheaton was hired, Leslie Crusher became Wesley Crusher. Roddenberry, Berman, and company were thrilled to add Wheaton, who was one of the most sought-after young actors in Hollywood at the time. Both Burton and Wheaton, coincidentally, were devoted fans of the classic series.

On May 15, 1987, Paramount issued a press release to introduce the show's freshly signed cast. The announcement mentioned that *The Next Generation* had been sold to 150 stations across the U.S., serving 90 percent of American households. Millions of viewers were eager to see how the new show—and the new cast—stacked up against the old one. Before a single script had been written, it was clear that *Next Gen* would be walking in the footsteps of giants. This was a far more intimidating prospect than going where no man had gone before.

7

Rightful Heirs

The Pre-*Trek* Careers of the *Next Generation* Cast

The ensemble assembled by Gene Roddenberry, Bob Justman, and casting director Junie Lowry to star in *The Next Generation* included no major stars, but it boasted many gifted and seasoned performers. Most had delivered outstanding work in vehicles that were soon eclipsed by *Star Trek*. Although little remembered today, these prior efforts—along with their performances in auditions and interviews—helped actors win their career-defining roles on the new series.

Patrick Stewart

For many reasons, Captain Jean-Luc Picard was the most difficult role to cast. (For an overview of the *Next Generation* casting process, including other performers considered for major roles, see the preceding chapter.) After scores of auditions and much debate, Roddenberry selected forty-seven-year-old British actor Patrick Stewart, even though Stewart wasn't what he had in mind when he first imagined the character. Roddenberry chose wisely.

Born in Mirfield, Yorkshire, on July 13, 1940, Stewart enrolled in his first acting course at age eleven. For the young performer, acting was both a creative outlet and a means of escape from his physically and emotionally abusive father. Stewart quit school at age fifteen and, after short stints as a newspaper reporter and a furniture salesman, enrolled in Bristol's Old Vic Theatre School in 1957. During his two years at the Old Vic, Stewart lost both his thick Northern accent and most of his hair. Surprisingly, however, baldness often worked in the actor's favor. After graduating from the Old Vic program, the versatile Stewart was often hired because he could play two characters in the same production— one bald and one wigged, usually of widely disparate ages. At age twenty-one, he joined the Old Vic touring company, which played theaters throughout England, Australia, South America, and elsewhere. Throughout this period, he appeared in countless Shakespearean and classical roles, and met his first wife, choreographer Sheila Falconer. In 1966, Stewart joined the Royal Shakespeare Company, where he performed until 1982, rising from supporting parts to leading roles. During his tenure with the RSC, he became involved with the Alliance for Creative Theater Education and Research (ACTER), teaching classes and hosting workshops in the U.S.

Although performing with the Royal Shakespeare Company was prestigious, it was not well paying. In the mid-1970s, Stewart (who by then was supporting a wife and two children) made just $400 per week. To supplement his income he appeared in British film and television productions. Among other roles, he played Vladimir Lenin in *The Fall of Eagles* (1974), a thirteen-part BBC miniseries about the collapse of the Romanov, Habsburg, and Hohenzollern dynasties of Russia, Germany, and Austria-Hungary; he appeared (under a toupee) as the romantic lead in *North and South* (1975), a four-episode BBC miniseries not to be confused with the later ABC miniseries of the same title; and he portrayed Sejanus in *I, Claudius* (1976), another well-received BBC miniseries set in ancient Rome. He is particularly impressive as Sejanus, the conniving, power-hungry commander of the imperial guard who ruthlessly murders political rivals and curries favor with but then plots against the emperor. When Sejanus's plots are discovered and he's taken captive in the chambers of the Roman Senate, he accepts his fate with an insolent smirk.

Star Trek wasn't Stewart's first TV series. He starred in the BBC's *Maybury* (1981–83), playing a psychiatric consultant employed at the provincial Maybury General Hospital. When the series concluded, Stewart decided to leave the RSC permanently and seek more lucrative employment in Hollywood. At first, however, his career seemed to take a step backward. He was excited to win the role of Gurney Halleck in director David Lynch's much-anticipated adaptation of the science fiction masterpiece *Dune* (1984), but all of Stewart's best scenes were deleted and the movie flopped. After playing major roles in prestigious British television productions and secondary characters in major features such as *Excalibur* (1981), Stewart found himself confined to forgettable supporting parts in low-rent pictures such as *Lifeforce, The Doctor and the Devils, Code Name: Emerald,* and *Wild Geese II* (all 1985). Although he was no longer associated with the RSC, Stewart continued to work with ACTER, which in 1986 offered a workshop and performance at UCLA. The workshop, titled "The Changing Face of Comedy," was led by Stewart and attended by producer Bob Justman, who came away convinced he had discovered the next captain of the *Enterprise*.

Brent Spiner

Brent Spiner, born February 2, 1949, in Houston, Texas, took up acting while attending Bellaire High School in suburban Houston, where his classmates included Randy and Dennis Quaid. At a 2012 convention appearance, Spiner credited his success to his high school drama teacher, Cecil Pickett. After graduation he enrolled at the University of Houston but never completed his degree.

Instead, he dropped out to pursue a theatrical career in New York. Spiner began landing small off-Broadway parts and worked as a cab driver between plays. Eventually the talented actor and vocalist worked his way up the ladder to Broadway shows, including James Lapine and Stephen Sondheim's Pulitzer Prize- and Tony Award-winning *Sunday in the Park with George* (1984). Spiner played a pair of minor roles in this play, which was inspired by a famous painting by French impressionist Georges Seurat and starred Mandy Patinkin and Bernadette Peters. As his theatrical career progressed, Spiner gave up taxi driving and worked in movies and TV series between stage productions. After playing uncredited bits in a handful of films including director Woody Allen's *Stardust Memories* (1980), Spiner decided to move to California and pursue movie and television roles full time.

In 1984, he landed the starring role in the offbeat comedy *Rent Control* and a handful of guest parts on TV series, including *The Paper Chase* and *Tales from the Darkside*. He later appeared on *Hill Street Blues* (1985) and the revamped *Twilight Zone* (1986), among other programs. In 1986, PBS's *American Playhouse* broadcast a filmed performance of *Sunday in the Park with George*, featuring Spiner and the rest of the original cast. Spiner's excellent comedic timing helped him land guest spots on sitcoms, including *Cheers*, *Mama's Family*, and *Sledge Hammer* in 1987, and a recurring role on *Night Court* from 1985 to '87. On *Night Court*, Spiner made a half-dozen uproarious appearances as displaced dullard Bob Wheeler, whose family stumbled into one misadventure after another after relocating to New York City. Spiner made an excellent foil for stars Harry Anderson, who played eccentric judge Harry Stone, and John Larroquette, who portrayed condescending prosecutor Dan Fielding. Wheeler, who Stone once described as a "recidivist knucklehead," was repeatedly charged with bizarre offenses such as "illegal detonation of poultry." Spiner's droopy-eyed, slack-jawed facial expressions and nasaly Southern drawl—although they initially claimed to be from West Virginia, the Wheelers were later revealed to be from Yugoslavia—were side-splittingly funny, and the Wheeler family's sporadic appearances rank among the funniest moments in the history of the series, which ran from 1984 to 1992. In the interim between the third and fourth seasons of *Night Court*, producers offered Spiner a regular role on the series, but the actor elected to accept the role of Lieutenant Commander Data instead.

Jonathan Frakes

Jonathan Frakes was born August 19, 1952, in Bellefonte, Pennsylvania. His father, John Frakes, taught English at nearby Lehigh University. Jonathan became involved with off-campus professional theatrical productions while studying psychology at Penn State. He soon changed his major to theater arts and, after graduation, studied drama at Harvard University for two summers. In the early 1970s, he moved to New York to pursue a stage career and joined the Impossible Ragtime Theater Company, which staged off-Broadway productions at various locations. He was also hired by Marvel Comics to appear at conventions and comic shops costumed as Captain America. Eventually, he matriculated to Broadway productions, including the Tony-nominated musical *Shenandoah* (1975). Like Stewart and Spiner, Frakes moved to California in pursuit of television work and landed the role of Tom Carrol on the daytime soap *The Doctors* (1977–78). After leaving that series, Frakes became an in-demand prime-time guest star, appearing on eight different series in late 1978 and 1979, including a two-episode arc on *The Waltons*. Frakes was generally cast as dashing romantic characters, often in period pieces. In 1983, he won a regular role on the short-lived prime-time soap *Bare Essence*, where he met his future wife, actress Genie Francis. He also played recurring guest roles on *Paper Dolls* (1984) and *Falcon Crest* (1985), and supporting parts in the star-studded ABC miniseries *North and South* (1985) and *North and South, Book II* (1986), both based on John Jakes's historical novels (and of no relation to the Patrick Stewart series of the same title). Frakes appeared as Stanley Hazard, the weak-kneed brother of protagonist Virgilia Hazard (Kirstie Alley). In all, Frakes had amassed appearances in nearly forty TV series—including several leading or recurring parts, making him one of the more experienced members of the *Next Generation* cast.

Of all Frakes's early roles, the one that garnered the most attention were his appearances in the two *North and South* miniseries as the dandyish Stanley Hazard. In a memorable sequence from the first series, Stanley assumes control of the family business, an iron works, but bungles it. He ignores his younger brother's safety concerns, leading to a catastrophic explosion at the foundry that kills several immigrant workers. Frakes is brilliant in an ensuing sequence, squirming with a queasy mix of shame and indignation as his brother (James Read) demands he accept responsibility and make amends, and then staring in doe-eyed disbelief as his mother (Inga Swenson) removes him from control of the company. Frakes's thoughtful, multifaceted performance stands in contrast to the bombastic, soapy hamming of most of the rest of the cast, which also includes David Carradine, Patrick Swayze, Lesley-Anne Down, Morgan Fairchild, and Genie Francis. The miniseries also featured cameos by stars Elizabeth Taylor, Robert Mitchum, Jean Simmons, Hal Holbrook, and Johnny Cash, among others. Frakes's appearances as Stanley Hazard also demonstrate the actor's range; the character could not be more different from the forceful, self-possessed William T. Riker.

Marina Sirtis

Marina Sirtis was born March 29, 1955, in London to conservative, working-class Greek immigrants who did not want their daughter to date and were adamantly opposed to her pursuing her interest in acting. In high school, Sirtis applied in secret to the Guildhall School of Drama and was accepted. After completing her training at Guildhall in 1976, she joined the Connaught Theater, a repertory company in Sussex, where she appeared in various roles, including Ophelia

Promotional head shot of Marina Sirtis, from her pre-*Trek* days. The British actress was preparing to give up on Hollywood and return to England when she was offered the role of counselor Deanna Troi.

in *Hamlet*. She later played Magenta in a touring production of *The Rocky Horror Show* and began making occasional appearances on British TV programs and telefilms, and in commercials. Between 1977 and 1985, she appeared in eleven English television productions and had bit parts in two films, playing a hooker in the thriller *Blind Date* (1984), and Maria, one of Charles Bronson's neighbors, in *Death Wish 3* (1985). With her raven hair and exotic features, the actress was often cast in various "ethnic" roles—playing Greek, Italian, and Hispanic characters. In the British sitcom *Up the Elephant and Round the Castle* (1985), she made two appearances as Linda, a gorgeous but ditsy "Vestonian" waitress who struggles to understand British customs and master

the intricacies of pouring a draft beer and making change. The actress showed her dramatic chops in "The Six Napoleons," a 1986 episode of *The Return of Sherlock Holmes*, in which she played an Italian woman who's part of a mafia family. The actress's emotionally charged performance is even more impressive since all her dialogue is in Italian. Later in 1986, Sirtis traveled to Hollywood in search of higher-profile work but earned just one role, a guest spot on the detective series *Hunter*, in six months. She was preparing to return to London when, following a series of auditions, she was offered the role of Counselor Deanna Troi on *The Next Generation*.

LeVar Burton

LeVar Burton, the best-known cast member hired for *The Next Generation*, had appeared in twenty-five film and television roles prior to *Star Trek*, including an Emmy-nominated performance as Kunta Kinte in the landmark miniseries *Roots* (1977). He was also widely recognized as the host of the PBS children's series *Reading Rainbow*, which began in 1983 and continued until 2006 and was relaunched as an iPad app in 2012. Burton has remained the host of the show throughout. Levardis Martin Robyrt Burton was born February 16, 1957, on a U.S. military base in West Germany, where his father was serving in the Army Signal Corps. He was raised in Sacramento and, at age thirteen, entered St. Pius X Seminary in Galt, California, to prepare for the priesthood. But he found his true calling as a student at Christian Brothers High School, where he became involved in school plays. After graduation in 1974, Burton studied theater at the University of Southern California. Kunta Kinte in *Roots* was his first professional role. Burton was a sophomore at USC when he auditioned for the part. The miniseries aired in January 1977. Critical acclaim and a flood of offers followed. The actor worked steadily for the next three years, appearing in several made-for-TV movies and two theatrical features, director Richard Brooks's *Looking for Mr. Goodbar* (1977) and the Steve McQueen thriller *The Hunter* (1980). While none of these performances matched the deathless brilliance of his work in *Roots*, Burton's acting was uniformly strong. He gave a particularly affecting performance as a deaf-mute young man accused of murder in the 1979 telefilm *Dummy*, costarring Paul Sorvino. By the time *Reading Rainbow* premiered in 1983, however, work had begun to dry up for the actor. The roles he was offered started to shrink, and he began making guest appearances on TV series such as

LeVar Burton gave a heartrending performance as a deaf-mute teenager wrongfully charged with murder in the TV movie *Dummy*, one of many fine performances the actor delivered prior to *The Next Generation*.

The Love Boat and *Fantasy Island*. During this period, he appeared in *Emergency Room*, a failed TV pilot (which later ran as a Movie of the Week) produced by once and future *Star Trek* insider Bob Justman. Four years later, Justman urged Roddenberry to hire Burton for the role of engineer Geordi La Forge.

Michael Dorn

Michael Dorn, born December 9, 1952, in Luling, Texas, grew up in Pasadena and began his career as a musician, playing bass and keyboards in several rock bands in San Francisco and Los Angeles in the early 1970s. In 1970 a bandmate's father who worked on the staff of *The Mary Tyler Moore Show* helped Dorn land a job playing the background character "Stan the Newsman." In 1976, Dorn made his big-screen debut in an uncredited bit role as one of boxer Apollo Creed's bodyguards in *Rocky*. After playing another uncredited bit in *Demon Seed* (1977), Dorn won his first recurring speaking part, portraying Officer Jebediah Turner in thirty-one episodes of *CHiPs* (1979–82). During his tenure on the show, Dorn studied with acting coach Charles Conrad for six months, his

first formal training. After *CHiPs*, Dorn tallied guest appearances on a dozen series and played a supporting role on the daytime soap *Days of Our Lives* for a season (1986–87). None of the actor's early work suggests he possessed the depth and range he would bring to his role as Lieutenant Worf. The artistic growth and maturation audiences witnessed throughout Dorn's seven seasons on *The Next Generation* and beyond was nothing short of astounding.

Promotional head shot of actor Michael Dorn, dating from his tenure on the series *CHiPS*. Dorn's early work provided little indication of the ability he would demonstrate on *The Next Generation*.

Gates McFadden

Gates McFadden, without question, had the most diverse training and background of any of the performers hired for *The Next Generation*. Born March 2,

1949, in Cuyahoga Falls, Ohio, McFadden had studied theater at Brandeis University, and acting with instructor Jacques Lecoq in Paris, and had worked as a choreographer and puppeteer with Jim Henson, contributing to *The Dark Crystal* (1982), *The Muppets Take Manhattan* (1984), and *Labyrinth* (1986). When working in nonacting roles, McFadden is typically credited as Cheryl McFadden (Gates is her middle name). Prior to *Star Trek*, McFadden worked primarily in theater. At first she declined the role of Dr. Beverly Crusher because the shooting schedule conflicted with a play (*The Matchmaker* at the La Jolla Playhouse) she had already agreed to do. She joined *Next Gen* after producers assured her that the schedule would accommodate both projects. Although she played Dr. Crusher off and on for the next fifteen years (through *Nemesis* in 2002), the role never gave her the opportunity to display the full spectrum of her talents.

Denise Crosby

Before she became known as Tasha Yar, model and actress Denise Crosby was known primarily as Bing Crosby's granddaughter. Born November 24, 1957, in Hollywood, her parentage was the subject of a much-publicized paternity suit involving her mother, Marilyn Scott, and actor Dennis Crosby, the son of the legendary actor and crooner. Denise began modeling as a teenager. After appearing in *Playboy* in 1979, she landed an uncredited role in the Blake Edwards comedy *"10"* (1979). She also began dating Edwards's son, Geoffrey, whom she married in 1983 (the couple divorced seven years later). Crosby played minor roles in three more Blake Edwards movies (*Trail of the Pink Panther*, 1982; *The Man Who Loved Women*; and *Curse of the Pink Panther*, both 1983) and appeared in the comedy smash *48 HRS.* (1982). In all, she tallied fifteen pre-*Trek* screen appearances. She had so little to do in these early roles that it's difficult to assess her work. She also played the recurring role of Lisa Davis on the daytime soap *Days of Our Lives* in 1980. Winning the part of the *Enterprise*'s chief of security marked a major breakthrough for the actress. Nevertheless, she quit the series after less than a season because she felt her character was being undervalued and underdeveloped.

Wil Wheaton

Other than LeVar Burton, the most famous and acclaimed actor hired as part of the *Next Generation*'s original cast was fifteen-year-old Wil Wheaton, whose résumé included sixteen film and television projects, among them director Rob Reiner's critically lauded *Stand by Me* (1986), in which Wheaton starred alongside River Phoenix. Born July 29, 1972, in Burbank, California, Richard William Wheaton III made his screen debut in a Jell-O commercial with Bill Cosby. At age nine he landed his first significant role in the TV movie *A Long Way Home* (1981). Wheaton began a long and ongoing career in voice work with his next project, the animated feature *The Secret of NIMH* (1982). His subsequent pre-*Trek* roles included guest appearances on hit TV series such as *Highway to Heaven* (1985), *St. Elsewhere* (1986), and *Family Ties* (1987). But his calling card was *Stand by Me*, a brilliant, dark, coming-of-age story based on a Stephen King novella. The film unfolds from the point of view of Wheaton's character, Gordie LaChance, an introverted but imaginative and intelligent boy who enjoys writing stories. His bittersweet, doe-eyed performance as a likeable kid coping with the loss of his beloved older brother and the inattention of his disinterested father drives the entire movie. The picture's best moments are Wheaton's emotionally charged scenes with costar River Phoenix. Few actors of any age have delivered a more powerful performance.

8

Identity Crisis

The Next Generation, Season One (1987–88)

T he crossover success of *Star Trek IV: The Voyage Home* (1986), combined with the steadfast devotion of the franchise's core fans, created an enormous built-in audience for *Star Trek: The Next Generation*, one of the most anticipated new shows in television history. This was a tremendous advantage for the fledgling series, but with it came unique and daunting challenges. Gene Roddenberry and his creative team realized that *Next Gen* had to establish a separate identity because fans would reject a simple retread of the classic program. Yet the new show had to remain instantly recognizable and credible as *Star Trek*, so it couldn't depart radically from the established setting and philosophy of the original. To succeed, *Next Gen* needed to thread a needle between these paradoxical expectations. Also, the show would have to be good. Despite a hit-and-miss final season, the majority of the original *Star Trek* episodes had been of extraordinarily high quality, with endearing characters, exciting science fiction scenarios, and daring commentary on contemporary political and social issues. Fans wouldn't accept less from the sequel.

There were plenty of doubters. Many fans, while excited by the prospect of a new *Star Trek* series, were disappointed that the beloved original crew would not be involved. "The Trekkies loved the original cast, cared for each and every one of them very much, and felt in a way betrayed by the fact that they wouldn't be coming back," said supervising producer Bob Justman in an interview included on the *Star Trek: The Next Generation Season One* DVD collection. Others, including many cast members, believed that *Star Trek* was an inimitable, once-in-a-lifetime phenomenon and that trying to duplicate it was futile. "One of the reasons I signed on was that I assumed that the six-year [actually five-year] contract that I was signing was meaningless, that this series would do one, perhaps two years at the most because nobody expected it to be successful," confessed Stewart, in Paul M. Block and Terry J. Erdmann's book *Star Trek: The Next Generation 365*. Spiner, in a DVD interview, admits that he shared this gloomy outlook. "I thought we would do our year and then we would go home," he said. "Because, after all, no one can do another *Star Trek* was my feeling. And many of the fans shared that feeling." So did other franchise insiders, including Leonard Nimoy, who turned down the opportunity to create and executive produce the sequel series. "I felt the original *Star Trek*'s success was due to many factors—the themes, the characters, the chemistry between the actors, the timing," Nimoy wrote in his memoir *I Am Spock.* "There was simply no way that anyone could duplicate those things and be successful with a second *Star Trek* show. And so I opted out." Other original cast members including William Shatner and James Doohan were openly dismissive of the new series.

Roddenberry made a difficult task even more challenging with a pair of edicts to his writing staff. First, he discouraged direct references to the original *Trek,* including contact with or even mention of alien species encountered by the previous generation. At first, the only exception was the addition of "a Klingon marine" to the *Enterprise* crew and the establishment of an alliance between the United Federation of Planets and the Klingon Empire. Second, Roddenberry decreed that the highly evolved Starfleet of the twenty-fourth century must remain free of interpersonal conflicts—no personality clashes, petty jealousies, competing personal ambitions, romantic triangles, or other such story elements would be tolerated. This was a particularly exasperating limitation because such conflicts have been essential building blocks of drama as far back as Sophocles. "Gene did not want conflict between the regular characters on *TNG,*" writer-producer Ronald D. Moore commented during an AOL chat in 1997. "This began to hamstring the series and led to many, many problems. To put it bluntly, this wasn't a very good idea." In an interview published on the ING.com site, Moore went further. "The original series didn't work like this!" he said. "I mean, the original series people were not perfect. My god, Spock and McCoy were at each other's throats for big chunks of time, and sometimes McCoy thought Kirk was an idiot. They were flawed people. . . . You were never allowed to go there with *Next Gen.*"

A revolving roster of writers struggled to devise compelling plots and flesh out the show's ensemble of characters, without recourse to forbidden plot devices. As a result, most Season One episodes seemed to value ideas more than people. Captain Picard and his crew went underdeveloped, their personalities, relationships, and backgrounds largely unexplored. Meanwhile, as he had during the first two seasons of the classic *Trek* series, Roddenberry oversaw or personally undertook uncredited rewrites on many teleplays, usually to the irritation of the credited authors. Regardless, the Great Bird of the Galaxy once again held final say over what was and wasn't *Star Trek.*

The perhaps inevitable result was that *The Next Generation* came together more slowly than the classic *Trek* series, never consistently hitting its stride until Season Three. Although some outstanding episodes (including "Arsenal of Freedom," "Hide and Q," "The Big Goodbye," "Datalore," and "Conspiracy") aired during the first season of *Next Gen,* so did several forgettable ones, and a few memorably awful ones (including "Code of Honor" and "Angel One"). Curiously, despite Roddenberry's injunction against references to the first series, when push came to shove, *Next Gen* seemed to revert to familiar approaches. The show's debut season contained a myriad of concepts and scenarios that mirror or borrow from classic *Trek* episodes. In Edward Gross and Mark Altman's book *Captains' Logs*, screenwriter Katharyn Powers says that "even though it's a new cast, they still wanted the same kind of stories." It showed.

"Encounter at Farpoint"

For the series' premiere, associate producer Dorothy ("D.C.") Fontana developed a fresh and imaginative scenario: The *Enterprise* crew discovers that a palatial star base on a remote planet is actually a giant, shape-shifting life-form that has been captured and enslaved by the planet's residents. However, when Paramount executives demanded the pilot be expanded from one hour to two (to accommodate more commercials), Roddenberry grafted a far more familiar yarn onto Fontana's teleplay. In this story, which brackets Fontana's "Farpoint" adventure, Captain Picard and company are captured and placed on trial for the sins of the human race by an apparently omnipotent alien known as Q (John de Lancie). The Q material revived one of Roddenberry's favorite themes. A half-dozen times during the original seventy-nine episodes, Captain Kirk and his crew had, as representatives of humanity, endured testing by more advanced aliens. Human beings were repeatedly judged to be an exceptional species. (For a full rundown of these encounters, see Chapter 31 of the original

When *The Next Generation* pilot, "Encounter at Farpoint," was expanded from one hour to two, a touching cameo was added featuring DeForest Kelley as Admiral McCoy.

Yareena (Carole Selmon, left) and Tasha Yar (Denise Crosby) battle to the (apparent) death in the climax of "Code of Honor," one of Season One's most notorious failures.

Star Trek FAQ.) For his part, Q seemed to be a (slightly) more grown-up version of Trelaine from "The Squire of Gothos," one of several godlike aliens featured on the original program. "Encounter at Farpoint" made a direct link with classic *Trek* when, to further pad its runtime, a delightful throwaway sequence was added in which Admiral McCoy (DeForest Kelley) tours the new, Galaxy Class *Enterprise-D*. Despite this reversion to familiar themes, "Encounter at Farpoint" made a favorable first impression. It scored high ratings, earned a Hugo nomination for Best Dramatic Presentation, and, most importantly, inspired most fans to return the following week.

"The Naked Now"

Roddenberry broke his own rule by requesting a direct sequel to, and very nearly a remake of, writer John D. F. Black's "The Naked Time." This is the classic adventure in which an inhibition-loosening illness causes Captain Kirk's usually disciplined crew to run amok. (Famously, a bare-chested Sulu takes up a fencing foil and attacks Kirk like a mad musketeer.) "The Naked Time" provided a window into the psychological inner workings of characters including

Spock, Nurse Chapel, and, of course, Sulu, helping viewers bond with the crew. Roddenberry hoped "The Naked Now" would do the same for the new cast of characters. Although it contains at least one famous scene (in which security chief Tasha Yar trysts with Data), many viewers were disappointed by the results. Producer Maurice Hurley and cast members Jonathan Frakes and Wil Wheaton, among others, later expressed antipathy for the episode in interviews. And in his autobiography, *To the Stars*, George Takei wrote that "The Naked Now" was like watching "young children putting on their parents' clothes and trying to act like grown-ups."

"Code of Honor"

Still, "The Naked Now" looks like "The City on the Edge of Forever" next to "Code of Honor," one of *Next Gen*'s most notorious installments. On Planet Ligon II, Picard and Tasha Yar become ensnared in the machinations of Lutan (Jessie Lawrence Ferguson), a tribal chieftain who dupes Tasha into engaging in a battle to the death with his wife, Yareena (Karole Selmon), as part of a surreptitious power grab. The climactic battle is highly reminiscent of the ritual combat between Kirk and Spock from "Amok Time." At the conclusion of that episode, the apparently dead Kirk was beamed back to the *Enterprise* and revived by Dr. McCoy. At the conclusion of "Code of Honor," the dead Yareena is beamed to the *Enterprise-D* and revived by Dr. Crusher. At best, this episode would have played like a predictable rehash of a classic adventure, but director Russ Mayberry steered the installment toward infamy when he unilaterally decided to cast only dark-skinned African American actors as the tribal Ligonians, adding unpleasant racial connotations to the scenario. When Roddenberry learned of this casting decision midway through production, he fired Mayberry immediately. The episode was completed by Les Landau, but the damage was done. Several cast members (including Brent Spiner, LeVar Burton, Frakes, and Wheaton) later disowned "Code of Honor." At a *Star Trek* convention in Las Vegas in 2011, Frakes called the episode "a racist piece of shit."

"The Last Outpost"

Once again *Enterprise* crew members, on behalf of the human race, are tested by a superadvanced alien. In this case, landing parties from both the *Enterprise* and a Ferengi starship are examined by an entity known as the Portal, a vestige of the long-vanished Tkon Empire. As usual, the humans are deemed to be exceptional. Not so the Ferengi. The basic scenario—the *Enterprise*, while pursuing an enemy vessel, strays into the space of a more advanced civilization, which halts the starships in their tracks and brings crew members planetside for testing and judgment—is remarkably similar to the setup for the classic episode "Arena," in which the Metrons force Kirk to battle the reptilian Gorn. "The

Last Outpost" introduced viewers to the Ferengi, who were originally intended as *Next Gen*'s answer to the Klingons. However, the sawed-off, bubble-headed aliens proved too comical in appearance and behavior to be taken seriously as a recurring adversary. It didn't help that director Robert Colla instructed the Ferengi actors to "jump up and down like crazed gerbils." That's according to Armin Shimerman, as quoted in Garfield and Judith Reeves-Stevens's book *Star Trek: The Next Generation—The Continuing Mission*. Shimerman played a Ferengi here and later portrayed Quark on *Deep Space Nine*, where he belatedly brought some dignity to the species.

"Where No One Has Gone Before"

Despite its familiar title, "Where No One Has Gone Before" features one of the most innovative story lines devised for *Next Gen*'s first season. Based on an original crew novel, Diane Duane's *The Wounded Sky*, the scenario involves the *Enterprise* being hurtled to the far reaches of the galaxy and beyond by a mysterious alien known as the Traveler (Eric Menyuk). This premise was so fertile that a similar idea was used as the basis for the later series *Voyager*, in which a federation starship is flung (via a different contrivance) to a distant quadrant of the galaxy and cut off from Starfleet. "Where No One Has Gone Before" was intended as a foundational episode for teenager Wesley Crusher, whom the Traveler identifies as a human with extraordinary gifts and potential. In the next episode, Captain Picard would appoint Wesley an Acting Ensign, giving him a logical reason to take part in the crew's adventures, but writers would continue to struggle to craft believable dialogue and situations for the young character. "Where No One Has Gone Before" benefits greatly from a finely nuanced guest performance by Stanley Kamel as an arrogant warp-drive engineer. After sputtering for three episodes, the series was finally gathering steam. This episode earned an Emmy nomination for sound mixing.

"Lonely Among Us"

Like the classic episode "Journey to Babel," "Lonely Among Us" tasks the *Enterprise* with transporting a pair of unruly diplomatic delegations to a key summit. Along the way, the ship passes through a strange energy cloud, and Captain Picard becomes possessed by a noncorporeal life force. Picard begins acting strangely, and soon Dr. Crusher and other crew members realize something is amiss. The possession subplot sometimes plays like "Turnabout Intruder," in which Captain Kirk's body is taken over by a jealous ex-lover with access to fantastic alien technology. In *Captains' Logs*, screenwriter Dorothy Fontana acknowledges borrowing from her "Babel" teleplay for this episode, but stresses that she "switched it around" to be played for comedy rather than drama. While the Picard story line is played straight, the scenes involving the cobra-like Selay and the mongoose-like Anticans are wickedly funny. For instance, at one point Riker learns that the Anticans have asked the *Enterprise* chef to cook what looks like a murdered Selay delegate!

"Justice"

Crew members are enjoying shore leave on a newly discovered but apparently peaceful planet when Wesley Crusher is sentenced to die for an unknowing infraction of local laws. Commander Riker, who's leading the landing party, belatedly learns that on this world every offense (no matter how petty) is punishable by death. Meanwhile, in orbit, Captain Picard discovers that the planet is under the care and protection of a fantastically powerful orbital supercomputer, which the natives worship as a deity. It's a relationship much like that between the computer-"god" Vaal and the docile denizens of Gamma Triangulai VI in the classic episode "The Apple." Once again, the striking similarities to the original program originated with a Roddenberry rewrite. Screenwriter John D. F. Black is credited under the pseudonym "Ralph Willis" because he was so displeased with the alterations to his original teleplay, which featured no god-machine. Black originally intended the episode as an indictment of capital punishment, a theme diluted in the broadcast version.

"The Battle"

Bok (Frank Corsentino), a vengeance-crazed Ferengi, plots to dupe Picard into destroying the *Enterprise*. He uses a thought-projecting machine to place Picard under his mental control and forces the captain to relive a battle from his youth, in which he destroyed a Ferengi cruiser. In Bok's re-creation, however, the *Enterprise* will stand in for the doomed Ferengi vessel. Like a few classic episodes, most memorably "Obsession," "The Battle" addresses the self-destructive folly of revenge. But the plot of "The Battle" provides an original (albeit highly implausible) variation on its familiar theme. This installment marked the final attempt to present the Ferengi as a credible menace to the Federation. In their subsequent appearances, they would be portrayed as amusing nuisances, along the lines of Harry Mudd. They wouldn't appear at all for the remainder of Season One and figured in only one Season Two adventure.

"Hide and Q"

Q returns, this time to share his godlike abilities with Commander Riker. Humanity is put to the test yet again, this time through the temptation of near-omnipotence. In several classic episodes—including the series' second pilot, "Where No Man Has Gone Before"—humans gained godlike powers, always with disastrous consequences. Perhaps this story line, coauthored by Hurley (credited as C. J. Holland due to another rewrite dispute) and Roddenberry, was intended by the Great Bird to demonstrate how superior these *Next Generation* Starfleet officers were to their twenty-third-century counterparts. Riker becomes the first human to attain godhood and use his new power constructively. He is also wise enough to ultimately relinquish it. "Hide and Q" marks another example of *The Next Generation* offering a new twist on a familiar theme rather than a simple recapitulation. It's a terrific early installment. Already, de Lancie's Q was emerging as one of the show's most popular recurring characters. Moving forward, an appearance by Q virtually guaranteed an excellent installment.

"Haven"

"Code of Honor" appropriated the finale of "Amok Time," but "Haven" swipes the setup of that classic episode. The *Enterprise* crew—especially Riker—is shocked to learn that Counselor Troi is engaged to Wyatt Miller (Rob Knepper), a handsome young doctor who she's never met. Her since-deceased father arranged the marriage when she was a child, and now Deanna feels compelled to honor the agreement. Her overbearing mother, Lwaxana (Majel Barrett-Roddenberry), arrives with Wyatt and his parents in tow. While Wyatt and Deanna like one another, the young man remains obsessed with a mysterious blonde woman who has haunted his dreams since childhood. Then Wyatt's dream girl turns up aboard a ship of plague victims. After its disappointingly familiar first act, "Haven" plots a course quite different than "Amok Time." The presence of former Nurse Chapel Barrett-Roddenberry invites further comparisons with the original program, but in this instance the comparison benefits *Next Gen*. The brassy, bawdy Lwaxana (who Roddenberry described as "the Auntie Mame of outer space") is a far more colorful and interesting character than Chapel ever was, and Barrett-Roddenberry demonstrates comedic talents untapped during her original *Trek* appearances. Screenwriter Tracy Tormé created "Haven," with its stigmatized plague victims, to serve as an allegory for the AIDS epidemic. The episode is an effective blend of social commentary, romance, and comedy. It also earned an Emmy nomination for hairstyling.

"The Big Goodbye"

In the first of many holodeck-centered yarns, Picard, Data, Dr. Crusher, and Dr. Whalen (David Selburg), an expert on the twentieth century, are trapped in a program devoted to the adventures of hard-boiled gumshoe Dixon Hill. As the Sam Spade–like Hill, Picard must unravel a mystery inspired by Dashiell Hammett's *The Maltese Falcon*. But with the safety protocols off-line, Whalen is shot and grievously wounded. In subsequent seasons, and subsequent series, episodes based on the virtual realities of the holodeck became a cliché, but the idea was still fresh at this point. Some viewers—notably the unnamed critic from *TV Guide*, who panned "The Big Goodbye"—thought this episode seemed too similar to "A Piece of the Action," the classic *Trek* comedy in which Kirk, Spock, and

Patrick Stewart (left) and Brent Spiner model a pair of William Ware Theiss's Emmy-winning costumes in this publicity still for the holodeck noir "The Big Goodbye," one of the first season's finest episodes.

McCoy encounter an entire civilization that emulates Chicago gangsters of the 1920s. While it's true that both tales place Starfleet personnel in the noir milieu (not to mention in pinstripe suits), "The Big Goodbye" is entirely different in tone and intent than "A Piece of the Action." Both are fine episodes, unlikely to be confused with one another. "The Big Goodbye," which remains perhaps the most satisfying of *Next Gen*'s holodeck tales, earned the George Foster Peabody Award for Excellence in Television Broadcasting and an Emmy for costume design. Its cinematography was also Emmy nominated. Despite his difficulties in this installment, Picard returned to the Dixon Hill program in two more episodes ("Manhunt" and "Clues") and in the feature film *Star Trek: First Contact.*

"Datalore"

At its heart, "Datalore" is an Evil Twin story, like "The Enemy Within." In that classic *Trek* adventure, written by the great Richard Matheson, a transporter malfunction splits Captain Kirk into two people—one compassionate but weak-willed, the other ruthless but decisive. In "Datalore," the *Enterprise* discovers and assembles Data's twin brother, Lore. Unlike Data, Lore can experience human emotions, but has no affection for human beings and lusts for power. Coincidentally, the climaxes of both "Datalore" and "The Enemy Within" take place on the transporter pad. The scenario also contains echoes of "Space Seed," with the *Enterprise* crew unwittingly reviving a superpowered villain. "The Enemy Within" was a tour de force for William Shatner, and "Datalore" proved to be an equally impressive showcase for Brent Spiner. This episode, another Season One highlight, was the final *Star Trek* teleplay credited to Roddenberry (with Robert Lewin).

"Angel One"

In another of the series' most reviled installments, Commander Riker leads an away team to a planet where aggressive women dominate passive, servile men. While possibly intended as a corrective to the often chauvinistic gender politics of the classic series (see Chapter 34 of the original *Star Trek FAQ*), "Angel One" seems misguided and is often unintentionally laughable. The basic scenario recalls *Planet Earth*, one of Roddenberry's failed pilots from the 1970s. *Planet Earth*'s Dylan Hunt (John Saxon), a twentieth-century man reawakened in the postapocalyptic future after a suspended animation experiment goes haywire, stumbles across a matriarchal society where women keep drug-addled men as manual laborers and sex slaves. It's "Women's Lib gone mad," as Hunt describes it. So is planet Angel I, where Riker allies himself with a band of antifeminist radicals out to restore "equality" to the repressive matriarchy. Many fans, cast members, and insiders rank "Angel One" among *Next Gen*'s weakest efforts. During production, Frakes, Patrick Stewart, and Marina Sirtis complained about the teleplay, to no avail. Producer Maurice Hurley, in *Captains' Logs*, called it "one of the ones you'd just as soon erase."

"11001001"

In a handful of classic *Trek* adventures, including "By Any Other Name" and "Let That Be Your Last Battlefield," aliens hijacked the *Enterprise*. The same thing happens here, but the Bynars, pairs of twins who communicate directly with computers through a cybernetic link, are unlike any classic *Trek* species. And the Bynars' ultimate goal—saving their civilization, rather than the conquest of the galaxy or some other nefarious purpose—is refreshingly different as well. Despite a silly subplot in which Riker falls in love with a comely holodeck-generated barfly named Minuet (Carolyn McCormick), "11001001," written by Hurley and Lewin, remains a satisfying installment. Too bad the Bynars were never seen again. This episode won an Emmy award for Outstanding Sound Editing.

"Too Short a Season"

To *Trek* fans with long memories, "Too Short a Season" may seem like a near-sequel to the classic episode "A Private Little War." In that adventure, Captain Kirk discovers that the Klingons have armed the city dwellers of planet Neural, who are waging a genocidal civil war against the neighboring Hill People. Kirk's solution is to create a balance of power by arming the Hill People, too. "Too Short a Season" reveals that aged Admiral Jameson (Clayton Rohner) played a similar gambit while negotiating the resolution to a hostage crisis on Mordan IV decades earlier, agreeing to provide weapons to the oppressive government but secretly arming the planet's dissidents as well. Now the governor of Mordan IV has taken a Federation diplomat hostage in an attempt to gain revenge against Jameson, whose actions led to a bloody, forty-year civil war. To prepare for the negotiations, Jameson takes an experimental de-aging drug and rapidly grows younger. This plot point recalls the animated adventure "The Counter-Clock Incident," which also featured a rapidly de-aging Starfleet admiral. "Too Short a Season" contains the core of an effective episode but is undone by Rohner's grandiose barnstorming as Jameson and some lamentable old age makeup. Don Ingalls's "A Private Little War" teleplay, extensively rewritten by Roddenberry, served as a thinly veiled commentary on the Vietnam War. Screenwriters Michael Michaelian and Dorothy Fontana intended "Too Short a Season" as a statement about the Reagan-era Iran-Contra arms-for-hostages scandal.

"When the Bough Breaks"

This episode begins with a fascinating concept: the discovery of an outer space Shangri-La, a mystery planet fabled in the songs and stories of many civilizations. The world in question is Aldea, which is protected by a massive invisibility cloak and an impenetrable force field. Unfortunately, the rest of screenwriter Hannah Louise Shearer's teleplay proves far less intriguing than this initial idea. Like the aliens from the classic *Trek* tales "For the World Is Hollow and I Have Touched the Sky" and "Spock's Brain," the denizens of Aldea have forgotten how to control or maintain the machinery that remains central to their way of life. The Aldeans call their supercomputer "the Custodian," similar to "the Oracle"

Mordock, the Benzite whom Wesley befriends in "Coming of Age," was immortalized (after a fashion) as an action figure.   *Photo by Preston Hewis, East Bank Images*

from "For the World Is Hollow" and "the Controller" from "Spock's Brain." The Aldeans have also become sterile, and so kidnap a clutch of children from the *Enterprise* (including Wesley Crusher) to try to perpetuate their civilization. Eventually, Picard and Crusher make a discovery that forces the Aldeans to pursue another course of action. With its scintillating setup and so-so follow-through, "When the Bough Breaks" remains better than a handful of other Season One installments—but only a handful.

"Home Soil"

The *Enterprise* is called in to probe a series of deadly, unexplained "accidents" that have struck a terraforming operation on planet Velara III. The investigation reveals that the scientists have unearthed a unique, sentient, but inorganic life-form on a world believed to be lifeless. Eventually, communication is established with the life-forms, which refer to humans as "ugly giant bags of mostly water." Many fans and critics have noted this episode's similarities with the classic adventure "The Devil in the Dark," in which miners are menaced by an entity known as the Horta, which is ultimately revealed to be a mother protecting her unhatched offspring. However, the lukewarm "Home Soil" is nowhere near as powerful as "The Devil in the Dark." "Home Soil" was written by Robert Sabaroff, who also penned the classic *Trek* adventure "The Immunity Syndrome" and the original story for the later *Next Gen* episode "Conspiracy."

"Coming of Age"

"Coming of Age" was one of the first *Next Generation* episodes to use the "A/B" structure, featuring two parallel stories, which in later years became the standard approach. The A-story—in which Picard comes under investigation by a Starfleet admiral and his abrasive adjutant, Remmick (Robert Schenkkan)—recalls "Court Martial," in which Captain Kirk is falsely accused of negligence in the apparent death of a crewman. The B-story follows Wesley as he endures a series of strenuous exams required to qualify for admission to Starfleet Academy. The Picard plot lacks drama until the very end, when, after Picard is cleared, Admiral Quinn (Ward Costello) reveals that he is trying to identify loyal officers because he believes Starfleet may be threatened from within. He refuses to reveal more, but his comments set up the later episode "Conspiracy." The Wesley story is more compelling but begs credulity. Is Starfleet so overburdened with exceptional candidates that it can afford to accept only one new student from a group with at least three applicants possessing extraordinary skills and aptitude? Wesley is rejected but told he can reapply next year. A scene cut from this episode would have introduced the *Enterprise*'s bar and lounge, then known as "Twenty-One-Forward," which finally debuted in Season Two as Ten-Forward. "Coming of Age" won an Emmy nomination for makeup but lost the award to another *Next Gen* installment, "Conspiracy."

"Heart of Glory"

This is precisely the sort of Klingon-centered story Roddenberry initially wanted to avoid. Nevertheless, like most of *Next Gen*'s Klingon episodes, it's an exciting, rewarding adventure. "Heart of Glory" divulges Worf's background—he was adopted and raised by humans after his family was killed in a Romulan attack— and reveals that not all Klingons are pleased with the Empire's alliance with the Federation. A pair of rogue Klingons attempt to coax Worf into abandoning his crewmates and joining them in an effort to splinter the alliance and start a glorious new war with humankind. This was the first installment to demonstrate the potential of both the Worf character and actor Michael Dorn. Producers took note and soon began featuring both more prominently.

"The Arsenal of Freedom"

One of the finest episodes from the first season of *The Next Generation*, "The Arsenal of Freedom" recalls one of the best classic *Trek* adventures, "The Doomsday Machine." Both stories involve superweapons still wreaking destruction even though the wars they were created to fight are long over. Investigating the disappearance of a Federation starship, Riker, Yar, and Data beam down to an unexplored world and soon come under fire from the deadly drones of an automated, planet-wide defense system. When Riker is trapped in an energy bubble, Picard and Crusher beam down to assist, leaving Geordi in charge of the *Enterprise*. Picard and Crusher become separated from the rest of the group, and Crusher is seriously injured. Meanwhile, Geordi finds himself battling both the weapons system's orbital defenses and Chief Engineer Logan (Vyto Ruginis), who believes he should assume command because he outranks La Forge. (During Season One, Geordi was only a lieutenant.) Eventually, Picard learns that this planet was once the home to a civilization of weapons makers who developed a perfect, unstoppable killing machine, then loosed it on themselves to test it. (Oops!) Writer Robert Lewin had envisioned "The Arsenal of Freedom" as a Picard-Crusher love story, with Crusher revealing her hidden affection for the captain after Picard (not she) is seriously wounded during the away mission. But this was nixed in heavy rewrites (Lewin wound up with a cocredit for the story) as the episode evolved into a full-tilt action piece. Geordi's struggles with Logan represent a rare, and exhilarating, example of interpersonal tension on *Next Gen*.

"Symbiosis"

"Symbiosis" tackles the issue of drug abuse with about as much subtlety as the classic series had tackled the issue of racism in "Let That Be Your Last Battlefield"— which is to say, with none at all. During a scientific mission to the Delos System, the *Enterprise* responds to a distress signal and finds itself in the middle of a trade dispute between a planet, Brekka, whose entire economy is built around manufacturing a single pharmaceutical, felicium, and a neighboring world, Ornara, that is wholly dependent on the drug for survival. The Ornarians believe they suffer from an incurable plague that can only be treated with felicium, which can only be produced on Brekka. But Dr. Crusher discovers the Ornarians have been misled. The "disease" they suffer from is addiction, and felicium is a powerful narcotic. In other words, Ornara is Junkie World and Brekka is Planet Pusher. If this wasn't heavy-handed enough, Tasha Yar delivers a "just say no" lecture to Wesley to further hammer home the message. "Symbiosis" is also static, talky, and tedious—like "Let That Be Your Last Battlefield." Merritt Butrick, who played Captain Kirk's son David in *The Wrath of Khan* and *The Search for Spock*, plays one of the drug-addicted Ornarians.

"Skin of Evil"

"Skin of Evil" was designed to invoke, then deconstruct, audience expectations established by the original *Trek*— namely, the familiar clichés that only red-shirted extras die and that stars who are "killed" always somehow return by the end of the episode. In at least a

Tasha Yar met an ignominious fate in "Skin of Evil," killed by a living oil slick, as depicted on this videotape box.

half-dozen installments of the classic program, crew members, including Dr. McCoy ("Shore Leave"), Scotty ("The Changeling"), and Chekov ("Spectre of the Gun"), apparently died but were later revived. So when, twelve minutes into "Skin of Evil," Tasha Yar was struck down by a bitter, lonely alien that looked like a living oil slick, most viewers probably expected her to magically return by the conclusion of the story. Instead, the tale ends with the rest of the crew attending a memorial service for their fallen comrade on the holodeck. Perhaps the audience should have known something was up when the teleplay credits included the name Joseph Stefano, who knocked off star Janet Leigh's character during the first act of Alfred Hitchcock's *Psycho*. Unfortunately, aside from Tasha's shocking demise and touching funeral, there's little else of interest in

"Skin of Evil," which suffers from a grindingly slow pace and inept visual effects. Tasha was eliminated because Denise Crosby, frustrated by the writing staff's inability or unwillingness to flesh out her character, asked to be released from her contract. Originally, Crosby had auditioned as Counselor Troi and Marina Sirtis as the *Enterprise* security chief. If Roddenberry hadn't flipped Crosby and Sirtis's roles, then Deanna, rather than Tasha, probably would have been killed off during Season One.

"We'll Always Have Paris"

Like the classic episode "The Alternative Factor," "We'll Always Have Paris" involves opening a gateway to another dimension, with perilous consequences. For most of the story, however, the sci-fi elements take a backseat to a will-they-or-won't-they romance between Captain Picard and a former lover, Jenice Manheim (Michelle Phillips), who's now married to the injured scientist whose interdimensional experiments have gone awry. Ultimately, Jean-Luc and Jenice don't, but they might have. In Deborah Dean Davis and Hannah Louise Shearer's original story, Picard and Manheim consummated their long-simmering attraction, but Patrick Stewart objected to this scene, arguing that Picard would never bed another man's wife. The reappearance of a woman from the captain's past was another frequently used story device from the classic series, but it was seldom utilized on *Next Gen*. (Apparently Kirk got around more than Picard.) Phillips remains best known as one of the "Mamas" from sixties folk group the Mamas and the Papas.

"Conspiracy"

Screenwriter Tracy Tormé 's dark, paranoid, and at times gruesome "Conspiracy" is unlike anything else dating from Season One, and little like anything else in the entire run of *The Next Generation*. Originally, working from a story submitted by Robert Sabaroff and inspired by John Frankenheimer's political thriller *Seven Days in May* (1964), Tormé wanted to have right-wing elements in Starfleet leadership, unhappy with the Klingon alliance and chafing under the Prime Directive, stage an attempted coup. When that idea was shot down by Roddenberry, Tormé returned with a creepy, *Invasion of the Body Snatchers*–like scenario with parasitic alien invaders taking possession of a group of admirals and other key Starfleet personnel. The episode follows up on the previous "Coming of Age," with Admiral Quinn (now a puppet of the aliens) reappearing, along with the abrasive Lieutenant Merrick, who is revealed to be the host of the alien queen. Merrick meets a controversial demise when Picard and Riker blow his head off and then disintegrate the bug-like alien that arises from his smoldering corpse. It's *Scanners* meets *Alien*, in a gross-out bonanza with an off-the-charts ick factor. "Conspiracy" is gripping SF, suspenseful and hard-hitting, but it feels a bit rushed, especially its conclusion, in which the enemy is vanquished with unlikely speed. "Conspiracy," which won an Emmy for Outstanding Achievement in Makeup, is a rare story that might have been improved by expansion into two episodes.

"The Neutral Zone"

Maurice Hurley's teleplay for "The Neutral Zone" was thrown together quickly—reportedly, in just two days—due to an impending Writers Guild strike that went on to cause major problems for *Next Gen*'s second season. Haste made waste, forcing an ambitious, multipart story line to be truncated and resulting in a less than fully gratifying Season One finale. As it stands, "The Neutral Zone" seems to have been assembled from pieces and parts borrowed from the classic adventures "Space Seed" and "Balance of Terror." The *Enterprise* discovers an ancient starship full of cryogenically frozen humans, who Data rescues and Dr. Crusher revives. But instead of genetically engineered supermen, the unfrozen passengers prove to be a bunch of twentieth-century doofuses (including a greedy financial baron and an alcoholic country music singer) who seem to exist only to annoy Captain Picard and to demonstrate by contrast how much humanity has advanced in the past four hundred years. Meanwhile, Picard has more serious problems: Federation outposts along the Neutral Zone have been wiped out, and Starfleet fears the Romulans may be on the attack. Originally, Hurley intended "The Neutral Zone" as the first installment of a two- or three-part story arc that would introduce the Borg. In a later episode, the Federation and the Romulans would have fought side by side to repulse a common enemy. Due to the strike, however, this concept was abandoned, and the twentieth-century characters, who were supposed to provide comedy relief, became the primary focus of the episode. The disappearance of outposts along both sides of the Neutral Zone is left unexplained, and relations between the Federation and the Romulans remain strained. The debut of the Borg was pushed back until midway through Season Two, and Season One went out with a whimper instead of a bang.

Despite the scattershot quality of the product, *The Next Generation*'s first season was a rousing success where it mattered most: in the Nielsen ratings. During its inaugural season, the show attracted a 10.6 rating and an average viewership of around nine million households per episode, becoming the highest-rated syndicated drama on television and earning the third-highest rating among all syndicated series, trailing only game show titans *Wheel of Fortune* and *Jeopardy!* In later years, its ratings would surpass those of all other syndicated programs. *Next Gen* was the highest-rated program on television among viewers between the ages of eighteen and forty-nine, a highly desirable demographic with advertisers. It would retain this distinction throughout its seven-season run. *TV Guide* reported that thirteen ABC affiliates and two CBS stations had dumped prime-time network programming in favor of *Next Gen*. Perhaps just as importantly for its ongoing viability, the new show also won over many of those fans who at first were reluctant to embrace a *Star Trek* without Kirk, Spock, and McCoy. In an early example of marketing synergy between the movies and the series, printed advertisements for *The Next Generation* were placed in the home video boxes for *Star Trek IV: The Voyage Home*, which was released shortly before the initial broadcast of "Encounter at Farpoint."

Back in 1967, Roddenberry surreptitiously helped mount a write-in campaign to pressure NBC to grant the classic series a second season. This time around, despite the early trepidation of Stewart, Spiner, and others, there was never any doubt that *The Next Generation* would be renewed. The program would make major strides during Season Two, despite handicaps both circumstantial and self-inflicted.

9

The Captain's Chair

Next Generation Directors

No one has greater influence over a motion picture than its director. But in the realm of television, producers and writers are the true authors of the work, guiding the course of the series while directors come and go from week to week. Still, directors play a vital role in the crafting of individual episodes, which remain the basic units in which TV shows function. Good ones are even more valuable to series such as *Star Trek*, which do not rigorously enforce a "house style" but give directors relatively free reign. A gifted, imaginative filmmaker can elevate a mediocre teleplay, while a poor one can sink even brilliant material.

The original *Star Trek* benefitted greatly from the work of two talented directors, Marc Daniels and Joseph Pevney. Between the two them, Daniels and Pevney helmed twenty-nine of the first fifty-six episodes of the program, including most of the show's best-loved adventures. The quality of the series dropped off precipitously in its third season in part because Daniels directed only one installment that year and Pevney none. One of the crucial tasks facing Roddenberry, Berman, and company in the early days of *Star Trek: The Next Generation* was recruiting—or, in some cases, developing—a stable of reliable directors capable of delivering high-quality episodes on a regular basis. Over the course of the program's seven seasons and 176 episodes, the series' brain trust accomplished the task by hiring seasoned veterans such as Cliff Bole and Winrich Kolbe, spotting up-and-coming talents like Les Landau and Rob Bowman, and nurturing the directorial aspirations of cast members including Jonathan Frakes and Patrick Stewart. By the time the series hit its stride, beginning with Season Three, most of these directors (and a handful of other talented filmmakers) were helming multiple episodes each year. The timing was not coincidental.

Les Landau

Although he had a handful of other directorial credits on his résumé (including episodes of *MacGyver*, *Seaquest 2032*, and *Lois & Clark: The New Adventures of Superman*), Les Landau joined *The Next Generation* as an assistant director and worked on thirteen installments in that capacity. This speaks to the many complexities involved in directing *Next Gen*, including its large cast, unique setting and nomenclature, ambitious story lines (sometimes involving stunt work), and extensive visual effects—variables few television directors often encounter, especially in combination. Landau made an inglorious, uncredited *Star Trek* directorial debut when Gene Roddenberry fired director Russ Mayberry midway through the production of the Season One episode "Code of Honor." Landau finished this notorious installment, widely reviled as one of the worst of the entire series. Landau's first credited episode as director was "The Arsenal of Freedom," a Season One highlight. He went on to helm another twenty episodes, including series landmarks "Sins of the Father," "Deja Q," "Sarek," "Half a Life," "Ensign Ro," the cliff-hanger "Time's Arrow, Parts I and II," and the intense "Chain of Command, Part II." Landau had a knack for subtle but powerful camera setups that underscored the impact of each scene. Scattered throughout his *Trek* filmography are some of the series' most emotionally charged sequences. For instance, for the climax of "Sarek" (when Picard hosts the Vulcan ambassador's raging emotions) Landau's camera begins in ultra-close-up on Patrick Stewart, then glides around the actor's face as he shudders with sorrow, fear, and rage. Finally, the camera pulls back to reveal Gates McFadden's Dr. Crusher seated nearby, comforting Captain Picard. Moving into close-up on an actor delivering such a fraught performance was risky, but it paid off with an unforgettable scene. Landau, who later directed installments of *Deep Space Nine*, *Voyager*, and *Enterprise*, is now retired.

Cliff Bole

Cliff Bole was a television veteran who had directed installments of more than two dozen series prior to his association with *Star Trek*, working extensively on action-oriented shows such as *The Six Million Dollar Man*, *Charlie's Angels*, and *MacGyver*. Coincidentally, he helmed seventeen episodes of William Shatner's *T. J. Hooker* and eighteen of Ricardo Montalban's *Fantasy Island*. Bole oversaw twenty-five episodes of *The Next Generation*, directing at least three episodes each of the show's seven seasons. His work included "Hollow Pursuits"; "First Contact"; "Unification, Part II," which guest starred Leonard Nimoy; and the watershed "Best of Both Worlds, Parts I and II." Bole had an instinctive grasp of pacing—his episodes never seemed to stall—and he displayed special flair with action-oriented scenarios of any sort. He was equally at home shooting Barclay's comedic holodeck swordfight with Picard, Data, and Geordi in "Hollow Pursuits" and the nail-biting space battles of "The Best of Both Worlds." Bole also oversaw the two-fisted Season One episode "Conspiracy" (the blue-skinned "Bolians," who first appeared in this installment, were named in his honor). He later directed seven *Deep Space Nine*s and ten *Voyager*s along with many other series including *The X-Files*. He last worked in 2007, on the series *Supernatural*.

Winrich Kolbe

German-born Winrich ("Rick" for short) Kolbe was another veteran television director who had worked on nearly two dozen different series prior to *The Next*

Generation, helming multiple episodes of shows such as *Magnum, P.I., Knight Rider*, and *Spenser: For Hire*. One of his earliest credits was "Baltor's Escape," an episode of the original *Battlestar Galactica*. His *Next Gen* work includes the brilliant series finale "All Good Things . . ." and edgy, atmospheric adventures such as "Where Silence Has Lease," "Pen Pals," and "The Galaxy Child." Kolbe often used stark lighting schemes and unorthodox compositions to lend his installments a distinct sense of atmosphere. In "Where Silence Has Lease," for instance, when Worf and Riker explore the ghostly, empty galaxy-class starship USS *Yamato*, Michael Dorn and Jonathan Frakes were simply walking through the same, instantly recognizable corridor and bridge sets from the *Enterprise*. But through the use of shadowy, chiaroscuro lighting and oblique camera angles, Kolbe makes these familiar trappings seem eerie and otherworldly. In all, Kolbe helmed sixteen *Next Generation* installments and later worked on all the other *Star Trek* spin-off series. He left television in the mid-2000s to take a teaching position at the Savannah College of Art and Design in Georgia. He resigned that post in 2007 for health reasons.

Rob Bowman

Like almost everything else about *Next Gen*, the quality and stability of the show's pool of directors increased as the series progressed. In the early seasons, many directors came and went after a (usually substandard) episode or two. But Rob Bowman was an early stalwart of the program, directing thirteen episodes during the show's first four seasons, including the foundational adventures "Datalore," "Heart of Glory," "Elementary, Dear Data," and "Q Who," which introduced the Borg. For this episode, Bowman and producer Maurice Hurley supplied the voice of the Borg. Bowman, the son of TV producer-director Chuck Bowman, had directed scattered episodes of a dozen series prior to *The Next Generation* and worked with writer-producer Michael Piller on *Probe*. Bowman was a talented and versatile director who seemed to excel at everything (except perhaps clip shows—his filmography also includes the woeful "Shades of Gray"). Working in a variety of registers, from the comedic to the horrific, Bowman seldom failed to deliver a remarkable hour of television. His "Q Who" was the most ambitious episode of the series produced during its first two seasons, and also one of the best. Bowman rose to greater prominence after *Star Trek*, directing thirty-three episodes of *The X-Files* as well as the 1998 *X-Files* feature film. He remains active and, as of this writing, is serving as executive producer (and sometimes director) for the ABC mystery series *Castle*.

Robert Scheerer

Robert Scheerer's lengthy television career began in the early 1960s when he directed episodes of programs like *The Bell Telephone Hour* and *The Danny Kaye Show*. The journeyman director worked on nearly sixty different series in his career, including *Kolchak, the Night Stalker*, several nighttime soaps; and thirty episodes of *The Love Boat*. He joined *Star Trek* during the twilight of his career, helming eleven episodes, including the fan favorites "The Measure of a Man," "The Defector," "The Outcast," and "True Q." Scheerer's eye for dramatic compositions helped enliven static, dialogue-heavy teleplays, and his rapport with actors helped him elicit remarkable work from regular cast members and guest stars alike. In the hands of a lesser director, talky episodes like "The Measure of a Man" and "The Defector" might have devolved into lifeless philosophical blather, but Scheerer mined the interpersonal and moral tension of these scenarios and others like them for powerful dramatic impact. Scheerer, who is now retired, later directed a *Deep Space Nine* installment. His final credit was a 1997 episode of *Star Trek: Voyager*.

Jonathan Frakes

Although he will forever be recognized as Commander William Riker, Jonathan Frakes also made important contributions to *The Next Generation* behind the camera. He was the first *Next Gen* regular to direct an episode and only the second actor to direct a *Star Trek* project (following Leonard Nimoy). Before gaining approval to helm an episode, Frakes endured an arduous apprentice-

ship during which he logged three hundred hours observing nearly every aspect of the creative process. He made an auspicious directorial debut with "The Offspring," a deeply moving Season Three installment in which Data creates an android "daughter." Eventually, Frakes directed a total of eight episodes, displaying an affinity for emotionally charged material with "Reunion" and "The Drumhead," among other installments. Frakes took his work seriously and prepared meticulously for each directorial opportunity. Prior to helming "The Drumhead," for instance, he studied classic courtroom dramas such as *Judgment at Nuremberg* and *The Caine Mutiny*, and later

Actor-director Jonathan Frakes, seen here on the set of *Star Trek: Insurrection*, helmed some of *The Next Generation*'s best episodes and the blockbuster movie *Star Trek: First Contact*. His directorial career continues to thrive.

admitted to lifting shots from those films. Frakes faced his greatest challenge with the Season Five installment "Cause and Effect," in which the same events are repeated five times because the *Enterprise* is trapped in a "temporal causality loop." He worked with cinematographer Marvin Rush to shoot each pass through the cycle in a slightly different way, with lighting schemes and camera placements growing more off-kilter as the show progressed to suggest the continued warping of time and space. Perhaps the greatest testament to Frakes's prowess is that he was selected to direct two of the four *Next Generation* feature films, *First Contact* and *Insurrection*. He also oversaw three episodes each of *Deep Space Nine* and *Voyager*. Since the turn of the millennium, Frakes has worked more frequently as a director than as an actor, helming episodes of twenty different television series, including frequent assignments for the TNT drama *Leverage*.

Gabrielle Beaumont

London-born Gabrielle Beaumont has the distinction of being the first woman ever to direct a *Star Trek* episode (Season Three's "Booby Trap"). Like Bole and Kolbe, she was a seasoned professional, who had worked on nearly fifty other programs—including prestigious dramas such as *Hill Street Blues* and *L.A. Law*—in a career that stretched back to the early 1970s. She directed a total of seven episodes scattered throughout the final four seasons of *Next Gen*, including such outstanding installments as "Disaster" and "Lower Decks." Like Frakes, she excelled with episodes that placed an emphasis on interpersonal drama and usually elicited fine performances from the cast. "Lower Decks," which was told from the perspective of the show's junior officers (played by youthful guest stars with little previous *Star Trek* experience), presented a unique challenge. Beaumont later worked on *Deep Space Nine* and *Voyager*, among other series, but retired in the early 2000s. She now lives in Spain.

David Carson

David Carson directed only four episodes of *The Next Generation*, but all were memorable: "The Enemy," "Redemption, Part II," "The Next Phase," and "Yesterday's Enterprise," widely considered among the greatest single episodes of the series. He was also selected to helm the pilot episode of *Deep Space Nine* and the first *Next Gen* feature film, *Generations*. Carson consistently zeroed in on the human (or Klingon) drama in any screenplay, no matter how fantastic the scenario. He deftly handled the budding romance between Tasha Yar and Lieutenant Castillo in the action-packed time-travel adventure "Yesterday's Enterprise" and the moral dilemmas faced by Worf during "The Enemy" (in which he refuses to save the life of an injured Romulan) and "Redemption II" (when he jeopardizes his career to reclaim his family honor). Carson's pre-*Trek* résumé included work for twenty other series, including the critically renowned *L.A. Law*, *Northern Exposure* and *Homefront*. His career remains active.

Patrick Stewart

Following the lead of Jonathan Frakes, Stewart became the second *Next Generation* regular to begin directing for the series. He made a promising debut with "In Theory," a seriocomic yarn in which Data enters a romantic relationship with a fellow crew member. (At times, the episode plays like a parody of classic sitcoms like *I Love Lucy* and *The Honeymooners*.) Stewart later directed four more installments, most of them prominently featuring Brent Spiner. Although Stewart has no other film or television directing credits, he showed promise with his work for the series, working in a variety of styles and hues—from comedy ("A Fistful of Datas") to horror ("Phantasms") to high drama ("Hero Worship," "Preemptive Strike")—without a single clunker. During the production of "Hero Worship," it fell to Stewart to inform the cast and crew of the death of Gene Roddenberry. During his tenure on *Next Gen*, Stewart also wrote and directed a one-man version of *A Christmas Carol* that played on Broadway to rave reviews, and directed and starred in a touring revival of the play *Every Good Boy Deserves Favour*, about Russian political dissidents, which starred fellow *Next Gen* cast members Brent Spiner, Jonathan Frakes, Colm Meaney, and Gates McFadden.

More Directors

Other noteworthy *Next Generation* directors:
- **Alexander Singer** was one of the final pieces of the *Next Generation*'s directorial puzzle to fall into place. He directed six episodes during the show's final two seasons, including such treasured installments as "Relics" (guest starring James Doohan), "Descent, Parts I and II," and "Ship in a Bottle." Like Scheerer, Singer was among the most experienced directors to work for the series. His career began in the early 1960s and included multiple episodes of *The Fugitive*, *Mission: Impossible*, and *The Monkees*, among many other programs, mostly police dramas and nighttime soap operas. He also directed a *Lost in Space* adventure. His final credits were for episodes of *Deep Space Nine* and *Voyager*. He has since retired.
- **Corey Allen** directed the *Next Generation* pilot, "Encounter at Farpoint," and four later installments spanning the show's seven seasons. By coincidence or by design he directed three of the best Wesley Crusher episodes: "Final Mission," "The Game," and "Journey's End." He later made four *Deep Space Nines*.
- **Adam Nimoy**, the son of Leonard Nimoy, directed a pair of *Next Generation* episodes, the offbeat "Rascals," in which a transporter accident turns Picard, Ro, Guinan, and Keiko into children, and "Timescape," a more traditional *Trek* adventure in which the *Enterprise* is frozen in time.
- **LeVar Burton**, like Frakes and Stewart, also helmed episodes of *The Next Generation*. Although he directed just two installments ("Second Chances" and "The Pegasus"), both were excellent and helped launch a successful directorial career. He later oversaw ten episodes of *Deep Space Nine*, eight

of *Voyager*, and nine of *Enterprise*. He also directed on a half-dozen other series, as well as the TV movie *The Tiger Woods Story* (1998) and the theatrical features *Blizzard* (2003) and *Reach for Me* (2008).

- **Gates McFadden**, like Frakes, Stewart, and Burton, decided to try her hand at directing but helmed just one installment, the disappointing "Genesis."
- **Peter Lauritson** was one of the few writer-producers who also directed occasional episodes of *The Next Generation*. Of this group, Lauritson had the most success, directing both "Gambit, Part I" and "The Inner Light." The latter installment, hailed by many fans and critics as one of the series' best episodes, won a Hugo Award. Lauritson later worked extensively as a producer (and occasionally director) on *Deep Space Nine*, *Voyager*, and *Enterprise*, and coproduced all four *Next Generation* feature films (*Generations*, *First Contact*, *Insurrection*, and *Nemesis*).
- **Richard Compton** has the rare distinction of having acted in the original *Star Trek* series and directed an episode of *The Next Generation*. Early in his career Compton played small roles in a pair of classic *Trek* adventures—he was Washburn in "The Doomsday Machine" and an unnamed Romulan officer in "The Enterprise Incident." These were among his first screen credits. By the end of the decade Compton had moved from acting to directing, working for producer Roger Corman making low-budget drive-in fare like *Macon County Line* (1974). Compton also helmed installments of nearly sixty different series over thirty-five years, including "Haven" for *Next Gen*. His later credits include multiple episodes of *Babylon 5*, *The X-Files*, and *Sliders*. Compton, who was married to actress Veronica Cartwright (*Invasion of the Body Snatchers* [1978], *Alien* [1979]), died in 2007.

10

The Masterpiece Society

Sets, Costumes, Makeup, Special Effects and Music

lthough they appear quaint today, the original *Star Trek*'s sets, costumes, makeup, and visual effects were groundbreaking for a television
production of the era. If you doubt this, compare the production
values from any episode of *Star Trek* with those from any episode of *Lost in Space*,
which was produced concurrently at CBS on a *larger* budget. *Star Trek* earned
eight Emmy nominations in various technical categories during its three-season
broadcast run. The genius of legendary *Trek* craftsmen such as production
designer Matt Jefferies and makeup artist Fred Phillips set a lofty standard for
their *Next Generation* successors. Yet, while the producers and writers of *The Next
Generation* struggled to match the brilliance of the original during the show's
early years, the technical departments swiftly surpassed the achievements of the
classic program, racking up fifteen Emmy nominations (and five wins) during
the first two seasons of *Next Gen* alone. Over the complete run of the show, they
amassed a whopping forty-one Emmy nominations and nineteen wins.

From the outset, *The Next Generation* was one of the best-looking and most
polished productions on television, thanks to a peerless team of behind-the-
scenes professionals. However, crediting individual contributors for their work
is more difficult with *Next Gen* than with the classic series because the two
shows functioned on entirely different scales. While it employed many gifted
craftsmen, the original *Trek* was a mom-and-pop operation compared with the
sequel series. The *Next Gen* production staff was not limited to the names listed
in an episode's end credits; most of those who received on-screen credit were
department heads in charge of large creative teams. The production of a single
Next Generation installment required the combined effort of between 120 and
150 people, not including the forty-member orchestra that played the show's
musical scores. As many as seven crew members shared credit for many of the
series' Emmy Awards. Nevertheless, a handful of individuals in each of several
key departments must be singled out for their outstanding contributions to the
success of *The Next Generation*—and, in some cases, to that of the entire franchise.

Production Design

Few people left a larger imprint on *Star Trek* than production designer Herman Zimmerman. Born April 19, 1935, Zimmerman studied acting at Northwestern University before joining NBC as an assistant art director on the soap opera *Days of Our Lives* in 1965. Over the next forty years, he worked as a set decorator, art director, and production designer on more than fifty movies and TV series. In the 1970s, Zimmerman did wildly creative work on tiny budgets as the art director for a handful of Sid and Marty Krofft children's programs, including *Sigmund and the Sea Monsters* (1973) and *Land of the Lost* (1974–76). He eventually graduated to prime time with series such as *Cheers* (1983–86) before joining *Star Trek*. Zimmerman, more than anyone else, defined the look of the twenty-fourth-century *Trek* universe. He created the spacious, finely appointed *Enterprise-D* interiors, including the elaborate engineering set, and, working with production artist Andrew Probert, built the ship's sleek, bi-level bridge. Although Zimmerman left *Next Gen* midway through its second season, he served as the production designer for six *Trek* feature films (*The Final Frontier* through *Nemesis*) and created the primary sets for *Deep Space Nine*, *Voyager*, and *Enterprise*. He teamed with production illustrator John Eaves to design the Ten-Forward lounge and with designer Rick Sternbach to create space station Deep Space Nine. Zimmerman won four Emmy nominations and an Art Director's Guild Award for his work on *Deep Space Nine*, but his greatest achievement may be the life-size Ba'ku village he designed and constructed for *Star Trek: Insurrection*

The sleek, Galaxy-class *Enterprise-D* starship was designed by production artist Andrew Probert.

(1998), a project of staggering scale and surpassing elegance that would never even be attempted today (it would be computer animated instead). Actor-director Jonathan Frakes, in a DVD interview, ventured that the Ba'ku village "shows what an artist Herman Zimmerman really is."

Production designer Richard James, whose previous credits included the original *Battlestar Galactica* (1978), briefly worked alongside Zimmerman before succeeding him on *The Next Generation*. Week after week, James, who remained with the series for the rest of its run, devised inventive solutions to many challenges involved in designing alien worlds and other sci-fi settings. After *Next Gen* ended, he moved to *Star Trek: Voyager*. Other key production design contributors include Andrew Probert, whose association with *Star Trek* began with the failed *Phase II* series in the late 1970s and continued through the creation of *The Next Generation*. Probert designed the exterior of the Galaxy Class *Enterprise-D* and the ship's bridge before leaving to work for Disney. Designer Rick Sternbach designed twenty-four different *Star Trek* spacecraft, as well as handheld weapons and equipment used by Starfleet officers and alien races. Set decorator Jim Mees, who joined *Next Gen* during Season Two, became a trusted ally of James and a franchise stalwart, working on every subsequent *Trek* series. His many responsibilities included designing the various circuitry panels (which the technical crew nicknamed "Mees panels") often opened aboard the *Enterprise*.

Scenic art supervisor Michael Okuda designed various esoteric elements seen on *Star Trek*, including the characters of written alien languages, the ancient artifacts collected by Captain Picard, and (in most cases) the readouts displayed on computer screens visible throughout the *Enterprise*. When data such as star charts or personnel files was retrieved from the *Enterprise* computer library, Okuda often hid references to fellow members of the production team or to his favorite TV shows (*M*A*S*H* and *Gilligan's Island*) within the displays. Affectionately known by fans as "Okudagrams," these inside jokes can be found if the viewer freeze-frames the picture and carefully examines the information displayed. The most elaborate of these gags, created for "The Naked Now," features a parrot with Gene Roddenberry's head labeled "Great Bird of the Galaxy."

Costumes

At Gene Roddenberry's behest, costume designer William Ware Theiss, who designed the original gold, blue, and red Starfleet uniforms for the classic series, returned to create the look of the twenty-fourth-century Starfleet. His sleek spandex bodysuits provided the futuristic look Roddenberry wanted but were extremely uncomfortable for the cast. Although forever identified with the iconic *Trek* uniforms, Theiss earned his greatest accolades for period costumes, winning an Emmy Award for "The Big Goodbye" (all fedoras and pin-striped suits) and an Emmy nomination for "Elementary, Dear Data" (featuring gaslight-era suits and dresses). Theiss left *The Next Generation* after its second season due to declining health (he died of AIDS in 1992) and was replaced by Robert

Blackman. (For more on Theiss, see the original *Star Trek FAQ*.) Blackman immediately won over the cast with a redesign of the Starfleet uniforms, switching the men from spandex bodysuits to far more comfortable two-piece wool outfits. He subsequently undertook another redesign, introducing the Starfleet uniforms worn in *Deep Space Nine*, *Voyager*, and the final two *Next Gen* movies. But Blackman's contributions went far beyond uniforms. Like Theiss before him, Blackburn also created the wardrobe for all the alien visitors and civilian personnel seen on *Star Trek*. Blackman earned Emmy Awards for two *Next Gen* episodes, "Cost of Living" and "Time's Arrow, Part II" (the latter featured an array of stylish nineteenth-century garb), and earned eight additional nominations for his work on various *Trek* series. In 2009, he won a third Emmy Award for his work on the series *Pushing Daisies*.

Makeup and Hairstyling

The work of *Star Trek*'s makeup and hairstyling departments consistently earned the franchise praise and admiration. *The Next Generation* earned six Emmy nominations and won three awards for makeup, and tallied six nominations— including two victories—for hairstyling. The series' makeup department was overseen by supervisor Michael Westmore, whose legendary family has led Hollywood makeup departments for decades. Michael's grandfather, George (1879–1931), a former British wigmaker, traveled to Hollywood and became the first Westmore to work in the film industry as a makeup artist. He sired three generations of makeup professionals, including Michael Westmore's father, Monte, who worked on *Gone with the Wind* (1939), among other classic productions. Michael Westmore took part in every *Star Trek* project from *The Next Generation* through *Enterprise*, including six movies, and earned an Oscar nomination for *Star Trek: First Contact* (1996). He and his team developed the concept of alien makeups based primarily on forehead and nose appliances, which became the standard approach when creating extraterrestrials within the *Star Trek* universe. The beauty of this method was that it gave actors playing Klingons, Cardassians, Ferengi, and other species a decidedly unearthly appearance but left the performers' eyes visible and facial muscles uncovered to allow a free range of expression. The hairstyling team, including key stylists Richard Sabre and Joy Zapata, worked in concert with Westmore's makeup artists to design hairstyles or apply wigs that completed the transformation. Sabre won two of *Next Gen*'s hairstyling Emmys, and Zapata won the third. The hair and makeup departments also ensured that the regular cast members and guest cast looked their best in each episode. The work of these departments was most evident in flashy adventures that featured large numbers of Klingons or other aliens, such as "Redemption, Parts I and II" and the Emmy-winning "A Matter of Honor." But they provided equally impressive yet more subtle work on numerous other installments, such as the Emmy-winning "The Inner Light," in which Patrick Stewart and a handful of guest stars seem to age forty years.

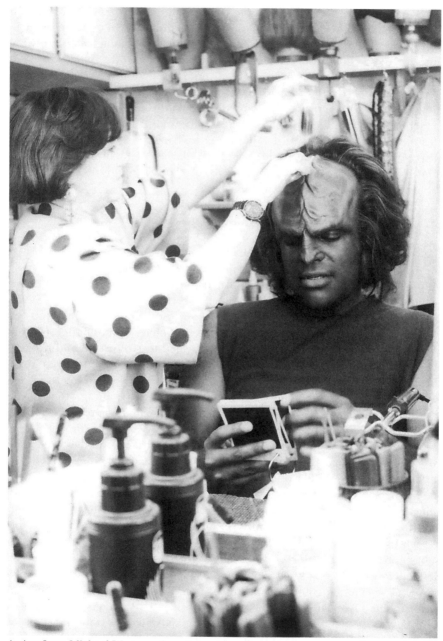

Artists from Michael Westmore's makeup team spent hours every morning turning the amiable Michael Dorn into the fierce Worf. Dorn later said that the process of transforming into a Klingon "was always a pain."

Special Visual and Sound Effects

No technical specialty requires greater concerted effort than visual effects. The imaginative but meticulous work of dozens of artists, including coordinators Rob Legato and Ronald B. Moore (who is not to be confused with writer-producer Ronald D. Moore), enabled *The Next Generation* to establish a new standard in visual effects for television science fiction. Legato won an Emmy Award for overseeing "Conundrum" and earned nominations for "Tin Man" and "Best of Both Worlds, Parts I and II." After *Next Gen*, Legato worked on *Deep Space Nine*—scoring a second Emmy for the pilot "Emissary" (and won Oscars for his work on director Rob Reiner's *Apollo 13* in 1995 and Martin Scorsese's *Hugo* in 2011). Throughout his tenure with the franchise, Moore earned a total of thirteen Emmy nominations, including five wins for various *Trek* series. For *The Next Generation*, he claimed one Emmy Award (for "A Matter of Time") and two nominations (for "Q Who" and "Deja Q").

Visual effects supervisor Dan Curry oversaw the entire operation, serving in this capacity not only on *Next Gen* but on all the subsequent *Trek* series as well. However, he may be best known as the creator of many elements of Klingon culture, including the bat'leth weapon. A devotee of tai chi, Curry also helped choreograph Worf's Klingon exercise routines, which were based on the Chinese martial art. He also directed the Klingon-focused episode "Birthright, Part II." Curry's contributions to Klingon mythology went above and beyond the call of duty; they were not part of his regular responsibilities.

Given the consistent excellence of *The Next Generation*'s visual effects, it's surprising that the series won just two Emmys in that category, among a total of six nominations. Legato's masterful work on "Best of Both Worlds, Part II," including the stunning sight of a space battlefield cluttered with wreckage from starships destroyed by the Borg, lost—maddeningly—to a CBS special starring magician David Copperfield.

The visual effects team worked hand in glove with the series' sound department, which provided the hum of the *Enterprise* engines, the whir of the transporter, the zap of phaser fire, and endless other sound effects. The show's sound design was among the most sophisticated on television. In fact, *Next Gen* won more Emmys for sound mixing and sound editing—a total of nine, amid fourteen nominations—than in any other category. As with visual effects, sound recording, editing, and mixing were a group effort. Nevertheless, one of the unsung heroes of the franchise is sound mixer Alan Bernard, who earned eight Emmy nominations and won four awards for his work on *The Next Generation*, along with five Cinema Audio Society awards. Bernard's most striking achievement is probably the eerie, mechanized soundscapes he helped create for various Borg episodes, including "Q Who" and "The Best of Both Worlds, Parts I and II." Another major contributor was Bill Wistrom, who served as supervising sound editor for *The Next Generation* from its inception through Season Six's "Chain of Command, Part II." After that episode, he moved to *Deep Space Nine*, eventually working on all the *Trek* sequel and prequel series. Sound rerecording mixer Chris Haire was another important team member, working on eight episodes that earned Emmy recognition.

Music

As it is for most successful movies and television programs, *Star Trek*'s finishing touch was its music. *The Next Generation*'s evocative orchestral scores subtly enriched the drama unfolding on-screen. Acclaimed composer Jerry Goldsmith penned scores for five *Trek* feature films and earned an Oscar nomination for his work on *Star Trek: The Motion Picture* (1979). His "Star Trek Theme," written for the movie, was later employed as the main title music for *The Next Generation*. He also composed the title theme for *Star Trek: Voyager*, which won an Emmy, and wrote music for more than 250 movies and TV series during a legendary career. Goldsmith died in 2004 at age seventy-five. Although it couldn't afford talent like Goldsmith—or even James Horner, who was a relative unknown when director Nicholas Meyer hired him to score *Star Trek II: The Wrath of Khan* (1982), but went on to a distinguished career that includes six Oscar nominations—*The Next Generation* also boasted a fine stable of composers, who wrote stirring and often inventive music for the series.

The most prolific and accomplished of the group was Dennis McCarthy, who earned five Emmy nominations. His Emmy-honored work included the tender, delicate scores for "The Child," "Half a Life," and "All Good Things . . ." as well as the moody, grim music of "Unification I" and "Yesterday's Enterprise." McCarthy also composed the main title theme for *Deep Space Nine*, which also won an Emmy, and the music for *Star Trek Generations*. In all, he scored eighty-eight episodes of *Next Gen*, seventy-eight of *DS9*, sixty-four of *Voyager*, and thirty-eight of *Enterprise*.

Aside from McCarthy, the series' other go-to composer was Ron Jones, who penned forty-three scores during the first four seasons of *The Next Generation*. His work tended to be edgier and more experimental, as exemplified by the creepy "Borg music" he composed for "Q Who" and "The Best of Both Worlds, Parts I and II." He also wrote memorable themes for "The Offspring," "Reunion," and many other episodes. Unfortunately, Jones's work was *too* distinctive for executive producer Rick Berman, who fired the composer at the conclusion of *Next Gen*'s fourth season, complaining that Jones's scores were "too noticeable." Afterward, Jones became a vocal critic of Rick Berman's management of the franchise and especially of *Star Trek*'s music. He once quipped that "Faith of the Heart," the Diane Warren–penned power ballad used as the opening theme for *Star Trek: Enterprise*, would better serve as the theme song of the WNBA. After *Trek*, Jones continued to write excellent music, winning two Emmy nominations for his work on the animated series *Family Guy*.

Composer Jay Chattaway replaced Jones and penned forty-two *Next Gen* scores during the show's final three seasons, including the inventive "The

Inner Light," with its haunting flute theme. Other memorable Chattaway scores include "Relics" and "Chain of Command, Parts I and II." He went on to write music for all the subsequent *Trek* spin-offs, winning an Emmy for the *Voyager* series finale "Endgame" and claiming five other nominations.

In addition to those mentioned above, a pair of other little-recognized behind-the-scenes personnel made invaluable contributions to the success of *The Next Generation*, and of the franchise in general. Junie Lowry-Johnson oversaw casting of every episode of every *Star Trek* series from *The Next Generation* through *Enterprise* and all four *Next Gen* feature films. It was her job to put actors in front of producers, including Gene Roddenberry and, later, Rick Berman, to be considered not only for the series' starring and recurring roles, but also for the multitude of guest, supporting, and background parts to be filled each week. Lowry-Johnson has worked on many other, non-*Trek* series and movies, and has won seven Emmy awards (although none for *Star Trek*).

Eric Stillwell also deserves special commendation. He joined the staff of *Next Gen* as a production assistant during Season One. Beginning with the second season, he advanced to the post of script supervisor, serving ably in one of the most important yet least glamorous roles on the staff of any TV series—ensuring scene-to-scene continuity and making sure actors and directors were

Ron Jones's eerie music for "The Best of Both Worlds, Parts I and II" was released on CD by Crescendo Records. Despite the popularity of the composer's work, Rick Berman fired him, complaining that Jones's scores were "too noticeable."

in possession of the most current version of the teleplay. The parameters of Stillwell's job changed dramatically when supervising producer Michael Piller instituted *The Next Generation*'s unheard-of open submission policy for screenplays. Soon the show was flooded with teleplays—as many as three thousand per year—mostly from enthusiastic but clueless amateurs. It fell to Stillwell, who was eventually promoted to the post of preproduction supervisor, to sift through this mountainous slush pile and identify usable teleplays—or at least teleplays with usable elements, which could be purchased and reworked by the show's writing staff. Stillwell unearthed gems such as Melinda Snodgrass's "The Measure of a Man." As a writer himself, he cocreated the original story for the venerated "Yesterday's Enterprise." Stillwell left the series in 1992 to make a career of organizing fan conventions. From 1995 to 2001, he teamed with *Cruise Trek* to organize *Star Trek*–themed vacation cruises but returned to serve as script coordinator on *Star Trek: Insurrection* in 1998.

11

Too Short a Season

The Next Generation, Season Two (1988–89)

B y most accountings, the debut season of *Star Trek: The Next Generation* was a resounding success. The show earned high Nielsen ratings, generated tens of millions of dollars in revenue for Paramount, and won over many fans who were leery of a *Trek* absent Kirk, Spock, and McCoy. Yet no one was entirely satisfied with Season One of *Next Gen*. Viewers grumbled about the uneven quality of the stories—some thrilling, others groan-inducing. Writers and producers recognized this weakness and aspired to deliver a more consistent product. The cast groused about their characters, which remained underdeveloped. Paramount, while delighted with Season One's ratings and earnings, believed the show was capable of more and pushed for even bigger numbers in Season Two. In the end, everyone got what they wanted, but not without great difficulty.

The problems with Season Two began while Season One was still in production. An impending Writers Guild of America strike forced writer-producer Maurice Hurley to take a sweeping, multiepisode story arc—intended to span the end of Season One and the beginning of Season Two, and to introduce the Borg—and reduce the concept to an awkward single installment ("The Neutral Zone"). The strike dragged on for six months and delayed the start of the 1988–89 TV season. Although the labor dispute wreaked havoc on every series, it was particularly damaging to *Star Trek* due to the unique demands of *The Next Generation*. During its first two seasons, *Next Gen* was nearly the only science fiction program on TV, and its script development cycle was protracted and rewrite-heavy. As a result of the strike, *Next Gen*'s sophomore campaign was shortened from twenty-six episodes to twenty-two. In order to meet even that modest number, however, producers were forced to open with a ten-year-old story excavated from the scrap heap of the scuttled *Star Trek: Phase II* series ("The Child") and to close with a glorified clip show ("Shades of Gray").

Meanwhile, turmoil and turnover roiled the program's writing staff and creative leadership. Classic *Trek* veterans David Gerrold and Dorothy Fontana, tapped by creator-producer Gene Roddenberry to help launch *The Next Generation*, bolted before Season One was over due to conflicts with Roddenberry over his dictatorial rewrites of their teleplays. In the hiatus between seasons, screenwriters Robert Lewin and Hannah Louise Shearer bailed for the same reason. Supervising producer Bob Justman, Roddenberry's right-hand man on the original program, left *The Next Generation* midway through Season One, citing health issues. In his absence, Rick Berman became the show's de facto first officer. For Season Two, Berman was officially elevated to the title of Co-Executive Producer. Roddenberry continued to steer the series to the best of his ability. In an interview filmed in 1988 and included on the *Star Trek: The Next*

Diana Muldaur (pictured) replaced Gates McFadden in sick bay for Season Two, but fans never warmed to her crusty Dr. Pulaski. By the start of Season Three, Muldaur was out and McFadden was back.

Generation Season Two DVD collection, writer-producer Maurice Hurley stressed that every script had to receive Roddenberry's blessing. "Is this *Star Trek?* Until he [Roddenberry] puts his thumbprint on it, it's not," Hurley said. "Once he does, we know we have a *Star Trek* show and we move forward."

With the Great Bird at the helm, the series' creative staff continued to abandon ship. At the beginning of Season Two, the staff included writers Hurley, Peter Lauritson, David Livingston, John Mason, Mike Gray, Burton Armus, and Tracy Tomé. Of that group, only Hurley, Lauritson, and Livingston remained for the entire season. The rest quit midway through, unhappy with the direction of the series and with ongoing, heavy-handed rewrites by Roddenberry, often assisted by Hurley, who also departed at the year's end. Producer Richard Manning, who joined the series the following season, created a large poster labeled the "The Star Trek Memorial Wall" that listed the names of all the writers who had left the show. Manning placed his own name on the Memorial Wall and left the series later that season, handing off the poster to Ronald D. Moore, who continued to update it throughout the remainder of the series.

The turnover wasn't restricted to the writing staff, however. The show's most visible change was in sick bay, where Diana Muldaur's Dr. Katherine Pulaski replaced Gates McFadden's Dr. Beverly Crusher. Throughout the first season, the *Next Gen* brain trust, when unsure of how to proceed, had fallen back on concepts from the original program. The change in Chief Medical Officers was the final but most profound example of this unfortunate tendency. Roddenberry decided the crew needed a new doctor with a personality more akin to DeForest Kelley's crusty "Bones" McCoy, and wanted to introduce playful bickering between Dr. Pulaski and Data, emulating the Spock-McCoy relationship. It didn't work. Although Muldaur is a fine actress—she had made memorable guest appearances in two classic *Trek* adventures and would later earn a pair of Emmy nominations on *L.A. Law*—her Dr. Pulaski came across as cold and stern, especially compared to the warm, approachable Dr. Crusher. Her attitude toward Data (whom she only grudgingly accepted as a sentient being) seemed hard-hearted. She also clashed repeatedly with Captain Picard, putting her continually at odds with the show's two most popular characters. Fans never warmed to the character and flooded Paramount with cards and letters pleading for the return of Dr. Crusher.

Following the departure of Denise Crosby in the middle of Season One, actress Whoopi Goldberg approached Roddenberry and asked to join the cast of *Next Gen*. Goldberg had been a *Trek* fan since childhood and was inspired to pursue a career in acting by Nichelle Nichols's portrayal of Lieutenant Uhura. By the time *The Next Generation* entered its second season, Goldberg, originally known as a stand-up comedian, had proven her dramatic skills with an Oscar-nominated appearance in director Steven Spielberg's *The Color Purple* (1985). She also won a Golden Globe and an NAACP Image Award for her work in that film. Roddenberry created the recurring character of Guinan—the *Enterprise-D*'s mysterious, centuries-old alien barkeep—especially for her. Although she wasn't involved every week (she appeared in twenty-nine episodes scattered throughout Seasons Two through Six), Guinan proved to be a fascinating character, and Goldberg played her brilliantly. The acclaimed actress's presence also boosted the show's prestige.

In another cast development, actor Colm Meaney, who was seen as an unnamed background character in a pair of Season One episodes ("Encounter at Farpoint" and "Lonely Among Us"), earned a recurring role as transporter chief Miles O'Brien. Meaney quickly became another fan favorite, appearing in fifty-two *Next Gen* episodes before transferring to the crew of *Star Trek: Deep Space Nine* in 1993, where O'Brien became a leading character.

"The Child"

Strapped for teleplays due to the writer's strike, producers dusted off this relic, penned by Jon Povill for the abandoned *Star Trek: Phase II* television series of the 1970s and updated by writers Jaron Summers and Maurice Hurley. Deanna Troi is impregnated by a noncorporeal life force and gives birth to a child that matures with amazing speed. Meanwhile, the lives of the crew are jeopardized when the containment field surrounding a shipment of frighteningly dangerous biological agents begins to break down. Surprisingly, given its desperate origins, "The Child" supplied a promising start for Season Two, combining nail-biting *Wages of Fear*–like suspense with affecting human (or, rather, Betazoid) drama. Originally created to feature Ilia, the bald female Deltan played in *Star Trek: The Motion Picture* by Persis Khambatta, "The Child" was retrofitted for Counselor Troi and became the first of many Season Two installments designed to explore a single character in greater depth. Marina Sirtis has more to do in this single adventure than she had in all of Season One combined, and she handles it well. She is particularly touching in the story's final moments, following the loss of her superhuman offspring. The episode benefits from a moving, Emmy-nominated score by Dennis McCarthy. "The Child" also shows off Sirtis's new, softer hairstyle, which replaced the severe bun she had worn throughout the previous season. "The Child" reveals Geordi La Forge's promotion to Chief Engineer and Worf's promotion to Chief of Security. It also introduces both the *Enterprise*'s Ten-Forward lounge and bartender Guinan (Goldberg), and is the first installment to show Commander Riker wearing a beard.

"Where Silence Has Lease"

"Where Silence Has Lease" has a terrific premise: The *Enterprise* is trapped by an apparently omnipotent alien life-form that uses the ship's crew as lab rats in a series of twisted psychological experiments. It also features some outstanding sequences, such as Worf telling a Klingon legend about a giant monster that eats spaceships, and Riker and Worf nervously exploring the abandoned USS *Yamato*, an eerily empty twin of the *Enterprise*. This installment also introduced the

Klingon's brutal, monster-filled holodeck calisthenics program. Unfortunately, however, screenwriter Jack Sowards was unable to devise a satisfactory ending to the story, which suffers from a feeble final act. Patrick Stewart later quoted from Picard's speech about death, written for this episode, during his eulogy for Gene Roddenberry.

Data (Brent Spiner) as Sherlock Holmes, Geordi (LeVar Burton) as Dr. Watson, and Dr. Pulaski (Diana Muldaur) as herself, venture into the realm of Sir Arthur Conan Doyle in the holodeck yarn "Elementary, Dear Data," a Season Two highlight.

"Elementary, Dear Data"

While participating in an elaborate holodeck story based on the adventures of Sherlock Holmes, Geordi overrides security protocols and accidentally grants sentience to a holographic realization of the genius supervillain Dr. Moriarty (Daniel Davis). It's up to Data (impersonating Holmes) and Geordi (Dr. Watson), aided by Picard (himself), to rescue the kidnapped Dr. Pulaski and prevent Moriarty from taking over the *Enterprise*. Like "The Big Goodbye," "Elementary, Dear Data" ranks among the series' most engrossing holodeck-centered stories. Enjoyable on many levels, "Elementary, Dear Data" boasts an excellent, tension-rich teleplay; outstanding costumes and production design; and a scintillating guest performance by Davis as Moriarty. Brian Alan Lane's script has a light, playful tone but touches on weighty issues that would be explored in later installments such as "The Measure of a Man." The Moriarty character anticipates the Doctor (Robert Picardo) from *Star Trek: Voyager*, another hologram who gains self-awareness. The episode earned Emmy nominations for its art direction and costume design. Data's fascination with Holmes began the previous season when Riker introduced the android to the works of Sir Arthur Conan Doyle during "Lonely Among Us." "Elementary, Dear Data" was well liked by fans but not by the Doyle estate, which fired off a letter to *Next Gen*'s producers explaining that it retained a partial interest in the Holmes character. Although the estate took no legal action, *Star Trek* would have to obtain permission and pay a fee if it wanted to use Doyle's characters again.

Saturday Night Live comedian Joe Piscopo (left) made one of the season's least-loved guest appearances in "The Outrageous Okona." This publicity shot also features new cast member Whoopi Goldberg (center), who was greeted warmly by fans, and Brent Spiner.

"The Outrageous Okona"

"The Outrageous Okona" is so dominated by its guest stars that the regular cast members seem like background color. The central focus of the story is Captain Okona (William O. Campbell), a rakish adventurer and interstellar Don Juan who seeks refuge on the *Enterprise* from two rival civilizations, both of whom want his head (for different reasons). While Picard tries to negotiate a solution, Okona beds a succession of female crew members. Meanwhile Data, struggling to understand the concept of humor, trades one-liners with a twentieth-century stand-up comedian (Joe Piscopo) on the holodeck. Many fans recoiled at the sight of *Saturday Night Live*'s Piscopo on *Star Trek*, but Campbell's Okona was only slightly less irksome. The fan website Agony Booth named this episode one of the worst in the history of the franchise, calling it "pretty damn excruciating" and comparing Burton Armus's teleplay with bad fan fiction. "The Outrageous Okona" may not be *that* bad, but it's certainly not very good.

"Loud as a Whisper"

The *Enterprise* delivers legendary diplomat Riva (Howie Seago) to planet Solais V, where he will try to end a centuries-old civil war. Riva is mute and "speaks" through a trio of interpreters he refers to as his "chorus." The mission seems doomed when violence breaks out during the first bargaining session, and all three members of Riva's chorus are disintegrated. Counselor Troi and Data are forced to improvise in order to save the negotiations. Seago, who is deaf, proposed the idea of an episode featuring a nonspeaking character to knock down stereotypes about those who can't hear or speak. The impulse was noble, but the resulting episode is lackluster. Ironically, most of its problems stem from the Riva character. As written, Riva seems pompous and smarmy. He is imperious and dismissive with everyone except Deanna, who he tries to seduce. His behavior is so off-putting and boorish that viewers may find themselves rooting for the negotiator to fail. And Seago monopolizes "Loud as a Whisper" nearly as much as Campbell did "The Outrageous Okona." In an interesting subplot, Dr. Pulaski suggests an experimental medical procedure could grant Geordi normal human eyesight. The chief engineer says he'll think it over. This possibility was written in for the benefit of actor LeVar Burton, who disliked working with his marvelously expressive eyes covered. Nevertheless, Geordi would retain his VISOR for the remainder of the series.

"The Schizoid Man"

Dr. Ira Graves (W. Morgan Sheppard), an irascible, terminally ill cybernetics genius, downloads his mind into Data's body. Quickly Data starts exhibiting Graves's personality traits, becoming vain and insubordinate, and begins romancing Graves's former assistant, a young woman named Kareen (Barbara Alyn Woods). Screenwriter Tracy Tomé adapted the teleplay from an original treatment by Richard Manning and Hans Beimler, integrating several ideas from an unrelated story of his own creation. The resulting script is uneven but gives Spiner the opportunity to play a wide range of emotions usually off-limits for Data. Suzie Plakson, who later portrayed Worf's love interest, K'Eheyr, among other *Trek* characters, appears here as the Vulcan Dr. Selar.

"Unnatural Selection"

The *Enterprise* encounters a derelict starship whose crew has been wiped out by a mysterious illness that causes rapid aging. Dr. Pulaski traces the disease back to

Darwin Station, a Federation outpost where geneticists have engineered a brood of telepathic human children. The scientists there are also dying, but the children—who have superhuman immune systems—seem unaffected. Pulaski risks her life to try to find a cure for the disease and save the children, but winds up contracting the illness herself. Following four plot-driven and guest-star-oriented episodes, "Unnatural Selection," written by John Mason and Mike Gray (and extensively rewritten by Hurley), was intended as a showcase for the series' new chief physician. It's a medical mystery (not unlike a science-fictionalized episode of *House*) that recalls the classic episode "The Deadly Years," in which several crew members, including Kirk, Spock, McCoy, and Scotty, suffer from rapid aging. "Unnatural Selection" is tense and hard-hitting and includes Muldaur's best work for *Next Gen*. It also earned an Emmy nomination for hairstyling. However, the scenario also represents a rare violation of *Star Trek*'s carefully guarded franchise continuity. The Federation had supposedly banned the kind of genetic experimentation being conducted at Darwin Station, as stated in the classic episode "Space Seed" and later reiterated in the *Next Gen* adventure "The Masterpiece Society" and on installments of *Deep Space Nine* and *Enterprise*.

"A Matter of Honor"

Continuing a welcome trend toward character-driven adventures (as opposed to plot-driven or guest-star-oriented episodes), screenwriter Burton Armus's "A Matter of Honor" places Commander Riker in the spotlight. He volunteers to serve as second-in-command on the Pagh, a Klingon Bird of Prey, as part of a Federation exchange program, and becomes entangled in a conflict of loyalties when Klingon captain Kargan (Christopher Collins), whom Riker has sworn to obey, decides to attack the *Enterprise*. (Kargan believes Picard has sabotaged his ship.) Riker devises a clever solution to the crisis, averting a catastrophic attack without sacrificing the honor of the Pagh and its captain. "A Matter of Honor" is full of shining moments for actor Jonathan Frakes, as Riker eats repulsive-looking Klingon food (twice), jokes and brawls with his Klingon crewmates, and flirts with Klingon women. After staying tight-lipped through most of the first season, Riker's sense of humor and joie de vivre were emerging, bringing the character more in line with the actor's ebullient personality. Stories like this one also underscored the growing friendship between Riker and Worf, which would continue in later stories. This episode earned an Emmy nomination for makeup and the highest Nielsen ratings of any *Next Gen* installment yet to air. No Season Two episode is more pure fun than this one.

"The Measure of a Man"

With "The Measure of a Man," *The Next Generation* delivered its first masterpiece, an installment that could stand side by side with the best episodes of the original *Trek*—or any other series—in terms of writing, performance, and production. Thought-provoking yet unpretentious, exciting but character centered, it marked an astonishing *Star Trek* debut for rookie screenwriter Melinda Snodgrass, who wrote the teleplay on spec and was quickly hired as a story editor on the strength of this script. Cyberneticist Bruce Maddox (Brian Brophy) arrives with orders to take possession of Data, who he plans to disassemble and study in order to help create a legion of similar android officers. To avoid this fate, Data attempts to resign his commission, but is told he cannot because he is the property of Starfleet. Picard protests, and a hearing is scheduled to determine whether or not Data is a sentient being with human rights or merely a highly advanced computer mechanism. Since they are at a remote starbase without a full judge advocate general staff, Picard represents Data's interests at the hearing, while Riker is forced to argue against his friend's humanity.

Snodgrass's screenplay abounds with interpersonal drama, as members of the crew struggle with the potential loss of their android friend and grapple with weighty moral and philosophical issues. Spiner, Stewart, Frakes, and Goldberg all have outstanding moments. Picard's stirring final argument aside, the episode's finest scene is the captain's illuminating conversation with Guinan, who helps Picard realize the dark implications of a ruling against Data: the potential creation of a race of android slaves. Guest star Brophy supplies a rich, carefully shaded supporting turn as Maddox, who honestly believes he's doing the right thing. This episode also introduced the bridge crew's on-again, off-again poker games, which would recur throughout the remainder of the series. "The Measure of a Man" was a rare instance of the writer's strike working in the show's favor. It was the first spec script purchased for the program. Producers wouldn't have been looking at spec work if not for the strike. "The Measure of a Man" was nominated for a Writers Guild of America award. Director Robert Scheerer and producers Rick Berman and Michael Piller have all named it one of *Next Gen*'s best episodes, echoing the sentiment of countless fans.

"The Dauphin"

Wesley Crusher romances Salia (Jamie Hubbard), a lonely alien princess returning from exile to assume leadership of her home world. His attentions draw the ire of Salia's attendant and jealous protector, Anya (Paddi Edwards), who turns out to be a shape-shifting alien. "The Dauphin," yet another character-driven piece, has its moments, including Wheaton's tender scenes with Hubbard and the amusingly useless advice on women the young ensign receives from his male superior officers. In one hilarious sequence, Riker demonstrates his flowery romantic approach by wooing Guinan, to the bartender's delight. At last the writers found something believable for Wesley to do (namely, fall for a girl) and allowed Wheaton to better demonstrate the talent he had displayed in his pre-*Trek* roles.

"Contagion"

The *Enterprise* contracts what is essentially a debilitating alien computer virus and becomes immobilized during a risky mission to a planet in the Neutral Zone. A pursuing Romulan warship is struck by the same virus. While trying to solve the problem, Picard and Data discover a secret capable of shifting the balance of power in the galaxy. "Contagion" is a workmanlike effort with greater emphasis on plot than character. Its best sequence comes early on, when the USS *Yamato*, infected with the virus, suffers a critical system failure and explodes with all hands on board. This shocking event registers a jarring emotional impact on the *Enterprise* crew and with viewers.

"The Royale"

On the otherwise uninhabitable planet Theta VII, the *Enterprise* discovers a tiny habitable zone containing a large, man-made structure. Riker, Worf, and Data beam down to investigate and discover the Royale, a twentieth-century hotel and casino populated by characters out of a cheap detective novel. They also find the desiccated, 283-year-old remains of an early Earth astronaut—which is puzzling since Earth ships of that vintage lacked warp drive and were incapable of venturing so far into the galaxy. Although it boasts an intriguing mystery premise, "The Royale" is more interested in placing Riker, Worf, and Data into comical fish-out-of-water situations with the Royale's dime-novel inhabitants. At one point, Data joins a high-stakes craps game. "Baby needs a new pair of shoes!" he says as he rolls the bones. Unfortunately, most of the (intended) comedy falls flat. Tracy Tomé wrote "The Royale" but later disowned it because he was so displeased with Maurice's Hurley's rewrites. Tomé removed his name from the episode and is credited as "Keith Mills." Soon, Tomé would disown the entire series. Following a similar dustup over Hurley's changes to his teleplay "Manhunt," Tomé joined the parade of miffed writers who stormed out on *The Next Generation* during its first two seasons.

"Time Squared"

In the first time-travel story featured on *The Next Generation*, the *Enterprise* recovers a damaged shuttlecraft only to discover that it's one of their own—piloted by a wounded duplicate Captain Picard. Eventually, Geordi, Data, and Dr. Crusher piece together that this Picard, who is unable to speak, has traveled into the past from six hours in the future, when the *Enterprise* will be destroyed. The only hope for survival is that this sketchy knowledge of these future events will somehow help the crew avert catastrophe. Maurice Hurley's teleplay suffers from some dull stretches (as when Picard attempts to interrogate his insensible doppelganger in sick bay) and is riddled with the headache-inducing logical conundrums characteristic of time-travel yarns. Nevertheless, "Time Squared" remains a diverting entry. The central concept of trying to alter an apparently established timeline would be put to far more imaginative use a season later in the superb "Yesterday's Enterprise." Originally, "Time Squared" was planned as a two-parter that would tie directly into "Q Who," but the two teleplays were decoupled.

"The Icarus Factor"

While Riker weighs whether or not to leave the *Enterprise* and accept his first command, he receives an unwelcome visit from his estranged father, who he hasn't seen in fifteen years. Meanwhile, Worf sulks, feeling isolated as an important Klingon cultural milestone approaches and dreading the imminent loss of his friend, Riker. "The Icarus Factor" is a rare *Star Trek* character study with no action sequences at all. Moreover, the only mystery element (other than Wesley, Data, and Geordi trying to figure out what's bothering Worf) is a puzzling series of readout anomalies in the engineering section that are resolved without incident. Director Robert Iscove wanted to take the episode even further afield by playing up the tortured, conflicted emotions of Riker and Worf, but Roddenberry nixed this approach. As a result, Iscove, a long-time *Trek* fan, refused offers to return to the series. Future episodes would integrate the kind of character-enriching, soul-searching scenes found here into more action-oriented scenarios.

"Pen Pals"

Data begins a subspace correspondence with Sarjenka (Nikki Cox), an adolescent female humanoid from a technologically primitive planet with no knowledge of extraterrestrial life. When a geological survey reveals that Sarjenka's planet will soon be blown apart by seismic instabilities, Picard must decide whether or not to violate the Prime Directive in order to save Sarjenka and her civilization from destruction. Sharply written by Snodgrass, based on a story by Hannah Louise Shearer, "Pen Pals," like "The Measure of a Man," skillfully combines a provocative moral dilemma with affecting interpersonal drama. Both Stewart and Spiner are excellent here, and Frakes and Meaney have an enjoyable scene in the transporter room when Riker, in a blatant violation of Starfleet regulations, beams Data down to the planet to search for Sarjenka. "O'Brien, take a nap," Riker says. "You didn't see any of this. You're not involved." "Right, sir," Meaney replies. "I'll just be standing over here dozing off." The episode also features a handful of small but illuminating character moments. Picard's passion for riding (holographic) horses is revealed, and the captain drinks Earl Grey tea (hot) for the first time.

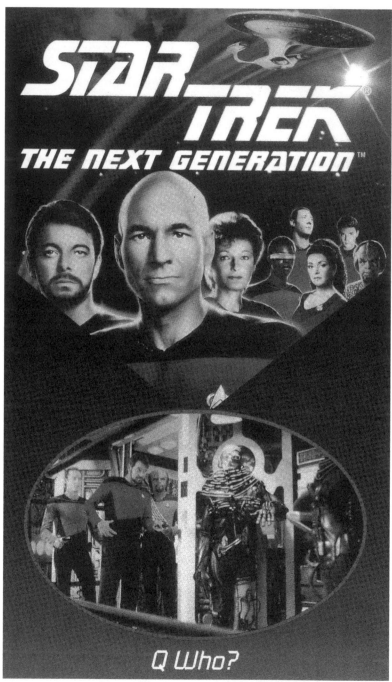

The implacable Borg first menaced Captain Picard and his crew in the Season Two thriller "Q Who." The Borg was created by writer-producer Maurice Hurley with input from Gene Roddenberry and Rick Berman.

"Q Who"

In a watershed installment, Q returns and the Borg make their belated entrance. To prove to Picard that the Federation is ill prepared for the dangers that await it as it ventures into more distant corners of the galaxy, Q transports the *Enterprise* to a region dominated by the Borg, whose implacable determination to assimilate every culture they encounter, combined with their technological superiority, make them an adversary more dangerous than any Picard and his crew have faced before. The Borg, created by Maurice Hurley with input from Roddenberry and Berman, were the fearsome adversary *Star Trek*'s brain trust had been searching for since *Next Gen* premiered. They remain arguably the most daunting foes in the history of the franchise. In fact, the Borg were so powerful and intimidating that they made just five more appearances in the show's remaining five seasons, in part because writers struggled to find credible ways for Picard to defeat them. (In this instance, when destruction of the *Enterprise* seems assured, Q simply whisks the ship back home.) "Q Who" was lavishly produced, loaded with costly visual and sound effects, and elaborate sets and costumes. According to Larry Nemecek's *Star Trek: The Next Generation Companion*, this episode ran $50,000 over budget, but it was money well spent. The installment was rewarded with a pair of Emmys for sound editing and sound mixing, and an additional nomination for visual effects. The unsettling appearance of the Borg, who resemble cyberpunk Nosferatu, was inspired by the work of artist H. R. Giger, best known for his contributions to Ridley Scott's *Alien* (1979).

"Samaritan Snare"

Picard and Wesley travel in a shuttle to Starbase 515, where the captain will have his malfunctioning artificial heart replaced. Meanwhile, Geordi is taken captive by dimwitted, unscrupulous aliens out to steal technology from more advanced civilizations. The Geordi story line is tough to swallow. It's predicated on Riker behaving like an idiot, ignoring Worf's advice and sending his chief engineer to the alien spacecraft to attend to routine repairs. Couldn't any ensign have handled the job as easily? Rather than menacing, the aliens come off as comically stupid. However, the Picard-Crusher scenes on the shuttle are excellent. Given something to work with, Wheaton offers his finest work of the season during a heart-to-heart with his captain on the long shuttle flight to Starbase 515. For once, Wesley comes across as authentic and likeable. The excellent Season Six episode "Tapestry" grew out of events from Picard's youth, which the captain recalls in this story.

"Up the Long Ladder"

Responding to an old-fashioned distress signal, the *Enterprise* discovers two civilizations that have arisen on neighboring worlds, both stemming from a single, ill-fated spaceship containing two groups of colonists. The first, settlers with a Luddite, antitechnology bent, live like Irish peasants from the nineteenth century. The others have developed a technologically advanced civilization made up entirely of clones. Unfortunately, the clone race is nearing extinction due to overuse of the limited genetic material in their gene pool. (Only five settlers survived a tragic crash landing on their planet.) To survive, they must acquire new genetic material, but Riker, Pulaski, and others from the *Enterprise* refuse to donate it and treat the clones with disdain, which forces the colonists to take desperate measures. Screenwriter Melinda Snodgrass, who hit a home run with "The Measure of a Man" and belted a double with "Pen Pals," struck out with this teleplay, which was intended as a commentary on U.S. immigration policy, a connection difficult to discern in the completed episode. She also envisioned this installment as a comedy (her original title was "Send in the Clones"), but most of the humor was eliminated in rewrites, and what's left isn't very amusing. Perhaps worse, the *Enterprise* crew's sneering attitude toward the clones is difficult to reconcile with Starfleet's usual open-mindedness toward alien cultures.

The foremost of those two fishy-looking aliens is Fleetwood Mac drummer Mick Fleetwood, an avid Trekker who made a cameo appearance (under heavy makeup) in the episode "Manhunt."

"Up the Long Ladder" drew fire from Irish Americans, who resented its stereotypical depiction of the Irish (the only missing cliché is a leprechaun hawking Lucky Charms breakfast cereal), and from anti-abortion groups, due to a scene in which Riker disintegrates incubating clones of himself and Pulaski. Politics aside, there remains no shortage of other reasons to dislike this episode. Writer-producer Ronald D. Moore, in a 1997 AOL chat, called it "embarrassing."

"Manhunt"

Lwaxana Troi returns, this time looking for a new husband as she enters a hypersexualized Betazoid form of menopause. Her preferred new mate is Captain Picard, who hides out in the Dixon Hill holodeck program to try to avoid her. After the disastrous "The Royale" and "Up the Long Ladder," Season Two finally delivered an enjoyable comedy with this lighthearted romp. Screenwriter Tracy Tormé wrote "Manhunt" to serve as a sequel to two of his Season One episodes, "Haven" and "The Big Goodbye," but removed his name from this teleplay (he's credited as "Terry Devereaux") because he felt the Dixon Hill sequences were "mutilated" in rewrites. This was Tomé's final *Trek* script; he left the show soon after. Mick Fleetwood, the drummer and cofounder of rock band Fleetwood Mac, makes a guest appearance under heavy makeup as one of two fishlike alien dignitaries traveling to a diplomatic summit.

"The Emissary"

A special Federation representative—the half-Klingon, half-human K'Ehleyr (Suzie Plakson)—beams aboard the *Enterprise* to assist as Captain Picard and his crew race to meet a Klingon sleeper ship full of recently reawakened Klingons who don't realize the war between the Federation and the Empire is over. Along the way, Worf and K'Ehleyr, who were previously acquainted, indulge in a physical encounter on the holodeck. Afterward Worf proposes to marry her, which is required according to Klingon custom. But K'Ehleyr, who has rejected Klingon ways, also rebuffs Worf's overtures. "The Emissary" is a minor marvel of sustained tension, within both its sleeper ship story line and its romantic subplot. K'Ehleyr returned in the fourth-season installment "Reunion," and repercussions of events from this episode were felt throughout the remainder of the series. Both Dorn and Plakson are superb in "The Emissary" and display sensational chemistry. Plakson was a favorite of producers and played several characters of various species on *Next Gen* and other *Trek* series, including the Vulcan Dr. Selar in "The Schizoid Man," a female Q in the *Voyager* episode "The Q and the Gray," and the Andorian Terah in the *Enterprise* adventure "Cease Fire."

"Peak Performance"

Captain Picard grudgingly agrees to participate in war games designed to test the tactical ingenuity of his bridge crew. Kolrami (Roy Brocksmith), a preening, smug Federation master strategist, is dismissive toward the chances (and abilities) of Commander Riker, who must stage a mock assault on the *Enterprise* using a derelict spaceship with extremely limited firepower and no operative warp drive. But the exercise is thrown for a loop when a real adversary intervenes—a Ferengi warship. Eventually, of course, the Ferengi are defeated, and Kolrami gets his comeuppance, but along the way David Kemper's teleplay works in enjoyable character scenes for several crew members, including Riker, Data, Geordi, and Wesley. These moments make the episode fun, even though the *Enterprise* never seems to be in any real danger. Armin Shimerman, who portrayed a Ferengi in "The Last Outpost" and later played Quark on *Deep Space Nine*, guest stars as the captain of the meddling Ferengi vessel.

"Shades of Gray"

During a routine away mission, Commander Riker is infected by alien microbes that induce paralysis. He soon lapses into a coma. When traditional treatments prove ineffective, Dr. Pulaski, flanked by Counselor Troi, stimulates Riker's cerebral cortex, triggering memory flashbacks that release endorphins capable of combatting the microbes. The first twelve minutes of "Shades of Gray" seem fairly promising, but its final thirty minutes are excruciating. The episode devolves into a parade of library footage, interrupted only by shots of Frakes lying on his back while Muldaur spews medical Treknobabble and Sirtis corkscrews her face in empathic agony. Clips from no fewer than twenty previous installments are incorporated, including scenes from "Up the Long Ladder," which premiered just four episodes before this one. Some adventures, including "The Last Outpost" and "Skin of Evil," are sampled more than once. Curiously, some of the clips are from scenes in which Riker does not even appear! The dearth of quality screenplays played a factor in this debacle, but budget constraints were the larger problem. Several episodes, most notably "Elementary, Dear Data" and "Q Who," had run over budget. The bargain-basement "Shades of Gray" was intended to make up for some of the overage, since it would require only a few days' worth of new footage. But in television production, you get what you pay for, and "Shades of Gray" is widely considered one of *Next Gen*'s weakest entries. In *Captains' Logs*, Hurley, who developed the original story, dismissed "Shades of Gray," his last work on the series, as a half-hearted effort. "Terrible, just terrible," he said of the episode. "I was on the way out the door."

For the second year in a row, *The Next Generation* concluded with a subpar entry, but overall the show's second season represented a major improvement over its first. While the quality of its teleplays remained uneven, it featured higher high points and fewer low points. Installments such as "The Measure of a Man," "Elementary, Dear Data," "A Matter of Honor," "Q Who," and "The Emissary," among others, pointed the way forward as the program stepped out of the shadow of its classic predecessor and established a fascinating mythology of its own. Not coincidentally, writers finally began to develop the *Enterprise* crew more fully. None of these advances were lost on the audience. Viewership increased by a half-million viewers per episode from Season One. Both on the screen and in the ratings, *The Next Generation* was improving. It would make a quantum leap forward in Season Three.

12

And the Children Shall Lead

Gene Roddenberry's mastery of *Star Trek: The Next Generation* was even shorter-lived than his stewardship of the *Trek* movie franchise. Roddenberry had worked for nearly five years to bring *Star Trek: The Motion Picture* to the screen. But the film's disappointing performance (and capricious studio politics) quickly reduced him to a mere figurehead. Roddenberry reclaimed his primacy when he was granted total creative control over *The Next Generation* but remained fully in command of the series for only two seasons. Then, as age and illness began to take their toll, he was forced to cede ever greater authority to younger producers, led by Rick Berman. By the time of Roddenberry's death in 1991, the man affectionately known as the Great Bird of the Galaxy no longer had any day-to-day involvement in production of either the *Trek* movies or the TV series. What's more, most of the producers hired by Roddenberry had also departed. The franchise was now largely controlled by the previously little-known Berman and personnel hired by Berman. For the next twenty-two years, these creators—many of whom had no affinity for *Star Trek* before signing on with *Next Gen*—steered the franchise. Under their guidance, *Star Trek* achieved its greatest popular success. Then the roof caved in, and a third generation of franchise leadership took over.

Rick Berman

Richard Keith Berman, the son of Edward and Alvira ("Chickie") Berman, was born Christmas Day, 1945, in New York City. His father was a painter who in the 1950s moved out of fine art and into advertising, and ran the ad department at the Abraham & Straus department store in New York for many years. Young Rick grew up surrounded by art and literature (he describes his mother as a "voracious reader"). In junior high school Berman became fascinated with movies—discovering Italian and Swedish art films of interest to few other boys his age—and he soon set his heart on a career in the movie industry. After graduating from the Wheatley School, a private high school on Long Island, Berman studied film at the University of Wisconsin from 1963 to 1967. His first job after college was as a page and tour guide at NBC in New York.

From there Berman landed a job with a small, nonunion company that made documentaries and industrial films. "I learned everything about film because I was the guy who had to do it all," Berman said in a 2006 interview for the Archive of American Television. In 1970, he served as a production assistant on John Lennon and Yoko Ono's experimental film *Fly*. Throughout the early and middle 1970s, Berman worked as assistant director to documentary filmmaker Dick Young, helping make a series of short films commissioned by the United Nations. Together, Young and Berman traveled to more than eighty countries and shot nonfiction shorts on a myriad of subjects. That experience helped Berman secure positions producing nature and science documentaries in the late 1970s, including the syndicated children's series *The Big Blue Marble*, for which Berman won an Emmy in 1977.

Berman married his wife, Elizabeth, in 1980. The couple eventually had three children—sons Tom and Eddie and daughter Molly. To better provide for his growing family, Berman left documentary filmmaking and moved to Hollywood in 1984. He accepted a job as producer of the ABC program *Ripley's Believe It or Not*, hosted by Jack Palance, but resigned after one day to take what he considered a better position at Warner Brothers as Director of Drama Television. In this role Berman worked with Warner vice president Cindy Dunn listening to pitches from writers and selecting some of them to take to the networks and try to secure script development funds, the first step in the process of piloting a new series. But Berman, who bought a house shortly after signing on with Warner Brothers, was laid off four months later in a corporate belt-tightening move. Fortunately, three weeks after that, near the end of 1984, he was offered a job in the programming department at Paramount. He suddenly found himself working for John Pike, executive vice president of Paramount Television, and overseeing all the Paramount-produced series currently airing on all networks, including the hits *Cheers*, *Family Ties*, and *MacGyver*, plus two more series and two miniseries. "It was kind of overwhelming," Berman told the Archive. Nevertheless, he performed well and was soon promoted to vice president in charge of long form (industry jargon for TV movies and miniseries) and special projects.

The next year, when Paramount began developing the series that would become *Star Trek: The Next Generation*, studio supervision of the program fell to Berman. He was assigned to the show ostensibly because he was in charge of special projects but actually because he was the lowest-ranking, shortest-tenured vice president on staff, and nobody else at Paramount wanted to work with Gene Roddenberry. "The general opinion was that Roddenberry was a cranky old bastard and nobody wanted to have anything to do with him," Berman told the Archive interviewer. But Berman and Roddenberry hit it off immediately, and shortly afterward Roddenberry asked Berman to leave Paramount and come to work for him, producing the series. Even though Berman, coming from a background in documentary filmmaking, knew virtually nothing about *Star Trek*,

Rick Berman (center), Gene Roddenberry's hand-picked successor, began to assume control of *The Next Generation* during its third season. Eventually, Berman would cocreate three *Star Trek* series, oversee hundreds of episodes, and produce four movies, a larger legacy (in terms of sheer bulk) than that of the Great Bird of the Galaxy.

he agreed. After experiencing life as a network executive, he yearned to move back into the creative side of the business.

Berman was hired to replace Ed Milkis, a holdover from the classic series who left after a disagreement with Roddenberry, and worked alongside original program veteran Bob Justman for a year as Supervising Producer. Berman was much younger than Roddenberry, Justman, and Milkis. "I think he [Roddenberry] wanted a younger ear and a younger voice in the mix," Berman said in the same Archive interview. Roddenberry also reasoned that since Berman knew almost nothing about *Star Trek*, he could provide a fresh perspective. Originally, Berman handled casting and editing for *The Next Generation*, while Justman led most of the other day-to-day production responsibilities. When Justman left near the conclusion of the show's first season, Berman assumed the title of Co-Executive Producer and took over all responsibilities previously held by Justman. Already Roddenberry's right-hand man, Berman was now officially the show's second-in-command. After Season Two, Roddenberry began ceding ever-greater control to Berman, who became the de facto leader of the series. In 1991, following Roddenberry's death and the completion of the final *Star Trek* film featuring the original cast, Berman gained total creative control of the franchise. Eventually, he would cocreate three new *Star Trek* series and oversee more than six hundred television episodes and four feature films, a much larger legacy (in terms of sheer volume) than that of Roddenberry.

Berman shouldered much of the blame as the franchise's fortunes fell in the early and mid-2000s, with sagging ratings for *Star Trek: Voyager* (1995–2001) and *Star Trek: Enterprise* (2001–2005), and the box-office failure of *Star Trek Nemesis* (2002). But if he is charged with responsibility for *Star Trek*'s decline during those years, he must also be credited for its ascendance in the 1990s, when *The Next Generation* achieved the highest ratings in the history of the franchise.

Michael Piller

Producer Maurice Hurley worked with Roddenberry, Justman, and Berman to create *Star Trek: The Next Generation* and led the show's writing staff (serving as the "show runner," in industry parlance) during its turbulent first two seasons. But Hurley operated more as Roddenberry's proxy than his successor. When Hurley left the series after Season Two, Berman eventually hired Michael Piller as his replacement. Piller quickly became a trusted ally of Berman's, helping change the course of *Next Gen* and cocreate *Star Trek: Deep Space Nine* and *Star Trek: Voyager.*

Berman and Piller shared the bond of beginning their careers in nonfiction fields. Piller was born May 30, 1948, in Port Chester, New York. His father was a screenwriter and his mother a songwriter, and Michael aspired to become a screenwriter like his father. But after one of his professors at the University of North Carolina discouraged his creative ambitions, Piller transferred into journalism school. After he graduated from UNC, Piller launched a successful career as a producer of news programs, first at WBTV in Charlotte, then WBBM in Chicago, and finally with CBS News in New York, where he won a pair of Emmys.

Despite his success as a journalist, Piller remained drawn to the creative side of the industry. In the late 1970s, he transferred to the CBS West Coast offices, where he worked as a network censor. He began writing screenplays in the early 1980s. His first produced teleplay was a 1982 episode of the detective series *Simon & Simon.* He also wrote installments of *Cagney & Lacy* and *The Dukes of Hazzard* before leaving his network day job to serve as story editor for *Simon & Simon.* During these years, Piller also penned episodes of *Miami Vice* and the short-lived series *Sidekicks* and *Hard Time on Planet Earth.* The latter was his first science fiction show. In 1989, Piller and Michael Wagner served as producers on another quickly cancelled series, the science-themed mystery series *Probe*, cocreated by mystery writer William Link and SF legend Isaac Asimov.

When Hurley decided not to return for the third season of *The Next Generation*, Berman hired Wagner, who had also worked on the prestigious *Hill Street Blues*, as show runner. But Wagner, overwhelmed by the magnitude of the problems facing the program early in Season Three, resigned after only three episodes. Wagner recommended Piller—who had co-written one *Next Gen* teleplay, "Evolution"—as his replacement. Piller brought order to the show's chaotic writing staff, discovered many talented young writers (in part by establishing the show's unique open submission policy, which encouraged fans to submit spec teleplays), and shifted the emphasis away from plot-driven scenarios toward more character-focused stories. More than any other writer, he charted the course the series followed during its most successful years. "In the third year Michael Piller came in and it was shaky at first and then started to stabilize and it was very stable on all fronts ever since," Patrick Stewart told a *TV Guide* interviewer. "It was a well-oiled machine and it got better and more consistent."

In 1991, when Paramount asked Berman to create a *Next Generation* spin-off and eventual replacement series, he and Piller joined forces to cocreate *Star Trek: Deep Space Nine*. Piller left *Next Gen* to serve as an executive producer on *DS9* for two seasons and then left that series to cocreate *Star Trek: Voyager* with Berman and Jeri Taylor. Piller also wrote the screenplay for the movie *Star Trek: Insurrection* (1998), from a story by Berman.

During his tenure with *Star Trek*, Piller cocreated the offbeat sci-fi Western series *Legend*, starring John ("Q") de Lancie, which ran for two episodes on the UPN network in 1995. After his association with the franchise ended, Piller and his son Shawn developed *The Dead Zone*, based on the Stephen King novel, which ran on the USA Network from 2002 to 2007. With Christopher Teague, Piller cocreated *Wildfire*, a family drama set in the world of horse racing and starring *Deep Space Nine* alum Nana Visitor, which ran on the ABC Family channel from 2005 to 2008. Piller died in 2005 after a long battle with cancer. He was survived by his wife, Sandra, and sons Brent and Shawn.

Jeri Taylor

Jeri Taylor, born June 30, 1938, in Evansville, Indiana, earned a bachelor of arts from Indiana University in 1959 and then a Master's degree in English from Cal State-Northridge. From 1963 to 1973 she was married to sportscaster Dick Enberg, with whom she had three children: Alexander, Andrew, and Jennifer. She began writing teleplays in the late 1970s, selling scripts to little-remembered series such as *The Secret Empire* and *California Fever* (both 1979). Although Taylor later insisted she had little experience writing science fiction prior to her association with *Star Trek*, one of her earliest credits was a teleplay for *Salvage 1*, which starred Andy Griffith as a man who builds his own spaceship to recover space junk, including equipment left on the moon by the Apollo space missions. This bizarre show ran for sixteen episodes on ABC in 1979. Later, Taylor wrote for more successful programs such as *Little House on the Prairie, Magnum P.I.,* and *In the Heat of the Night*. She also served as a writer-producer on the medical-mystery series *Quincy M.E.* (1980–83).

In 1990, Piller asked Taylor to revise the teleplay for "Suddenly Human," her first work for *Star Trek*. Piller was pleased with Taylor's work and invited her to join the show's writing staff. When he left *Next Gen* to executive produce *Deep Space Nine* at the end of Season Five, Piller selected Taylor as his successor. Piller and Taylor shared similar screenwriting philosophies, both placing great value on character development, so the transition was seamless. Taylor, the series' final show runner, was credited as Co-Executive Producer during the penultimate season of *Next Gen* and as Executive Producer during its final year. When *Next Gen* concluded, she joined with Berman and Piller to create *Star Trek: Voyager* and served as executive producer and show runner of that series for its first four seasons. Then she took a step back, serving as a creative consultant on the show for its final three seasons before retiring from the industry when the show left the air in 2001. Her son, Alexander Enberg, had a recurring role on *Voyager* as the Vulcan Ensign Vorik. Since 1986, Taylor has been married to television producer-director David Moessinger.

Brannon Braga

Brannon Braga, born August 14, 1965, in Bozeman, Montana, studied film at Kent State University in Ohio and at the University of California-Berkeley. After briefly working as a producer of music videos, Braga earned an eight-week internship (sponsored by the Academy of Television Arts and Sciences) on *Star Trek: The Next Generation* in 1990. Like Berman, Piller and Taylor, Braga had never been a fan of *Star Trek* before joining its staff. Yet he quickly adapted to the idiom and was invited to join the show's regular staff when his eight weeks ended. In his first season, Braga wrote the intriguing "Identity Crisis," cowrote the landmark Worf episode "Reunion," and made uncredited contributions to numerous other episodes.

Braga rose quickly through the ranks and went on to write twenty-two episodes of *The Next Generation*. He collaborated with Ronald D. Moore to pen the landmark series finale "All Good Things . . . ," as well as the screenplays for the first two *Next Gen* movies, *Generations* and *First Contact*. Like Taylor, he moved to *Voyager* when *The Next Generation* ended, serving as a writer-producer and penning forty-eight episodes. When Taylor left the series, Braga took over as show runner and served as executive producer of the series during its final three seasons. In 2000, Braga cocreated the prequel series *Star Trek: Enterprise* with Berman. (Writer-producer Ken Biller served as show runner during the final season of *Voyager*.) Braga executive produced the first three seasons of *Enterprise* before stepping back into a smaller role, primarily as a writer, during its final year, when writer-producer Manny Coto took over the series. Like Berman, Braga has been pilloried by many fans, who blame him for the inconsistent quality and poor ratings suffered by *Voyager* and *Enterprise* on his watch. Braga seemed to take the criticism in stride. "Who can blame them?" he said in an interview with The Fandom website in 2006. "If you are indeed angry you are probably going to look to the person running the show, so it's not surprising. It's not a pleasant thing . . . [but] I'm sure I will take my share of the blame, creatively."

Braga's fifteen-year association with *Star Trek* ended with the cancellation of *Enterprise* in 2005. Since then he has worked as an executive producer on the CBS science fiction series *Threshold* (2005–2006), which costarred Brent Spiner. He accepted a reduced role during the final season of *Enterprise* in part to devote more time to the development of *Threshold*, about a secret government investigation into contact with extraterrestrials. But *Threshold* was cancelled after thirteen episodes. Braga served as a screenwriter and executive producer on the hit Fox series *24* during its seventh and eighth seasons (2009 and 2010). He also cocreated and executive produced the ABC sci-fi series *FlashForward* (2009–2010), about a mysterious incident that causes several people to black out and awaken with knowledge of the future. The program ran for one season but was not renewed. As of this writing, his most recent venture was the Fox SF series *Terra Nova*, about a group of time-traveling colonists who attempt to escape an overpopulated, environmentally wrecked Earth by resettling in the Cretaceous period. Like *FlashForward*, *Terra Nova* was cancelled after one season.

More Successors

Berman, Piller, Taylor, and Braga, the only people other than Roddenberry to create a live-action *Star Trek* series, were the franchise's primary power brokers in the post-Roddenberry era. But Ira Steven Behr, Kenneth Biller, and Manny Coto also earned executive producer credit on various *Trek* series.

Born October 23, 1953, in New York City, Behr began his screenwriting career in the early 1980s and served as a writer-producer on the TV series *Fame*, *Once a Hero*, and *Bronx Zoo*. He joined the writing staff of *The Next Generation* during its pivotal third season, then left to pursue opportunities in feature films. He was lured back to the franchise to serve as a writer-producer, and later as executive producer, on *Deep Space Nine*. He wrote or cowrote fifty-three episodes of the series and helped develop the epic Dominion War story line.

Kenneth Biller, an established Hollywood screenwriter whose previous credits included an episode of *The X-Files*, joined the writing staff of *Voyager* during its first season. He progressed steadily through the ranks, becoming an executive producer when Jeri Taylor semiretired after Season Four.

Veteran writer-producer Manny Coto had extensive experience with science fiction prior to joining *Star Trek*. He served as executive producer on Showtime's revived *Outer Limits* and on ABC's *Strange World*. Coto wrote fourteen episodes of *Star Trek: Enterprise* during the show's final two campaigns and was the architect of the epic Xindi Weapon story line that dominated its third season. He was promoted to executive producer for the show's final year. Unlike many of the show's leaders, Coto was an avid *Star Trek* fan since childhood.

J. J. Abrams

Immediately following the cancellation of *Enterprise* in 2005, Paramount began planning to resurrect the suddenly moribund franchise with an eleventh feature film. Although initial reports indicated that Rick Berman and possibly Brannon

Braga would be involved in this project, Paramount leadership decided their services were no longer required. After flirting with Sam Raimi, executives began wooing writer-director-producer J. J. Abrams as their chosen successor to Roddenberry's successors. Abrams didn't officially announce that he had agreed to direct the picture until February 2007, but he was the unquestioned creative force behind the reboot of *Star Trek*.

Jeffrey Jacob Abrams was born June 27, 1966, in New York City and moved to Los Angeles as a small child. His parents, Gerald and Carol Abrams, were both film producers. Abrams earned his first industry credit in high school, creating sound effects for the low-budget horror film *Night Beast* in 1982. During his senior year at Sarah Lawrence College, he sold his first screenplay, *Taking Care of Business* (1990), which was produced with stars Charles Grodin and Jim Belushi. His other early screenplays included the Harrison Ford vehicle *Regarding Henry* (1991) and the Mel Gibson picture *Forever Young* (1992). Over the next decade, Abrams enjoyed success as a writer-producer both on television and in feature films. He served as executive producer on the college drama *Felicity* (1998–2002) and created the action-SF series *Alias* (2001–2006), before scoring a major breakthrough with the almost unclassifiable *Lost* (2004–2010), which he cocreated with writing partners Damon Lindelof and Jeffrey Leiber. Abrams cowrote director Michael Bay's blockbuster *Armageddon* (1998), among other feature films, and made his directorial debut with *Mission: Impossible III* (2006).

Paramount's belief in Abrams proved well founded. The 2009 film titled simply *Star Trek*, which Abrams directed and coproduced, became the highest-grossing and most-honored feature film in the history of the franchise. (For more on the 2009 movie, see Chapter 40, "*Star Trek* Lives!") As of this writing, Abrams and the other principal creators of that picture, coproducers Bryan Burk and Damon Lindelof and screenwriters Roberto Orci and Alex Kurtzman, were preparing a sequel titled *Star Trek into Darkness*, which is scheduled to premiere at about the same time as this book.

13

Shatner's Folly

The *Final Frontier* Debacle (1989)

Star Trek IV: The Voyage Home returned the *Trek* universe to perfect harmony, with our heroes reunited and restored to health, ready to pursue further adventures aboard a gleaming new starship *Enterprise*. The movie had attracted the largest audience of any in the series so far, and many of those viewers were eager to join in the next voyage. After *Star Trek IV*, the film series could have gone anywhere. Then William Shatner took it straight to hell.

Motivated by a combination of jealousy (of Leonard Nimoy's growing influence over *Star Trek*) and ambition, Shatner invoked the "favored nations clause" in his contract, which guaranteed him parity with Nimoy in terms of pay and perks, up to and including the opportunity to write and direct a film. Under the terms of his agreement, Shatner could have demanded to direct the fourth film in the series, but he was unavailable due to his obligations to the TV series *T. J. Hooker*. When that show was cancelled in 1986, Shatner was free to direct *Star Trek V*. (If *T. J. Hooker* had been renewed, the fifth *Star Trek* movie would have been entirely different.) Nimoy, who found the experience of simultaneously directing and starring in *Star Trek IV* exhausting, had no interest in helming the new film. Since *The Voyage Home*, he had directed the cuddly comedy *Three Men and a Baby*, which became the top-grossing movie of 1987. Nimoy wanted to maintain the forward momentum of his directorial career, and returning to *Trek* may have seemed like a step backward. Shatner had limited experience—he had overseen ten episodes of *T. J. Hooker*—but more directorial credits than Nimoy had amassed before making his debut with *Star Trek III: The Search for Spock*. So Paramount Pictures executives crossed their fingers and handed *Star Trek V* to Shatner.

"Too Much Exuberance and Too Little Discernment"

As it turned out, the real problem wasn't that Shatner wanted to direct the film—it's that he wanted to write it, too. The story he concocted, originally titled *An Act of Love*, involved a messianic, unicorn-riding Vulcan named Zar who telepathically beguiles the crew of the *Enterprise* (all except the iron-willed Captain Kirk) and convinces them to take him on a journey to the center of the universe to meet God. When they arrive at the fabled God-planet, however, "God" turns out to be the Devil in disguise, and heaven suddenly turns into

Dante's inferno. A chorus of angels morph into demons and try to kill Kirk and company, who barely escape with their lives. Afterward, however, Kirk realizes that if Satan exists, so must God. Shatner was deeply invested in this concept, which he considered profound. "This was the story I wanted to do," Shatner said in the book *Captain's Log: William Shatner's Personal Account of the Making of Star Trek V: The Final Frontier*, written by his daughter, Lisabeth Shatner. "I felt like I had been searching for a philosophy, a way of thinking, and I wanted to express what my search had been like, and some of my thoughts, in dramatic form."

However, Shatner stood alone in his enthusiasm for *An Act of Love*. Paramount was unimpressed with the concept, and Gene Roddenberry was aghast, not least because he loathed the idea of *Star Trek* endorsing belief in a divine being. Producer Harve Bennett considered walking away from the franchise, in part because his relationship with Nimoy had deteriorated during the making of *Star Trek IV* but mostly because he thought Shatner's concept was fundamentally flawed. Shatner realized he needed Bennett's help and made some important concessions to convince the producer to remain on board. Bennett suggested that rather than dealing with God and Satan overtly, which would offend many moviegoers, the story should feature an alien who *pretends* to be God. Even though this radically altered Shatner's spiritual-philosophical premise, the writer-director agreed, and Paramount approved the revised concept.

Why did the studio back this idea when in 1975 it had rejected Gene Roddenberry's screenplay *The God Thing*, which also concerned an alien entity that pretends to be God, as "too anti-religious"? Executive producer Ralph Winter chalks it up to hubris ("too much exuberance and too little discernment") following the astounding success of *Star Trek IV*. "Maybe we were smoking our own publicity, I don't know," Winter said in an interview included on the *Star Trek V: The Final Frontier* DVD. "We thought we could do anything."

Development Hell

The next step in the process was fleshing out Shatner's treatment into a screenplay. Everyone's first choice for that job was Nicholas Meyer, who had directed *The Wrath of Khan* and collaborated on the screenplay for *The Voyage Home*. But Meyer declined because he thought Shatner's basic concept was hopeless. Eventually, Shatner and Bennett engaged young screenwriter David Loughery, recently hired by Paramount. As the screenplay began to take shape, however, the studio demanded more comedy. *Star Trek IV* had appealed to a wider audience primarily because it was funny, the executives believed, so Paramount wanted *Star Trek V* to be funny, too. Loughery, with input from Bennett and Shatner, inserted sarcastic one-liners and other comedic business into nearly every scene.

Despite its surface similarities to his earlier *God Thing* screenplay, Roddenberry remained adamantly opposed to the scenario and fired off angry missives to Shatner and Bennett when the first draft of Loughery's script arrived on his desk. "In my opinion, a film made to this story or anything similar will destroy much of the value of the *Star Trek* property," he wrote to Bennett in a letter reprinted in David Alexander's authorized biography of Roddenberry, *Star Trek Creator*. The Great Bird mounted a vehement and sustained campaign against *The Final Frontier*, and even contacted his attorney, Leonard Maizlish, regarding potential legal action. Roddenberry also shared a draft of the screenplay with distinguished science fiction author Isaac Asimov, who wrote back that he was "appalled" by the proposed story. But Paramount ignored Roddenberry, who had lost credibility by raising equally passionate objections to earlier films, including the smash *Star Trek II: The Wrath of Khan*.

Nimoy and DeForest Kelley wielded greater influence. After seeing an early draft of the script, they protested that Spock and McCoy would never turn against Captain Kirk. So the ending was rewritten, with the trio facing off against the devil-god instead of Kirk standing alone. This was only the first in a series of revisions that would significantly alter, and weaken, Shatner's planned finale. To assuage other complaints by Nimoy and Kelley, the film's two flashback scenes—to Spock's birth and to the death of McCoy's father—were also reworked. The unicorn was eliminated from the story, too. The picture was drifting further and further away from Shatner's original vision. "Little by little, I retreated," Shatner said in an interview included on the *Star Trek V* DVD.

The final version of the script introduces a dissident Vulcan named Sybok, later revealed as Spock's half-brother, who uses his telepathic abilities to heal psychological wounds and bend his followers to his will (or something—it's never made clear). Exiled on planet Nimbus III, which (inconceivably) has no spacecraft, Sybok leads his ragtag, brainwashed "army" in a raid that results in the capture of the planet's Federation, Klingon, and Romulan administrators. The Federation sends the *Enterprise* to rescue the bureaucrats and capture Sybok, who has rejected logic and views himself as a messianic figure on a holy quest. The hostage ordeal proves to be an elaborate ruse to get Sybok and his followers aboard Kirk's ship, which they promptly commandeer. Sybok tries to exert his will over Kirk, Spock, and McCoy, but fails. However, the rest of the crew follows Sybok without reservation and takes him and his followers through the Great Barrier (whatever that is) to the center of the galaxy and the legendary planet Sha Ka Ree, which Sybok believes is the home world of the Almighty. All the while, the *Enterprise* is being pursued by a Klingon Bird of Prey led by an ambitious young captain who wants to advance his career by destroying Kirk.

Time and Money

Loughery's screenplay remained unfinished when the 1988 Writers Guild strike began. The strike lasted for six months, wreaking havoc on both *Star Trek: The Next Generation* (see Chapters 11 and 14 for details) and the film now officially known as *Star Trek V: The Final Frontier*. During the ensuing delay, Nimoy signed on to direct *The Good Mother* (1988), a searing drama about a woman mired in a

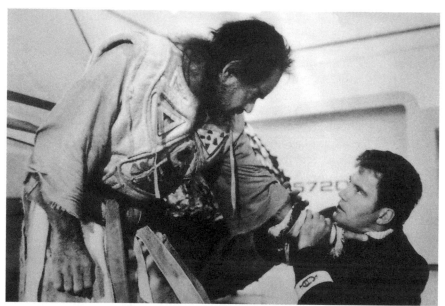

Larry Luckinbill, as Sybok, tries to wring William Shatner's neck in *Star Trek V: The Final Frontier*. After viewing the film, many fans wanted to do the same thing.

bitter child-custody battle. Loughery completed the script once the strike ended, but Paramount decided to abbreviate the preproduction schedule and slash the budget of *Star Trek V*. The budget cuts only exacerbated a glaring problem with Shatner's concept—it was simply too ambitious. Realizing Shatner's grandiose, epic vision—half *Lawrence of Arabia*, half *2001: A Space Odyssey*—would have cost tens of millions more than Paramount was willing to spend on a *Star Trek* film. The studio remained convinced that thrifty budgets were the cornerstone of the franchise's profitability. Although *The Final Frontier* was assigned a $30 million bottom line, the highest since *Star Trek: The Motion Picture*, corners had to be cut.

The trimming began with special effects. Industrial Light & Magic, the industry's gold standard, had provided visuals for the previous four *Trek* films, but for *The Final Frontier* Winter elected to hire Associates and Ferren, Bran Ferren's modest New Jersey–based shop, which had supplied visual effects for *Altered States* (1980) and other films. ILM was already committed to two other projects (*Indiana Jones and the Last Crusade* and *Ghostbusters II*), and Winter feared the shop wouldn't be able to give *The Final Frontier* the same TLC it had shown earlier *Trek* films.

Budget constraints also caused casting problems. The role of Sybok was written for Sean Connery. (The name of the god-planet, Sha Ka Ree, was derived from the actor's name.) But by the time *Star Trek V* was ready to cast, Connery was already committed to *Indiana Jones and the Last Crusade*. Shatner's second choice was Swedish film legend Max von Sydow, but his asking price was too high. So instead of Connery or von Sydow, Shatner wound up with little-known journeyman Larry Luckinbill in this pivotal role.

Shatner's finale also continued to wither. His original idea of angels that transform into demons was ruled out early on as too costly. In its place, he and Loughery devised a sequence where monsters emerge from the volcanic rocks on the surface of Sha Ka Ree. Shatner pictured Kirk battling ten giant "rock men." But the cost of building each latex rock man suit ran to nearly a third of a million dollars, so Shatner was forced to make due with a single creature. Later, after the monster suit looked laughable in test footage, the rock man concept was dropped entirely. When Paramount rejected a request for more money to punch up the sequence, Shatner's bravura climax was reduced to footage of Kirk running around frantically and dodging lightning bolts.

Production began in mid-October 1988 and wrapped in late December, on budget and two days ahead of schedule. Shatner made some rookie mistakes. While shooting the opening mountain-climbing sequence, which was being faked with a man-made climbing wall, Shatner left the top of a tree in frame. This ruined the illusion of great height and forced an entire day's worth of location footage to be reshot. Additional difficulties arose when a teamster strike forced the production to use nonunion truck drivers for location work in Yosemite National Park and the Mojave Desert.

Worse problems developed in postproduction. Paramount wanted fifteen minutes trimmed from Shatner's rough cut, which ran two hours (too long to guarantee multiple prime-time showings), and Bennett and Shatner clashed over where the trims should be made. Then the effects footage from Ferren began to arrive, and proved disappointing. Although Winter, Bennett, and Shatner had been pleased with Ferren's test product, the small shop struggled to maintain quality while producing visuals in the quantity needed for the effects-heavy *Final Frontier*. To save time, Ferren used rear screen projection—a more primitive but faster process—instead of blue screen compositing to create the spaceship effects. The resulting footage was usable but beneath the standard of previous *Trek* features. Whenever possible, Bennett and Shatner reused stock footage from the earlier films. The movie's initial test screening was a disaster, forcing the film to be recut yet again. One new scene was also shot—an expository sequence on the bridge of the *Enterprise* that makes clear why the Klingon Captain Klaa rescues Kirk at the conclusion of the story. The lone bit of good news was that Bennett and Shatner were able to secure the services of composer Jerry Goldsmith, who had earned an Oscar nomination for his work on *Star Trek: The Motion Picture*. Goldsmith's rousing score would emerge as the single, unassailably good element in *Star Trek V*.

Reception

Released June 9, 1989, *The Final Frontier* opened well but faded fast, becoming the least-profitable and worst-reviewed film of the series so far. The movie grossed $52 million in the U.S. and $70 million worldwide (that's about $129 million in inflation-adjusted figures). It earned $17 million in its first week, but its receipts dropped by 59 percent in week two and by nearly 50 percent each of the next three weeks. Previous *Star Trek* features had enjoyed theatrical runs of up to four months, but *The Final Frontier* was gone from many theaters within six weeks. It was lost in a summer packed with blockbusters, including *Batman, Indiana Jones and the Last Crusade, Lethal Weapon II,* and comedy hits *Look Who's Talking, Honey, I Shrunk the Kids,* and *Ghostbusters II,* all of which grossed more than $100 million in the U.S. alone. Based on its disappointing American box-office results, and given the weak international performance of previous *Trek* movies, *Star Trek V* was released directly to home video in many foreign markets. The contrast with its predecessor was striking: *Star Trek IV* had raked in $133 million and was the fifth-highest-earning film of the year. Twenty-four films outgrossed *Star Trek V.*

As bad as the box-office receipts were, however, the reviews were even worse. *Chicago Sun-Times* critic Roger Ebert called *The Final Frontier* "a mess." Reviewers at *Variety,* the *New York Times, Washington Post, Newsweek,* and other influential outlets agreed. Even those rare critics who praised the film griped about its subpar special effects. *Star Trek V* became the first *Trek* film *not* nominated for a Hugo Award. At the 1990 Golden Raspberry Awards, presented as a counterpoint to the Academy Awards by "honoring" the worst in Hollywood moviemaking, *Star Trek V: The Final Frontier* won three Razzies: Worst Picture, Worst Director (Shatner), and Worst Actor (also Shatner). It was also nominated for Worst Supporting Actor (Kelley), Worst Screenplay (Loughery, Shatner, and Bennett), and as Worst Picture of the Decade.

The Final Frontier was a crushing disappointment to Trekkers, many of whom came into the picture with great expectations, only to leave befuddled and irritated. The film is still reviled by many fans. *Mystery Science Theater 3000* alums Mike Nelson and Kevin Murphy lampooned *Star Trek V* with a downloadable audio track from Nelson's RiffTrax service in 2006. Roddenberry tried to disown the film, labeling it "apocryphal." As a result, even though everything that occurs on-screen in *Star Trek* films and TV series is regarded as "canon" within the franchise's carefully guarded continuity, the events and characters depicted in *The Final Frontier* have been ignored by the writers of subsequent *Trek* productions. Sybok, in particular, has been virtually erased from the *Trek* memory banks.

Assessing *The Final Frontier*

Years later, Harve Bennett attributed *Star Trek V: The Final Frontier*'s disappointing box-office performance to *Star Trek: The Next Generation,* arguing that the new show siphoned viewers away from the film. Shatner placed the blame on budget cuts and poor quality special effects. But the real reason for the film's failure was simple: It stinks.

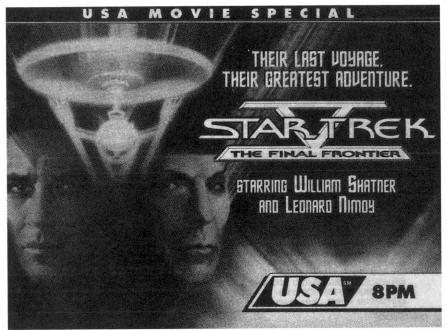

TV Guide ad for a cable rebroadcast of *Star Trek V: The Final Frontier*. The movie performed so poorly that it was released directly to home video in many foreign markets.

The problems with *Star Trek V: The Final Frontier* are plentiful and pervasive, but they begin with Shatner's original concept. The premise of a quest to discover a mythical land and meet a divine being owes more to epic fantasy than to *Star Trek*. In a science-fictional setting, the idea becomes utterly transparent because it's obvious from the outset that this "God" must be a fake. Worse yet, the prime mover in Shatner's story is Sybok—Kirk, Spock, McCoy, and the rest of the gang are merely dragged along for the ride. Structurally, the film shares many of the flaws that plagued *Star Trek: The Motion Picture*—a methodical pace, ponderous philosophical posturing, and a transparent anticlimactic finale—but with bad jokes and lousy special effects as well.

While the fish-out-of-water comedy in *Star Trek IV* arose organically from the film's time-travel scenario and the series' established character relationships, the jokes in *Star Trek V* are shoehorned into the action and often work against established characterizations. We laugh *with* the *Enterprise* crew in *The Voyage Home*, but we're supposed to laugh *at* them in *The Final Frontier*. The most notorious example of this is the moment when Scotty assures Captain Kirk, "I know this ship like the back of my hand," and then immediately knocks himself out by clonking his head on an exposed pipe. The problem with this gag is that Scotty *would* know the ship like the back of his hand. He's a talented engineer who loves his ship, who delights in poring over technical schematics and has spent weeks running all over the vessel trying to stem the tide of mechanical malfunctions. The idea that Scotty would knock himself unconscious through simple carelessness is not only improbable but insulting. Throughout the film, crew members behave in ways that seem wrong. For instance, Uhura reveals a secret crush on Scotty (where did this come from?). Sometimes it's difficult to tell which moments are intended to be dramatic and which are supposed to be humorous. Uhura doing a fan dance to distract Sybok's sentries? Spock felling a horse with his Famous Vulcan Nerve Pinch? Are we supposed to take these moments seriously?

The movie's plot amounts to little more than a collection of contrivances. Events happen because the screenwriters want them to, not because they make any logical sense. It's hard to believe that the new *Enterprise* (the flagship of the Federation) would be so riddled with breakdowns and glitches, or that Scotty and his team—who performed ship-saving miracles on a weekly basis for years—couldn't set things right in short order. The real reason for these technical difficulties is that if the ship's transporters worked, Kirk would simply beam the hostages off of Nimbus III and leave Sybok and his followers behind. End of movie. But there are dozens of more believable ways to set the Sybok story in motion. It's also difficult to accept the ease with which Sybok hijacks the *Enterprise*—Kirk's crew puts up only token resistance. The list of story problems is endless. Nearly every sequence in the film collapses under even the mildest scrutiny.

None of these shortcomings are improved by Shatner's direction, which is prosaic at best. Ferren's visual effects look outdated, almost like throwbacks to the TV show. The film's production values are also chintzy. When Sybok's army storms the capital of Nimbus III, for instance, the same handful of extras runs past the camera over and over again. Even the work of the film's cast proves disappointing. It's perhaps understandable that Doohan and Nichols seem off, since they are asked to behave in ways that are wildly out of character. But the usually reliable Kelley has an unaccountably poor outing as well (in fairness, he's stuck with some of the film's worst clunker one-liners), and Nimoy seems disinterested. Shatner usually performed best when led by a skilled director such as Joseph Pevney, Marc Daniels, or Nicholas Meyer. Left to his own devices, he delivers a performance that's simultaneously too big and too shallow. The film's best acting comes from Larry Luckinbill as Sybok, even though the role cries out for a more charismatic screen presence (like Connery or von Sydow).

For once, Roddenberry's gloomy forecast proved correct. As the Great Bird predicted, *Star Trek V* damaged the *Star Trek* brand severely. The wide audience the franchise had won with *Star Trek IV* immediately defected. Disgruntled Trekkers vented their frustration at conventions and drowned their sorrows in episodes of *The Next Generation*, or returned wistfully to reruns of the classic series. Fans and industry insiders alike assumed this would be the final voyage for the cast of the original program—and it very nearly was.

14

The Bonding

The Next Generation, Season Three (1989–90)

T he third season of *Star Trek: The Next Generation* brought less drama behind the scenes and more drama to TV screens. Although the show once again endured wholesale changes to its writing staff, this time many of the newcomers (including Ronald D. Moore and Ira Steven Behr) would become key contributors to the franchise, bringing sorely needed creative continuity to the program. Age and declining health forced Gene Roddenberry to delegate more of his responsibilities to co-executive producer Rick Berman. The Great Bird of the Galaxy occasionally consulted on scripts and retained veto power over all decisions, but Berman assumed control of the show's day-to-day operations and began to put his signature on the series. As a result, *Next Gen* started to back away from Roddenberry's restrictive screenwriting mandates and prohibitions. Not coincidentally, the creative and interpersonal conflicts that wreaked havoc throughout Seasons One and Two were greatly reduced.

Meanwhile, Diana Muldaur was dismissed and Gates McFadden rehired. Berman, who in his words "was not a fan" of the decision to replace McFadden in the first place, believed it made more sense to rehire the original actress than bring in the show's third doctor in as many seasons. This decision pleased fans and enabled the cast to finally gel as a unit. Plus, new costumer Robert Blackman redesigned the Starfleet uniforms—eliminating the spandex jumpsuits worn during the show's first two seasons—so the actors could literally breathe easier. In another milestone, Jonathan Frakes became the first *Next Gen* actor to direct an episode. Before approving Frakes as a director, the studio required him to endure an arduous apprenticeship the actor jokingly called "Paramount University," during which he logged three hundred hours observing nearly every aspect of the creative process, from initial story conferences through postproduction. Over the course of the show's final five seasons, Frakes and future "Paramount University" graduates Patrick Stewart and LeVar Burton would direct some of the series' finest installments.

None of this means that Season Three was easy. In fact, it was a struggle—a tooth-and-nail battle simply to develop filmable material from week to week. The show was still reeling from the Writers Guild strike that truncated the previous campaign. Although the creative team had managed (barely) to produce twenty-two episodes the previous season, there was almost nothing left in the pipeline for Season Three. Originally, *Hill Street Blues* veteran Michael Wagner was tapped to replace burned-out producer Maurice Hurley as *The Next Generation*'s lead writer, but the overwhelmed Wagner resigned after only three episodes. In turn, Wagner recommended his friend Michael Piller for the job. Berman hired Piller, who had worked for four seasons on the detective show *Simon & Simon*, and who, with Wagner, had cowritten the *Next Gen* teleplay "Evolution."

Piller took extraordinary measures to fill the cavernous story deficit. He sorted through discarded material from the previous seasons in search of concepts that could be resuscitated and reworked, sifted through the show's slush pile of spec scripts, and initiated the program's unique open submission policy. Although hopeful fans had always submitted teleplays and story ideas, *Star Trek: The Next Generation* became the only series in production to actively solicit submissions from nonprofessionals. From such humble origins came some of the season's best moments and greatest screenwriting discoveries. Piller insisted that stories remain character centered, even as he pushed the staff (which also included holdovers Richard Manning, Hans Beimler, and Melinda Snodgrass) for imaginative sci-fi concepts. Piller himself wrote the watershed season finale "The Best of Both Worlds."

It was hectic and stressful business—pages were sometimes delivered to the set just in time to be memorized and filmed. But the quality of the material was consistently first-rate, and the cast responded with its finest and most cohesive work so far. The result was a twenty-six-episode campaign some fans consider the finest in the history of the series. The timing was providential. *The Next Generation* found its mojo just in time to reassure fans shaken by the wretched *Star Trek V: The Final Frontier* (1989). Even if Captain Kirk and friends were finished—as suddenly seemed likely—the future of *Star Trek* remained bright.

"Evolution"

The shift in creative leadership was apparent from the Season Three premiere, which concerns tiny, adaptive nanites (designed by Wesley Crusher as a biology experiment and accidentally released when he falls asleep in the lab), which infiltrate the *Enterprise* computer system. The story begins with the crew struggling to diagnose an epidemic of puzzling breakdowns and glitches—the kind of mechanical problems it was forbidden to depict in previous seasons. The nanite mishap creates additional anxiety for Wesley, who, after living on his own for a year, is struggling with mixed emotions over the return of his mother. "Evolution" is one of Wil Wheaton's best episodes, but guest star Ken Jenkins has too much screen time as a single-minded scientist whose decades-long experiment is jeopardized by the nanite infestation. While diverting, this episode only hints at the excellence of many later Season Three adventures. It remains a historically important installment, however, because this teleplay—cowritten by Piller and Wagner—brought Piller to *Star Trek*.

"The Ensigns of Command"

The *Enterprise* is dispatched to relocate a human settlement on Tau Cygna V, which the Federation ceded to the nonhumanoid Sheliak in a treaty a century ago because the planet's atmosphere contains deadly radiation. The Sheliak are on their way to belatedly claim their property and will annihilate any humans left on the planet. But the colonists, who have developed resistance to the radiation, refuse to leave. While Picard attempts to negotiate an extension from the Sheliak, the radiation-immune Data beams down to the planet to try to convince the colonists to abandon the settlement, testing the android's ability to interact with human beings. Produced before "Evolution" but aired afterward, "The Ensigns of Command," written by Melinda Snodgrass, is a so-so entry but includes some outstanding sequences for Brent Spiner. The Sheliak look similar to the rocklike Excalbians from the classic *Trek* episode "The Savage Curtain"—and the Excalbians looked hokey in the first place. This deficiency is likely the result of budget cuts. According to director Cliff Bole, $200,000 was slashed from the episode's budget in preproduction.

"The Survivors"

Responding to a distress signal, the *Enterprise* discovers that a Federation colony on Delta Rana IV has been completely obliterated by alien invaders—except for a tiny patch of land containing the home of two survivors, a kindly old couple who are not quite what they seem. Structured as a mystery, "The Survivors" is a model of sustained tension with a devastatingly powerful revelation held in reserve for its climax. This emotionally gripping installment also features a pair of winning guest performances from John Anderson and Anne Haney in the title roles. Overall it ranks as a major improvement over the first two installments of Season Three. Anderson, whose wife had died recently, brings a profound sense of loss and regret to his performance. This was the final teleplay written by Wagner before the writer-producer left the series.

"Who Watches the Watchers"

Containing elements remarkably similar to the movie *Star Trek Insurrection* (1998), "Who Watches the Watchers" concerns a team of Federation anthropologists secretly observing a preindustrial Vulcanoid civilization on Mintaka III when a power failure reveals their presence to a pair of impressionable natives. The situation is worsened when Dr. Crusher saves the life of one of the Mintakans, who believes he has been resurrected by divine beings. Religious fervor begins to sweep through the previously atheistic civilization. "Who Watches the Watchers," written by Manning and Beimler, contains both a thought-provoking exploration of the moral complexity inherent in the Prime Directive and the most vitriolic expression of the series' guiding atheism since the classic episode "Who Mourns for Adonais?" Location footage for this episode was filmed at Vasquez Rocks, where four classic *Trek* episodes, including "Arena," were shot. This was the last installment overseen by Wagner; Piller took over with the next episode.

"The Bonding"

Twelve-year-old Jeremy Aster (Gabriel Damon) is orphaned when his mother is killed during a routine away mission. (Jeremy's father was killed in the line of duty years before.) As the child struggles to come to grips with his loss, a powerful, shape-changing alien appears in the guise of the dead mother. Meanwhile, Worf, who commanded the ill-fated mission, is riddled by guilt, and Wesley is reluctant to reach out to the boy and offer advice because the situation brings up difficult memories of the death of his father. Piller unearthed writer Ronald D. Moore's affecting, emotionally complex "The Bonding" from the series' slush pile. On the strength of this script, Moore was asked to join the show's staff. He quickly became a franchise stalwart, going on to write or co-write twenty-seven more *Next Generation* adventures (including the Hugo-winning series finale "All Good Things . . ."), two movies (*Generations* and *First Contact*), as well as episodes of *Deep Space Nine* and *Voyager*. The teleplay's careful balance of a sci-fi mystery (who is this alien and what is it up to?) and character-driven drama points in the direction where Piller would steer the series.

"Booby Trap"

The *Enterprise* discovers a thousand-year-old starship and, when it approaches to investigate, stumbles into an ancient, energy-draining weapon left over from a forgotten war. Unless it can escape this trap, Captain Picard's ship will be reduced to a lifeless hulk. It's up to Geordi to solve the problem. To help him sort through possible solutions, he orders the computer to construct a holographic duplicate of the designer of the *Enterprise*'s engines—Dr. Leah Brahms, who turns out to be an attractive young woman. Although heavily laden with Treknobabble, "Booby Trap" (a script begun by Wagner but completed by Ron Roman) supplies both nail-biting tension and enriching character material in equal measure. The scenario contrasts Geordi's ineptitude with women with his genius for solving technological riddles in amusing and surprisingly affecting ways. LeVar Burton is wonderful both in his misbegotten attempt to woo crewmate Christy Henshaw (Julie Warner) and his romantically charged sequences with the holographic Dr. Brahms. Whoopi Goldberg also has a memorable scene in which Guinan comforts Geordi after his disastrous date with Christy.

"The Enemy"

A Romulan spy ship crashes on a Federation planet. One grievously wounded survivor is beamed aboard the *Enterprise* for treatment, but Geordi is stranded on the planet's surface with a second Romulan. The planet is swept by violent electromagnetic storms that inhibit the transporter, but Geordi and the Romulan work out an uneasy truce that enables them to survive. Meanwhile Worf, whose parents were killed by Romulans, refuses to donate cellular material needed to save the other Romulan, who eventually dies. "The Enemy," written by Piller and David Kemper, brings the differences between Worf's Klingon outlook and morals and those of his human (and android and Betazoid) shipmates into sharp relief. "My Starfleet training tells me one thing, but everything I am tells me another," Worf says. This episode proved foundational for the many Klingon-centric stories that followed. Piller came up with the idea of Worf standing his ground and allowing the Romulan to die, a concept that was highly controversial among the show's writers and cast (and later among viewers). At first Michael Dorn balked at the idea, but then realized it was perfectly in character for Worf. The actor delivers a powerful, fully committed performance. Rick Berman also backed the idea, which would never have passed muster during *Next Gen*'s first two seasons. "The Enemy" stands as an uncommonly effective and hard-hitting installment, one of the highlights from a season almost overflowing with his memorable adventures.

"The Price"

The *Enterprise* hosts multilateral negotiations with several civilizations, including the Federation and the Ferengi, bidding for control over what appears to be the galaxy's first stable wormhole, connecting the Alpha Quadrant with the distant Gamma Quadrant. Counselor Troi finds herself attracted to Devinoni Ral (Matt McCoy), the unctuous human negotiator representing the Chrysalians, and the two fall madly in bed with each other. But skullduggery is afoot, involving both the Ferengi and Ral. This installment, written by Hannah Louise Shearer, focuses primarily on Deanna, who once again displays extremely suspect taste in men (her affection for Riker notwithstanding). Like many early Troi episodes, "The Price" generates only middling interest. Although the show's other characters were coming along nicely, writers remained unsure what to do with Deanna. This in turn left Marina Sirtis (never the cast's strongest performer) adrift, with only a nebulous idea of where her character was headed. "The Price" remains notable for the franchise's first (tastefully executed) sex scene. While this wormhole turns out to be worthless (exploration reveals that it's stable on only one end), the concept of a wormhole that serves as a galactic gateway later provided the premise for *Star Trek: Deep Space Nine*. Two Ferengi stranded in the Gamma Quadrant in this episode later turned up in the *Voyager* installment "False Profits."

"The Vengeance Factor"

A band of nomadic raiders known as the Gatherers launch a series of attacks on Federation targets. To end the raids, Picard attempts a rapprochement between these space pirates and their mother civilization, the Acamarians, who have turned away from violence after centuries of tribal warfare. But an ancient blood feud threatens to resurface and foil the potential agreement. "The Vengeance Factor," written by Sam Rolfe, represents a step up from "The Price" but remains one of the least memorable third-season installments. Fortunately, the series quickly returned to form.

"The Defector"

Captain Picard takes in Jarok (James Sloyan), a Romulan admiral who defects in order to warn the Federation of an impending Romulan sneak attack that will plunge the galaxy into war. To confirm Jarok's tip, Picard must take his ship into the Neutral Zone, where the Romulans are supposedly massing an invasion fleet. But is Jarok—who at first claims to be a low-level logistics officer—telling the truth, or is he trying to lure the *Enterprise* into a trap? "The Defector" ranks among the season's most spell-binding tales, with white-knuckle suspense tempered by an aching awareness of the cost of war—even cold wars. Sloyan delivers a haunting performance as the conflicted Jarok, who has abandoned his home and family, and his personal honor as well, to preserve peace in the galaxy. After being relegated to the background in several recent installments, Picard returns to the forefront of the action in "The Defector"; Patrick Stewart responds in typically vibrant style. The events of this episode tie in directly with those from "The Enemy." Ronald D. Moore received sole credit for this teleplay, which the writer has described as "the Cuban Missile crisis in outer space," but the entire writing staff collaborated on extensive revisions. At one point, the story involved a romance between Jarok and Dr. Crusher, which was wisely jettisoned. The rewrites continued to the very end. A teaser sequence featuring Data as Sherlock Holmes had to be abandoned just two days prior to shooting to avert legal action by the Arthur Conan Doyle estate, and was replaced with Data performing a scene from Shakespeare's *Henry V.*

"The Hunted"

On a mission to Angosia III, a planet that has applied for entry into the Federation, the *Enterprise* crew apprehends an escaped Angosian prisoner. However, the renegade turns out to be no common criminal but a genetically engineered and psychologically programmed supersoldier created by Angosians to fend off an alien attack. Angosia III is now an idyllic, peaceful world, and its residents want nothing to do with the cunning, aggressive warriors they manufactured to win their freedom and security. The ex-soldiers are now confined to Lunar 5, an orbiting gulag. "The Hunted," penned by Robin Burger (under the name Robert Bernheim), is a full-tilt action yarn that serves as a parallel with the plight of Vietnam War veterans who struggled to reacclimate to civilian life. The guest cast includes James Cromwell, who would later portray warp-drive pioneer Zefram Cochrane in *Star Trek: First Contact*, as the Angosian prime minister. While not top-tier *Trek*, "The Hunted" is another solid, thought-provoking entry.

"The High Ground"

While delivering medical supplies to Rutia IV, Dr. Crusher is kidnapped by separatist rebels, drawing the *Enterprise* into a civil conflict that has transformed a once-peaceful world into a police state. Riker coordinates a search with the bitter Rutian security chief (Kerrie Keane), who is bent on wiping out the terrorists who have repeatedly bombed civilians, even children. Meanwhile, Crusher begins to understand the perspective of the insurgents, who see themselves as freedom fighters. "The High Ground" boasts electrifying action sequences, affecting character moments, and some outstanding work by Gates McFadden. Writer Melinda Snodgrass's gutsy teleplay, her best since "The Measure of a Man," paints in shades of gray and offers no easy answers to the complex issues it raises. At the conclusion of the episode, the crew seems delighted to warp away from Rutia IV and be free of the planet's horrifying violence and heart-wrenching moral conundrums. Puzzlingly, Moore and Piller both slagged "The High Ground" in later interviews, complaining that Snodgrass's teleplay had nothing meaningful to say about the problem of terrorism. This isn't entirely true. By virtue of its mere existence within the framework of *The Next Generation*, Snodgrass's story suggests that terrorism will continue to vex humanity into the twenty-fourth century and beyond—a depressing but probably valid statement. The issue of terrorism would reappear with the Bajoran-Cardassian conflict, depicted in later *Next Gen* episodes and on *Deep Space Nine*.

"Deja Q"

Captain Picard and his crew are working furiously to save planet Bre'el IV from a catastrophic collision with its own moon, when suddenly Q appears, naked, on the bridge. He claims to have been thrown out of the continuum and stripped of his omnipotent powers (along with his clothes, apparently). Given the choice to serve out his banishment in any mortal form, Q has chosen to become a human. Data, ironically, is assigned to help Q make the adjustment to human life. Although he no longer possesses his godlike powers, Q tries to help Data and Geordi find a way to save the civilization on Bre'el IV, but then aliens arrive to take revenge on the now-mortal Q. "Deja Q," written by Richard Danus, is arguably the funniest of all the series' many highly amusing Q stories. The teleplay sparkles with bons mot from Q (he asks Worf, "Eat any good books lately?" and tells Riker, "You're so stolid. You weren't like that before the beard!") as well as amusing situations, such as Q experiencing hunger, pain, and sleepiness for the first time—and enjoying none of it. The scenario playfully examines the nature and meaning of human life through the eyes of two nonhuman characters. John de Lancie contributes a zesty but well-considered performance as Q. Spiner matches him with an equally thoughtful but also very funny turn as Data, who patiently explains the mundane mechanics of human existence. This episode also features the first Q not played by de Lancie (a fellow member of the continuum portrayed by Corbin Bernsen). No *Next Gen* episode is more pure fun than this one.

"A Matter of Perspective"

"A Matter of Perspective," written by Ed Zuckerman, is a Trekian variation on the theme of director Akira Kurosawa's *Rashomon*. Commander Riker is charged with murder when a space station explodes, killing an alien scientist. Picard oversees a hearing to determine whether or not his first officer should be extradited to Tanuga IV, the scientist's home world, where criminals are guilty until proven innocent and the penalty for murder is death. A series of witnesses, including Riker, the scientist's widow, and his assistant, all testify and give wildly different accounts of the events leading up the explosion, realized through holodeck simulations. None of them are lying, Troi explains. They are telling "the truth as each of you remembers it." The similarly structured *Rashomon* offers no answer to the puzzlingly conflicted versions it gives of a single event; the film is a rumination on the subjective nature of truth, and even of reality itself. However, since "A Matter of Perspective" is a *Star Trek* episode rather than an art film, it features a more conventional ending: Picard, aided by research from Data, Geordi, and Wesley, uses bits and pieces of the various accounts to reveal what actually happened—something different from anything any single witness observed. While not a top-drawer episode, "A Matter of Perspective" remains a satisfying mystery with some amusing interludes. It also enables Frakes to show more range than usual.

"Yesterday's Enterprise"

A battle-scarred starship emerges from a wormhole near the *Enterprise-D*, and suddenly everything changes: Picard and his crew—including tactical chief Tasha Yar (Denise Crosby)—aren't on a peaceful mission of exploration. They are on the run from Klingon battle cruisers, as the Federation's war with the Klingon Empire stretches into its second decade. The damaged ship turns out to be the *Enterprise-C*, which vanished twenty-two years earlier. Only Guinan realizes something is amiss. Nothing is as it should be, including Tasha. To set things right, Guinan tells Picard, the *Enterprise-C* must go back through the wormhole and prevent the Federation-Klingon war, which has cost billions of lives. But going back means certain death to the lost-in-time crew.

"Yesterday's Enterprise" is imaginative and suspenseful. Although fast-paced and tightly plotted, it contains moments of powerful emotional resonance, especially for Tasha—who, belatedly, receives the heroic send-off fans felt her character deserved. The entire cast performs commendably, especially Crosby, Goldberg, and guest stars Tricia O'Neill as Captain Garrett, the courageous commander of the displaced *Enterprise-C*, and Christopher McDonald as Lieutenant Castillo, one of Garrett's officers, who strikes up a doomed romance with Tasha. Director David Carson and cinematographer Marvin Rush lend the episode a darker look, while re-dressed sets and subtle costume changes (for instance, officers wear phasers at all times) create a more militaristic atmosphere. Dennis McCarthy's brooding score provides the finishing touch. In every aspect, "Yesterday's Enterprise" is a masterpiece. The concept originated with a spec teleplay submitted from a fan, Trent Christopher Ganino, which Piller purchased and then combined with a story from writer Eric Stillwell (who came up with the idea of reviving and re-killing Tasha Yar). The show's entire writing

Tasha Yar (Denise Crosby) returned from the dead, only to be killed again in "Yesterday's Enterprise," widely regarded as among the greatest episodes in the history of the series.

staff collaborated on the teleplay, which was written in just three days to accommodate the limited schedule availability of Crosby and Goldberg. Originally, the episode featured a much more gruesome climax, with the alternate-timeline Data being electrocuted and Wesley being decapitated during the final confrontation with the Klingons.

The initial broadcast of "Yesterday's Enterprise" drew just over thirteen million viewers, making it the third-highest-rated single telecast of the series. Many fans and critics now consider it the single greatest episode of *The Next Generation*. It was selected as such in six different fan polls taken over the years and was named one of the series' best installments by both *TV Guide* and *Entertainment Weekly*. Rick Berman lists it and "The Measure of a Man" as his personal favorite *Next Gen* episodes. "Yesterday's Enterprise" also earned three Emmy nominations, winning for Outstanding Sound Editing and losing in the categories of Sound Mixing and Music (score). By any yardstick, it stands among the greatest works in the history of not only *The Next Generation*, but the entire franchise.

"The Offspring"

Data shocks his crewmates by assembling an android child named Lal (Hallie Todd), whom he intends to raise as his daughter. This is not an experiment, he insists, but "procreation." Despite Data's best efforts to teach Lal how to interact with humans, she remains a misfit—teased by the ship's teenagers (who should be her peer group) and shunned by younger children, who find her scary. Data's progeny also attracts the attention of Starfleet researchers, who try to take control of Lal as they did Data in "The Measure of a Man." Although her neural network was copied from Data's, Lal displays abilities beyond those of her father, including the use of contractions and short bursts of emotion. Then things begin to go wrong.

The unenviable task of helming the episode to immediately follow "Yesterday's Enterprise" fell to first-time director Jonathan Frakes. Luckily, Frakes was assigned an excellent teleplay, submitted on spec from newcomer Rene Echevarria. Like Ronald D. Moore, Echevarria became a key contributor to the franchise, penning fourteen more *Next Gen* installments and twenty-three *DS9* episodes. "The Offspring" also features superb performances from Spiner and guest star Todd, who is heartbreakingly convincing as Lal. For his part, Frakes made smart but subtle choices (like using a gently gliding camera to add visual interest to dialogue-heavy scenes) that serve the story and performers without drawing undue attention to the director. The end result was a quietly poignant installment that remains, in its own fashion, just as emotionally intense as "Yesterday's Enterprise." Michael Dorn has named "The Offspring" and "The Drumhead" as his personal favorite *Next Gen* episodes. "The Offspring" is also a favorite of Frakes, for obvious reasons. He has every right to be proud; this is a sensational directorial debut.

"Sins of the Father"

Worf's long-lost brother Kurn (Tony Todd), serving aboard the *Enterprise* through the Federation-Klingon officer exchange program, informs his sibling that their deceased father, Mogh, has been named a traitor to the Empire. Newly discovered evidence supposedly reveals that Mogh was complicit in the Romulan attack on Khitomer, which resulted in his death along with thousands of other Klingons. Worf and Kurn return to the Klingon home world to challenge the ruling, while Captain Picard leads an investigation aimed at finding out what really happened at Khitomer. But the Starfleet officers become embroiled in Klingon High Council political machinations, which could result in civil war and threaten the alliance with the Federation.

"Sins of the Father" is another watershed episode. Written by Moore, with W. Reed Moran, and based on a spec scenario submitted by writer Drew Dieghan, it gave *Star Trek* fans their first look at the Klingon home world, Qo'noS (pronounced "Kronos"), and initiated story lines that would continue to unspool throughout the remainder of the series and on *Deep Space Nine*. It offers a lively combination of action and mystery, and a stunning performance by Dorn. Although his work had been improving throughout the first two and a half seasons, the actor makes a quantum leap forward with his judiciously gauged,

Worf (Michael Dorn, center) sacrifices his family honor to preserve the Klingon Empire in "Sins of the Father," a sensational Season Three installment. Worf is flanked by his brother Kurn (Tony Todd), left, and Captain Picard, right.

splendidly nuanced portrayal here. "You look at Worf in a different light, and I've played him in a different light since that episode," Dorn said in Edward Gross and Mark A. Altman's book *Captains' Logs*. The show's production artists outdid themselves, bringing the Great Hall, High Council chambers, and other Klingon sights to vivid life, and earning a well-deserved Emmy for Outstanding Art Direction. Like "Yesterday's Enterprise," "Sins of the Father" is often named among the finest installments in the history of the series. *Entertainment Weekly* listed it as one of the series' ten best entries in its twentieth anniversary tribute to the series in 2007. The episode lives up to its lofty reputation. Patrick Stewart once described it as "pure Shakespeare."

"Allegiance"

In the midst of an incredible roll, *The Next Generation* hit a speed bump with the formulaic "Allegiance." While resting in his cabin, Captain Picard suddenly vanishes and reappears in a holding cell with three other prisoners of various species, including one other human (a Starfleet cadet). Picard tries to organize the other abductees and formulate an escape plan. Meanwhile, an exact duplicate of the captain—possessing even his memories and knowledge of his crewmates—takes Picard's place on the *Enterprise* and begins issuing unusual orders and behaving strangely. "Allegiance," written by Manning and Beimler, contains echoes of classic *Trek* episodes such as "The Empath" and "Turnabout Intruder,"

The chemistry in "Captain's Holiday" between Patrick Stewart and guest star Jennifer Hetrick was real. The two soon began a well-publicized affair.

and harkens back to the bad old days of Season One, when *Next Gen* often aped the original program. Its premise is shopworn and implausible, and its logic flimsy (for instance, the aliens behind Picard's disappearance/replacement seem to command powers on the scale of those wielded by Q, yet can be trapped by a simple force field). The only real point of interest is the bogus Picard, who reveals thoughts and feelings the captain has kept hidden (including his romantic interest in Dr. Crusher) and gives Patrick Stewart an opportunity to stretch (he even leads his shipmates in a drinking song in Ten-Forward). "Allegiance" earned an Emmy nomination for Outstanding Makeup, mostly on the strength of a furry, snaggle-toothed alien that is incarcerated alongside Picard. According to Piller, the teleplay's primary selling point was that it could be produced cheaply, since the action was limited to one simple set and the existing *Enterprise* interiors. Berman needed an inexpensive installment to balance the season's budget following cost overruns on "Yesterday's Enterprise" and "Sins of the Father." As usual, however, you get what you pay for.

"Captain's Holiday"

Captain Picard, reluctantly taking much-needed shore leave on Risa, crosses paths with a beautiful flimflam artist named Vash (Jennifer Hetrick), two alien time travelers, and a pesky Ferengi, and becomes involved in the search for the priceless Tox Uhtat, a legendary artifact supposedly capable of rendering a sun lifeless. Throughout the life of the series, Patrick Stewart lobbied for stories where Picard did more than simply give orders to the crew or negotiate with aliens. His wish was granted with "Captain's Holiday," written by Ira Steven Behr, which plays like a cross between *The Maltese Falcon* and *Raiders of the Lost Ark*. The scenario removes Picard from his usual environs and reveals his inner swashbuckler. Stewart sparkles throughout, demonstrating tremendous range and dexterity as the grumpy Picard becomes engrossed in the mystery and begins having a grand time in spite of himself. Eleven episodes after *Star Trek*'s first sex scene (involving Deanna Troi and Devinoni Ral, in "The Price"), Picard beds—or, more precisely, sleeping bags—Vash. The roguish adventuress (charmingly played by Hetrick) reappeared a season later in "Qpid" and in the *Deep Space Nine* yarn "Q-less." Max Grodenchik, who plays a Ferengi in this episode, later earned the recurring role of Quark's brother, Rom, on *DS9*. This refreshing change-of-pace episode began another string of memorable Season Three adventures.

"Tin Man"

The *Enterprise* and two Romulan vessels race to intercept a mysterious alien entity—apparently a living spaceship—in orbit around a star that's about to go supernova. To assist Picard and his team in communicating with the life-form, code-named "Tin Man," Starfleet sends powerful but abrasive Betazoid telepath Tam Elbrun (Harry Groener), whose actions may have contributed to the deaths of forty-seven Starfleet officers during a previous botched first contact. "Tin Man" was adapted by Dennis Bailey and David Bischoff (with the uncredited Lisa Putnam White) from their Nebula Award–nominated short story "Tin Woodman." The episode boasts a fertile sci-fi premise, an edgy guest performance by Groener, and finally gives Deanna something meaningful to do, as she struggles to help Tam and her shipmates overcome their mutual disdain for each other. The "Tin Man" itself—intended to resemble a giant flying peach pit—is a highly original creation, and the ship's interiors—created with copious amounts of spray-on foam rubber to remove all right angles—look truly, weirdly alien. This underrated, highly entertaining episode earned an Emmy nomination for special visual effects, and deserved, but failed to receive, a second nomination for Art Direction.

"Hollow Pursuits"

The reclusive, nebbish Lieutenant Reginald Barclay (Dwight Schultz), a low-profile diagnostician on Geordi's engineering team, is assigned to investigate a series of puzzling mechanical breakdowns. But Barclay shirks his duties to engage in elaborate holodeck fantasies involving re-creations of his fellow officers. In one of his programs, Barclay fences with Picard, Geordi, and Data (pictured as the Three Musketeers), romances Deanna (transformed into "the Goddess of Empathy"), and reduces Riker to a pint-sized mascot. His superiors are not amused when these programs are discovered, but Barclay eventually finds the source of the increasingly dangerous breakdowns, narrowly averting the ship's destruction.

With "Hollow Pursuits," *The Next Generation* broke all the rules and gained its humanity. Sarah Higley's hilarious, insightful, and fleet-footed teleplay (written under the pseudonym Sally Caves) centers on technical malfunctions, which were explicitly banned by Roddenberry. More significantly, the introduction of the neurotic, holodeck-addicted Lieutenant Barclay shatters the Great Bird's carefully cultivated image of twenty-fourth-century Starfleet officers as bastions of virtue and competence. Schultz brings Barclay to life with a vivid, multifaceted performance, with quirky humor overlaying deep pathos. Although fans admired the heroic crew of the *Enterprise*, Barclay was the first character that seemed fully human. Barclay became an instant fan favorite, and Schultz reprised the character in four more *Next Gen* episodes, in *Star Trek Generations*, and in six *Voyager* adventures. (For more on Schultz, see Chapter 15, "Heroes.") "Hollow Pursuits" earned an Emmy nomination for hairstyling, but should have been honored for its teleplay and for Schultz's performance. Although popular with fans, this episode has never received the acclaim bestowed on other Season Three entries such as "Yesterday's Enterprise," "Sins of the Father," "The Best of Both Worlds," or even "The Offspring"—probably because it's (gasp!) funny. That's unfortunate, because "Hollow Pursuits" is an extraordinary achievement.

"The Most Toys"

Data is kidnapped by a venal collector (Saul Rubinek) who wants to keep him prisoner, displaying him as part of his private collection of unique and priceless artifacts, including the *Mona Lisa* and the only surviving Roger Maris baseball card. Like "Captain's Holiday," "The Most Toys" separates a lead character from the rest of the cast and unveils hidden attributes. The scenario reveals Data's toughness and resolve as he struggles to gain freedom from his nefarious captor. How far will he go to break free from one of the most ruthless and despicable villains in the history of the series? Will Data kill? This episode features brilliant performances by both Spiner and Rubinek, who was a last-minute replacement. Originally, producers hired British actor David Rappaport, but he attempted suicide shortly into production. Two days' worth of footage featuring Rappaport had to be scrapped and reshot with Rubinek. Rappaport fatally shot himself two months later. Despite its troubled production, "The Most Toys" emerged as another excellent adventure.

"Sarek"

Sarek, the legendary Vulcan diplomat (and father of a certain well-known half-Vulcan Starfleet officer), beams aboard the *Enterprise* to help negotiate an important treaty with the reclusive Legarans. This is to be the final assignment in the distinguished career of the 202-year-old Vulcan. Unfortunately, it soon becomes clear that Sarek is not well. He has developed a disorder that causes older Vulcans to lose control of their emotions. Because he's a telepath, this problem spreads throughout the ship, with crew members suddenly suffering fits of irrational anger. To complete his vital mission, Sarek mind-melds with Picard, who temporarily hosts the diplomat's raging emotions. This episode was undertaken with some trepidation, since it made the most direct link yet between *The Next Generation* and the classic series, but the results proved well worth the risk. The finely wrought, elegiac teleplay by fantasy author Peter S. Beagle delivers a series of wrenching moments (like Sarek, shockingly, tearing up during a chamber music performance). As Sarek, Mark Lenard delivers a masterful performance—arguably the best among all nine of his *Trek* appearances. Stewart is also very impressive, especially during the climactic sequence in which he fights to contain Sarek's emotional turmoil. Stewart's sweaty, bug-eyed, laughing-crying freak-out is positively Shatnerian (in a good way). This outstanding episode had special meaning for the show's writers and producers. The tale of a great man coping with an inescapable decline was intended as a coded tribute to Roddenberry. Michael Piller, in Judith and Garfield Reeves-Stevens's book *Star Trek: The Next Generation—The Continuing Voyage*, says, "If you go back and look at 'Sarek' closely, what that character is, is Gene Roddenberry."

"Ménage a Troi"

In Season Three's Lwaxana Troi episode, an unscrupulous Ferengi (is there such a thing as a scrupulous Ferengi?) kidnaps Lwaxana (and Deanna and Riker along with her) because: a) he is smitten with Lwaxana, and b) he wants to use her telepathic powers to gain an advantage in negotiations. Written by Fred Bronson and Roddenberry's longtime secretary Susan Sackett, "Ménage a Troi" is frothy and funny, like all the early Lwaxana stories. Majel Barrett-Roddenberry is delightful throughout, especially during an icky but amusing lobe-stroking sexual interlude with her Ferengi captor. However, the episode's funniest moment belongs to Patrick Stewart when Captain Picard, feigning devotion to Lwaxana, recites a mishmash of Shakespearian sonnets with mock romantic ardor. Trekkers will note the presence of Ethan Phillips (later to play Neelix on *Voyager*) in a secondary role as a sadistic Ferengi scientist.

"Transfigurations"

Dr. Crusher treats an alien grievously wounded in a starship crash. The patient, who Crusher refers to as "John Doe" because he suffers from amnesia and can't recall his name, exhibits a miraculous healing power and other extraordinary abilities. Just as the alien's memory is beginning to return, a vessel from John Doe's home world arrives and informs Picard that the patient is a dangerous criminal who must be turned over for immediate execution. Written by Rene Echevarria, who had earlier penned "The Offspring," "Transfigurations" is one of *The Next Generation*'s most blatantly spiritual/metaphysical stories, guest starring a thinly veiled Christ figure (Doe) and featuring a wonder-inspiring finale. The episode also boasts a standout performance by McFadden.

"The Best of Both Worlds"

Since the events of "Q Who" the season before, Starfleet has been preparing for an attack by the Borg. But the incursion happens sooner than anyone anticipated, and Starfleet still lacks an effective defense. The *Enterprise* is dispatched to try to repel the Borg, or at least slow their advance, but the effort is fruitless. Captain Picard is apprehended and assimilated, transformed into Locutus of Borg, spokesman for the collective as it prepares to consume humanity, beginning with Earth. *The Next Generation* struck out with its first two season finales (the badly compromised "The Neutral Zone," followed by the barely watchable "Shades of Gray"). But for Season Three, Piller wrote a walk-off grand slam home run—and one of the greatest cliff-hangers in television history.

As ever, Piller's aim was to balance human interest with sci-fi action, and he certainly hit the target. The scenario is almost unbearably suspenseful, but makes room for outstanding moments for Frakes, Sirtis, Stewart, and Goldberg, as well as guest star Elizabeth Dehanny's Commander Shelby, an ambitious young officer snapping at Riker's heels. Like "Q Who," "The Best of Both Worlds" was mounted on a spectacular scale (by TV standards), with eye-popping sets, costumes, and Emmy-winning visual effects, and an ominous score by Ron Jones. Initially, this installment left fans spooked—some feared the cliff-hanger ending signaled that Stewart, or Frakes, or both, wanted off the show. But even so, "The Best of Both Worlds" was a tremendous hit and is now widely ranked as one of the series' finest moments (especially when considered in combination with Season Four's "The Best of Both Worlds, Part II"). Ronald D. Moore points to this episode as the turning point in the history of the program. "Suddenly everyone was talking about *TNG*," he writes in his foreword to Paula M. Block and Terry J. Erdmann's *Star Trek: The Next Generation 365*. "Suddenly, we weren't 'the new *Star Trek* series,' we were *the Star Trek* series. . . . We never felt like the new kids again." This nearly perfect episode also served as the ideal finish to a phenomenal season.

The classic *Star Trek* was cancelled following its third season. Such a fate never threatened *The Next Generation*. Its already strong ratings climbed even higher during Season Three, when it attracted an average of 9.77 million viewers per week. The series, now carried by 235 stations nationwide (the most of any syndicated program), would top 10 million viewers per week during each of its next three seasons. Just as importantly, the show finally delivered the kind of week-in, week-out excellence achieved by its parent program during its glory days. However, the original *Trek* had functioned at this high level for barely a season and a half (coming together in the middle of Season One and continuing throughout Season Two, only to fall off badly during its final campaign). *The Next Generation* would remain in peak form for the next three seasons. In terms of ratings performance, longevity, and sustained excellence, the offspring was about to surpass its parent.

The thrilling "Best of Both Worlds" epic, depicted on this Franklin Mint commemorative plate, marked a turning point in the history of the series, and of the franchise.

Photo by Preston Hewis, East Bank Images

15

Heroes

Guest Stars and Secondary Cast Members, Part One

William Shatner, Leonard Nimoy, Patrick Stewart, and Brent Spiner were the big guns (or, if you prefer, big phasers) of the *Star Trek* franchise. But performers such as Whoopi Goldberg, John de Lancie, and Dwight Schultz were its secret weapons. One of the greatest strengths of *The Next Generation* and the *Trek* movies was the richness and depth of its supporting characters—Guinan, Q, Lieutenant Barclay, and so on—all of whom brought something unique, refreshing, and in some cases badly needed to the *Trek* dynamic. Propelled by adventurous screenwriting and high-quality acting, these "minor" figures grew into personalities as dynamic as any of the show's leads—arguably more compelling than some of the regulars.

Over the course of 176 *Next Gen* episodes and eleven feature films, dozens of actors created unforgettable supporting characters. Some were major stars, some later became stars, while others were simply jobbing character actors. Whatever they accomplished in their other work, however, these performers became indelibly etched in fans' memories for their superb performances as the allies, enemies, love interests, and family members who appeared alongside the iconic *Enterprise* crews. This book celebrates their achievements with three chapters—this one, Chapter 16 ("Villains"), and Chapter 18 ("Friends and Family"). As the titles indicate, these chapters are organized thematically based on the nature of the characters portrayed. This chapter is devoted to the work of actors whose characters worked alongside Captains Kirk or Picard and, in some manner or another, embodied *Star Trek*'s ideals and virtues. Performers within each chapter are listed alphabetically.

Even with three full chapters devoted to the task, however, not every outstanding guest star could be included here. Other memorable performers are noted in the entries for individual movies and episodes in which they appeared. The careers and performances of Denise Crosby and Wil Wheaton are covered in Chapters 7 ("Rightful Heirs"), 35 ("The High Ground"), and 36 ("Thine Own Self") because they were members of the show's original starring cast.

Kirstie Alley

Kirstie Alley, born January 12, 1951, in Wichita, Kansas, had just one television appearance on her résumé prior to winning the role of the half-Vulcan, half-Romulan Lieutenant Saavik in *Star Trek II: The Wrath of Khan* (1982). She declined to return as Saavik for *Star Trek III: The Search for Spock* (1984) because she had several lucrative television offers, including the miniseries *North and South* and *North and South, Book II*, in which she appeared opposite Jonathan Frakes. Alley brought underlying warmth and likeability to the coolly logical Saavik, qualities that stand out in comparison with the stiff, bland performance of her successor, Robin Curtis. In 1987, Alley replaced Shelley Long as the love interest of barkeeper Sam Malone (Ted Danson) on *Cheers*, winning both fame and three Emmy nominations (taking home the prize in 1991). She later appeared in movies such as the popular *Look Who's Talking* series opposite John Travolta and many TV shows, headlining in the highly rated sitcom *Veronica's Closet* (1997–2000). The actress has waged a well-publicized battle with her weight in recent years. Alley has married and divorced twice and has two children, William True and Lillie Price, who she adopted during her second marriage, to actor Parker Stevenson.

Ronny Cox

Veteran character actor Ronny Cox, born July 23, 1938, has one of the most instantly recognizable faces in Hollywood—even if viewers can't immediately remember his name. By the time he was signed to play Captain Jellico in "Chain of Command," from *The Next Generation*'s sixth season, Cox had already appeared in hits such as *Beverly Hills Cop* (1984), *Robocop* (1987), and *Total Recall* (1990). His first major movie role was in *Deliverance* (1972), in which he played guitar during the famous "Dueling Banjos" sequence. Later in his career, Cox was usually cast as politicians, police captains, and other authority figures, often corrupt. He brought an edge to his role of Captain Jellico (who assumes command of the *Enterprise* while Captain Picard takes part in a covert mission) that goes beyond toughness and borders on meanness. Much of the tension (especially during the first half of the two-part story) has to do with Commander Riker and the rest of the senior staff chafing under Jellico's unbending, dictatorial rule. But the iron-fisted Jellico ultimately secures Picard's safe return, which earns him the crew's grudging respect. Cox, a native of New Mexico, remains active and has garnered roles in more than 130 films and television series so far. He was married to his wife, Mary, from 1960 until her death in 2006. The couple had two children. Cox is also an accomplished folk musician who has released eight CDs.

James Cromwell

Like Ronny Cox, veteran character actor James Cromwell had appeared in scores of movies and TV shows prior to his *Star Trek* roles. Born January 27,

1940, in Los Angeles, Cromwell launched his career in the mid-1970s with guest appearances on shows such as *The Rockford Files* and *All in the Family*. One of his earliest jobs was on William Shatner's short-lived TV series *Barbary Coast*. In all, he has appeared in nearly 160 movies and TV shows so far, including memorable performances as Farmer Hoggett in the family comedy *Babe* (1995), for which he earned an Oscar nomination, and *L.A. Confidential*, in which he played police chief Dudley Smith. The versatile Cromwell has great comedic timing but can also believably radiate menace and has often played villains. For *Star Trek: First Contact*, Cromwell supplied a zesty comic performance as the alcoholic, self-aggrandizing warp-drive pioneer Zefram Cochrane, whose enthusiasm wavers when he learns that he will someday be regarded as a hero. Cromwell's is generally regarded as the definitive take on the character, who was previously played by Glenn Corbett in the classic episode "Metamorphosis." Cromwell reprised the role in two episodes of *Star Trek: Enterprise* (the pilot "Broken Bow" and the Mirror Universe story "In a Mirror, Darkly"). The actor also appeared as three other *Star Trek* characters. On *Next Gen* he played Prime Minister Nayrock in "The Hunted" and mysterious trader Jaglom Shrek in "Birthright, Parts I and II," and on *Deep Space Nine* he appeared as Minister Hanock in "Starship Down."

James Doohan

Doohan's life and career were discussed in depth in the original *Star Trek FAQ*, but the actor's lone *Next Generation* appearance earns him a spot on this list. As Scotty in "Relics," Doohan made by far the most satisfying and memorable *Next Gen* appearance by a classic *Trek* star. Rematerialized by Geordi after spending more than seventy years locked in the pattern buffer of a crashed starship's transporter, the usually indomitable Scotty feels useless and out-of-date. In one unforgettable sequence, Scotty visits a holographic re-creation of the original *Enterprise*, where he commiserates with Captain Picard before sinking into despair. "This was my home, this was where I had a purpose," he muses wistfully. Doohan's deeply moving performance is arguably his single finest *Star Trek* portrayal.

Shannon Fill

Born June 13, 1971, Shannon Fill graduated from Cal State-Northridge with a degree in the theater and enjoyed a brief career in film and television, tallying eight credits from 1992 to 1995, including guest roles on *Murder, She Wrote*; *Silk Stalkings*; and *Walker, Texas Ranger*. She remains best known for her powerful performances as Bajoran Sito Jaxa, seen first as a Starfleet Academy classmate of Wesley Crusher in "The First Duty" and later as a young ensign under the command of Lieutenant Worf (and the scrutiny of Captain Picard) in "Lower Decks." Although Fill, a former Olympic class ice skater, displayed impressive talent in both of her *Star Trek* appearances, she gave up acting to pursue other interests.

Michelle Forbes

Michelle Renee Forbes Guajardo, born January 8, 1965, in Austin, Texas, trained as a ballet dancer at Performing Arts High School in Houston but elected to pursue acting instead after graduation. In 1987, she landed a dual role as twins Solita and Sonni Carrera on the daytime soap opera *Guiding Light.* She remained with the series for two seasons and was nominated for a Daytime Emmy. In her first two years after leaving *Guiding Light,* she played supporting roles in three prime-time television series, including a brief appearance as Dara, the daughter of an eminent scientist who falls in love with Lwaxana Troi in "Half a Life." *Next Gen* producers were impressed with Forbes and later hired her for the recurring role of the Bajoran Ensign Ro Laren.

Like Schultz's Lieutenant Barclay, Forbes's edgy Ro was created to shake up the uniformly convivial *Enterprise* crew. The headstrong Ro, a Bajoran, clashed with Captain Picard and Commander Riker over whether or not the Federation should intervene on behalf of her people, an oppressed minority fighting a guerrilla campaign against their Cardassian overlords. The Prime Directive prevented the Federation from aiding the Bajoran insurgents, known as the Maquis, since they were residents of Cardassian space. In the last of Forbes's eight appearances as the character (Season Seven's "Preemptive Strike"), Ro defects to join the Maquis. Introducing a character who questioned the Prime Directive brought a greater dimension of moral complexity to the series' story lines. Ro's cool and direct demeanor made her interactions with crewmates interesting viewing. And the extraordinarily talented Forbes's authoritative work strengthened every episode in which she appeared. As a result, Ensign Ro remains one of the show's most enduringly popular supporting characters. The Bajoran/ Cardassian conflict would continue to play out over the run of *Star Trek: Deep Space Nine* and provide the backdrop for *Star Trek: Voyager.*

After "Preemptive Strike," Forbes twice declined opportunities to return to the franchise as Ro. She was offered a

Producers were so wowed by Michelle Forbes's Ensign Ro Laren that they offered the actress leading roles on two later *Star Trek* series, but she declined both times.

leading role on *Deep Space Nine* but turned it down because she wanted freedom to pursue feature film opportunities. Nana Visitor's character, Major Kira Nerys, was created as a replacement for Ro. Forbes also was offered a leading role on *Voyager* but again declined. Over the next few years she appeared in a handful of movies, including *Swimming with Sharks* (1994) and *Escape from L.A.* (1996), but soon returned to television, where she has held recurring or costarring roles—usually as strong, commanding characters—in nine different series, including *Homicide: Life on the Street* (1996–98), *24* (2002–2003) and *Battlestar Galactica* (2005–2006). She is currently appearing in AMC's critically acclaimed mystery series *The Killing* (2012). In the 1990s, she was married to Ross Kettle, but the couple is now divorced. Her friends call her "Mishka."

Colm Meaney

Colm Meaney seemingly has led two careers—one as a busy character actor and the other as Chief Miles O'Brien, among the most popular and most-seen characters in the history of the *Star Trek* franchise.

Meaney (whose first name is pronounced "column") was born May 30, 1953, in Dublin, Ireland, and took up acting as a teenager while in secondary school (the equivalent of high school). Upon graduation he studied with the Irish National Theater School of Acting and later performed with several professional touring companies in Great Britain. In the mid-1980s, he moved to the U.S. to pursue a film and television career, making his American TV debut in an episode of the Bruce Willis-Cybill Shepherd detective series *Moonlighting* in 1986. He has worked almost constantly ever since, appearing in scores of feature films, including hits like *Under Siege* and *The Commitments* (both 1991), and dozens of television series, ranging from *Remington Steele* to *Law & Order* to *The Simpsons*. In 1993, he was nominated for a Golden Globe Award for his appearance in director Stephen Frears's movie *The Snapper*.

To Trekkers, however, Meaney will always be the stalwart O'Brien. After making a pair of appearances as a background character during the first season of *Star Trek: The Next Generation*, Meaney was given the recurring role of transporter chief Miles O'Brien during *Next Gen*'s second season. The affable but tough-minded and resourceful O'Brien gradually emerged as one of the show's most popular supporting characters. With the launch of *Star Trek: Deep Space Nine* in 1992, O'Brien (and Meaney) transferred from the *Enterprise* to *DS9*, where he was elevated from supporting status to a leading role. Meaney appeared in 52 *Next Gen* installments and 211 total *Trek* episodes between the two series, the second most of any actor in the history of the franchise, trailing Michael Dorn's record 281 appearances. (That is, unless you count Majel Barrett-Roddenberry's ubiquitous voice-over work as the *Enterprise* computer. Adding her vocal appearances to her work as Nurse Chapel and Lwaxana Troi, Barrett-Roddenberry was seen or heard in more than three hundred *Trek* episodes and movies.)

Many actors who have appeared in far fewer *Star Trek*s became inescapably linked with the franchise, but Meaney was never typecast. This is a testament to the actor's formidable talent and tireless work ethic, exemplified by the number and variety of his non-*Trek* roles. "I'd meet people that knew me from features that I did, and didn't even know I did *Star Trek* because they didn't watch it," Meaney said in a recent interview published on the Collider.com website. "It was almost like *Star Trek* was a world unto itself. But it was a great show." Meaney, who has moved back to Ireland, remains active and appeared in four movies in 2010 alone. He married actress Bairbe Dowling in 1977, but the couple split in 1994. Meaney is now married to Ines Glorian and is active in Irish politics as a vocal supporter of the Sinn Fein party. He has two daughters, Brenda and Ada.

Colm Meaney's Chief Miles O'Brien began as a background character, but was later promoted to a leading role on *Deep Space Nine*. Eventually, Meaney tallied the second-most on-camera appearances of any *Star Trek* actor, trailing only Michael Dorn.

Diana Muldaur

Diana Charlton Muldaur was born August 19, 1938, in New York City. Following her graduation from tiny Sweet Briar College, an all-female school located in rural Virginia, she launched a theatrical career in New York and began accepting occasional television guest roles four years later. By the end of the decade, Muldaur had emerged as a busy guest star, appearing on numerous programs, including producer Quinn Martin's short-lived alien invasion series *The Invaders* (1968) and two classic *Trek* episodes. She portrayed astrobiologist Dr. Ann Mulhall in the Season Two adventure "Return to Tomorrow" and returned the following season as telepathic psychologist Dr. Miranda Jones in "Is There in Truth No Beauty?" She excelled in both parts but is particularly memorable in the latter, playing a blind woman who "sees" by wearing a garment interwoven with a web of censors. She remained an in-demand performer throughout the 1970s and '80s, racking up guest appearances on scores of TV series and in feature films, including the horror classic *The Other* (1972) and the John Wayne picture *McQ* (1974). Gene Roddenberry hired her for a guest role in his failed pilot *Planet Earth* (1974). Muldaur secured starring roles in two series—*Born Free* (1974) and *Hizzoner* (1979)—but both were quickly cancelled. She also enjoyed a recurring part as journalist Chris Coughlin on the detective series *McCloud*, appearing in fifteen episodes between 1970 and 1977.

In 1988, Muldaur joined the cast of *Star Trek: The Next Generation* as Dr. Katherine Pulaski. Although she was signed to replace Gates McFadden's Dr. Beverly Crusher, Muldaur declined to be listed with the regular cast and, like Goldberg, received "Special Guest Appearance" credit. Roddenberry brought in Muldaur to add some fire to the crew, envisioning Dr. Pulaski as the latter-day equivalent of DeForest Kelley's crusty Dr. McCoy. Muldaur appeared in twenty of twenty-two Season Two episodes and handled her role well (she is especially strong in "Unnatural Selection," an episode written as a showcase for her), but fans never warmed to Dr. Pulaski. Writers went overboard in making the doctor seem gruff. In her exchanges with Data (intended to recall McCoy's verbal jousts with Spock), Pulaski often seemed to be bullying the childlike android, whom she was reluctant to accept as a sentient being, let alone as an equal. She also repeatedly clashed with Captain Picard, putting her at odds with the show's two most popular characters. Fans deluged Paramount with letters demanding the return of Dr. Crusher, and eventually producers acquiesced to the will of Trekdom. Muldaur was let go after the season, and McFadden returned.

After leaving *Trek*, Muldaur enjoyed her greatest success with a recurring role as ruthless, double-dealing attorney Rosalind Shays on *L.A. Law* (1989–91), for which she won a pair of Emmy nominations. Over her long career, which continued into the mid-1990s, she became one of the most respected women in television, serving as a board member of the Screen Actors Guild and becoming the first female president of the Academy of Television Arts and Sciences. She has survived the deaths of two husbands, actor James Vickery, who passed away in 1979, and writer-producer Robert Dozier, who succumbed to cancer in 2012. She has no children, but is a prominent breeder and judge of Airedale terriers.

Dwight Schultz

In his film and television career, Dwight Schultz has specialized in playing quirky, offbeat characters—including the neurotic Lieutenant Reginald Barclay on *The Next Generation*. He was born November 24, 1947, in Baltimore and, after graduating from Maryland's Towson University in 1970, launched a successful theatrical career in New York. By the end of the decade, he was starring in Broadway productions, including David Mamet's *The Water Engine* (1978), which ran for sixty-three performances. He also had a supporting role in *The Crucifer of Blood* (1978), adapted from Sir Arthur Conan Doyle's Sherlock Holmes tale "The Sign of Four," which ran for 236 performances and earned four Tony nominations. When the play moved to Los Angeles in late 1980, Schultz moved with it and never moved back, remaining in California to pursue film and television opportunities. He quickly found work in TV movies and gained fame playing Captain H. M. "Howlin' Mad" Murdock on *The A-Team* (1983–87).

Whoopi Goldberg, a friend of Schultz and a fan of his work, lobbied for producers to bring him on board *The Next Generation* when *The A-Team* left the air. The character of Lieutenant Barclay was created specifically for Schultz. As Barclay, Schultz made twelve scattered appearances from 1990 to 2001, five times on *The Next Generation* and in *Star Trek Generations*, then six more times on *Star Trek: Voyager*. He also provided Barclay's voice for a *Star Trek* video game. But Schultz's impact on *Next Gen* proved profound, much greater than his relatively modest number of appearances might indicate. The timid, insecure, holodeck-addicted yet endearing Barclay became the first *Next Generation* character with serious flaws, and went a long way toward humanizing a crew that, during its first two seasons, seemed a bit *too* perfect. Also, like Goldberg, Schultz elevated the work of everyone around him through his superb performances.

During and after his *Trek* tenure, Schultz kept active in other film and television projects. He remains busy and is now in demand as a voice actor. In all, he's collected on-screen or vocal appearances in more than 160 movies, TV shows, and video games, and is currently a

Dwight Schultz's Reginald Barclay (left) crosses swords with Captain Picard during one of Barclay's holodeck fantasies from "Hollow Pursuits." Barclay helped humanize the idealized *Next Gen* crew.

regular on the *Ben 10* animated series, playing Dr. Animo. Schultz married therapist Wendy Fulton in 1983 and has a daughter named Ava.

Patti Yasutake

Originally, Patti Yasutake auditioned for the role of Meaney's on-screen spouse, Keiko Ishikawa O'Brien. That didn't work out, but the actress won the recurring role of Nurse Alyssa Ogawa, appearing in sixteen *Next Generation* episodes over the series' final four seasons and in the movies *Generations* and *First Contact*. Born September 6, 1953, in California, the Japanese-American actress made her television debut in a 1985 episode of William Shatner's *T. J. Hooker*. She has appeared in more than fifty films and television series in her career, most recently in a recurring role on the TNT crime drama *The Closer* (2008–2011). Although her role was minor, her presence enhanced every episode in which she appeared, especially the excellent "Lower Decks."

Others

By far the most celebrated (or at least massively hyped) guest star in the history of *The Next Generation* was Leonard Nimoy, whose appearance as Spock in "Unification, Parts I and II" helped the series climb to a new ratings peak. Nimoy's career, of course, was covered extensively in the first *Star Trek FAQ*. Less ballyhooed but, on balance, more impressive was the work of virtual unknowns Elizabeth Dennehy, Tricia O'Neill, and Christopher McDonald. Dennehy left an enduring impression as Lieutenant Commander Shelby, the ambitious young officer who hopes to replace Commander Riker as the *Enterprise*'s second-in-command in "The Best of Both Worlds, Parts I and II." The actress's only screen credit prior to her appearances on *Next Gen* was a one-season recurring role on the daytime soap *Guiding Light*. She went on to earn small parts in numerous film and television projects, and had a recurring role on the light fantasy series *Charmed* from 2004 to 2006. She is the daughter of well-known actor Brian Dennehy. O'Neill and McDonald appeared together in "Yesterday's Enterprise," as the battle-hardened Captain Rachel Garrett and her courageous tactical officer, Lieutenant Castillo. Both contributed outstanding performances to this excellent episode. O'Neill is a veteran actress whose screen career began in the early 1970s and has included (mostly minor) roles in nearly seventy movies and TV shows. She played two other *Star Trek* characters—Kurak, a Klingon scientist in the *Next Generation* episode "Suspicions," and Korinas, a member of the Cardassian Obsidian Order in *Deep Space Nine*'s "Defiant."

Star Trek: The Motion Picture also contained a pair of colorful supporting characters. Persis Khambatta was a supermodel and former Miss India who was hired to play the bald, Deltan Lieutenant Ilia in *Star Trek: The Motion Picture*. Although her performance was awkward, Khambatta was an intriguing screen presence and became the face of the movie. Khambatta went on to appear in at least fourteen other film and television roles, including the Sylvester Stallone thriller *Nighthawks* (1981). She died of a heart attack in 1998, at age forty-nine, in Bombay, India. Stephen Collins played Ilia's former lover, Captain Willard Decker, in *The Motion Picture*. Although his screen career was just three years old at the time, he had more than a dozen screen credits on his résumé, including a small role in the blockbuster *All the President's Men* (1976). More than thirty years and sixty credits later, Collins remains active. He starred in the family drama *7th Heaven* (1996–2007) as Reverend Eric Camden. His most recent appearance, as of this writing, was in the Farrelly Brothers' *The Three Stooges* (2012).

16

Villains

Guest Stars and Secondary Cast Members, Part Two

"The more successful the villain, the more successful the picture."
—*Alfred Hitchcock*

Hitchcock's simple equation has been proven many times in many places, including the *Star Trek* universe. Although creator Gene Roddenberry tried to dissuade writers from penning stories with clear-cut heroes and villains, many of the most satisfying *Trek* tales featured clashes between the noble Federation and the fearsome Klingons, Romulans, or the Borg, among other adversaries. These and other antagonists—such as Khan Noonien Singh, Q, and Lore—broadened the appeal of the franchise, since everyone (except maybe Roddenberry) loves a powerful, dynamic villain. Just as importantly, the franchise's villains helped define what *Star Trek* stood for by personifying ideologies the Federation stood against.

Behind every great *Trek* villain, however, was an actor—usually a guest star. Villains are famously enjoyable to play, but creating a truly memorable one takes skill and nuance. "A villain must be a thing of power, handled with delicacy and grace," wrote essayist Agnes Repplier. "He must be wicked enough to excite our aversion, strong enough to arouse our fear, [yet] human enough to awaken some transient gleam of sympathy." The eleven performers considered in this chapter accomplished this tricky feat with dexterity and style.

This is the second of three chapters devoted to actors who contributed sterling work in supporting and secondary roles. The others are Chapters 15 ("Heroes") and 18 ("Friends and Family").

John Anderson

John Anderson delivered one of the finest guest performances from the early seasons of *The Next Generation* with his haunting portrayal of Kevin Uxbridge in "The Survivors." The elderly Uxbridge and his wife, Rishon (Anne Haney), appear to have mysteriously survived an alien attack that devastated the rest of their planet, but it's later revealed that he committed a horrific act of vengeance. Anderson, born October 20, 1922, in Clayton, Illinois, was a veteran television actor whose career began in the early fifties, during the dawn of the medium.

By the time he was cast on *Star Trek*, Anderson had already appeared in more than two hundred other series, including numerous Westerns and crime dramas, and four episodes of *The Twilight Zone*. Although he usually played one-off guest parts, Anderson landed recurring roles on a few series, including *Dallas* (1988) and *MacGyver* (1986–91, as MacGyver's grandfather). He also took small roles in feature films, and played the dealer who sells a used car to Marion Crane in Alfred Hitchcock's *Psycho* (1960). Anderson's wife passed away shortly before his appearance on *The Next Generation*, lending his performance singular depth and authenticity. The actor later said that, due to the circumstances, the role was the most difficult of his long career. Anderson died in 1992 at age 69.

Kim Cattrall

Kim Cattrall, born August 21, 1956, in Liverpool, England, played the duplicitous Vulcan officer Valeris in *Star Trek VI: The Undiscovered Country*. She brought surprising depth and nuance to what could have been a one-note role, and is especially effective in her final scene with Leonard Nimoy's Spock. Originally, director Nicholas Meyer wanted Saavik to be revealed as a traitor but created the Valeris character when Kirstie Alley declined to reappear as Saavik. Apparently Robin Curtis was not considered a viable option, even though she had appeared as Saavik twice. Cattrall, who trained at the London Academy of Music and Dramatic Art, was an experienced Hollywood actress who had appeared in more than forty films and television shows, and had costarred in both *Police Academy* (1984) and *Big Trouble in Little China* (1986) before her role in *Star Trek VI*. She has continued to work regularly and is now best known as the promiscuous Samantha Jones from the *Sex and the City* TV series and films. Cattrall has been married and divorced three times, and was once romantically linked with Alexander Siddig, Dr. Bashir from *Deep Space Nine*.

Daniel Davis

Daniel Davis relished the opportunity to play one of the most charismatic and fascinating villains not only in *Star Trek* but anywhere—Sherlock Holmes's nemesis Professor James Moriarty, or rather a holographic depiction of him, as seen in "Elementary, Dear Data" and "Ship in a Bottle." Davis approached the role with zest and conviction, engendering fear and sympathy in nearly equal measure as the self-aware hologram fighting for his continued existence. Davis, born November 26, 1945, in Gurdon, Arkansas, also affected a convincing British accent for the role (his normal speaking voice has a distinctly Southern twang). His parents owned and operated the local movie theater, and Davis grew up idolizing Hollywood stars like Tyrone Power. Classically trained at the Arkansas Art Center, Davis worked with several theatrical companies including six years with the American Conservatory Theatre before beginning his film and television career in the early 1970s. Since then, he has appeared in many sitcoms, crime dramas and nighttime soaps. He landed recurring parts on *Texas* (1980–82) and *Dynasty* (1987–88), and a costarring role (as Niles, the butler) on the Fran Drescher comedy *The Nanny* (1993–99). He has also maintained his theatrical career, earning a Tony nomination for his work in *Wrong Mountain* in 2000. The actor claims to have performed in thirty-one of William Shakespeare's thirty-seven plays.

Alice Krige

Viewers are unlikely to forget Alice Krige's unsettling portrayal of the Borg Queen in *Star Trek: First Contact* (1996). Her menacing yet seductive performance inspired reviewer Roger Ebert to quip that the Krige "looks like no notion of sexy I have ever heard of, but inspires me to keep an open mind." For her work in *First Contact*, Krige was named Best Supporting Actress at the 1997 Saturn Awards. Krige, born June 28, 1954, in Upington, South Africa, moved to London in 1976 to pursue a theatrical career. She made one of her earliest screen appearances in the Academy Award–winning *Chariots of Fire* (1981). Later that year she played the twin roles of Eva Galley and Alma Mobley in *Ghost Story*, the performance that inspired Rick Berman, director Jonathan Frakes, and casting director Junie Lowry to hire Krige to play the Borg Queen. The versatile actress has appeared in scores of movies and television episodes since then, including several sci-fi and horror projects, and played Mary Shelley in *Haunted Summer* (1988). She reprised her role as the Borg Queen in the *Star Trek: Voyager* series finale, "Endgame," and for the filmed portions of the *Star Trek: The Experience* attraction at the Las Vegas Hilton.

Malcolm McDowell

With more than two hundred movie and TV appearances on his résumé, including his iconic starring performance in director Stanley Kubrick's *A Clockwork Orange* (1971), Malcolm McDowell is one of the most accomplished screen actors of his generation. But *Trek* fans remember him as the man who killed Captain Kirk in *Star Trek Generations*. Born June 13, 1943, in Leeds, England, McDowell trained at the London Academy of Music and Dramatic Art and later joined the Royal Shakespeare Company. After several forgettable television appearances, McDowell made a memorable movie debut in director Lindsay Anderson's acclaimed *If. . .* (1968). Three years later, he starred as the maladjusted Alex in *A Clockwork Orange*, a role that colored his later career. Although he sometimes played heroic parts (including an outstanding performance as H. G. Wells in director Nicholas Meyer's *Time After Time*, 1979), he was more frequently cast as villainous or unstable characters. His title role in the controversial *Caligula* (1979) was a more typical part for McDowell. He was excited to be offered the role of Dr. Soran—reportedly telling Berman, "I want to be the man to kill Kirk!"—and delivered a delightfully venomous performance. His work is one

B'Etor (Gwynyth Walsh) takes a word with Dr. Soran (Malcolm McDowell) in *Star Trek Generations*. Screenwriter Brannon Braga later said he received more hate mail for blowing up B'Etor and her sister Lursa in *Generations* than for killing Captain Kirk.

of the liveliest elements in the film. As of this writing he had a costarring role on the TNT courtroom dramedy *Franklin & Bash*. Surprisingly, despite his long and distinguished career, McDowell has never earned an Oscar, BAFTA (British Oscar), or Emmy nomination. He has been married three times and has four children, two from his second wife (*Time After Time* costar Mary Steenburgen) and two by his current spouse, Kelly Kuhr. He is an uncle of *Deep Space Nine* actor Alexander Siddig.

John de Lancie

No performer, outside of the series' principal cast, made a greater contribution to the success of *The Next Generation* than John de Lancie, whose guest appearances as the impish, superpowered Q invariably became season highlights. The series' writers enjoyed writing for Q, who presented endless story possibilities, and for the gifted de Lancie, who could be both amusing and frightening—often at the same time. Both Q and de Lancie's approach to the character evolved over the years, becoming less menacing and more sympathetic. Nearly every Q episode ranks among the series' best, but de Lancie's richest performance came in the Season Three installment "Deja Q," in which he takes refuge on the *Enterprise* after losing his powers. While he hurls some hilarious, scathing insults at Worf and Riker, and throws out his typically dismissive comments about the human race, de Lancie laces his portrayal with a note of anxiety that lends Q an

John de Lancie posed for this publicity still to promote his appearance in the 1995 Sci-Fi Channel movie *The Evolver*. But the actor remains best known as the omnipotent Q.

appealing vulnerability. He seems genuinely confused and unnerved as Q experiences hunger, pain, and sleepiness for the first time. De Lancie also delivers a surprisingly endearing performance in "Tapestry," in which Q enables a dying Captain Picard to relive his life and undo the mistakes of his impulsive youth—with unforeseen consequences.

In all, de Lancie played Q in eight *Next Generation* adventures, including the series premiere ("Encounter at Farpoint") and finale ("All Good Things . . ."), in one episode of *Deep Space Nine* and three installments of *Voyager*. No matter the series, de Lancie's name in the credits virtually guaranteed a good episode. In interviews during the early stages of preproduction for the ninth *Star Trek* feature film, producer Rick Berman reported that the upcoming picture would feature Q. This made sense, since Paramount Pictures had urged Berman to produce a lighter, more comedic movie following the intense *Star Trek: First Contact* (1996), but the idea was abandoned before writer Michael Piller began work on what became *Star Trek: Insurrection* (1998). This is too bad, since a Q movie would almost certainly have been more successful than the poorly received *Insurrection*.

De Lancie, born March 20, 1948, in Philadelphia, suffers from dyslexia and didn't learn to read until age twelve, yet appeared in his first play (a high school production of *Henry V*) at age fourteen. He attended Kent State University and studied at Juilliard. His film and television career began in the mid-1970s with small roles on shows like *McMillan & Wife* and *The Six Million Dollar Man*. Although best known as Q, he has appeared in nearly 150 movies and TV series and many theatrical productions, including a great deal of voice work. He played kooky inventor Eugene Bradford on the daytime soap *Days of Lives* from 1982 to 1986. With Leonard Nimoy, de Lancie cofounded Alien Voices, which produced several audio plays, including a pair of humorous "Q vs. Spock" dialogues. Voice work has always been an important outlet for de Lancie, who was sometimes bypassed for roles due to his height (he stands a towering six-foot-four).

For de Lancie, *Star Trek* is a family business. He is married to actress Marnie Mosiman, who had a supporting role in the *Next Gen* episode "Loud as a Whisper." The couple has two sons, both of whom have portrayed Q's offspring. Keegan de Lancie, born in 1984, played "Q Jr." in the *Voyager* installment "Q2," while Owen de Lancie, born in 1987, played that role in the filmed segment of *Star Trek World Tour*, a traveling museum exhibit. De Lancie and Mosiman's daughter, Nicole de Lancie, made a cameo appearance in the *Voyager* episode "Death Wish." In addition, de Lancie is close friends with actress Kate Mulgrew, *Voyager*'s Captain Janeway. He has participated in many other *Trek* projects over the years, including video games and audio books, and coauthored a *Star Trek* novel (*I, Q*) with writer Peter David.

Barbara March and Gwynyth Walsh

Barbara March and Gwynyth Walsh took similar paths into show business, and became inexorably linked in the imaginations of *Star Trek* fans for their appearances as the ruthless Duras Sisters, Lursa and B'Etor. Both March and Walsh hail from the same place—not the Klingon home world, but Canada. March was born October 9, 1953, in Toronto and earned a BFA in dramatic arts from the University of Windsor. She began her career at the prestigious Stratford Shakespeare Festival and became well known in Canadian theatrical productions. She also landed small roles on a handful of TV series and has written novels and screenplays. In 1995, she served as story editor for *Mysterious Island*, a short-lived Canadian TV series based on the Jules Verne novel and starring her husband, Alan Scarfe. Coincidentally, Scarfe appeared in two episodes of *Next Gen* (including a memorable turn as Tokath, administrator of a Romulan penal colony in "Birthright, Part II") and one of *Voyager*. Walsh was born in 1958 in Winnipeg and raised in Vancouver. She earned a BFA from the University of Alberta and appeared in many Shakespearean and classical roles for various Canadian companies. She launched her screen career in the mid-1980s and has earned many more film and television credits than March, including a recurring supporting role on the Canadian crime drama *Da Vinci's Inquest* (1998–2005).

In 1991, March and Walsh were cast in "Redemption, Parts I and II" as Lursa and B'Etor Duras, who instigate a Klingon Civil War to try to install their young nephew as a puppet High Chancellor. The characters proved extremely popular, in part because the evil-but-alluring sisters appeared in provocatively cut outfits with plenty of exposed cleavage. Both actresses attacked their roles with aplomb, turning Lursa and B'Etor into what March later characterized as "Klingon sex goddesses." The Duras Sisters returned in the *Next Gen* episode "Firstborn" and the *Deep Space Nine* installment "Past Prologue" before finally being dispatched in *Star Trek Generations*, in which the sisters are blown to smithereens in a space battle with the *Enterprise*. March also appeared as different characters in two *Voyager* episodes. Lursa and B'Etor might have appeared more often, but it was difficult to coordinate the actress's schedules. As a twisted sort of testament to the enduring popularity of March and Walsh's characters, writer Brannon Braga, in a 2006 interview with The Fandom website, revealed that following the release of *Star Trek Generations*, he received more hate mail and death threats for blowing up the Duras Sisters than for killing Captain Kirk.

Ricardo Montalban

The first *Star Trek FAQ* covered the career of Ricardo Montalban in detail, but his work as Khan Noonien Singh in *Star Trek II: The Wrath of Khan* must be acknowledged here as well. The actor's importance in the history of the franchise cannot be overstated. The blockbuster success of *Wrath of Khan* assured the future of the *Trek* franchise, which was left in doubt by the shaky performance of *Star Trek: The Motion Picture*. Montalban's dynamic, iconic performance in the title role was a major factor in the film's wide appeal. Although less subtle and actorly than his first turn as the character (in the classic episode "Space Seed"), Montalban's full-throttle portrayal of the unhinged movie Khan provided the perfect foil for William Shatner's Captain Kirk and established the character as *Star Trek*'s single greatest villain. Montalban was an enormous talent who seldom found roles equal to his abilities; *Star Trek II* was one of the rare instances when the actor was able to truly shine. Director Nicholas Meyer, in his memoir *The View from the Bridge*, wrote, "I've never driven a Lamborghini, but I imagine directing Ricardo Montalban is as close as I will ever come."

Terry O'Quinn

Terry O'Quinn, born July 15, 1952, in Sault Sainte Marie, Michigan, has made a career out of playing mysterious and sometimes reprehensible characters. He first gained notoriety in the title role of *The Stepfather* (1987), in which he played a serial killer who murders entire families, and is best known as the enigmatic John Locke on J. J. Abrams's smash television series *Lost* (2004–2010). But *Star Trek* fans remember him for his superb portrayal of Admiral Erik Pressman in "The Pegasus." Riker's former commanding officer, Pressman arrives on the *Enterprise* with a secret agenda—to revive a forbidden experiment that led to the loss of his former ship, the USS *Pegasus*. O'Quinn brings a deep sense of misplaced moral authority to the obsessive admiral, who truly believes his unscrupulous actions are in the best interests of the Federation. Like all the best villains, Pressman thinks he's a hero. He's unconcerned by the death of nearly his entire crew; only reviving the project matters. Even though Pressman was supposed to be many years older than Commander Riker, O'Quinn is actually only a month older than actor Jonathan Frakes. Like Patrick Stewart, O'Quinn began balding in his early twenties. Since 1979, O'Quinn has been married to Lori O'Quinn. They have two sons, Oliver, born in 1984, and Hunter, born in 1986. He earned three Emmy nominations for his work on *Lost* and was named Outstanding Supporting Actor in a Drama Series in 2007.

Jean Simmons

Jean Simmons, a legendary star from Hollywood's golden age, delivered a sensational performance as another dangerously misguided Starfleet admiral, Norah Satie, in "The Drumhead." Satie, searching for Romulan sympathizers on board the *Enterprise*, begins an ever-expanding witch hunt based entirely on rumor and guilt by association. Her actions are even more threatening than those of Admiral Pressman in "The Pegasus" (they could destabilize all of Starfleet), but Simmons's carefully shaded performance underscores the sadness (stemming from the loss of her idolized father) behind Satie's paranoia, making the character seem damaged and in pain rather than simply crazed and evil. Simmons, born January 31, 1929, in London, was a major figure in British cinema in the 1940s and '50s. At the height of her stardom she moved to Hollywood and became a naturalized American citizen. She starred in many prestigious productions by major filmmakers, including David Lean's *Great Expectations* (1946), Michael Powell and Emeric Pressburger's *Black Narcissus* (1947), Laurence Olivier's *Hamlet* (1948), and Stanley Kubrick's *Spartacus* (1960). She earned two Academy Award nominations as Best Actress and won an Emmy for her work in the miniseries *The Thorn Birds* (1983). She died in 2010.

David Warner

Refined villainy is the stock-in-trade of British actor David Warner, who played three *Star Trek* characters, including Gul Madred, Captain Picard's brutal Cardassian inquisitor in "Chain of Command, Parts I and II." Madred and Picard engage in an epic battle of wills that consumes nearly an entire episode. Warner's icy performance is one of the most unnerving of his career (which is full of unsettling characters); Madred not only strips Picard naked, humiliates, and tortures him, but is so comfortable doing so that he even allows his young daughter into the room afterward. Warner's work is even more remarkable considering that the actor was a late addition to the cast and had only three days to prepare for the role. Because the dialogue contained so much Treknobabble, Warner was forced to perform from cue cards. "I got the makeup on, read the lines and hoped for the best. And it turned out to be a classic episode," Warner told a StarTrek.com interviewer. "Isn't that nice?"

Previously, Warner had appeared in two *Star Trek* movies. He played Starfleet administrator John Talbot in *Star Trek V: The Final Frontier*, a forgettable role in a forgettable film, and Chancellor Gorkon in *Star Trek VI: The Undiscovered Country*, a far more memorable role in a much better picture. He brought gravitas and dignity to his brief role as the soon-to-be-assassinated Klingon leader.

Warner, born July 29, 1941, in Manchester, England, trained at the Royal Academy of Dramatic Arts and performed with the Royal Shakespeare Company, where he acted with a young Patrick Stewart. His film and television career began in the early 1960s (appropriately enough, his first film role was as the underhanded Blifil in *Tom Jones*, 1963). At first he played all sorts of roles, but

Gul Madred

OFFICER

Ruthless Obsidian Order officer. **Madred's** torture of Jean-Luc Picard quickly degenerated into a desperate attempt to break Picard's will. A pitiable man.

- Obsidian Order ● SECURITY ● Treachery
- Archaeology ▼ Torture

| INTEGRITY | 2 | CUNNING | 8 | STRENGTH | 6 |

This card, from a *Star Trek* card game, features David Warner's Gul Madred from the "Chain of Command" epic, one of the series' most reprehensible villains.

by 1979, when he played Jack the Ripper in director Nicholas Meyer's *Time After Time*, Warner had been typed as the villain. He went on to portray antagonists in movies including *Time Bandits* (1981) and *Tron* (1982), and was offered the role of Freddy Krueger in *A Nightmare on Elm Street* (1984) but turned it down. His résumé includes several sci-fi, horror, and fantasy vehicles, and he is one of few actors to have appeared on both *Star Trek* and *Doctor Who*. He is also a prolific voice actor and portrayed the nefarious Ra's al Ghul on *Batman: The Animated Series*. He won an Emmy for his work in the miniseries *Masada* (1981). His career remains active.

Others

Journeymen performers Saul Rubinek and Marta Dubois delivered two of the most delightfully wicked, rococo performances in the entire run of *The Next Generation*—Rubinek as crazed collector Fajo from "The Most Toys" and Dubois as the demonic Ardra in "Devil's Due." Without ever gaining true stardom, Rubinek, the son of Polish Holocaust survivors, has so far tallied more than 140 screen credits, appearing most memorably as dime novelist W. W. Beauchamp in director Clint Eastwood's Oscar-winning Western *Unforgiven* (1992). He was offered his *Star Trek* role after David Rappaport, originally cast as Fajo, attempted suicide. Dubois has racked up appearances in nearly sixty movie and TV series since 1979, including a costarring role in the *McBride* series of made-for-TV movies, alongside John Larroquette.

Former Academy Award winner (for his performance as Salieri in *Amadeus*) F. Murray Abraham brought enormous talent and flair to his underwritten role as Son'a leader Ru'ofo in *Star Trek: Insurrection*.

Then there's Robin Curtis, who replaced Kirstie Alley as Lieutenant Saavik in *Star Trek III: The Search for Spock* and *Star Trek IV: The Voyage Home* (1986). Her performances in those pictures were less than impressive, but she fared far better in the *Next Generation* two-parter "Gambit," in which she portrayed Romulan mercenary Tallera (later revealed to be a Vulcan extremist). She retired from acting in 1999 and is now working as a real estate agent in Upstate New York.

17

New Ground

The Next Generation, Season Four (1990–91)

I n its fourth season, *Star Trek: The Next Generation* continued to improve and to break new ground, in part because executive producer Rick Berman and his team were unencumbered by the creative conflicts, personality clashes, story deficits, and budget woes that afflicted the series in previous years. At the season-ending wrap party, Gene Roddenberry called Season Four "the most untroubled season we've ever had." As a consequence, it was also the most consistent. "Arguably you could say there were better shows during the third season, but week after week we maintained a much higher consistency of quality than we had [before] or most shows ever achieve," said writer-producer Michael Piller, as quoted in James Hatfield and George Burt's *Patrick Stewart: The Unauthorized Biography*.

For the first time, there were no changes or additions to the show's cast during the summer hiatus, although Wil Wheaton asked to leave in mid-season. Wheaton was increasingly frustrated by the writing staff's inability to flesh out his character and believed his career was stagnating. After being denied leave to appear in director Milos Forman's *Valmont* (1989), Wheaton wanted greater freedom to pursue movie roles. Shooting of *Valmont* would have extended into the first week of production for Season Four of *Next Gen*. Wheaton asked to be excused from the premiere episode. Producers refused, forcing him to decline the movie, but later cut Wesley's only major scene. The rest of the cast, encouraged by the more character-based teleplays Piller had brought forward the prior season, entered Season Four reenergized. Patrick Stewart had enrolled in "Paramount University" and was preparing to begin directing episodes, following the lead of Jonathan Frakes.

The series once again turned over a significant percentage of its writing staff, but this time the departures were mostly by writers who wanted to capitalize on their success the year before. For instance, Hans Beimler and Richard Manning left the show to create a science fiction series of their own, *Beyond Reality* (1991–93). Ira Steven Behr departed to pursue feature film opportunities, but was lured back to write the memorable teleplay "Qpid." All three later returned to the franchise and were important contributors to *Star Trek: Deep Space Nine*. Talented newcomers stood ready to fill any vacancies. Veteran screenwriter Jeri Taylor and fresh-faced intern Brannon Braga both joined the show during Season Four. Taylor would eventually succeed Piller as the show's chief writer and later cocreated *Star Trek Voyager* with Berman and Piller. Braga went on to write or coauthor twenty *Next Gen* teleplays as well as the *Star Trek* films *Generations* and *First Contact*. He also worked extensively on *Voyager* as a writer-producer and cocreated *Star Trek: Enterprise* with Berman.

As Roddenberry receded further into the background, the show's writers and producers pushed further into terrain previously unexplored on *Star Trek*, bending format and breaking rules on an almost weekly basis. Berman kept a small bust of Roddenberry on his desk, which he blindfolded whenever a writer proposed a story idea that violated one of the Great Bird's decrees. Led by Piller, writers opened up the characters' private lives (eleven of the first thirteen fourth-season episodes dealt in some manner with family ties) and began to introduce subplots that couldn't be resolved in a single episode (for instance, the emotional and political fallout of the Worf's decision to forsake his Klingon heritage in "Sins of the Father" the prior season). Previously, *Star Trek* intentionally had steered clear of serialized stories because they made it more difficult for new viewers to follow the ongoing plotlines and understand character relationships. But the show's cast feasted on this meatier, more mature material. Also, Piller wanted greater emphasis placed on the series' female characters. As a result, Deanna Troi and Dr. Crusher each received two showcase teleplays and were used more effectively in several other episodes. Finally, Piller encouraged writers to leverage the series' coalescing mythology. As a result, the show became more self-referential, and several popular supporting characters from previous years reappeared.

All these risks paid off in a season that proved to be adventurous and unpredictable. "That's what was so great about the fourth season," Piller said. "Each week you were never quite sure what was going to come on." However, as Season Four approached, Piller's first priority was figuring out how to resolve the nail-biting cliff-hanger that had concluded the previous season.

"The Best of Both Worlds, Part II"

Piller penned a spellbinding finale for Season Three with "The Best of Both Worlds," in which Captain Picard was assimilated by the Borg and Earth seemed destined for destruction at the hands of the apparently unstoppable alien menace. There was just one problem: He had no idea how to resolve the conundrum he had created. Piller figured that concluding the cliff-hanger would be somebody else's problem. Originally, he planned to leave the show after its third season. When Roddenberry talked Piller into staying, suddenly Piller had to find a way out of the corner he had written himself into. It wasn't easy. When new intern Brannon Braga met his coworkers during his first day on the job, Piller was holed up in his office, sweating it out. "He introduced himself and said 'I'm trying to figure out how to beat the Borg. I have no idea how to do it,'" Braga said in an interview published in *Cinefantastique*. Yet, eventually, Piller hit upon a clever yet plausible answer, turning the interconnectedness that was the Borg's greatest strength into their Achilles heel. Once the teleplay was complete, Paramount went to great lengths to keep it secret, even leaking a bogus script in which the events of "The Best of Both Worlds" were explained away as an illusion created by Q.

Videotape box for "The Best of Both Worlds, Part II," the thrilling conclusion to the cliffhanger finale of Season Three. Screenwriter Michael Piller had great difficulty coming up with a plausible way for Picard to defeat the Borg.

"The Best of Both Worlds" was a landmark episode, but the second half of the two-parter was even more impressive in scope and profound in its impact on the series. Although remembered primarily as the episode where Picard is transformed into Locutus of Borg, Piller's Part I teleplay focused primarily on Commander Riker and his reaction to being thrust into the captaincy of the *Enterprise* after Picard's abduction. "Part II" returns the story's focus to Picard, with scenes that permanently changed the way fans viewed the captain. "It was a show in which Picard became more human than ever before. He was the indestructible captain, untouchable, above all risk and danger, and suddenly, in this two-parter, he is a man who's been raped by the Borg and has to deal emotionally with huge consequences," Piller said in an interview included on the *Star Trek: The Next Generation Season Four* DVD collection. "After that, Picard was more complex, never the same. He was a far more interesting character after that."

"The Best of Both Worlds, Part II" also contains some of the series' most exhilarating action sequences. The episode was mounted on a cinematic scale, with astounding visual effects (including the haunting image of an outer space battle field full of charred and splintered starships), sound effects, and production design, and an unnerving score by Ron Jones. "Best of Both Worlds, Part II" was nominated for four Emmys, winning in the categories of Sound Editing and Sound Mixing and losing in the categories of Special Visual Effects and Art Direction. Numerous fan polls and publications, including *Entertainment Weekly*, have named this episode one of the best in the history of the series. The accolades are well deserved.

"Family"

Piller and screenwriter Ronald D. Moore followed the fire-breathing action finale of "The Best of Both Worlds" with one of the most offbeat installments in the history of the series—"Family," in which Picard visits his brother in provincial France as the captain struggles with the emotional fallout of being assimilated and forced to help kill thousands of people. The episode is set on Earth, which is unusual, and includes no major sci-fi elements, and no footage shot on the bridge, which makes it unique. This is also the only *Next Gen* installment in which Commander Data does not appear. Two subplots involve a visit to the orbiting *Enterprise* by Worf's adoptive Earth parents and Wesley viewing a recorded message from his dead father. All three story lines are emotionally gripping and cast familiar characters in a new light. Stewart and Dorn deliver sterling performances, ably assisted by guest stars Jeremy Kemp (as Picard's surly older brother), and Theodore Bikel and Georgia Brown (as Worf's doting parents). Piller lobbied passionately to convince Berman and Roddenberry to risk an episode absent any typical *Trek* action or suspense. In *Star Trek: The Next Generation 365*, writer-producer Ronald D. Moore explains that Roddenberry believed "Family" was "too much 'art'" and "too little adventure." Maybe he was right. "Family" is a superbly written and performed piece, and its cinematography earned an Emmy nomination. But it was also the poorest Nielsen-rated episode of Season Four.

"Brothers"

Fans who were disappointed by Brent Spiner's absence from the episode "Family" were rewarded with "Brothers," in which the actor plays three roles: Data, Data's brother Lore, and their creator, Dr. Noonian Soong. The *Enterprise* is transporting a gravely ill child to Starbase 416 for treatment when Data, responding to an automated signal from Soong, commandeers the ship and steers it to the remote planet Terla III, where he beams down for a secret meeting with his elderly human "father," long believed dead and now truly dying. However, Soong's signal also attracts the murderous Lore, whom the scientist doesn't know has been reassembled. "Brothers," the first of five *Next Gen* teleplays written personally by Rick Berman, introduced the emotion chip, a MacGuffin that would feature in future episodes and movies. It's a tension-packed, emotionally and psychologically complex scenario, but the episode is most enjoyable as a vehicle for Spiner. For two and a half days, the actor worked entirely alone on the set, shooting sequences that would be cut together so that Data, Lore, and Soong would appear to be speaking with one another. "Brothers" earned an Emmy nomination for Best Makeup, primarily on the strength of Spiner's transformation into the aged Dr. Soong.

"Suddenly Human"

Responding to a distress call, an *Enterprise* away team rescues a handful of young survivors from a Talarian military training ship—including a young human known as Jono (Chad Allen). Captain Picard and Dr. Crusher try to determine whether the adolescent has been adopted or abducted, loved or abused—matters that are hard to judge due to stark differences between human culture and that of the war-mongering Talarians. "Suddenly Human" is a solid installment but remains most notable as the episode that brought Jeri Taylor to *Star Trek*. Piller asked Taylor, a seasoned writer-producer who had worked on series such as *Little House on the Prairie*, *Quincy M.E.* and *Magnum, P.I.*, to punch up the interpersonal "character" material in freelancer John Whelpley's teleplay. When her work emerged as the strongest component in the episode, Piller invited her to join the *Next Gen* writing staff.

"Remember Me"

This episode offered one of the season's most intriguing mystery plots and the series' best outings for Gates McFadden. Dr. Crusher's mentor, Dr. Quaice (Bill Erwin), is apparently winked out of existence when a Wesley Crusher warp-bubble experiment goes awry. Not only does Quaice vanish from the *Enterprise*, which he was visiting, but so does all evidence that he ever lived. Soon members of the crew begin disappearing, too. Only Dr. Crusher retains any memory of their existence. "Remember Me" began as a subplot for the episode "Family," intended to introduce a traditional sci-fi story line in counterpoint to the human drama of Picard's visit with his brother, Robert, in France. When it became apparent that the stories simply didn't work together, they were decoupled. The scenario puts Beverly Crusher center stage and gives McFadden a rare opportunity to stretch. The story also featured the return of the mysterious Traveler

(Eric Menyuk), last seen in Season One's "Where No One Has Gone Before."
"Remember Me" was the only teleplay penned by Lee Sheldon, who worked as
a staff writer-producer for the first eight episodes of Season Four, then left to
launch a career designing video games. Jeri Taylor was hired as his replacement.

The popular Ambassador K'Ehleyr, depicted in this action figure, made a final appearance
in the gripping "Reunion," one of the series' most emotionally powerful installments.

Photo by Preston Hewis, East Bank Images

"Legacy"

A Federation freighter crashes on the lawless Turkana IV, home planet of the late Tasha Yar. The survivors are taken hostage by one of the ruthless gangs that vie for dominance of the anarchic planet. Commander Riker leads a rescue party and gains assistance from an unexpected source—Tasha's sister, Ishara Yar (Beth Toussaint). Ishara befriends Data, but does she have an ulterior motive for aiding the Starfleet officers? The first of sixteen *Next Gen* episodes written by Joe Menosky, "Legacy" is one of the season's most psychologically complex teleplays and contains choice material for both Frakes and Spiner. Guest star Toussaint contributes a deft, nuanced performance that is muted by her hair and makeup, which seem calculated to make her look as much like Linda Hamilton from *The Terminator* as possible (and, strangely, nothing at all like Denise Crosby's Tasha Yar). Director Robert Scheerer brings visual flair to the action-oriented yarn with his dynamic compositions and smooth, flowing dolly shots. "Legacy" represents a minor landmark in the history of the series: It was the eightieth installment of *The Next Generation*. The new series had officially surpassed the original program's seventy-nine episodes.

"Reunion"

The half-human, half-Klingon Ambassador K'Ehleyr (Suzie Plakson) returns with a surprise for Worf—his son, Alexander (Jon Steuer), the result of a sexual encounter between the two in Season Two's "The Emissary." Worf yearns to marry K'Ehleyr and form a family, but cannot because he sacrificed his Klingon honor to preserve peace in the Empire (in the previous season's "Sins of the Father"). K'Ehleyr arrives in the company of the Klingon High Chancellor K'mpec (Charles Cooper), who has been slowly poisoned and is now dying. The Chancellor asks Picard to oversee the selection of his replacement from among two candidates, Gowron (Robert O'Reilly) and Duras (Patrick Massett), one of whom may be K'mpec's assassin. Rich in both interpersonal and political tension, the suspenseful, emotionally harrowing "Reunion" is one of the best episodes of Season Four, if not the entire series. Written by committee (six different writers receive teleplay or story credit), the episode dives deeper into the blood-tainted waters of Klingon politics and psychology and takes risks seldom ventured in previous *Trek* tales. The most daring turn is K'Ehleyr's shocking murder midway through the story, which outraged many fans of the adored character. Worf's decision to set aside his Starfleet oath and take retribution also proved controversial. Jonathan Frakes, who made his directorial debut with Season Three's excellent "The Offspring," tops himself with this episode, which packs a visceral wallop. He elicits superb work from the guest cast, especially Plakson, O'Reilly, and Massett, and perhaps the single best performance of Michael Dorn's career. "Reunion" marks young Steuer's only appearance as Alexander. In future installments, the character was played by the more experienced Brian Bonsall.

"Future Imperfect"

While performing a security sweep near the Neutral Zone, the *Enterprise* detects a possible secret Romulan base on an unpopulated Federation planet. Commander Riker—on his birthday!—beams down with a security team to investigate and is knocked unconscious by methane gas. He awakens in sick bay sixteen years later, with no memory of the intervening time. Now-Captain Riker has a son and a deceased wife, neither of whom he remembers. Shortly afterward, Ambassador Picard arrives with a Romulan dignitary, and the two inform Riker that the Federation and the Romulans are on the verge of a historic alliance. "Future Imperfect," penned by J. Larry Carroll and David Bennett Carren, is an elaborate shaggy dog story. It's obvious from the outset that someone is trying to dupe Riker, but the tale is well crafted and slyly entertaining, with a clever payoff. Although clearly intended as a vehicle for Frakes, the scenario also allows Stewart, McFadden, Sirtis, and other cast members to demonstrate range by playing older versions of their familiar characters. "Future Imperfect" also marks the first appearance of Nurse Alyssa Ogawa (Patti Yasutake), who would become a fixture in sick bay alongside Dr. Crusher, appearing in fifteen additional episodes and two movies (*Generations* and *First Contact*).

"Final Mission"

Young Wesley Crusher, who repeatedly saved the *Enterprise* during Season One, saves his captain's life when he and Picard are marooned on a desolate desert moon. As the title indicates, this is Wesley's final mission before leaving to enroll at Starfleet Academy. Written by Jeri Taylor and Kacey Arnold-Ince specifically to serve as actor Wil Wheaton's swan song, "Final Mission" is a tense survival drama with a sci-fi twist involving an alien life force. But it's also a finely tuned character piece that features strong moments for both Wheaton and Stewart. Coupled with Taylor's deft handling of the young character Jono in "Suddenly Human," "Final Mission" suggests that the show had finally hired someone who understood how to write for young people. Unfortunately, the frustrated Wheaton had already decided to leave. Although Wesley left the *Enterprise* following this episode, Wheaton returned for guest appearances as the character in four later adventures and (briefly) in the feature film *Star Trek Nemesis*. Rick Berman has named "Final Mission" among his personal favorite episodes.

"The Loss"

The *Enterprise* discovers, and becomes trapped within, a swarm of two-dimensional life-forms. Simultaneously, Deanna Troi begins suffering from severe headaches and loses her empathic abilities. Frightened and frustrated by her inability to read her shipmates' emotions, she resigns as ship's counselor, yet plays a vital role in saving the ship from destruction. Hilary Bader, Alan Adler, and Vanessa Greene wrote "The Loss" to highlight Counselor Troi. Marina Sirtis responds with one of her most unaffected and touching performances. She's particularly strong in a scene with Gates McFadden, in which Deanna lashes out at the doctor for failing to respond promptly when the counselor first fell ill. In later interviews, Piller said the idea of removing Deanna's empathic powers had been on the table since Season One. The writing staff considered making the loss permanent but decided against it.

"Data's Day"

In another change-of-pace episode, Commander Data compiles a report of his daily activities for the benefit of Dr. Bruce Maddox (the cyberneticist who attempted to have the android declared property of Starfleet in "The Measure of a Man"). During this twenty-four-hour slice of Data's life, a Romulan spy is discovered on board, and Chief Miles O'Brien (Colm Meaney) marries botanist Keiko Ishikawa (Rosalind Chao). Written by Harold Apter and Ronald D. Moore, "Data's Day" features a charming blend of sweet-natured humor (as Keiko gets cold feet) and interstellar intrigue surrounding Vulcan ambassador T'Pel (Sierra Pecheur). Like "The Loss," "Data's Day" utilized a concept that had been circulating for years—or, actually, two concepts: a day-in-the-life story and a marriage involving one of the recurring characters. Rosalind Chao joined the cast with this installment. Her loving but tempestuous marriage to Chief O'Brien would provide rich story fodder throughout *Next Gen*'s next two seasons and on *Deep Space Nine* (when the O'Brien family relocated to the spin-off series). Captain Picard presides over the marriage and uses the same ceremonial language employed by Captain Kirk in the classic episode "Balance of Terror," which (coincidentally) introduced the Romulans. This episode also features the debut of Data's cat, Spot.

"The Wounded"

Starfleet Captain Ben Maxwell, formerly Chief O'Brien's commanding officer, goes rogue and launches a series of unprovoked attacks on Cardassian installations and vessels along the Federation-Cardassian border. Captain Picard is assigned to bring in Maxwell, whose actions threaten a fragile agreement that ended decades of war between the Federation and Cardassia. But many *Enterprise* crew members (including O'Brien and Worf) remain wary of the unscrupulous Cardassians and seem sympathetic to Captain Maxwell. Screenwriter Jeri Taylor credits Joseph Conrad's *Heart of Darkness* as the inspiration for "The Wounded." (Conrad's classic novel also inspired director Francis Ford Coppola's *Apocalypse Now*.) Taylor also may have been influenced by current events. While Taylor wrote this script, the United States and Iraq were on the brink of conflict over Iraqi claims on oil fields in Northern Kuwait. By the time the episode aired, the U.S. had plunged into the first Gulf War. In any case, this episode emerged as one of the richest of the season. Chief O'Brien plays a pivotal role in the story, struggling to overcome his own prejudice against Cardassians and to come to grips with the unconscionable behavior of his admired former captain. Actor Colm Meaney takes full advantage, delivering a scintillating performance. The depiction of Starfleet officers plagued by festering hatred of a bitter enemy also anticipates *Star Trek VI: The Undiscovered Country*, which premiered ten months after the initial broadcast of "The Wounded." This episode introduces the Cardassians, who would create problems in future *Next Gen* installments and serve as one of the primary adversaries on *Star Trek: Deep Space Nine*. Marc Alaimo, seen here as Cardassian Gul Macet, later had a recurring role as Gul Dukat on *DS9*. Alaimo had previously guest starred as a Romulan in "The Neutral Zone" and as a dog-faced Antican in "Lonely Among Us." The actor would return, sans alien makeup, as gambler Frederick La Roque in "Time's Arrow."

"Devil's Due"

In this science-fictional derivative of "The Devil and Daniel Webster," Captain Picard defends the residents of Ventax II against a woman who claims to be Ardra (Marta DuBois), a satanic figure who (according to legend) entered into a Faustian bargain with the Ventaxians millennia earlier. Ardra, the Ventaxians believe, granted a thousand years of peace and prosperity but has now returned to claim the planet as her own. Even though Ardra appears to have superhuman powers (she can transform into various persons and creatures, can make people appear and disappear, and can cause seismic tremors), Picard is convinced she's a phony and coaxes her into entering an arbitration (essentially, a trial) to prove it. Like Season Two's "The Child," "Devil's Due" was a scenario reclaimed from the slag heap of teleplays left over from the failed *Star Trek: Phase II* series from the 1970s. Written by Philip LaZebnik, it's a lively, lighthearted entry, especially considered in contrast with the high drama of "The Wounded." The sharply written episode features a wickedly amusing guest performance by Dubois as Ardra. "Devil's Due" earned an Emmy nomination for Best Costume Design and scored the series' highest ratings yet for a single episode. This installment also recalls the animated adventure "The Magicks of Megas-Tu," in which Captain Kirk and company become embroiled in a sort of reverse "Devil and Daniel Webster" scenario on a planet populated by demon-like beings.

"Clues"

The entire crew of the *Enterprise* (except Data) is simultaneously rendered unconscious. When they awaken, Data informs them that the ship passed through a wormhole, which knocked out all nonandroid crew members for thirty seconds. But subsequent discoveries indicate that the crew members have been unconscious for much longer—an entire day—and cast doubt on other aspects of Data's story. Is Data lying, and if so, why? "Clues" began as a spec script submitted by fan Bruce D. Arthurs, which was reworked by Joe Menosky. Unlike most Season Four episodes, it's plot driven rather than character focused. But it's also an engrossing mystery. Michael Piller named it as one of his favorite installments.

"First Contact"

Not to be confused with the *Star Trek* feature film of the same title, "First Contact" represents another major break from franchise orthodoxy, and another spellbinding Season Four adventure. While on a reconnaissance mission to the prewarp planet Malcor III, Commander Riker is severely injured and rushed to a Malcorian hospital. His true nature is quickly discovered, which creates a potentially explosive situation on a planet that has historically denied the existence of alien beings and considers itself the center of the universe, but which is now on the verge of achieving warp drive. Captain Picard has been assigned to make first contact with the Malcorians and invite them to join the United Federation of Planets, but his efforts are complicated by Riker's capture. Although the Malcorian Chancellor and a distinguished warp scientist are sympathetic, others, including the planet's Minister of Security, fear that Malcoria faces an alien invasion.

Guest star Bebe Neuwirth played Nurse Lanel, who has an unusual request for Commander Riker in the format-bending episode "First Contact."

"First Contact" is told primarily from the Malcorian point of view, and was the first episode to depict Starfleet from an outsider's perspective. It also cleverly inverts familiar plot points from classic science fiction films of the 1950s (particularly *The Day the Earth Stood Still*), with humans serving as the mysterious extraterrestrials—or, in this case, extra-Malcorials. Screenwriter Marc Scott Zicree first pitched this intriguing scenario during Season Three but found "First Contact" a tough sell. It wasn't typical *Trek* by any measure, and once Zicree's story was purchased, the *Next Gen* writing staff struggled to develop it (five different writers share credit for the teleplay; Zicree receives story credit). Early drafts were told from the perspective of the *Enterprise* crew, because Roddenberry had demanded this always be *Star Trek*'s point of view. Eventually, Piller went to Berman and requested permission to break the rules. "I went to Rick and said that even though I know he doesn't like to break format, this could be a special show if he would let me write it from the alien point of view. He did, as long as I let everyone know that we weren't going to ever break this rule again," Piller said in Edward Gross and Mark A. Altman's book *Captains' Logs*. Granted this indulgence, Piller considered expanding the tale to serve as Season Four's two-part cliff-hanger finale.

Given its unusual structure, the adventure succeeds largely on the strength of its excellent guest cast, including George Coe as the Chancellor, Carolyn Seymour as a warp scientist, Michael Ensign as the paranoid security minister, and a delightful cameo by *Frasier* regular Bebe Neuwirth as a Malcorian nurse with a fetish for aliens. In 2007, *Entertainment Weekly* named "First Contact" one of the ten best episodes of *The Next Generation*. Zicree later wrote one of the most memorable *Deep Space Nine* episodes—"Far Beyond the Stars," in which Captain Sisko dreams of being a science fiction writer during the 1950s.

"Galaxy's Child"

In another departure from standard practice, this episode's science fiction story—about an infant space-creature that thinks the *Enterprise* is its mommy, latches on to it, and begins suckling energy from the starship—is diverting, but remains secondary to its character-oriented "subplot," in which Geordi meets the real-life Dr. Leah Brahms (Susan Gibney). In the previous season's "Booby Trap," Geordi became infatuated with a holodeck-generated simulation of Brahms, an eminent Starfleet warp-drive engineer. But the true Dr. Brahms proves to be very different than her holographic twin. Written by former producer Maurice Hurley from a story by Winrich Kolbe, and polished by Jeri Taylor, the teleplay crackles with wit. LeVar Burton displays impressive range as Geordi's romantic anticipation to turns to disappointment, embarrassment, and anger before the engineer establishes a working rapport, and finally a friendship, with Dr. Brahms. Guest star Gibney also delivers an outstanding performance, particularly when taken in contrast with her diametrically opposed take on (basically) the same character from "Booby Trap." Geordi later recounts the events of "Galaxy's Child" to Scotty in the episode "Relics."

"Night Terrors"

The *Enterprise* discovers the USS *Brattain* adrift in space. It appears that the ship's crew killed one another. Shortly afterward, Picard learns that his ship, like the *Brattain*, has become trapped in a space-time anomaly. After ten days drifting in space, Picard's crew begins to lose the ability to think clearly and starts exhibiting paranoid, aggressive behavior. The *Enterprise* seems destined to suffer the same fate as the *Brattain*, until Counselor Troi realizes that a solution may be found in the strange, recurring nightmares she has suffered since the crisis began. "Night Terrors," written by Pamela Douglas and Shari Taylor from a story by

Shari Goodhartz, was designed as another vehicle for Marina Sirtis. But the actress hated the episode because she had to be strapped into an uncomfortable harness to "fly" during the story's dream sequences. "Night Terrors" is strikingly different than most *Trek* fare, with an eerie, almost supernatural undercurrent (although eventually everything is explained through scientific Treknobabble), but it was not well received. Usually reliable director Les Landau let scenes play out so languidly that nine minutes had to be trimmed to reduce the episode to the standard 42-minute runtime. Even so, its tempo remains dirgelike. The episode also suffers from some uncharacteristically poor visual effects. Jonathan Frakes reportedly called the episode "a yawner." However, it features one of production artist Michael Okuda's funnier inside jokes. The Brattain's motto, visible on a plaque, is a quote from the theme song of *Gilligan's Island*: "A three hour tour, a three hour tour."

"Identity Crisis"

While visiting the site of a mysterious incident five years earlier, Geordi begins to transform into an alien life-form. "Identity Crisis," another creepy, horror-tinged teleplay (written by Brannon Braga from a fan-submitted story by Timothy DeHaas), proved far more effective than "Night Terrors." "Identity Crisis" boasts another fine performance from Burton, atmospheric direction by Winrich Kolbe, outstanding visual effects, and Emmy-nominated creature makeup. This was one of the most difficult episodes of the season to shoot, since it involved a high number of effects shots and heavy use of tricky-to-film blue-light effects. The blue lighting was necessary to make the shadowy alien creatures appear to have glowing blue veins running all over their bodies.

"The Nth Degree"

Lieutenant Reginald Barclay (Dwight Schultz) returns. This time the neurotic engineer, introduced in Season Three's "Hollow Pursuits," is knocked unconscious by an alien space probe and awakens with greatly expanded and ever-growing mental faculties. At first, his newfound intellect and confidence seem harmless, even beneficial, but the situation quickly turns. Like "Hollow Pursuits," "The Nth Degree" was written (by Joe Menosky) specifically as a vehicle for guest star Schultz. The teleplay went through several revisions, in part to downplay similarities with *Star Trek V: The Final Frontier* (in "The Nth Degree," as in that misbegotten film, a starship *Enterprise* travels to the center of the galaxy and encounters a godlike alien intelligence). As Piller reportedly said, "The absolute last thing we wanted to remind anyone of was *Star Trek V*." In its final form, "The Nth Degree" is a frothy comedic tour de force for Schultz, whose superpowered, supersuave version of Barclay is hilarious, yet retains the core of vulnerability that makes the character so appealing.

"Qpid"

Season Four's Q episode reunites Captain Picard with Vash (Jennifer Hetrick), the alluring con artist with whom he had an adventure (and a fling) in "Captain's Holiday" the previous season. To settle the lingering romantic tension between Picard and Vash, Q (John de Lancie) transports Picard and his senior staff to a re-creation of Sherwood Forest, where they reenact *The Adventures of Robin Hood*, with Robin (Picard) rescuing Maid Marion (Vash) from the clutches of the evil Sheriff of Nottingham. Ira Steven Behr, a die-hard Robin Hood fan, was enticed back to *The Next Generation* to write this playful, wildly amusing yarn. The mere sight of the *Enterprise* crew transformed into Robin's band of do-gooding bandits (Riker costumed as Little John, a bald-headed Data as Friar Tuck, and a mandolin-toting Geordi as Alan-a-Dale) is side-splittingly funny. Worf, wearing the absurd red tights of Will Scarlet, protests, "I am not a Merry Man!" The production of the episode wasn't all laughs, however. Jonathan Frakes had to be rushed to the hospital after his forehead was gashed while filming the story's swordfight climax. Despite this incident, Patrick Stewart, in an interview included on the *Star Trek: The Next Generation Season Four* DVD collection, reports that, "That episode probably gave us as a group more fun than any other."

"The Drumhead"

Retired Admiral Norah Satie (Jean Simmons) beams aboard the *Enterprise* after a Romulan agent is discovered among the crew. Satie launches an ever-expanding investigation, based entirely on rumor and guilt by association. Picard is increasingly troubled by Satie's actions, especially when they threaten the career of a young, part-Romulan medical technician whose only crime seems to be falsifying his Starfleet application (listing his grandfather as Vulcan, rather than Romulan). Soon several other *Enterprise* crew members come under suspicion, including Picard himself. This splendid episode, crafted to consciously evoke the "Red Scare" paranoia of the 1950s and the horror of the Salem witch trials, was written by Jeri Taylor as a cost-saving measure. Originally, Paramount executives suggested a clip show, but no one wanted to reprise the "Shades of Gray" debacle. Filmed entirely on standing sets, "The Drumhead" came in under budget by a quarter-million dollars. Jonathan Frakes, who directed, admits to lifting shots from films including *Judgment at Nuremberg* and *The Caine Mutiny* for the story's climactic courtroom scenes. Stewart delivers a riveting, heartfelt performance, one of his best in the entire series, but Simmons nearly steals the show with her intimidating yet pathetic turn as the obsessive, fear-consumed Admiral Satie. Hiring Oscar winner Simmons, the distinguished British actress best known for her work in prestige pictures such as David Lean's *Great Expectations* and Laurence Olivier's Oscar-winning *Hamlet*, was a major coup for the program. Both Stewart and Frakes list "The Drumhead" among their personal favorite episodes, as does Michael Dorn. Taylor considers it the best of her *Next Generation* teleplays.

"Half a Life"

Until now, the appearance of Lwaxana Troi signaled the arrival of a frothy comedy. But, in another departure from convention, "Half a Life" emerges as a three-hanky tearjerker. Lwaxana falls deeply in love with Dr. Timicin (David Ogden Stiers), an eminent scientist from Kaelon II. Timicin returns Lwaxana's affection but sees no future for the relationship because in just a few days, according to the custom of his people, he will celebrate his sixtieth birthday by committing ritual suicide. Written by Peter Allan Fields from a story by Fields and Ted Roberts, "Half a Life" reveals new depths in the Lwaxana character. Majel Barrett-Roddenberry takes full advantage, delivering a multilayered, fully effective dramatic portrayal, arguably the single finest of her career. Stiers, best remembered for playing snooty Dr. Charles Emerson Winchester III on *M*A*S*H*, also gives a brilliant, against-type performance as the shy, sensitive Timicin. Michelle Forbes, who would later portray Ensign Ro Laren, has a cameo as Timicin's oddly coiffured daughter. This episode's mournful score, composed by Dennis McCarthy, was nominated for an Emmy.

"The Host"

In the second doomed romance in as many weeks, Dr. Beverly Crusher falls for Ambassador Odan (Frank Luc), who turns out to be a Trill. When Odan is severely injured in an assassination attempt, Crusher removes the Trill (a wormlike symbiotic life-form that lives for hundreds of years, passing from one humanoid host body to the next) and temporarily implants it in Commander Riker. The physician battles conflicted feelings, but eventually resumes her romance with Riker-Odan. Then Odan's new, permanent host arrives—and turns out to be female. "The Host," a spec script written by Michael Horvat, was the first *Star Trek* teleplay to brush (lightly) on the subject of homosexuality. Even in a female body, Odan loves Crusher and wants to continue their relationship, but Beverly rebuffs her. Some viewers complained that Crusher's rejection of Odan was homophobic. However, if we take Beverly at her word, she rebuffs Odan not because of her new gender, but because Crusher found the process of her lover moving from body to body to body emotionally traumatic. "The Host" introduced the Trill, a species that would be featured prominently on *Deep Space Nine* (Worf would eventually marry the Trill Jadzia Dax). Director Marvin Rush had a difficult time shooting Crusher's love scenes because McFadden was several months' pregnant at the time. The actress mustered one of her most memorable performances, despite her physical discomfort.

"The Mind's Eye"

Romulans kidnap and brainwash Geordi, turning the trusted engineer into an unknowing assassin programmed to kill a Klingon official and rupture the alliance between the Federation and the Klingon Empire. "The Mind's Eye" was written by Rene Echevarria, from a story by Echevarria and Ken Schafer, and directed by David Livingston, all of whom acknowledge that the episode was an homage to director John Frankenheimer's classic *The Manchurian Candidate*. Livingston used equipment and copied techniques (including wide-angle lenses and oblique camera angles) Frankenheimer had employed, lending this episode an unsettling look and feel atypical of *Star Trek*. He also tried unsuccessfully to secure a cameo appearance by a cast member from the 1962 movie. Like the Frankenheimer original, "The Mind's Eye" is an unnerving, white-knuckle thriller.

"In Theory"

Patrick Stewart made his directorial debut with this seriocomic story about Data's first romantic relationship. After Data comforts security officer Jenna D'Sora (Michele Scarabelli) following the breakup of her relationship with a shipmate, D'Sora initiates a new romance with Data. From there, it's the age-old story of android-meets-girl, android-loses girl, full of broad comedic business for Spiner. "Darling, you remain as aesthetically pleasing as the first day we met," Data tells Jenna, in an attempt to be romantic. "I believe I am the most fortunate sentient in this sector of the galaxy." Another sequence, in which Data calls upon Guinan, Geordi, Deanna, Worf, Riker, and eventually Picard for dating advice, is side-splittingly funny. Screenwriters Joe Menosky and Ronald D. Moore also shoehorn in an extraneous sci-fi subplot, in which the *Enterprise* is threatened by subspace anomalies while exploring a "dark matter nebula." This is one of Spiner's funniest and best performances. Guest star Michele Scarabelli, who provides an ideal rom-com foil for Spiner, is best remembered for her work on the *Alien Nation* TV series and TV movies. Stewart selected "In Theory" for the *Star Trek: Fan Collective—Captain's Log* DVD collection, which gathered together the favorite episodes of each of the series' captains.

"Redemption"

The *Enterprise* travels to the Klingon home world so Picard can oversee the installation of Gowron as Klingon High Chancellor, but the Duras family rebels and civil war breaks out in the Empire. When Picard insists the Federation remain neutral, Worf resigns his commission to fight alongside Gowron and try to reclaim his family honor. Meanwhile, the Duras family is receiving aid from Romulan allies—one of whom bears a striking resemblance to the late Tasha Yar. It was a testament to producers' growing appreciation for the abilities of Michael Dorn and fans' ardor for all things Klingon that a Worf story was chosen for the season-ending two-part cliff-hanger. ("The Best of Both Worlds" had focused on Riker and Picard. The series' two remaining cliff-hanger finales both centered on Data.) Written by Ronald D. Moore, "Redemption" balances large-scale action sequences against intimate character moments, with plenty of ruthless political skullduggery. The episode, which introduces the villainous Duras Sisters, brings a daring, brilliant season to a rip-snorting climax. Former president Ronald Reagan visited the set during the production of this episode and quipped that the Klingons "remind me of Congress."

Fans had to wait until the start of Season Five to learn that the shadowy Romulan who looks so much like Tasha Yar, seen in the final frame of "Redemption," was actually Sela, Tasha's half-Romulan daughter. The character was considered action-figure worthy.

Photo by Preston Hewis, East Bank Images

"Reunion" was the one hundredth episode of the series produced—the magic number, according to conventional wisdom, for success in syndication, since it enabled the program to be "stripped"—industry lingo for running Monday through Friday. However, reruns of *The Next Generation* were already being stripped in many markets. During Season Five, the show, which had already surpassed all expectations, climbed to new heights in the Nielsen ratings, topping ten million viewers per installment for the first time. But the series would reach the zenith of its popularity the following season, when classic *Trek* and *Next Gen* came together to unify a mourning franchise.

18

Friends and Family

S tar Trek rose and fell on the strength of its heroes and villains, but the franchise was enriched greatly by its supporting characters—wives, lovers, parents, children, allies, even a friendly bartender—which humanized its protagonists and added emotional depth to the stories. The brilliant work of performers including Majel Barrett-Roddenberry, Mark Lenard, and Whoopi Goldberg all added meaningful threads to the *Star Trek* tapestry. This is the last of three chapters devoted to guest stars who delivered unforgettable performances in supporting and secondary roles. The others are Chapters 15 ("Heroes") and 16 ("Villains").

Majel Barrett-Roddenberry

Like Mark Lenard, the life and career of Majel Barrett-Roddenberry were considered in detail in the first *Star Trek FAQ*. However, it must be noted that the actress was much more impressive as Lwaxana Troi than in her previous *Trek* roles (as Nurse Christine Chapel, as the nameless first officer referred to as Number One in the failed pilot "The Cage," and as the *Enterprise* computer voice). The colorful, lusty Lwaxana became one of *The Next Generation*'s most beloved recurring characters, thanks in large part to Barrett-Roddenberry's flair and comedic timing. In her early appearances, such as "Haven" and "Manhunt," Lwaxana is presented simply as a comic irritant for Captain Picard. Barrett-Roddenberry was hilarious and charming in these installments, but later episodes enabled her to demonstrate greater range and depth. In "Half a Life," Lwaxana falls deeply in love with the Kaeloni scientist Timicin, only to learn that he must soon commit ritual suicide, as is the custom for all sixty-year-olds on his planet. Lwaxana seems at first giddy, then (when she learns of his impending suicide) panicked, distraught, angry, and finally quietly resolute. Throughout, Barrett-Roddenberry's performance remains believable and unaffected. Her heartrending portrayal is arguably the single best performance of her career. But all nine of her appearances as Lwaxana (six on *Next Gen* and three on *DS9*) remain impressive.

Brian Bonsall

Brian Bonsall, born December 3, 1981, in Torrance, California, was a Hollywood veteran when he joined *The Next Generation* at age ten. Bonsall played Worf's son, Alexander, in seven *Next Generation* episodes scattered throughout the show's final three seasons. He did not originate the role, however; when first seen, as a toddler in the Season Four episode "Reunion," Alexander was played by Jon Steuer. Prior to *Next Gen*, Bonsall had accumulated more than a dozen film and television credits, including a recurring role as Andy Keaton, the younger brother of Alex (Michael J. Fox), Mallory (Justine Bateman), and Jennifer (Tina Yothers) on the highly rated sitcom *Family Ties* (1986–89). His acting career ended in 1994 after he starred in the Walt Disney comedy *Blank Check*. Then he launched an unsuccessful career as a punk rock musician. Bonsall has also joined the long line of former child stars to run afoul of the law, with a string of arrests for various alcohol- and drug-related offenses and alleged domestic violence.

Rosalind Chao

Rosalind Chao was born September 27, 1957, in Anaheim, California. Her parents, who for many years operated a restaurant across the street from Disneyland, had appeared in productions by California's Peking Opera and helped five-year-old Rosalind win a role in one of the company's productions. She went on to appear in commercials and TV shows during her pre-teen years and in 1970, at age thirteen, won a guest role on *Here's Lucy*. Two years later, she earned a regular supporting part as Yul Brynner's daughter on the short-lived series *Anna and the King* (1972). After graduation from USC with a journalism degree in 1978, Chao launched her career in earnest, appearing in dozens of television series over the next decade, including a recurring part as Miss Chung on the sitcom *Diff'rent Strokes* (1981–83). Then she was cast as Soon-Lee, Corporal Max Klinger's Korean wife, in the final episodes of *M*A*S*H* (1983) and the sequel series *After M*A*S*H*, which lasted only one season (1984–85). Guest performances on many more series followed, including recurring roles on both the nighttime soap *Falcon Crest* (1986) and the quirky comedy *Max Headroom* (1987).

In 1987, Chao auditioned for the role of the *Enterprise*'s chief of security. She lost that part to Denise Crosby but subsequently won the role of botanist Keiko Ishikawa, who weds transporter chief Miles O'Brien (Colm Meaney) in the episode "Data's Day." Over the course of eight *Next Generation* appearances, Keiko and Miles built a loving but sometimes tempestuous life together and produced a daughter (Molly, delivered by Worf in the Ten-Forward lounge during a ship-wide power outage in the episode "Disaster"). When Meaney transferred to *Deep Space Nine*, Chao moved with him and made nineteen additional appearances as Keiko there. Miles and Keiko had a second child, under even more bizarre circumstances, during their tenure on *DS9*. Chao had wonderful chemistry with Meaney and perfectly matched his finely tuned, naturalistic approach. Together, especially during their tenure on *Next Gen*, Miles and Keiko brought a warm, familial dimension to the show that enriched the texture of its stories. Her presence, and Molly's, also made O'Brien seem even more likeable.

Throughout and after her association with *Star Trek*, Chao remained busy with other endeavors, including work in motion pictures, such as *The Joy Luck Club* (1993), *What Dreams May Come* (1998), and *I Am Sam* (2001). Although she is best known for playing Korean and Japanese characters, Chao is Chinese American. She is married to British voice actor Simon Templeman, who made an on-screen appearance in the *Next Generation* episode "The Defector."

Jonathan Del Arco

Jonathan Del Arco is a workaday actor who has cobbled together a career for the last twenty-five years through theatrical work and minor roles in more than thirty movies and television series. Lately he has played the recurring character of Dr. Morales on the TNT series *The Closer* and its spin-off *Major Crimes*. But *Star Trek* fans know him as Hugh, the Borg who gains a sense of personhood and befriends Geordi in the *Next Generation* episode "I Borg." Del Arco reappeared as Hugh in "Descent, Part II" and played a different character in the *Voyager* adventure "The Void." Born March 7, 1966, in Uruguay, Del Arco brought a disarming, childlike quality to Hugh (also known as Third of Five) that was revolutionary—and controversial—for the species. (Jeri Taylor suggested that Del Arco model Hugh after Johnny Depp's *Edward Scissorhands*.) His wonderstruck delivery, as Hugh slowly awakens to the concepts of individuality and friendship, is deeply touching. Although the Borg had previously been portrayed as monstrous automatons, Del Arco's haunting performance helped humanize the species, making each drone seem as much a victim of the Collective as those they assimilate. This didn't sit well with some fans, who preferred the Borg remain faceless and implacable, but it made for gripping television. According to an interview with the actor included on the *Star Trek: The Next Generation Season Five* DVD collection, Del Arco was a confessed Trekker who had auditioned unsuccessfully for the role of Wesley Crusher. He later supplied Borg voices for three *Star Trek* video games.

Whoopi Goldberg

Whoopi Goldberg is one of the few performers to have won an Oscar, an Emmy, a Grammy, and a Tony, among numerous other honors and awards, during her distinguished career. But to *Star Trek* fans she will always be Guinan, the mysterious, centuries-old barkeep from the *Enterprise-D*'s Ten-Forward lounge.

Goldberg, born Caryn Elaine Johnson in 1955 in New York City, was eleven years old when *Star Trek* debuted and was inspired to pursue a career in acting by Nichelle Nichols's portrayal of Lieutenant Uhura. She began her career as a stand-up comic, using the stage name Whoopi Cushion (pronounced coo-SHAWN), switching her pseudonymous surname to Goldberg after her mother

Acclaimed actress and comedian Whoopi Goldberg, who was inspired to take up acting after watching Nichelle Nichols on *Star Trek*, asked to join the cast of *The Next Generation* following the departure of Denise Crosby. Gene Roddenberry created the character of Guinan especially for her.

complained that Whoopi Cushion sounded ridiculous. After training at New York's HB Studio under the direction of renowned instructor Uta Hagen, she landed a few minor film roles but made her first real splash with her one-woman play *The Spook Show* in 1984. A year later, retitled simply *Whoopi Goldberg*, the play moved to Broadway, where it ran for 156 performances and earned Theatre World and Drama Desk awards for Outstanding One Person Show. Also in 1985, director Stephen Spielberg cast the actress in his adaptation of Alice Walker's Pulitzer Prize–winning novel *The Color Purple*. For her heartbreaking portrayal of the pitilessly abused Cellie Johnson, Goldberg earned an Oscar nomination as Best Actress and won a Golden Globe Award and an NAACP Image Award. She followed *The Color Purple* with several film and television appearances, including a headlining role in the comedy *Jumpin' Jack Flash* (1986), which also featured Stephen Collins, formerly Captain Decker from *Star Trek: The Motion Picture.*

In 1987, following the departure of Denise Crosby from *Star Trek: The Next Generation*, Goldberg approached Gene Roddenberry and asked to join the cast of *Next Gen*. Roddenberry, once he realized Goldberg was serious, created the recurring character of Guinan especially for her. Named for notorious New York City speakeasy proprietor Mary Louise Cecilia "Texas" Guinan, Guinan quickly became one of the series' most likeable and intriguing personalities. The actress appeared in twenty-nine episodes scattered throughout the show's final six seasons and had cameos in the *Star Trek* feature films *Generations* (1994) and

Nemesis (2002). Her addition to the cast was a game-changer in certain respects, bringing a new degree of critical respect to the series and, through Goldberg's vibrant performances, inspiring the other cast members to improve their work.

Goldberg remained active in other endeavors throughout her *Trek* tenure. She won an Oscar for her portrayal of psychic Oda Mae Brown in *Ghost* (1990) and appeared in several other hits, including the *Sister Act* films (1992 and '93). She also resumed her stand-up career, wrote best-selling books, and lobbied for political causes, including AIDS research and assistance for the homeless. Today Goldberg cohosts the popular daytime talk show *The View* and accepts occasional film and television roles. She has married and divorced three times and has a daughter, Alexandrea Martin, born in 1973.

Jennifer Hetrick

Model and actress Jennifer Hetrick created one of *Star Trek*'s most appealing supporting characters as Vash, the conniving adventuress who romances Jean-Luc Picard in "Captain's Holiday" and "Qpid." Vash was likeable without being trustworthy, and Hetrick played her with verve and playful insolence. She was a perfect foil for the prim and proper Picard, helping the captain reconnect with his inner swashbuckler. The chemistry between Hetrick and Patrick Stewart was real. The couple soon began a torrid affair that was reported in the Hollywood tabloids and led to the breakup of Stewart's twenty-five-year marriage to Sheila Falconer. Hetrick, born May 12, 1958, reappeared as Vash in the *Deep Space Nine* episode "Q-Less." At the time of her casting on *Next Gen*, she was best known for her recurring role as the ex-wife of attorney Arnold Becker (Corbin Bernsen) on *L.A. Law* and as the "face" of Oil of Olay beauty products. Since *Star Trek*, the actress has remained busy with television guest roles (including appearances on *The X-Files, Buffy the Vampire Slayer,* and *Sliders*) and commercials (including spots for Tylenol and the cholesterol-reducing drug Crestor).

Mark Lenard

The career of Mark Lenard was covered in the original *Star Trek FAQ,* but his ongoing contributions to the franchise deserve commendation. The actor reprised his role as Spock's father Sarek in three *Star Trek* movies (*The Search for Spock, The Voyage Home,* and *The Undiscovered Country*) and two *Next Generation* installments ("Sarek" and "Unification I"). He was especially impressive in his *Next Generation* performances, beautifully playing an aging and infirm version of the proud, stoic Vulcan first seen in the classic episode "Journey to Babel." His masterful, pathos-rich work in "Sarek" remains arguably the finest of his nine *Star Trek* appearances. The actor makes the most of a marvelous screenplay, full of wrenching moments like Sarek shockingly tearing up during a chamber music performance. Lenard also had a cameo as the captain of the Klingon Bird of Prey destroyed at the beginning of *Star Trek: The Motion Picture.*

Mark Lenard (left) reprised his role as Sarek, Spock's father, in two *Next Generation* episodes including "Unification I," in which he discusses his son with Captain Picard.

Robert O'Reilly

Robert O'Reilly's fierce, pop-eyed glare and forceful demeanor made Klingon Chancellor Gowron seem like a powerful friend and fearful enemy. He played the recurring character for nine years, appearing in four installments of *The Next Generation* (beginning with "Reunion" in 1990) and seven of *Deep Space Nine* (concluding with "Tracking into the Wind" in 1999). He also provided the voice of Gowron for three *Trek* video games. O'Reilly portrayed other characters in an episode each of *Next Gen*, *DS9*, and *Enterprise*. Born March 25, 1950, in New York City, O'Reilly began his screen career in 1979 with a guest appearance on *Fantasy Island*. Since then, he has appeared in more than sixty movies and TV shows (covering a variety of genres, everything from *CHiPs* to *Cheers* to *Dr. Quinn, Medicine Woman*), as well as numerous plays.

Suzie Plakson

Suzie Plakson played four different *Star Trek* characters but is best remembered by fans as K'Ehleyr, Worf's lover and mother of his son, Alexander. Her bold, provocative take on the freethinking character (and sizzling chemistry with Michael Dorn) made K'Ehleyr, first seen in Season Two's "The Emissary," so appealing that fans were shocked by her death in "Reunion" the following season. Previously, Plakson had appeared as the Vulcan Dr. Selar in "The Schizoid Man." Later, she portrayed a female Q in the *Voyager* installment "The Q and the Grey" and the Andorian Tarah in the *Enterprise* adventure "Cease Fire." All of her *Trek* performances are exemplary. Plakson, born June 3, 1958, in Buffalo, New York, is a multitalented actress, writer, singer, and sculptor. In addition to many stage roles, the statuesque (six-foot-one) actress has collected credits for more than thirty movies and TV series, including recurring roles on sitcoms *Love & War* (1992–95), *Mad About You* (1996–99), and *How I Met Your Mother* (2005–present). In 2008, she released a country-rock album titled *DidnWannaDoit!*, produced by singer-songwriter Jay Ferguson. Samples of her prose and poetry and photographs of her sculpture are available at her website, SuziePlakson.com.

James Sloyan

Like Plakson, actor James Sloyan played several *Star Trek* characters, but none with quite as much depth and emotional resonance as Jarok, the Romulan admiral who defects to avert a war in "The Defector." He delivered a riveting, unforgettable performance as the conflicted Jarok, who sacrifices his relationship with his beloved wife and daughter, as well as his prized personal honor, to preserve peace in the galaxy—with bitterly ironic consequences. Sloyan later appeared as K'mpec, a "family advisor" to Worf in "Firstborn"; a Bajoran scientist who studies Odo in two installments of *Deep Space Nine*; and as a Haakorian scientist in an episode of *Voyager*. He was born February 24, 1940, in Indianapolis, Indiana, but raised in Europe—his family lived in Italy, Switzerland, and Ireland during his formative years. He moved back to the U.S. in his late teens and earned a scholarship to the American Academy of Dramatic Arts. After graduation, he performed with the New York Shakespeare Festival until he was drafted in 1962. After four years in the army, he resumed his theatrical career and performed in the original off-Broadway production of *One Flew over the Cuckoo's Nest*. His screen career began in 1970 and continued until 2000, with roles in nearly ninety movies and TV series, including starring roles on the short-lived series *Westside Medical* (1977) and *Oh, Madeline* (1983–84), and a recurring part on *Murder, She Wrote* (1986–91). In recent years, he has concentrated on voice work and commercials. From 1989 until 2009, he served as the "voice" of carmaker Lexus. He is married and has two adult children, Dan and Samantha Sloyan, both actors.

David Ogden Stiers

The rest of the galaxy recognizes David Ogden Stiers from his costarring role as the stuffy Dr. Charles Emerson Winchester III on *M*A*S*H* (1977–83), but *Star Trek* fans remember his superb, against-type performance as Timicin in "Half a Life." Stiers supplied a quietly moving, emotionally rich portrayal of the scientist from Kaelon II who falls in love with Lwaxana Troi shortly before his society demands he commit ritual suicide. It's a finely tuned performance of extraordinary restraint and depth. Stiers was born on Halloween of 1942 in Peoria, Illinois, but moved to Eugene, Oregon, in high school. After graduation, he studied acting at Juilliard and appeared in theatrical productions on both coasts. His screen career began in 1971 with a small part in *Drive, He Said*,

David Ogden Stiers (left) and Majel Barrett-Roddenberry both delivered brilliant, against-type performances in the romantic tearjerker "Half a Life."

directed by Jack Nicholson, and voice work in George Lucas's *THX 1138*. He has worked on more than 150 movies and TV shows, and won two Emmy nominations for *M*A*S*H*. The towering (six-foot-four) actor has often appeared in minor roles in films directed by Woody Allen. Stiers remains a busy voice actor who has contributed to more than twenty Disney films, perhaps most memorably as Cogsworth, the talking clock from *Beauty and the Beast* (1991). He is also an experienced orchestra conductor who has led more than seventy different orchestras. He is currently associate conductor with the Newport Symphony Orchestra in Newport, Oregon.

Hallie Todd

Hallie Todd made a single, unforgettable *Star Trek* appearance, delivering a finely shaded and deeply moving performance as Lal, Data's ill-fated android "daughter" in "The Offspring." It was an unusually demanding role: Over the course of the forty-five-minute teleplay, Lal grows, mentally, from childhood to maturity; after developing the ability to experience emotions, she grapples with anger, fear, love, and loss; and all the while she moves and speaks with the stiff physicality and flat vocal delivery of an android. Todd plays it all beautifully. Both costar Brent Spiner and director Jonathan Frakes credit her for the episode's success. Todd was born Hallie Eckstein on January 7, 1962, in Los Angeles. Her first film appearance was an uncredited walk-on in *Fast Times at Ridgemont High* (1982). She landed supporting or recurring roles on several TV shows, beginning with *Brothers* (1984–89) and including *Murder, She Wrote* (1989–91). She may be best known (to non-Trekkers) as Jo McGuire, the mother of the titular character from the Disney series *Lizzie McGuire* (2001–2004). Since 1991, she has been married to actor-director Glenn Withrow. They have a daughter named Ivy.

Paul Winfield

The distinguished Paul Winfield made a pair of memorable *Star Trek* appearances—first as Captain Terrell, who falls under the nefarious influence of Khan Noonien Singh in *Star Trek II: The Wrath of Khan*, and later as Captain Dathon in "Darmok." While he's impressive in both parts, his work in "Darmok" is mildly miraculous. His character, a member of the enigmatic Tamarian species, communicates entirely through the use of metaphors derived from the planet's mythological heritage, which cannot be resolved by the Universal Translator. Despite this handicap, Dathon and Captain Picard, trapped on an alien planet, must find a way to collaborate in order to defeat a fearsome creature. Winfield's screen time is limited; he appears under heavy, disfiguring makeup; and his dialogue consists entirely of gibberish like "Darmok and Jalad at Tanagra." Nevertheless, Winfield manages to create a fully realized character with a discernible arc. It's simply marvelous work. Winfield, born May 24, 1939, in Portland, Oregon, began his theatrical career in the mid-1960s and signed a contract with Columbia

Pictures in 1966. He made a creative breakthrough with his starring role in *Sounder* (1970), becoming the third African American nominated as Best Actor (following Sidney Poitier and James Earl Jones). In 1978, he earned an Emmy nomination for his portrayal of Dr. Martin Luther King Jr. in the TV miniseries *King*. He won an Emmy for a guest appearance on *Picket Fences* in 1995 and won an NAACP Image Award in 1982. Winfield was also a prolific voice actor. In all, he contributed to more than 120 films and TV series. Winfield was openly gay and, in his later years, often played homosexual characters. He suffered a fatal heart attack March 7, 2004, at age sixty-four. He is interred in Forest Lawn Memorial Park in Los Angeles alongside his romantic partner of more than thirty years, architect Charles Gillan Jr., who passed away in 2002.

Others

Other guest performers who created memorable characters include Eric Menyuk as the alien known as the Traveler. Menyuk, who was beginning his acting career while *The Next Generation* was being cast, unsuccessfully auditioned for the role of Data. He played the Traveler in three episodes that spanned the series' seven seasons with a tenderheartedness that served the character well. Menyuk has earned sporadic credits in twenty-three movies and TV series from 1987 to 1998.

Susan Gibney made a pair of memorable appearances, playing very different versions of the same character—warp-drive theorist Dr. Leah Brahms. In the Season Three episode "Booby Trap," she played Geordi's holographic re-creation of Brahms, with whom the romance-starved engineer becomes emotionally involved; in the following season's "Galaxy's Child," Gibney guest starred as the real Dr. Brahms, who turns out to be very different than Geordi's idealized hologram. Gibney is an asset to both episodes, but her prickly, wary performance in "Galaxy's Child" is priceless. The actress later appeared as Commander Erika Benteen in two episodes of *Deep Space Nine*. Her résumé includes work for nearly fifty movies and television shows, including a recurring role as a district attorney on the crime drama *Crossing Jordan* (2002–2007).

Margot Rose delivered an achingly beautiful performance as Eline, the beloved wife of "Kamin" (Captain Picard) in "The Inner Light." Rose displayed excellent chemistry with Patrick Stewart and effectively portrayed a wide range of emotions in a challenging part that spanned forty years of her character's life and required her to perform under heavy makeup much of the time. She also made a far less memorable appearance on *Deep Space Nine* as an alien judicial administrator. Her career began in the late 1970s and includes nearly sixty film and television roles. Rose, who is also a composer, was seen most recently on *Desperate Housewives*.

Australian actress Wendy Hughes made another memorable romantic interest for Captain Picard in "Lessons," a sort-of sequel to "The Inner Light" in which Picard falls in love with his new chief of astrophysics, an amateur musician. Her career began in the early 1970s and includes more than seventy film and television roles, often cast as strong, educated women. She played medical examiner Dr. Carol Blythe during the first season of *Homicide: Life on the Street* (1993).

Alfre Woodard, who played Lily in *Star Trek: First Contact,* ranks among the franchise's most acclaimed guest stars. Her crowded trophy case includes four Emmys (and thirteen more nominations), an Oscar nomination, a Grammy nomination, a Golden Globe, three Screen Actors Guild Awards, and three NAACP Image Awards, among numerous other honors. Her career began in the late 1970s and remains active, with more than a hundred film and television credits. She is close friends with actor-director Jonathan Frakes, who insisted on casting her in *First Contact* (not that anyone was going to argue with selecting the brilliant Woodard). Screenwriters Moore and Braga created Lily as a point-of-view character for non-Trekkers in the audience; she exists to enable Picard to explain what the Borg is and other fine points of *Trek* lore. But Woodard's rich, fiery performance brings Lily to vivid life. She transforms what on the page had been a simple expository device into a believable, three-dimensional character.

19

The Trek Not Taken

The Academy Years

The disappointing returns for *Star Trek V: The Final Frontier* left Paramount Pictures' leadership flummoxed and the future of the film series uncertain. Many insiders thought the film's poor showing indicated that the series had reached the point of diminishing returns. Many fans believed that the *Final Frontier* title was intended as a subtle hint that *Star Trek V* would be the last go-round for the original cast. The picture's dismal box-office numbers only reinforced this gloomy theory. *The Final Frontier* grossed nearly $70 million worldwide but netted less than $40 million after production and promotional costs were subtracted from the ledger—which was about $68 million less than *Star Trek IV: The Voyage Home*. *Star Trek V* was the least-profitable film in the series so far, and future installments (if any) figured to be even more expensive to produce, as cast salaries and special effects costs continued to escalate.

This left Paramount in a tricky spot. On the one hand, executives, including production chief Ned Tanen, wanted to maximize the promotional value of *Star Trek*'s upcoming twenty-fifth anniversary by issuing another feature film in 1991 (just two years after *The Final Frontier*). On the other hand, executives were leery of making another big-budget picture with the original cast, who were expensive and whose age was a frequent subject of parody for stand-up comedians and sketch comedy shows. Paramount was already looking ahead to a possible *Next Generation* movie but didn't want to launch that vehicle while the TV show, now in its third season, remained in production. The studio needed a stopgap solution.

Harve Bennett believed he had the answer: a prequel, originally titled *Star Trek: The Academy Years*, set during Kirk, Spock, and McCoy's tenure at Starfleet Academy. The film (later renamed *Star Trek: The First Adventure* and sometimes referred to simply as *Starfleet Academy*) would feature younger, hunkier, and (most importantly) cheaper actors as youthful versions of Kirk, Spock, McCoy, and the other characters. Bennett had floated this idea previously during preproduction of *The Voyage Home*. It failed to gain traction then, but in 1989 it seemed like a viable alternative. Tanen gave Bennett the resources to develop a screenplay in collaboration with David Loughery, who had penned *The Final Frontier*.

The Story

The screenplay Bennett and Loughery created revealed the origins of the Kirk-Spock-McCoy team. At the beginning of the film, seventeen-year-old Jim Kirk is a rowdy Iowa farm boy who busies himself chasing girls and buzzing cornfields in a futuristic crop duster until word arrives that he's been admitted to Starfleet Academy. (The film's early scenes would also have introduced Kirk's brother, George, who is killed in the classic episode "Operation—Annihilate!") Jim's Academy roommate is the thirty-year-old McCoy, still distraught after euthanizing his father (as depicted in *Star Trek V*). Kirk meets Cassandra Hightower, a female cadet, and Spock, who is treated as a pariah by his fellow cadets due to his half-Vulcan parentage. It's love at first sight for Kirk and Hightower, but it takes longer for friendship to develop between Kirk and Spock. At first the two are rivals, but they bond after Kirk rescues Spock from a savage beating at the hands of another cadet—an alien named Kalibar—and his cronies. Kalibar, the scion of a wealthy and powerful family (essentially, he's an alien prince), is expelled from the Academy.

Cassandra and McCoy are assigned to a training mission aboard the *Enterprise*, but Kirk and Spock are forced to remain behind. Both have been suspended for cheating on an exam (presumably, the Kobayashi Maru test mentioned on the TV series and depicted in *Star Trek II*). The revenge-crazed Kalibar and his followers seize control of the *Enterprise* and take a Federation official hostage. Kirk and Spock disobey orders and race to the rescue, stealing an antique warp vessel from the Academy museum. Their classmate Scotty, a whip-smart engineering student, helps them get the vintage vessel up and running, and accompanies them on their rogue mission to save the *Enterprise*. McCoy and the Federation dignitary are rescued, but Cassandra is killed during the battle. The story ends with Kirk and Spock reluctantly parting ways, assigned to serve as midshipmen on separate star craft, with no knowledge of the further adventures that lay in their future.

Bennett was deeply invested in this screenplay, which he hoped to direct himself. He was convinced of both its emotional power and its commercial appeal. He estimated that *The Academy Years* could be produced for a frugal $27 million ($3 million less than *The Final Frontier*). He also believed that it would be the perfect movie to release in conjunction with the series' twenty-fifth anniversary, since it would take fans back to the very beginning. "*Starfleet Academy*, like *Star Trek IV*, would have reached beyond the cult," Bennett told authors Mark A. Altman, Ron Magid, and Edward Gross for their book *Charting the Undiscovered Country: The Making of Star Trek VI*. "It would have interested people who had never seen a *Star Trek* film, which did not exclude the regulars, but simply said, 'If you don't understand what it's all about, come see how it all began.'" If successful, *The Academy Years* could have formed a new branch of the film series, with the adventures of the young Kirk and Spock appearing in parallel with the planned *Next Generation* movies.

However, many other franchise insiders were vehemently opposed to the idea.

The Outrage

By the time Bennett and Loughery's screenplay was completed, the concept's original champion, Ned Tanen, had been replaced by Sid Ganis, who was less enthusiastic about the prequel concept. He and Paramount CEO Frank Mancuso were worried about the commercial prospects of a *Star Trek* film not starring the original cast. Mancuso asked Bennett if the picture could be shot with Shatner and Nimoy in their familiar roles. Bennett was adamant that it could not. There was simply no way the then-fifty-nine-year-old Shatner and Nimoy could pass for teenagers.

However, in an effort to involve Shatner and Nimoy in some capacity, Bennett and Loughery added a framing sequence in which the now-legendary Admiral Kirk, accompanied by Ambassador Spock, returns to the Academy to speak at commencement ceremonies. They begin to reminisce about their days as cadets, and the picture flashes back to the main story. At the close of the film, Kirk would have placed flowers on Cassandra's grave and beamed back to the *Enterprise* with Spock.

Ganis and Mancuso seemed satisfied with this compromise and authorized more preproduction funds. Bennett scouted locations and began looking for potential cast members. Had the film moved forward, it probably would have been shot, in part, on the campus of Washington and Lee University in Lexington, Virginia. As for casting, in 2010 Bennett told a StarTrek.com interviewer that "I had an eye on John Cusack for Spock, which would have been great. Ethan Hawke could have been Kirk. There were so many possibilities."

But the idea of recasting the roles was anathema to many of the franchise's power brokers, including Gene Roddenberry and most of the cast members who would have been replaced. James Doohan and Walter Koenig denounced the proposed film publically and vociferously. Roddenberry badly damaged the movie's prospects during an interview published in the magazine *Cinefantastique*. He misleadingly compared Bennett's screenplay with the puerile *Police Academy* films, leading many fans to believe *The Academy Years* would be a lowbrow spoof. In fact, Bennett and Loughery drew their inspiration from director Michael Curtiz's classic cavalry film *The Santa Fe Trail* (1940), starring Errol Flynn as a young J. E. B. Stuart and Ronald Reagan as a young George Armstrong Custer. The Bennett-Loughery screenplay also recalls Robert A. Heinlein's 1948 novel *Space Cadet*, in which an expelled cadet emerges as the story's primary villain. Roddenberry often cited *Space Cadet* as an inspiration for *Star Trek*. Based on Roddenberry's spurious comments, however, outraged fans inundated Paramount with cards and letters demanding that the studio scrap *The Academy Years*.

Rejection and Redemption

Eventually, in May 1990, news of the controversy surrounding *The Academy Years* reached Martin Davis, head of Paramount's parent company, corporate conglomerate Gulf + Western. In response, Davis reportedly insisted that the next *Trek* picture star the original cast. This decision felled the prequel like a phaser set on heavy stun. Ganis and Mancuso broke the news to Bennett, who the studio wanted to retain to produce the original-cast film. They insisted the studio could still make *The Academy Years* following *Star Trek VI*, but Bennett doubted this would actually happen—and, of course, it didn't. Bennett was also extremely dubious that a viable movie could be conceived, written, and produced in time to meet the planned Thanksgiving 1991 release date, which was only eighteen months away. Since Bennett's contract with Paramount was nearly up, the studio offered him a $3 million, two-picture renewal as an inducement. But the skeptical, bitterly disappointed, and emotionally drained Bennett declined. He walked away from Paramount and *Star Trek*, the franchise he had revived with *The Wrath of Khan*.

This turn of events sent Bennett into an alcoholic tailspin. "For the first time in my life, I drank excessively," Bennett told William Shatner for his book *Star Trek Movie Memories*. "Thank God I got over that. I got a life back, but I was terribly hurt." Bennett still speaks wistfully about *The Academy Years*. "It was the best script of all and it never got produced," Bennett told StarTrek.com. "All the possibilities were open, the script was beautiful, and the love story was haunting, but it didn't happen."

Still, Paramount kept the idea of a *Trek* prequel bubbling on the back burner. In 2004, Paramount chairman Sherry Lansing met with Bennett about possibly reviving *The Academy Years*. But ultimately, the studio decided the prequel might create further problems for its struggling series *Star Trek: Enterprise*, which was set in an even earlier era, prior to the foundation of the United Federation of Planets. *Star Trek* fell dormant for four years following the cancellation of *Enterprise* in 2005. The vehicle the studio chose to relaunch the franchise was director J. J. Abrams's *Star Trek* (2009), which depicted Kirk, Spock, and friends as cadets at Starfleet Academy.

Written by Roberto Orci and Alex Kurtzman, Abrams's film shares many concepts with Bennett's *Academy Years* screenplay, but is very different in structure and tone. Most importantly, the doomed romance that would have provided the emotional core of *The Academy Years* is absent. Also, Abrams's film adds a new layer of complexity with its time-travel/alternate timeline setup, a clever device that enabled the filmmakers to retain whatever elements of classic *Trek* mythology they liked and to abandon any they considered inconvenient.

Bennett panned the 2009 movie, describing it as "rapid cuts, explosions, [and] gore for the sake of gore," in another StarTrek.com interview. Nevertheless, the picture's breathtaking success bolsters Bennett's contention that *The Academy Years* was a potential blockbuster. Although some Trekkers complained about the casting of Chris Pine as Kirk and Zachary Quinto as Spock, Abrams's film grossed more than $385 million worldwide (and earned another $100 million-plus in DVD sales). Even adjusting for inflation, and factoring in the 2009 picture's hefty $140 million budget, it remains by far the most profitable *Star Trek* movie ever made, blowing away *Star Trek IV: The Voyage Home*.

Bennett may be correct that *The Academy Years* could have been a smash. However, its success would have meant that *Star Trek VI: The Undiscovered Country* would never have been produced. As it turned out, the film Bennett refused to make recaptured the charm of the series and enabled the original cast to make a graceful exit.

20

The Big Goodbye

By May 1990, when Paramount Pictures committed to making a final *Star Trek* movie with the original cast, the picture's projected release date was only eighteen months away. Although its premiere was eventually pushed back from November 1991 to December of that year, the development window for *Star Trek VI* remained tighter than for any other entry in the series. Executives were adamant that the film had to be released in 1991 to capitalize on the franchise's much-ballyhooed twenty-fifth anniversary. Cross-promotion between the two projects would benefit the new movie and help propel *Star Trek: The Next Generation* to new ratings heights. Previously, the most speedily produced *Trek* picture had been *Star Trek III: The Search for Spock*, which went from conception to release in just twenty-two months. In that case, however, the tentpoles of the plot were self-evident, and a producer was already in place. Neither of those conditions applied with *Star Trek VI*, since a dejected Harve Bennett left the studio after the scuttling of his originally planned prequel (see the preceding chapter for details), and nobody had a clue what this new movie might be about.

To fill this gaping void of leadership and imagination, Paramount CEO Frank Mancuso turned to Leonard Nimoy. Over lunch, Mancuso asked Nimoy to assume control of the project as executive producer. Like Bennett before him, Nimoy at first was skeptical that a worthwhile film could be made so quickly, but he promised to consider it. Three days later, he called Mancuso and pitched his concept for a *Trek* story that would mirror current events—the collapse of the Soviet Union and the normalization of relations between Russia and the United States—by chronicling the formation of the alliance between the Klingon Empire and the United Federation of Planets. Nimoy described his idea as "the Berlin Wall comes down in outer space." Mancuso was enthusiastic. Nimoy asked for and received permission to contact Nicholas Meyer about writing and directing the picture.

In his memoir *I Am Spock*, Nimoy recalls warning Mancuso that in order to deliver a quality product so quickly, "everything will have to fall into place perfectly." Mancuso assured Nimoy that the studio would "do everything necessary for that to happen." But that's not the way it played out.

A Walk on the Beach

Nimoy's next step was to fly to Cape Cod, where Meyer was vacationing. During a walk on the beach, the two men hashed out most of the story's major plot points: The Klingon Empire, brought to its knees by an environmental disaster (inspired by the Chernobyl catastrophe), petitions for peace. A skeptical Kirk is assigned to accompany the Klingon High Chancellor (modeled after Mikhail Gorbachev) to Earth for a summit, but on the way the Klingon leader is assassinated by a human-Klingon cabal with a vested interest in continuing the decades-old war. Kirk and McCoy are blamed for the murder and exiled to the Klingon equivalent of Siberia. Spock rescues his friends. Finally, the reunited crew of the *Enterprise* must stop a second assassination that would extinguish all hope for peace.

Both Nimoy and Meyer left their Cape Cod meeting brimming with optimism about the project, but Paramount, despite Mancuso's assurances, hesitated to hire Meyer to write the script. Instead, the studio insisted that Nimoy meet with screenwriters Lawrence Konner and Mark Rosenthal, who were already under contract (so their services were available at no additional cost). Nimoy dutifully took a meeting with Konner and Rosenthal, who proposed a story featuring the Romulans that Nimoy rejected out of hand. Then he recounted the tale he and Meyer had envisioned and asked the duo to respond with notes. Nimoy considered Konner and Rosenthal's notes "useless"—he claimed they simply recapped the story he had outlined, with no new concepts or suggestions. Later, Paramount executives convinced Meyer to meet with Konner and Rosenthal, too, which created friction between Nimoy and Meyer. Paramount leadership never told Nimoy that it was flying Konner and Rosenthal to England (where Meyer lives) to meet the director. Nor did it tell Meyer than Nimoy was unaware of the meeting. The end result was that Nimoy and Meyer each thought the other had gone behind his back, and both felt their authorship of the film, or at least of the story, was being threatened.

(As it turned out, they were right to feel threatened—but by Konner and Rosenthal, not by each other. Postproduction was marred by an ugly credit dispute. Initially, the Writers Guild awarded Nimoy sole story credit for *Star Trek VI*, but Konner and Rosenthal appealed, and produced the "useless" notes from their meeting with Nimoy as evidence that they had written the story. Nimoy, it seems, had never written anything down. On appeal Konner and Rosenthal were granted the film's story credit. After the irate Nimoy threatened to sue the Guild, the decision was amended again and story credit was shared by Konner, Rosenthal, and Nimoy.)

Following their meeting with Meyer, Konner and Rosenthal wrote a screenplay that was deemed unusable. Meyer never even bothered to read this version. Only after all this had transpired did the studio finally authorize Meyer to begin a script of his own, and even then executives balked at hiring Meyer's friend Denny Martin Finn as cowriter. Paramount eventually caved when Meyer threatened to walk away unless Finn was brought in on the screenplay. Since

Director Nicholas Meyer consults with stars Leonard Nimoy and William Shatner on the set of *Star Trek VI: The Undiscovered Country.*

Finn was in Los Angeles and Meyer in England, the team worked by e-mail, with Finn writing pages by day (California time) and e-mailing them to Meyer, who revised and polished them while Finn slept. The screenplay was completed in late 1990, and Meyer took out a six-month lease on a Hollywood bungalow, where he planned to reside during production and postproduction. Then the real problems started.

Budget Battle and Other War Stories

Since *Star Trek: The Motion Picture*, Paramount had kept the *Star Trek* movies on a short budgetary leash. The disappointing returns for *Star Trek V* convinced executives that further retrenchment was necessary. Shortly after Meyer arrived in Hollywood, he learned that the budget for *Star Trek VI* had been slashed from $30 million (the same price as its predecessor) to an austere $25 million. Meyer, feeling he had been bamboozled, was livid. At a meeting with producers Ralph Winter and Steven-Charles Jaffe and Paramount executives David Kirkpatrick and John Goldwyn, Meyer insisted that the planned film simply could not be made for less than $30 million. When Kirkpatrick and Goldwyn tried to haggle with him over the budget, Meyer (as he recalls in his memoir, *The View from the Bridge*) informed them that "I am not negotiating. I am giving you reality." Faced with this reality, Kirkpatrick, Goldwyn, and Mancuso cancelled the film altogether.

A few days later, however, Mancuso was fired and replaced by Meyer's old friend Stanley Jaffe, who promptly revived the project. Meyer agreed to cut an elaborate opening sequence (originally, the movie began with the already-retired crew of the *Enterprise* being rounded up for a final mission), and the picture was assigned a $27 million budget. To save money, the film was shot mostly on standing sets from *The Next Generation* and leftovers from previous *Trek* features. For example, *Star Trek VI* used the bridge from the previous film, along with re-dressed versions of the *Next Gen* transporter room, sick bay, and engineering sets. The office of the Federation president was a redress of the Ten-Forward lounge. In another money-saving choice, Meyer bypassed the expensive Jerry

Goldsmith and signed little-known young composer Cliff Eidelman, who delivered one of the most strikingly original and emotionally powerful scores of the entire series. One area where Meyer and Nimoy refused to cut costs was special effects. Industrial Light & Magic, which had provided special visuals for the first four *Trek* films, was hired back, after being passed over for *Star Trek V*.

While all this was going on, Meyer was defending his screenplay from attacks by Gene Roddenberry. The Meyer-Finn script adhered closely to Nimoy and Meyer's original story but included material to which Roddenberry objected strongly, including the idea that Kirk has grown to hate and distrust Klingons since the murder of his son (by Commander Kruge in *Star Trek III*), as well as the depiction of other Starfleet officers who harbor racist (or species-ist) prejudice against the Klingons. "Mr. Roddenberry really believed in the perfectibility of man, of humans, and I have yet to see the evidence for this," Meyer said at the Hero Complex film festival in 2011. "So [*Star Trek*] *VI* is a film in

When Kirstie Alley declined to return as Saavik, Kim Cattrall was hired to appear as the Vulcan Lieutenant Valeris.

It was Meyer's idea to have Michael Dorn appear in *Star Trek VI* as Worf's grandfather, the defense attorney who represents Kirk and McCoy during their Klingon show trial.

which the crew of the *Enterprise* has all kinds of prejudice, racial prejudice, vis-à-vis the Klingons. And some of their remarks, including how they all look alike and what they smell like, and all the xenophobic things which we grappled with—that was all deeply offensive to him because he thought there isn't going to be that."

Consumed with budget concerns, casting choices, and other decisions, all of which had to be dealt with at warp speed to meet an inflexible release date, Meyer was openly dismissive of Roddenberry. Meyer walked out a meeting with Roddenberry, who was now gravely ill, after only five minutes. Later, the two met again, and Meyer promised to make corrections based on Roddenberry's input, but he never made a single revision. In retrospect, Meyer regrets his behavior. "There are moments in one's life where you look back and you say, 'Well, I wish I had done this differently,'" he said in the same film festival interview. "I came out of it feeling not very good, and I've not felt good about it ever since. He was not well, and maybe there were more tactful ways of dealing with it. . . . Not my finest hour."

Hiring the Cast and Bridging the Generations

Star Trek VI, now officially subtitled *The Undiscovered Country* (the same moniker the studio rejected for Meyer's *Star Trek II*), gathered together arguably the finest supporting cast ever assembled for a *Trek* feature. The lineup included Christopher Plummer as a duplicitous Klingon general, David Warner as the Gorbachev-like Klingon Chancellor, Kim Cattrall as Vulcan science officer Valeris, supermodel Iman as a shape-shifting alien, and Mark Lenard as Spock's father, Sarek. William Shatner and fellow Canadian Plummer worked together early in their careers at the Stratford Festival in Ontario. Shatner, then serving as Plummer's understudy, took over the lead role in Shakespeare's *Henry V* when Plummer was stricken with a kidney stone. It was Shatner's first big break. Originally, Meyer wanted to hire Kirstie Alley to appear as Lieutenant Saavik in *Star Trek VI*, but Alley (now a star on TV's *Cheers*) wasn't interested in returning to *Trek*, so the character of Valeris was created as a substitute. Apparently, Robin Curtis, who had played Saavik in the third and fourth *Star Trek* films, was not considered for the role.

Although it played no part in Nimoy's original conception of the story, the film's plot enabled Meyer to begin merging the disparate realms of classic *Trek* and *The Next Generation*. In showing how the Federation and the Klingons came to be allies, *The Undiscovered Country* provided important backstory for the sequel series. Meyer and Finn's screenplay integrated elements of *Next Gen* mythology to further whet fans' appetite for the big-screen debut of the *Next Generation* crew. For example, the story's climax takes place on the planet Khitomer, which would play an important role in several *Next Gen* story lines. It was Meyer's idea to give Michael Dorn an extended cameo as a Klingon defense attorney (although it's never mentioned on-screen, the character is supposed to be Worf's grandfather). To further integrate the two *Treks*, Nimoy agreed to make a historic appearance on *Next Gen*. Finally, Meyer penned Kirk's final Captain's Log entry, which plainly refers to handing the *Enterprise* over to a new crew: "This ship and her history will shortly become the care of another crew. . . . They will continue the voyages we have begun, journey to all the undiscovered countries, boldly going where no man—or no one—has gone before."

Honoring the Great Bird of the Galaxy

Despite a compressed schedule (filming began April 16 and wrapped July 2), shooting and postproduction ran smoothly. During production, some of the film's more racist dialogue was dropped, revised, or reassigned. For instance, Nichelle Nichols flatly refused to deliver a line in which Uhura was supposed to ask, "But would you want one [a Klingon] to marry your daughter?" Even though some of this content was softened, Gene Roddenberry remained vehemently opposed to any depiction of racism within Starfleet. After viewing the film at a private screening October 21, 1991, Roddenberry contacted his attorney and dictated fifteen minutes' worth of trims and revisions he wanted made to the film. But no action was taken because Roddenberry died three days later.

The passing of the Great Bird of the Galaxy inspired an outpouring of heartfelt tributes. At his memorial service, he was eulogized by members of both *Star Trek* casts and by science fiction author Ray Bradbury. Nichelle Nichols sang Paul McCartney's "Yesterday." Fans all over the world honored Roddenberry at informal gatherings, or by writing poetry or drawing portraits. Many seemed to be compelled to express how profoundly their lives had been shaped by *Star Trek* and Roddenberry's uplifting vision of the future. Meyer decided *Star Trek VI* had to include some sort of acknowledgment of Roddenberry's death. Although

Paramount executive Brandon Tartikoff argued for a longer, more flowery tribute, Meyer opted for the simple (and, in light of the Great Bird's feelings about the film, ironic) dedication "for Gene Roddenberry."

Roddenberry's passing also underscored the finality of the sixth *Star Trek* film. "When he died after we completed *VI*, essentially *Star Trek* died with him," William Shatner said in an interview included on the *Star Trek VI: The Undiscovered Country* DVD. "The *Star Trek* we [original cast members] knew died with him."

Reception

Star Trek VI: The Undiscovered Country, released December 6, 1991, pleased ticket buyers and critics alike. Despite the sour taste left by its predecessor, the picture opened No. 1, grossing $18 million in its first week, and remained among the Top 10 weekly money-earners for more than a month. The picture benefitted from Paramount's yearlong ballyhoo for *Star Trek*'s twenty-fifth anniversary and from the broadcast of the monumental, two-part *Next Generation* "Unification" saga, guest starring Leonard Nimoy as Spock, which ran November 4 and 11, 1991, and earned the highest Nielsen ratings in the history of the franchise so far. (For more on "Unification," see the next chapter.) *Star Trek VI* went on to rake in nearly $75 million in the U.S. and nearly $97 million worldwide (that's almost $164 million when adjusted for inflation). It was a far better showing than *Star Trek V: The Final Frontier*, and the critical response was much more favorable, too. Most reviewers rated the film highly. Janet Maslin of the *New York Times* wrote that the movie "gets almost everything right," and Desson Howe of the *Washington Post* described the zero-gravity assassination sequence as "space-age Sam Peckinpah." *The Undiscovered Country* garnered two Oscar nominations, for its sound effects and makeup. It also earned a Hugo nomination for Best Dramatic Presentation but lost to *Terminator 2: Judgment Day*. However, it won the Saturn Award for Best Science Fiction Film, beating *T2*. *The Undiscovered Country* was somewhat controversial among fans, some of whom shared Roddenberry's discomfort with the depiction of anti-Klingon prejudice within Starfleet. However, everyone agreed *Star Trek VI* was a tremendous improvement over *Star Trek V*.

Assessing *The Undiscovered Country*

Everyone knew that *Star Trek VI* would be the final mission for the beloved original cast. A nostalgia-tinged teaser trailer for *Star Trek VI* featured a montage of images from classic TV series (and from earlier feature films) and announced that, "Now you're invited to join them for one last adventure." Nearly everyone involved in making *Star Trek VI* had the same top priority: sending the series' beloved regular cast off with a worthy swan song. "They said they were not happy going out on [*Star Trek*] *V*," Meyer said in an interview included on the *Star Trek*

The tagline of this *TV Guide* ad, for a cable rebroadcast of *The Undiscovered Country*, sums up the movie's central theme succinctly.

VI: The Undiscovered Country DVD. Meyer's film helped the series conclude on a high note, rather than a sour one.

The Undiscovered Country is the biggest of the three *Star Trek* films Meyer wrote and/or directed. It functions on a grand, operatic scale (it's nothing less than a clash of civilizations) and grapples with weighty, timeless issues (war and peace, prejudice and tolerance, enmity and reconciliation). Yet, at its heart, like all of Meyer's work, it's an intimate story about one character's journey to enlightenment—in this case, Captain James T. Kirk. Meyer's *Star Trek II* showed Kirk wrestling with aging and mortality. *Star Trek VI* finds him battling even fiercer demons—the fear and loathing that have infested the place in his heart formerly reserved for his son, David.

The virulence of the anti-Klingon sentiment expressed in *Star Trek VI* is jolting—even more so when taken in contrast to *Star Trek: The Next Generation*, where Lieutenant Worf had emerged as one of the franchise's most popular and sympathetic characters. When Spock informs Shatner that the Klingons, as a species, are dying, Kirk snaps, "Let them die!" Shatner initially balked at this line. Later, after meeting the daughter of the slain Klingon High Chancellor,

Scotty ventures, "I'll bet that Klingon bitch killed her father." It's understandable that Gene Roddenberry and many fans recoiled at such material. But what Roddenberry and others seemed to miss was that, while Kirk may have succumbed to hatred and prejudice following David's murder, he eventually comes to realize his good judgment, and even his love for his son, has become a prisoner of this rancor. He regains both by overcoming his blind animosity toward the Klingons. Although it may muddle the Great Bird's vision of a future where human beings no longer participate in such intolerance, Meyer's film offers an instructive, even inspirational, illustration of the healing power of reconciliation. Rather than showing us a world free of hatred, *The Undiscovered Country* demonstrates how we might create such a place.

If the thematic content of *Star Trek VI* remains controversial, its cinematic merits are beyond reproach.

Meyer and Finn's marvelously constructed screenplay thrusts viewers immediately into the action—and delights us with the sight of Captain Sulu commanding his own ship, the USS *Excelsior*—quickly establishing political and interpersonal tension that is sustained throughout. It boasts showstopping set pieces, including the imaginatively conceived and brilliantly staged zero-gravity assassination scene and Kirk's two-fisted battle with himself (or actually with a shapeshifting alien that has taken on his appearance). The scenario doubles down on suspense in the third act, as Spock and company comb the *Enterprise* looking for a traitor, while Kirk and McCoy try to escape from Klingon penal colony Rura Penthe. The dialogue sparkles with witty repartee and Shakespearean quotes. The Klingon General Chang (Plummer) spouts dialogue from at least eight different Shakespeare plays.

As usual, Meyer elicits finely tuned performances from his cast. Shatner, Nimoy, and Kelley are all in top form, rekindling the old Kirk-Spock-McCoy chemistry one last time. Plummer gnaws the scenery with reckless abandon and delightful aplomb. Cattrall contributes a carefully measured portrayal of surprising depth. Other than Kirk, Valeris has a greater breadth and richer mix of (repressed) emotions stewing within her than any other character; she functions largely as a foil to Kirk. David Warner, given little to do in *Star Trek V*, makes a strong impression here as Klingon Chancellor Gorkon. Dorn is solid in what amounts to an extended cameo. Meyer even makes effective use of supermodel Iman, who was never much of an actress. Avowed Trekker Christian Slater makes a brief appearance, and sharp-eyed fans will notice Rene Auberjonois, who would later play Constable Odo on *Deep Space Nine*, in an uncredited role as Colonel West. Although billed as the final voyage for the original cast, only DeForest Kelley, Nichelle Nichols, and Grace Lee Whitney (who makes a brief appearance) make their last official *Star Trek* appearances in *The Undiscovered Country*.

The film's production values are also impressive. Although made for less money, *Star Trek VI* looks like a far more expensive movie than *Star Trek V*. Its Klingon sets—particularly the nightmarish courtroom where Kirk and McCoy are tried, in Kafkaesque fashion, and convicted of murder—are particularly arresting. The visual effects sequences are well crafted and exciting, as well. Thrilling, touching, thought-provoking, *The Undiscovered Country* rivals *The Wrath of Khan* as the most satisfying *Trek* feature. It was a rousing climax to the franchise's triumphant twenty-fifth anniversary year.

21

Resistance Is Futile

The Next Generation, Season Five (1991–92)

The behind-the-scenes continuity and cohesion that helped *Star Trek: The Next Generation* explore new terrain and expand its audience during Season Four continued into the series' fifth campaign. In fact, there was even less turnover among the show's writers and producers during Season Five. Michael Piller remained in the fold (but was increasingly distracted by preparations for the spin-off *Star Trek: Deep Space Nine*). So did Jeri Taylor, now promoted to Supervising Producer and taking over more of Piller's duties. Writers Ronald D. Moore and Joe Menosky became producers, while talented scribes including Brannon Braga, Peter Allan Fields, Joe Menosky, and Rene Echevarria remained in the fold. Yet the season was hardly devoid of backstage drama. After devoting most of the past two years to character-driven stories, Rick Berman, Piller, and Taylor wanted to juice up the show's science fiction elements for Season Five. To this end, Berman rehired SF specialist Herbert Wright, who had stormed off the show during its first season due to conflicts with Gene Roddenberry. Wright served as a writer-producer for a half-dozen mid-season episodes before leaving the series again, citing creative differences.

Despite the carryover of personnel, *Next Gen*'s reservoir of teleplays in development was running low. Throughout the season, the writing staff struggled to generate story ideas up to the lofty standard set during recent years. (This troubling sign forecast greater problems in future seasons.) As a result, a fistful of concepts abandoned in previous years were revived for Season Five. Unsolicited scripts continued to pour in (about three thousand per year) as a result of the program's open submission policy, but nearly all of those—penned by star-struck neophytes—proved unusable. Even those script coordinator Eric Stillwell deemed salvageable normally required extensive revisions. In mid-season, a desperate Piller invited the writing staff to a weekend brainstorming session at his home in Mexico, which proved astoundingly productive. Removed from their usual habitat, the staff dreamed up five of the season's final six episodes, including the game-changing "I Borg," the Season Five cliff-hanger "Time's Arrow," and the Hugo-winning masterpiece "The Inner Light." Although the writing staff struggled mightily from week to week, their efforts produced another season filled with consistently engrossing and daring episodes.

Meanwhile, the show's on-camera talent continued to improve, both individually and as a unit. *The Next Generation* cast was never vexed by the kind of interpersonal feuds and petty jealousies that roiled the original *Star Trek*. Wil Wheaton, in his memoir *Just a Geek*, reports that "believe it or not, nobody was a dick. Everyone was very, very cool." In fact, many *Next Gen* cast members forged lasting friendships and sometimes collaborated on side projects. For instance, Patrick Stewart, LeVar Burton, Jonathan Frakes, and Michael Dorn formed a band called the Sunspots, which played on Brent Spiner's 1991 album of Sinatra standards, *Ol' Yellow Eyes Is Back*. And in 1992, Stewart, Frakes, Spiner, Gates McFadden, and Colm Meaney appeared together in a touring production of Tom Stoppard and Andre Previn's play *Every Good Boy Deserves Favour*. "We've all become each other's best friends," said Marina Sirtis in a DVD interview.

Marina Sirtis made a major breakthrough during the fifth season of *The Next Generation*, when writers finally began to craft worthwhile material featuring Counselor Troi.

Over the past four seasons, the cast had also become a precision-tuned instrument that delivered pitch-perfect performances week in and week out. Season Five marked a breakthrough for Sirtis, who (perhaps due to the influence of Jeri Taylor) finally received worthwhile material and responded with the least affected and most enjoyable work of her tenure on the show.

For the first (and only) time, Q failed to appear during Season Five. But the headstrong Ensign Ro Laren, played by Michelle Forbes, joined the series early in the season and quickly became one of the show's most popular supporting characters. Although Wesley Crusher left the series a year prior, now-Cadet Crusher (and actor Wil Wheaton) returned for a pair of episodes, including the thought-provoking "The First Duty." Wheaton received better scripts as a guest star than he did as a regular. But the highest-profile guest star of Season Five was Leonard Nimoy, whose heavily hyped appearance as Spock in the aptly titled two-part adventure "Unification" helped *The Next Generation* score its highest Nielsen ratings to date.

Coming in November, toward the end of a yearlong Paramount Pictures publicity blitz honoring the franchise's twenty-fifth anniversary, Spock's presence represented both a benediction of the sequel series (once dismissed by Nimoy and other original cast members) and a passing of the torch. In his memoir *I Am Spock*, Nimoy ventured that "Unification" healed, once and for all, any festering animosity between fans of *The Next Generation* and holdouts devoted to the original program. The episode "did away with any friction between these groups, and brought them together for the first time," Nimoy wrote. "It was as though a breach had been healed. There were no longer two *Star Treks*, or two groups of fans—only one." "Unification I and II" carried the simple dedication, "Gene Roddenberry, 1921–1991." The Great Bird of the Galaxy passed away October 24, 1991. The two-part epic served as a fitting tribute. Its underlying theme of reconciliation through a sense of brotherhood, played out both on-screen and among the show's fans, underscored one of Roddenberry's core convictions and the franchise's central messages, dating back to the original program.

"Redemption II"

In the first part of "Redemption," which concluded Season Four, Worf resigned his commission to fight alongside Chancellor Gowron (Robert O'Reilly) in the Klingon Civil War, in hopes of restoring his family honor. Audiences also learned that a Romulan bearing a striking resemblance to Tasha Yar (and played by Denise Crosby) was supporting Gowron's rivals, the Duras Sisters, Lursa (Barbara March) and B'Etor (Gwynyth Walsh). In "Redemption II," Data prevents the Romulans from resupplying the Duras clan, handing victory to Gowron and helping Worf win back his family name. The mysterious Romulan is revealed as Tasha's half-Romulan daughter Sela, the unexpected result of Lieutenant Yar traveling into the past during the climax of "Yesterday's Enterprise." Written by Ronald D. Moore, "Redemption II" expertly balances interpersonal tension, political intrigue, and military brinksmanship. While the first half of the saga focused primarily on Worf, the second half concentrates largely on Picard, Data (who receives his first command), and the story's trio of splendid villainesses, the Duras Sisters and Sela. Michael Dorn later complained that the "Redemption II" teleplay was too crowded with ideas, arguing that the Data story and the Sela story both could have sustained entire episodes. Nevertheless, the action-packed "Redemption II" kick-started Season Five with a jolt of excitement.

"Darmok"

What we have here is a failure to communicate. Captain Picard is whisked away to the surface of an uninhabited planet, where he and Captain Dathon, a member of the enigmatic Tamarian species, must find a way to collaborate in order to defeat a fearsome creature. But the Tamarian language, based on metaphors derived from the planet's mythological heritage, cannot be resolved by the Universal Translator. The basic scenario for "Darmok," submitted by Phillip LaZebnik, had been floating around for two years, passing from hand to hand until writer Joe Menosky came up with the idea of a language based on metaphor. After that, the teleplay came together quickly. This installment features a pair of notable guest stars: Oscar nominee and Emmy winner Paul Winfield, unrecognizable beneath his heavy Tamarian makeup, and rising starlet Ashley Judd, who has a minor role as Lieutenant Lefler, a member of Geordi's staff. Winfield, who had appeared as Captain Terrell in *Star Trek II*, manages to create a believable, well-rounded character as the Tamarian captain, even though his dialogue consists entirely of nonsensical phrases like "Darmok and Jalad at Tanagra." Both Piller and Berman have named this episode among their favorite *Next Generation* installments. "There is no better *Star Trek* episode, I think, than 'Darmok,'" Piller opines in an interview included on the *Star Trek: The Next Generation Season Five* DVD collection.

"Ensign Ro"

Ensign Ro Laren (Michelle Forbes) of Bajor is released from the Starfleet stockade to help the *Enterprise* track down a band of Bajoran terrorists believed to have bombed a Federation outpost. Commander Riker and other members of the crew aren't happy about having Ro aboard, and Ro is no more pleased with the situation. But Guinan connects with her, and eventually the much-reviled ensign proves her true mettle, helping avert a miscarriage of justice. Written by Piller, "Ensign Ro" was designed to introduce its assertive, freethinking title character, intended to spice up the cozy, agreeable crew of the *Enterprise-D*. "The other characters in the cast are relatively homogeneous—some might even say bland," said Rick Berman, in author Larry Nemecek's *Star Trek: The Next Generation Companion*. "So we wanted a character with the strength and dignity of a Starfleet officer but with a troubled past, an edge." It worked.

Instantly, Ro became one of the series' most popular characters. The episode also introduced the Bajorans and their long-standing conflict with Cardassia, story elements that were foundational to *Star Trek: Deep Space Nine*. Originally, it was hoped that Forbes would join the regular cast of that show. When she refused (Forbes wanted freedom to pursue film roles), Nana Visitor was hired to portray Commander Kira Nerys, a Ro Laren substitute. Forbes won the role of Ensign Ro based on her memorable cameo in the previous season's "Half a

Dathon, the Tamarian captain who befriends Picard in "Darmok" despite an apparently insurmountable language barrier, was recreated for this action figure.

Photo by Preston Hewis, East Bank Images

Life." The actress appeared as Ro in five further Season Five adventures and one episode apiece during Seasons Six and Seven.

"Silicon Avatar"

The Crystalline Entity—the giant, planet-eating creature that wiped out Data's home world —returns to ravage a colony on Melona IV. Afterward, Dr. Kila Marr (Ellen Geer), whose son was devoured by the Entity, beams aboard the *Enterprise* to assist as Captain Picard and his crew attempt to pursue the mysterious beastie, which roams open space. But Dr. Marr has a secret agenda. Written by Jeri Taylor from a story by Lawrence V. Conley, "Silicon Avatar" is one of the season's most emotionally charged scenarios. Like the classic *Trek* adventure "The Doomsday Machine," "Silicon Avatar" was inspired by Herman Melville's *Moby Dick*, with Marr as the story's Captain Ahab. Geer delivers a heart-wrenching performance as the grief-haunted, revenge-obsessed Dr. Marr. Although both Piller and Brent Spiner have expressed disappointment with it, "Silicon Avatar" is a solid entry that maintained the season's positive momentum.

"Disaster"

The *Enterprise* collides with a "quantum filament," crippling the ship and killing several crew members. In the aftermath, Counselor Troi finds herself in command, while Captain Picard is trapped in a turbolift with three schoolchildren. Geordi and Dr. Crusher are stuck in a cargo hold. Several more crew members gather in Ten-Forward, where Worf helps Keiko O'Brien give birth. Ron Moore wrote this episode, from a story by Ron Jarvis and Philip A. Scorza, as a paean to the disaster films of the 1970s. He even tried to talk his fellow producers into casting Shelley Winters and Red Buttons from *The Poseidon Adventure* as guest stars. Cooler heads prevailed, preventing the installment from crossing the line into parody. As it stands, "Disaster" is a brilliantly structured thriller and a turning point for both Marina Sirtis and Counselor Troi. Unexpectedly forced to make life-or-death decisions, Deanna proves to be a capable and, when necessary, forceful leader rather than an empathic shrinking violet. Sirtis's carefully shaded performance suggests that Deanna is as surprised as anyone else to discover this inner strength. In another unforgettable vignette, Riker is forced to remove Data's head and carry it to engineering.

"The Game"

Just when Wesley Crusher haters thought they had seen the last of the junior ensign, now-Cadet Crusher returns to save the *Enterprise* one last time. On a break from Starfleet Academy, Wesley visits his mother and former shipmates, only to discover the crew is becoming obsessed with an addictive video game. Only he and Lieutenant Robin Lefler (Ashley Judd) fail to become entranced by the game, mostly because they are too busy being enchanted with each other. When Wesley and Robin discover that the game has mind-controlling properties, the story takes on shades of *Invasion of the Body Snatchers*. Like "Darmok" (which, coincidentally, features Judd's only other appearance as Lefler), "The Game" had been in development for more than a year. Originally proposed by Susan Sackett and Fred Bronson, it languished until Brannon Braga took over and recast the story—originally a statement about addiction—into a spellbinding, horror-tinged alien-possession yarn. The episode remains one of Wheaton's favorites, not least because it allowed him to give Judd her first screen kiss. "The Game," first aired October 28, 1991, was the first new *Star Trek* episode broadcast after Roddenberry's death.

"Unification I and II"

Spock (Leonard Nimoy) secretly travels to Romulus to aid a band of dissidents who, in defiance of Romulan law, want to learn the way of logic and pursue

Leonard Nimoy guest starred as Spock in the furiously hyped "Unification" two-parter, commemorated on this Franklin Mint collectible plate.

Photo by Preston Hewis, East Bank Images

reunification with their ancient home world, Vulcan. Captain Picard, assigned by alarmed Starfleet brass to determine what Spock is doing, becomes entangled in a web of political intrigue also involving Sela (Denise Crosby), the half-Romulan daughter of Tasha Yar introduced in "Redemption." The "Unification" saga was conceived by Rick Berman and Michael Piller during the production of *Star Trek VI: The Undiscovered Country*, which debuted less than a month after the initial broadcast of these episodes. It was a clever cross-promotional gambit that drove *Next Gen*'s ratings to a new peak during the November sweeps period and helped build anticipation for the upcoming theatrical feature. It's not a bad story either, even though its first half (written by Jeri Taylor) is little better than a protracted preamble, focusing primarily on Picard's relationship with Spock's father, Sarek (the two shared a mind meld during Season Three's "Sarek"). Spock's presence is limited to the installment's final shot. Due to Nimoy's schedule, most of the footage for "Unification II" was actually shot prior to "Unification I." The second part, written by Michael Piller, offered a great deal more action than the first and included the scenes fans most wanted to see, as Spock interacts with Picard and with Data. (He tells Picard, "In your own way, you are as stubborn as another captain of the *Enterprise* I once knew.") During the story's climax, Data employs the Famous Spock Nerve Pinch. Dennis McCarthy's score for "Unification I" received an Emmy nomination, while "Unification II" earned an Emmy nomination for art direction. The "Unification" saga gave fans their first look at Romulus and their last look at both Sarek (Mark Lenard), who dies, and Sela, who was never heard from again. This installment also marked Nimoy's final appearance as Spock for eighteen years, until he returned in director J. J. Abrams's reboot *Star Trek* (2009).

"A Matter of Time"

A mysterious, eccentric time traveler, who claims to be a historian from the future, arrives to observe Captain Picard and his crew as they attempt to avert an ecological disaster on planet Penthara IV. But Professor Burlinghoff Rasmussen (Matt Frewer) may not be what he claims to be. This slight but diverting episode represented a refreshing change of pace after the string of heavy dramas that opened Season Five. Frewer (best remembered for his title role on the short-lived, offbeat sitcom *Max Headroom*) supplies the kind of oddball, seriocomic performance needed to sustain the story. But "A Matter of Time" might have played better with its originally intended guest star—self-described "Trekkie" Robin Williams. Unfortunately, even though screenwriter Rick Berman had tailored the teleplay for Williams, the actor had to decline the role due to conflicts with the shooting schedule for director Steven Spielberg's *Hook* (1991). Frewer's portrayal is charming but doesn't approach the heights of inspired lunacy Williams is capable of reaching. "A Matter of Time" and "Conundrum" shared an Emmy Award for special visual effects.

"New Ground"

Worf's troubled son, Alexander, comes to live with him on the *Enterprise* after Worf's adoptive Earth parents realize they are no longer up to the task of raising a Klingon child. Meanwhile, the test of an experimental new propulsion system goes haywire. A throwback to the kind of character-driven stories that dominated the show's previous two seasons, "New Ground" features outstanding performances from both Dorn and Brian Bonsall, who took over the role of Alexander with this episode. He would appear as the character in six more *Next Gen* installments. Written by Grant Rosenberg from a story by Sara and Stuart Charno, it's essentially a family drama, with the lonely, isolated Alexander acting out by stealing, lying, and generally making a nuisance of himself, all to Worf's horror. Helped by Dorn and Bonsall's finely tuned performances, it's a gripping episode that reaches a tense climax when the two disparate story lines finally merge.

"Hero Worship"

A young boy begins to mimic Data after the android rescues him from a starship disaster that killed his entire family. Like "New Ground," "Hero Worship" is a character-focused piece in which a member of the bridge crew unexpectedly finds himself caring for a child. Fortunately, also like "New Ground," "Hero Worship" is compellingly written and performed. Penned by Joe Menosky from a story by Hillary J. Bader, "Hero Worship" is heartwarming but never cloying. During production of this installment, word reached the soundstage that Gene Roddenberry had died. It fell to Patrick Stewart, who was directing, to inform the cast and crew. He was also forced to decide whether or not to suspend shooting for the rest of the day. Even though the news hit cast members hard (especially Sirtis, who had developed close ties with Gene and Majel Barrett-Roddenberry), Stewart elected to finish the day's work. He reasoned that it was what Roddenberry, the consummate producer, would do.

"Violations"

After telepathic alien researchers beam aboard the *Enterprise*, several crew members—including Counselor Troi, Commander Riker, and Dr. Crusher—suffer bizarre nightmares and slip into mysterious comas. Eventually it's revealed that all three have endured a form of telepathic rape. Written by Pamela Gray and Jeri Taylor, "Violations" was extrapolated from ideas left over from the previous season's "Night Terrors." Yet "Violations" proves far more rewarding than that Season Four snooze-fest. It's a harrowing, hard-hitting episode marked by strong performances (including stellar work from Frakes and, again, Sirtis) and directorial flash. Director Robert Wiemer used a variety of special lenses to achieve the distorted visuals in the arresting dream sequences. The installment also features a rare glimpse of Patrick Stewart in his seldom-used toupee (in Dr. Crusher's dreams, it seems, Captain Picard has hair). Coauthored by two women, "Violations" is the only *Next Generation* teleplay to deal overtly with the subject of rape. If nothing else, it serves as a long overdue corrective to the original *Trek* episode "The Enemy Within," which treated sexual assault as something to be laughed off. (See the original *Star Trek FAQ* for details.)

"The Masterpiece Society"

The *Enterprise* rushes to the aid of a reclusive civilization that practices genetic engineering (which is banned on Federation planets). Although at first reluctant to accept help, the colonists on Moab IV have no choice but to allow Captain Picard and his crew to assist them in averting an astronomical calamity that would destroy all life on their planet. However, interacting with the *Enterprise* crew has unintended effects on the colony, whose residents have existed (literally and figuratively) inside a protective bubble for two centuries. "The Masterpiece Society," written by Adam Belanoff and Michael Piller from a story by James Kahn and Belanoff, is sociological science fiction (not unlike the work of acclaimed author Ursula K. Le Guin) reinforced with interpersonal drama. It's a particularly strong episode for LeVar Burton, who seems genuinely insulted, even horrified, by the colonists' practice of screening out children with genetic defects (such as Geordi's congenital blindness). "The Masterpiece Society" was yet another story that had lingered on the shelf for more than a year. Five other writers tried to develop it before Piller finally finished the teleplay himself. Although Piller was pleased with the resulting episode, most other series insiders—including Berman, Taylor, and Ron Moore—have stated they consider it one of the year's weakest entries. If it is, then the worst of Season Five is still pretty good.

"Conundrum"

An alien vessel wipes the memories of the *Enterprise* crew, who awaken with no idea of their identities or ranks. Records indicate that the Federation is at war with a civilization known as the Lysians, and that the ship has been assigned to destroy the Lysian Central Command. "Conundrum" (credited to Barry Schkolnick but heavily rewritten, without credit, by Joe Menosky) was yet another Season Four leftover. The episode's action story line seems perfunctory; the installment's primary purpose is to enable the cast to explore new dimensions of their characters, freed by amnesia to express themselves and interact with one another in new and unexpected ways. For instance, Riker and Ro, instead of bickering, become lovers; Picard defers to Worf, who assumes command of the ship. The cast seems thrilled by the chance to monkey around with their familiar roles. Unfortunately, Erich Anderson's heavy-handed, one-note performance as an alien ringer hidden among the crew takes this installment down a notch. This episode shared an Emmy Award for special visual effects with "A Matter of Time."

"Power Play"

Responding to a distress signal, Deanna, Data, and O'Brien beam down to an M-Class moon of planet Mab-Bu VI. There they are taken over by noncorporeal entities that claim to be the immortal spirits of the crew of a Federation starship that crashed there two hundred years earlier. The possessed trio, led by Deanna, attempt to take control of the *Enterprise* but are beaten back to Ten-Forward, where a hostage crisis ensues. "Power Play," a rousing action yarn written by committee (five different writers share screenplay or story credit), emerges as one of the most exciting adventures of the season and features delightfully malevolent performances by Sirtis, Spiner, and Meaney as the brutal, ruthless alien villains. In a particularly twisted flourish, the prisoners in Ten-Forward include Keiko and baby Molly, who the possessed O'Brien offers up as potential targets for execution. Although it contains little in the way of character development or social commentary, "Power Play" remains the most pulse-quickening installment of the season.

"Ethics"

Worf is paralyzed in a shuttle bay accident. Dr. Crusher doesn't believe he can regain the use of his legs, but visiting Dr. Toby Russell (Caroline Kava) thinks she can restore the Klingon to full health with an experimental procedure. Crusher argues that Russell's research is too flimsy to support testing with a live patient, making the procedure too risky and ethically inappropriate. But Crusher acquiesces once the despondent Worf begins planning to commit ritual suicide. This rather static and dialogue-heavy episode, written by Ronald D. Moore from a story by Sara and Stuart Charno, was intended as a vehicle for Gates McFadden and as a think piece about the ethical complexities of medical research. Unfortunately, neither are served well by the scenario. Crusher comes off as oddly unsympathetic—more concerned with esoteric philosophical dilemmas than her patient's well-being. And the underlying ethical concerns are rendered moot by Worf's desire for death. Surely any experiment, no matter how ethically dodgy, is preferable to suicide. The teleplay also lacks believable tension. Few viewers seriously entertained the idea that the show's writers would kill Worf or leave him a paraplegic. As soon as Dr. Russell proposes the experimental procedure, all the drama goes out the airlock. The episode's few redeeming moments arise from Frakes, Sirtis, and Bonsall's touching performances as Worf's gravely concerned friends and family.

"The Outcast"

While helping locate a missing shuttlecraft belonging to the J'naii, an androgynous race, Riker falls in love with Soren (Melinda Culea), a J'naii with a secret, forbidden female sexual orientation. When the relationship is exposed, Soren is convicted of deviance and sentenced to sexual reprogramming, but Riker attempts to rescue her. After brushing gingerly against the subject of homo-sexuality in the previous season's "The Host," *Star Trek* finally takes up the cause of gay, lesbian, and transgender rights (albeit in coded form) with this story. Jeri Taylor's teleplay turns the issue on its head by introducing a society where heterosexual relations are considered perverse, but the script states its case clearly enough. "What makes you think you can dictate how people love each other?" Soren asks during her trial. Through various crew members' discomfort with the J'naii (especially Worf, who admits that they "bother him"), Taylor's teleplay suggests that homophobia (or its equivalent) survives into the twenty-fourth century, even among the elite of Starfleet. Frakes and Culea deliver fully committed performances, but the script offers little explanation why Riker becomes so deeply attached to Soren, in contrast to his superficial relationships with women of many species in numerous other episodes. Despite the earnest efforts of its creators, "The Outcast" generated angry letters from fans who believed the story didn't go far enough in support of the cause. Frakes later argued that the episode would have been more powerful if the androgynous Soren had been played by a male actor. Rick Berman told a reporter from the *San Jose Mercury News* that this was considered but ruled out because the sight of Frakes passionately kissing another man would have been "unpalatable" for many viewers. Still, "The Outcast" represented a bold step forward for *The Next Generation*, compared to its previous silence on the issue.

"Cause and Effect"

The *Enterprise* becomes trapped in a "temporal causality loop," reliving the same twenty-four-hour period over and over again. The cycle invariably ends with the destruction of the starship. Written by Brannon Braga, "Cause and Effect" is brilliant, high-concept science fiction. It's intriguing, imaginative, and well acted, but it presented unique challenges for director Jonathan Frakes. Due to the elliptical structure of the teleplay, the same events occur (with subtle varia-tions) five different times in the course of the story; much of the dialogue is repeated in each iteration. Frakes, working with cinematographer Marvin Rush, shot each pass through the cycle in a slightly different way, with lighting schemes and camera placements growing more off-kilter as the show progressed to sug-gest the continued warping of time and space. "Cause and Effect" also features a memorable cameo: Kelsey Grammer, star of *Cheers* and *Frasier*, briefly appears as the captain of the USS *Bozeman*, which has been trapped in the same time loop for a much longer period. Grammer, a die-hard *Trek* fan, also arranged for Patrick Stewart and Brent Spiner to make separate guest appearances on *Frasier*.

"The First Duty"

Captain Picard returns to Earth to deliver the commencement address at Starfleet Academy, only to discover Wesley Crusher is embroiled in a scandal surrounding a training accident that resulted in the death of a fellow cadet. Wesley must decide whether to follow his conscience and reveal all he knows about the incident, or to protect his classmates, whose careers may be destroyed if the truth comes out. "The First Duty," penned by Ronald D. Moore and Naren Shankar, ranks as the best Wesley episode ever made and boasts an assured, mature performance by Wil Wheaton. Patrick Stewart, who usually excelled when paired with Wheaton, provides heartfelt, empathetic support. The episode's moral quandary (to whom does Wesley owe the greater loyalty—Starfleet or his friends?) sparked fiery debate between Moore and Piller, with Piller ultimately enforcing his belief that viewers would lose respect for Wesley if the cadet did not eventually tell all. Robert Duncan McNeill, who would play Lieutenant Tom Paris on *Star Trek: Voyager*, guest stars as the reckless classmate actually responsible for the cadet's death. "The First Duty" also features the only *Next Generation* appearance of Boothby, the Starfleet Academy groundskeeper played by former *My Favorite Martian* star Ray Walston. The episode was enthusiastically received by critics and fans, as well as staff members, including Berman, Piller, Taylor, and Moore. It also helped freelancer Shankar win a staff position on the show. In 2007, *Entertainment Weekly* named "The First Duty" one of the series' ten best episodes. According to Piller, "The First Duty" has been shown at the U.S. Air Force Academy as part of cadets' honor code training.

"Cost of Living"

Lwaxana Troi returns with plans to marry a man she's never met, then forces herself into counseling Deanna is conducting to ease the ongoing familial tension between Worf and Alexander. Lwaxana decides somebody needs to teach the boy how to have fun—"Life's true gift is the capacity to enjoy enjoyment," she says—but she winds up learning more from Alexander than he does from her. Also, in a completely disposable subplot, the *Enterprise* becomes infested with metal-eating parasites. Although Lwaxana's mood remains wistful, "Cost of Living" is a far more lighthearted entry than Season Four's mournful "Half a Life." Still, Majel Barrett-Roddenberry's appearance as the lonely Lwaxana seems especially poignant because this installment was filmed barely four months after her husband's death. Written by Peter Allan Fields, "Cost of Living" features sharply written scenes for both Barrett-Roddenberry and Brian Bonsall, and utilizes Sirtis and Dorn to good advantage. (The episode's final shot, featuring Dorn up his neck in a mud bath, is a riot.) Barrett-Roddenberry would make only one more on-screen appearance on *Next Gen*, in the Season Seven episode "Dark Page." She continued to provide the voice of the *Enterprise* computer, however. At one point in "Cost of Living," when Lwaxana converses with the computer, Barrett-Roddenberry is talking to herself. This episode won a pair of Emmys, for costume design and makeup.

"The Perfect Mate"

The *Enterprise* is hosting a reconciliation between two rival planets when meddling Ferengi try to steal a priceless gift from one civilization's leader to the other. The prize turns out to be a strikingly beautiful empathic woman capable of transforming herself into her mate's ideal wife. Unfortunately, since her intended husband hasn't yet arrived, she becomes fixated on Captain Picard. Aside from the tantalizing chemistry between Patrick Stewart and Famke Janssen (who plays the title role in "The Perfect Mate"), this remains an unremarkable episode. However, Berman and Piller were so impressed with Janssen that they offered her the leading role of Jadzia Dax on *Star Trek: Deep Space Nine*. When she turned them down, actress Terry Farrell was hired instead. Stewart and Janssen were reunited in the *X-Men* films, which starred Stewart as Professor Xavier and Janssen as Jean Grey. "The Perfect Mate" was the first of five Season Five episodes to emerge from the writing staff's brainstorming sessions at Piller's home in Mexico.

"Imaginary Friend"

Elementary school girl Clara (Noley Thornton) believes her imaginary friend (Shay Astar) has magically come to life. But her playmate is actually an alien scout preparing the way for an invasion of the ship. As indicated by its convoluted writing credits (five writers share partial credit for the teleplay or story), "Imaginary Friend" took a long and torturous path to production, passing through several writers until Brannon Braga finally produced a usable version. It was hardly worth the effort. Not only is its plot transparent and toothless, but the episode is entirely reliant on a pair of juvenile guest performers, neither of whom were well cast. Braga dismissively nicknamed this installment "Romper Room: The Next Generation." Among the final six episodes of Season Five, this was the only one that did not originate from the writing staff's Mexican retreat.

"I Borg"

After rescuing a single injured Borg, Captain Picard hatches a plan to infect the alien with a computer virus capable of wiping out the entire Borg collective. But, isolated from the rest of the collective, the young Borg (who Geordi nicknames "Hugh") discovers individuality and begins to form friendships with members of the *Enterprise* crew. Soon, Geordi, Crusher, and others begin to question the morality of using a living being—even a Borg—as a weapon of mass destruction. Written by Rene Echevarria, "I Borg" annoyed some fans, who were displeased that the episode humanized and softened the previously monolithic, implacable Borg. In author Larry Nemecek's *Star Trek: The Next*

Generation Companion, Jeri Taylor admitted that after this episode "we can never treat the Borg the same way again." But the story remained perfectly in keeping with the series' Roddenberrian ideals. Picard's attempts to overcome his (fully understandable) hatred of the Borg echo Captain Kirk's efforts to break through his prejudice against Klingons in *Star Trek VI*. Provocatively written and power-fully performed—nearly everyone is terrific here, especially Stewart, Whoopi Goldberg, and guest star Jonathan Del Arco as Hugh—"I Borg" ranks among the season's finest installments. Piller named it his favorite episode of the year.

"The Next Phase"

While beaming back to the *Enterprise* during a humanitarian mission to aid a damaged Romulan vessel, Geordi and Ro are believed lost in a transporter accident. But they're not dead; instead, they have been "phased"—trapped on the ship, floating around like ghosts. The two learn that the Romulans have sabo-taged the *Enterprise*, but they cannot communicate with or even be seen by their shipmates. Written by Ron Moore, "The Next Phase" is another high-concept SF yarn, laced with philosophical ruminations on mortality—but much more fun than such a description would indicate. It's fast-paced and full of nifty visual effects, and includes razor-sharp performances by Burton and Forbes. Although originally conceived as a cost-saving "ship show," "The Next Phase" became one of the season's most expensive installments due to its extensive special effects. It also earned an Emmy nomination for sound mixing.

"The Inner Light"

According to Ronald D. Moore, the writing staff knew "The Inner Light" was special even before the teleplay was complete. "Each of us would have *killed* to write that script, because we knew how great it was going to be, that it was destined to become a part of *Star Trek* history," Moore reports in *Star Trek: The Next Generation 365*.

After an alien space probe knocks Picard unconscious, the captain experi-ences forty years in the life of Kamin, an everyman resident of the planet Kataan. As Kamin, Picard has a wife, children, friends, and a career as an artisan and public servant. He even learns to play the flute. Alas, he also discovers that Kataan is dying. "The Inner Light" rivals such masterworks as "Yesterday's Enterprise" and "The Best of Both Worlds" as the single greatest achievement in the history of the series, and ranks among the high points in the history of the entire franchise. Morgan Gendel and Peter Allan Fields's absorbing, emotion-ally resonant teleplay offered Patrick Stewart a showcase like no other. "It was a fascinating script, and it gave me the opportunity to explore a whole different kind of Picard," said Stewart (as quoted in *Patrick Stewart: The Unauthorized Biography*). The actor responded with his single finest *Star Trek* performance, a fully invested, richly nuanced, wistful portrait of the man Picard might have been. Stewart's work is all the more impressive since he delivers most of it under heavy (but excellent, Emmy-nominated) old-age makeup. Adding to the poignancy of the episode was the appearance of Stewart's son, Daniel, as Kamin's son, Batai. It was the first time the two Stewarts had performed together. The installment also benefits from Jay Chattaway's superb score, including a haunting flute melody. "The Inner Light" became the first television episode to win a Hugo Award since "The City on the Edge of Forever" from the classic *Trek* series in 1968. Numerous magazines, including *Entertainment Weekly*, and endless fan polls have selected "The Inner Light"

Patrick Stewart's son, Daniel (right), guest starred in "The Inner Light," one of the series' greatest episodes. It was the first time the two Stewarts performed together.

as one of the best episodes of *The Next Generation*. The installment's non sequitur title was borrowed by Gendel from a Beatles song by George Harrison. *Star Trek* does not get better than "The Inner Light." Neither does television.

"Time's Arrow"

Season Five's cliff-hanger finale sends Data, Picard, Riker, Geordi, Deanna, and Crusher back to late 1800s San Francisco to stop time-traveling alien predators, who are preying on the helpless humans of the era, and to try to avert Data's apparent death. (In the precredit teaser sequence, the android's severed head is uncovered in an archaeological dig dating back to the era.) During the adventure, our heroes cross paths with Samuel Clemens (alias Mark Twain, played by Jerry Hardin) and a much younger Guinan. "Time's Arrow," written by Joe Menosky and Michael Piller, is a relatively light entry in comparison to the series' last two season finales. But it's a delectable confection—quickly paced, funny, and relentlessly entertaining. The story allowed Piller to incorporate another idea that had been percolating for some time: Data trying to pass for human. In "Time's Arrow" the android explains that he is French, recalling Kirk's ruse that Spock is Chinese from "The City on the Edge of Forever." Like most of the series' season finales, "Time's Arrow" was lavishly produced, with extensive location shooting, sumptuous costumes, elaborate sets, and complex makeup (especially Hardin's transformation into Clemens). Goldberg contributes the episode's most memorable performance, offering a subtly different, more ebullient Guinan. (The character, as depicted here, dates from an era prior to her civilization's destruction at the hands of the Borg.) Like most of *Star Trek*'s time-travel stories, "Time's Arrow" scores a bull's-eye.

In its fifth season, *Star Trek: The Next Generation*—a show many believed would never work—became an unstoppable force. Due to Paramount Pictures' year-long ballyhoo surrounding the twenty-fifth anniversary of the franchise, Leonard Nimoy's appearance in the much-anticipated "Unification" epic, the commercial and critical success of *Star Trek VI: The Undiscovered Country*, and the many tributes and general outpouring of goodwill that followed the death of Gene Roddenberry, *The Next Generation* (and *Trek* in general) soared to the apex of its popularity and cultural impact. Paramount even entered a *Star Trek* float, featuring a forty-five-foot replica of the *Enterprise-D*, in the January 1992 Tournament of Roses Parade. *Star Trek* was everywhere; resistance was futile.

Even though, since it was a syndicated program, the series aired on different days and times in different markets, sometimes out of prime time, *Next Gen* was now drawing an average of nearly twelve million viewers per episode, and it remained the most popular program on television with viewers aged eighteen to thirty-four, a highly desirable and difficult-to-reach demographic. The "Unification" saga earned the series' highest Nielsen ratings so far, attracting nearly twenty million viewers. As a result, Paramount was able to sell a thirty-second commercial for up to $150,000. The studio was clearing more than $30 million per year in profit. In every way, the series had exceeded its creators' wildest aspirations.

And yet Paramount was already planning to cancel it. (See Chapter 24.)

22

New Life and New Civilizations

The Next Generation of *Star Trek* Aliens

One of the most attractive aspects of *Star Trek* is that it imagines a galaxy teeming with life and depicts weekly encounters with extraterrestrial civilizations—some friendly, others hostile. The classic series introduced audiences to many allies and enemies of the United Federation of Planets—the coolly logical Vulcans and their belligerent cousins the Romulans, along with the jingoistic Klingons, among many other species. Even though many of these aliens—particularly the Vulcans and Klingons—were cherished by fans, at first creator Gene Roddenberry wanted to write them out of *The Next Generation*. Since human exploration was expanding into new corners of the galaxy, Roddenberry reasoned, the crew of the *Enterprise-D* should meet different species than those already featured on the original program. Like many of Roddenberry's early mandates, however, this prohibition was enforced only intermittently. Vulcans played no significant role in *The Next Generation*, and other original *Trek* aliens (such as the Orions, Andorians, Tellarites, and Tholians) were barely even mentioned. However, the Klingons and Romulans returned to participate in many story arcs. In addition, writers dreamed up a myriad of new civilizations, including the apparently omnipotent Q, the implacable Borg, the venal Ferengi, the ruthless Cardassians, and the deeply spiritual Bajorans, all of which became important components in the continuously expanding mythology of the *Star Trek* universe.

Klingons

The overall quality of *The Next Generation*'s teleplays, and the show's ratings, surged when writers began to flesh out the character of Lieutenant Worf and explore the Klingon culture. During its first two seasons, the series offered only three Klingon-centric episodes ("Heart of Glory" in Season One, and "A Matter of Honor" and "The Emissary" in Season Two). Throughout the series' final five seasons, the Klingons were featured much more prominently, as writers deftly crafted colorful, tension-rich scenarios stemming from political upheavals within the Klingon Empire and Worf's conflicted loyalties as both a Klingon warrior and a Starfleet officer. Along the way, the Klingon species was radically redefined.

The *Next Generation* Klingons bore little resemblance to their original *Trek* forebears. As the first *Star Trek FAQ* details, the twenty-third-century Klingons not only looked strikingly different (they were played by actors with bronzed skin and Fu Manchu mustaches, without the prominent forehead and nose prosthetics seen in later movies and TV series), but they behaved quite differently, as well. On the original program, Klingons were usually depicted as amoral and unsympathetic, merciless oppressors who murdered unarmed hostages and stabbed their adversaries in the back. But *Next Generation* writers, including Ronald D. Moore, Rene Echevarria, and Burton Armus, reimagined the Klingons, borrowing from Japanese, Norse, and other cultures and recasting them as a warrior civilization with a deeply ingrained honor code similar to the *bushido* way of the samurai, a tribal society organized into distinct "houses" that compete for political influence, and a deeply spiritual culture. These Klingons wrote operas and built baroque temples and palaces. They worshipped Kahless, founder of the Klingon Empire, and believed that if they died honorably, they would join their spiritual leader in the Valhalla-like Sto-Vo-Kor. They valued courage and loyalty and loathed deceit and betrayal.

The differences between these two generations of Klingons were so glaring and profound that writers eventually felt compelled to explain them away. The *Next Generation* episode "Rightful Heir," along with several installments of *Deep Space Nine* and *Enterprise*, revealed the backstory piece by piece: During the twenty-second and twenty-third centuries, it seems, Klingon culture turned its back on traditional beliefs, adopted a totalitarian government, and even pursued a misguided genetic engineering program that accidentally resulted in Klingons with smooth foreheads and humanlike features. In any case, however, most fans loved the New Look Klingons, and especially Lieutenant Worf, who emerged as one of the franchise's most popular characters. Klingon-based episodes such as "Sins of the Father," "Reunion," "Redemption, Parts I and II," "Birthright, Parts I and II," and "Rightful Heir" thrilled fans and scored high Nielsen ratings.

Romulans

By turning the Klingons into allies, *Star Trek* sacrificed its most popular and daunting villains. Throughout the show's first season, writers struggled to create a worthy adversary to replace them. In desperation, Roddenberry approved reviving classic *Trek*'s other best-known antagonists, the Romulans, who returned in the Season One finale "The Neutral Zone." While the Klingons were almost completely reimagined for *The Next Generation*, the Romulans were presented in the same light as their twenty-third-century predecessors—as cagey, merciless conquerors bent on crushing the Federation. Only their appearance was modified (slightly) by the introduction of a thickened brow that physically differentiated Romulans from Vulcans.

Many story lines, such as "Redemption, Parts I and II," revolved around Romulan attempts to shatter the alliance between the Federation and the Klingons and shift the balance of power in the galaxy. It was also revealed (in episodes including "The Enemy") that the Romulans and Klingons were long-standing and bitter rivals. The two-part "Unification" story during Season Five marked a turning point, revealing that at least some Romulans had grown weary of military rule, these dissidents wanted to learn the way of logic and to pursue reunification with Vulcan. This development made the Romulan civilization seem less monolithic and more believable, but the Romulans remained a serious threat throughout the remainder of the series, and later on *Deep Space Nine* and in *Trek* movies, including *Nemesis* (2002) and *Star Trek* (2009).

The Ferengi, introduced in "The Last Outpost," were originally envisioned as *The Next Generation*'s answer to the Klingons. Pictured are, left to right, original Ferengi Mordoc (Jack Dengel), Kayron (Tracey Walter), and Letek (Armin Shimerman).

Ferengi

Originally, the Ferengi were envisioned as major recurring adversaries—the *Next Generation*'s replacement for the Klingons. But the stubby, bulbous-headed, jug-eared aliens, whose entire society was driven by greed, were simply too comical to be taken seriously. After two early episodes ("The Last Outpost" and "The Battle"), the Ferengi vanished for the rest of the first season and most of the second (briefly appearing in "Peak Performance") before reemerging in Season Three, transformed from serious threats into comedic irritants in episodes such as "The Price," "Captain's Holiday," and "Ménage a Troi." Had audiences accepted the Ferengi as credible villains, the Romulans' presence in the series likely would have been dramatically reduced, if not eliminated entirely. In all, Ferengi appeared in fifteen *Next Gen* episodes, Romulans in twenty-one.

Armin Shimerman, who played one of the original Ferengi in "The Last Outpost," went on to portray Ferengi barkeep Quark on *Deep Space Nine*. The mythology associated with the Ferengi culture was largely developed on *DS9* rather than *Next Gen*. The information about Ferengi society revealed in their *Next Generation* appearances was extremely unflattering: They pursued financial profit to the exclusion of all other concerns and were (by human standards) extremely unethical. They considered it praiseworthy to trick or cheat someone and would acquiesce to fair deals only when necessary. They were cowardly. Ferengi considered females inferior, and kept their wives at home, servile and naked. Ferengi women were expected to pre-chew food for male offspring and sometimes their husbands and to caress their mate's giant ear lobes, which were erogenous zones. In short, by the time *Deep Space Nine* appeared, they were a civilization in dire need of a rewrite. Eventually, on that series, characters such as Quark, his brother Rom, mother Ishka, and nephew Nog (the first Ferengi to join Starfleet) helped bring some dignity to the species.

The Q

The first major new species invented for *Next Gen* was the apparently omnipotent and immortal Q, although at first it wasn't clear that they comprised an entire civilization. In the beginning, there was simply Q (John de Lancie), the godlike alien who places Captain Picard and his senior staff on trial for the alleged crimes of humanity in the series pilot "Encounter at Farpoint." In the pilot and in his next two appearances ("Hide and Q" and "Q Who"), Q was presented as purely menacing, but he soon evolved into something more ambiguous—a trickster figure who threatened the *Enterprise* mainly through careless use of his awesome powers and indifference to human suffering. Although he claimed to despise human beings, Q clearly harbored a secret, if tenuous, affection for them—or at least for select members of the species. Q saved the captain's life (or at least taught Picard the true value of his existence) in Season Six's "Tapestry" and helped humanity avert destruction in the series finale "All Good Things . . ." Even at his best, however, Q was, as Picard once warned, "devious and amoral and unreliable and irresponsible and definitely not to be trusted." However, he was also wickedly funny, brimming with caustic observations about human society and insults for Picard and his crew (especially Worf). Viewers loved watching him, de Lancie loved playing him, and writers loved writing him. A title containing a "Q" pun became a virtual guarantee of a good episode—and of high ratings.

Q turned up in one or two episodes every year except for Season Five, in which he failed to appear. Although Q told Picard at the conclusion of "All Good Things . . ." that the two might meet again, the character was never utilized in any of the *Next Gen* movies. However, he was featured in the *DS9* installment "Q-Less," in three *Voyager* adventures, as well as four video games, at least fifteen novels, dozens of comic book stories, and untold reams of fan fiction. Although

At first, the puckish, omnipotent Q seemed to be one of a kind, but in "Deja Q," another member of the Continuum played by Corbin Bernsen (right) finally appeared.

Q often mentioned that he was a member of a civilization known as the Q Continuum, it took a while for fans to meet another member of his species. That finally happened when Corbin Bernsen appeared as another Q in the Season Three episode "Deja Q." The Season Six installment "True Q" introduced a young Earth woman who is revealed to be a female Q. The inner workings of the Continuum were never revealed, but several other members of the species were featured on *Voyager*. "Colonel Q" and a female Q played by Suzie ("K'Ehleyr") Plakson in "The Q and the Grey"; Q's son Q Junior (in "The Q and the Grey" and "Q2"); and a human named Quinn who is a former Q (in "Death Wish"). However, the original remains the best. Accept no substitutes.

The Borg

The Next Generation's search for a worthy adversary ended with the Season Two episode "Q Who," in which Q whisked the *Enterprise* to a distant corner of the galaxy dominated by the apparently unstoppable cybernetic, hive-minded Borg. Unlike the Klingons and Romulans, the Borg could not be reasoned with, appeased, tricked, or intimidated. They possessed massively superior weapons and technology, and assimilated other civilizations with a pitiless, unbending sense of purpose. They were, in short, utterly terrifying—exactly the kind of bloodcurdling foe *Next Gen* lacked, and arguably the most intimidating villain in all of *Trek* mythology. Fans loved them, but the Borg were so powerful that they made only five more appearances in the show's remaining five seasons, primarily because writers struggled to find believable ways for Captain Picard to defeat

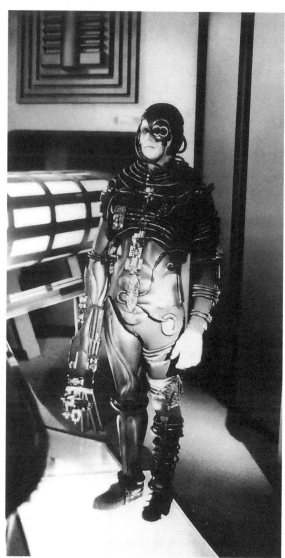

The Next Generation's quest for a worthy adversary ended with the Season Two adventure "Deja Q," which introduced the Borg.

them. In "Q Who," Q simply blinks the *Enterprise* to safety when the ship's destruction seems imminent. The Borg returned with a vengeance in the Season Three cliff-hanger "The Best of Both Worlds," in which Picard was assimilated into, but later rescued from, the Borg Collective. In that adventure, Picard's connection to the Borg proves the Collective's undoing.

The Borg were created for "Q Who" by writer-producer Maurice Hurley, with input from Roddenberry and Rick Berman, and were developed in later episodes by writers Michael Piller, Rene Echevarria, and Ronald D. Moore. Originally, Hurley envisioned the Borg as a race of insectoids, but when the makeup was deemed too expensive, they were changed to cybernetic beings. Many basic "facts" about the Collective remained a mystery. The exact origin of the Borg was never revealed, nor was it clear which of the hundreds of civilizations the Collective had assimilated represented its original, organic race (assuming one existed). During their first three appearances, the Borg were presented as more machinelike than truly living, a nightmarish phalanx of emotionless, robotic invaders.

The Borg were softened with the Season Five episode "I Borg," in which a lone, injured drone captured by an *Enterprise* away team developed a sense of individuality and befriended Geordi. This story led directly to the events of the Season Six cliff-hanger "Descent, Parts I and II" (in which disaffected Borg leave the Collective and rally behind Data's android brother, Lore), and indirectly to the creation of Seven of Nine, the rehumanized Borg drone played by Jeri Taylor on *Star Trek: Voyager*. Although they were seldom employed on *Next Gen*, the Borg returned in the movie *Star Trek: First Contact* (1996) and as recurring adversaries on *Voyager*, where they made twenty-one appearances. The Borg were also featured in the clever (and scary) *Enterprise* episode "Regeneration." Visitors to the *Star Trek: The Experience* attraction at the Las Vegas Hilton take part in a mock battle with the Borg.

Cardassians

They were popular and imposing, but the Borg were too formidable to serve as regularly featured antagonists, at least in the opinion of the *Next Generation* writing staff (the *Voyager* team apparently held a different opinion). So writer-producer Jeri Taylor invented the Cardassians, who debuted in the fourth season *Next Gen* episode "The Wounded." The Cardassians arrived complete with a backstory: Apparently the Federation had waged a decades-long border war with them but had recently negotiated a peace treaty. Over the course of the final two and a half seasons of *The Next Generation*, Captain Picard and his team would become embroiled in a series of disputes with the Cardassians, who grew increasingly important within the mythology of the franchise, appearing in nine *Next Gen* episodes. In the hair-raising sixth-season adventure "Chain of Command, Parts I and II," Picard was captured and tortured by the Cardassians. Later, they served as one of the primary antagonists on *Deep Space Nine*, figuring in 71 of the series' 173 episodes.

Although a great deal of the franchise's elaborate Cardassian mythology derives from *DS9*, the basics were established on *Next Gen*, in episodes such as "Chain of Command," "Journey's End," and "Preemptive Strike." The Cardassians were vaguely reptilian in appearance, with a distinctive spoon-shaped indentation in the middle of their foreheads. They were an intensely xenophobic species, convinced of their own racial superiority and suspicious of outsiders, with a militaristic culture at least as tightly wound as that of the Romulans. Their weapons and technology were on par with those of Starfleet, but the Cardassians deployed them with utter disregard for the lives of those beings they considered inferior.

In the distant past, Cardassia boasted an enlightened culture, with an emphasis on religion, literature, and architecture, but the planet's natural resources could not sustain its population, leading to chaos and famine. A dictatorship took hold and launched a war of conquest to feed the Cardassian populace. The Cardassians' cultural achievements crumbled over the centuries as resources were drained from those pursuits to develop the military and fund a totalitarian government. Eventually the Cardassians came to rule a large swath of the galaxy and brutally oppressed the civilizations they conquered, committing atrocities on a planetary scale. They pursued victory at any cost and had no compunction about using torture, genetic engineering, biological weapons, or other tactics banned by interstellar law. In a 1997 AOL chat, writer Ronald D.

Moore admitted that Nazi Germany was one of the models the writing staff used for the Cardassians.

Bajorans

One of the peoples subjugated by the Cardassians were the Bajorans, one of the oldest and most sophisticated cultures in the Alpha Quadrant of the galaxy. The Cardassians withdrew from Bajor as part of their treaty with the Federation, but several Bajoran colonies remained in Cardassian territory or in a demilitarized buffer zone between Federation and Cardassian space. Bajoran insurgents known as the Maquis (named for the French resistance that fought the Nazis in World War II) battled both the Cardassians and the Federation in the demilitarized zone. Most of this was established by writer-producer Michael Piller in "Ensign Ro," which simultaneously introduced both the Bajoran people and the episode's title officer, one of *The Next Generation*'s most popular recurring characters, played by Michelle Forbes. At first, the popularity of the Bajorans was linked to that of Ro, but eventually, as further episodes revealed more about Bajor and its culture (Bajorans were featured in twelve episodes), the Bajorans emerged as one of the most sympathetic and fascinating alien civilizations ever imagined for *Star Trek*, and the only one since the Vulcans to be so fully fleshed out that wasn't (at some point) an enemy.

The Bajorans were also one of the most human-looking *Trek* species, identifiable by ridges at the bridge of the nose and by their distinctive dangling earrings, a symbol of Bajoran religious faith. Makeup supervisor Michael Westmore went light on the Bajoran makeup at the behest of executive producer Rick Berman. In a DVD interview, Westmore recounts that Berman told him, "We've hired a pretty girl [Forbes] and I want to keep her that way." The Cardassian-Bajoran conflict became an important backdrop for both *Deep Space Nine* and *Voyager*.

Many fans saw the Bajorans as metaphoric Jews, presented in opposition to the Nazi-like Cardassians, but it was possible to draw parallels between the Bajorans and numerous other disenfranchised peoples, such as the Palestinians, Kurds, or Native Americans. "While these parallels do enter our discussions and sometimes are more overt than others, we don't really try to make Bajor a direct analogy to any specific contemporary country or people," Moore explained in that 1997 AOL chat. "Blending the experiences of many Earth peoples and races into our storytelling allows us to comment on these subjects without advocating a particular political point of view, while at the same time allowing us to view the topics in a different light without the baggage of contemporary politics."

Betazoids

Even though the *Enterprise* boasted a half-Betazoid member of its senior staff in Counselor Deanna Troi, and despite the fact that Deanna's fully Betazoid mother, Lwaxana, often visited the ship, the Betazoid culture remained surprisingly unexplored. In the pilot episode, "Encounter at Farpoint," viewers learned that residents of Betazed were fully telepathic (as a half-Betazoid, Deanna's abilities are merely empathic—she can sense emotions but cannot read minds). Later episodes revealed that Betazoid philosophy was epicurean and that their marriages took place in the nude, but little was divulged beyond these basic points. Only ten *Next Gen* episodes featured appearances by Betazoids other than Deanna (and eight of those were Lwaxana stories). The species was employed sparingly on subsequent series, appearing just three times on *DS9*, eight times on *Voyager*, and once on *Enterprise*.

El-Aurians

This was the incredibly long-lived species of which Guinan was a member. El-Aurians were physically indistinguishable from humans and extremely tight-lipped about their origins. In "Q Who," viewers learned that the once-thriving El-Aurian civilization was nearly wiped out by the Borg. Guinan was one of the few members of her race left alive, scattered across the galaxy. Guinan also once said that her people were a civilization of "listeners." Often, the audience was left with the impression that there was much more to know about Guinan and her people than would ever be revealed—and that was just what writers and producers wanted. Roddenberry and Berman desired to create an aura of mystery and power around Guinan, and succeeded masterfully. At times (as in "Q Who" and "Deja Q"), even Q seemed intimidated by her. Dr. Soran, the villain from *Star Trek Generations* played by Malcolm McDowell, was also an El-Aurian.

Others

The preceding assortment of *Next Generation* aliens remains far from complete. Over the course of 176 episodes and four feature films, scores of new species were introduced, although few were developed to any meaningful extent. Some other notable *Next Gen* extraterrestrials include:

- **Benzites**—Bald, blue-skinned aliens who required an inhaler to breathe human air. They prized accuracy and attention to detail and followed regulations scrupulously. In the Season One episode "Coming of Age," Wesley Crusher befriended a Benzite named Mordock. A different Benzite (played by the same actor) appeared in the Season Two installment "A Matter of Honor."
- **Bolians**—Another bald, blue-skinned race, with a distinctive seam running vertically down the middle of their face. The Bolians were generally used as background characters. The highest-profile Bolian on *Next Gen* was Mot, the *Enterprise* barber. The species was named after *Next Gen* director Cliff Bole.
- **Neural Parasites**—The nameless race of insectoid parasites that took over the bodies of several Starfleet Admirals and attempted to seize control of the Federation in the Season One episode "Conspiracy." Although they

appeared only once, they left an indelible impression as one of *Next Gen*'s most dangerous—and ickiest—adversaries.

- **The Crystalline Entity**—The giant, snowflake-like alien that destroyed Data's home world and threatened the *Enterprise* in "Datalore" and "Silicon Avatar." Although it was more a monster than a species, presumably the Entity could not have been one of a kind.
- **The aliens from "Galaxy's Child" and "Tin Man"**—Giant, spacefaring creatures (the former looks like an enormous pierogi, the latter like a giant peach pit) who travel the vast expanse of interstellar space without need of starcraft.
- **Nausicaans**—Surly, long-haired, snaggle-toothed humanoids, one of whom stabbed young Ensign Jean-Luc Picard through the heart during a bar fight, resulting in the future *Enterprise* captain's dependence on an artificial heart. They were featured in just two *Next Gen* installments ("Tapestry" and "Gambit, Part I"), but also turned up on *DS9* and *Enterprise*.
- **Tamarians**—Bald, leathery humanoids with ridged foreheads and piggish noses. A reclusive civilization that communicated entirely through the use of metaphors drawn from their unique cultural mythology. Captain Picard established friendly relations with the Tamarians under trying circumstances in the episode "Darmok."
- **Remans**—The Nosferatu-like slave race that inhabited the Romulan vassal state Remus. The Remans were central villains in *Star Trek Nemesis* (2002).

23

Prime Directives

Social Commentary and Recurring Themes on *The Next Generation*

From the beginning, social commentary was Gene Roddenberry's prime directive. The Great Bird of the Galaxy created *Star Trek* after being frustrated by network censors in his attempts to express his progressive, humanist philosophy through his first series, the short-lived peacetime military drama *The Lieutenant* (1963–64). He created *Star Trek* to address political and social issues under the cover of fantasy, as Jonathan Swift had done with *Gulliver's Travels*. "Censorship was so bad that if he could take things and switch them around and maybe paint somebody green and perhaps put weird outfits on them and so forth, he could get some of his ideas across," said Majel Barrett-Roddenberry, in an interview featured on the *Star Trek: The Motion Picture* DVD. "He got lots of ideas through and that's how *Star Trek* was born."

Although Roddenberry was only fully in control of *The Next Generation* for two seasons, and his power dwindled rapidly in later years, the impulse to speak out on moral and ethical issues remained. It was an inextricable part of the franchise's DNA. Executive producer Michael Piller, in an interview included on the *Star Trek: Insurrection* DVD, says that Roddenberry "taught me the fundamentals of *Star Trek*," which included "an optimistic view of the future" and stories "about moral and ethical dilemmas, which I felt was the heart of Roddenberry's philosophy for *Star Trek*. . . . Great heroes are people who respond to those moral and ethical challenges and triumph." Not only did *Next Gen* continue to tackle such topics, but many of Roddenberry's overarching concerns, explored in numerous classic *Trek* episodes, returned as recurring themes on the sequel series. (For a detailed discussion of recurring themes in the original program, see Chapters 31 through 34 of the first *Star Trek FAQ*.)

The Human Touch

Above all else, *Star Trek* was a reflection of Roddenberry's guiding conviction that the human race was continually improving, advancing slowly but inexorably toward perfection. This was the core of his optimistic vision of the future, more important (to Roddenberry, at least) than fantastic technologies such as warp drive and the transporter. The original program established his vision of a future society free of ancient evils such as greed, famine, and racism, and even suggested (in episodes such as "Arena") that humans might someday develop far greater, nearly divine, abilities. *The Next Generation* continued along this path. Roddenberry insisted (to the consternation of his writing staff) that the twenty-fourth-century *Enterprise* crew be even more agreeable and self-actualized—in other words, more perfected—than their twenty-third-century counterparts; and in "Where No One Has Gone Before" and "Journey's End," Wesley Crusher evidenced the godlike ability to warp space and time through the power of his mind. Captain Picard learned a similar skill during his visit to the Ba'ku planet in *Star Trek: Insurrection.* Thankfully, however, *The Next Generation* usually furthered Roddenberry's optimistic humanism in more subtle ways. Toward this end, two important story threads were woven through the *Next Gen* narrative during its seven seasons—Data's quest to become more human and Q's fascination with our species.

The mere fact that a being like Data, superior to homo sapiens in most respects, would desire to become human made a powerful statement in and of itself. Data's ongoing struggle to grasp the subtleties of human interaction and learn more about concepts like love, courage, and humor provided the platform for the series to celebrate those elusive qualities that comprise the better parts of our nature. His interest in human art forms—classical music, painting, drama,

Data is left to the tender mercies of the Borg in *Star Trek: First Contact.* His quest to become more human revealed the better parts of human nature, while the Borg lacked those qualities that, in Roddenberry's view, make our species special: personal initiative, compassion, and imagination.

and literature—suggested that the creative impulse was another priceless human virtue; Data attempted to validate his growing humanity by creating his own works of art and literature. In "The Offspring," Data's android "daughter," Lal, asks him why he struggles to emulate humans even though he can never become truly human. "We must strive to be more than we are, Lal," Data explains. "It does not matter that we will never reach our ultimate goal. The effort yields its own rewards." This exchange suggests that the android Data possesses a human soul, since in the Roddenberrian understanding of our species the desire for self-improvement is *the* signature trait of humankind.

Although Q claims to despise human beings, the omnipotent alien's ongoing interest in our species belies his true feelings. At the very least, he is fascinated with them, or else he wouldn't spend so much time in their company; Q is not easily amused. Over time, his behavior toward human beings became more overtly supportive. He saved Captain Picard's life in "Tapestry," and in "All Good Things . . ." he helped Picard prevent humanity from being obliterated. The Data and Q metanarratives crossed, memorably, in the episode "Deja Q," in which Q takes refuge on the *Enterprise* after losing his powers. Data, ironically, is assigned to help Q make the adjustment to human life. The android does his best to explain human nature—"The human race has an enduring desire for knowledge and for new opportunities to improve itself," he says—and models the human values of compassion and self-sacrifice when he risks his life to save Q. "There are creatures in the universe who would consider you the ultimate achievement, android. No feelings, no emotion, no pain. And yet you covet those qualities of humanity," Q marvels. "If it means anything to you, you're a better human than I." Nevertheless, Q later tries to sacrifice his own life to save the *Enterprise*, and after regaining his powers uses them to help avert the destruction of a populated planet. "Perhaps there is a residue of humanity in Q after all," Picard muses.

In the original *Star Trek FAQ*, I wrote that Roddenberry's humanism finds *some* form of expression in every installment of the classic series. The same is true of *The Next Generation*. Many episodes—such as "The Child," "Where Silence Has Lease," "A Matter of Honor," and "Suddenly Human," among others —brought Captain Picard or members of his crew into contact with extraterrestrials who were puzzled or intrigued by humankind. These aliens always left favorably impressed. *The Next Generation* also considered the nature of humanity by introducing its opposite—the Borg. Especially in their first three appearances, in which they were portrayed as a monolithic menace, the Borg were not merely inhuman but antihuman. They had no sense of individuality and thus no independent will. They were capable only of consuming, not of creating. This is what made them so frightening, and what made Captain Picard's assimilation (in "The Best of Both Worlds") so horrifying. The qualities the Borg lack are also those that, at least according to *Star Trek*, make us truly human: personal initiative, compassion, and imagination.

Diversity and Fraternity

Perhaps the most celebrated theme of classic *Trek* was its steadfast opposition to racism. When *Star Trek* premiered, it was still illegal for blacks and whites to marry in many states, and some Southern schools were not yet desegregated. Yet Roddenberry put his vision of a postracial future center stage by placing an African American woman and an Asian man on the bridge of his starship, and produced episodes such as "Let That Be Your Last Battlefield" that emphatically opposed segregation and bigotry. The show's commitment to interracial harmony was expressed most eloquently in the Vulcan concept of IDIC (Infinite Diversity in Infinite Combinations), introduced in "Is There in Truth No Beauty?"

The Next Generation proudly carried forward the franchise's commitment to diversity and expanded it to minorities not directly addressed on the original show, such as differently abled persons (represented by blind engineer Geordi La Forge) and Native Americans (in "Journey's End" and later on *Star Trek: Voyager*). Although *Star Trek* has been timid regarding the full inclusion of all sexual orientations (no *Trek* movie or TV show has yet introduced a gay or lesbian Starfleet officer), *Next Gen* made a coded argument for LGBT equality in "The Outcast." This episode featured a lengthy speech in which Soren, a character with a female sexual orientation born into an androgynous species, argued forcefully for the acceptance of persons regardless of their sexuality. "I have had those feelings, those longings, all of my life," Soren explains. "It is not unnatural. I am not sick because I feel this way. I do not need to be helped. I do not need to be cured. What I need, and what all of those who are like me need, is your understanding and your compassion. . . . What right do you have to punish us? What right do you have to change us? What makes you think you can dictate how people love each other?"

The Next Generation also employed *Star Trek* mythology to underscore the franchise's commitment to diversity in metaphoric terms. By introducing the Federation-Klingon alliance, for instance, the series modeled the values of reconciliation and of overcoming prejudice. Although the relationship was sometimes unsteady, humans and Klingons—after decades of war and bitter rivalry—came to understand one another and to recognize both were stronger together than apart. This was a remarkable political statement, especially considering that on the original *Trek* the Klingons functioned as allegorical surrogates for the Soviet Union, while the Federation represented the United States, and that *The Next Generation* premiered in 1987, four years before the dismantling of the Berlin Wall. As the series progressed, the Federation continually reached out in friendship to even its most bitter rivals. In "Unification, Parts I and II," Spock traveled to Romulus to aid dissidents who wanted to reunify with Vulcan—a move that, it was hoped, might lead to normalized relations between the Federation and the Romulan Empire. Captain Picard's crew even befriended a Borg drone, nicknamed Hugh, in "I Borg," proving that, separated from the Collective, even Borg drones can discover individuality—and humanity.

The most overt expression of this recurring theme was the Season Six adventure "The Chase," in which Captain Picard, along with rival Klingon, Cardassian, and Romulan factions, uncovers an ancient secret—that most of the major civilizations in the galaxy stem from a common ancestor. Early drafts of Joe Menosky and Ronald D. Moore's teleplay also featured the Ferengi and Vulcans. But even without involving those civilizations directly, the episode's message was clear: We are all brothers. The classic series had consistently prescribed fraternity as the antidote to fear and hatred. That's why director Jonathan Frakes described the episode as "Roddenberry-esque."

Golden Years

Roddenberry was forty-three years old when he dreamed up the original *Star Trek*. He created *The Next Generation* at age sixty-six. Perhaps inevitably, aging emerged as another central concern of the sequel series. In numerous episodes, including "Too Short a Season," "The Schizoid Man," "The Survivors," "Brothers," and "Sarek," characters struggled with diminished capacity or grappled with end-of-life issues. Consistently in these stories, older characters are treated with dignity and honor, and shown continuing to make important contributions, often despite increasing physical and even mental infirmities. In "Sarek," for instance, the 202-year-old Vulcan diplomat negotiates a vital treaty between the Federation and the reclusive Legarans, despite a disorder that causes older Vulcans to lose control of their emotions. Executive producer Michael Piller later revealed that "Sarek" was written as a veiled tribute to the increasingly ill Roddenberry.

The single most powerful story on the subject of aging was "Half a Life," in which Lwaxana Troi falls in love with Timicin, a scientist from Kaelon II, only to learn that Timicin is about to turn sixty, the age at which in Kaelon society citizens commit ritual suicide. Using another common *Next Gen* ploy, the teleplay makes its thematic point by demonstrating the inverse proposition—a society where the elderly are not merely marginalized but eliminated. "He's just going to die, and for no good reason," Lwaxana sobs to Deanna. "Because his society has decided that he's too old, so they just dispose of him, as though his life no longer had any value or meaning." Later, Lwaxana argues eloquently that younger people have a responsibility to care for the elderly.

The Next Generation also demonstrated its commitment to older persons by placing one in command of the *Enterprise*. This was a controversial move. At first, Paramount Pictures executives were skeptical about hiring Patrick Stewart as the captain of the *Enterprise*, largely because he was bald, and what hair he had was gray. Stewart was forty-seven—but looked even older—when *The Next Generation* debuted, nine years senior to the next-eldest cast members, Brent Spiner and Gates McFadden. Episodes such as "Future Imperfect," "The Inner

Light," and "All Good Things . . ." featured older versions of Captain Picard or other members of the crew. During her tenure as executive producer, Jeri Taylor (who was fifty-four when she took the reins of the program) insisted on hiring more background actors who appeared to be older than thirty. All of this was remarkable. As the original *Trek* cast increased in years, aging had also emerged as a theme in the *Star Trek* movies, beginning with *The Wrath of Khan* and continuing through *The Undiscovered Country*. But, in general, this remained an unusual topic for science fiction films and TV series, which normally were the province of dashing young men and nubile starlets. That *Star Trek* stood apart from this prevailing ageism can also be seen as another expression of the franchise's commitment to diversity.

Family Values

In addition to aging, *The Next Generation* took up another topic seldom addressed in sci-fi movies and TV shows—parenting. This aspect of the series also began with Roddenberry, who decreed that in the twenty-fourth century, Starfleet officers would travel though space with their wives and children. Although some fans never warmed to this concept, Roddenberry believed it introduced rich new story possibilities—and eventually he was proven correct, although not through the means he imagined.

At first, the vehicle for these family drama story lines was supposed to be Dr. Beverly Crusher and her teenage son, Wesley. But Wesley was portrayed as a brainiac superkid who seldom seemed to need any parenting at all, and Beverly was exiled from the series for the duration of Season Two. The show might have fared better—and Gates McFadden and Wil Wheaton would certainly have had more interesting material to play—if Wesley had been portrayed as a typical fifteen-year-old. Instead, it took until Season Four, and the introduction of Worf's troubled son Alexander, for the series to begin to explore the potential pitfalls of raising children while serving in Starfleet. But it was worth the wait, since the eight Worf-Alexander stories in the series' final four seasons included some of the best episodes of the entire series, such as the emotionally gripping "Reunion" and the wildly enjoyable holodeck Western "A Fistful of Datas." The franchise introduced more family drama following the birth of Miles and Keiko O'Brien's daughter Molly in "Disaster."

Over the course of the show's seven seasons, every major character became a parent at some point, or at least appeared to. In "The Child," Deanna gave birth to a short-lived alien son, whom she named Ian. In "The Offspring," Data created a daughter he named Lal, who also soon expired. In the possible future of "All Good Things . . . ," Geordi had a wife and two children. In "Future Imperfect" and "Bloodlines," Riker and Picard, respectively, were duped into thinking they had sons. Although the relationships proved to be false, the parental concern Riker and Picard demonstrated was real. In other episodes, such as "Suddenly

Majel Barrett-Roddenberry, as Lwaxana Troi, comforts her daughter, Deanna (Marina Sirtis), in "Manhunt." Parenting and family dynamics became one of *The Next Generation*'s most prevalent recurring themes.

Human," "The Bonding," and "Hero Worship," Picard, Worf, and Data become father figures for displaced or orphaned children.

Throughout these and other stories, the series suggested that, even in the twenty-fourth century, nothing was more cherished than the life of a child, and that no trust was more sacred than that between parent and offspring. This point was driven home forcefully (albeit clumsily) in the early episode "When the Bough Breaks," in which Picard risks the *Enterprise* and the lives of its entire crew to rescue a clutch of children, including Wesley, kidnapped by the denizens of the planet Aldea. The often tense but loving relationship between Lwaxana and Deanna Troi also reflected this idea. After all, the meddling Lwaxana always had Deanna's best interests—or at least what Lwaxana considered Deanna's best interests to be—at heart. Meanwhile, Riker's chilly relationship with his father Kyle (seen in "The Icarus Factor" and mentioned in a few other episodes) stemmed from Will's perception that his father had abandoned him to focus on his career following the death of Will's mother. Other *Next Generation* episodes explored other rocky family dynamics, including the strained relationships between Captain Picard and his brother Robert (in "Family") and Worf and his adoptive brother (in "Homeward"). At no point did *The Next Generation* threaten to become a spacefaring *Long Day's Journey into Night*, but the series eventually became a program that dealt with realistic family problems in a science fiction setting. Roddenberry's insistence on including families on the starship was vindicated, belatedly, by the success of these stories, which enhanced the realism and emotional resonance of the series and its characters.

Justice and Jurisprudence

In addition to carrying forward themes from the original *Trek*, *The Next Generation* introduced several recurring motifs of its own. One of the most prevalent was the subject of justice and jurisprudence—exploring how societies decide what is right or wrong and who is innocent and guilty. Numerous episodes, including the premiere "Encounter at Farpoint" and the finale "All Good Things . . . ," featured legal proceedings, and several ("Justice," "The Measure of a Man," "Sins of the Father," "The Drumhead," "The Outcast," "The First Duty," and "Devil's Due") climaxed with courtroom showdowns. Captain Picard usually served as the voice of moral authority in these proceedings. In "The Measure of a Man," Picard describes the courtroom as "a crucible. In it, we burn away irrelevancies until we are left with a pure product—the truth, for all time." That episode ends with a just outcome: Data, although a machine, is deemed to be a sentient being and entitled to human rights.

More often than not, however, *The Next Generation* demonstrated the value of proper jurisprudence by presenting scenarios involving outrageous miscarriages of justice. In "Justice," Wesley Crusher accidentally ran afoul of a society where every legal infraction, no matter how petty, was punishable by death. In "Sins of the Father," Worf, to avert a Klingon Civil War, was forced to accept punishment for crimes his family never committed. "The Outcast" (as already mentioned) features an alien trial in which a character is sentenced to be reprogrammed due to her sexual orientation. And in "The Drumhead," Picard combats a Starfleet investigation conducted by the paranoid Admiral Norah Satie, which devolves into a witch hunt. Maintaining a just society takes constant effort and attention, Picard tells Worf at the conclusion of the episode. "She or someone like her will always be with us, waiting for the right climate in which to flourish, spreading fear in the name of righteousness," Picard says. "Vigilance, Mr. Worf. That is the price we have to continually pay." Picard's remarks represent a succinct summary of *Star Trek*'s stance on the subject.

Other Themes

The preceding covers only a handful of the many recurring themes that run through the 276 episodes of *The Next Generation* and the four *Next Gen* feature films. There are numerous others. For instance, several episodes explore the dilemmas presented by conflicting loyalties—such as Wesley Crusher in "The First Duty," torn between his friends and his Starfleet oath, or Worf in "Redemption I and II," pulled in different directions by his identity as a Klingon warrior and his station as a Starfleet officer. Another recurring theme is that financial gain, in and of itself, is not a mature or enlightened goal. "A lot has changed in the past three hundred years," Picard says in "The Neutral Zone." "People are no longer obsessed with the accumulation of things. We've eliminated hunger, want, the need for possessions. We've grown out of our infancy." Repeatedly, the greedy Ferengi are held up to ridicule. There is no more repulsive *Star Trek* villain than Fajo, the insatiable collector from "The Most Toys." More comprehensive discussions of the moral themes of the series can be found elsewhere, including Judith Brand and Ed Robertson's book *The Ethics of Star Trek*.

24

Peak Performance

The Next Generation, Season Six (1992–93)

T he die was cast. As it entered its sixth season, *Star Trek: The Next Generation* was the most successful syndicated program on television. It had earned its highest-ever Nielsen ratings the prior year and cleared more than $30 million in profit for Paramount Pictures. Nevertheless, although few people knew it yet, the studio had already decided to cancel the series. The question was when, not if, the show would have to go.

To understand why, it's necessary to recall how *The Next Generation* came about in the first place: Stations running the original seventy-nine *Star Trek* episodes day after day for more than a decade had begun to see the original program's ratings decline and demanded new product. Now they had it. By the conclusion of its fifth season, 126 episodes of *The Next Generation* had been produced, more than enough for its repeats to be "stripped" (run nightly, Monday through Friday). In fact, many stations were already paying a syndication fee for older episodes of *Next Gen* and running them nightly in addition to broadcasting the new episodes in a different, weekly time slot. Although stations paid no syndication fee to carry new *Next Generation* episodes, Paramount made only five minutes of commercial time available for local advertising during current season broadcasts (it sold the rest to national customers). Local stations could sell all twelve minutes of advertising during nightly reruns. This made repeats more profitable for individual stations, despite the syndication fee. "After about seven years, the show, even as successful as it was, was probably going to have to be taken off the market, just because stations already had too many episodes," said Brandon Tartikoff, chairman of Paramount at the time, as quoted in Judith and Garfield Reeves-Stevens's *Star Trek: The Next Generation—The Continuing Voyages*.

Paramount, too, was losing its appetite for new installments of the series. Production costs continued to escalate and jumped significantly after Season Five, when the show's cast reached the end of their original contracts. All agreed to return, but at significantly higher salaries, which cut into the studio's profit margin. Also, Paramount wanted to continue the highly successful *Star Trek* feature film franchise with a series of *Next Generation* movies. Executives reasoned that this would only work if the show were off the air. Why would fans go to theaters and pay for something they could receive at home for free? And yet no one wanted *Star Trek* left out of the lucrative first-run syndication market, which *The Next Generation* had revitalized. So, in the summer of 1991, Paramount decided to launch a third live-action *Star Trek* series. "I was asked to create and develop a series that would serve as a companion piece to *The Next Generation* for about a year and a half, and then *TNG* would go off the air and this new show would continue," said Rick Berman in Terry J. Erdman and Paula M. Block's *Star Trek: Deep Space Nine Companion*. According to Berman, Gene Roddenberry gave his blessing to the idea of developing a spin-off but passed away before any of the details could be worked out.

Throughout the fifth season of *The Next Generation*, Berman and Piller divided their attention between *Next Gen* and creating and casting what would become *Deep Space Nine*. This workload became unsustainable once *DS9* entered production, and a game of musical chairs ensued. For Season Six of *The Next Generation*, Jeri Taylor was elevated to co-executive producer—essentially replacing Piller as *Next Gen*'s lead writer and show runner, although both Berman and Piller retained veto power over all story concepts. Other staffers, including David Livingston and J. P. Farrell, assumed many of Berman's day-to-day responsibilities. When Livingston was promoted to supervising producer of both shows, Merri Howard took over as line producer of *Next Gen*.

Taylor immediately set about placing her own stamp on *The Next Generation*, doing away with certain conventions introduced by Piller. In particular, she was keen to eliminate (or at least reduce) teleplays with A/B plotlines—those in which the primary narrative was intercut with a secondary story, especially when the A plot was a character study and the B plot was a token sci-fi yarn introduced to place the ship in jeopardy, such as Season Five's "Conundrum" and "Cost of Living." The A/B structure is a common one for ensemble cast series, but Taylor believed it had been overworked on *Next Gen* during the past few seasons. Under her leadership, the show became less character driven and issue oriented, and placed a greater emphasis on action and humor. Taylor also pushed for scripts with less Treknobabble. As a result, while Season Six maintained the series' high standard of week-to-week quality, it included a much higher percentage of peppy, lighthearted mysteries and action-adventures. The change in tone and style pleased writers, actors, and viewers alike.

"I think our sixth season was actually our best year," said Brent Spiner in an interview included on the *Star Trek: The Next Generation Season Six* DVD collection. There are "more good episodes in the [sixth] season than any other." Elsewhere on the same DVD, writer Ronald D. Moore opines that "Season Six is when the show was at its best. We did interesting, fresh work that year."

"Time's Arrow, Part II"

Once again, however, the writing staff struggled to generate promising story ideas. Heading into Season Six, the staff had only four teleplays in the pipeline. One of those was the second half of the two-part time-travel yarn that capped

Season Five. In the conclusion, Samuel Clemens (aka Mark Twain, played by Jerry Hardin) causes nearly as many problems as the time-traveling Devidians, who are feeding on the life forces of human victims in nineteenth-century San Francisco. Eventually, Picard and friends overcome Samuel's meddling and save the world, while Data survives being decapitated.

"Time's Arrow, Part II," written by Taylor from a story by Joe Menosky, set the tone for the entire season. It's a lively, up-tempo adventure with some highly amusing comic interludes. For instance, when Clemens first sees Worf, the startled author cries "Werewolf!" Taylor's teleplay also reveals some of the previously hidden history between Picard and Guinan. Whoopi Goldberg was so excited by this script that she cleared her schedule to make herself available for multiple days of shooting. Typically, Goldberg's appearances on the show remained brief because the actress only worked one day per installment. As a result, "Time's Arrow" is the closest thing to a "Guinan episode" ever produced. Taylor hired her son, Alexander Enberg, to play the small role of a reporter who converses with Clemens. This episode won Emmy Awards for costume design and hairstyling.

"Realm of Fear"

Another of Taylor's goals was to use familiar characters in unfamiliar ways— like the unexpected dramatic turn Lwaxana Troi took with "Half a Life," or Deanna Troi's emergence as a credible commander in "Disaster." "Realm of Fear" transplants Lieutenant Reginald Barclay (Dwight Schultz) from his usual light comedy milieu into a straightforward sci-fi adventure with distinct horror trappings. The transporter-averse Barclay encounters wormlike alien life-forms while transporting from the *Enterprise* to the USS *Yosemite*, which is trapped in a plasma field and whose crew has mysteriously disappeared. At first, everyone—even Barclay—believes he imagined the transporter beam creatures, but eventually Reg becomes convinced that the aliens are real and may be behind the disappearance of the *Yosemite* crew. "Realm of Fear" enabled guest star Schultz to stretch as the shaken but grimly determined Barclay. The scenario prominently features transporter chief O'Brien, and Colm Meaney demonstrates why he was selected for a leading role on *Deep Space Nine*. Piller nearly vetoed Brannon Braga's story idea because he thought "Realm of Fear" was too similar to "Nightmare at 20,000 Feet," the classic *Twilight Zone* episode in which an airplane passenger played by William Shatner spots a gremlin on the wing of the plane. Braga's finished teleplay downplays any such resemblance. This was the first *Star Trek* episode to show transport process from the point of view of the person being transported.

"Man of the People"

Deanna strikes up a friendship with Ambassador Alkar (Chip Lucia), who the *Enterprise* is transporting to an important diplomatic summit. She attempts to comfort Alkar following the death of his elderly mother. But soon afterward Troi's personality changes: She becomes testy, cruel, and sexually predatory. She also begins to age rapidly. "Man of the People," a *Star Trek* version of "The Picture of Dorian Gray," was rushed into production when "Relics" (originally slated as Season Six's third episode) was pushed back due to scheduling difficulties with guest star James Doohan. Although newly hired writer-producer Frank Abatemarco received sole teleplay credit for "Man of the People," the entire writing staff collaborated on the hastily assembled script, which accounts for the jumbled nature of the episode's final scenes. The installment's major attraction is the exemplary and often hilarious performance of Marina Sirtis, who relished the opportunity to portray a Troi who seduces random crewmen and crushes the spirit of a counseling patient.

"Relics"

The *Enterprise* discovers an old Starfleet ship that has crashed onto the surface of a Dyson Sphere (a massive artificial structure encasing a star). On board the crashed ship, Geordi rematerializes Captain Montgomery Scott (James Doohan), preserved for more than seventy years in the pattern buffer of the vessel's transporter. Scotty is relieved to be rescued but feels useless and out-of-date in the twenty-fourth century. Then the *Enterprise* becomes trapped in the Sphere, and Scotty and Geordi must work together to save the ship. Although less heralded than Leonard Nimoy's much-hyped appearance in "Unification" the season prior, "Relics" is by far the most satisfying *Next Generation* appearance by a classic *Trek* star. And Doohan's wistful, touching performance is arguably his single finest *Star Trek* portrayal. The episode not only gives fans a chance to see Scotty interact with the *Next Gen* crew, but includes numerous references to the original program. Scotty recounts events from the classic episodes "Elaan of Troyius," "Wolf

The popular "Relics," featuring the return of James Doohan as Scotty, was novelized by author Jan Michael Friedman.

in the Fold," and "The Naked Time," and Spiner and Doohan reenact a comedic interlude from "By Any Other Name" involving a bottle of green liquor. Scotty also visits a holodeck simulation of the original *Enterprise* bridge. "It's really a love poem to the old show," writer Ron Moore said in an interview included on the *Star Trek: The Next Generation Season Six* DVD collection.

The production team went all out to create this loving tribute, which featured an extraordinary number of visual effects shots and unusual production design challenges. For the holodeck re-creation of the original *Enterprise*, the staff worked from classic *Trek* production chief Matt Jefferies's original specs and rebuilt a single pie-shaped bridge section. The captain's chair and helm were homemade replicas loaned to the show by fan Steve Horch, and the rest of the bridge was created through computer graphics. Nearly every critical survey and fan poll has named "Relics" among the best installments of *The Next Generation*. The episode was so popular that Pocket Books published an extended novelization of it, written by Michael Jan Friedman. In the novelization, Scotty converses with holographic versions of the young Kirk and Spock, an idea originally considered for the episode (stock footage would have been used to pull this off) but later nixed to cut costs. Also deleted from the episode was a scene in which Troi attempts to comfort the despondent Scotty. This sequence, which was filmed but never aired, "basically has Troi coming to counsel Scotty, and at first he's very friendly to her, but then realizes she's a therapist and gets pissed that Geordi thinks he's crazy," Moore explained in an AOL chat in 1998. "It was this scene that sent him to Ten-Forward to get a drink."

"Schisms"

In another horror-tinged, high-concept sci-fi tale, Commander Riker begins suffering from memory gaps and strange nightmares. Eventually it's revealed that he and other crew members are being abducted by aliens from subspace and subjected to bizarre experiments. "Schisms," written by Brannon Braga from a story by Jean Louise Matthias and Ron Wilkerson, has a fertile premise and contains some arresting sequences, yet it failed to wow audiences. Braga blamed the episode's chilly reception on Paramount's preview, which gave away virtually the entire plot. During this episode, Data reads his "Ode to Spot." Spiner's staccato delivery of this literary gem, penned by Braga about Data's cat, provides the highlight of the episode. The poem concludes: "O Spot, the complex levels of behavior you display/ Connote a fairly well-developed cognitive array/ And though you are not sentient, Spot, and do not comprehend/ I nonetheless consider you a true and valued friend."

"True Q"

After skipping Season Five in its entirety, Q (John de Lancie) made a pair of memorable appearances in Season Six. In the first of these, Q arrives to investigate a young woman who has won an internship aboard the *Enterprise*. Her deceased parents, Q reveals, were outcasts of the Q Continuum who chose to live on Earth as humans. Q must determine if their offspring represents a threat. For much of this fresh, imaginative episode, written by Rene Echevarria, Q seems less playful and more menacing, like the sinister figure he appeared to be in his earliest appearances. Still, Q remains full of scathing, funny, and eminently quotable assessments of the human race and the *Enterprise* crew. He tells Captain Picard, "Sometimes I think the only reason I come here is to listen to these wonderful speeches of yours." Later he momentarily turns Dr. Crusher into a dog. In addition to this episode and the later "Tapestry," de Lancie also appeared on the *Deep Space Nine* episode "Q-Less" (alongside Picard's former love interest Vash) during the 1992–93 season.

"Rascals"

A transporter mishap turns Captain Picard, Ensign Ro, Guinan, and Keiko into twelve-year-old versions of themselves. When a band of Ferengi raiders seize control of the ship, the suddenly youthful quartet (who retain their memories and adult mental faculties) help take it back. Written by Allison Hock from a story suggested by Michael Piller, "Rascals" is an airy action-comedy, nimbly directed by Adam Nimoy and featuring a charming performance by David Tristan Birkin as the young Picard. Previously, Birkin played Picard's nephew Rene in "Family." "Rascals" remains diverting, even though its premise requires viewers to not merely suspend their disbelief but send it into orbit. As if the age-reducing transporter accident weren't improbable enough, the audience must also buy the idea that a handful of Ferengi—*Ferengi?*—are able to capture the *Enterprise* with little effort. "I still cringe when I think of that episode," said Ron Moore, who was assigned to polish "Rascals." Adam Nimoy had been approached about directing his father in the prior season's "Unification" epic. When that fell through, he was brought in to direct this entry. "Rascals" was the final *Next Generation* episode to feature Colm Meaney and Rosalind Chao as Miles and Keiko O'Brien before the duo moved to *Deep Space Nine*. Meaney returned to appear in the *Next Gen* finale, "All Good Things . . ." This was also Michelle Forbes's only Season Six appearance as Ensign Ro. She returned in Season Seven's "Preemptive Strike." "Rascals" recalls the animated *Star Trek* episode "The Counter-Clock Incident," in which Kirk, Spock, and the rest of the original crew regress in age, eventually becoming toddlers.

"A Fistful of Datas"

While "Rascals" drew a mixed reception, fans and critics universally embraced the offbeat, seriocomic "A Fistful of Datas," a sci-fi-Western hybrid. Worf, Alexander, and Deanna, trapped in an out-control holodeck program, must defeat an apparently unstoppable android gunslinger, the accidental by-product of an experiment by Geordi and Data. Eventually, all the holographic characters in the program become imitation Datas. Directed by Patrick Stewart, "A Fistful of Datas" was a challenging episode in many respects. It involved many complicated special effects shots and required location work (on the Universal Studios back lot). As importantly, it demanded a great deal of creative dexterity to keep its humorous elements from completely obliterating the drama of the scenario. Stewart handles it all brilliantly. To prepare for this assignment, he studied classic Westerns including George Stevens's *Shane* (and even quotes a shot from that film in "A Fistful of Datas"). This is arguably his most impressive directorial effort. Written by Robert Hewitt Wolfe and Brannon Braga, the story was modeled after director Howard Hawks's *Rio Bravo*, with Worf in the John Wayne role. It also contains echoes of director Michael Crichton's *Westworld* (1973). Both Dorn and Sirtis (as Durango, a mysterious, rifle-toting stranger) are excellent here. "A Fistful of Datas" won an Emmy for sound mixing.

"The Quality of Life"

Data becomes convinced that small industrial robots known as Exocomps, created by Dr. Farallon (Ellen Bry) to assist in the creation of an experimental "particle fountain," have gained sentience. When the fountain malfunctions, threatening the lives of the human engineers, Dr. Farallon devises a plan that will shut down the fountain but destroy the Exocomps. Data intervenes, arguing that the Exocomps qualify as a new life-form and should be protected. "The Quality of Life" was written by Naren Shankar, who joined the show's staff for Season Six after penning the excellent Season Five teleplay "The First Duty." Although entertaining, the underlying premise of "The Quality of Life" repeats Season Two's classic "The Measure of a Man." Data even refers to the events of that episode during a meeting with Captain Picard. Director Jonathan Frakes does what he can to enliven things, but this remains one of the season's more forgettable installments.

"Chain of Command, Parts I and II"

The string of breezy, humor-laced action-adventure stories that opened Season Six came to a screeching halt with the one-two gut-punch that is "Chain of Command." The first half of this grim epic focuses primarily on the crew's discomfort with no-nonsense Captain Edward Jellico (Ronny Cox), who assumes command of the *Enterprise* while Picard prepares for a secret mission. In the second half, Picard is captured by the Cardassians and tortured. Both episodes are riveting, but the deeply disturbing "Part II" proves indelible. Written by Ron Moore and Frank Abatemarco, "Chain of Command" originally was intended as a single installment. It was split into two parts because the story's second half—much of which plays out on a single set, where Picard and his Cardassian inquisitor (David Warner) engage in a brutal battle of wills—could be expanded into a cost-saving episode along the lines of "The Drumhead." Amnesty International consulted on the teleplay, providing psychological profiles of and videotaped interviews with torturers and their victims. Stewart, a committed supporter of Amnesty, was keen to do an episode on the subject of torture and, as a method actor, insisted on appearing nude (rather than being doubled) during the first torture sequence. The resulting episode upset many fans, especially its final revelation that Picard was about to crack under sustained physical and psychological torment. But Stewart insisted that it would be both dishonest and insulting to real-life victims to portray Picard as immune to torture. "Ultimately, the victory for Picard is just surviving," said Michael Piller, as quoted in *Patrick Stewart: The Unauthorized Biography.*

"Chain of Command" boasts superb, carefully textured work from guest stars Cox and David Warner, who plays Gul Madred, Picard's Cardassian tormentor. Neither Jellico nor Madred seem purely good or evil; both are richly shaded, multifaceted characters. Warner and Picard had worked together before in the Royal Shakespeare Company. Warner had also appeared in both *Star Trek V: The Final Frontier* and *Star Trek VI: The Undiscovered Country*, playing different characters. Despite the exemplary work of Cox and Warner, the episode's most gripping performance is Stewart's. Producers were so impressed with his inspired work in "Chain of Command" that Paramount took out a full-page ad in *Variety* to lobby for an Emmy nomination on the actor's behalf, but the effort failed. "It's probably his finest performance," said Jeri Taylor in author Larry Nemecek's *Star Trek: The Next Generation Companion.* "He literally threw himself, physically and mentally, into that." Stewart remains justifiably proud of the episode, calling it "the very best of what *Star Trek* could do." *Entertainment Weekly*, among many others, concurred, ranking it one of the ten best episodes of *The Next Generation.*

"Chain of Command, Part II" was the final *Next Gen* installment to air prior to the debut of *Deep Space Nine*, which featured the Cardassians prominently. Events depicted in this episode tie directly into those of "Emissary," the *DS9* pilot. Patrick Stewart made a guest appearance as Captain Picard in the *DS9* premiere.

"Ship in a Bottle"

The final few seasons of *The Next Generation* were marked by the reappearances of characters first seen in the show's early episodes—Lore, the Traveler, and the revenge-crazed Ferengi Bok, to name a few. But none seemed less likely to return than evil genius Professor Moriarty, a holographic version of Sherlock Holmes's archenemy first seen in Season Two's "Elementary, Dear Data." After that episode aired, the estate of Sir Arthur Conan Doyle contacted Paramount Pictures and warned that the Holmes characters remained under copyright. Any future unauthorized use of them (which is to say, any more episodes produced without paying a license fee to Doyle's heirs) would result in legal action. Four seasons later, producers finally decided to spend the money and create a story that would resolve the fate of *Star Trek*'s Moriarty, a hologram that accidentally gained sentience in the previous episode.

In this sequel, Lieutenant Barclay unwittingly reactivates the Moriarty program. Moriarty (Daniel Davis), incensed after spending four years stored in memory, seizes control of the *Enterprise* and demands that Captain Picard develop a solution that will enable the professor and his holographic sweetheart (Stephanie Beacham) to leave the holodeck. But this appears to be physically impossible. Rene Echevarria's clever teleplay offers a pair of wildly enjoyable twists, and Davis delights once again as the crafty, charismatic Moriarty. Like "Elementary, Dear Data" before it, "Ship in a Bottle" became a much-loved adventure. Brannon Braga named it one of his favorite *Next Gen* episodes. Although Moriarty was never seen again, the concept of a sentient hologram was revived to create the Doctor (Robert Picardo) for *Star Trek: Voyager*.

"Aquiel"

An away team sent to deliver supplies to a remote subspace relay station finds the outpost abandoned and at least one crew member killed (reduced to a puddle of goo). When another assumed victim, Lieutenant Aquiel Uhnari (Renee Jones), is found alive, she becomes the prime suspect in the murder. But Geordi, who has fallen in love with Aquiel while reviewing her personal logs, becomes determined to prove her innocence. "Aquiel," a sci-fi whodunit penned by Brannon Braga and Ron Moore from a story by Jeri Taylor, was modeled after the film noir classic *Laura*, in which a detective falls in love with a murder victim, who becomes a suspect when she is later discovered alive. Unfortunately, LeVar Burton and guest star Renee Jones display little of the chemistry shared by Dana Andrews and Gene Tierney in that classic film. Despite this weakness, and although it was not well liked by the show's production staff (in a 1997 AOL chat, Moore said he wished that he had never written this episode), "Aquiel" remains an engrossing mystery with an imaginative SF twist.

"Face of the Enemy"

Deanna Troi is kidnapped and forced to impersonate an officer of the Tal Shiar (the Romulan equivalent of the Gestapo) as part of an elaborate scheme to rescue dissidents from Romulus. Written by Naren Shankar from a story by Rene Echevarria, "Face of the Enemy" is another full-tilt action yarn and a direct follow-up to the previous season's "Unification" saga. Although he does not appear in the episode, Spock is supposedly behind a plan to create an outer space version of the Underground Railroad and help Romulans committed to reunification escape to Vulcan. This is an outstanding installment for Marina Sirtis, as Troi displays admirable courage and ingenuity, staring down and outwitting a strong-willed, sharp-eyed Romulan commander (Carolyn Seymour). Joanne Linville, who had portrayed a female Romulan commander in the classic episode "The Enterprise Incident," was considered for the role of Troi's nemesis, but the actress was unavailable.

"Tapestry"

Q appears to Picard, who is hovering near death after being attacked on an away mission, and grants the captain the opportunity to relive his life. Given this second chance, Picard decides to avoid some youthful mistakes—including a barroom brawl in which he was impaled through the chest, requiring him to receive an artificial heart. But Picard finds that these changes alter the entire course of his life, leaving him trapped in a dull, dead-end career as a nondescript astrophysics officer. Although screenwriter Ron Moore insists that "Tapestry" had autobiographical origins, the story nevertheless recalls holiday classics such as "A Christmas Carol" and "It's a Wonderful Life" in which characters are forced to reexamine their lives and values. Picard's ill-fated barroom brawl was first mentioned in the Season Two episode "Samaritan Snare." Stewart is marvelous here, playing the reinvigorated, youthful Picard, while de Lancie delivers an unusually restrained performance as Q. Coincidentally, a week before this episode was first aired, de Lancie appeared in the *Deep Space Nine* installment "Q-Less." The poignant and thought-provoking "Tapestry" is widely regarded as another milestone in the history of the series. In 2007, *Entertainment Weekly* named it one of the ten best episodes of *The Next Generation*. "I still think it's one

Picard relives his days as a young ensign, with friends Cortan Zweller (Ned Vaughn) and Marta Batanides (J. C. Bandy), in "Tapestry."

of the best things I wrote and one of *TNG's* finest episodes," Moore stated in a 1997 AOL online chat.

"Birthright, Parts I and II"

Worf discovers a colony where disgraced Klingons (apprehended during the Khitomer massacre, where his parents were killed) live in harmony with their Romulan captors, but at the cost of their cultural heritage. Worf's pride in his Klingon identity reignites the captives' sense of honor but threatens their peaceful lives. In a subplot restricted to the first half of this two-part adventure, Data experiences a vision of his "father," Dr. Noonian Soong, after being zapped by an alien device. "Birthright," credited to Brannon Braga and Rene Echevarria but including contributions from four other writers, was the third of a record four multichapter stories to air in part or in their entirety during Season Six. The first half of the story takes place mostly on Deep Space Nine and includes a guest appearance by Alexander Siddig as Dr. Julian Bashir. James Cromwell, who previously played the Angosian prime minister in "The Hunted" and would later portray warp-drive pioneer Zefram Cochrane in *Star Trek: First Contact*, appears under heavy makeup as the mole-like alien Jaglom Shrek, who tells Worf that the Klingon's father may still be alive in the secret Romulan camp. Originally the Shrek character played a larger role in the story's resolution, but his screen time was reduced when Cromwell broke his leg in an offstage accident. The thought-provoking "Birthright" saga remains a favorite of many staff members, including Michael Piller (who compared it to director David Lean's *The Bridge on the River Kwai*) and Rick Berman.

"Starship Mine"

After the *Enterprise* is evacuated for routine maintenance, Picard becomes trapped on board the empty ship with a band of terrorists. Written by Morgan Gendel, "Starship Mine" is another high-octane action piece, intended as the *Star Trek* equivalent of blockbusters like *Die Hard* (1988) and the then-recent *Under Siege* (1992). In the latter film, Steven Seagal claims to be a cook; in "Starship Mine," Picard tells the villains he is Mot, the barber. Although Gendel's unusually violent teleplay received a green light, it inspired heated debate among the writing staff as to whether or not the story "was *Star Trek.*" To resolve lingering concerns, Michael Piller assigned Ron Moore to do a last-minute polish. Revised pages reached the set daily, just in time to be filmed. Tim Russ, who would later portray Vulcan security officer Tuvok on *Voyager*, plays a terrorist who Picard incapacitates with what appears to be the Famous Spock Nerve Pinch. (Maybe Picard learned this trick during his mind meld with Sarek.) Although derivative, the fast-moving, hard-hitting "Starship Mine" remains exciting television and represents a breath of fresh air for *Next Gen*. Patrick Stewart ranks it among his favorite episodes.

"Lessons"

Captain Picard falls in love with his new chief of stellar sciences, Lieutenant Commander Nella Daren (Wendy Hughes), who shares his passion for music. After playing a flute-and-piano duet of "Frere Jacques," Picard opens up and tells her about the events of Season Five's "The Inner Light," which have clearly made a profound impact upon him. Perhaps Picard sees a chance for the kind of family life he enjoyed as "Kamin" in the earlier episode. If so, he soon reconsiders when he's forced to order Daren to risk her life on an away mission. "Lessons," written by Ron Wilkerson and Jean Louise Matthias, is a bittersweet romance featuring tender, heartfelt performances from Stewart and guest star Hughes. Gates McFadden also shines as a jealous Dr. Crusher. Smart, dedicated, courageous, and resourceful, Daren emerges as the most believable romantic interest Picard would encounter during the series (except perhaps Beverly Crusher).

"The Chase"

When Picard's former archaeology professor (Norman Lloyd) is killed, the captain investigates and becomes embroiled in a cutthroat competition with Klingon, Cardassian, and Romulan agents to recover artifacts that may reveal an ancient secret. Written by Joe Menosky from a story by Ron Moore and Menosky, "The Chase" was born out of a desire by the show's writing staff to come up with a reasonable explanation for why so many *Star Trek* species are bipedal humanoids. The classic episode "Return to Tomorrow" offered a possible answer, suggesting that life on many planets, including Earth and Vulcan, may stem from a common ancestor. "The Chase" verifies this and climaxes with a holographic message from the now-deceased aliens who seeded the galaxy. Curiously, the aliens look remarkably like the shape-shifting Founders later seen on *Deep Space Nine*. Coincidentally, Salome Jens, who plays the holographic alien, later portrayed a Founder on *DS9*. Early drafts of "The Chase" also featured the Vulcans and the Ferengi and were more comedic in tone. Director Jonathan Frakes was pleased with the episode, which he considered extremely "Roddenberry-esque."

"Frame of Mind"

Commander Riker is undergoing intensive therapy in an alien insane asylum after murdering a civilian. Or is he only appearing in a play on board the *Enterprise*? Or is something else going on? To reveal more would undercut the visceral impact of screenwriter Brannon Braga's eerie, unsettling "Frame of Mind,"

At the climax of "The Chase," Worf, Captain Picard, and Dr. Crusher, along with competing Klingon, Cardassian, and Romulan agents, meet a holographic recreation (far left)
of the aliens who seeded life throughout the Alpha Quadrant.

which was carefully calculated to screw with viewers' heads. Director James L.
Conway and cinematographer Jonathan West employ a host of unorthodox
camera setups and stark lighting schemes to enhance the bizarre ambiance of
the story, which was inspired by director Roman Polanski's brooding, surreal
Repulsion (1963). In a DVD interview, Jonathan Frakes named the "wonderfully
dark" "Frame of Mind" as his favorite Riker episode.

"Suspicions"

Dr. Crusher suspects foul play in the death of a Ferengi scientist who apparently
committed suicide after the failure of an important experiment. Picard suspends
her from duty when she performs an autopsy on the deceased researcher in
violation of Ferengi burial customs, but Crusher remains determined to find
the truth. Jeri Taylor—whose previous experience included a staff position on
Quincy, M.E., which starred Jack Klugman as a crime-solving coroner—encouraged the development of this medical mystery, intended as a showcase for
Gates McFadden. Written by Joe Menosky and Naren Shankar, "Suspicions"
is a credible whodunit, although mystery buffs may find the story's "surprise"
resolution predictable. "Suspicions" has an unusual flashback structure, with
Crusher relating the first half of the story to Guinan. This episode also marked

the final *Next Generation* appearance of Whoopi Goldberg, although she returned as Guinan in two *Next Gen* feature films.

"Rightful Heir"

In the midst of a faith crisis, Worf travels to a Klingon holy site in search of a mystical vision. Instead of the ethereal experience he expects, Worf witnesses the flesh-and-blood return of Kahless the Unforgettable, founder of the Klingon Empire. "Rightful Heir," written by Ron Moore from a story by James E. Brooks, is far more sympathetic to spiritual exploration than most previous *Star Trek* teleplays, which tended to dismiss religion as childish superstition. The episode stirred discussion among the writing staff about their own spiritual beliefs (or lack thereof) and debate over the proper place (if any) for religion in *Star Trek*. Yet "Rightful Heir" remains in keeping with the relatively positive portrayal of the Bajoran faith on *Deep Space Nine*. Guest star Kevin Conway offers a far more righteous and inspiring Kahless than the underhanded, venal version of the character played by Robert Herron in the classic episode "The Savage Curtain." (However, that episode featured an Excalbian re-creation of the Klingon leader rather than the real Kahless.) "Rightful Heir" also features one of Michael Dorn's finest performances.

"Second Chances"

Returning to a Federation outpost he helped evacuate eight years earlier, Commander Riker is shocked to discover that a freak transporter accident created a duplicate of himself, who remained stranded alone on the deserted station. After beaming aboard the *Enterprise*, the castaway Lieutenant Riker tries to renew his romance with Deanna Troi, who he still loves passionately. Rene Echevarria's brilliant teleplay uses a familiar plot device (a transporter malfunction) to unusually potent effect. Jonathan Frakes delivers one (or, actually, two) of his best performances in his dual roles as Commander Riker and Lieutenant Riker. Sirtis also acquits herself well. LeVar Burton made his directorial debut with this complex entry, which featured many tricky visual effects shots. Burton would helm one more *Next Gen* episode and multiple installments of later *Star Trek* series, and launch a successful second career as a filmmaker. "Second Chances" features former astronaut Mae Jemison,

Astronaut Mae Jemison, the first African American woman in space, made a cameo appearance in "Second Chances."

the first African American woman in space, in a minor role. Nichelle Nichols visited the set in honor of Jemison's appearance on the show. At one point, the writing staff considered killing off Commander Riker and having Lieutenant Riker join the *Enterprise* crew, with Data taking over as first officer. When that intriguing idea was abandoned, it was decided that both Rikers should live. Lieutenant Riker—who, to avoid confusion, finally decides to go by his middle name, Thomas—was never seen again on *Next Gen* but returned in the *Deep Space Nine* adventure "Defiant."

"Timescape"

Captain Picard, Data, Geordi and Troi encounter temporal distortions while traveling in a "runabout" shuttle. Then they find the *Enterprise* frozen in time, a split-second away from being destroyed by a Romulan Bird of Prey. This was the second and final *Star Trek* episode directed by Adam Nimoy, following the offbeat "Rascals." Although his work here is slick and stylish, Nimoy was not invited back. "Timescape" was Brannon Braga's attempt to top his Season Five time-travel story "Cause and Effect," in which the *Enterprise* is trapped in a "causality loop" and events are repeated again and again. Although entertaining, "Timescape" lacks the inventiveness and snap of the earlier episode.

"Descent"

In the now-obligatory season-ending cliff-hanger, the *Enterprise*, responding to a distress call, discovers that the Federation outpost on planet Ohniaka III has been wiped out by rogue elements of the Borg, who now function as individuals and appear to possess emotions. After interrogating a captured drone, Data defects and joins the enemy—who, it is revealed at the episode's conclusion, are led by his android brother, Lore. With most of the crew off-ship to search for Data, Picard turns command of the *Enterprise* over to Dr. Crusher. The tense, fleet-footed "Descent" is a rousing, fun episode, but Picard is unbelievably slow to realize that the change in the behavior of the Borg is the result of the *Enterprise* crew's actions in Season Five's "I Borg." "Descent" also includes one of the series' most memorable opening scenes, in which Data plays a game of poker with holographic re-creations of Sir Isaac Newton, Albert Einstein, and Professor Stephen Hawking. Hawking remains the only person to appear on *Star Trek* as himself (albeit, in this case, as a holographic duplicate of himself). After shooting his cameo, Hawking received a tour of the show's sets. When he saw the warp engine, he reportedly quipped, "I am working on that."

In its penultimate season, *Star Trek: The Next Generation*'s performance in the Nielsen ratings slipped for the first time. Although the series remained an unqualified smash, drawing nearly eleven million viewers per week and continuing its reign as the most popular syndicated drama on television, its viewership declined slightly from Season Five's record peak. Profitability also decreased, due to higher salaries and heftier expenses. With higher cast salaries factored in, production costs jumped to nearly $2 million per episode (up from $1.2 million in Season One). In May 1993, shortly before the conclusion of the sixth season, Paramount announced at the ShoWest film exhibitors convention in Las Vegas that the *Star Trek* feature film series would resume with the first big-screen appearance of the *Next Generation* crew. The as-yet-untitled film was slated to debut in December 1994. Three months later, the studio announced that the seventh season of *Star Trek: The Next Generation* would be the last. The news disappointed and angered fans, especially since *Next Gen* remained popular and profitable. Many Trekkers, unaware of or unconcerned with the financial rationale behind

Physicist Stephen Hawking, the only person to appear as himself on *Star Trek*, played poker with Data, Albert Einstein, and Sir Isaac Newton in Part One of the Season Six cliffhanger finale, "Descent."

Paramount's decision, argued that another five or six seasons of new episodes would be preferable to a single movie every two or three years. But the studio never considered this a viable option. As it turned out, completing even one additional season proved extremely difficult.

25

Mess Call

The Food and Beverages of *Star Trek*

I n *The Real Frank Zappa Book*, a memoir written by the iconoclastic musician, satirist, and free-speech advocate, the author seems puzzled that fans and interviewers often asked questions about his diet. Nevertheless, Zappa obligingly sprinkled his book with food-related anecdotes "since it seems to matter so much to certain people in the audience." (As a boy his favorite foods were blueberry pie, oysters, and fried eels; as a struggling young musician in 1960s San Francisco, for a full week he consumed nothing except red beans and rice and Miller High Life.) Zappa should not have wondered why the public was interested in what he ate. Dining is a foundational cultural activity, and meals are often central to family, social, business, and religious functions. Since everybody eats, food also serves as a common denominator between artist and audience. Some dietary choices make a statement. For instance, it might interest readers of this book that strapping actor Michael Dorn is a vegan.

Many science fiction stories have offered imaginative solutions to civilizations' need for nourishment (including tales by Isaac Asimov, Philip K. Dick, Harry Harrison, Robert A. Heinlein, and George R. R. Martin, among many other authors). However, in most classic sci-fi movies and TV shows, space travelers never seemed to eat, or subsisted exclusively on vitamin pills. One of the subtle but effective ways that creator Gene Roddenberry enhanced the realism of *Star Trek* was by showing his crew taking meals together. On the classic series, the crew often dined together in the recreation room or had food delivered to their cabins. Captain Picard sometimes ate in his ready room or breakfasted in Dr. Crusher's cabin. The *Enterprise-D*'s Ten-Forward Lounge was created to present a relaxed space where crew members could eat, drink, and interact on an unofficial, social basis. Quark's Bar served the same function on *Deep Space Nine*, while the mess hall became an important setting on both *Voyager* and *Enterprise*. To solve the problem of explaining how a starship could store enough food to feed a crew of hundreds on a long space voyage, Roddenberry invented the replicator, capable of producing ice cream sundaes for young refugees (in "And the Children Shall Lead") or a bowl of chicken soup for a captured twentieth-century MP (in "Tomorrow Is Yesterday"). The replicator was capable of producing any type of food, yet Captain Kirk and his crew most often ate multicolored food cubes that looked like diced melons mixed with chunks

Yeoman Janice Rand appeared on the cover of the unofficial *Trekker Cookbook*, self-published by fan Johanna Cantor in 1977.

of Play-Doh. As the franchise mythology grew richer and more detailed in the 1980s and '90s, a more sophisticated menu was developed, including distinctive cuisine for each of the major cultures featured on the show (or at least for those that served aboard the *Enterprise*).

Like virtually every other aspect of the franchise lore, the food of *Star Trek* has long been a subject of interest for devoted fans. In 1977, Johanna Cantor self-published *The Trekker Cookbook*, which compiled recipes from fans across the country, including the Terran equivalent of delicacies such as Vulcan Plomeek

Soup (made with potatoes, carrots, and beets). A year later, Bantam Books published *The Official Star Trek Cooking Manual*, by the presciently named Mary Ann Piccard. Actor Ethan Phillips, who played cook Neelix on *Voyager*, coauthored *The Star Trek Cookbook*, published by Pocket Books in 1999. For the sake of brevity, this discussion will remain limited to those foodstuffs shown on classic *Trek*, *The Next Generation*, and in the movies. Recipes will be omitted. (Sorry.)

Human Food

Perhaps the most shocking fact *Star Trek* revealed about the twenty-third century is that two hundred years from now people will still eat meat loaf. In "Charlie X," that's the meal the *Enterprise* chef is preparing for Thanksgiving Dinner. (Kirk instructs the cook to shape the loafs so they look like turkeys.) In fact, human appetites and diets seem to have changed little over the centuries, despite assumed advances in nutrition and encounters with numerous alien cultures. In the classic episode "The Trouble with Tribbles," the *Enterprise* was assigned to protect a shipment of the experimental grain quadro-triticale, but Starfleet officers were never shown eating the stuff themselves. Their preferred dishes remained staples like, for breakfast, bacon and eggs or croissant and coffee. In *Star Trek Generations*, Kirk prepares a breakfast of Ktarian eggs spiced with dill weed and toast. Of course, cultural differences emerged. In *Next Gen*'s "The Wounded," newlywed Miles O'Brien blanches when his wife Keiko serves him her preferred breakfast of kelp buds, plankton loaf, and sea berries in place of his usual corned beef, eggs, and oatmeal. Although occasionally forced to consume field rations (as mentioned in "Silicon Avatar"), humans usually dined on familiar standbys like hamburgers, pizza, pasta, and salad.

Curiously, for such a physically fit group, the *Enterprise* crew consumed many desserts—mostly traditional choices such as sundaes, banana splits, and chocolate cake. Ice cream was a particular favorite and was consumed in numerous classic and *Next Gen* episodes. In "And the Children Shall Lead," the *Enterprise* computer reports that the replicator has been programmed to produce ice cream in the following flavors: vanilla, strawberry, peach, chocolate, chocolate wobble, coconut, Rocky Road, and pistachio. The chocoholic Counselor Troi, in a fit of decadence, ordered a bowl of chocolate ice cream, chocolate chips, chocolate fudge, and a cherry in "The Price." Along with their meals, *Enterprise* crew members were seen drinking water, milk, coffee, lemonade, orange juice (or perhaps Tang), and, of course, tea—Earl Grey, hot.

Vulcan Cuisine

Vulcans were vegetarians. Spock ate relatively little other than the generic food cubes, but in "Amok Time" nurse Christine Chapel prepared him a bowl of Plomeek Soup, which the *pon farr*-addled Vulcan hurled at her. Later, Spock apologized and asked her to prepare another serving. The Vulcan commitment to vegetarianism was part of the rule of logic and pacifism introduced by the great Surak five millennia ago. In "All Our Yesterdays," Spock travels to the ancient past, where he reverts to primitive ways, including eating meat. "I have eaten animal flesh and I have enjoyed it," he states with revulsion. "What is wrong with me?" *Voyager* and *Enterprise* revealed more details about Vulcan dietary habits, including the fact that they loathed to touch their food, preferring to always eat with utensils.

An interior illustration from *The Trekker Cookbook*. In both the twenty-third and twenty-fourth centuries, ice cream remained the favored dessert of Starfleet's finest.

Klingon Chow

Of all the alien civilizations the Federation encountered, the diet of the Klingons was by far the most explored—and the most sickening. Writers and art directors seemed to take great pleasure in imagining and preparing the most revolting cuisine possible for the proud warrior race. Klingons preferred to eat their food while it was still alive, or else freshly killed. Gagh (a writhing saucer of live worms) was a popular dish. Riker eats gagh in "A Matter of Honor," and Picard consumes it in "Unification I." Other delicacies included heart of targ (a kind of Klingon pig), bregit lung, pipius claw, rokeg blood pie, and octopus. Klingon feasts containing many of these items are consumed in "A Matter of Honor" and *Star Trek VI: The Undiscovered Country* (1998). In interviews included on the *Star Trek: The Next Generation Season Two* DVD collection, prop master Alan Sims revealed how these Klingon treats were created for "A Matter of Honor." Gagh was actually long brown noodles; rokeg blood pie was red-dyed pumpkin pie and turnips; pipius claw was chicken feet; and various animal organs were used as heart of targ and bregit lung. The octopus was actual octopus, purchased along with assorted fish eyes, squid and other items from a local Asian market. In battle, Klingons often survived on generic food packs, as revealed in *Star Trek IV: The Voyage Home* (1986). Worf was fond of prune juice, a beverage he considered worthy of a warrior.

Potent Potables

Starfleet officers apparently work up a mighty thirst exploring the galaxy. Both the twenty-third and twenty-fourth-century *Enterprise* crews spent a good deal of time consuming alcoholic beverages. In the original pilot "The Cage," Dr. Boyce "prescribes" a martini for the melancholic Captain Christopher Pike. The crews' drinking habits were sometimes less than exemplary. Chief engineer Montgomery Scott's consumption of Scotch whiskey and other potent potables was legendary. In "By Any Other Name" he waged an epic drinking contest with the Kelvan Tomar. In *Star Trek IV: The Undiscovered Country*, Kirk and his senior staff engaged in a night of binge drinking with the Klingon chancellor and his party, resulting in acute hangovers the next morning. Counselor Troi got plastered with warp-drive pioneer Zefram Cochrane in *Star Trek: First Contact* (1996).

Given the obvious dangers posed by drunken phaser-wielding officers, in the more enlightened era of *The Next Generation*, Starfleet replaced alcoholic beverages with "syntheholic" equivalents, which duplicated the flavor of the original drink without the debilitating and addictive properties of the real McCoy. Devotees of authentic spirits (such as Scotty, and Picard's brother Robert) loathed synthehol, but Captain Picard insisted in "Family" that drinking synthehol increased his appreciation of real wine. Most Starfleet vessels stocked a limited supply of authentic alcoholic spirits for special occasions, and intoxicating beverages remained popular among the general population of the Federation. Some of the more notable libations included:

- **Blood wine**—A Klingon liquor often consumed during celebrations following a glorious battle, usually served in large barrels, into which warriors dip oversized flagons. Introduced in "A Matter of Honor" and mentioned again in "Gambit, Part II," blood wine was supposedly twice as potent as whiskey.
- **Romulan Ale**—One of the more notorious spirits in *Star Trek* lore, this drink looked like pale blue Kool-Aid but apparently packed a wallop. Although it was technically illegal in the Federation, Starfleet officers seemed to have little difficulty acquiring it. Dr. McCoy gave Captain Kirk a bottle for his birthday in *Star Trek II*. Captain Kirk and his senior staff overindulge in Romulan Ale with Chancellor Gorkon and friends in *Star Trek VI*. At Riker and Troi's wedding reception in *Star Trek Nemesis*, Worf, hung over from Riker's bachelor party the night before, complained that Romulan Ale should be illegal. "It is," Geordi replied. (Originally the scene continued with Worf groaning, "Then it should be *more* illegal.") In the past, the Star Trek Experience at the Las Vegas Hilton sold six packs of "Romulan Ale," a blue lager brewed exclusively for Paramount Pictures by the Central American Cerveceria la Constancia. As a tie-in with the 2009 *Star Trek* movie, Boston America manufactured a Romulan Ale energy drink.
- **Saurian Brandy**—Another famous *Star Trek* drink, Saurian Brandy was stored in an elegant, curved bottle and was a favorite of Scotty. The beverage was featured in five classic *Trek* episodes and an animated adventure, as well as

Star Trek VI and two episodes of *The Next Generation.* While Saurian Brandy was a fiction, the "powder horn"-shaped bottles were real, originally produced as commemoratives by Tennessee's George Dickel Distillery in 1964. The Dickel distillery remains in business, but the bottles are long out of manufacture. They were scarce by the time *Star Trek VI* was filmed and now fetch upwards of a hundred dollars apiece on eBay.

- **Scotch**—The drink of choice for Montgomery Scott, Scotch whiskey remained popular into the twenty-fourth century and was featured in multiple episodes of both the classic series and *The Next Generation.*

- **Tequila**—In *Star Trek: First Contact* (1996), warp-drive pioneer Zefram Cochrane and Counselor Deanna Troi binge on tequila shots.

- **Wine and champagne**—Wine and champagne were consumed in many episodes of both series. The Picard family operated a vineyard, and Robert regularly sent Jean-Luc bottles of Chateau Picard. A bottle of Dom Perignon (vintage 2265) was used to christen the *Enterprise-B* in *Star Trek Generations.*

- **Beer**—Not only did beer remain popular, but many twentieth-century breweries were apparently still in business into the twenty-third and twenty-fourth centuries. Brands mentioned by name on *Star Trek* include Budweiser (*Star Trek*, 2009) and Schlitz (*Next Gen*'s "The Big Goodbye"). Also, Guinness turned up on *Voyager.* While visiting the twentieth century in *Star Trek IV,* Captain Kirk downed a Michelob.

- **Green stuff**—Finally, there was the mysterious green liquor that Scotty consumed in "By Any Other Name" during his drinking contest with Tomar. Scotty could not identify the spirit, nor could Data when he discovered a bottle of the stuff in Ten-Forward during "Relics." Later in that episode, however, Captain Picard revealed that the drink was Aldebaran whiskey, a favorite of his. "Who do you think gave it to Guinan?" he asked.

26

"Make It So"

The Quotable *Next Generation*

Star Trek: The Next Generation coined a few phrases that gained popular currency, including Captain Picard's terse commands, "Make it so" and "Engage" (to say nothing of "Earl Grey—hot") and the Borg's warning that "resistance is futile." But *Next Gen* never produced a catchphrase as instantly recognizable and widely quoted (or parodied) as the classic series' iconic "Live Long and Prosper" or the illusory "Beam Me Up, Scotty" (a phrase never actually uttered on the show). Nevertheless, like its predecessor, the show remained eminently quotable, and numerous lines and dialogue exchanges have gained currency among fans over the years. As a companion to the classic *Trek* quotes provided in the original *Star Trek FAQ*, we submit the following topically grouped sampling of *Next Generation* humor and insight.

On the Human Condition

"It's hard to be philosophical when faced with suffering."
                                                    —Dr. Crusher, "Symbiosis"

"Maybe if we felt any loss as keenly as we felt the death of one close to us, human history would be a lot less bloody."
                                                    —Riker, "The Bonding"

"Oh, your species is *always* suffering and dying."
                                                    —Q, "Hide and Q"

"I've noted that some people use humor as a shield. They talk much, yet say little."
                                                    —Worf, "The Emissary"

"You can't rescue a man from what he calls his home."
                                —Ramsey (Sam Hennings), "Angel One"

"The quest for youth, Number One. So futile."
                                                    —Picard, "Too Short a Season"

"Thinking about what you can't control only wastes energy and creates its own enemy."
                                                    —Worf, "Coming of Age"

"Things are only impossible until they're not."

—Picard, "When the Bough Breaks"

"Ugly giant bags of mostly water."

—The crystal life-form describing humans in "Home Soil"

"As I learn more and more what it is to be human, I am more and more convinced that I would never make a good one."

—Q, "Deja Q"

"I know human beings. They are all sopping over with compassion and forgiveness. They can't wait to absolve almost any offense. It's an inherent weakness of the breed."

—Q, "Deja Q"

On Humanity in the Twenty-Fourth Century

Captain Picard's command, "Make it so," has been emblazoned on shirts, hats, stickers, buttons, coffee mugs and nearly everything else in the galaxy.   *Photo by Preston Hewis, East Bank Images*

"I'm with Starfleet; we don't lie."

—Wesley Crusher, "Justice"

"Genetic manipulation or not, nobody's perfect."

—Picard, "The Masterpiece Society"

Samuel Clemens (Jerry Hardin): "Young lady, I come from a time when men achieve power and wealth by standing on the backs of the poor, where prejudice and intolerance are commonplace and power is an end unto itself, and you're telling me that isn't how it is anymore?!"

Deanna Troi: "That's right."

Clemens: "Hmm. Maybe it's worth giving up cigars for, after all."

—"Time's Arrow, Part II"

"A lot has changed in the past three hundred years. People are no longer obsessed with the accumulation of things. We've eliminated hunger, want, the need for possessions. We've grown out of our infancy."

—Picard, "The Neutral Zone"

"Don't you people from the twenty-fourth century ever pee?"

—Zefram Cochrane (James Cromwell), *First Contact*

On Other Life-forms

"We are more alike than unlike, my dear captain. I have pores. Humans have pores. I have fingerprints. Humans have fingerprints. My chemical nutrients are like your blood. If you prick me, do I not . . . leak?"

—Data, "The Naked Now"

"If there's one thing I've learned over the years it's never to underestimate a Klingon."

—Picard, *Star Trek Generations*

"I did not faint. Klingons do not faint."

—Worf, "Up the Long Ladder"

"As you humans say, 'I'm all ears.'"

—Kazago (Doug Warhit), a Ferengi, "The Battle"

Riker: "Yes, it's something Troi warned me about when we first started to see each other. A Betazoid woman, when she goes through this phase, quadruples her sex drive."

Deanna: "Or more."

Riker (eyebrow raised): "Or more? You never told me that."

Deanna: "I didn't want to frighten you."

—Riker and Counselor Troi, about women from Betazed, in "Manhunt"

"The chance to study you is, frankly, provocative, but you are next of kin to chaos."

—Picard, to Q, in "Q Who"

"The Borg are the ultimate user. They're unlike any threat your Federation has ever faced. They're not interested in political conquest, wealth, or power as you know it. They're simply interested in your ship, its technology. They've identified it as something they can consume."

—Q, "Q Who"

"The Borg have neither honor nor courage. That is our greatest advantage."

—Worf, "The Best of Both Worlds, Part II"

On Crime and Punishment

"Your Honor, a courtroom is a crucible. In it we burn away irrelevancies until we are left with a pure product: the truth, for all time."

—Picard, "The Measure of a Man"

"When has justice ever been as simple as a rulebook?"

—Riker, "Justice"

"The prisoners will not be harmed . . . until they're found guilty."

—Q, "Encounter at Farpoint"

"'A matter of internal security'—the age-old cry of the oppressor."

—Picard, "The Hunted"

"I have never subscribed to the idea that political power flows from the barrel of a gun."

—Picard, "The High Ground"

"There are times, sir, when men of good conscience cannot blindly follow orders."

—Picard, "The Offspring"

"Captain, I believe I speak for everyone here sir, when I say to hell with our orders."

—Data, *Star Trek: First Contact*

"The first time any man's freedom is trodden on we're all damaged."

—Picard, "The Drumhead"

"No being is so important that he can usurp the rights of another!"

—Picard, "The Schizoid Man"

On War and Peace

"Here on Minos, we live by the motto, 'Peace through superior firepower.'"

—The Peddler (Vincent Schiavelli), "The Arsenal of Freedom"

"One world's butcher is another world's hero."

—Jarok (James Sloyan), "The Defector"

"The difference between generals and terrorists is only the difference between winners and losers. If you win you are called a general, if you lose . . ."

—Finn (Richard Cox), "The High Ground"

"In a world where children blow up children, everyone's a threat."

—Alexana (Kerrie Keane), "The High Ground"

"People blame the military for the wars we are asked to fight."

—Toreth (Carolyn Seymour), "Face of the Enemy"

"How much innocent blood has been spilled for the cause of freedom in the history of your Federation, Doctor? How many good and noble societies have bombed civilians in war? Wiped out whole cities. And now that you enjoy the comfort that has come from their battles, their killing, you frown on my immorality? I am willing to die for my freedom. And, in the finest tradition of your own great civilization, I'm willing to kill for it too."

—Finn, "The High Ground"

"Starfleet is not a military organization. Its purpose is exploration."

—Picard, "Peak Performance"

"The true test of a warrior is not without, it is within."

—Worf, "Heart of Glory"

"Diplomacy! Oh, I adore diplomacy! Everyone dresses so well!"

—Lwaxana Troi, "Half a Life"

On Metaphysics

Data: "Where is your mother?"

Gia (Kimberly Cullum): "She died about a year ago. Father said she went to a beautiful place, where everything is peaceful and everyone loves each other and no one ever gets sick. Do you think there's really a place like that?"

Data: "Yes. I do."

—"Thine Own Self"

"Sharing an orbit with God is no small experience."

—Deanna Troi, "Justice"

"If we're going to be damned, let's be damned for what we really are."

—Picard, "Encounter at Farpoint"

Q (dressed as a monk): "Let us pray for understanding and for compassion."

Picard: "Let us do no such damn thing!"

—"Hide and Q"

"Dr. Barron, your report describes how rational these people are. Millennia ago they abandoned their belief in the supernatural. Now you are asking me to sabotage that achievement, to send them back into the dark ages of superstition and ignorance and fear? No!"

—Picard, "Who Watches the Watchers"

On Romance and Gender Politics

"My love is a fever, longing still for that which longer nurseth the disease, in faith I do not love thee with mine eyes for they in thee a thousand errors see; but 'tis my heart, that loves what they despise, who in despite of view, are pleased to dote. Shall I compare thee to a summer's day?"

—Picard, quoting a mash-up of Shakespeare's sonnets, in "Ménage a Troi"

"I prefer to be acquainted with the women that I kiss."

—Picard, "Captain's Holiday"

"She's found a vulnerability in you, a vulnerability I've been looking for for years. If I had known sooner, I would have appeared as a female."

—Q, to Picard, in "Qpid"

"I would be delighted to offer any advice I can on understanding women. When I have some I'll let you know."

—Picard, "In Theory"

"Klingons do not pursue relationships. They conquer that which they desire."

—Worf, "In Theory"

"Darling, you remain as aesthetically pleasing as the first day we met. I believe I am the most fortunate sentient in this sector of the Galaxy!"

—Data to Jenna (Michele Scarabelli), "In Theory"

Geordi: "Did you ever think about getting married again?"

Guinan: "No. Twenty-three was my limit."

—*Star Trek Nemesis*

Picard: "Beverly, may I take off the uniform for a moment?"

Dr. Crusher: "Captain!"

—"The Perfect Mate"

Troi: "And have you noticed how your boobs have started to firm up?"

Crusher: "Not that we care about such things in this day and age."

Deanna: "Uh-huh."

—*Star Trek: Insurrection*

Soren (Melinda Culea): "Commander, tell me about your sexual organs."

Riker: "Uhhh . . ."

—"The Outcast"

"You work with your females, arm them, and force them to wear clothing."

—Ferengi officer, "The Last Outpost"

"Women aren't people, they're women!"

—Dr. Graves (Morgan Sheppard), "The Schizoid Man"

Soren: "On my planet we have been taught that gender is primitive."

Riker: "Primitive?"

Soren: "Less evolved."

Riker: "Maybe so, but sometimes there is a lot to be said for an experience that's
. . . primitive."

—"The Outcast"

"Ladies and gentlemen, and invited transgendered species . . ."

—Data, *Star Trek Nemesis*

"I have had those feelings, those longings, all of my life. It is not unnatural. I am not sick because I feel this way. I do not need to be helped. I do not need to be cured. What I need, and what all of those who are like me need, is your understanding. And your compassion. We have not injured you in any way. And yet we are scorned and attacked. And all because we are different. What we do is no different from what you do. We talk and laugh. We complain about work. And we wonder about growing old. . . . And for that we are called misfits, and deviants and criminals. What right do you have to punish us? What right do you have to change us? What makes you think you can dictate how people love each other?"

—Soren, "The Outcast"

On the Prime Directive . . .

"The Prime Directive is not just a set of rules. It is a philosophy, and a very correct one. History has proved again and again that whenever mankind interferes with a less developed civilization, no matter how well-intentioned that interference may be, the results are invariably disastrous."

—Picard, "Symbiosis"

Picard: "We were saddened by those events, but they occurred within the borders of the Cardassian Empire."

Ro: "And the Federation is pledged not to interfere with the internal affairs of others. How convenient that must be for you. To turn a deaf ear to those who suffer behind a line on a map."

—"Ensign Ro"

...and Other Words to Live By

"Captain, the most elementary and valuable statement in science, the beginning of wisdom, is 'I do not know.'"

—Data, "Where Silence Has Lease"

"Wishing for a thing does not make it so."

—Picard, "Samaritan Snare"

"Respect is earned, not bestowed."

—Deanna Troi, "The Icarus Factor"

"Friendship must dare to risk, Counselor, or it isn't friendship."

—Picard, "Conspiracy"

"We must strive to be more than we are, Lal. It does not matter that we will never reach our ultimate goal. The effort yields its own rewards."

—Data, "The Offspring"

"The game isn't big enough unless it scares you a little."

—Riker, "Pen Pals"

"The more difficult the task, the sweeter the victory."

—Riker, "Captain's Holiday"

"I think, when one has been angry for a very long time, one gets used to it. And it becomes comfortable like . . . like old leather. And finally it becomes so familiar that one can't remember feeling any other way."

—Picard, "The Wounded"

"Mr. Worf, villains who twirl their mustaches are easy to spot. Those who clothe themselves in good deeds are well-camouflaged."

—Picard, "The Drumhead"

"I've been told that patience is sometimes a more effective weapon than the sword."

—Worf, "Redemption"

"This is just a thing . . . and things can be replaced. Lives cannot."

—Data, "The Ensigns of Command"

On Health and Fitness

"Swimming is too much like . . . bathing."

—Worf, with disdain, in "Conspiracy"

"Vitamins . . . they do wonders for the body."

> —The elderly Admiral Quinn (Ward Costello), possessed by an alien symbiote, as he mops up the floor with Riker in "Conspiracy"

On Children

"What the hell? Children are not allowed on the bridge!"

> —Picard, "Encounter at Farpoint"

"The bridge will be sending a rescue party as soon as possible, so I want you all to stop crying!"

> —Picard, to the children, in "Disaster"

Keiko O'Brien: "I'm going into labor!"

Worf: "You cannot! This is not a good time, Keiko!"

> —"Disaster"

"Of course he's unreasonable, he's a child!"

> —Lwaxana Troi, to Worf, in "The Cost of Living"

On Dessert

"I never met a chocolate I didn't like."

> —Deanna Troi, "The Game"

"I would gladly risk feeling bad at times, if it also meant that I could taste my dessert."

> —Data, "Hero Worship"

On Literature

Q: "Hear this, Picard, and reflect: 'All the galaxy's a stage.'"

Picard: "'World,' not 'galaxy'; 'all the world's a stage.'"

Q; "Oh, you know that one. Well, if he was living now, he would have said 'galaxy.'"

> —"Hide and Q"

"A great poet once said 'All spirits are enslaved that serve things evil.'"

> —Picard, quoting from Percy Shelley's "Prometheus Unbound" in "Skin of Evil"

"It's elementary, my dear Riker . . . sir."

> —Data, "Lonely Among Us"

On Picard (and Other Starship Captains)

Wesley Crusher: "He wants the impossible!"

Geordi: "That's the short definition of 'captain.'"

—"The Ensigns of Command"

"Starship captains are like children. They want everything right now and they want it their way. The secret is to give them what they need, not what they want."

—Scotty, "Relics"

"Jean-Luc, sometimes I think the only reason I come here is to listen to these wonderful speeches of yours."

—Q, "True Q"

Spock: "In your own way, you are as stubborn as another captain of the *Enterprise* I once knew."

Picard: "Then I am in good company, sir."

—"Unification II"

"I was out saving the galaxy when your grandfather was in diapers."

—Kirk to Picard in *Generations*

"In your position it's important to ask yourself one question: 'What would Picard do?'"

—Riker to Wesley Crusher in "Pen Pals"

On the Crew's Interpersonal Dynamics

"I think we shall end up with a fine crew . . . if we avoid temptation."

—Picard, "The Naked Now"

"This is the worst-run ship I have ever been on. You should take lessons from the *QE2*. Now that's an efficient operation."

—Ralph Offenhouse (Peter Mark Richman) to Picard in "The Neutral Zone"

"Would you like to talk about what's bothering you, or would you like to break some more furniture?"

—Deanna Troi to Worf in "Birthright I"

"If you're looking for my professional opinion as ship's counselor . . . he's nuts!"

—Deanna Troi, *Star Trek: First Contact*

"Don't go criticizing my counseling techniques!"

—Deanna Troi, while drunk, in *First Contact*

The Borg warning that "resistance is futile" became one of *The Next Generation*'s most repeated (and parodied) catchphrases, as witnessed by this Christmas card by cartoonist Matt Wuerker.

"Androids do not have fun."

—Data, *Insurrection*

"My hair does not require trimming, you lunkhead."
        —Data, experimenting with "friendly insults and jibes" in "Data's Day"

"Captain, we've got a problem with the warp core or the phase inducers or some other damn thing."—Geordi, "All Good Things . . ."

Geordi: "I told the Captain I would have this diagnostic done in an hour."

Scotty: "And how long will it really take you?"

Geordi: "An hour!"

Scotty: "Oh, you didn't tell him how long it would *really* take, did you?"
                        —"Relics"

"A blind man teaching an android how to paint? That's got to be worth a couple of pages in somebody's book!"
                —Riker to Geordi and Data in "11001001"

"Doctor, God knows I'm not one to discourage input, but I would appreciate it if you'd let me finish my sentences once in a while."
                —Picard to Pulaski in "Unnatural Selection"

"We are losing our professional detachment, Doctor."

—Captain Picard to Doctor Crusher in "Symbiosis"

"My great-grandfather was once bitten by a rattlesnake. After three days of intense pain, the snake died."

—Riker in "Shades of Gray"

"Oh, you're so stolid. You weren't like that before the beard."

—Q to Riker in "Deja Q"

"Shut up, Wesley!"

—Picard and Dr. Crusher, at different times, in "Datalore"

"Maybe I am sick of following rules and regulations! Maybe I'm sick of living up to everyone else's expectations! Did you ever think of that?!"

—Wesley Crusher, "Journey's End"

On the Final Frontier

"If you can't take a little bloody nose, maybe you ought to go back home and crawl under your bed. It's not safe out here. It's wondrous, with treasures to satiate desires both subtle and gross, but it's not for the timid."

—Q in "Q Who"

"Fate. It protects fools, little children, and ships named *Enterprise*."

—Riker, "Contagion"

"Let's see what's out there. Engage!"

—Picard, "Encounter at Farpoint"

27

All Good Things

T he behind-the-scenes stability that helped foster four years of consistently excellent television disintegrated during the final season of *Star Trek: The Next Generation*. Executive producer Rick Berman, in an interview included on the *Star Trek: The Next Generation* Season Seven DVD collection, described the 1993–94 season as "the most chaotic time I have ever experienced." That's because the seventh season of *The Next Generation* overlapped with both the second season of *Deep Space Nine* and preproduction of *Star Trek Generations*. Meanwhile, Berman, Michael Piller, and Jeri Taylor were also developing *Star Trek: Voyager*, set to premiere in January 1995. Amid this frenzy of activity, *The Next Generation* became the producers' lowest priority. Their top concern was the movie and making the tricky transition from the original crew to the *Next Gen* characters. Ensuring the continued success of *DS9* and paving the way for *Voyager* were also deemed more important than shepherding *The Next Generation* through a season that, in the grand scheme, amounted to little more than a victory lap. Consequently, most of the series' veteran writers and other key personnel were moved to other *Trek* projects or asked to pull double or triple duty. Executive producer Jeri Taylor, for instance, was helping develop *Voyager*. Michael Piller was executive producing both *The Next Generation* and *DS9* while cocreating *Voyager*. Writers Ronald D. Moore and Brannon Braga were hired to pen *Generations* in addition to their ongoing *Next Gen* responsibilities. Rick Berman remained involved in everything.

In order to accommodate the schedule for *Generations*, which began filming during production of the *Next Gen* series finale, the cast and crew's summer hiatus was cut short by a month. Lack of rest only worsened writers' ongoing difficulty with generating fertile story ideas. Everyone was so overextended that for several weeks producers stopped listening to pitches from freelance screenwriters, exacerbating the problem. In previous seasons, producers had purchased several stories and sometimes complete teleplays from freelancers. Now the creative workload fell entirely on the show's exhausted, distracted, written-out staff. At one point, Taylor approached Patrick Stewart and Brent

Spiner to solicit ideas. Stewart suggested a story later developed as "Bloodlines." The fact that Taylor took this step at all indicates the severity of the problem. In the early days of the series, according to Wil Wheaton, Gene Roddenberry expressly forbade writers from discussing story ideas with cast members.

The inevitable result of all this was a steep decline in quality. Teleplays became increasingly far-fetched and gimmicky, and often seemed jumbled or underdeveloped. Although Season Seven featured a clutch of episodes as good as any in the show's history (including "Parallels," "The Pegasus," "Lower Decks," and the epic finale "All Good Things . . ."), it also included a handful of the worst installments of the series and many mediocre entries. After the particularly dire "Force of Nature," Piller gathered the writing staff for a series of lengthy meetings aimed at correcting the course of the season. "I felt we were letting it slip away," Piller said in Edward Gross and Mark A. Altman's book *Captains' Logs.*

Piller insisted that writers refocus on the characters and try to wrap up dangling plot threads. Curiously, this led to an unintentional and, in the words of staff writer Naren Shankar, "embarrassing" proliferation of stories concerning the crew's relatives. The final season began with a story involving Data's brother, Lore. Later Season Seven tales introduced Data's mother, Geordi's mother, Worf's adoptive brother, and Picard's "son." "It was like, 'Oh no, who's next? Is it Guinan's third cousin?'" quipped screenwriter Nick Sagan in an interview on the Trek Today website. Other Season Seven teleplays dealt with the ongoing family drama between Lwaxana and Deanna Troi, Worf and his son Alexander, and Beverly and Wesley Crusher. In another controversial development, Worf and Deanna Troi became romantically involved, creating interpersonal tension between Worf and Commander Riker. This story arc irritated many fans and even a few of the show's writers, such as Shankar, who had pushed for Riker and Troi to resume their relationship and perhaps even get married. Berman and Piller, however, both supported the Worf-Troi romance.

The final season was further depleted by the loss of secondary cast members who had made important contributions in recent years. Colm Meaney and Rosalind Chao were now playing Miles and Keiko O'Brien on *DS9*. Michelle Forbes's Ro Laren appeared in just one episode during the final *Next Gen* campaign. Most damaging, Whoopi Goldberg's Guinan failed to appear at all in Season Seven. *Next Generation* regulars had mixed reactions to the series' imminent cancellation. Some, including Patrick Stewart and Brent Spiner, expressed relief, while others, including Jonathan Frakes and Marina Sirtis, voiced regret. But the ensemble soldiered on together and delivered another season of mostly exemplary work. So did the show's platoon of gifted technicians and artisans. Despite the struggle and controversy, Season Seven improved as it progressed and closed in bravura style with an eagerly awaited and entirely satisfying two-hour finale.

"Descent, Part II"

The nail-biting Season Six finale left Data allied with Lore and a ship full of renegade Borg in an attempt to destroy the Federation. In the rousing conclusion, Captain Picard, Geordi, and Deanna manage to break Lore's hold over Data, while Riker and Worf renew acquaintances with the Borg nicknamed Hugh. Dr. Crusher, left in command of the *Enterprise*, battles the Borg starship. An early draft of Rene Echevarria's teleplay concluded with Data destroying Lore. In the final version, Data's problematic brother is merely deactivated and disassembled. This enables Data to gain possession of the Emotion Chip, first introduced in the Season Four adventure "Brothers" and featured in the first two *Next Generation* movies. Spiner, as always, impresses in his dual roles as Data and Lore, and Gates McFadden effectively sells Dr. Crusher as an effective commander. Jonathan Del Arco reprises his fine work as Hugh from Season Five's "I Borg." "Descent, Part II" launched *Next Gen*'s final campaign with great promise, but it would take a while for Season Seven to equal this exciting beginning.

"Liaisons"

Captain Picard, stranded in a shuttle crash, falls into the clutches of a mentally unstable woman who has been marooned on the same remote planet for seven years. Meanwhile, Deanna Troi and Worf host a pair of irritating dignitaries aboard the *Enterprise*. "Liaisons," a freelance submission credited to Jeanne Carrigan-Fauci and Lisa Rich (from a story by Roger Eschbacher and Joq Greenspon), was originally intended as a *Star Trek* spin on Stephen King's *Misery*, with a wounded Captain Picard imprisoned by an obsessed admirer. When producers became concerned that the scenario was a bit *too* similar to *Misery*, Brannon Braga reworked the teleplay extensively. Braga, who declined a screen credit, added the comedic subplot involving Troi and Worf and their annoying guests. The resulting episode betrays its troubled origins: It's slow-moving and clumsily structured, a ponderous collection of mismatched parts.

"Interface"

Geordi is testing an experimental device that enables him to control an exploratory probe through mental commands when word arrives that his mother has been killed in a starship crash. Later, his presumed-dead mom appears to him while he's linked to the probe and pleads with her son to rescue her. "Interface," written by Joe Menosky, had been gathering dust for two seasons. It's easy to see why the story had been bypassed previously. This glacially paced installment needed more plot twists or a B-story; there was simply not enough action to fill an entire episode. Three weeks after "Interface" wrapped production, a hastily written filler scene, in which Riker tries to comfort Geordi, was filmed to get the installment up to acceptable length. An early draft of "Interface" featured

Commander Riker and his father instead of Geordi and his mom. In its broadcast form, the episode includes Madge Sinclair as Geordi's mother and a cameo by Ben Vereen as Geordi's father. Coincidentally, Sinclair had already played Burton's mother in two made-for-TV movies (*One in a Million: The Ron LaFlore Story*, 1978, and *Guyana Tragedy*, 1980). Writer-producer Ronald D. Moore, in an interview with ign.com, said that "Interface" was one of the episodes that suggested Season Seven was on the wrong track. "We all kind of looked at each other and we were like, 'This is sad. This is the best we can do—Geordi's mother?'" Moore said. "It was such a 'Who cares?' idea that we were just sort of, 'Oh, man, this show has *got* to end.'"

"Gambit, Parts I and II"

Commander Riker is captured while investigating the apparent murder of Captain Picard, perpe-

Ben Vereen made a cameo appearance as Geordi's father in "Interface," one of several Season Seven installments to introduce the relative of an *Enterprise* crew member.

trated by a band of cutthroat mercenaries who are stealing ancient Romulan artifacts. This leaves Data in charge of the *Enterprise*, with Worf as his second-in-command. However, Riker soon discovers that Picard isn't dead—he's working undercover as one of the mercenaries. "Gambit," written by Naren Shankar and Ron Moore from a story by Christopher Hatton, broke one of Gene Roddenberry's cardinal rules—a prohibition against stories involving "space pirates." It's a diverting yarn but the least impressive of *The Next Generation*'s eight multipart adventures. Again, the major problem is a dearth of story. The scenario lacks the complexity and scope needed to carry two full installments. Many sequences seem needlessly protracted, and the story's resolution proves anticlimactic. "Gambit" remains notable primarily for its guest cast, including Robin Curtis, who had played Lieutenant Saavik in *Star Trek III* and *Star Trek IV*, as Vulcan mercenary Tallera; Los Angeles Lakers star James Worthy as Klingon mercenary Koral; and Sabrina La Beauf (formerly Sondra Huxtable on *The Cosby Show*) as Ensign Giusti.

In "Gambit," the least engaging of *The Next Generation*'s two-part adventures, Captain Picard infiltrated a gang of space pirates, including Vekor (Caitlin Brown).

"Phantasms"

Data, while exploring his dream program (introduced in the previous season's "Birthright, Part I"), begins suffering bizarre nightmares and hallucinations. At first Deanna thinks Data may be developing a neurosis, but the truth turns out to be far more disturbing. Brannon Braga wrote this dark, surreal, horror-laced episode, which is full of unnerving imagery and shocking plot twists, including Data attacking Deanna with a knife. Spiner contributes a spellbinding and at times terrifying performance to "Phantasms," one of the few praiseworthy episodes to emerge during the early part of *Next Gen*'s seventh season.

"Dark Page"

Lwaxana Troi lapses into a sort of mental coma while teaching a group of telepathic aliens known as the Cairn to communicate verbally. Deanna enters her mother's mind to investigate and learns a dark secret about her childhood. The downbeat "Dark Page," written by Hilary J. Bader, is another slow-footed, thinly plotted episode. Like "Liaisons," this teleplay—originally written to feature Dr. Crusher—had been on the shelf for years and required extensive revisions (by the uncredited Rene Echevarria). Majel Barrett-Roddenberry, making her final

Next Gen on-screen appearance, contributes an unusually subdued performance and spends half the episode unconscious. Kirsten Dunst, who would later costar in director Sam Raimi's three *Spider-Man* films, appears as a young alien girl. "Dark Page," "Liaisons," and "Family" are the only *Next Generation* episodes to include no scenes set on the bridge.

"Attached"

On a diplomatic mission gone awry, Captain Picard and Dr. Crusher are captured by xenophobic aliens, imprisoned, and implanted with devices that force the two to remain in close proximity to one another. The two linked inmates stage a breakout but, as they make their escape, discover that they can hear each other's thoughts. This forces Jean-Luc and Beverly to finally address their long-simmering romantic attraction. Written by Nick Sagan, son of famed astronomer Carl Sagan, "Attached" also includes a satirical subplot in which Riker attempts to negotiate the release of Picard and Crusher from the planet's two paranoid, rival civilizations. Director Jonathan Frakes does a commendable job of handling disparate elements—romance and satire—and of helping foster touching performances from Patrick Stewart and Gates McFadden. Originally, Sagan wanted to take the Picard-Crusher romance in a more serious (and sexy) direction, but Michael Piller reportedly nixed that idea. As a result, their relationship ultimately remained unchanged, which irked many fans who had spent the last seven years rooting for the captain and the doctor to become lovers. Later, Jeri Taylor explained that the show's executive producers were leery of any Season Seven stories that limited screenwriters' options in creating the forthcoming *Next Generation* movies.

"Force of Nature"

While searching for a missing medical ship, the *Enterprise* is waylaid by alien dissidents who claim that warp drive is destabilizing the fabric of space in their sector of the galaxy. Another dull, flat entry, writer Naren Shankar's "Force of Nature" overflows with pseudo-scientific mumbo jumbo, ham-handed ecological posturing, and risible ideas such as the imposition of an interstellar speed limit. (This installment explains why, in a few later episodes, Starfleet has to grant the *Enterprise* special permission to travel at speeds faster than Warp Five.) Like many other Season Seven teleplays, the plot of "Force of Nature" is too thin to carry a full episode. As a result, the story is padded out with filler scenes, including an absurdly protracted, five-minute sequence in which Geordi and Data realign various pieces of equipment while discussing Data's cat. "Force of Nature" disappointed everyone involved in its creation, not to mention the show's fans. Michael Piller singled it out as the season's worst episode.

"Inheritance"

While helping the residents of planet Atrea IV avert a geological disaster, Data meets a woman who claims to be his "mother"—Juliana Tainer (Fionnula Flanagan), the ex-wife of his creator, Dr. Noonian Soong. She dotes on her android son, but Data begins to suspect she may not be exactly who she seems. "Inheritance," written by Dan Koeppel and Rene Echevarria, isn't perfect, but it marks a major step up from "Force of Nature" and most previous Season Seven installments. The episode moves briskly and is peppered with gripping character moments for both Data and Tainer. Flanagan, who also appeared on *Deep Space Nine* and *Enterprise*, supplies a warm and moving performance as Data's loving but guilt-plagued parent. The teleplay also fills in some of the backstory involved in Data's creation, including the revelation that there were three failed prototypes constructed prior to Data and his brother Lore, an idea later exploited by *Star Trek Nemesis*.

"Parallels"

Worf begins moving through a series of alternate realities, including one in which he is married to Deanna Troi and another in which Captain Picard was killed by the Borg. In the Picard-less parallel universe, the Federation and the Cardassians are allied in a war against the Bajorans, and Lieutenant Wesley Crusher serves aboard the *Enterprise*. Written by Brannon Braga, "Parallels" intentionally grows more disorienting as Worf moves through a dizzying variety of alternate realities, but the tale remains consistently engrossing. The art and costume departments introduce a series of subtle but telling variations between universes, including slightly different uniforms and a modified bridge set. Also, Data's eyes change color, from gold to blue and back. This episode also features one of the most spectacular visual effects shots in the history of the series, showing scores of various starships *Enterprise* gathered around a "quantum fissure." Michael Dorn's superb, and at points very funny, performance as the confused yet resolute Klingon holds the trippy, fractured narrative together. "Parallels" began the controversial Worf-Troi romance that would continue, off and on, throughout the remainder of the season. That element aside, this remains one of the most absorbing episodes of the seventh—or any other—season.

"The Pegasus"

Commander Riker's former captain beams aboard to oversee a salvage mission to locate the USS *Pegasus*, an experimental vessel that was lost under mysterious circumstances twelve years earlier, during Riker's first tour of duty. The *Enterprise* must recover or destroy the *Pegasus* to prevent it from falling into Romulan hands. As the mission proceeds, Picard grows suspicious of Riker's former commanding officer, now-Admiral Pressman (Terry O'Quinn), while Riker struggles with a grim secret from his past. Written by Ron Moore, "The

Pegasus" is a fiery, exquisitely cut jewel of an episode—rich in both interpersonal and political tension, populated by believable characters grappling with complex ethical issues. Everything in this installment works brilliantly, including a humorous opening sequence involving preparations for "Captain Picard Day," celebrated by the ship's children. Moore wrote this bit to show off Frakes's hilarious Patrick Stewart imitation. Stewart, Frakes, and guest star O'Quinn (who later gained fame as the enigmatic John Locke on writer-producer J. J. Abrams's *Lost*) all deliver razor-sharp performances. Moore's teleplay also explains why Federation starships do not have cloaking devices—they are forbidden under the treaty that ended the sixty-year war with the Romulans. The series finale of *Star Trek: Enterprise*, which guest starred Frakes and Marina Sirtis, and unfolds in a holodeck-created flashback, ties in with the events of "The Pegasus."

With a good episode ("Inheritance") followed by back-to-back great ones, *The Next Generation*'s seventh season was finally on track. A couple of clunkers remained, but most of the series' remaining installments would meet fans' high expectations.

"Homeward"

Worf's adoptive brother, Federation cultural observer Nicholai Rozhenko (Paul Sorvino), violates the Prime Directive (and tricks Captain Picard) in order to save a village of primitives when an environmental disaster wipes out all life on planet Boraal II. Rozhenko transports the Boraalans to an *Enterprise* holodeck, where they will live in a holographic re-creation of their home world while being ferried to a new planet. Unfortunately, the holodeck begins to malfunction. Written by Naren Shankar from stories by Spike Steingasser and William N. Stape, "Homeworld" features a fertile premise but presents an extremely hard-hearted, doctrinaire interpretation of the Prime Directive. The behavior of Captain Picard, who tries to prevent Rozhenko from saving the Boraalans, runs counter to his actions in the Season Two installment "Pen Pals," wherein Picard risked his career to save another, less advanced civilization from a similar planetary natural disaster. Sorvino, best known for playing gangsters in movies such as *GoodFellas*, was a devoted *Star Trek* fan who contacted producers and asked to make a guest appearance on the show. Penny Johnson, who appears as Rozhenko's Boraalan wife, later landed the recurring role of Kasidy Yates, Commander Sisko's love interest on *Deep Space Nine*. The classic *Trek* episode "For the World Is Hollow and I Have Touched the Sky" also involved primitive people who are unaware they are traveling aboard a starship. A similar plot device turned up in *Star Trek: Insurrection*.

"Sub Rosa"

Dr. Crusher is seduced by a mysterious entity who claims to be a centuries-old ghost, and who has carried on secret affairs with Beverly's female parentage for generations. Written by Brannon Braga from material by Jeri Taylor and Jeanna F. Gallo, the offbeat "Sub Rosa" is bodice-ripping romance disguised as *Star Trek.* It's set almost entirely on a Federation colony constructed to resemble gaslight-era Scotland, and director Jonathan Frakes drenches the proceedings in thick shadows to enhance the scenario's gothic ambiance. According to Taylor, "Sub Rosa" was an homage to Henry James's classic *The Turn of the Screw* and director Jack Clayton's 1961 film *The Innocents,* which was based on the James novel. She denies any connection with the Anne Rice book *The Witching Hour,* which contains a similar premise. According to Brannon Braga and Rene Echevarria, "Sub Rosa" split *Star Trek* fans along gender lines: Women loved it and men hated it. Gates McFadden delivers a daring performance—at one point, she writhes in ecstasy with an invisible lover. The actress has named "Sub Rosa" her favorite episode of the season.

Shannon Fill appeared as Sito Jaxa (pictured on this *Next Generation* game card) in two excellent episodes, Season Five's "The First Duty" and Season Seven's "The Lower Decks."

"Lower Decks"

This format-bending episode unfolds from the perspective of four junior officers and a civilian friend—the kind of characters that serve as "background color" in other episodes. The plot, about a secret mission to transport a Cardassian double agent back home, remains secondary; the episode concerns itself primarily with exploring the aspirations and anxieties of these fresh-faced, idealistic young people who represent *The Next Generation*'s next generation. Rene Echevarria's teleplay, based on a story by Ron Wilkerson and Jean Louise Matthias, also reveals how the ship's senior staff is viewed by their subordinates. The charming young characters are all vividly played. They include ambitious ensign Sam Lavelle (played by Dan Gauthier), resourceful Vulcan engineer Taurik (Alexander Enberg), courageous Bajoran ensign Sito Jaxa (Shannon Fill), love-struck nurse Alyssa Ogawa (Patti Yasutake), and gossip-mongering Ten-Forward bartender Ben (Bruce Beatty). The greatest testament to the work of these five actors is that the story's tragic climax registers with stunning emotional impact. Previously, Fill appeared as Jaxa in Season Five's "The First Duty," and events from that episode are referenced here. Years later, the writers of *Deep Space Nine* considered reviving Jaxa, but the idea was eventually scrapped. Enberg, the son of executive producer Jeri Taylor, later earned a recurring role as the Vulcan ensign Vorik on *Star Trek: Voyager*. The refreshing and deeply moving "Lower Decks" provides another Season Seven highlight.

"Thine Own Self"

Data, marooned and amnesia stricken on a world with a preindustrial civilization, seeks help from the planet's residents, with disastrous consequences. Meanwhile, Deanna struggles with the exams necessary to become a full commander, with occasional bridge duties. "Thine Own Self" was written by Ron Moore from a story pitched by Christopher Hatton, who sold producers on the simple idea of "Data as the Frankenstein monster." Moore's teleplay integrates numerous *Frankenstein* elements, including the presence of a young girl who befriends the misunderstood "monster" and the threatening presence of angry villagers. The episode remains memorable for Brent Spiner's vulnerable, open-hearted performance and notable for Patrick Stewart's near absence. Stewart, granted leave to perform his one-man production of *A Christmas Carol* in London, appears only in the episode's final scene and has just one line. "Thine Own Self" earned an Emmy nomination for art direction.

"Masks"

An ancient intelligence seizes control of the *Enterprise* computers, as well as Data's neural net, and begins using the transporter and replicator to transform the ship into a replica of a lost civilization. Screenwriter Joe Menosky's "Masks" is so far-fetched that it borders on fantasy and so convoluted that it perplexed even Menosky's fellow writers. It was produced in the absence of any other filmable material. The scenario calls on Spiner to portray four different characters (possessed by the alien intelligence, Data develops multiple personalities). Ordinarily, the actor would have relished this challenge, but coming on the heels of the exhausting "Thine Own Self" and with very little time to prepare, Spiner merely slogs his way through the confusing teleplay. Not surprisingly, "Masks" was poorly received by the cast and crew. In an interview on the TrekMovie.com website, Spiner called the installment "preposterous." Michael Dorn named it his least favorite *Next Generation* episode.

"Eye of the Beholder"

While investigating the suicide of a young officer, Deanna begins suffering from telepathic flashbacks that suggest one of the *Enterprise*'s nacelles may have been the site of a murder back when the ship was being constructed. Written by Rene Echevarria, based on a story by Brannon Braga, "Eye of the Beholder" might have been called "The Haunted Nacelle." It's an engrossing and offbeat ghost story-mystery-sci-fi hybrid with a fascinating premise and a twisty plot. Braga's story was initially rejected but revived and reworked by Echevarria due to the ongoing dearth of viable stories. Director Cliff Bole uses off-kilter camera setups and evocative lighting schemes to enhance the episode's dreamy atmosphere. For better or worse, this installment also furthers the budding Worf-Troi romance.

"Genesis"

Dr. Crusher's attempt to treat Lieutenant Barclay for a garden-variety illness accidentally unleashes a retrovirus that causes the ship's crew to devolve into lower forms of life. Riker becomes a caveman, Troi turns into a frog-woman, Barclay changes into a spider creature and Worf regresses into a prehistoric Klingon predator. Only Data and Picard, who are off-ship, remain unaffected. They return to the vessel and find it overrun with mutated monsters. "Genesis," written by Braga, is a grim, queasy horror yarn, stylishly realized by Gates McFadden, the final *Next Gen* cast member to take a turn in the director's chair. Makeup supervisor Michael Westmore created a variety of startling creatures for this episode, the most memorable being Schultz's ghastly spider-man. In order to create the extensive prosthetics required for "Genesis," Westmore's staff worked through Christmas break. This episode marked Schultz's final appearance on the series, although he returned as Barclay in *Star Trek: First Contact* and in six *Voyager* episodes. "Genesis" won an Emmy Award for sound mixing and also earned nominations for sound editing and makeup. Westmore was robbed in the makeup category.

"Journey's End"

Cadet Wesley Crusher returns to the *Enterprise* in the middle of a personal crisis. Although he's nearing the end of his tenure at the Academy, he has lost his passion to serve in Starfleet. Meanwhile, Captain Picard is ordered to relocate a group of American Indian settlers whose adopted planet has been ceded to Cardassia in a peace treaty. With the help of an Indian medicine man, Wesley has a vision that sets his life on a very different path. "Journey's End," written by Ronald D. Moore from a story by Shawn Piller and Antonio Napoli, was created to wrap up the saga of Wesley Crusher and to set up the forthcoming series *Star Trek: Voyager*. The episode introduces the Maquis, an anti-Cardassian resistance movement named after French guerrillas who fought the Nazi occupation during World War II. The presence of American Indians in outer space was intended to establish a background for *Voyager*'s Commander Chakotay (Robert Beltran). "Journey's End" features the final appearance of both Eric Menyuk as the Traveler and Wil Wheaton as Wesley (other than a nonspeaking cameo in *Star Trek Nemesis*). It also reveals the beginnings of the superhuman abilities the Traveler suggested Wesley would someday command, way back in Season One's "Where No One Has Gone Before." In a 1997 AOL chat, Moore said it was his idea to have Wesley walk away from Starfleet. "I was tired of everyone in the twenty-fourth century saying, 'All I want to do is wear the uniform and serve on a starship.' Hey, it's cool, but it's not for everyone."

"Firstborn"

New tensions arise in Worf's relationship with his son when Alexander announces that he does not want to take part in the First Rite of Ascension, the initial step toward becoming a Klingon warrior. Then a Klingon named K'mtar (James Sloyan), who claims to be a trusted advisor to Worf's family, arrives to warn that the Duras Sisters are plotting to kill the remaining members of the Mogh clan. He also offers to help kindle Alexander's interest in Klingon culture, but K'mtar is not what he seems. "Firstborn" originated with a story by Mark Kalbfeld, which was rewritten extensively by Rene Echevarria (Kalbfeld's story didn't include Alexander). In its final form, the teleplay concludes with Worf and Alexander finally reaching an understanding. "Firstborn" features cameos by Gwynyth Walsh and Barbara March as the Duras Sisters and Armin Shimerman as Quark. Brian Bonsall makes his final appearance as Alexander. The character, then much older, returned in a pair of *Deep Space Nine* installments ("Sons and Daughters" and "You Are Cordially Invited") but was played by Marc Worden. "Firstborn" earned an Emmy nomination for hairstyling. It's an agreeable, imaginative episode that was well received by the show's staff and fans alike.

"Bloodlines"

Bok (Lee Arenberg), the revenge-crazed Ferengi from Season One's "The Battle," reappears with a twisted plot to exact revenge on Picard by killing the son the captain never knew he had. Picard's progeny, the apparent result of a youthful tryst, is a smirking petty criminal. Picard takes the young ne'er-do-well, Jason (Ken Orlandt), into protective custody and tries to establish a rapport. But Jason responds with cynicism and resentment. Although it's not top-tier *Trek*, "Bloodlines" features a first-rate performance by Patrick Stewart. Picard's efforts to connect with Jason—including a rare joke about his baldness—are touching. "Bloodlines" stemmed from an idea suggested by Stewart. It was the second of two Season Seven teleplays penned by Nick Sagan, following the earlier "Attached." In addition to these two stories, Sagan pitched several ideas that were rejected, including one involving Charlie Evans from the classic episode "Charlie X" and another featuring Armis, the oil-slick monster from Season One's "Skin of Evil." Sagan later wrote five episode of *Star Trek: Voyager*.

"Emergence"

Mysterious new wires and nodes begin appearing in various *Enterprise* systems. Soon the ship stops responding to human commands, hurtling through space toward an unknown destination. To regain control of the vessel, the crew must interact with a bizarre holodeck program that seems to be the nerve center of the phenomenon. Written by Joe Menosky, based on a story by Brannon Braga, the fast-paced "Emergence" is never dull, although its underlying premise remains more than a little silly. It was Braga's idea to mount a final holodeck-centered yarn—the more outlandish the better. His goal was to create "the ultimate holodeck episode." The train set used in "Emergence" was a leftover from director Francis Ford Coppola's film *Bram Stoker's Dracula* (1992). This was the last of director Cliff Bole's record twenty-five episodes of *The Next Generation*.

In retrospect, entertaining but slight episodes like "Bloodlines" and "Emergence" seem like wasted opportunities. As Michael Dorn complains in *Captains' Logs*, "I wish they had taken the last six episodes or even the last four episodes and made it more about us [the characters]. . . . I would have liked the last four episodes to tie up loose ends."

"Preemptive Strike"

The penultimate episode of *The Next Generation*, like the previous "Journey's End," was created to provide closure for one of the series' secondary characters—in this case, Ro Laren (Michelle Forbes)—and to establish backstory for the upcoming *Star Trek: Voyager*. Now-Lieutenant Ro agrees to infiltrate the Maquis, a Bajoran-led anti-Cardassian resistance movement that operates illegally within the Federation-Cardassian demilitarized zone. She is supposed to bait the insurgents into a Federation ambush that will crush the movement. After spending time with the Maquis, however, Ro begins to question the mission. In her final *Star Trek* appearance, Forbes delivers a riveting, unaffected performance. The actress had already declined a leading role on *Deep Space Nine* and would later pass on a similar opportunity on *Voyager*, but her scintillating work here demonstrates why producers badly wanted to retain her. Written by Rene Echevarria from a story by Naren Shankar, and directed by Patrick Stewart, "Preemptive Strike" ranks among the season's strongest installments.

"All Good Things . . ."

Picard begins shifting in time, slipping back and forth between the present, the past (his first mission aboard the *Enterprise*), and a possible future in which, after developing an incurable brain disorder, he has retired from Starfleet to tend the family vineyards. In all three time periods, events draw Picard to the same distant star system. It turns out that Q is behind Picard's time-shifting, but the captain (and the rest of the human race) faces a far more serious threat than the puckish, superpowered extraterrestrial.

Ronald D. Moore and Brannon Braga were completing rewrites to their screenplay for *Star Trek Generations* when they began coauthoring *The Next Generation*'s greatly anticipated and furiously promoted two-hour series finale. It was a tricky assignment. They needed a big finish, something that would live up to Paramount's hype, but it couldn't really be a finish at all, due to the forthcoming feature films. Also, the teleplay had to be written in about two weeks. Braga introduced the concept of Picard shifting back and forth in time (shades of Kurt Vonnegut's *Slaughterhouse-Five*), while Moore suggested the final episode should include Q and bookend the series premiere, "Encounter at Farpoint." In the first draft of the teleplay, Picard also revisited the traumatic events of "The Best of Both Worlds," including his assimilation by the Borg, but this element was dropped to streamline the story and create the elegant past-present-future structure of the finished piece. Executive producer Michael Piller, who hadn't penned a *Next Gen* teleplay since Season Five, irked Moore and Braga by stepping in at the last minute and reworking their script. Piller eliminated some character interludes and beefed up the plot because he feared that "All Good Things . . ." didn't contain enough action to sustain viewers' attention for two full hours.

Although Moore and Braga labored over their *Generations* screenplay for many months and had only two weeks to write "All Good Things . . . ," the series finale proved far more satisfying than the feature film. However, as Brannon and Moore have pointed out in interviews, "All Good Things . . ." would not have worked as a movie because it wasn't accessible enough to average filmgoers. "It was a love letter to the show," said Ron Moore in an interview included on the *Star Trek: The Next Generation Season Seven* DVD collection. "It's really for people who have followed these characters, who lived with them and loved them and knew their quirks and backstories." The teleplay is packed with offhand references to characters, places, and incidents from earlier episodes. Denise Crosby (as Tasha Yar), Colm Meaney (as Miles O'Brien), and John de Lancie (as Q) returned to reprise their roles from "Encounter at Farpoint."

The future depicted in this episode presents some stunning outcomes. Picard and Crusher married but are now divorced; Captain Beverly Picard now captains a Starfleet medical vessel. Worf, now a Klingon governor, and Riker, a Starfleet admiral, suffered a rancorous falling-out over Worf's relationship with Deanna Troi, who is now deceased. Data is teaching at Cambridge. And Geordi gave up engineering to become a novelist. This was rich, exciting material, and the entire cast delivered inspired work, even though many of them were approaching exhaustion after the long, taxing season. The actors were also distracted by the making of a TV documentary, *Journey's End: The Saga of Star Trek the Next Generation*, which was filmed during production of "All Good Things . . ." and first broadcast immediately prior to the series finale.

The complex and ambitious "All Good Things . . ." also demanded a herculean effort from the show's production staff. The set decoration, costume, and makeup departments went to extraordinary lengths to present three different versions of the series' familiar settings and characters within the same story. To name just a few of the challenges: scenes in the past required sets such as the bridge, which had been subtly altered over the years, to be re-dressed so they resembled their original configuration; costumes worn during Season One, including Deanna Troi's "skant" jumper, also had to be recreated; and sequences set in the future required labor-intensive age makeup and yet another set of costumes. Production designer Richard James and director Winrich Kolbe masterfully oversaw all these variables and brought in the huge show on time and on budget.

"All Good Things . . ." attracted a huge audience, earned rave reviews, and delighted fans. It garnered a 15.4 rating and a 26 share, which means than more

This Franklin Mint collectible plate commemorated "All Good Things . . . ," the historic, two-hour finale of *The Next Generation*, which scored stratospheric Nielsen ratings.

Photo by Preston Hewis, East Bank Images

than a quarter of all households watching television during the episode's original broadcast were watching *Star Trek*. The double-length episode finished No. 2 for the week, outdrawing major hit series like *Seinfeld*. These remain the franchise's highest-ever Nielsen numbers. Insiders including Rick Berman, publications such as *Entertainment Weekly*, and endless fan polls have all included the series finale among the finest *Next Generation* adventures. Braga named "All Good Things . . ." as his best *Star Trek* teleplay. The episode won an Emmy for special effects and earned three other nominations for its score, editing, and costume design. "All Good Things . . ." also won a Hugo Award, becoming the final *Star Trek* episode so honored. By any standard, it was a glorious finish.

Despite the lofty numbers for "All Good Things . . ." ratings for *The Next Generation* dipped again in its final season, although the series still attracted an average of better than ten million viewers. Profitability remained solid, as well. Paramount charged a whopping $700,000 for a thirty-second commercial during the heavily promoted series finale. Ironically, given the show's drop-off in quality from recent years, the television industry finally accorded *Next Gen* some respect. It was nominated as Outstanding Drama Series at the 1994 Emmy Awards, becoming the only *Star Trek* series to receive this honor since the original, which was nominated as Outstanding Drama during its first two seasons. Also, Patrick Stewart earned a Screen Actors Guild Award nomination. Despite these honors, it seemed for long stretches that *The Next Generation* was treading water during its final season. But perhaps this was inevitable, since the series finale represented the turning of a page, not the closing of a book. Less than two weeks after "All Good Things . . ." wrapped, the cast reassembled to begin work on *Star Trek Generations*.

28

The Next Phase

From the perspective of franchise insiders, the seventh *Star Trek* movie was the most important since *Star Trek II: The Wrath of Khan* in 1982. A box-office hit would assure the ongoing viability of the *Trek* brand and bolster the careers of its creative leaders and stars; a flop would be catastrophic for all concerned. *Star Trek Generations* represented a high-stakes gamble on the part of Paramount Pictures executives, who bet that moviegoers would accept the transition from the beloved original crew to a new cast of characters as yet untested with film audiences. The studio doubled down its wager by cancelling the most successful syndicated program on television to improve the movie's chances, venturing that *Next Gen*–starved fans would gobble up the new movie. To Rick Berman, who had been handed the keys to the franchise following Gene Roddenberry's death, the picture represented an opportunity to validate his vision for *Star Trek*. For the film's director, writers, and most of its cast, it was a chance to make a huge leap in terms of industry prestige, moving from the lowly medium of syndicated TV to the rarefied realm of major motion pictures.

Tentative plans to retire the original cast and replace it with the younger, cheaper *Next Generation* crew had been in place at least as far back as 1991, when Berman obtained permission from Roddenberry, shortly before his death, to create a new *Star Trek* series (what became *Deep Space Nine*) as an eventual replacement for *Next Gen*. *Star Trek VI: The Undiscovered Country* (1991) was filled with none-too-subtle hints that the next *Trek* film would feature the *Next Generation* characters. In late 1992, Paramount CEO Sherry Lansing made it official, assigning Berman to oversee the creation of the first film featuring Captain Picard and friends. Berman, perhaps looking to hedge his bets, suggested that the new movie could feature an appearance by Captain Kirk and company as well, to "pass the baton." Lansing approved, and assigned the picture a $30 million budget (slightly higher than *Star Trek VI*) and a target release date of Thanksgiving weekend, 1994.

"What if we kill Kirk?"

Next, Berman took the unusual step of soliciting story concepts from three different sources: writer-producer Maurice Hurley, who had overseen the *Next Generation* writing staff during the show's first two seasons; Michael Piller, who

William Shatner's Captain Kirk hits the trail with Patrick Stewart's Captain Picard in *Star Trek Generations*. But Kirk was headed for the last roundup.

took over for Hurley and was now executive producing both *Next Gen* and *DS9*; and writers Ronald D. Moore and Brannon Braga, who had penned some of the best *Next Generation* adventures. Piller declined to participate in the competition to develop a screenplay. Berman worked with Hurley and with Moore and Braga to generate separate story concepts, both of which were later developed into first-draft screenplays. Eventually, both Berman and Paramount leadership agreed that the Moore-Braga script was superior.

Before composing the draft script, Moore and Braga kicked around other discarded ideas. At first, the duo envisioned a story that would pit the twenty-third and twenty-fourth-century *Enterprise* crews against one another. "We all tried our best, but we were never able to come up with any scenario that made both crews look heroic," Moore explained in William Shatner's book, *Star Trek Movie Memories*. "No matter how we played around with this thing, somebody was going to come off looking like the bad guy." Even if a workable story could have been devised, the *Trek*-versus-*Trek* scenario would have faced numerous other obstacles, not least of which was that hiring both casts in their entirety would have blown the movie's budget. Once this idea was shelved, Moore and Braga took up Berman's suggestion of "a mystery that spans two generations." The centuries-old Guinan, they reasoned, could serve as a hinge for the story. It was a fertile idea, but the screenwriters believed that, in lieu of their originally planned battle between the Kirk and Picard teams, the picture still needed a hook. Then "one of us threw out, 'What if we kill Kirk?'" Moore reports in Shatner's book.

"We all kinda looked at each other and said, 'Wow.'" Surprisingly, although many fans were upset when word leaked that Kirk would die, no one involved in the creation of the film—not Paramount executives, not even William Shatner—objected to the idea.

So Moore and Braga began to flesh out the bare-bones story. In an effort to avoid a traditional time-travel scenario—since sending Kirk forward to the twenty-fourth century or Picard back to the twenty-third both created potential problems for the franchise's carefully guarded continuity—the writers dreamed up the Nexus, a sort of interdimensional Shangri-La, where time has no meaning and residents live in a state of perpetual bliss. The Nexus idea helped Moore and Braga avoid continuity conundrums and enabled Kirk and Picard to meet on neutral ground, giving both characters equal footing.

The original Moore-Braga screenplay opened in the late twenty-third century with three retired dignitaries—Captain Kirk, Ambassador Spock, and Admiral McCoy—attending the ceremonial maiden voyage of the *Enterprise-B*. The journey is an elaborate photo op rather than a real mission, but the vessel's leisurely cruise around the solar system is interrupted by distress calls from two Federation starships, which are threatened by a mysterious "energy distortion" later revealed as a gateway to the Nexus. While attempting to rescue the crews of the trapped ships, the *Enterprise* accidentally beams a handful of people out of the Nexus, including Guinan and the ruthless Dr. Soran, both members of the same long-lived species. During the incident, Kirk is lost in the rift and presumed dead.

Seventy-eight years later, Soran—aided by the unscrupulous Duras Sisters and their Klingon henchmen—uses a forbidden weapon to destroy a star. Soran plans to destroy a second star—and wipe out an entire civilization—as part of a scheme to reenter the Nexus. Since being ripped away from paradise by the *Enterprise-B* transporter almost eighty years earlier, he has become obsessed with returning to the Nexus. Aided by Guinan, Picard attempts to stop Soran but fails, and is pulled into the Nexus along with him. In the Nexus, again with Guinan's assistance, Picard finds Kirk and enlists his help to defeat Soran.

"You have a great movie, but a bad ending."

With a screenplay in hand, Berman set about hiring a director. His first choice was Leonard Nimoy, whose *Trek* credentials were impeccable and who had met and liked the *Next Generation* cast while guest starring in the two-part adventure "Unification." But Nimoy, who was used to playing a leading role in story development, wanted to make major revisions to the screenplay. There was no time for extensive changes, and Nimoy was unwilling to shoot the film as written. So Berman turned to David Carson, a veteran television director with no feature film experience. Carson had directed four episodes of *The Next Generation*, including the brilliant "Yesterday's Enterprise," considered by many the single best installment of the series. He had also helmed the two-hour *Deep Space Nine* pilot, "Emissary."

With a script and a director in hand, the next task was securing a cast, which proved tougher than expected. Nimoy not only declined to direct *Generations*, but passed on appearing in the film, as well, since Spock's role amounted to little more than a cameo. DeForest Kelley also demurred. Kelley saw no point in appearing in *Generations*, since he had said his goodbyes to *Star Trek* in *The Undiscovered Country* and had appeared in the *Next Generation* pilot, "Encounter at Farpoint." So James Doohan and Walter Koenig—ironically, the two cast members who had, over the years, been most vocal in their disdain for William Shatner—were hired to appear as Scotty and Chekov, alongside Captain Kirk. To play the nefarious Soran—the movie's only important new character—Berman signed British actor Malcolm McDowell, still best known for his starring role in director Stanley Kubrick's *A Clockwork Orange* (1971). Although he played the heroic H. G. Wells in director Nicholas Meyer's *Time After Time* (1979), by the early nineties he was most often cast as the villain—a role he relished. McDowell, in *Star Trek Movie Memories*, recalls that when Berman offered him the role, "I was thrilled. I said, 'I'd love to do it. I want to be the man to kill Kirk!'"

Production of *Star Trek Generations*, which included an unusually large amount of location work for a *Trek* picture (including shoots in Marina del Rey, Pasadena, Lone Pine, and Nevada's Valley of Fire State Park), opened on March 24, 1994. Carson began filming the sequence featuring Kirk, Scotty, and Chekov aboard the *Enterprise-B* while, on a separate Paramount soundstage, director Winrich Kolbe was shooting "All Good Things . . . ," the *Next Generation* series finale. In early April, two weeks after "All Good Things . . ." wrapped, the *Next Gen* cast reported for duty on the film, beginning on location aboard the sailing ship *Lady Washington* in Santa Monica's Marina del Rey. Hollywood tabloids ran stories about friction between the movie's two starship captains, but these reports were erroneous. Earlier in the year, Shatner and Stewart had struck up a friendship—or at least a collegial working rapport—on a flight aboard the Paramount corporate jet to Los Angeles from the ShoWest theater exhibitors convention in Las Vegas, where they had appeared together and met for the first time. Despite oppressive heat during filming of the climactic fight scenes involving Kirk, Picard, and Soran on location in the appropriately named Valley of Fire, where temperatures soared to 110 degrees, production wrapped in August without major setbacks.

Everything was going splendidly. Then preview audiences got a look at the film.

Generations bombed with test viewers, who hated the movie's climax—the sequence shot in sweltering heat in the Valley of Fire. In particular, they were unhappy with the manner of Captain Kirk's demise (in the movie's original version, Soran shoots him in the back) and with the interaction of the two captains, or the lack thereof. Moore, in a 1997 AOL chat, said the audience's response was disheartening but not surprising. "By the time of the test screening, we knew

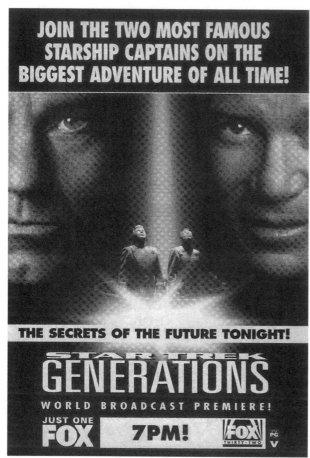

JOIN THE TWO MOST FAMOUS STARSHIP CAPTAINS ON THE BIGGEST ADVENTURE OF ALL TIME!

THE SECRETS OF THE FUTURE TONIGHT!

STAR TREK GENERATIONS

WORLD BROADCAST PREMIERE!

JUST ONE FOX   7PM!   FOX

This *TV Guide* ad, promoting the broadcast premiere of *Generations*, plays up the historic meeting of Captains Kirk and Picard, which Leonard Nimoy later dismissed as a marketing gimmick.

that this sequence wasn't working—we'd already seen dailies, of course, and had watched several rough cuts of the picture and everyone knew this wasn't playing the way we thought it would," Moore said. "The test audience reaction pretty much confirmed what we all suspected."

Lansing called Berman, Moore, and Braga into her office and informed them that, "You have a great movie, but a bad ending," as Moore and Braga recount in a DVD commentary. Fortunately, Paramount—which refused director William Shatner's request to film a revised ending to *Star Trek V: The Final Frontier*, with disastrous results—approved a whopping $5 million to reshoot the *Generations* finale, as well as an earlier sequence in which Picard spends Christmas with a dream family inside the Nexus. The fact that Lansing and other Paramount power brokers were willing to invest the extra money (one-sixth of the film's original $30 million cost) indicates how vital the studio considered the success of this picture, and the continuation of the *Trek* film series. In the revised version of the finale, Kirk and Picard operate more as a team. Kirk dies in heroic fashion, crushed under a collapsing bridge while working with Picard to save an entire species as well as the crew of the *Enterprise-D* from obliteration.

Reception

Star Trek Generations, released November 18, 1994, earned a promising $23 million in its opening weekend. Receipts fell off dramatically over the next few weeks, but the film nevertheless grossed nearly $76 million in the U.S. and $118 million worldwide (that's about $183 million in inflation-adjusted terms). Although most previous *Trek* movies fared poorly overseas, *Generations* raked in $42 million outside the U.S., a respectable showing. Even though the picture ran nearly $5 million over budget, due to the reshoots, it still turned a handsome profit for Paramount. As part of its promotional campaign for the film, the studio launched an official website devoted to *Star Trek Generations*. It was the first website created to market a movie.

Generations' critical reception was less impressive than its box-office performance. Despite excellent visual and sound effects and other technical merits, the movie failed to garner a single Oscar nomination. At the 1995 Hugo Awards, *Generations* was nominated as Best Dramatic Presentation (a category open to movies, TV shows, and other media), but lost, ironically, to "All Good Things . . . ," the series finale of *Star Trek: The Next Generation. Generations* divided movie critics. *Chicago Tribune* film critic Gene Siskel gave *Generations* a thumbs-up, while Roger Ebert, his colleague from the *Chicago Sun-Times*, voted thumbs-down. Michael Medved of *Sneak Previews* sneeringly derided *Generations* as "Star Dreck" and claimed it was worse than *Star Trek V.* Some of reviewers' harshest criticism was directed at star Patrick Stewart. Mark A. Altman, reviewing the film for *Sci-Fi Universe*, wrote that "William Shatner's charismatic Kirk blows the more subdued Stewart off the screen." The film's detractors also included Nimoy, who publically derided *Generations* as pointless and the meeting of the two captains as a facile marketing gimmick. Fan reaction was mixed, as well. Although many Trekkers found things in it to enjoy, *Generations* seemed to fully satisfy no one. Although it was the first *Star Trek* film since *The Motion Picture* without a roman numeral in its title, many fans now dismiss *Generations* as one of the bad, odd-numbered installments of the film series.

Assessing *Generations*

Sherry Lansing's assessment that "you have a great movie, but a bad ending" was generous, but fairly accurate. *Star Trek Generations* is at least a *good* movie up until Picard enters the Nexus. Although it has some other problems, none of these seem insurmountable until the Nexus scenes begin. Then the movie falls to pieces. The opening sequence on the *Enterprise-B* is gripping and filled with small but enjoyable flourishes, such as Chekov introducing Kirk to Sulu's daughter (the vessel's young helmsman) and Kirk visibly trying to fight against the urge to take control when the crisis arises. Shatner is excellent here, and Doohan's quietly devastated reaction to the loss of Captain Kirk is superb, as well.

Curiously, considering that Berman, Moore, and Braga all viewed *Generations* as a *Next Gen* movie with classic *Trek* guest stars rather than as a full-blown franchise crossover, and since all three had a vested interest in establishing the new crew as viable protagonists, the film fumbles in its introduction of the *Next Generation* characters. The picture cuts away from the stunning scene of Kirk's assumed death to a humorous sequence in which Picard and company gallivant around the holodeck in frilly Napoleonic naval uniforms to celebrate Worf's overdue promotion to lieutenant commander. Shortly after this sequence, exasperated with his ongoing inability to comprehend humor, Data installs his Emotion Chip. For the rest of the film, the android struggles with emotions that threaten to overwhelm him. This plot device gives Brent Spiner the opportunity to display greater range than usual and fulfills *Next Gen* fans' desire to see an emotional Data. But the team is weakened by the presence of a Data who cracks bad jokes and cowers when danger threatens. Picard, after learning that his brother and nephew have died in a fire, sobs openly—something Kirk didn't do, even after the murder of his son. Marina Sirtis's Deanna Troi and Gates McFadden's Beverly Crusher have almost nothing to do. The sum of these and other accumulated minor points is to make the *Next Gen* crew, and especially Picard, seem weak and ineffectual compared to the swashbuckling, two-fisted Kirk. Mark Altman's assertion that Shatner/Kirk blows Stewart/Picard off the screen is correct, but this is due mostly to the way the characters are written, rather than to the relative quality of the actors' performances.

The film's most exciting moments are contained in the story's midsection. The *Enterprise-D*, led by Riker, engages the Duras Sisters' Bird of Prey in the most thrilling space battle seen in any *Trek* film since Kirk's climactic encounter with Khan from *Star Trek II*. Although the Klingons are defeated, the *Enterprise* is mortally wounded and—in a spectacular climax to this sequence—crashes on planet Veridian III. Elsewhere on Veridian III, Picard slugs it out with Soran to try to prevent the villain from launching a missile that will enable Soran to enter the Nexus but destroy all life in the solar system. But Soran defeats Picard with deflating ease, and the two are sucked into the Nexus. Then the movie's real problems start.

Picard's Dream World turns out to be a stuffy neo-Victorian Christmas with a servile wife and five beaming, well-mannered children wearing starched shirts and spotless frocks. This sequence was shot twice, but it's still groan inducing. Next, Picard goes pleading for help from Captain Kirk, who—also trapped in the Nexus—spends his time chopping wood, riding horses, and renewing romance with a former girlfriend. At first, Kirk refuses to help save the galaxy one more time. "The galaxy owes me one," he says. But eventually he agrees to accompany Picard on a trip back in time to stop Soran. There are many problems with this sequence. Although he comes off better than Picard, it's hard to swallow the idea that Kirk, even in paradise, wouldn't jump at the chance for one last adventure.

Like the Picard family Christmas, the climactic Kirk-Picard-Soran fight scene, even in its reworked form, still doesn't play well. Simply put, it's a letdown— nowhere near as exciting as the battle between the *Enterprise* and the Duras Sisters. As a result, Kirk's death registers surprisingly little impact. All things considered, the captain would have met a far more dramatic and fitting demise by taking a phaser blast to preserve the budding Federation-Klingon alliance in the finale of the preceding film, *Star Trek VI: The Undiscovered Country*. Kirk's death should have happened in that sort of way and on that sort of stage, the culmination of a long build-up throughout the film, during an event of great significance within the mythology of the franchise. While it's better than being shot in the back, Kirk's death in the revised climax of *Generations* nevertheless seems too cheap.

Ultimately, although it stemmed from an understandable impulse, Rick Berman's decision to include original cast members in the first *Next Generation* movie backfired. Shatner didn't receive enough screen time to develop a satisfactory story arc, let alone an event as galaxy-shaking as Kirk's death. Yet Kirk remained a more dynamic and appealing character than any of his twenty-fourth-century counterparts, at least as they are depicted here. In hindsight, the franchise would have been better served had Berman, Moore, and Braga simply authored a kick-ass *Next Generation* story and let the new cast prove its mettle on its own—which is exactly what happened next.

29

I Borg

Star Trek: First Contact (1996)

S tar Trek Generations proved to be a poor vehicle for the big-screen debut of the *Next Generation* crew, who were upstaged by William Shatner's Captain Kirk. The film earned mixed reviews and was seen by many fans as a disappointment. But it accomplished the one thing it absolutely had to do: It made money for Paramount Pictures, returning a robust $83 million above its production costs. So, in February 1995, less than three months after the release of *Generations*, Paramount CEO Sherry Lansing instructed producer Rick Berman to begin preparing the eighth *Star Trek* feature film. The studio wanted the new movie to debut Thanksgiving weekend, 1996, to coincide with the franchise's thirtieth anniversary. Despite the lukewarm results of their first collaboration, producer Rick Berman once again teamed with writers Ronald D. Moore and Brannon Braga (who had signed a two-picture deal) to craft a follow-up. All three were committed to delivering a movie that could stand alongside the best previous entries in the film series.

In their initial story conferences, Berman suggested that the upcoming film should be a time-travel story. The most successful *Trek* movie (*The Voyage Home*) had involved time travel, as had many cherished TV episodes, including "The City on the Edge of Forever," from the original program, and "Yesterday's Enterprise" and "All Good Things . . . ," from *The Next Generation*. But Moore and Braga were keen to do a story involving the Borg, which, through episodes such as "Q Who" and the two-part "Best of Both Worlds" epic, had emerged as the most popular, and most terrifying, antagonists in the mythos of *Next Gen*—or arguably the entire franchise. The two ideas quickly merged into a single, novel concept: A Borg time-travel adventure.

Back to the Future

But in what historical period would the story take place? Various eras, including Imperial Rome and the American Civil War, were considered. Moore and Braga developed extensive notes for a story set during the Italian Renaissance, featuring Leonardo da Vinci and a swordfight sequence, but eventually discarded the concept because it seemed (in Moore's words) too "campy and over-the-top." Finally, Braga devised a unique twist on the time-travel concept, suggesting a journey back from the twenty-fourth century to an era that remains in the future for audiences—namely, the beginnings of the Federation. The Borg would travel to postapocalyptic Earth to try to stop Zefram Cochrane's first warp flight and prevent mankind from meeting its Vulcan allies. Although the underlying concept smacked a bit of *The Terminator*, the future-historic setting made the idea seem fresh and offered Trekkers the chance to visit a time and place much discussed but never actually shown in any previous *Trek* film or TV episode. Captain Picard and friends would fight for nothing less than the survival of the uplifting future envisioned by Gene Roddenberry. If the Borg win, Braga explained in an interview included on the *Star Trek: First Contact* DVD, "*Star Trek* would never be born."

It was a promising idea, but additional story problems remained. In the first-draft screenplay, titled *Star Trek: Resurrection*, most of the action took place on Earth, with Captain Picard and Dr. Crusher tending to an injured Cochrane and ensuring the success of his historic flight. Meanwhile, Riker battled the Borg on the orbiting *Enterprise*. No one liked this script. When Patrick Stewart suggested that Picard should be on his ship battling his nemesis, the Borg, Moore and Braga immediately realized he was right and reworked the entire scenario. Picard's struggle to save his ship from the Borg became the primary focus of the film, while Riker and Deanna's attempts to assist Cochrane became a humorous B-story. Originally, the Borg had merely served as a mechanism to set up the primary story on Earth. With the change in structure, the Borg now had much more screen time. This worried Paramount executives, who complained that the Borg seemed like "bionic zombies" (a phrase Moore and Braga incorporated into their screenplay) with no personality. To allay these concerns, Moore and Braga invented the Borg Queen to serve as the face of the Collective and present a more traditional movie villain.

From that point, the screenplay came together quickly. The finished version, which was retitled to avoid confusion with Fox's recently announced *Alien Resurrection* (1997), opens with Picard enduring a nightmare-flashback to his assimilation by the Borg. He awakens to learn that the Borg is once again moving against the Federation. Starfleet, wary of a captain who was previously taken over by the Collective, orders the *Enterprise* to patrol the faraway Romulan Neutral Zone. Once the Borg near Earth, however, Picard defies orders and rushes back to join the battle. Aided by a mysterious mental connection with the Collective, he coordinates an attack that destroys the invading Borg Cube, but not before the vessel launches a probe that escapes into the past, where the aliens change history and assimilate humankind. Picard follows the probe back in time and surmises that the Collective will try to sabotage Cochrane's historic warp flight. A team led by Commander Riker, Counselor Troi, and chief engineer La Forge beams down to protect and assist Cochrane. Cochrane's gal pal, Lily, is beamed aboard the *Enterprise* for medical treatment. But soon afterward, Picard realizes that the Borg have infiltrated the *Enterprise* and are trying to take over the ship. Data holds the enemy at bay by encrypting access to the main computer. A pitched battle ensues, with Picard seemingly obsessed with preventing the Borg

When Paramount leadership complained that the Borg seemed like a bunch of "bionic zombies" without any personality, writers Ronald D. Moore and Brannon Braga dreamed up the Borg Queen (played by Alice Krige) to serve as a more traditional movie villain.

from capturing his ship. Then Data is taken captive by the Borg Queen, who tries to seduce the android into joining the Collective (and unlocking the computer). If she succeeds, all will be lost.

Star Search

During his tenure with the franchise, producer Harve Bennett hired a director early in the creative process and empowered the filmmaker to collaborate in the writing of the screenplay. Perhaps to protect his authorship of the films and maintain greater control over the production, Berman preferred to wait until the screenplay was finished to begin recruiting a director. With an unusually generous budget ($45 million, $15 million more than the original budget for *Generations*), Berman hoped to lure an A-list action filmmaker. Moore and Braga's screenplay was sent to Hollywood heavyweights, including John McTiernan (*Die Hard*) and Ridley Scott (*Alien*), but neither was interested in doing "*Star Trek 8*," as Jonathan Frakes explained in a DVD interview. So Berman turned to "inside" talent—directors who had worked previously on the *Next Generation* series. It's unclear if David Carson, who had helmed *Generations*, was considered, but actor-directors Frakes, Stewart, and LeVar Burton were all candidates. Finally, Berman selected Frakes, who had the most directorial experience of all the cast members; had helmed outstanding episodes such as "The Offspring," "Reunion," and "The Drumhead"; and had limited screen time in the film. It would be Frakes's first movie as a director. He had never even acted in a theatrical film prior to *Generations*. To prepare for the assignment, Frakes studied the work of McTiernan, Scott, and James Cameron.

Berman, Frakes, and casting director Junie Lowry next set about finding actors for the key supporting roles of Zefram Cochrane, Lily, and the Borg Queen. Originally the Cochrane role was to be played by two-time Oscar winner and devoted Trekker Tom Hanks, but Hanks had to bow out due to conflicts with the production of his directorial debut, *That Thing You Do!* (1996). So Berman and friends turned to the ever-reliable James Cromwell, who had already appeared twice on *The Next Generation* (playing different characters in "The Hunted" and "Birthright, Parts I and II") and once on *Deep Space Nine* (in "Starship Down"), and who recently had earned an Academy Award nomination for his work in *Babe* (1995). No one was concerned that Cromwell was much older and looked nothing like Glenn Corbett, who had played Cochrane in the classic episode "Metamorphosis." Cromwell's portrayal is generally regarded as the definitive take on the character. He reprised the role in two episodes of *Star Trek: Enterprise* (the pilot "Broken Bow" and the Mirror Universe story "In a Mirror, Darkly"). For the role of Cochrane's friend, Lily, Frakes insisted on hiring his close friend Alfre Woodard (who he refers to as his "godmother"). Woodard's credentials were impeccable. She had already won three Emmys (and notched another five nominations), earned an Oscar nomination, and claimed three NAACP Image Awards, among numerous other honors. The intimidating yet alluring Borg Queen proved the most difficult role to cast. Eventually, Berman, Frakes, and Lowry settled on South African actress Alice Krige, based primarily on her work in *Ghost Story* (1981). Krige later reprised her role as the Borg Queen in the series finale of *Star Trek: Voyager* and for the filmed segments of the "Borg Invasion: 4-D" exhibit at the Las Vegas Hilton's *Star Trek: The Experience*.

In addition, *Next Gen* semiregulars Dwight Schultz and Patti Yasutake were signed to appear as Lieutenant Barclay and Nurse Ogawa, respectively. *Voyager*'s Robert Picardo made a cameo as an emergency medical hologram, and Ethan ("Neelix") Phillips appeared briefly as the holographic maître d' in the Dixon Hill holodeck program. Oddly, Whoopi Goldberg's Guinan, who had played an important part in most previous Borg stories and was featured prominently in *Generations*, was overlooked. She would not return until *Star Trek Nemesis* (2002).

Assimilate This!

Paramount didn't grant *First Contact* a $45 million budget in a sudden fit of benevolence. It did so because the project required the greatest effort in many years by the studio's production design and costume departments, as well as many elaborate visual effects. Since the *Enterprise-D* had been destroyed in the previous film, *First Contact* necessitated the design and construction of the new *Enterprise-E*—not only a new starship's exterior but its interiors as well. Production designer Herman Zimmerman and illustrator John Eaves created a sleek but fierce-looking vessel. Among other notable changes, Zimmerman and Eaves replaced the familiar circular saucer section with an oval, lending the craft a more sharklike appearance. The redesigned interiors were less luxuriously appointed and more military in effect. Although some *Voyager* sets were re-dressed for the film, many—including the new bridge—were built from scratch. Along with the new ship, the crew received redesigned uniforms more in keeping with those now seen on *Deep Space Nine* and *Voyager*. Meanwhile, makeup designer Michael Westmore and costume designer Deborah Everton completely revised the Borg, creating a far more elaborate, detailed, and convincing look for the species compared to the simplistic designs seen previously on TV. Once again, Paramount engaged Industrial Light & Magic to provide special visual effects. For *First Contact*, ILM employed much more computer animation than had been seen in any previous *Trek* film. The larger budget also enabled Berman to hire esteemed composer Jerry Goldsmith—who had worked on *The Motion Picture* and *The Final Frontier* and had written the title theme for *Voyager*—to score *First Contact*.

According to all reports, production, which ran from to April 8 to July 2, 1996, was congenial and crisis-free. Rookie director Frakes strived to create a working atmosphere he later described as "comfortable, jocular, [and] silly," and relied on cinematographer Matthew Leonetti to help evaluate his work as an actor. The film was shot at the Titan Missile Museum in Tucson, Arizona, in the Los Angeles National Forest, and on the series' familiar Paramount soundstages. During the production of *Generations*, the fan press had obtained a copy of the script. To prevent this from happening again, *First Contact* screenplays were printed on red paper, making them difficult to photocopy but also hard to read. Postproduction also ran smoothly, and the film played extremely well with test audiences. Even before it reached theaters, insiders were convinced that they had produced something special.

Reception

Star Trek: First Contact, which opened November 22, 1996, scored with ticket buyers and movie critics alike. The film earned $92 million in the U.S. and another $54 million overseas (the highest international gross for any *Trek* film to date), for a total of $146 million worldwide. That's more than $213 million in inflation-adjusted dollars. It was the second-best box-office performance for a *Trek* movie so far, trailing only *Star Trek IV: The Voyage Home* (1986).

The film pleased most reviewers, earning a thumbs-up from both Gene Siskel and Roger Ebert, and enthusiastic endorsements from many important media outlets, including *Variety* and the *Los Angeles Times*. Ebert opined that *First Contact* ranked among the best entries in the *Star Trek* movie series. Many reviewers singled out Patrick Stewart, the guest cast, and the film's visual effects for praise. *First Contact* earned an Oscar nomination for Best Makeup but lost to *The Nutty Professor*. It was also nominated for a Hugo Award but lost to TV's *Babylon 5*, and for a Saturn Award as Best Science Fiction Film, losing to *Independence Day*. For her work in *First Contact*, actress Alfre Woodard was nominated for another NAACP Image Award. The movie was immensely popular with fans, and its creators were proud of it. "*Star Trek* was at its apex," Braga ventured in a DVD interview. "Everything was clicking."

Assessing *First Contact*

In every respect, *First Contact* represents a vast improvement over the clumsy, stilted *Generations*. Its opening scenes—including the thrillingly executed space battle—grab viewers' attention and hurl the narrative forward with propulsive energy. Compared to *Generations*, which seemed to limp along at half-impulse, *First Contact* zooms by at warp eight. Once the Borg are discovered aboard the *Enterprise*, suspense mounts inexorably, relieved only by occasional comic interludes involving Zefram Cochrane (Cromwell) and the away team. A handful of first-rate action sequences follow, as well, including a brilliantly conceived scene in which Picard, Worf, and a redshirt bridge officer fight a zero-gravity skirmish with the Borg on the hull of the spaceship, and another clever passage in which Picard confuses Borg drones by leading them into his Dixon Hill holodeck program.

Despite the breakneck pace, the picture finds small moments for all the major cast members to shine and includes absorbing story arcs for Picard and Data, both of whom seem tougher yet more likeable here than in *Generations*. After spending most of the previous film weeping or begging for help, Picard comes off as hell-bent, and nearly unhinged, in his determination to save his ship—and take vengeance against the Borg. "I will make them pay for what they've done!" he bellows during a charged (and brilliantly acted) exchange with Lily (Woodard), who compares Picard with *Moby Dick*'s revenge-crazed Captain Ahab. Meanwhile, the Borg Queen (Krige) grafts human skin onto Data's body and uses every means at her disposal to try to seduce him into joining the Collective. Stewart, Spiner, Woodard, and Krige contribute uniformly high-caliber portrayals. Moore and Braga admit they created Lily in an attempt to widen the film's appeal; she represents the non-Trekkers in the audience, providing someone to whom Picard can explain what the Borg are. But the gifted Woodard elevates Lily into a fully realized character rather than a simple expository device. Critic Roger Ebert wrote that Krige's Borg Queen "looks like no notion of sexy I have ever heard of, but inspires me to keep an open mind." The rest of the cast perform capably, as well. Cromwell lays it on a bit thick as Cochrane but remains fun to watch.

Thanks to Leonetti's gorgeous cinematography, Herman Zimmerman's handsome sets, and ILM's eye-popping visual effects, *First Contact* is the best-looking of all the *Star Trek* films. Director Jonathan Frakes skillfully coordinates all these elements. His clean, subtle, but evocative work—including graceful dolly shots employed throughout the scenes shot on the *Enterprise* sets—is extremely impressive for a rookie filmmaker. His camera prowls the corridors of the Borg-ized *Enterprise*, underscoring the ship's transformation into a spacefaring house of horrors. The cast loved working for Frakes (who, despite his technical acumen, is known as an actor's director), and Paramount executives

Promotional artwork for *Star Trek: First Contact*, like this newspaper ad, prominently featured Captain Picard, Data, and the Borg Queen.

were delighted with his results. Looking at the finished product, Frakes doesn't seem to have wasted a penny of the studio's $45 million.

First Contact isn't perfect. Its comedic interludes are too broadly played, and some of the screenplay's intended laugh lines fall flat, such as Cochrane's observation that the Federation officers "are all astronauts, on some kind of star trek." Also, the movie's Picard seems very different from the cool, unflappable leader seen on the television series. After weeping openly in the previous film, here Picard suffers fits of uncontrollable rage. Two entries into the *Next Generation* film series, the captain of the *Enterprise* was beginning to seem like an emotional basket case. But these liabilities are far outweighed by the picture's many impressive assets. *Star Trek: First Contact* is not merely the best *Next Gen* movie (by a light year), but one of the best *Star Trek* films period, and a first-rate sci-fi action-adventure. At this distance, it holds up much better than the vacuous alien invasion romp *Independence Day*, also released in 1996, which became a runaway blockbuster, earning $817 million worldwide.

First Contact gave fans reason to be optimistic about the future of the *Trek* film series. As *Daily Variety* critic Joe Leydon wrote in his review of the film, "If *First Contact* is indicative of what the next generation of *Star Trek* movies will be like, the franchise is certain to live long and prosper." Unfortunately, it was not.

30

Descent

Star Trek: Insurrection (1998)

T he blockbuster success of *Star Trek: First Contact* ensured that the *Trek* film series would continue. But discerning where to take the franchise next proved to be a daunting task. As actor-director Jonathan Frakes admitted, *First Contact* was "a tough act to follow." As a result, producers and writers decided to veer off in another direction entirely. "How do you out-Borg the Borg? How do you create a villain or adversary that will be their equal?" asked Michael Piller, in Terry J. Erdman's book *The Secrets of Star Trek: Insurrection*. "The answer is, don't try. Make a different kind of movie." Brent Spiner, in an interview included on the *Star Trek: Insurrection* DVD, underscored this. "There was a real intention on the part of the powers that be to do something very different than we did last time," Spiner said.

Unfortunately, although the "powers that be" agreed that the ninth *Trek* film should take a new direction, there was no consensus regarding what that new direction should be. As a result, the project soon became mired in a tangle of conflicted ideas and inspirations. Paramount development executives pushed producer Rick Berman to make the next *Trek* movie brighter and more humorous, more akin to the frothy *Star Trek IV: The Voyage Home* than the brooding *Generations* and dark *First Contact*. Berman, however, suggested a story based loosely on novelist Joseph Conrad's grim *Heart of Darkness*, which had previously inspired Jeri Taylor's *Next Generation* episode "The Wounded" (as well as director Francis Ford Coppola's *Apocalypse Now*). Screenwriter Piller—chosen to pen the upcoming film because Ronald D. Moore and Brannon Braga were busy writing *Mission: Impossible II*, in addition to their production duties on *Deep Space Nine* and *Voyager*—had a separate agenda. He wanted to spin a tale that would restore Gene Roddenberry's original, guiding optimism, while subtly indicting what he saw as the franchise's gradual drift away from Roddenberry's intent. "I wanted to do one for Gene," said Piller in a DVD interview. "I wanted to do one that got back to the values he taught me in the earliest days" [of Piller's tenure as a writer-producer on *Star Trek: The Next Generation*]. A grueling screenwriting process ensued, resulting in a product that was a mélange of these disparate approaches. Although each of these stakeholders could lay claim to isolated moments and story elements, the film as a whole reflected no single, unifying vision.

From *Stardust* to *Insurrection*

More is known about the creation of the *Star Trek: Insurrection* screenplay than any other in the history of the series. That's because, before his death in 2005, Piller penned a meticulously detailed book titled *Fade-In: The Writing of Star Trek: Insurrection*, which contained multiple story drafts, variant screenplays, and even correspondence with producers and cast members. In the book, Piller explains his original concept for the picture and argues that studio interference forced him to author a compromised, muddled film. Paramount suppressed the book's publication, but the TrekCore website published the manuscript posthumously online, where it was widely downloaded before Piller's heirs requested it be removed. "Through the book you can see how the movie went from something that sounded very cool and would've been a worthy *Star Trek* movie to something that ended up being just a mediocre two hour episode of the series that happened to be released in theaters," wrote an unnamed contributor to the Furious Fanboys website.

Piller's first-draft screenplay combined Berman's *Heart of Darkness* idea with Piller's more Roddenberrian concept, which explored the moral dilemmas that arise from the discovery of an extraterrestrial fountain of youth. This version, titled *Star Trek: Stardust*, involved a Starfleet Academy classmate of Picard's named Duffy who has gone rogue and is attacking Romulan starships in a distant corner of the galaxy known as the Briar Patch. As the *Enterprise* crew travels deeper and deeper into the Briar Patch in pursuit of Duffy, they begin to slowly regress in age. Finally, they arrive at a planet populated entirely by children. "In that script, we got to meet Picard at the Academy, one of his best friends (who played a huge part in the movie), [Academy groundskeeper] Boothby, and the planet of ten-year-olds," Piller reported in a 1997 AOL online chat. But neither Berman nor Paramount executives liked this draft, so Piller wrote a second version that (at Berman's insistence) dropped his Fountain of Youth concept and replaced Duffy with Data. In this iteration, Picard eventually learns that Data is battling an "unholy alliance" of Starfleet and Romulan military leaders, led by an unscrupulous half-Romulan, half-Klingon agent named Goff. But this version didn't pass muster either, mostly because executives were leery of making Starfleet the bad guys. Berman complained that the scenario was "too political."

Piller undertook a third draft that combined elements of the first two, with Picard again pursuing an out-of-control Commander Data, who is later revealed to be protecting the Ba'ku, a race of children who reside on a planet whose atmosphere functions as a fountain of youth. The Ba'ku are threatened by the designs of the Federation and its new allies, the Son'i. Although closer to the final version, this third draft was also deemed unacceptable. Piller solicited input from his friend Ira Steven Behr, executive producer of *Star Trek: Deep Space Nine*, and from actor Patrick Stewart. Behr pointed out structural problems with the screenplay, while Stewart pushed for Picard to play a more important role in the film's action sequences and requested a love interest for the captain. Piller's

Former Oscar winner F. Murray Abraham appeared as the villainous Ru'afo in *Star Trek: Insurrection*. Here, Ru'afo is attended to by his nurse (played by an uncredited actress identified only as Katrina).

fourth draft of the screenplay truncated Berman's *Heart of Darkness* material and changed the Ba'ku from a race of children to a race of deathless adults. This version included more action sequences and portrayed the villains (now known as the Son'a) in much more monstrous fashion. Piller wrote in the character of Anij to satisfy Stewart's request for a romantic subplot. Piller also peppered the script with one-liners and other comic interludes to appease Paramount executives, who wanted the movie to be funny. This draft, now titled *Star Trek: Insurrection*, finally earned studio approval.

In the finished screenplay, Data appears to go berserk while visiting the planet of the Ba'ku, a primitive civilization of peaceful farmers and artisans being studied by the Starfleet and its new allies, the Son'a. Starfleet Admiral Dougherty informs Captain Picard of the incident but insists the *Enterprise*'s assistance is not required. Undaunted, Picard races to the Ba'ku planet and apprehends Data. The android's memory is damaged, so Picard and his team beam down to investigate the cause of Data's malfunction. During the course of the inquiry, Picard and other crew members begin to feel physically rejuvenated and regain the exuberance of youth. Commander Riker and Counselor Troi rekindle their long-dormant romance. Geordi's eyes heal themselves, and he gains normal human vision. Anij, a Ba'ku woman with romantic feelings for

Picard, explains that radiation from the planet's rings perpetually regenerates the inhabitants' DNA, giving their world incredible healing and life-extending powers. She also reveals that the Ba'ku are an ancient, warp-capable civilization that has rejected technology and that, despite her youthful appearance, she is more than three hundred years old. Eventually, Picard discovers that Data was trying to defend the Ba'ku from a plot to forcibly resettle them on a new planet. The conspiracy involves both Admiral Dougherty and Ru'afo, the heartless leader of the Son'a. When Dougherty reports that this plan has been endorsed by the highest levels of the Federation government, Picard and most of his senior staff strike out on their own, disobeying orders and beaming down to the planet to fight against the removal of the Ba'ku.

Under Construction

In a departure from its usual penny-pinching strategy for the *Trek* films, Paramount Pictures empowered Berman to mount *Insurrection* on a lavish scale. Production costs eventually reached $58 million, the most of any in the series so far in raw terms. (*Star Trek: The Motion Picture* remained more expensive in inflation-adjusted dollars). The ambitious scenario required extensive location work, hundreds of extras, many new sets, and some 288 special visual effects shots. The picture was filmed at various California sites (Lake Sherwood, Mammoth Lakes Park, San Gabriel Canyon in Los Angeles National Forest, and Bishop, California), as well as on the usual Paramount soundstages. Although some sets (including sick bay) were re-dressed from *Voyager*, production designer Herman Zimmerman designed and built fifty-five entirely new sets for *Insurrection*, eighteen more than he had for *First Contact*. The largest undertaking was the design and construction of the Ba'ku village, built full scale from the ground up near Lake Sherwood. Nearly four hundred extras were hired to portray the Ba'ku villagers, all of whom had to be costumed in native garb. With Industrial Light & Magic consumed with production of *Star Wars, Episode I: The Phantom Menace*, Paramount hired Blue Sky Studios and Santa Barbara Studios, which had contributed to *Deep Space Nine* and *Voyager*, to create the film's visual effects. For *Insurrection*, nearly all the special visuals were computer generated. Once again, Jerry Goldsmith was hired to score the film.

To oversee this grand undertaking, Berman stuck with actor-director Jonathan Frakes, whose work on *First Contact* had been first-rate. Once again, Berman, Frakes, and casting director Junie Lowry were tasked with locating actors to fill three key guest roles. Former Oscar winner F. Murray Abraham was signed to play the villainous Ru'ofo. Although primarily a stage actor, Abraham won an Academy Award for his work in *Amadeus* (1984). Donna Murphy, who was engaged to play Picard's Ba'ku love interest, Anij, also worked primarily in theater and had recently earned a Tony for her performance in Stephen Sondheim and James Lapine's *Passion*. Hollywood veteran Anthony Zerbe was hired to play Admiral Dougherty. Zerbe's film and television career dated back to the early 1960s and included projects ranging from the sublime (*Cool Hand Luke*, 1967) to the ridiculous (*Kiss Meets the Phantom of the Park*, 1978). He won an Emmy for his work on the David Janssen TV series *Harry-O*.

With Frakes at the helm, production again ran easily, despite the complexities involved with some of the picture's locations. The Mammoth Lakes shooting site was so remote that cast, crew, and supplies had to be flown in by helicopter. A cameo featuring *Deep Space Nine*'s Quark (Armin Shimerman) and Rom (Max Grodenchik) vacationing on the Ba'ku planet was shot but prudently deleted. Another deleted scene would have revealed that the Son'a have lost the ability to procreate, providing a more understandable motivation for their actions. Test audiences disliked the film's climax, so this sequence was reshot. In the original version, Ru'ofo is catapulted into the planet's rings, where he rapidly regresses in age and eventually vanishes. In the final version, the villain is blown to smithereens.

Reception

Star Trek: Insurrection, released December 11, 1998, opened No. 1 at the box office, earning $22 million its first weekend. But receipts quickly plummeted. Ultimately, the picture grossed about $70 million in the U.S. and about $112 million worldwide, a disappointing return on the studio's $58 million investment, not counting money spent promoting the picture. *First Contact* had earned $142 million against its $41 million production cost. In raw dollar terms (without adjusting for inflation), *Insurrection* remains the third-lowest-grossing movie in the series.

Reviews of the film were mixed. Gene Siskel of the *Chicago Tribune* gave the picture a thumbs-up, while Roger Ebert of the *Chicago Sun-Times* voted thumbs-down. The *New York Times*, the *Los Angeles Times*, and *TV Guide* all praised the picture, while other influential outlets, including *Variety* and the *Village Voice*, panned it. *New Yorker* critic Bruce Diones described *Insurrection* as "perhaps the most colorful and relaxed of the series." *Austin Chronicle* reviewer Marc Savlov called it "a muddled, gimpy mess." Fan reaction was lukewarm. While many liked the film, most considered it a comedown after the high of *First Contact*. Many (like the unnamed writer from the Furious Fanboys website) complained that *Insurrection* seemed more like an extended TV episode than a feature film. In recent years, Frakes and other members of the cast and crew have blasted the film. In an interview on the TrekMovie.com site, Sirtis said that the film "sucked. . . . I fell asleep during the premiere of *Insurrection*." The picture earned a Hugo nomination but lost to *The Truman Show*.

Assessing *Insurrection*

Star Trek: Insurrection has its share of problems but remains a better movie than its lackluster box-office performance would indicate. It's an entertaining, thought-provoking picture that might have been more enthusiastically received had it followed the clunky *Generations* instead of the spectacular *First Contact*.

The charge most frequently leveled at *Insurrection* is that it seems more like a long television episode than a feature film. This is a fair assessment. The movie's visual effects, created by shops that usually supplied footage for various *Trek* series, look more like those seen on TV than those created by ILM for previous *Trek* movies. Also, the makeups Michael Westmore designed for the two Son'a slave races, the Tarlac and the Ellora, recall the baroque look of various aliens on *Star Trek: Voyager*. More importantly, the plot of *Insurrection* does not involve a major franchise "event," such as Spock's death (or his resurrection), Kirk's death, the formation of the Federation-Klingon alliance, or the defeat of the Borg. And *Insurrection* is one of the few *Star Trek* movies where the Earth is never placed in jeopardy. As a result, even though it was a larger-scale production than any previous *Trek* movie, *Insurrection* seems smaller—less cinematic—in scope.

But if *Insurrection* plays like a TV episode, at least it's a good episode. Taken in two-part, episodic form, *Insurrection* would have rivaled all but the very finest *Next Generation* installments.

Paramount's demands for a lighter scenario helped make the PG-rated *Insurrection* more family-friendly than most *Trek* movies. However, the comic interludes are hit-and-miss. For instance, Data's revelation that he is programmed to function as a flotation device is very amusing, but it seems ridiculous for Picard and Worf to break into a Gilbert and Sullivan number in the middle of an otherwise thrilling shuttle chase scene. It's unfortunate that Worf, in this film, serves almost entirely as comedy relief. Originally, the screenplay included a few lines referring to Worf's recently deceased wife, Jadzia Dax, but this dialogue was cut because producers didn't want

Gates McFadden strikes a tough pose in this publicity still for *Star Trek: Insurrection*.

to confuse viewers who didn't watch *Deep Space Nine*. It's delightful to see Riker and Troi resume their long-stalled romance, mostly because it inspires Frakes and Sirtis to deliver playful, unaffected performances. Both supply their best work in any *Trek* movie. Although Gates McFadden's Dr. Crusher is again underutilized, LeVar Burton enjoys some splendid moments, especially when Geordi regains his eyesight. Patrick Stewart and Brent Spiner, as always, are excellent throughout; their work anchors the film. Picard finally seems like the captain of the TV series—a forceful, principled leader capable of taking bold action without becoming emotionally unglued.

Unfortunately, perhaps due to the screenplay's convoluted history, the story's supporting characters are under-written, leaving the guest cast little to work with. Abraham attacks his part with gusto, but Ru'afo remains a one-note villain. Anij (Murphy) and the rest of the Ba'ku come off as hippie-dippie New Age granola zombies, living a lifestyle that would never have tempted Captain Kirk and his crew. (In certain respects, *Insurrection* recalls the classic episode "This Side of Paradise," in which a small group of settlers live in a state of perpetual bliss thanks to happiness-inducing spores produced by native flowers. Kirk eventually yanks the colonists out of their reverie.) *Insurrection*'s most interesting guest performance comes from Zerbe as Admiral Dougherty, who projects a sense of regret even while rationalizing his actions.

Even though it was reshot, the climactic slugfest between Picard and Ru'afo remains uninspired. However, Riker's space battle with a pair of Son'a starships, the shuttle chase scene (Gilbert and Sullivan notwithstanding), and most of the action sequences on the surface of the Ba'ku planet are inventive and gripping. The best material in the film, though, is that which most clearly arose from Piller's intent to write a *Star Trek* movie "about moral and ethical dilemmas" and to comment on the state of the franchise, seven years past the death of Gene Roddenberry.

Insurrection is arguably the most thematically complex and intellectually challenging of all the *Star Trek* films. The scenario presents a vexing moral quandary. Although eventually Ru'afo is revealed to have darker motives, the initially stated goal of the Son'a and the Federation—to use the healing powers of the Ba'ku planet to benefit billions of people across the galaxy—is a worthy end. The plan, while underhanded, certainly aligns with Spock's philosophy that "the good of the many outweighs the good of the few." Although Picard takes up arms to oppose the forced relocation of the Ba'ku, he was reluctantly willing to forcibly relocate American Indian settlers in the Federation-Cardassian demilitarized zone in the Season Seven episode "Journey's End." This contradiction underscores the depth of the film's moral ambiguity.

The story also offers wry commentary on our youth- and beauty-obsessed culture, satirized by the grotesque efforts of the Son'a—including genetic manipulation and habitual plastic surgery—to extend their lives and remain "attractive." Finally, through Starfleet's uneasy alliance with the Son'a, Piller lashes out at the perceived drift of the franchise away from Roddenberry's founding ideals. Starfleet, weakened after its battles with the Borg (in the previous film) and the Dominion (on *DS9*), needs all the help it can get, and so joins with the militarily strong but morally bankrupt Son'a, who practice slavery and employ banned weapons. The situation parallels the franchise's move toward darker, more militaristic stories and themes in the face of increased competition from grittier sci-fi TV series and movies. At one point, Picard tells Dougherty that by siding with the Son'a against the Ba'ku, "We are betraying the principles upon which the Federation was founded. It is an attack upon its very soul." Substitute "*Star Trek*" for "the Federation," and you have a perfect encapsulation of Piller's sentiments.

Alas, Piller's coded warning went unheeded. The next *Star Trek* film would stray even further from Roddenberry's founding vision, with disastrous consequences.

31

Journey's End

Star Trek Nemesis (2002)

P aramount Pictures cranked out a new *Star Trek* movie every two or three years for the better part of two decades, releasing nine *Trek* pictures from 1979 to 1998. But the disheartening returns for *Star Trek: Insurrection*, combined with sagging ratings for the *Trek* television series, gave the studio pause. A four-year gap, the longest so far in the history of the film series, ensued. During the interim, it became clear that the franchise was in decline (see Chapter 37 for details). *Deep Space Nine* ended its seven-season run in 1999 amid a ratings nosedive. *Voyager* was limping through its final season, and the ill-fated prequel *Enterprise* was in preproduction when in early 2001, after much hand-wringing, Paramount nervously approved a tenth *Star Trek* feature film.

Producer Rick Berman decided to pivot away from the kinder, gentler *Insurrection*, the most classically Roddenberrian of the *Next Generation* films. He wanted a grittier, edgier, more action-oriented picture, which he believed would appeal to moviegoers beyond the franchise's devoted but shrinking core audience. The most successful *Next Gen* movie, *First Contact* (1996), had also been the darkest. Berman's three previous films were written and directed by talent groomed on *The Next Generation* TV series. This time, to ensure a fresh approach, Berman ventured outside the *Trek* "family" and hired a screenwriter and a director with no franchise experience. These radical shifts, intended to inject new life into the *Next Gen* movie series, instead sealed its doom.

New Blood

The movie that became *Star Trek Nemesis* originated with newcomer John Logan, who in the early 2000s was an up-and-coming screenwriter. After penning several successful plays, Logan launched a film and television career in the late 1990s. His HBO telefilm *RKO 281* (1999), about the production of director Orson Welles's *Citizen Kane*, earned an Emmy nomination and led to more lucrative assignments, including writing the screenplay for director Ridley Scott's *Gladiator* (2000), which earned Logan an Oscar nomination. Logan, a lifelong *Star Trek* fan, and actor Brent Spiner were friends. So when Berman began casting about for someone to write the tenth *Trek* feature, Spiner suggested Logan. Berman, Logan, and Spiner collaborated on the story for *Nemesis*, and Logan finished the script.

Star Trek Nemesis featured the final voyage for (from left) Michael Dorn, Brent Spiner, Jonathan Frakes, LeVar Burton, Patrick Stewart, and the rest of the *Next Gen* cast.

With the breakup of Captain Picard's crew imminent (Riker has finally accepted his own command, the USS *Titan*, where he will transfer along with his new wife, Deanna Troi), the *Enterprise* rushes to investigate a positronic signal emanating from planet Kolarus. There, an away team discovers a disassembled android—one of Dr. Noonian Soong's early prototypes, named B-4, created prior to Data and his "brother," Lore. While Data and Geordi reassemble B-4 (who turns out to be a relative simpleton), Captain Picard receives orders to travel to Romulus, where a mysterious new leader named Shinzon has seized control of the Romulan government. On Romulus it's revealed that Shinzon is a clone of Picard, raised on the Romulan vassal planet of Remus by its Nosferatu-like inhabitants, previously treated as indentured servants by the Empire. Now the Remans have assumed control, and Shinzon claims they want peace—but he's lying. Geordi discovers that Shinzon's giant, bat-like spaceship, the *Scimitar*, houses a devastating weapon capable of wiping out life on a planetary scale. Although they don't realize it yet, Picard and friends are playing into a convoluted scheme to destroy life on Earth. A frantic series of action sequences ensue, with Picard being captured and taken aboard the *Scimitar*, rescued by Data, and returned to the *Enterprise*, then beaming back to the *Scimitar* to be rescued by Data once again. Logan's screenplay also includes the longest space battle in the history of the franchise and concludes with the apparent destruction of Data, who sacrifices his life to save his friends.

According to Spiner, he, Berman, and Logan considered ending *Nemesis* with Picard's death. Instead, they chose to kill Data—but to do so in such a way that the character could be revived through various means. "Data's not dead. You know that, right?" Jonathan Frakes said during an interview at the Canada Comic-Con in 2011. Frakes insisted that Data would have returned in the next movie, had there been one. Although the picture would be promoted as "a generation's final journey," the script leaves the table set for a possible sequel (*Star Trek XI: The Search for Data?*).

Frakes, who had directed both *First Contact* and *Insurrection*, was bypassed for *Nemesis*. Instead, Berman signed Stuart Baird, a veteran editor who had cut action blockbusters such as *Superman* (1978) and the first two *Lethal Weapon* movies, but whose only directorial credits were the Kurt Russell thriller *Executive Decision* (1996) and *U.S. Marshalls* (1998), a sort-of sequel to *The Fugitive* (1993) starring Tommy Lee Jones. Baird was unfamiliar with *Star Trek*, although he reviewed the previous *Next Gen* films to prepare. "I'm not a Trekkie," the director admitted in an interview included on the *Star Trek Nemesis* DVD. "I have no knowledge of the backstory. . . . It's not necessarily my genre." Baird went on to explain that his goal was to make *Nemesis* "as big as possible, and dark and edgier."

"Laverne" and Sirtis

Logan's *Nemesis* screenplay included a pair of notable guest roles. As Shinzon, Berman and Baird eventually selected British actor Tom Hardy, who had only a handful of minor television and film roles to his credit at the time. According to Baird, Hardy was chosen primarily because with his head shaved he looked like a young Patrick Stewart. To portray Shinzon's viceroy, Berman and Baird hired former *Beauty and the Beast* star Ron Perlman, who was used to performing under heavy makeup and was a personal friend of Stewart. Denise Crosby contacted Berman and asked if she could appear in the film as the half-Romulan Sela, but was told the character would not fit into the story. Nevertheless, *Nemesis* features a female Romulan commander played by Dina Meyer, who had costarred in *Bats*, a low-budget horror movie written by Logan. Bryan Singer, who would later direct Stewart's first two *X-Men* movies, has a nonspeaking walk-on as a tactical officer on the bridge.

Paramount, wary of letting Baird's "as big as possible" ambitions grow *too* big, assigned *Nemesis* a $60 million budget. This was the largest in raw numbers (not adjusting for inflation) of any *Star Trek* film to date, but still conservative given that *Insurrection*—made four years earlier—had cost $58 million. There was very little location shooting required for *Nemesis*, but production designer Herman Zimmerman and his team had to build nearly all the sets from scratch. For previous films, standing television sets had been re-dressed to reduce costs, but that wasn't possible this time. The *Voyager* sets used in *Insurrection*, for instance, had been torn down to make room for *Star Trek: Enterprise*. The first season of that series was produced concurrently with *Nemesis*. In another costly move, Baird insisted phasers, tricorders, and other props be redesigned and made more "realistic." Unhappy with the efforts of Blue Sky Studios and Santa Barbara Studios on *Insurrection*, Berman turned to visual effects house Digital Domain. While not as widely known as Industrial Light & Magic, Digital Domain was a well-respected shop that earned Academy Awards for its work on *Titanic* (1997) and *What Dreams May Come* (1998). The company would later create visual effects for director J. J. Abrams's *Star Trek* (2009), the *Transformers* movies, and many other pictures.

Production opened on November 28, 2001, and wrapped on March 9, 2002. Baird brought in the picture on time and on budget, but irritated some members of the cast with his directorial style, which he describes as "hands on." Marina Sirtis and LeVar Burton both trashed Baird in a 2006 interview posted on the TrekMovie.com site. Sirtis said she resented that Baird didn't bother to watch a single episode of *The Next Generation* before reporting for duty on *Nemesis*, and claims he didn't understand the series' characters. Burton—who reports that for the first few weeks of production, Baird repeatedly called him "Laverne"—blames Baird for the film's many flaws. In other interviews, Frakes has ventured that *Nemesis* would have turned out better if he had been allowed to direct.

Baird's background in editing came in handy when his rough cut of *Nemesis* ran nearly three hours. Almost fifty minutes of footage was excised, mostly character moments that provided additional information about various crew members. Through these deleted scenes (many of which are included on the *Nemesis* DVD), the audience would have learned that Wesley Crusher has returned to Starfleet and will serve under Captain Riker aboard the USS *Titan*, and that his mother, Beverly, is leaving the *Enterprise* for a promotion to Starfleet Medical. A longer ending to the film would have introduced Riker's replacement, new first officer Martin Madden, played by Steven Culp, who later appeared as Major Hayes in several third-season episodes of *Enterprise*. These and several more sequences were deleted in favor of more action footage.

Reception

Star Trek Nemesis was released December 11, 2002, to an apathetic reception. The movie premiered at No. 2, earning $18 million but trailing the Jennifer Lopez comedy *Maid in Manhattan*. It was the first *Star Trek* movie to debut outside the No. 1 slot, and the returns only worsened from there. Receipts for *Nemesis* dropped a then-record 76 percent in its second week. Ultimately, it grossed an anemic $43 million in the U.S. and $67 million worldwide, becoming the first (and only) *Star Trek* picture to lose money. Paramount had invested $60 million in its production and another $33 million in prints and advertising. *Nemesis* was trounced at the box office by other action and fantasy fare, including *Harry Potter and the Chamber of Secrets*, the James Bond entry *Die Another Day*, and *The Lord of the Rings: The Two Towers*. Critics didn't like *Nemesis* any better than audiences did. The movie was widely panned. *Chicago Sun-Times* critic Roger Ebert spoke for many when he opined that the *Trek* film series seemed to be "out of gas." Stephen Hunter of the *Washington Post* described *Nemesis* as "an ordeal for all save the most ardent Treksters." But many devoted fans also disliked the film, complaining (with good reason) that it seemed un-*Trek*-like. Several cast members have blasted the movie in recent years. In that 2006 TrekMovie.com interview, for instance, Burton and Sirtis both say that *Nemesis* "sucked." The picture failed to earn a single Oscar, Hugo, or Saturn Award nomination.

Assessing *Nemesis*

In an interview included on the *Star Trek Nemesis* DVD, Patrick Stewart asserts that a *Trek* picture "must be a *Star Trek* film first and foremost. It cannot be a film that happens to be a *Star Trek* film." *Nemesis* isn't a terrible movie, but it's a *Star Trek* picture in name only. In key respects, it more closely resembles George Lucas's *Star Wars* than Gene Roddenberry's *Star Trek*. Its prolonged phaser rifle shootouts, one aboard the *Scimitar* and later aboard the *Enterprise*, play like outtakes from Lucas's space operas. One shot, in which a rifle-toting Picard dives into an access chute, is a direct quote from the Detention Block escape sequence in *Star Wars, Episode IV: A New Hope* (1977). And the underlying MacGuffin of a planet-destroying weapon recalls the Death Star. This more *Star Wars*-y approach works, up to a point, thanks to the picture's amped-up action quotient. The film boasts a terrific sequence in which Picard and Data fly a two-man attack shuttle through the hallways of the Reman warship, and an epic space battle concludes in spectacular fashion with the *Enterprise* ramming the *Scimitar*. These scenes and others benefit greatly from Digital Domain's beautifully rendered visual effects.

But in its attempts to emulate *Star Wars* and other sci-fi action blockbusters, *Nemesis* loses focus on the recurring characters, which are poorly written and often reduced to window dressing. This is particularly galling in a picture billed as the last go-round for the beloved *Next Generation* ensemble. Baird confesses in a DVD interview that "the interesting part for me was this Shinzon character." No kidding. The picture is so tilted toward Shinzon that Captain Picard and his crew seem like extras in their own movie. This weakness is compounded because, as Logan explains in yet another DVD interview, Shinzon is incapable of growth. This means that *Nemesis* focuses primarily on a character that has no arc. Perhaps inevitably, saddled with such a role, Hardy's performance is flat and one-dimensional, hardly compelling enough to merit his character's copious screen time. Perlman makes a far more memorable impression as Shinzon's vampiric viceroy.

Michael Dorn, LeVar Burton, and Gates McFadden have almost nothing to do as Worf, Geordi, and Dr. Crusher. Adding insult to injury, Dorn's voice (along with those of the actors playing the Remans) was electronically "enhanced" in postproduction to make him sound more "alien." Burton fares marginally better as Geordi, who appears here with his mechanical eyes from *First Contact* (apparently the healing effects of his visit to the Ba'ku planet in *Insurrection* wore off). Frakes and Sirtis give a good accounting and again display appealing chemistry as the newlywed crew members. Counselor Troi is busier than most of the supporting characters; her telepathic abilities are used as a weapon during the battle between the *Enterprise*

Paramount's promotional department had to scour papers from across the country and selectively edit reviewers' quotes to come up with copy for this *Nemesis* newspaper ad. Most critics hated the movie.

and the *Scimitar*—a fresh and effective twist. Patrick Stewart's work here is unusually subdued. At times, he seems to be functioning on autopilot. But Brent Spiner is terrific in his dual roles as Data and B-4. The movie's single most emotionally powerful scene is the one in which Data is forced to deactivate his "older brother." The entire cast suffers from cinematographer Jeffrey Kimball's harsh lighting schemes. Although in vogue at the time for action movies, the film's washed-out color palate makes the actors look sallow and puffy-eyed.

Nemesis runs counter to *Trek* orthodoxy in several respects. The Riker-Troi on-camera sex scene (which turns into a Reman mind-rape of Deanna) is more overt than anything from any previous *Star Trek* film or episode. More jarring is the sequence on Kolarus, where Picard, Data, and Worf tool around in a dune buggy with a rear-mounted phaser cannon. (This scene must have sent Roddenberry spinning in his grave.) The spectacle of *Enterprise* crew members brandishing sidearms and withdrawing phasers from hidden weapons lockers throughout the ship (even in sick bay!) makes it seem as if *The Next Generation* has somehow crossed over into the grim alternate future of "Yesterday's Enterprise." But Logan and Baird's unfamiliarity with the *Star Trek* idiom and characters is most troubling at the story's climax, when Picard—apparently stunned by the death of his clone, Shinzon—simply stands around like a dope while Data tags him with a small transporter device, beams Picard to safety, and then sacrifices himself to save his friends. This is all wrong. *Picard* should be the one trying to sacrifice himself to save the *Enterprise*. Data should tag Picard from behind and transport him to safety before the captain realizes what has happened. Only then should the android trade his life for that of his friends.

From beginning to end, *Nemesis* simply seems off. As a generic sci-fi action piece, it's acceptable (though hardly exceptional), but as *Star Trek* it's substandard. And as the final appearance of the *Next Generation* crew, it is exasperating. Berman's attempts to break the *Trek* mold and attract a wider audience resulted in a movie that failed to deliver what harcore Trekkers yearned for in a series finale, yet it still wasn't fresh or exciting enough to draw crowds away from the latest exploits of Harry Potter, James Bond, or Frodo Baggins. In short, *Nemesis* was the worst of both worlds.

Aftermath

Nemesis ended the *Next Generation* movie series with a sickening thud. Many members of the *Next Gen* cast have expressed regret that their last tour of duty came aboard such an ignominious vehicle. Following *Star Trek V: The Final Frontier*, the original cast had the chance to redeem itself with *Star Trek VI: The Undiscovered Country*. The *Next Gen* ensemble, regrettably, never enjoyed such an opportunity. The franchise's loyal fans were forced to endure an agonizing six and a half years with no new *Trek* movie. The *Nemesis* debacle didn't slow screenwriter John Logan, however, who continued his rapid rise through Hollywood's ranks. He later penned screenplays for two Oscar-nominated films by director Martin Scorsese (*The Aviator*, 2004, and *Hugo*, 2011), the Academy Award-winning animated film *Rango* (2011), and the recent James Bond picture, *Skyfall* (2012). Logan also wrote a Tony-winning play, *Red* (2009). On the other hand, *Nemesis* snuffed out Stuart Baird's directorial aspirations. Although he remains in demand as an editor, he has yet to helm another film. As of this writing (in the fall of 2012), his most recent project was *Skyfall*, written by Logan. Combined with the rapidly eroding ratings for the *Star Trek* television series, the failure of *Nemesis* also destabilized Berman's position as master of the *Trek* universe. His last hope for maintaining control of the franchise was the prequel series *Star Trek: Enterprise*. When that program failed to engage audiences, Berman's days were numbered. While not all the problems with *Nemesis* and the various *Trek* spin-offs were his fault, Berman was intimately involved in the development of every *Trek* project and ultimately accountable for the success or failure of the franchise. With great power comes great responsibility.

32

Starship Mine

Patrick Stewart's Finest Moments

The success of *Star Trek: The Next Generation* can be attributed to many factors, including the ability of writers and producers to recapture the spirit of the cherished original program while updating the product for a new era; the show's groundbreaking, nearly cinematic production values; and the providential timing of the series' debut, when it had almost no competition from other science fiction or fantasy TV series, and while the franchise was riding a crest of popularity following *Star Trek IV: The Voyage Home* (1986). But another of the major reasons *The Next Generation* went over so well was that it starred Patrick Stewart. In a 2006 interview with the Archive of American Television, executive producer Rick Berman called the casting of Patrick Stewart as Captain Picard "the most critical element of the show."

Although he was unknown to most viewers, Stewart brought both charisma and gravitas to his pivotal role, lending badly needed charm and credibility to the fledgling series. His leadership was just as valuable backstage, where he quickly established himself as the leader of the large and high-spirited cast, setting the tone with his professionalism, work ethic, and consistently high-caliber performances. Stewart was completely unfazed by the prospect of replacing the iconic Captain Kirk. "I knew that what we were doing had a totally different personality," Stewart said, as quoted in James Hatfield and George Burt's *Patrick Stewart: The Unauthorized Biography*. "We are not replacing anyone; we simply are what we are. For twenty-seven years I played roles in Shakespeare actors had been playing for four hundred years before me and that will be played by actors long after I'm dead. So what is there to get upset about?"

According to some reports, Stewart's fellow cast members knocked him off his high horse when the former Royal Shakespeare Company performer began to put on airs early on in the show's first season. By all accounts, however, Stewart soon lightened up and became what Wil Wheaton, in his memoir *Just a Geek*, describes as a "mirthful presence." Elsewhere in Hatfield and Burt's biography, assistant director Chip Chalmers recalls the rehearsal in which Stewart first appeared in his grotesque makeup as Locutus of Borg. "He looked so creepy and spooky, and he said, 'I am Locutus of Borg. Have you considered buying a Pontiac?' And everyone was on the floor."

Stewart was famously short-tempered with critics who belittled *The Next Generation*. To name just one of several incidents, he was forced to make a public apology in 1992 after walking off the set to avoid an interview with *Good Morning America*. On February 12, 1992, the ABC morning talk show was broadcast live from the set of *Next Gen* as part of the ballyhoo surrounding the twenty-fifth anniversary of *Star Trek*, but Stewart became miffed when hosts Charlie Gibson and Joan Lunden, and meteorologist Spencer Christian, began clowning around with props and costumes and, in Stewart's view, mocking the show. "I thought it was disrespectful," Stewart later explained to a *TV Guide* reporter. His relationship with the press was stormy, but Stewart's fellow cast members appreciated the star's fierce loyalty to the program and belief in its artistic worth.

Executive producer Rick Berman later said that the casting of Patrick Stewart as Captain Picard was "the most critical element" in the success of *The Next Generation*.

Offscreen and on, Stewart anchored *The Next Generation*. He instantly became the face of the series and delivered superb performances week in and week out. One testament to Stewart's inestimable value is that a review of his finest *Star Trek* work could almost double as a list of *The Next Generation*'s greatest episodes. When Stewart was at his best, so was *Next Gen*.

"The Inner Light"

Of all the outstanding performances Patrick Stewart delivered on *The Next Generation*, none surpassed "The Inner Light," in which Captain Picard, after contacting an alien probe, experiences forty years in the life of an alien named Kamin from the planet Kataan. Morgan Gendel and Peter Allan Fields's engrossing, heart-wrenching teleplay, Stewart said, "gave me the opportunity to explore a whole different kind of Picard." It also gave him the chance to demonstrate the full range and depth of his abilities with a deft, unaffected, deeply moving portrayal of the man Picard might have been—a craftsman and musician with a wife and family. The actor, laboring under increasingly heavy (Emmy-winning) old-age makeup, gradually slows his delivery and changes his posture and gait as the episode progresses, seeming to visibly shrink and become frail. He also subtly transforms in less visible ways. As Kamin gradually accepts that his former life as Captain Picard was "only a dream," Stewart's unmistakable Picard persona seems to fade out, leaving only Kamin. But what makes his performance truly special is the vulnerability and tenderness Stewart brings to his scenes with Margot Rose as Kamin's wife Eline, and with his real-life son Daniel as Kamin's son Batai. Kamin, who grows to deeply love Eline, weeps bitterly at her death, only to enjoy an improbable (and highly dramatic) reunion with her at the episode's climax. In *Star Trek Generations*, Captain Picard enters the paradise-like Nexus and spends Christmas with a prim, all-too-perfect Dream Family. His life as Kamin remains much more believable and touching. (Perhaps in the Nexus Picard should have returned to Kataan and Eline!) "The Inner Light" has reduced many viewers to tears. It is, unquestionably, one of the most emotionally powerful of all *Star Trek* episodes, and the source of that power is Stewart's masterful work.

"Chain of Command, Part II"

If "The Inner Light" represents Stewart's most skilled performance, then "Chain of Command, Part II" features his most courageous work. Most of this episode takes place on a single set where Picard, captured by the Cardassians, endures physical and psychological torture at the hands of interrogator Gul Madred (David Warner). Stewart was deeply invested in this episode on many levels. As an ardent advocate for Amnesty International, he saw the two-part "Chain of Command" epic as a chance to make a powerful statement against torture and prisoner abuse. He reviewed psychological profiles of and videotaped interviews with torturers and their victims, provided by Amnesty, and insisted that, in the end, Picard must reveal he had been "broken" by Madred. Depicting the captain as immune to torture, he felt, would be both dishonest and demeaning to real-life torture victims.

Stewart's extraordinary commitment to the subject matter naturally carried over to the portrayal itself, resulting in an emotionally supercharged performance. He insisted on appearing nude (rather than being doubled) during the first torture sequence. The talented Warner, with whom Stewart had worked during his tenure with the Royal Shakespeare Company, also performs impeccably. Although other story lines are in play in this concluding installment of a two-part adventure, the battle of wills between Madred and Picard becomes the overriding concern of the episode, and at points seems like a third character in the room, hovering like a demon between the two men. At first Picard seethes with indignation at Madred's behavior, but the captain's proud front slowly crumbles. In the end he fights merely to survive and retain his sanity. Producers Rick Berman and Jeri Taylor were so impressed with Stewart's work in "Chain of Command, Part II" that they took out a full-page ad in *Variety* to urge Emmy voters to nominate him as Best Actor. That honor eluded him, but fans, critics, and franchise insiders all rave about his work here, as they should. Due in large part to Stewart's excellence, "Chain of Command" continues to thrill and unsettle audiences.

"The Best of Both Worlds, Parts I and II" and "Family"

Although spread across three episodes spanning two seasons, Captain Picard's assimilation by the Borg (in "The Best of Both Worlds"), his rescue and de-assimilation (in "The Best of Both Worlds, Part II"), and his struggle with the emotional aftermath of those events (in "Family") represent a coherent story arc and a single, superb performance by Stewart. Part one of "The Best of Both Worlds" focuses more on Commander Riker than Captain Picard, but Stewart's chilling transformation into Locutus of Borg is the installment's unrivaled highlight. The actor's cold, blank-faced delivery of the familiar Borg warning, "Resistance is futile," is terrifying. A major element in "Part II" is Picard's inner battle against his Borg reprogramming. In an unforgettable early scene, Locutus is receiving a cybernetic implant when the camera dollies in for a close-up; although his face remains impassive, a single tear leaks from Stewart's eye. The episode concludes with the rescued but still Borg-connected Picard fighting back against the Collective, relaying signals to Data through a sort of computerized mind meld. Once again, Stewart conveys deep emotions with almost no change of outward expression.

However, "Family" represents the pinnacle of Stewart's work in the assimilation story cycle. Although physically back to normal, Picard is still struggling with the emotional aftereffects of his Borg experience—and with the guilt of knowing that, as Locutus, he helped kill eleven thousand people. Searching for solace, Picard returns home to France, visiting his older brother, Robert, with whom he has long-standing grievances. Eventually, Jean-Luc's conflicts with Robert trigger an emotional breakdown. At first, Stewart remains a model of restraint, reading lines with clipped efficiency and tense body language. But once the Picard brothers finally come to blows—duking it out in a muddy vineyard—the actor uncorks a full-blown meltdown, weeping bitterly, racked with remorse and self-doubt. "They used me to kill. . . . I should have been able to stop them!" he sobs. It's a wrenching moment that wouldn't work so well if not preceded by two and a half episodes worth of tight-lipped emotional restraint. The "Best of Both Worlds" saga was a turning point for Captain Picard. As executive producer Michael Piller points out, the character was never the same afterward; he became more vulnerable—and more interesting. The story seems to have helped Stewart unlock Picard's inner workings. Most of the actor's finest performances follow this one.

"Tapestry"

In "Tapestry," Picard—hovering near death—meets Q, who offers the captain a chance to relive his life and correct his youthful mistakes. Although at first leery, Picard accepts Q's offer. He's transported back to his days as a reckless young ensign and reunited with the friends of his youth, with ironic consequences. Stewart's performance in "Tapestry" is remarkable on two levels. First and most obviously, the actor makes an astounding transformation. Without benefit of special makeup or other physical alterations, he seems visibly younger in his scenes as the twenty-one-year-old Ensign Picard. He smiles more readily and moves with greater spring in his step. Stewart demonstrates some of the chameleonic abilities that enabled him to play every role from Scrooge to Tiny Tim in his one-man version of *A Christmas Carol*, without changes of makeup or costume. Perhaps more importantly, Stewart's richly nuanced, soul-searching performance vividly illuminates Picard's need to overcome deep-seated regrets in order to fully appreciate his (possibly ending) life. In "The Best of Both Worlds" trilogy and "Chain of Command," Stewart explored the mind of Captain Picard. In "The Inner Light," he revealed Picard's heart. In "Tapestry," he unveils the character's soul.

"The Measure of a Man" and "The Drumhead"

In both of these episodes, Captain Picard is the voice of moral authority, averting miscarriages of justice with brilliant philosophical arguments and soaring oratory. In the hands of a lesser actor, both "The Measure of a Man" (featuring a hearing to determine whether Data is a sentient being or merely a machine, property of Starfleet) and "The Drumhead" (in which Picard opposes a witch hunt to uncover supposed Romulan spies aboard his ship) might have come off as dogmatic and self-righteous. But they don't, mostly because Stewart's work is surprisingly understated. For most of both episodes, his delivery is quiet, even hesitant. Without questioning Picard's commitment to the righteousness of his actions, Stewart underscores the captain's anxiety about the outcome of the proceedings. Until the moment when he delivers his climactic speeches, Picard seems extremely dubious about his prospects for victory. In "The Drumhead," as Starfleet investigator Nora Satie's investigation devolves into baseless suspicion and guilt by association, Picard grows increasingly agitated. Stewart's body language becomes more coiled and tense, and at points he hisses lines almost through his teeth. But when he confronts Satie (Jean Simmons) to demand an end to the investigation, his tone is surprisingly gentle. "What you're doing here is unethical. It's immoral, and I will fight you," he says. Rather than shouting with indignation, Stewart's delivery remains quiet and calm, with a hint of sadness. Even during his electrifying monologues, Stewart never settles for simple bombast. His words flicker with shifting emotions, and his delivery is often surprising. In "The Measure of a Man," for instance, Picard argues that validating Starfleet's claim on Data could lead to the creation of a race of android slaves. "Are you prepared to condemn him and all that come after him to servitude and slavery? . . . You wanted a chance to make law. Well here it is. Make it a good one," Stewart concludes, with a note of contempt, as if Picard is almost daring the judge to rule against Data. Every performance by every actor is a collection of choices. Stewart's work in these two episodes highlights his tendency to make imaginative, character-illuminating choices that wouldn't even occur to most performers.

"Starship Mine"

Patrick Stewart—action hero? In this hard-hitting episode, modeled after the blockbuster movie *Die Hard*, Stewart proves that he could play the dynamic, devil-may-care man of action. Trapped alone aboard the *Enterprise* with a gang of terrorists, Picard singe-handedly battles to wreck their scheme—and to stay alive. The episode revealed a seldom-seen side of the captain, more noted for his diplomatic achievements than his hand-to-hand combat skills, but it also showed a seldom-seen side of Stewart. With this performance the actor proved he could have played the kind of brawling, bare-chested hero popularized by William Shatner, had Picard been written more along the lines of Captain Kirk. His performance is nimble and stylish, and never feels airy or tossed off. Even in a role as straightforward as this one, Stewart is simply incapable of delivering a flat, monochromatic performance. In order to prevail, Picard must not only defeat but kill the terrorists. This enables Stewart to introduce an edge of something akin to menace (at the very least, it might be called grim determination) that prevents his work from becoming cartoonish. The final effect is akin to Sean Connery's early appearances as James Bond. Perhaps because it was so bracingly different from most Picard episodes, or maybe because it includes more physical action than high-flying speeches, "Starship Mine" is seldom mentioned as one of Stewart's best performances, but it should be.

"All Good Things ..."

Stewart contributed another spectacular performance—or, more accurately, three of them—to the series finale, "All Good Things ... ," in which Picard becomes dislodged in time, slipping between present day, the future (after his retirement), and the past (during his first mission with the *Enterprise*). He's excellent in all three time periods, as Picard struggles to discover the cause of

The aged Picard from "All Good Things ... " was hardly an action hero, yet he became an action figure.   *Photo by Preston Hewis, East Bank Images*

a mysterious rift in the fabric of space-time that threatens human existence. But he's particularly effective as the aged, retired captain—bearded, stooped, irascible, and possibly out of touch with reality as a result of a brain disorder. It's yet another striking transformation, this time offering a fascinating (and often funny) glimpse of a possible Future Picard—crotchety yet endearing, and as resolute as ever. There is much to admire in the feature-length "All Good Things . . . ," one of the best produced and performed installments of the entire series, but Stewart's work remains one of the episode's primary strengths.

Others

It is an almost criminal oversight that Stewart never received an Emmy nomination for his work on *The Next Generation*, although he was nominated for a Screen Actors Guild Award following the show's final season. He very seldom gave a poor performance and always came through with something special when playing opposite a guest star he admired. In addition to "Chain of Command" with David Warner and "The Drumhead" with screen legend Jean Simmons, he also shined in "Darmok" opposite the acclaimed Paul Winfield and in *Star Trek: First Contact* with the great Alfre Woodard. His performance in *First Contact* plays like a distant echo of his work in the "Best of Both Worlds"/"Family" saga. Stewart also seemed to have a special rapport with Wil Wheaton, contributing outstanding dialogues with the young actor in episodes such as "Samaritan Snare" and "Final Mission." Picard's fatherly dressing-down of cadet Wesley Crusher in "The First Duty" remains one of the series' most searing emotional moments. Stewart also displayed enticing chemistry with actress Jennifer Hetrick as Vash in "Captain's Holiday" and "Qpid." Both of his appearances with Mark Lenard, in "Sarek" and "Unification I," proved outstanding as well. Stewart's deft handling of Picard's laughing-crying freak-out after his mind meld with the emotionally unstable Vulcan in "Sarek" brings off a very difficult scene that could easily have seemed overblown. Finally, Stewart supplied a devilishly delightful but often overlooked performance in "Allegiance," playing Picard's alien doppelganger, who makes overt sexual advances to Beverly Crusher and leads the crew in drinking songs in Ten-Forward. Whenever Stewart was on-screen, the potential for something extraordinary existed.

33

A Fistful of Datas

Brent Spiner's Finest Moments

A side from Patrick Stewart, no single cast member was more important to *The Next Generation* than Brent Spiner. In fact, when Paramount entered contract negotiations with the *Next Gen* ensemble following the expiration of the cast's original deals at the conclusion of Season Five, the actor producers were most concerned about retaining was Spiner, even more than Stewart. While Jonathan Frakes could conceivably have been promoted to Captain Riker, there was no way to replace Spiner's Lieutenant Commander Data. The android officer was unique, and from the beginning had ranked among the show's most popular characters.

Creator Gene Roddenberry envisioned Data as the *Next Generation*'s answer to Spock, an emotionless outsider who provided detached commentary on the foibles of the human race. Data was also a thinly veiled revival of Questor, the android protagonist of Roddenberry's failed 1974 pilot *The Questor Tapes*. But Spiner brought a special quality to Data—a childlike readiness to see the best in people—that was quite different from Spock or Questor, and remarkably endearing. Fans respected and admired (and some desired) Spock, but they adored Data.

The role was difficult to cast because it presented singular challenges. Since Data was unable to experience human feelings, the actor had to find ways to trigger an emotional response in viewers without appearing to express emotion himself, something Nimoy mastered while playing Spock (even though the Vulcan's feelings were merely suppressed, not nonexistent). After an arduous series of auditions, Spiner won the role and immediately made it his own.

Cast as an unfeeling android, Spiner was denied big emotional scenes and forced to play everything small. However, the actor understood that, since his role required so much restraint, even his smallest movements—the raise of an eyebrow, the turn of his head, a change in the lilt of his voice—would register a powerful impact on the audience. (As Spock, Nimoy took this same approach). Spiner established a collection of Data-isms he utilized throughout the series: a sharp, slight turn of the head (resembling the expression of the dog from the old RCA/Victor logo) to express interest; a furrowed brow and pursed lips to indicate confusion; and so on. Spiner's frequent use of the word "curious" became the equivalent of Nimoy's trademark "fascinating." Spiner subtly suggested that Data made up for being unable to feel by being more able to think. Although he was unable to cry for his deceased friend Tasha Yar, he puzzled over the meaning of her funeral. Even when he wasn't the center of attention, Spiner's Data was never simply present, but always seemed to be silently analyzing information or calculating an algorithm or something.

Before joining *Star Trek*, Spiner was best known for playing broadly comedic roles, and at first writers used Data as comedy relief. Throughout Season One, for instance, the android was perpetually confused by human figures of speech. Spiner was continually assigned dialogue along the lines of, "But Captain, why should it precipitate canines and felines?" This sort of cheap humor was gradually curtailed. Over the course of seven seasons and four movies, Data rounded into a complex and multifaceted character. Spiner's brilliant comic timing never left him, and he supplied many of *The Next Generation*'s funniest moments, but he also delivered moments of intense drama and heartrending pathos. Like Stewart, Spiner was an amazingly consistent performer. In fact, the overall quality of his work is so strong that it's difficult to select a handful of performances as his best. Nevertheless, a fistful of episodes stand out.

"The Offspring"

Hollywood lore contains many stories about the unadorned, laconic acting of star Gary Cooper—directors such as Henry Hathaway, Billy Wilder, and Howard Hawks all reported being worried about Cooper's work, because he seemed to be doing almost nothing. His performances seemed flat and lifeless—until the director saw the dailies. "In making a scene with Coop, why, you look at it and you wonder, there's nothing there," said Hawks, in *Conversations with the Great Moviemakers of Hollywood's Golden Age*. "Then you'd look at the film and it was great." Like Cooper, Spiner's approach to Data could be so subtle it was practically invisible. Like all fine actors, his most important work took place in his own mind and heart—believing in the scene, remaining present to the moment and available to his fellow performers. This is a praiseworthy quality, but it makes analyzing the actor's work particularly difficult. His performances were enriched in ways that are hard to quantify—by unexpressed thoughts that seem to be flashing through his head, or by a straightforward line reading that nevertheless seems laced with emotion. All of these qualities are on display in "The Offspring," arguably Spiner's best performance and certainly one of his most haunting.

In this episode, Data creates an android daughter named Lal and, against the misgivings of Captain Picard and interference from Starfleet brass, attempts to raise her as his child. Throughout the episode Spiner suggests a wide variety of emotions—joy, pride, concern, indignation, fear, love, and grief—without any overt expression of those states. "Lal is my child," Spiner says when Data introduces the android to Geordi, Deanna, and Wesley Crusher. Although Spiner's tone is not noticeably different from Data's usual gentle speaking voice, his words nearly vibrate with pride and the sense of wonder experienced by all new parents. Later, he seems resentful when Picard argues that he should have cleared Lal's creation with command. He frowns, pauses, and looks away before finally addressing Picard. "I do not recall anyone else on board consulting you about their procreation, Captain." Spiner and guest star Halle Todd, as Lal, have wonderful chemistry. Data at first dotes on his daughter, then worries about her when she has difficulty assimilating with the other *Enterprise* children. Eventually, Lal begins to exhibit abilities beyond Data's, including the capacity to experience emotions. In the end, however, she suffers a massive breakdown of her neural net and dies. Spiner's final scene with Todd is one of the most heartbreaking in the *Star Trek* canon, all the more devastating because Spiner's performance remains so dry and straightforward. When Lal tells her father that she loves him, Data can only respond, "I wish I could feel it with you." If Data cannot, Spiner clearly does, and it's this delicate quality that makes the scene, and "The Offspring," so resonant.

"The Measure of a Man"

"The Measure of a Man" may be the single most celebrated "Data episode." In it, Captain Picard defends Data against an order from Starfleet Research, which has declared that the android is not a sentient being and, as a result, has no legal rights. Data is the property of Starfleet and must submit to cybernetics experiments that may prove fatal. This episode boasts outstanding performances from nearly everyone involved, including Patrick Stewart as Picard, Jonathan Frakes as Commander Riker (forced by a quirk of jurisprudence to argue the case *against* Data), and Whoopi Goldberg as Guinan, who has a pivotal *tête-à-tête* with the Captain. But Spiner remains central, and the episode would collapse without his precision-tuned portrayal of the android officer, who can only wait anxiously as his shipmates fight for his life. Early on, Data believes he can escape the experiment by resigning his Starfleet commission. There's a short but beautifully played scene in which Data packs his belongings, including a holographic portrait of Tasha Yar, at which Spiner stares wistfully. Throughout the episode, the actor delivers Data's matter-of-fact dialogue with buried emotions. The clearest instance of this is when Data learns of Starfleet's ruling that he must submit to the experiment. "I see. From limitless options I am reduced to none. Or, rather, one," Spiner says, spitting out the words with stinging resentment. Later, during the hearing, Picard asks Data to explain why he keeps a portrait of Tasha but not any of his other shipmates. "She was special to me sir," he replies, with obvious discomfort. "We were . . . intimate." Spiner almost whispers the last word, accentuating Data's unease. At the conclusion of the episode, after his sentience has been confirmed and his rights restored, Data takes a surprisingly conciliatory attitude toward both the Starfleet cyberneticist and Commander Riker. In these scenes, too, Spiner subtly allows twinges of emotion to leak through, making Data seem sympathetic and even (toward Riker) grateful. The actor's ability to sell moments like this is what, above all else, made Data one of *Star Trek*'s most beloved characters.

"Data's Day"

Compared to "The Offspring" and "The Measure of a Man," "Data's Day" is *Star Trek* Lite. In this seriocomic episode, Data narrates an account of a typical day in his life aboard the *Enterprise*—for the benefit of Dr. Bruce Maddox, the cyberneticist from "Measure of a Man." The episode concerns itself primarily with Data struggling to comprehend the nuances of human behavior, as he prepares to serve as Father of the Bride at the wedding of Keiko Ishikawa and Miles O'Brien, and as the ship hosts a visiting Vulcan dignitary, Ambassador T'Pel. The scenario enables Spiner to demonstrate his range, coming off as hilariously clueless regarding the wedding but perceptively uneasy about T'Pel, who is ultimately revealed as a Romulan spy. In addition to his on-screen contributions, Spiner also provides voice-over narration throughout the episode. In one early scene, Data's ironclad logic leads him to believe that Miles will be pleased to learn that Keiko has decided to call off the wedding (since she says it will make her happy, and Data knows Miles wants her to be happy). Data beams as he reports the "good news" to Miles and is taken aback when O'Brien is hurt and angry. Later, however, he senses something is amiss with Ambassador T'Pel, although he refuses to allow that he may possess the sense humans refer to as "intuition." This moment underscores another nuance of Spiner's performances. Since he consistently gilded his work with tinges of emotion, viewers came to believe that Data was not nearly so limited as he thought. This was not a violation of the character (since Data had the capacity to learn and grow) but an enrichment of it.

"Data's Day" also includes a series of short scenes in which Data interacts individually with a succession of other regulars: He turns to Guinan and Deanna for advice on dealing with Miles and Keiko; Worf helps him pick out a wedding gift; Dr. Crusher teaches him how to dance. As is usually the case, his cast mates shine in these sequences. Another tribute to Spiner's talent is that he always seemed to inspire the best from his fellow actors. Finally, in that dance lesson, Spiner even gets to show off some of his tap skills. Although he and Gates McFadden were doubled for some of the more demanding steps, this scene was mostly them. Both McFadden and Spiner had backgrounds in dance and musical theater, and relished the chance to strut their stuff.

"Brothers"

From a bang-for-your-buck perspective, no *Next Generation* adventure delivers more Spiner than "Brothers," in which the actor plays three roles: Data, Data's brother Lore, and their creator, Dr. Noonian Soong. For long stretches, "Brothers" becomes the television equivalent of a one-man show, with Spiner (through the wonders of editing and visual effects) performing opposite himself. In this episode, Dr. Soong triggers an automated signal that draws Data to the remote planet Terla III—but also attracts Lore (who Soong didn't know had been reassembled), bringing unintended consequences. "Brothers" required extraordinary effort by Spiner in several respects. A week prior to shooting, he and director David Livington spent three days rehearsing and blocking the Spiner-only sequences, placing colored tape on the floor to indicate which character should be where during each scene. To allow time for these rehearsals, which greatly simplified shooting, Spiner was written out of the preceding episode, "Family." During production, Spiner spent long hours in the makeup chair and for two and a half days worked entirely alone onstage, shooting sequences that would be cut together so that Data, Lore, and Soong would appear to be speaking with one another.

The actor was rewarded with a unique showcase for his talents. Spiner was always good as the jealous, vindictive Lore, but this may be his best work as the character. Here, Lore gains some sympathy (at least viewers learn how *he* views the events surrounding his creation and disassembly), but remains as cruel and dangerous as ever, lashing out at his terminally ill father. Spiner's performance as Dr. Soong tends toward the baroque but accomplishes a difficult task—clearly delineating the character from his two "children," while also revealing traits good and bad, which are amplified in his disparate android offspring. The actor's most nuanced and touching portrayal is of Data, who is at first understandably thrilled to meet his believed-dead creator, but comes to the sobering realization that Dr. Soong has serious faults and weaknesses. The scenario crackles with emotional and psychological tension, all of it played out among the trio of Spiner characters. "Brothers" also stands as a testament to the supreme confidence producers had in Spiner. The entire teleplay, written by executive producer Rick Berman, was predicated on Spiner's ability to deliver a tour de force, three-in-one performance, something few producers would ask of any actor.

"In Theory"

Spiner's funniest performance came in the delightful "In Theory," in which Data enters a romantic relationship with Lieutenant Jenna D'Sora (Michele Scarabelli). Early on, Spiner plays the straight man during a hilarious sequence in which Data calls upon Guinan, Geordi, Deanna, Worf, Riker, and finally Picard for dating advice. Later, Data installs a new "romance program," based on a collection of literary and cultural models, which gives Spiner leeway to indulge some of his broader comic abilities. He turns Data into an unctuous, smarmy schmoozer who offers to mix her a (replicated) drink, to rearrange her closet, and says things like, "Darling, you remain as aesthetically pleasing as the first day we met. I believe I am the most fortunate sentient in this sector of the galaxy." Then, turning on a dime, he attempts to instigate a lover's quarrel but succeeds only in confusing the increasingly exasperated D'Sora. As amusing as it is, however, Spiner's "In Theory" performance contains an underlying note of pathos, which finally comes to the fore at the conclusion of the episode when D'Sora dumps her android boyfriend. Data stares for a lingering second at the cabin door through which Jenna just exited. What, the audience must wonder, is Data pondering in that moment, following the loss of his first sweetheart? Spiner and Scarabelli, who sci-fi fans may recognize from her work on the *Alien Nation* TV series and TV movies, have appealing comedic chemistry. It's unfortunate that Lieutenant D'Sora was never heard from again.

"The Most Toys"

On the opposite end of the spectrum from "In Theory" falls "The Most Toys," in which Spiner delivered his most unsettling dramatic performance. In this story, Data is kidnapped by the unscrupulous collector, Fajo (Saul Rubinek), who wants to keep him prisoner, displaying him as part of his private collection of unique and priceless artifacts, including the *Mona Lisa* and the only surviving Roger Maris baseball card. The scenario, written by freelancer Shari Goodhartz, was designed to showcase Data's inner strength. Early on, Data protests his capture by quietly refusing to go along with Fajo's request that he sit in a certain location or "perform" to impress visitors. The enraged Fajo then begins to torture Data, and to threaten to torture or kill other people, to bend the android to his will. How far will Data go to free himself from the clutches of one of the most ruthless and despicable villains in the history of *Star Trek*? Will he kill Fajo? Can he? Spiner's defiant, smoldering performance reveals aspects of Data seldom explored in other teleplays. Rubinek's domineering, gleefully sadistic Fajo provides an ideal foil. Together, Spiner and Rubinek push "The Most Toys" into dark frontiers seldom explored on *The Next Generation*.

Brent Spiner's subtle, brilliant work helped make Lieutenant Commander Data one of *The Next Generation*'s most beloved characters. Producers considered Spiner irreplaceable.

"A Fistful of Datas"

In the seriocomic "A Fistful of Datas," Worf, Alexander, and Deanna find themselves trapped in an out-of-control holodeck Western program. As the episode progresses, all the other characters begin transforming into versions of Data—played by Brent Spiner. As a result, Spiner winds up playing five characters, two more than in "Brothers." His work as menacing gunman Frank Hollander and as his simpering son Eli is especially strong. The actor is also seen as two nameless gunmen (identified as "bandito" and "cowboy") and, for the clincher, Miss Annie Meyers. Although the narrative remains focused on Michael Dorn, Brian Bonsall, and Marina Sirtis (Spiner doesn't carry the episode, or any of its individual scenes, as he does in "Brothers") "A Fistful of Datas" remains an impressive achievement for the actor and a showcase for his versatility.

Others

Perhaps because Data was such a childlike character, Spiner also seemed to thrive in scenarios where he played opposite young actors, such as "Pen Pals," in which Data begins a subspace correspondence with an adolescent girl from a planet with no knowledge of alien species; "Hero Worship," in which Data is idolized by a young boy after saving the child's life; and "Thine Own Self," in which Data, after losing his memory, is befriended by a young girl on a planet with a preindustrial civilization. Then again, he seemed capable of delivering sterling work regardless of the setting. Some of Spiner's other notable performances include: "Redemption II" and "Gambit, Parts I and II," which feature Data's only missions as the commander of a starship; "Datalore" and "Descent, Parts I and II," which boast dual appearances by Spiner as Data and Lore; the underrated "Silicon Avatar," in which Data serves as a conduit for a mother to contact her dead son; "Time's Arrow, Parts I and II," with Data as the crux of an elaborate time-travel yarn; "Elementary, Dear Data," with Data impersonating Sherlock Holmes and matching wits with Professor Moriarty; and "The Quality of Life," in which Data risks his reputation to defend robot laborers he believes have gained sentience.

34

Heart of Glory

The Emergence of Michael Dorn

ieutenant Worf was an afterthought. He didn't appear among the crew profiles in Gene Roddenberry's initial series prospectus, nor was he listed on the earliest casting sheets for *Star Trek: The Next Generation*. Unlike the other characters, Worf didn't spring from the mind of Roddenberry but originated from producer Bob Justman's suggestion that the bridge crew include "a Klingon marine." Roddenberry, after considering the idea for weeks, finally approved Justman's concept shortly before casting began. Even then, however, Worf was not expected to be a major factor on the show. The small importance Roddenberry placed on the character was reflected in the choice of the actor hired for the part: Michael Dorn, whose career to date had consisted primarily of glorified bits. Among other small, often uncredited roles, he toiled silently in the newsroom as a background character on *The Mary Tyler Moore Show* and spent three seasons milling around the barracks as officer Jebidiah Turner on *CHiPS*, where his dialogue was usually restricted to lines like, "Go get 'em, Ponch!" However, with the unanticipated departure of Denise Crosby near the end of the first season of *The Next Generation*, Worf became a more significant figure in the framework of *Star Trek* than anyone anticipated. Dorn seized the opportunity, revealing—or perhaps developing—abilities untapped in his prior roles.

With Crosby's Tasha Yar removed from the equation, Worf became more actively involved in the show's story lines. Slowly at first, writers began to craft episodes that prominently featured Dorn's character, fleshing out Worf's back-story and (along with it) revealing more about Klingon culture. As the material grew more complex and challenging, Dorn demonstrated greater and greater acumen. Over the course of seven seasons and beyond, he delivered increasingly skillful and subtle performances in every conceivable register, from broad comedy to swashbuckling adventure to romantic and family drama. His artistic development, coupled with the emergence of Worf, was one of the most remarkable and entertaining features of the show. *Next Gen*'s Klingon episodes always earned high ratings, and Worf became an integral part of the series' appeal.

"Heart of Glory"

Although it wasn't a true Worf episode (its first fifteen minutes focus on Geordi's use of a Visual Acuity Transmitter, which allows the bridge crew to view what La Forge "sees" through his VISOR), "Heart of Glory" gave Dorn his first

The development of Worf as a character and Michael Dorn as a performer was one of the most exciting and enjoyable features of *The Next Generation.*

meaningful time in the spotlight, and he took full advantage. In this late-Season One installment, two rogue Klingons try to lure Worf into joining their plot to fracture the Federation-Klingon alliance and start a glorious new war with humankind. "Listen to your blood," one of the renegades tells him. "You are not of these people!" Writer-producer Maurice Hurley's teleplay reveals Worf's background—explaining for the first time that he was adopted and raised by humans after his Klingon family was killed in a Romulan attack. It also introduces Worf's internal strife and conflicted loyalties—he's torn between his identities as a Klingon warrior and a Starfleet officer—which would resurface in later adventures. All this gave Dorn, for the first time, material he could sink his prosthetic fangs into. Even though his status as a Klingon would seem to give the actor license to bark and snarl in unmitigated fury (guest stars Vaughn Armstrong and

Charles Hyman gnaw the scenery as the Klingon outlaws), Dorn instead offers a carefully measured performance. He quietly broods throughout much of the episode, engulfing Worf in an enigmatic silence that, for a while at least, seems to suggest that he may be seriously considering joining the renegades. In the climax, Worf reiterates his loyalties in no uncertain terms—he's devoted both to Starfleet and to his Klingon ideals, which the outlaws have forgotten. "The true test of a warrior is not without, it is within," Dorn says, eyes blazing. He places a clinched fist over his heart. "*This* is where we meet the challenge." In addition to his fiery oratory, Dorn speaks Klingon for the first time and twice performs the Klingon death ritual, looking into the eyes of the deceased, then throwing his head back and howling in fury to warn the dead that a Klingon warrior is about to join them. He invests these moments (which might have seemed silly) with dignity and pride. Later episodes explored the Klingon culture more fully and served as better showcases for Dorn's gifts, but "Heart of Glory" was foundational for all that followed. It established that this Klingon thing had real potential and that this Dorn guy was pretty good.

"The Emissary" and "The Enemy"

Dorn received his second turn in the spotlight with the Season Two adventure "The Emissary," in which the beautiful, half-Klingon Ambassador K'Ehleyr (Suzie Plakson), who has rejected Klingon ways, tries to coax Worf into abandoning his Klingon heritage. Worf holds fast to his Klingon identity, but the physical attraction between Worf and K'Ehleyr proves irresistible. "The Emissary" is an outstanding installment with important repercussions in future episodes, and it boasts another fine performance by Dorn. His scenes with Plakson sizzle. However, aside from proving that (even in his heavy Klingon makeup) Dorn could pull off a romantic interlude, "The Emissary" did not represent a major advance; It merely inverted the formula of "Heart of Glory." In "The Emissary," Worf is tempted to give up his ties with Klingon culture, just as he was tempted to reject his ties with humanity in the earlier episode. The first major breakthrough, for both the actor and the character, arrived early in Season Three with "The Enemy."

Worf's role in "The Enemy" is secondary, but its impact was enormous. The story involves the discovery of a crashed Romulan spy ship on a Federation planet. One grievously wounded survivor is beamed aboard the *Enterprise* for treatment, while Geordi is stranded on the planet's surface with a second Romulan. The episode focuses primarily on Geordi's struggles on the planet's surface, but in the teleplay's B-story, Worf refuses to donate cellular material needed to save the life of the injured Romulan because Romulans killed his parents. Dr. Crusher, Commander Riker, and Captain Picard all appeal to Worf to save the Romulan, but he still refuses. When Dr. Crusher tells him that the Romulan will die without Worf's help, Dorn coolly replies, "Then he will die." Then he stands and walks calmly from the room. Dorn seems more agitated in his conversation with Riker. "I am asked to give up the very lifeblood of my mother and father to those who murdered them," he howls with outrage. Then he seethes, "My Starfleet training tells me one thing, but everything I am tells me another." Riker and Picard appeal to his sense of fairness and duty, and try to convince him he would be serving the greater good by making the donation. Worf says that he will donate the material if Picard orders him to do so, but Picard stops short of overriding Worf's conscience with a direct order. Even though Picard says, "I ask you, I beg you," still Worf refuses. Finally, in an outcome that shocked many viewers at the time, the Romulan dies. This subplot is so powerful, and Dorn's performance is so riveting, that even though it takes up less than fifteen minutes of screen time, it's what most viewers remember about "The Enemy."

It was producer/cowriter Michael Piller's shocking, counter-*Trek*-ish idea to have Worf stand his ground and let the Romulan die, and this plot point proved extremely controversial among the show's writers and cast. At first, even Dorn objected, but after further thought, he realized it represented a major development for Worf. He responded with a forceful yet nuanced, deeply moving performance that forever changed the way audiences viewed his character. Before "The Enemy," Worf seemed different from his shipmates mostly because of the way he looked and dressed; afterward, he stood apart because of the way he thought. Viewers saw, for the first time, that as a Klingon, Worf subscribed to a different system of values than his human (or android or Betazoid) shipmates. This seemed to unlock the character for both the series' writers and for Dorn. From this point forward, both *The Next Generation*'s Worf stories and Dorn's performances became much more complex and gripping.

"Sins of the Father"

"Sins of the Father" marked the arrival of another important figure in the development of Worf, writer Ronald D. Moore. Moore, who went on to pen many Klingon-focused episodes for both *Next Gen* and *Deep Space Nine*, always wrote excellent material for Dorn, and Dorn consistently responded with first-rate performances. Their first collaboration (cowritten by Moore) was a landmark episode ranked by many among the best in the history of *The Next Generation*. In "Sins of the Father," Worf learns that his dead father, Mogh, has been named a traitor to the Empire by the Klingon High Council. Newly discovered evidence supposedly reveals that Mogh was complicit in the Romulan massacre at Khitomer, in which Mogh was killed along with thousands of other Klingons. Worf returns to the Klingon home world to challenge the ruling, while Captain Picard and Data investigate what really happened at Khitomer. Picard and Data find evidence that exonerates Mogh, but revealing the truth behind the Khitomer attack could trigger a Klingon civil war. Rather than risk the possible collapse of the Empire and the dissolution of its alliance with the Federation, Worf agrees to be punished for crimes his father never committed.

"Sins of the Father" didn't demand great range from Dorn. For most of the episode, as Worf defends himself from Klingons who question his fealty to the Empire and to Klingon tradition, and as he angrily denounces the charges against his father, Dorn simply seems indignant. "My heart is Klingon, I am of this world!" he snarls. But if "Sins of the Father" is largely a one-note teleplay for Dorn, the actor hits that note like Enrico Caruso. His outrage seems not only authentic but deeply rooted, suggesting that the whole controversy stirs up the unimaginable pain of his parents' murder. And Dorn is magnificent in the episode's climax, in which Worf agrees to sacrifice his family's honor and his identity as a Klingon warrior (a fate worse than death for a loyal Klingon) in order to avert a catastrophic war. Suffering the shame of discommendation is an act of extraordinary self-sacrifice and patriotism, but it's also painful. Dorn seems visibly sickened during the ritual, as his fellow Klingons symbolically turn their backs on Worf. It's a stinging, bitter moment.

"Reunion"

Building on the events of "The Emissary" and "Sins of the Father," a writing team that included Moore penned "Reunion," arguably Dorn's single best episode. His performance covers far more range than "Sins of the Father" (or any other previous installment) and soars to seldom-scaled dramatic heights. Ambassador K'Ehleyr returns, accompanied by her son Alexander, the result of her sexual encounter with Worf in "The Emissary." Although he's angry she had not previously informed him about the child, the attraction between Worf and K'Ehleyr remains strong. Worf would like to marry K'Ehleyr and form a family, but doesn't dare because of his discommendation. Dorn's scenes with Plakson's K'Ehleyr crackle with sexual energy. He also has some warm, funny moments with young Jon Steuer as Alexander, as Worf grows irritated with his incessant "why?" questions and alarmed by the child's ignorance of Klingon traditions. Yet he clearly loves his son. In a surprisingly tender sequence, Worf teaches Alexander how to hold a bat'leth.

Soon, however, the story's romantic and familial elements intersect with Klingon politics. Captain Picard is asked to oversee the selection of a new ruler of the Klingon Empire by the dying High Chancellor K'mpec. One of the two rivals for the throne—Gowron (Robert O'Reilly) and Worf's enemy Duras (Patrick Massett)—has poisoned K'mpec, but the Chancellor doesn't know which one. Eventually, K'Ehleyr discovers the truth—and is murdered for it. In the episode's most haunting moment, Worf and Alexander discover the bloody, dying K'Ehleyr, who reveals the identity of her killer, then places Alexander's hand in Worf's, leaving the child in his care. When K'Ehleyr dies, Dorn throws back his head and howls—but this isn't the ceremonial Klingon death cry from "Heart of Glory." It sounds more like an eruption of primal agony and rage. Worf rushes away to take vengeance on her killer, striking him down despite the protests of Riker and Data, who race to the scene but are unable to stop him. Dorn's eyes are alight with fury and satisfaction as Worf delivers the death stroke. It's a stunning moment in a tour de force performance, but still more outstanding sequences remain, as Worf endures a dressing-down from Picard and later returns to the forlorn Alexander. "I miss her, too," Dorn says simply, even though Alexander hasn't spoken at all. The episode ends as Worf hugs his son, and it's difficult to tell who is comforting who. This poignant conclusion caps a magnificent outing for Dorn, whose superb work fuels one of *The Next Generation*'s most emotionally powerful installments.

"Redemption I and II"

The events of "The Emissary," "Sins of the Father," and "Reunion" build toward Moore's two-part "Redemption" epic, which closed Season Four and opened Season Five. It was indicative of the producers' confidence in Dorn and the escalating popularity of Worf that the character was selected as the centerpiece of a season-ending cliff-hanger. The show's other cliff-hanger finales centered on Picard, Data, or Riker. "Redemption" established Worf as an equal of those tentpole characters. His ascendance was complete. It also signified that Dorn's importance to the show was on par with that of Patrick Stewart, Brent Spiner, and Jonathan Frakes. "Redemption I and II" is a sprawling tale with major parts for Picard, Data, Gowron, the villainous Duras Sisters, and Tasha Yar's half-Romulan daughter Sela, but Worf remains central to everything else, and Dorn's fierce yet soul-searching performance serves as the engine for the entire piece. The episode also marks another major turning point for Worf. Through these events, he finally came to grips with the conflicting impulses arising from his human upbringing and his Klingon instincts, which had vexed him throughout the course of the series so far.

At the conclusion of the first episode, Worf, feeling hemmed in by Starfleet regulations and exasperated by Picard's refusal to take a stand in the Klingon conflict, resigns his commission to clear his family name and help save the Empire. Picard gives Worf a heroic farewell, with crew members lining the halls as the Klingon makes his way to the transporter room. Dorn seems genuinely choked up in this sequence. But in "Redemption II," Worf becomes increasingly frustrated with his fellow Klingons as well. He's baffled by the way rival Klingons, who try to kill each other in battle, meet in the neutral ground of the capital city to carouse and drink together, and incensed when Chancellor Gowron kills one of his own men when the officer challenges Gowron's leadership. In the end, the Empire is saved, Worf's family honor is restored, and Worf even has the chance to kill a member of the family truly responsible for the Khitomer attacks. But he cannot bring himself to take the life of the captive, a thirteen-year-old boy. "But it's our way, it's the Klingon way!" Worf's brother, Kurn, pleads. "Yes," Worf answers, "but it is not *my* way." Dorn's delivery of this line seems packed with meaning. It's the moment in which Worf gains his sense of self. A major reason Worf is such a fascinating character is that he claims two proud heritages, taking the best parts of each yet standing apart from both. He is unique. And this is the way Dorn would play the character in his many later *Next Gen* and *DS9* appearances.

"Parallels" and Others

Dorn gave many more terrific performances on *The Next Generation*. One of his greatest gifts is his melodious baritone, which, with slight alterations in lilt and tone, could seem either deadly serious or playful, sometimes from one moment to the next. With Worf's personality at last defined and his position as one of the show's major characters now firmly established, the character was used in new ways. The complexities of Worf's family situation and his troubles raising Alexander became a recurring theme in episodes both dramatic ("New Ground," "Homeward," "Firstborn") and comedic ("Cost of Living"). He continued as the focal point of Klingon-centered story lines, such as "Birthright, Parts I and II," in which Worf rekindles the fighting spirit of Klingon youngsters raised in a Romulan prison camp, and "Rightful Heir," in which Worf encounters what appears to be the resurrected Kahless, founder of the Klingon Empire. But, what's even more impressive, Worf (and Dorn) was also selected to star in stories that could just as easily have featured Riker or Geordi or Picard or any other member of the *Enterprise* crew. These included the seriocomic holodeck Western "A Fistful of Datas" (to which the actor contributed a rip-snorting, tongue-in-cheek performance) and "Parallels," a Season Seven outing in which Worf moves through a series of alternate realities. Dorn contributes a scintillating, multifaceted portrayal to "Parallels," which many fans name as their favorite Worf episode. Once again, the actor displays sweeping range and great subtlety, as Worf struggles to understand what's happening and then to decide what to do about it. Dorn's reaction—wary yet intrigued—to one of the parallel universes, in which he is married to Deanna Troi, is highly amusing. In another reality, his unfamiliarity with the alternate *Enterprise*'s suddenly strange controls nearly leads to the destruction of the ship. Dorn seems not only terrified but queasy and ashamed.

Curiously, none of the *Next Generation* movies featured Worf prominently. In the films, Worf was usually reduced to comedy relief. However, in 1995, Dorn joined the cast of *Deep Space Nine*, and continued to grow as a performer and to refine Worf as a character throughout that show's final four seasons. The "Klingon marine" tossed into the *Next Gen* crew as an afterthought eventually became one of the most prominent and popular characters in the history of *Star Trek*, and the center of an elaborate fan cult based on the franchise's Klingon mythology. In all, Dorn appeared in a total of 276 episodes of various *Trek* series and in five movies, the most on-camera appearances of any actor in the history of the franchise. (Only Majel Barrett-Roddenberry, as the voice of the *Enterprise* computer, contributed to more *Star Trek* projects in any acting capacity.) Dorn also voiced Worf for six *Trek* video games and has spoofed the character on shows such as *Webster*, *Family Guy*, and an HBO *Comedy Relief* special cohosted by Whoopi Goldberg. Dorn, originally hired to serve as little more than a bit player, grew into one of *Star Trek*'s main attractions.

35

The High Ground

Patrick Stewart and Brent Spiner were brilliant, and Michael Dorn's work was revelatory, but that wasn't enough to sustain *Star Trek: The Next Generation*. After all, *Next Gen* was an ensemble production. While many teleplays were written to highlight Captain Picard or Lieutenant Commander Data or, increasingly in later seasons, Lieutenant Worf, all the other characters received turns in the spotlight, too—which meant that all the cast members had to prove themselves worthy. Fortunately, they did. Every regular cast member, even those with short tenures on the show, contributed something unique and important to the blend of styles and personalities that comprised the *Enterprise* crew. Together, the cast developed a working chemistry that became one of the program's most likeable features. Fans tuned in because they wanted to spend time with this crew.

Jonathan Frakes

No *Next Generation* performer was more valuable yet less appreciated than Jonathan Frakes. During the show's first two seasons, Frakes's dynamic Commander William T. Riker seemed to be almost a cocaptain with Stewart's Picard. It was Riker, not Picard, who assumed Captain Kirk's mantle as Swashbuckler-in-Chief and Playboy of the Galaxy, leading dangerous away missions and/or scoring with extraterrestrial babes on an almost weekly basis. Although this relationship was realigned in later seasons, with Picard becoming a more active participant in his crew's adventures, Riker remained a central figure in most teleplays. The show simply could not have worked without a charismatic actor in the role. Frakes brought charm, humor, and style to the part, but these perpetually undervalued qualities led critics and even many fans to unfairly dismiss the actor as a lightweight talent. Frakes's effervescent approach to the character served as a needed counterbalance to Stewart's more somber take on Captain Picard, preventing the series from becoming too heavy-handed or downbeat. Yet, when assigned more substantial dramatic material, Frakes usually responded with outstanding work. A survey of some of the actor's best episodes demonstrates his underrated abilities.

"A Matter of Honor," in which Riker serves as first officer aboard a Klingon Bird of Prey as part of an officer exchange program, stands out as a prime example of Frakes's dashing, high-spirited approach to his role, especially during the show's early seasons. Frakes shines throughout, as Riker eats repulsive-looking Klingon food, brawls with his Klingon crewmates, flirts with Klingon women, and (more importantly) devises a clever, face-saving solution that averts a disastrous conflict with the *Enterprise* without sacrificing the honor of the Bird of Prey and its captain.

Although it's remembered primarily as the story of Captain Picard's transformation into Locutus of Borg, the groundbreaking two-part epic **"The Best of Both Worlds"** was actually more concerned with Riker than Picard. Riker is once again offered a chance to command his own ship but is unsure he wants to the leave the *Enterprise*, and resents the presence of the ambitious young Lieutenant Commander Shelby, who is eager to replace him as first officer. Then, after Picard is captured and assimilated, Riker finds himself thrust into command under the most dire conditions imaginable. Frakes is brilliant throughout "The Best of Both Worlds," tempering Riker's usual joie de vie with evident (but not overplayed) inner turmoil. "The Best of Both Worlds" is not only one of the great *Next Generation* episodes, but also one of the best Will Riker episodes.

Jonathan Frakes appeared clean-shaven during the first season of *The Next Generation*, and bearded throughout the remaining six seasons. Producers liked the beard the actor had grown over the summer hiatus and asked him to keep it. It remained until *Star Trek: Insurrection*, ten years later.

Yet the actor's finest work came in later adventures. Frakes's personal favorite Riker episode was Season Six's dark, surreal **"Frame of Mind,"** in which Riker appears to be undergoing intensive therapy in an alien insane asylum after murdering a civilian. It's certainly his most intense performance, revealing an edge few viewers realized he had in him. He also delivers a scintillating performance (or, actually, two of them) in **"Second Chances."** In this installment, Riker is shocked to learn that a freak transporter accident eight years earlier created a duplicate of himself, who has remained stranded alone on a deserted outpost ever since. After beaming aboard the *Enterprise*, the castaway Lieutenant Riker tries to renew his romance with Deanna Troi, who he still loves passionately. Meanwhile, Commander Riker tries to come to grips with his double, who looks at him with suspicion and resentment. Frakes's work as the two Rikers is, in many respects, even more impressive than Brent Spiner's dual appearances as Data and Lore, since the differences between his two characters are much more subtle and psychologically complex. Frakes is also terrific in **"The Pegasus,"** in which Riker's former captain beams aboard, uncovering a web of deceit surrounding secret experiments aboard their former ship, the USS *Pegasus*. Throughout the episode, as the *Enterprise* attempts to salvage the *Pegasus*, Riker struggles with conflicted loyalties and overwhelming guilt. The scenario also allows Frakes to do his hilarious Patrick Stewart imitation, already famous on the set, for the benefit of viewers at home.

LeVar Burton

Nobody questioned LeVar Burton's talent, but the actor's *Star Trek* teleplays seldom equaled his abilities. Early on, screenwriters established Geordi La Forge as resourceful and amiable but socially awkward. Thereafter the writing staff struggled to bring additional dimensions to the character, even after promoting him to chief engineer in Season Two. Although Geordi became a more integral part of many plots, he continued to serve primarily as a fountain of Treknobabble or a sidekick for Data. To his credit, Burton never let the rising tide of double-talk engulf Geordi, and prevented the dearth of romantic and familial attachments from dehumanizing the character. His warm, sensitive portrayal turned these potential pitfalls to his advantage and helped make Geordi one of the most endearing personalities on the show. Nothing seemed to keep him down—not seemingly impossible technical challenges, nor his sad-sack romantic life. Through it all, Geordi seemed to possess inexhaustible wells of ingenuity and kindness.

The episodes that most readily demonstrate these virtues are **"Galaxy's Child"** and **"Relics."** "Galaxy's Child," from Season Four, is a sequel of sorts from the third-season installment "Booby Trap." In "Booby Trap," Geordi had freed the *Enterprise* from an energy-draining device left over from a long-forgotten war with the help of a holodeck-generated simulation of eminent warp scientist Dr. Leah Brahms. Along the way, the love-starved Geordi became infatuated

Actor LeVar Burton was one of *The Next Generation*'s most consistent performers, but seldom received material that challenged his abilities.

with the holographic Brahms. In "Galaxy's Child," the real Dr. Brahms beams aboard—and proves to be very little like the hologram with whom Geordi is smitten. Over the course of the adventure, in which Geordi and Brahms again team to save the ship, Geordi's excitement over Brahms's impending visit turns to disappointment, embarrassment, and anger, but he eventually establishes a working rapport, and finally a friendship, with Dr. Brahms. Burton plays it all brilliantly, taking full advantage of the most complete showcase for his gifts he would enjoy on *The Next Generation*. Geordi follows a similar arc in "Relics," in which the legendary Montgomery Scott is recovered from the pattern buffer of the transporter aboard a crashed starship. At first, Geordi is overjoyed to find himself in the company of his counterpart from the twenty-third-century *Enterprise*, but his happiness fades into irritation as the eager-to-help but out-of-date Scotty becomes a nuisance in engineering. Ultimately, however, he and Scotty develop an understanding; their combined efforts prevent the destruction of the *Enterprise*. This episode was a particularly exciting one for Burton, who was a longtime *Star Trek* fan even before joining *Next Gen*. His enthusiasm translates into a spirited, richly nuanced performance too often overlooked, since it resides in the shadow of James Doohan's superb farewell appearance as Scotty.

Burton made the most of the few teleplays that stretched Geordi or placed him in unexpected situations. In **"The Mind's Eye,"** for instance, Geordi is kidnapped and brainwashed by Romulan agents, who transform him into an unknowing assassin. This paranoid thriller, an homage to director John Frankenheimer's 1962 classic *The Manchurian Candidate*, plays so well because it subverts Burton's carefully constructed Geordi persona. There was no more trustworthy, likeable, or easygoing character on the show, which only makes Geordi's appearance as a remorseless, homicidal automaton all the more chilling. In **"Identity Crisis,"** in which his character is transformed into an alien life-form, Burton again called upon seldom-tapped dimensions, as Geordi slowly breaks down, emotionally, mentally, and at last physically. For the most part, however, Burton's best work came in roles that aligned more closely with the established contours of the character. He also contributed outstanding performances to **"The Next Phase,"** in which Geordi remains the voice of optimism even after he and Ensign Ro are trapped in a quasi-corporeal state (and presumed dead) following a transporter accident; and to **"I Borg,"** in which the open-hearted engineer cannot prevent himself from forging a friendship with a captured Borg drone, who Geordi nicknames "Hugh." That the actor accomplished all this with his wonderfully expressive eyes hidden behind Geordi's VISOR (which was actually a repurposed, spray-painted hair clip) makes his work even more remarkable.

Marina Sirtis

For three and a half seasons, the empathic, half-Betazoid counselor Deanna Troi was *The Next Generation*'s most muddled character. Producers and writers seemed to have no idea what to do with her. The trouble began in preproduction when, as Sirtis has often recounted, Gene Roddenberry asked the actress if she could do an accent. Sure, she replied, where is the accent from? "Betazed," Roddenberry answered. So the actress invented a sort of vaguely Middle Eastern accent and an odd, elliptical speech pattern that she thought sounded exotic but not culturally specific. Sirtis was exasperated and resentful when Roddenberry's wife, Majel Barrett-Roddenberry (cast as Deanna's mother, Lwaxana), never even attempted the Betazed accent. For no good reason, she felt, she had been robbed of her own lovely, British-accented voice. Sirtis's difficulties continued for the next three seasons, as writers struggled to place Deanna in intriguing situations or develop her personality. She seemed to exist only to serve as a walking lie detector and to hook up with smarmy Lotharios from outer space.

Sirtis got a rare opportunity to display her abilities with the Season Two opener **"The Child,"** in which Deanna is impregnated by an alien life force and gives birth to a son who grows into adolescence but then dies, all in the span of a few days' time. The actress had more emotional range to cover in this single episode than in all of Season One combined, but she handled it beautifully. She is particularly effective in the story's touching final moments, mourning the loss of her alien child. Tellingly, however, "The Child" was not a creation of the regular *Next Gen* writing staff but a leftover from the scrapped *Star Trek: Phase II* series of the 1970s, resurrected and revised due to a writer's strike.

The actress's fortunes didn't significantly improve until the arrival of writer-producer Jeri Taylor, who eventually replaced Michael Piller as executive producer. On Taylor's watch, the hazily written Deanna finally came into focus, and Sirtis finally began receiving teleplays that advanced her character in meaningful and engrossing ways. Nearly all of Sirtis's best performances came in the show's final four seasons. She delivered one of her most heartfelt and least affected portrayals in **"The Loss"** (produced midway through Season Four), in which Deanna temporarily loses her empathic abilities. In one unforgettable scene, Deanna, shaken by her inability to read emotions, lashes out at Gates McFadden's Dr. Crusher. Season Five brought three excellent episodes for Sirtis. In **"Disaster,"** Deanna is thrust into command of the *Enterprise* when the ship is disabled in a freak accident. Sirtis's carefully shaded performance suggests that Deanna is as surprised as everyone else to discover that she has the fortitude to make life-or-death decisions under intense pressure. In **"Violations,"** Deanna endures a form of telepathic rape but later brings her attacker to justice. And in **"Power Play,"** Deanna is one of three crew members possessed by ruthless alien life-forms who attempt to seize control of the ship. Sirtis supplies an amusingly sadistic performance. The following season, Sirtis delivered another pair of terrific performances. In **"Face of the Enemy,"** Deanna is kidnapped and forced to impersonate a Romulan officer, matching wits with a cagey female Romulan commander. Sirtis rose to the challenge of another intense teleplay. And she came through with a delightful against-type performance in **"Man of the People,"** in which Deanna, again under the control of an alien agency, crushes the spirit of a distressed counseling patient and seduces a young crewman. Across the board, Sirtis's work was generally of a much higher caliber during the show's final few seasons than during its first three.

Gates McFadden

Producers and screenwriters dealt Gates McFadden a lousy hand, but she played her cards as well as possible. Like Marina Sirtis's Counselor Troi, McFadden's Dr. Beverly Crusher remained underdeveloped during the first few seasons of *The Next Generation*. Worse yet, McFadden was unceremoniously booted off the show

Early on, Paramount hoped to capitalize on the teen stardom of actor Wil Wheaton to sell products like this lunch box, featuring Wesley Crusher, Captain Picard, and Data.

Photo by Preston Hewis, East Bank Images

after its first season. Ironically, the qualities that fans admired in McFadden's Dr. Crusher—her warmth and compassion, both as a healer and as the mother of youthful ensign Wesley Crusher—seemed to bore Gene Roddenberry, who brought Diana Muldaur on board as the gruff Dr. Pulaski for the duration of Season Two. When the Pulaski experiment failed, Roddenberry and Rick Berman rehired McFadden. Even then, however, the actress was seldom given anything important to do. McFadden's lot improved dramatically over the course of *Next Gen*'s final four seasons, and especially after Taylor took over as executive producer.

McFadden received her first real showcase in the offbeat fourth-season installment **"Remember Me,"** in which *Enterprise* crew members begin to inexplicably wink out of existence. Not only do they vanish, but Dr. Crusher alone remembers they ever existed. Eventually, only Beverly is left aboard. McFadden is center stage throughout, as Dr. Crusher solves a mind-bending sci-fi mystery.

In **"The Host,"** also from Season Four, Beverly falls in love with Ambassador Odan, who turns out to be a Trill. When Odan is severely injured in an assassination attempt, Crusher removes the Trill (a wormlike symbiotic life-form that lives for hundreds of years, passing from one host body to the next) and temporarily implants it in Commander Riker. After initial misgivings, Crusher resumes her romance with Odan (in Riker's body)—until Odan's new, permanent host arrives and turns out to be female. During all the story's twists and emotional upheavals, McFadden's work remains completely convincing and deeply touching. McFadden is also remarkably good in the Season Six adventure **"Suspicions,"** in which Dr. Crusher risks her career to prove that a Ferengi scientist whose death appears to be a suicide was actually murdered.

While *The Next Generation*'s final season was disappointing in many respects, it was a banner year for McFadden, whose work was exemplary throughout. In the season opener, **"Descent, Part II,"** Dr. Crusher temporarily took command of the *Enterprise*, and McFadden's level-headed, steely-eyed performance made her seem like a surprisingly viable substitute captain. In **"Attached,"** Beverly and Captain Picard finally addressed their long-simmering sexual tension, affording McFadden some delicious, and sometimes amusing, romantic interludes. **"Sub Rosa"** went even further, with Beverly entering a heated sexual affair with a ghostly extraterrestrial. This is perhaps McFadden's most courageous *Trek* performance: During one memorable scene, she writhes in ecstasy with an invisible lover. And although the entire cast performed commendably in the series finale **"All Good Things . . . ,"** McFadden's work as Dr. Beverly Picard, the now-*ex*-wife of Jean-Luc, is particularly rich and resonant. It's no wonder that Sirtis and McFadden were among those cast members who wished the series could continue for an eighth season.

Wil Wheaton

In a question-and-answer session at the Calgary Comic Con in 2012, LeVar Burton, sharing the stage with Wil Wheaton, recalled meeting his young costar for the first time in 1987. "I thought, 'Wow, that's the kid from *Stand by Me*!' And I was very impressed," Burton said, adding in jest, "which was short-lived." What Burton jokingly described, however, mirrored the actual experience of many viewers. At the time of *The Next Generation*'s premiere, Burton and Wheaton were its most recognizable faces, and Wheaton was considered the group's hottest talent. After the initial excitement about the young star joining the series faded, audience interest in Wheaton's Wesley Crusher soon cooled. Over the years, Wheaton unfairly shouldered most of the blame for Wesley's tepid reception. The real culprits were the show's writers, who seemed incapable of crafting believable dialogue or realistic situations for the teenaged character. Wesley never seemed sullen or bored or horny or any of the other conditions endemic to teenage boys, and seldom socialized with kids his age. Instead, writers continually contrived far-fetched scenarios in which the fifteen-year-old wunderkind saved the *Enterprise* from destruction. Some fans wrote off Wesley as a "Mary Sue" for Gene Roddenberry. (The term is a reference to a fan fiction cliché in which a character serves as a thinly veiled stand-in for the author herself.) Others vehemently objected to the idea of placing children aboard a starship in the first place. Together, these factors created headwinds that made it almost impossible for Wheaton to develop a endearing character.

Still, on those rare occasions when screenwriters gave him something worthwhile to play (as in **"Coming of Age"** and **"The Dauphin"**), the actor always seized the opportunity and delivered a fine performance. He also shined whenever he had the opportunity to work one-on-one with Patrick Stewart. Wesley's heart-to-heart with Captain Picard aboard a shuttlecraft in **"Samaritan Snare"** is a brilliant moment in an otherwise dreary episode.

Wheaton, frustrated by poor scripts and a shooting schedule that prevented him from pursuing more rewarding work, and tired of being a target for fans' ire, left the series after four seasons but returned to guest star in four later episodes. Ironically, he received far better teleplays as a guest star than he ever did as a regular cast member. In **"The Game,"** Wesley (on leave from Starfleet Academy) returns to the *Enterprise* and discovers the crew is becoming obsessed with an addictive video game. With the help of Lieutenant Robin Lefler (Ashley Judd), with whom he establishes a romantic relationship, Wesley learns that the game is part of an elaborate alien invasion plot. The thrill-packed scenario puts Wheaton through his paces, as tensions (both dramatic and sexual) steadily build. The actor's work remains touching and unaffected, and Wheaton and Judd have appealing chemistry. But Wheaton outdid even this fine performance with **"The First Duty,"** in which Wesley becomes embroiled in a scandal surrounding a training accident that resulted in the death of a fellow cadet. Wesley is torn between his sense of loyalty to his fellow cadets and his sense of duty to Starfleet (and his own moral compass). Wheaton is spectacular here, seeming almost ready to erupt with inner turmoil. This was the caliber of work that viewers expected from "the kid from *Stand by Me*," six years after that career landmark.

Denise Crosby

Denise Crosby left the series midway through its first season. Like Wheaton, Crosby was dissatisfied with the development of her character. Ironically, however, her Lieutenant Tasha Yar was perhaps the best-sketched of the show's three regular female roles and was certainly the strongest personality. During her brief tenure on the show, Crosby never enjoyed a true showcase episode, although she had a few unforgettable moments, including her seduction of Data in **"The Naked Now"** ("You jewel!") and, ironically, Tasha's holographic farewell to her shipmates at the funeral in **"Skin of Evil."** Crosby also returned to the series for a handful of episodes, including two appearances as Yar and two as Sela, Yar's half-Romulan daughter. Her best *Star Trek* performance, without question, remains **"Yesterday's Enterprise,"** which takes place along an altered timeline in which Tasha never died. This acclaimed adventure was conceived to give Lieutenant Yar the hero's farewell fans wanted, instead of the ignominious demise she met in "Skin of Evil." The scenario also introduces a love interest for Yar in the time-shifted Lieutenant Castillo (Christopher McDonald). Everything in this episode works beautifully, including Crosby's pitch-perfect performance and her winning chemistry with McDonald. Crosby also returned as Yar in the series finale, "All Good Things . . . ," in which Captain Picard moves forward and backward in time.

Crosby's impulsive departure from the series altered the course of *The Next Generation* in profound ways. It created a void in terms of the cast dynamic and eliminated the series' lone assertive female character. As a result, Michael Dorn's Worf emerged as a major character, and Roddenberry was able to hire Whoopi Goldberg as Guinan. While those two characters made up for Tasha's absence in terms of story possibilities, the series never fully overcame the loss of its one assertive female character. Dr. Pulaski (Diana Muldaur) was tough enough, but fans hated her and she only lasted a season. Yar's true successor should have been Ensign Ro (Michelle Forbes), but she wasn't introduced until Season Five and appeared in only eight installments. Had Crosby stuck with the series, *Next Gen* would have retained the powerful and well-liked Lieutenant Yar, who might have developed along intriguing lines in future seasons. But it's unlikely that Worf would have become as prominent a figure, and Guinan would never have been created. It would be interesting to travel, like Captain Picard, to an alternate timeline where Crosby remained aboard, just to see what that *Next Generation* would have looked like.

36

Thine Own Self

The Post-*Trek* Careers of the *Next Generation* Cast

When the classic *Star Trek* series left the air in 1969, many cast members fell on hard times. Thankfully, the cast of *The Next Generation* never faced such adversity. They were much better compensated their original *Trek* counterparts in the first place, and, unlike their predecessors, all received residuals from syndicated reruns and home video sales. More importantly, when the series ended in 1994, the cast seamlessly transitioned into feature films with a series of *Next Gen* movies that continued until 2002. The ensemble also benefitted from a circuit of conventions and other fan events that offered lucrative speaking engagements. But, of course, what the former *Next Generation* cast members wanted most of all was to strike out in new creative endeavors and prove they could succeed in roles beyond *Star Trek*. Performers began pursuing such opportunities even while the series remained in production. Nearly every member of the *Enterprise-D* crew has established a new, post-*Trek* creative identity—some in front of the camera, others behind it.

Patrick Stewart

Patrick Stewart was among the cast members most eager to pursue projects outside *Star Trek*. Throughout the run of the series he took other work—both in film and television and onstage—that presented new challenges. The most successful of these endeavors was his one-man version of *A Christmas Carol*, which played on Broadway to rave reviews in 1991. Stewart adapted and directed the show and played all the characters (from Ebenezer Scrooge to Tiny Tim) himself, without changes of costume or makeup, on a virtually bare stage. Clive Barnes of the *New York Post* called the play "stunningly effective and deviously imaginative." *New York Times* critic Mel Gussaw said that Stewart's performance "reminds us not only of what an inventive actor he is, but also of Dickens' great theatricality." Stewart's *A Christmas Carol* won a Drama Desk Award for best solo performance 1991–92. In 1993, Stewart won a Grammy for his audio version of the show. Stewart later revived the show at his beloved Old Vic Theater in England and in London's West End. In 1992, he mounted a touring version of Tom Stoppard and Andre Previn's play *Every Good Boy Deserves Favour* that

Patrick Stewart tried to shatter his Captain Picard image by appearing as a homosexual interior decorator in the gay-themed romantic dramedy *Jeffrey* (1995).

costarred his *Trek* cast mates Brent Spiner, Jonathan Frakes, Gates McFadden, and Colm Meaney. In 1993, Stewart made hilarious cameo appearances in Steve Martin's movie *L.A. Story* as an imperious maître'd, and in Mel Brooks's *Robin Hood: Men in Tights* as King Richard.

Stewart's most famous post-*Trek* character was Professor Charles Xavier, whom he played in three blockbuster films based on Marvel Comics superheroes—*X-Men* (2000), *X2* (2003), and *X-Men: The Last Stand* (2006). The actor is a major asset to these pictures, bringing gravitas and credibility as the stalwart leader of a band of superpowered mutants. But Professor Xavier didn't represent a major stretch from his Captain Picard persona. Many of Stewart's other post-*Trek* roles have been more daring. In Year One A.T. (After *Trek*), Stewart played a homosexual interior decorator whose partner dies of AIDS in the gay romantic dramedy *Jeffrey* (1995). He also worked in many notable television productions. He earned an Emmy nomination for his performance as Captain Ahab in a miniseries adaptation of *Moby Dick* (1998); appeared as Scrooge in a 1999 television version of *A Christmas Carol* (this was *not* an adaptation of his one-man show); garnered another Emmy nomination for his work as King Henry II in a television version of *The Lion in Winter* that costarred Glenn Close; and portrayed Captain Nemo in a 2005 telefilm based on Jules Verne's *Mysterious Island*. He also performed in BBC productions of *Hamlet* (2009), *Macbeth* (2010), and *Richard II* (2012). Thanks to his sonorous baritone, Stewart has become an in-demand voice actor, working in many animated films and TV shows, and numerous commercials, in recent years.

Stewart's theatrical career has also continued to thrive. In 1996, he earned a second Drama Desk Award for his performance as Prospero in a Broadway production of Shakespeare's *The Tempest*. In 1999, he won a Drama Desk nomination for his work in the Broadway version of Arthur Miller's play *The Ride down Mt. Morgan*, about a bigamist insurance salesman. The actor may have cost himself a Tony nomination by blasting producers after taking his bows at the play's final curtain, accusing them of not fully supporting their own show. Despite excellent reviews, the play generated only lukewarm ticket sales and closed after 121 performances. Producers were not amused by Stewart's behavior and filed a protest with Actors Equity, which forced the actor to make a public apology. Since the turn of the millennium, Stewart has appeared in fourteen stage productions in the U.S. and the U.K., including a British production of *Macbeth* (2007), which eventually moved to Broadway; a Royal Shakespeare Company production of *Hamlet* (2008) that also featured former *Doctor Who* star David Tennant; and a 2009 Scottish production of Samuel Beckett's *Waiting for Godot* in which Stewart appeared alongside his *X-Men* costar Ian McKellan. In many interviews, the actor has stated that he still considers his theatrical work the most important aspect of his career. The complete list of awards, honors, and ceremonial degrees heaped on the actor would run on for pages, but the most significant of these arrived on June 2, 2010. On that date, in appreciation for his contributions to British drama, Stewart was knighted by Queen Elizabeth II.

Stewart's personal life was rockier going. He entered a torrid and very public affair with *Next Gen* guest star Jennifer Hetrick ("Vash" from "Captain's Holiday" and "Qpid"), which was widely reported in the Hollywood tabloids and led to the breakup of Stewart's twenty-five-year marriage to Sheila Falconer. Stewart and Falconer, who remained in England with the couple's two children while Stewart worked in America, divorced in 1990. Hetrick and Stewart's relationship ended after about a year. In 2000, Stewart married Wendy Neuss, the postproduction supervisor for *The Next Generation*. Stewart and Neuss divorced three years later. As this book was going to press, it was announced that Patrick Stewart would marry jazz vocalist Sunny Ozell.

Brent Spiner

Unlike Stewart, Brent Spiner concentrated on his role as Data—not to mention his appearances as Lore and Dr. Noonian Soong—during his tenure on *The Next Generation*. His non-*Trek* roles during this period were limited to cameos in the comedy *Miss Firecracker*, director Wes Craven's *Shocker* (both 1989), and the made-for-TV movie *Crazy from the Heart* (1991). He declined a screen credit for his work in the latter two projects. He also recorded an album of Frank Sinatra standards titled *Ol' Yellow Eyes Is Back* (1991). Following the series' cancellation, however, Spiner began pursuing other roles in earnest. Most of his nearly fifty subsequent film and television roles have showcased the actor's comedic and musical gifts. He appeared as the kooky Dr. Okun in the SF megahit *Independence Day* (1996) and was side-splittingly funny as tyrannical British cruise director Gil Godwyn, who berates and belittles Jack Lemmon and Walter Matthau in the underrated comedy *Out to Sea* (1997). He also made memorable guest appearances on several sitcoms, including *Frasier* (2003), *Friends* (2004), and *The Big Bang Theory* (2011). In 1997, he returned to Broadway to play John Adams in a Tony Award–nominated revival of the play *1776*. The actor reminded viewers of his dramatic range with his heartfelt performance in the Emmy-winning HBO movie *Introducing Dorothy Dandridge* (1999), in which he played the manager of African American singer-actress Dandridge (Halle Berry), fighting to promote

Brent Spiner (left) appeared memorably as the kooky Dr. Okun in the sci-fi blockbuster *Independence Day* (1996). Here Spiner is joined by star Bill Pullman (center) and Bill Rebhorn (right).

and protect his client in the segregated America of the 1940s. He was also a regular cast member on the short-lived science fiction series *Threshhold* (2005–2006).

Spiner continued his association with *Star Trek*, not only appearing in all four *Next Generation* movies, but doing voice work for three *Trek* video games and guest starring in a three-episode arc on *Enterprise* in 2005, playing the Dr. Arik Soong, the great-grandfather of Dr. Noonian Soong. The actor has also done a great deal of other voice work and was one of many *Star Trek* actors (including Jonathan Frakes, Marina Sirtis, LeVar Burton, Michael Dorn, Colm Meaney, and Nichelle Nichols) to perform on the Disney animated series *Gargoyles*. Currently, Spiner has a recurring role on the SyFy Channel comedy SF series *Warehouse 13*. The actor can also be seen in the web series *Fresh Hell*, in which he satirizes aspects of his own life. Spiner appears as himself—or perhaps as a Mirror Universe version of himself. After his career collapses due to an offensive but never revealed "incident," the actor struggles to find work, aided by his neighbor, a wannabe porn star (Kat Steel), her sleazy agent-boyfriend (Brian Palermo), and a "borderline delusional" psychic (Karen Austin). The often hysterically funny series, launched in 2011, has so far run two seasons and fifteen episodes. LeVar Burton guest starred in an especially amusing Season Two episode titled simply "LeVar." Episodes can be streamed, free of charge, at http://freshhellseries.com.

Jonathan Frakes

Jonathan Frakes took no outside work at all during the seven-season run of *The Next Generation* and has accepted relatively few acting jobs in the years since. His first post-*Trek* appearance came in the familiar role of Stanley Hazard in *Heaven & Hell: North and South, Book III*, a 1994 miniseries in which he reprised his role from the two popular *North and South* miniseries of the 1980s. Beyond that, Frakes has played minor roles in a smattering of series, including guest appearances on *3rd Rock from the Sun* (2000), *Criminal Minds*, and *NCIS Los Angeles* (both 2010). He also appeared, as Commander Riker or as Thomas Riker (his transporter-created duplicate), in episodes of *Deep Space Nine*, *Voyager*, and *Enterprise*. Frakes also served as the host of several fact-based series including *Paranormal Borderline* (1996), *Beyond Belief: Fact or Fiction* (1997–2002), and *That's Impossible* (2009–present).

Frakes has seldom pursued acting jobs because he discovered that his true calling was *behind* the camera. After directing eight episodes of *The Next Generation* (most of them excellent) and the first two *Next Gen* feature films, Frakes went on to helm episodes of twenty-seven other television series, including *DS9*, *Voyager*, *The Twilight Zone* (2002), and *V* (2010). He has become an important contributor to the TNT series *Leverage*, directing a dozen episodes from 2009 to 2012. Frakes executive produced and directed episodes of the teen-themed sci-fi series *Roswell* (1999–2002). He also helmed the feature films

Clockstoppers (2002) and *Thunderbirds* (2004), and the made-for-TV *Librarian* films (*The Librarian: Return to King Solomon's Mines* in 2006, and *The Librarian: Curse of the Judas Chalice* in 2008). Frakes has also taught directing classes at the Waterfall Arts Center and the Saltwater Film Society in Maine. The trombone-playing skills the actor sometimes demonstrated on *The Next Generation* are real. He performed with the jam band Phish, appearing on the track "Riker's Mailbox" from the group's 1994 album *Hoist.* Frakes and his wife Genie Francis also co-own a furniture store called The Cherished Home, located in Belfast, Maine. Frakes and Francis have two children.

Marina Sirtis

Marina Sirtis starred in the BBC *Studio One* telefilm *One Last Chance* (1990), which was shot during the summer hiatus between the third and fourth seasons of *The Next Generation.* The following summer she costarred in the horror-comedy *Waxwork II: Lost in Time* (1992). Since *Next Gen* left the air, Sirtis reappeared as Deanna Troi in episodes of *Voyager* and *Enterprise*, in addition to her work on the *Next Gen* feature films. The actress parlayed her *Trek* fame into guest roles on numerous sci-fi series, including *The Outer Limits, Stargate SG-1* (both 1999), and *Earth: Final Conflict* (2000), and in movies such as *Spectres* (2004) and *InAlienable* (2008), which was written by and costarred Walter Koenig. She has also played supporting roles in mainstream productions, including TV series such as *Diagnosis Murder* (1998), *The Closer* (2005), and *Grey's Anatomy* (2011), and the Oscar-winning movie *Crash* (2004). As in her pre-*Trek* career, Sirtis has played characters of various ethnicities (but no Betazoids). Like many other *Trek* performers, she has also done voice work, most recently supplying the voice of a supervillain known as the Queen Bee on the cartoon series *Young Justice* (2012).

LeVar Burton

Throughout the run of *The Next Generation*, Burton continued to host his PBS show *Reading Rainbow* and provided the voice of Kwame for the environmentally themed cartoon show *Captain Planet and the Planeteers* (1990–96). These three series (understandably) consumed nearly all of his time. Since *Next Gen* left the air, Burton, like Frakes, has built a new career as a director, working on movies and TV series including ten episodes of *Deep Space Nine*, eight of *Voyager*, nine of *Enterprise*, three of *Charmed* (2005–2006), and telefilms including *The Tiger Woods Story* (1998) and *Smart House* (1999). He also serves on the board of directors for the Directors Guild of America. His on-camera work has declined as his behind-the-camera assignments increased. *Reading Rainbow* continued on television until 2006 and was recently revived as an iPad app. He portrayed Dr. Martin Luther King Jr. in the biopic *Ali* (2001), directed by Michael Mann and starring Will Smith. He also guest starred on several TV series, including *Becker* (2000), *How I Met Your Mother* (2006), and *The Big Bang Theory* (2010), and currently has a recurring role on the TNT crime drama *Perception* (2012–present). Burton recently completed a film titled *Dead Walking* that has yet to be released. He's also active as a voice actor and can be heard as Doc Greene on *Transformers: Rescue Bots* (2011–present). The actor-director married makeup artist Stephanie Cozart in 1992. They have a daughter named Michaela. Burton also serves as an advocate for numerous charitable and philanthropic causes.

Michael Dorn

With the end of *The Next Generation*, most cast members were eager to move on and establish new creative identities, but not Michael Dorn. Instead, after a short hiatus away from *Trek*, he returned to the fold, joining the cast of *Deep Space Nine* for its final four seasons and resuming his role as Lieutenant Worf. Dorn made this surprising move not only to secure a steady paycheck, but because he believed that, even after seven seasons of steady development, Worf was a character with still-unrealized potential. In his four seasons on *DS9*, Dorn continued to deliver increasingly thoughtful and powerful performances, as Worf experienced triumph and tragedy both in political and military struggles (including a key role in the epic Dominion War), and his personal life (falling in love with and marrying Jadzia Dax, then coping with her death). The series offered the actor a great deal more opportunity for artistic growth than the four *Next Generation* feature films, in which Worf was often reduced to comedy relief. In the end, Dorn appeared in a total of 276 episodes of various *Trek* series and in five feature films (including his performance as Worf's grandfather in *Star Trek VI*), the most of any actor in the history of the franchise—unless you include Majel Barrett-Roddenberry's work as the voice of the *Enterprise* computer. Dorn and Worf represented a once-in-a-lifetime match of actor and character. Give Dorn credit for realizing this, and remember, by way of comparison, that nobody faulted James Arness for playing Marshall Matt Dillon for twenty seasons. Dorn also directed three *DS9* episodes and an installment of *Enterprise*.

Dorn, whose dulcet baritone served so well on *Star Trek*, has also built a lucrative career as a voice actor, contributing to scores of animated programs and video games. Some of his more notable roles include I. M. Weasel on the Cartoon Network's *Cow and Chicken* (1997–99) and the spin-off *I Am Weasel* (1997–99), and Kalibak, the son of supervillain Darkseid, on *Superman* (1996–2000) and *Justice League* (2003–2005). Dorn continues to make occasional on-screen appearances as well and plays the recurring character Dr. Carter Burke on the detective series *Castle* (2009–present). He also played the president of the United States in two episodes of *Heroes* (2008–2009). Dorn is an avid amateur pilot and has flown with both the Blue Angels and Thunderbirds. He has devoted more of his time to flying since his tenure on *Star Trek* ended. He was contractually obligated not to fly during his tenure on *The Next Generation* and *Deep Space Nine*.

Gates McFadden

Gates McFadden left *Star Trek* sooner than anyone anticipated. In an attempt to bring a new, more McCoy-like chief medical officer on board, Gene Roddenberry released McFadden and replaced her with Diana Muldaur as Dr. Pulaski. But the new character didn't work, and McFadden was hired back for Season Three. During her unexpected absence from *Star Trek*, McFadden played Caroline Ryan, the wife of CIA agent Jack Ryan (Alec Baldwin), in the smash *The Hunt for Red October* (1990). Unfortunately, most of her scenes were deleted when the film ran long. She also appeared in the Jim Belushi comedy *Taking Care of Business* (1990). Even after rejoining *Next Gen*, the actress continued to pursue other opportunities when her schedule allowed. She guest starred on *L.A. Law* in 1992 and on the HBO sitcom *Dream On* the following year, and also accepted theatrical roles. Aside from her appearances as Dr. Crusher, McFadden has worked primarily on the stage and has taught theater classes at eight different universities, including Harvard, Temple, and USC. Since 2009, she has served as the artistic director of the Ensemble Studio Theater of Los Angeles. She has also made a dozen sporadic film and television appearances, including guest roles on series such as *Mad About You* (1995–96), *The Practice* (2000), and *Franklin and Bash* (2012). She is married to producer John Talbot and has a son, James, who was born in 1991. To conceal McFadden's pregnancy, Dr. Crusher wore a lab coat throughout most of *The Next Generation*'s fourth season.

Denise Crosby

Denise Crosby abandoned her post as Lieutenant Tasha Yar two-thirds of the way through Season One of *The Next Generation* to pursue more gratifying opportunities. The actress has worked steadily in the years since, piling up more than sixty film and television credits, but true stardom evaded her. She costarred in the Stephen King chiller *Pet Sematary* (1989) and in *Dolly Dearest* (1991), a low-budget rip-off of the 1988 horror hit *Child's Play*. She also guest starred on more than two dozen TV series, including *The X-Files* (2001), *Dexter* (2006) and *Mad Men* (2008), although her roles have grown smaller and less frequent in recent years. She has also worked on the stage, and in 2011 appeared in a production of the George Moss play *House of Gold* mounted by the Ensemble Studio Theater of Los Angeles (directed by Gates McFadden). Ironically, Crosby remains best known as Tasha Yar. She returned as Tasha in the classic *Next Gen* episodes "Yesterday's Enterprise" and "All Good Things . . ." and played Yar's half-Romulan daughter, Sela, in three other episodes. She played Yar's grandmother in an episode of the fan-produced Internet series *Star Trek: New Voyages*. Crosby also produced the 1997 documentary *Trekkies* and the 2004 sequel *Trekkies 2*, about *Star Trek* fandom. After divorcing first husband Geoffrey Edwards in 1990, Crosby married actor Ken Sylk. They have one son, August William Sylk.

Wil Wheaton

Leaving *Star Trek* didn't immediately improve the prospects of Wil Wheaton, either, but in recent years he has developed a thriving career as a writer, actor, and geek culture personality. Wheaton decided to give up his unpopular and unfulfilling role as wunderkind ensign Wesley Crusher when *Next Generation* producers denied him a leave of absence to accept a part in director Milos Forman's *Valmont* (1989). Leaving *Trek* freed him to take other offers, but Wheaton, like many former child stars, struggled to find steady and rewarding employment as he outgrew juvenile roles. He costarred in the kid-themed action movie *Toy Soldiers* (1991), starred in the direct-to-video horror film *Mr. Stitch* (1995), and made guest appearances on TV series, including *Tales from the Crypt* and *The Outer Limits* (both 1993), but worked less often and in smaller roles as the 1990s wore on.

His fortunes began to change in 2001 when he launched his blog, Wil Wheaton dot Net. Wheaton poured out his thoughts and feelings, including his anxiety about his sagging career and his conflicted feelings about Wesley Crusher and *Star Trek*. His writing was wildly funny and deeply moving, often simultaneously. Soon Wheaton's blog, which also dealt with gaming, computer programming, and other nerdy topics, became a must-read for many web surfers, not only *Star Trek* fans. Encouraged by the success of Wil Wheaton dot Net, he published two books of fiction and a riveting, hilarious memoir, *Just a Geek* (2004), compiled in part from his soul-searching blog entries. All were well received, and Wheaton began to emerge as a respected humorist—a sort of Robert Benchley of geek culture. In 2008, he published *Memories of the Future, Volume 1*, a collection of acerbic reviews/memoirs about the first thirteen episodes of *The Next Generation*.

As his profile increased, so did offers for acting roles, both on-camera and as a voice artist. He voiced Aqualad on *Teen Titans* (2003–2005), Cosmic Boy on *Legion of Super-Heroes* (2007–2008), and Michael Morningstar on *Ben-10* (2009–2012); played a lead role on the comedic web series *The Guild* (2009–2011); and made guest appearances on various TV series including *Numb3rs* (2007) and *Criminal Minds* (2008). In 2009, Wheaton scored a major breakthrough when he began appearing as an evil parody of himself on the hit sitcom *The Big Bang Theory*. So far, Wheaton has appeared in five *Big Bang* episodes and finally may be more widely recognized as himself than as Wesley Crusher. He also played the recurring character of Dr. Isaac Parish during Seasons Four and Five of the SyFy Channel series *Eureka* (2010–2012). In 2012, he launched the web series *TableTop*, which features Wheaton and guests chatting and playing various tabletop games. He currently writes a column for *LA Weekly* and is developing a science fiction novel. He continues to blog at http://www.wilwheaton.net, and is also extremely active on Facebook and Twitter. Wheaton married Anne Prince in 1999. He later adopted her two sons from a prior relationship.

37

When the Bough Breaks

The Decline and Fall of the *Star Trek* Empire

Star Trek reached the pinnacle of its popularity and cultural currency in the early 1990s, when *The Next Generation* earned its highest average Nielsen ratings and the original cast wrapped up its tour of duty with the blockbuster *Star Trek VI: The Undiscovered Country* (1991). Soon afterward, the franchise fell into decline. This wasn't entirely evident for some time—ratings for the final seasons of *Next Gen* remained strong, the spin-off *Deep Space Nine* opened promisingly, and the next two *Trek* movies turned tidy profits. But each of the three series that followed *The Next Generation* attracted a smaller audience than its predecessor, and profits from the *Star Trek* feature films dropped off dramatically after *First Contact* (1996), an anomalous crossover success that fostered a false sense of security. The synergies between television, film, publishing, and merchandising that had resurrected *Star Trek* in the 1970s and empowered its emergence as a cultural phenomenon in the 1980s worked against the franchise as its fortunes began to erode. *Star Trek* began to buckle under its own weight, and the carefully constructed and fiercely defended continuity of the *Trek* universe (previously one of its greatest strengths) now only hastened its collapse. Since in the minds of fans everything was interconnected, each lackluster television episode and disappointing movie diminished interest in the entire oeuvre.

Star Trek: Deep Space Nine premiered January 3, 1993, with a two-hour pilot (guest starring Patrick Stewart) that earned stratospheric Nielsen ratings, drawing nearly as many viewers as Leonard Nimoy's feverishly hyped appearance on *The Next Generation* fourteen months earlier. But the series was unable to hold that massive audience, and ratings steadily declined. Even adding Michael Dorn as Worf to the *DS9* crew beginning with Season Four could not reverse the downward trend. By the time the show ended its seven-season life span in 1999, its ratings had dropped from its first season average of nearly nine million viewers to an average audience of barely five million.

Star Trek: Voyager, which debuted January 16, 1995, followed a similar trajectory. It opened relatively well, drawing more than nine million viewers, but ratings soon dipped and continued to atrophy. Adding Jeri Taylor's sexy Seven of Nine (and introducing the Borg as recurring villains) could not change the course of the franchise. In its seventh and final season, *Voyager* drew less than half of its Season One audience. However, those would have been good numbers for the poorly received prequel *Star Trek: Enterprise* (2001–2005), which premiered to mediocre ratings and also suffered a steady attrition of viewers. After just two seasons, Paramount considered cancelling the series. To appease the show's small but devoted audience, which mounted an old-fashioned write-in campaign to encourage the studio to keep *Enterprise* on the air, and to protect its investment by ensuring the series reached the requisite one hundred episodes necessary for syndication, Paramount continued producing *Enterprise* for two more seasons. But *Enterprise* was unable to complete its originally planned seven-year mission. Drawing fewer than three million viewers per episode in its final campaign (half its Season One audience), *Enterprise* became the franchise's first ratings casualty since the original *Star Trek.*

Ratings for both *Voyager* and *Enterprise* suffered because these programs were broadcast on Paramount's fledgling UPN network instead of in syndication like *The Next Generation* and *Deep Space Nine.* UPN, which premiered in 1995, was never able to compete with the major networks and didn't have affiliates in some parts of the country. In 2006, UPN merged with Warner Brothers' WB Network to form the CW Television Network, a cable channel. But there was more behind the franchise's deterioration than Paramount's failed UPN experiment.

Market Saturation

Actor Jonathan Frakes, interviewed during the waning days of *Star Trek: The Next Generation*, expressed concern that Paramount was ignoring the elementary law of supply and demand. "One wonders if they aren't going to the well one too many times," said Frakes, as quoted in *Patrick Stewart: The Unauthorized Biography.* "I hope not, but it's certainly got to be a fear the creators have." In recent years, his criticism of the studio has grown sharper. "I also think that Paramount with their infinite wisdom was really, incredibly greedy," said Frakes during an appearance at the Canada Comic-Con in 2011. "We had our show on the air, then they put *Deep Throat*, er, *Deep Space Nine* on the air . . . they put [on] *Voyager*, then *Enterprise*, and then we did *Generations* and *First Contact* and *Insurrection* and there was just too much *Star Trek.*"

As ratings sagged for *DS9* and *Voyager*, viewers abruptly abandoned the feature films. *Generations* returned a robust $80 million over its production costs, and *First Contact* earned a surprising $101 million more than its budget. But *Insurrection* returned just $54 million, and *Nemesis* became the first *Star Trek* film to lose money. It earned a paltry $67 million against a production budget of $60 million, and Paramount had sunk another $33 million into prints and advertising. Both Frakes and costar Brent Spiner blame the failure of *Nemesis* on Paramount's attempts to milk its cash cow dry. Viewers were simply Trekked out, they argue.

"I honestly think that for that period of time, the fans had had enough of us," said Brent Spiner, in an interview posted on the TrekMovie.com website. "I say that because the movie [*Nemesis*] didn't open the way the other movies opened. It wasn't about good or bad—nobody came, and that was significant. It was not the quality of the film. People go to bad films all the time. Every *Star Trek* movie opened bigger, and that [*Nemesis* didn't] spoke to how the fans were sick of us. Maybe if we waited a few more years and came back it would have been a different story."

In hindsight, it's clear that Paramount's decision to maintain two television programs and a feature film series, all drawing from a single (however large) fan base, was a recipe for audience fatigue. Paramount would have been wiser to hold *Voyager* in reserve until *Deep Space Nine* ended its run, but the studio wanted *Star Trek* to serve as the flagship series of its new network. Although it was hoped the two shows would help boost one another, instead they divided the attentions and loyalties of devoted Trekkers. The last thing *Star Trek* needed was competition from within the franchise; it had more than enough of that from outside.

Increased Competition

When *Star Trek: The Next Generation* debuted in 1987, it, the oddball sitcom *Max Headroom*, and the revived *Twilight Zone* (which moved from CBS into syndication that season) were the only science fiction programs on television. The only fantasy and horror shows were CBS's *Beauty and the Beast* and Fox's short-lived *Werewolf*. But the success of *Next Gen* spawned a horde of rivals, and not just on the major networks. Paramount's massive profits from *The Next Generation* inspired many other companies to enter the suddenly lucrative business of first-run syndication, and many cable networks also launched sci-fi and fantasy programs. By the time *Next Gen* wrapped up its final season in 1994, *Star Trek* was competing in a much more crowded field, which included formidable programs such as *The X-Files* (1993–2002) and *Babylon 5* (1993–98).

During the next decade, *Deep Space Nine*, *Voyager*, and *Enterprise* battled to hold fans' attention against more than a dozen insurgent sci-fi series. These included the underrated *Sliders* (1995–2000, created by *Trek* alum Tracy Tormé), *Earth: Final Conflict* (1997–2002, based on a concept by Gene Roddenberry), the long-running *Stargate SG-1* (1997–2007), the revived *Outer Limits* (1995–2002), and the "reimagined" *Battlestar Galactica* (2004–2009)—not to mention the SF sitcom *3rd Rock from the Sun* (1996–2001), which featured William Shatner in a recurring role. Fantasy and horror programs also proliferated, including such shows as *Highlander: The Series* (1992–98), *Hercules: The Legendary Journeys* (1995–99), *Xena: Warrior Princess* (1995–2001), and *Buffy the Vampire Slayer* (1997–2003), to name only a handful. The sheer volume of science fiction, fantasy, and horror programming reduced the audience for even the most successful of these series.

Decreased Accessibility

TV Guide critic Frank Lovelace, in his review of *Nemesis*, wrote that the *Star Trek* film series appeared to have "collapsed into the black hole of its own mythology." While accurate, Lovelace's analysis didn't go far enough. In reality, the entire franchise had plunged past that event horizon, trapped in a vortex of stifling continuity and serialized storytelling, and cut off from the rest of the galaxy.

Star Trek's commitment to continuity originated with creator Gene Roddenberry, who understood that consistency of terminology regarding the series' futuristic technology and coherence in its references to "future historical" events, such as World War III, would make the show's fantastic setting more believable. As the franchise expanded in the 1980s and '90s, it held fast to this strategy, creating an expansive yet coherent mythology rare among film and television science fiction, and more akin to literary SF, such as Robert A. Heinlein's Future History stories (one of Roddenberry's inspirations) and Isaac Asimov's generations-spanning *Foundation* saga. One of the most impressive aspects of the franchise was that it offered committed fans a panoramic dreamscape. However, as its mythology grew ever more dense and complex, *Star Trek* became less accessible to casual viewers, who could be confused and overwhelmed by it all.

Executive producer Michael Piller began introducing serialized story threads, which had been expressly forbidden by Roddenberry, during Season Four of *The Next Generation*. It was one of many groundbreaking, rule-bending decisions Piller made to provide greater creative flexibility and enable writers to explore character relationships in more depth. The series' teleplays were enriched by the ongoing drama of Worf's troubled relationship with his son Alexander, and by the recurring (mostly comedic) friction between newlyweds Miles and Keiko O'Brien, to cite just two of the series' many soap opera–like subplots. But in later seasons, and on later series, open-ended narratives gradually crept out of the subplots and into the primary story lines. *Star Trek* became increasingly serialized and self-referential.

Deep Space Nine's space-station setting invited this approach. Unlike Captain Kirk or Captain Picard, Commander Sisko couldn't make a decision and then simply warp off to another planet without facing the consequences of his actions. Everything that happened on *DS9* had (often unexpected) repercussions that were felt in future episodes. As a result, situations grew increasingly complex. Story lines such as Constable Odo's search for his origins spanned not just episodes but years, culminating in the Dominion War epic, which consumed nearly all of the series' fifth, sixth, and seventh seasons. The engrossing saga took full advantage of the sweeping canvas of the *Star Trek* universe, but became intimidating for newcomers. The reason Roddenberry rejected serialized stories was that they make it difficult for uninitiated viewers to understand the characters and situations. Since, for one reason or another, every show's core audience dwindles at least a bit each season, new viewers are required to improve or even maintain the program's ratings. Despite its excellence, the sprawling Dominion

War saga, which grew so complex that it became virtually incomprehensible to newbies, was a major factor in *Deep Space Nine*'s ratings slippage during its final few seasons.

Voyager wasn't as heavily serialized as *DS9* and took place in the distant Delta Quadrant, so that (at least initially) Captain Janeway's ship seldom encountered species from other *Star Trek* series. Yet the underlying scenario and the backstories of the characters were rooted in *Trek* mythology, especially the Cardassian-Bajoran conflict, introduced on *The Next Generation* and continued on *Deep Space Nine*. Beginning in Season Four, the Borg emerged as *Voyager*'s major recurring villain. As the series neared its climax, the story lines became more serialized, and ties with other *Trek* series grew stronger. *Next Gen*'s Lieutenant Reginald Barclay (Dwight Schultz) even appeared as a recurring character.

Throughout its four seasons, the prequel series *Enterprise* fleshed out, tweaked, or toyed with many elements of *Star Trek* mythology, often to the consternation of traditionalist fans. Executive producers Brannon Braga and, later, Manny Coto brilliantly utilized established but largely underdeveloped civilizations, such as the Andorians and the Orions, and delved deeper into events from *Trek*'s future history, such as the Eugenics Wars. The series concluded with the founding of the United Federation of Planets. Had it continued into a fifth season, *Enterprise* would have dealt with the Federation-Romulan War, mentioned in the classic episode "The Balance of Terror" and elsewhere. But *Enterprise* irked many fans by, among other things, presenting the (previously) saintly Vulcans in a less than flattering light. In its final two seasons the series also was heavily serialized. Coto's Xindi Weapon epic consumed Season Three in its entirety, and Season Four was comprised mostly of two- and three-episode story arcs, many of which were designed to fill in gaps in *Trek* mythology (explaining, for instance, why Klingons look different on the classic series than on *The Next Generation*). Rick Berman and Braga had created *Enterprise* in the hope that taking *Star Trek* back to its beginnings would attract new viewers. They were so invested in reaching beyond the franchise's core audience that, when first announced, the series wasn't even branded *Star Trek*; it was simply titled *Enterprise*. When Trekkers howled in protest, the show was retitled *Star Trek: Enterprise*. Yet, under any name, the increasingly insular, doctrinaire nature of its teleplays made the series arguably the least accessible of the five live-action *Star Trek* series. The series annoyed many die-hard fans but was too deeply invested in the franchise's mythology to appeal to casual viewers.

Blurred Vision

Under Berman's leadership, *Star Trek*, aside from its scrupulous devotion to continuity, slowly drifted away from the course originally charted by Roddenberry. The differences went beyond breaking Roddenberry's prohibitions against serialized stories, romantic triangles, and other screenwriting devices. Slowly but inexorably the franchise diluted the guiding optimism of Roddenberry's original vision and lost sight of his belief in the perfectibility of humankind. The Federation began to seem far less inspiring and utopian, battered by enemies (the Borg, the Cardassians, the Romulans, and the Dominion) from without, riven by conspiracies and controversies from within. The tone of the series grew increasingly dark and militaristic. For instance, Starfleet's spooky Section 31 espionage division (introduced on *DS9*) worked against the morally elevated, self-actualized future Roddenberry wanted *Star Trek* to model. Piller tried to correct the course of the franchise with his screenplay for *Star Trek: Insurrection*

The Season One cast of *Star Trek. Deep Space Nine.* Top row, left to right: Nana Visitor as Major Kira Nerys, Avery Brooks as Commander Benjamin Sisko, Alexander Siddig as Dr. Julian Bashir, Rene Auberjonois as Odo, and Colm Meaney as Chief O'Brien. Bottom row, left to right: Terry Farrell as Lieutenant Commander Jadzia Dax, Cirroc Lofton as Jake Sisko and Armin Shimerman as Quark. Michael Dorn joined as Worf beginning with Season Four.

(1998). Despite Piller's best intentions, however, there was no way to reverse the overall trend away from Roddenberrian optimism. *Insurrection*'s disappointing box-office performance undermined his entire argument. Nevertheless, the Great Bird's uplifting vision of the future was foundational to the franchise's success. It was unique and set *Star Trek* apart. As Roddenberry's vision became blurred, *Star Trek* became less distinct from *Babylon 5*, *Battlestar Galactica*, and the other sci-fi franchises with which it was competing.

Uneven Quality

Finally, it must be acknowledged that the quality of the *Star Trek* product began to deteriorate in the mid-1990s. Of the films that followed *The Undiscovered Country*, only *First Contact* lived up to the high standard set by *The Wrath of Khan* (1982) and *The Voyage Home* (1986). The later *Star Trek* television series struggled to duplicate the sustained excellence achieved by the classic series and *The Next Generation* in their primes. *Deep Space Nine* contained fundamental conceptual limitations, *Voyager*'s writers struggled to deliver consistently engaging teleplays, while *Enterprise* suffered from both of those problems and others. None of the later *Trek* series boasted a cast as impressive from top to bottom as those assembled for the original program or *The Next Generation*. Only the work of the franchise's production departments remained above reproach. The drop-off in quality began with the final season of *The Next Generation*, when the franchise's writing resources were spread too thin between Season Seven of *Next Gen*, Season Two of *DS9*, development of *Voyager*, and preproduction of *Star Trek Generations*. To a lesser degree, this problem persisted for years, as it proved difficult to replace key personnel when experienced writers left the franchise or moved up the ladder to assume larger roles.

Deep Space Nine was arguably the most consistently well written of all the *Star Trek* series and contained a handful of fascinating, well-drawn characters, especially Major Kira Nerys (Nana Visitor), Odo (Rene Auberjonois), and Quark (Armin Shimerman). Nevertheless, many fans simply never warmed to the series, in part because they found its space station setting unappealing. Berman and Piller opted for this locale to differentiate the series from *Next Gen*. The idea was to make station Deep Space Nine, located next to the galaxy's only known stable wormhole (a gateway to the Gamma Quadrant), a hub of commerce, scientific exploration, and political intrigue, placing Commander Sisko at the center of major, galaxy-shaking events. However, being at the center of such events is not the same thing as driving them, and the show's static setting often left Sisko and his crew in a relatively passive position, being acted upon rather than initiating the action themselves. They were often swept up in movements and machinations originating from Cardassia, the Dominion, or elsewhere in the Federation.

Voyager, created by Berman, Piller, and Jeri Taylor, boasted a more intriguing premise: A starship, manned by an uneasy alliance of former Federation and Maquis (anti-Cardassian terrorist) officers, is stranded in the faraway Delta

Quadrant, cut off from Starfleet. The makeshift crew must make peace amongst themselves and find their way home. The scenario was inherently dramatic, offering the same thrill of exploration and discovery found in earlier *Star Trek* series, but with a plausible rationale for the kind of internal, interpersonal conflict Roddenberry eschewed on *The Next Generation*. Unfortunately, the series seldom delivered on its fertile setup. All too quickly, Captain Janeway's team stopped squabbling and fell into line, becoming just as chummy as Captain Picard's senior staff. The series meandered for its first few seasons, as story threads were introduced, toyed with, and then inexplicably dropped. These included the idea that the ship's energy reserves were critically low (although this never prevented the crew from spending its spare time on the holodeck), a problem that was never resolved but merely forgotten. Also, the USS *Voyager* seemed to contain an inexhaustible supply of shuttlecraft. From Season Four on, the series became overreliant on the Borg, which had appeared in just six episodes of *The Next Generation* (spread out over seven seasons) but were featured in twenty-two *Voyager* installments. Most damaging of all, many of *Voyager*'s characters were never satisfactorily developed. The most fully realized character on the series was the Doctor (Robert Picardo), a hologram. According to writer-producer Ronald D. Moore, who worked briefly on the series following the end of *Deep Space Nine*, *Voyager* was torn by conflicting pressures on the writing staff, then led by co-executive producer Brannon Braga. "It was just a lot of acrimony, and I think Brannon was just taking it from all sides," said Moore, in an interview with ign.com. "I'm there, and I'm telling him, 'Let's change things and let's go in a different direction. . . . Rick [Berman] is saying, 'Play it safe. It's *Star Trek*, you have to be careful.' And Michael [Piller]'s on the outside saying, 'You guys are fucking up everything!' And then Brannon was just in an untenable position, I think."

Like *Deep Space Nine*, the basic premise of *Enterprise*—set in the future-past of the pre-Federation Starfleet—was off-putting to many die-hard Trekkers. *Star Trek* fans are forward-thinking people, and many of them couldn't get behind a backward-looking show. The prequel setting also placed the *Enterprise* writing staff in a tough spot. Writers strived to catch the imaginations of new viewers but feared alienating the franchise's core fans. The staff aspired to pen teleplays that were fresh and surprising, but they couldn't depict events that would conflict with established future history. It was a delicate balance, and one writers often failed to strike, especially during the series' uneven first two seasons. The series carried on the *Star Trek* tradition of commenting on current events with writer-producer Manny Coto's intense Xindi Weapon epic, which paralleled the 9/11/2001 terrorist attacks and subsequent War on Terror, but many viewers were troubled by the story's grim tone (at one point, Captain Archer threatens to kill a captured suspect to gain information about the whereabouts of the Xindi device, which is capable of destroying all life on Earth). The Xindi Weapon saga took audiences far off the optimistic, inspiring course charted by Roddenberry—although *Enterprise*, it must be noted, takes place prior to the founding of the Federation or the establishment of the Prime Directive. As on *Voyager*, many *Enterprise* characters remained thinly sketched. Fans also objected to the casting of Scott Bakula as Archer. Even though the talented actor contributed fine performances, many viewers were unable to look at him and not see Sam Beckett, his character from *Quantum Leap* (a role for which Bakula earned four Emmy nominations). Also, many fans disliked the Diane Warren–penned power ballad "Faith of the Heart" (originally written for the movie *Patch Adams*), which served as the series' theme song.

The Season Four cast of *Star Trek: Voyager*. Back row: Ethan Phillips as Neelix and Garret Wang as Ensign Harry Kim. Middle row: Jeri Ryan as Seven of Nine, Robert Picardo as the Doctor, Robert Duncan McNeill as Lieutenant Tom Paris, Robert Beltran as Commander Chakotay, and Tim Russ and Lieutenant Commander Tuvok. Foreground: Kate Mulgrew as Captain Kathryn Janeway and Roxann Dawson as engineer B'Elanna Torres. This season, Taylor's Seven of Nine replaced Jennifer Lein's Kes.

After the cancellation of *Enterprise* in 2005, four years elapsed with no new *Trek* film or television product at all, the longest dry spell since the 1970s. Many assumed that, after a historic forty-year run, *Star Trek* had finally crossed its final final frontier. But its mission wasn't over yet.

The cast of *Star Trek: Enterprise*. Top, from left: Connor Trinneer as Commander Trip Tucker, Scott Bakula as Captain Jonathan Archer, Jolene Blalock as Sub-Commander T'Pol. Bottom row, from left: John Billingsley as Dr. Phlox, Anthony Montgomery as Ensign Travis Mayweather, Linda Park Ensign Hoshi Sato, and Dominic Keating as Lieutenant Malcolm Reed.

38

Do It Yourself

In the early 1970s, when *Star Trek* was condemned to the purgatory of syndicated reruns with no new episodes or movies in sight, Trekkers starved for fresh stories featuring their cherished characters began writing their own *Trek* tales and self-publishing them in fanzines. In the early 2000s, with the franchise trapped in a deteriorating orbit, fans again stepped in and began creating their own product. This time, however, the franchise's decline coincided with the popularization of low-cost, high-quality digital film production equipment, including sophisticated editing and animation software. As a result, fans were able to do what Trekkers could only dream of thirty years earlier—actually produce their own *Star Trek* episodes and create entirely new series. Although homemade *Trek* films—shot on videotape or, before that, on 8 mm—had been around as long as the original program, the new technology enabled fans to mount productions on a larger scale, execute them with greater polish, and distribute them worldwide via the Internet. Paramount Pictures, which (surprisingly) had long tolerated the *Star Trek* fan press, took the same laissez-faire attitude toward fan films, granting Trekkers wide latitude in the creation and distribution of these works as long as they were undertaken on a not-for-profit basis.

A boom of *Star Trek* fan films ensued. The quality of these works varies widely, but at least a few of them are well worth a look. All of the series covered in this chapter are available free online, either from the websites indicated or on secondary sites such as YouTube. An exhaustive listing of these films can be found at the Star Trek Expanded Universe website (http://stexpanded.wikia. com/wiki/Main_Page), which is devoted to fan-created, unauthorized, and noncanonical *Trek* works.

Star Trek: New Voyages/Phase II

Easily the best known and most ambitious of these fan-made Treks is the series now known as *Star Trek: Phase II* (originally titled *Star Trek: New Voyages*), which is produced on a relatively large scale, often with the participation of cast members and writers from official *Trek* series. Cocreated by actor James Cawley and director Jack Marshall, the series tells stories set during the missing final two years of the *Enterprise*'s original Five Year mission, featuring new (nonprofessional) actors as the classic *Trek* characters. "We think of ourselves as Season Four," said Marshall in a 2004 interview with the Washington *City Paper*. "We pick up right where the original show left off."

Cawley, who stars as James T. Kirk, is a professional Elvis impersonator, which accounts for the captain's incongruous hairstyle. Aside from Kirk's coiffure, however, Cawley, Marshall, and a team of more than fifty volunteers have invested significant time and treasure in creating uncannily accurate re-creations of production designer Matt Jefferies's sets and props and costume designer William Ware Theiss's Starfleet uniforms. The episodes, which also feature impressive computer animated visual effects, are shot in a disused car dealership in Ticonderoga, New York. The pilot episode, "Come What May," was released in 2004, and new installments have appeared every twelve to sixteen months since then. As of this writing (in the fall of 2012), seven full adventures and one vignette have been completed, and four full-length episodes were in various stages of production or preproduction. Among the *Star Trek* alumna who have guest starred on the series are George Takei, Walter Koenig, Grace Lee Whitney, Majel Barrett-Roddenberry (as the computer voice), and Denise Crosby (as Tasha Yar's grandmother). In all, a dozen actors who appeared on the classic *Trek* series have also worked on *New Voyages/Phase II*. Rod Roddenberry, the son of Gene Roddenberry, served as a consulting producer on the pilot.

As the series has progressed, episodes have grown more polished and elaborate. What sets the series apart from other fan productions is the high quality of its teleplays. Original *Trek* screenwriters Dorothy ("D. C.") Fontana and David Gerrold both penned scripts for the show, as did Marc Scott Zicree and Michael Reaves, both of whom wrote memorable episodes of *The Next Generation* ("First Contact" and "Where No One Has Gone Before," respectively). Several other episodes were based on teleplays created for the aborted *Star Trek: Phase II* series from the late 1970s. For the most part, the scenarios are imaginative and engrossing. Some of the more notable installments include:

"World Enough and Time" (2007)—In the most acclaimed episode of the series—written by Zicree and Reaves, based on their original, unproduced *Star Trek: Phase II* teleplay—the *Enterprise* becomes trapped in a space-time distortion. Sulu is swept into the distortion by a transporter mishap. Although he is recovered seconds later (starship time), in those few moments he has lived thirty years in an alternate dimension and returns with an adult daughter. Takei guest stars as the aged Sulu, and Christina Moses contributes a surprisingly effective guest performance as his daughter, Alana. The story also features a framing sequence set much later, aboard the USS *Excelsior*, commanded by Captain Sulu (as seen in *Star Trek VI*), and featuring Whitney as Janice Rand. The fast-paced, tense and emotionally gripping "World Enough and Time," shot on a $25,000 budget, was nominated for both the Hugo and Nebula awards, and earned *New Voyages* a TV Guide Award for Best Web Series.

"In Harm's Way" (2004)—Written by Erik Korngold, this early installment features an imaginative premise: History as we know it has been altered, and the planet Vulcan destroyed, by an unknown enemy that sent a Planet Killer (the giant, planet-eating superweapon seen in "The Doomsday Machine") into the past. In this altered reality, James T. Kirk is now the captain of the USS *Farragut*, and his first officer is a Klingon named Kargh. To set things straight, Kirk uses the Guardian of Forever (the time portal seen in "The City on the Edge of Forever") to travel back to the era of the original *Trek* pilot, where the *Farragut* and the *Enterprise*, led by Captain Christopher Pike, must join forces to destroy the Planet Killer. The episode features a cameo by William Windom as Commodore Matt Decker, from "The Doomsday Machine," and appearances by two other classic *Trek* guest stars, Barbara Luna (from "Mirror, Mirror") and Malachi Throne (from "The Menagerie, Parts I and II").

"Blood and Fire" (2008–2009)—This two-part adventure, cowritten by Gerrold and Carlos Pedraza, was based on Gerrold's controversial, gay-themed teleplay of the same title, which was originally penned for *Next Gen*. When Gene Roddenberry heavily rewrote the script, eliminating the homosexual angle, Gerrold filed an injunction with the Writers Guild to prevent it from being produced on *The Next Generation*. *The New Voyages* restores the controversial content, which involves a romantic relationship between two male Starfleet officers (in this version, one of them is Captain Kirk's nephew) and a deadly alien plague (intended as an AIDS metaphor). Captain Kirk seems only momentarily fazed by the revelation that his nephew is gay and readily agrees to marry the young man and his partner.

"Enemy: Starfleet" (2011)—In this action-packed installment, the *Enterprise* battles an enemy force that has commandeered a Federation starship and reverse-engineered its technology, creating a shadow Starfleet. "Enemy: Starfleet," written by Dave Galanter (author of several *Star Trek* novels) and Patty Wright, is one of the most entertaining *New Voyages/Phase II* adventures, but is compromised by the casting of the seventy-two-year-old Barbara Luna as a supposedly alluring villainess named Alersa.

"To Serve All My Days" (2006)—Written by Fontana, "To Serve All My Days" is a blatant rehash of the classic episode "Journey to Babel" (also penned by Fontana): The *Enterprise* is threatened by a mysterious enemy (at first misidentified as the Klingons) while ferrying interstellar diplomats (including humans, Andorians, and Tellarites) home from a diplomatic summit on planet Babel. While only a so-so installment, the episode remains notable for the presence of Walter Koenig as Ensign Chekov, who contracts the rapid-aging illness that afflicted most of the ship's other senior officers in "The Deadly Years." Koenig appears opposite Mary-Linda Rapelye, who played Chekov's space-hippie love interest in the classic episode "The Way to Eden."

Even the best *New Voyages/Phase II* episodes contain major flaws. The acting is amateurish, with most cast members simply doing impressions of their counterparts from the original program. Only Cawley offers anything like an original interpretation of his character. The lighting, sound, and special effects, while outstanding for a do-it-yourself effort, remain well below professional standards.

Promotional artwork for the Hugo and Nebula Award–winning *Star Trek: New Voyages* episode "World Enough and Time," guest starring George Takei as Sulu. Also pictured are Christina Marie Moses as Sulu's daughter, Alana, and (bottom, from left) John M. Kelley as McCoy, James Cawley as Kirk, and Jeffery Quinn as Spock.

Still, making allowances for the financial realities behind its creation, the series is diverting and will certainly hold the interest of open-minded fans. Episodes are available as free downloads at http://startrekphase2videos.com/index.html or mirror sites such as http://phase2trek.com/home.html.

Star Trek: Of Gods and Men

Star Trek: Of Gods and Men, an unofficial, semiprofessional three-part miniseries, was created and directed by Tim Russ, who played Tuvok on *Star Trek: Voyager*. It was shot on the *Star Trek: New Voyages/Phase II* sets in Ticonderoga, New York, in 2006 and premiered in 2007–2008. Classic *Trek* stars Nichelle Nichols, Walter Koenig, and Grace Lee Whitney reprise their roles as Uhura, Chekov, and Rand, and Russ appears as Tuvok. Alan Ruck returns as Captain John Harriman of the *Enterprise-B*, the character he played in *Star Trek Generations*. Several other *Trek* regulars appear in new roles, including *Voyager*'s Garrett Wang and Ethan Phillips, and *Deep Space Nine*'s Cirroc Lofton. *Of Gods and Men*, penned by *DS9* screenwriters Jack Trevino and Ethan H. Calk, takes place in the late twenty-third century, following the apparent death of Captain Kirk in *Generations*. A revenge-crazed Charlie Evans, who menaced the crew of the *Enterprise* in the classic episode "Charlie X," uses the Guardian of Forever time portal to change history and create an alternate timeline akin to the Mirror Universe seen in "Mirror, Mirror." Altered versions of Uhura, Chekov, and Harriman (who retain vague memories of their former lives) form an uneasy alliance to overthrow the evil Galactic Order and restore the timeline. The story is inventive, full of clever twists and references to classic *Trek* episodes, but prone to dialogue-heavy lulls. Production values and performances are markedly better than any other fan film so far produced. William Wellman Jr. portrays Evans, a role originated by Robert Walker Jr. All the key roles are handled by professional performers, many of whom appeared in similar supporting parts on various *Trek* series (for example, Klingon commander Koval is portrayed by J. G. Hertzler, who played General Martok on *DS9*). *Of Gods and Men* is not only entertaining but of historical significance, since it contains the final appearances of Nichols as Uhura and Koenig as Chekov. It's available as a free download from http://startrekofgodsandmen.com/main/.

Starship Farragut

New Voyages/Phase II and *Of Gods and Men* are extraordinary ventures. Most *Star Trek* fan productions operate more along the lines of *Starship Farragut*, created and executive produced by John Broughton. The series is set during the classic *Trek* era but features wholly original characters and scenarios. Broughton plays John T. Carter, the inexperienced captain of the USS *Farragut*. The show is produced on a much lower budget than *New Voyages/Phase II* or *Of Gods and Men*, and its screenplays are more simplistic, but its computer-animated visual effects are astoundingly good for a homemade effort. Like many fan productions, episodes are shot primarily "on location" in local parks or other green spaces, which stand in for alien worlds. *Starship Farragut*'s pilot episode, "The Captaincy," released in 2004, features guest appearances by Crawley, Jeffery Quinn, and John Kelley from *New Voyages* as Kirk, Spock, and McCoy. So far, four full live-action episodes and a vignette have been completed. Broughton and friends have also created a pair of animated installments drawn in the style of the *Star Trek* Saturday morning cartoon show from the 1970s. These episodes brilliantly recapture the look and spirit of the classic animated series. They are much more impressive than the live-action adventures of the *Starship Farragut*—and most other live-action fan films. Both the animated and live-action episodes are available for download at http://www.starshipfarragut.com/index.php.

Starship Exeter

Starship Exeter, created by Jimm and Joshua Johnson, was one of the first fan productions to emerge during the early 2000s. Its pilot episode, "The Savage Empire," was issued in 2002 and was followed by another adventure, "The Tressaurian Intersection," in 2005. Like *Starship Farragut*, *Starship Exeter* is set in the classic *Trek* era but features original characters. Jimm Johnson stars as Captain John Quincy Garrovick. At this distance the series seems crude, but the pioneering production served as a pathfinder for later, higher-caliber fan productions. *Starship Exeter*'s website is no longer operational, but both episodes are available on YouTube.

Star Trek: Hidden Frontier

Like *Starship Exeter*, *Star Trek: Hidden Frontier* was another of the earliest Internet-released fan productions. It's also by far the longest-running and most prolific fan-made series, with fifty episodes released across seven "seasons," as well as several spin-off projects. Created and produced by Bob Caves, the series was shot almost entirely on a green-screen stage, with computer-animated sets and visual effects. *Hidden Frontier* is set during the *Next Generation* era, aboard the USS *Excelsior* and space station *Deep Space Twelve*, which orbits the Ba'ku home world in the "Briar Patch" region of space, as introduced in *Star Trek: Insurrection* (1998). Story lines involve several *Star Trek* civilizations, including the Ba'ku and Son'a (from *Insurrection*), the Andorians, the Romulans, the Klingons, the Tholians, and a new species known as the Grey. The cast of characters includes gay and lesbian Starfleet officers. *Hidden Frontier*, which debuted in 2000, grew out of an even earlier fan-created series, *Voyages of the USS Los Angeles*, created by members of a Southern California *Star Trek* fan club. In addition to the fifty-episode series, two feature-length *Hidden Frontier* movies were produced (*Orphans of War* and *Operation Beta Shield*). *Hidden Frontier* has also spawned numerous spin-off series, including *Star Trek: Odyssey*, *Star Trek: The Helena Chronicles*, *Star Trek:*

Federation One, Frontier Guard, Star Trek: Grissom, Star Trek: Diplomatic Relations, and *Henglaar, M.D.* As you might expect, the early *Hidden Frontier* episodes are primitive and clunky (the acting is especially poor), but the series improved significantly as it progressed. The greatest strengths of *Hidden Frontier* are its epic scale, complex story lines, and emphasis on character development. Along with *New Voyages/Phase II, Hidden Frontier* and its associated projects have developed the largest and most loyal following of all *Star Trek* fan-created programs. Episodes of all the various series are available free at http://www.hiddenfrontier.com.

Star Trek: Intrepid

The Scottish-made *Star Trek: Intrepid* is set in the same twenty-fourth-century milieu as *Hidden Frontier*. In fact, the two *Hidden Frontier* movies are "crossovers" involving characters from *Intrepid*. Created by Nick Cook, who stars as Captain Daniel Hunter of the titular USS *Intrepid*, the series premiered in 2007 with the episode "Heavy Lies the Crown." In addition to the two feature-length *Hidden Frontier* coproductions, a total of seven *Intrepid* installments have been released so far, and two more are in the works. The series skillfully integrates location footage (shot in real buildings and green spaces) with computer-generated backgrounds, and its acting is a notch better than most amateur productions. *Intrepid*'s overarching story line involves the settlement of the sparsely populated "Charybdis" sector of the galaxy, which is home to a mysterious race known as the Surai. Episodes are available free at http://www.starshipintrepid.net.

Other Fan Productions

The preceding is by no means a comprehensive listing of all fan-made Treks. In addition to the many straight-faced dramatic productions, there are a slew of Trekker-created parodies, mostly of the short, one-off variety. Some of the best of these include: "Redshirt Blues," in which a veteran security officer explains the dangers of serving aboard Captain Kirk's *Enterprise* to an eager new recruit; "Star Trek: The Pepsi Generation," which mercilessly lampoons *Next Gen*; and "Steam Trek," a steam punk riff on the classic series, done in the style of a Georges Méliès silent movie. All are available on YouTube. There are also Trekker-made audio dramas, fan-created role playing games, comic books, and—yes—fiction, which is still written in abundance and now published on the Internet.

39

Starfleet Commendations Revisited

Awards Won (and Lost) 1980–2010

S *tar Trek*'s critical reputation has always been mixed. The classic series was panned by most critics upon its debut but earned back-to-back Emmy nominations as Outstanding Drama following its first two seasons (losing both times to *Mission: Impossible*). Over time, the Emmy Awards became a litany of futility for the original *Trek*, which failed to claim a single trophy despite thirteen nominations in various categories. Later *Trek* series and films have won Emmys and Oscars, but only in technical categories such as sound mixing and makeup.

During its prime era (from Seasons Three through Six), *Star Trek: The Next Generation* consistently delivered elegantly produced, convincingly performed, character-driven stories enriched by imaginative, thought-provoking science fiction concepts. The series was as ambitious and well crafted as any on the air and overall one of the best shows on television. But *The Next Generation*, while collecting an impressive haul of Emmys in various technical categories, for many years was shut out of the more prestigious "creative" categories. This became a source of frustration for the show's producers and cast, who believed Emmy voters didn't take the program seriously because it was syndicated and because it was science fiction.

"Because our show doesn't air on one of the traditional networks, we continually face the frustration of being an anomaly," Berman complained to a reporter from Entertainment Tonight, in a story about the production of *Next Gen*'s landmark eightieth episode (one more than the original program). "We can only hope our show will be acknowledged by the industry, which an increasing number of viewers have obviously been enjoying for the past four seasons regardless of where they watch it."

In the same interview, Patrick Stewart was even blunter. "We're conscious that some people think of us as 'That syndicated kid's show,' and as far as a large part of the TV industry is concerned, we are," Stewart fumed. "Otherwise, how can you explain the total absence of Emmy nominations for directing, writing and acting?" Stewart went on to compare *Star Trek* with Shakespeare, pointing out that the Bard's plays were also considered escapist entertainment in their day, but "clearly his plays could be very serious, too."

Indeed, looking back, *Star Trek: The Next Generation* compares favorably with many of the programs that earned higher ratings and greater Emmy recognition during its prime years (from Season Three in 1989–90 through Season Six in 1992–93).

Situation comedies dominated this era in television. Shows such as *Cheers, Roseanne, The Cosby Show,* and *Murphy Brown* ruled the Nielsen ratings. For the 1989–90 season, no drama series finished in the Top 10. The most popular dramas were *L.A. Law* and *Murder, She Wrote,* which tied for No. 14. *In the Heat of the Night* (No. 17) and *Matlock* (No. 20) also cracked the Top 20. Over the next three seasons, only three dramas made the Top 20: *Murder, She Wrote* (all three seasons), *Matlock* (in 1990–91), and *Northern Exposure* (in 1991–92 and '92–93). Today, *Next Gen* boasts a far larger following than any of those series.

The critical darlings of the era were *L.A. Law* (which won the Emmy for Outstanding Drama Series in 1990 and '91), *Northern Exposure* (Emmy champion in 1992), and *Picket Fences* (the 1993 Emmy winner), along with frequent nominees *China Beach, thirtysomething,* and *Law & Order.* A science fiction series rubbed elbows with this distinguished company, but it wasn't *Next Gen;* it was *Quantum Leap,* Emmy nominated for three consecutive seasons from 1990 through 1992. Yet *The Next Generation* was arguably more innovative in form and adventurous in content than any of those more celebrated programs.

The Next Generation was belatedly honored with an Emmy nomination as Outstanding Dramatic Series following its final season in 1994. Although it failed to win (losing to *Picket Fences*), *Next Gen* became the first syndicated program ever nominated for the award. *Next Gen* won a George Foster Peabody Award for the Season One episode "The Big Goodbye." It was the first syndicated program ever to win the award. Over the next several seasons, the Peabody Award (not widely known outside the broadcasting industry but coveted within it) went to *China Beach, thirtysomething, Twin Peaks,* and *Northern Exposure.* Peabody voters, at least, considered *The Next Generation* on par with the finest dramas on TV.

Stewart's frustration with the Emmys, no doubt, had a personal edge. Although Leonard Nimoy was Emmy nominated following each of the classic show's three seasons, no *Next Generation* cast member ever earned an Emmy nomination. *Star Trek* fans might be surprised to learn that while Stewart never received a single Emmy nomination, Scott Bakula—himself a future *Enterprise* captain—earned four Best Actor nominations in a row for his work on *Quantum Leap* from 1990 through 1993.

However, the franchise's enormous number of awards and honors in technical categories bears witness to the extraordinarily high level of artistry routinely demonstrated by *Star Trek* movies and TV series. Here's a rundown of the major honors bestowed on the franchise from 1980 to 2010. For a look at awards won and lost by the classic program and by the animated series, consult the first *Star Trek FAQ.*

The Emmys

Television's highest honor, the Emmy Awards have been presented annually since the medium's infancy in 1949. They are administered by a triumvirate of trade organizations—the Academy of Television Arts and Sciences, the National Academy of Television Arts and Sciences, and the International Academy of Television Arts & Sciences. *Star Trek* won its first Emmy, after fourteen consecutive defeats, when the *Trek* animated series won Outstanding Entertainment Children's Series at the Daytime Emmys in 1975. It was the franchise's only victory in a major category. However, *Trek* programs have earned many nominations in the various technical disciplines.

The Next Generation cast, circa Season Four. Top, from left: Whoopi Goldberg, Gates McFadden, Michael Dorn, Marina Sirtis, and Wil Wheaton. Bottom, from left: LeVar Burton, Patrick Stewart, Jonathan Frakes, and Brent Spiner. The autographs greatly simplify identification.

- In 1988, following its premiere season, *Star Trek: The Next Generation* won three Emmys (for sound editing in the episode "11001001," for costume design in "The Big Goodbye," and for makeup in "Conspiracy") and earned four additional nominations (for cinematography in "The Big Goodbye," for makeup in "Coming of Age," for hairstyling in "Haven," and for sound mixing in "Where No One Has Gone Before").

- The next year the show collected two Emmys (for sound mixing and sound editing in "Q Who") and six more nominations (for visual effects in "Q Who," for art direction and costume design in "Elementary, Dear Data," for dramatic score in "The Child," for makeup in "A Matter of Honor," and for hairstyling in "Unnatural Selection"). "Q Who" and "Elementary, Dear Data" were lavish and sophisticated productions that deserved every nomination and more.

- In 1990, the series garnered two more Emmys and seven additional nominations. "Yesterday's Enterprise" won for its sound editing and was also nominated for its sound mixing and score. "Sins of the Father" won for its art direction. "Deja Q" was nominated for its editing and visual effects. Other nominees included "Tin Man" (for visual effects), "Allegiance" (makeup), and "Hollow Pursuits" (hairstyling). By all rights, the show could have won the makeup category every year.

- The following year, *The Next Generation* tallied two more awards and seven more nominations. "The Best of Both Worlds, Part II" won Emmys for its sound editing and sound mixing, and was also nominated for its art direction and visual effects. Other nominations went to "Devil's Due" (costume design), "Family" (cinematography), "Half a Life" (score), and "Brothers" and "Identity Crisis" (both makeup). While its dual wins and four nominations were impressive, "Best of Both Worlds, Part II"—one of the most ambitious single hours of television ever broadcast—was shortchanged. It could justifiably have been nominated for its cinematography, score, and makeup, at minimum. Patrick Stewart's brilliant performance also deserved recognition.

- For Season Five, *Next Gen* scored three wins and five additional nominations. The installment "Cost of Living" won a pair of Emmys for its costume design and makeup, and was also nominated for its hairstyling. Two episodes—"A Matter of Time" and "Conundrum"—tied and each received an award for visual effects. Other nominees included "Unification I" (score), "Unification II" (art direction), "The Next Phase" (sound mixing), and "Power Play" (sound editing).

- In 1993, following its penultimate season, *The Next Generation* claimed three wins (for costume design and hairstyling in "Time's Arrow, Part II" and for sound mixing in "A Fistful of Datas") and two more nominations (sound editing in "Time's Arrow, Part II" and makeup in "The Inner Light"). This year the series faced a daunting new rival to its mastery of the Emmy's technical awards—*Star Trek: Deep Space Nine*, which won an Emmy for its main title theme and another for its visual effects (in "The Emissary"), and earned additional nominations for its sound editing, sound mixing, makeup, and hairstyling (in various other episodes). This was the franchise's most successful year with Emmy voters.

- In 1994, following its final season, *Next Gen* won two final Emmys and garnered eight more nominations. The series finale, "All Good Things . . . ," won for its visual effects and was nominated for its score, editing, and costume design. "Genesis" won in the category of sound mixing and earned nominations for its sound editing and makeup. In addition, "Thine Own Self" was nominated for art direction and "Firstborn" for hairstyling. The highlight, of course, was the series' nomination as Outstanding Drama. That year, *DS9* earned two nominations (for makeup and hairstyling) but failed to notch a win.

- In subsequent years, the franchise racked up a dozen more Emmys (one more for *Deep Space Nine*, seven for *Star Trek: Voyager*, and four for *Star Trek: Enterprise*), plus seventy-four additional nominations (twenty-three for *DS9*, thirty-four for *Voyager*, and seventeen for *Enterprise*). Counting nominations and awards bestowed on the original program and the animated series, *Star Trek* amassed a staggering grand total of 33 Emmy Awards and 155 nominations. Not bad for a franchise that has seldom been the darling of TV critics.

Academy Awards

Star Trek has earned a total of fourteen Academy Award nominations (so far), but it took nearly thirty-nine years for the franchise to finally bring home an Oscar.

- In 1980, *Star Trek: The Motion Picture* was nominated for three Academy Awards but lost in the Art Direction category to director Bob Fosse's stylish musical *All That Jazz*, in the music (original score) category to director George Roy Hill's comedy *A Little Romance* and in the special visual effects category to *Alien*.

- *Star Trek II: The Wrath of Khan* and *Star Trek III: The Search for Spock* failed to receive any nominations. *Star Trek IV: The Voyage Home* earned four, the most of any film in the series, but struck out with Academy voters. It lost the cinematography award to director Roland Joffe's period piece *The Mission*, the music award to Herbie Hancock's jazzy compositions for *Round Midnight*, the sound mixing award to Oliver Stone's *Platoon*, and the sound effects award (which it fully deserved to win) to *Aliens*.

- Unsurprisingly, Oscar ignored *Star Trek V: The Final Frontier*. (Alas, the Golden Raspberry Awards did not.) However, *Star Trek VI: The Undiscovered Country* earned a pair of nominations for its makeup and sound effects. It lost both awards to *Terminator 2: Judgment Day*.

- The *Next Generation* feature films earned far less Academy respect than their original cast forebears. The four *Next Gen* movies earned just one Oscar nomination among them, in the category of Best Makeup for *Star Trek: First*

Contact. In one of the franchise's most galling defeats, it lost to the Eddie Murphy comedy *The Nutty Professor.*

- At the 82nd Annual Academy Awards in 2010, the series finally took home a statuette. Director J. J. Abrams's franchise reboot *Star Trek* won the Oscar for makeup and also garnered nominations for sound editing and sound recording (losing both to Best Picture winner *The Hurt Locker*) and for visual effects (losing to *Avatar*).

The Golden Raspberry Awards

The Golden Raspberry Awards, presented as a counterpoint to the Academy Awards, "honors" the worst in Hollywood cinema. These awards, commonly referred to as "Razzies," have been bestowed each year since 1981, when they were created by publicist John J. B. Wilson. At the 1990 Razzies, *Star Trek V: The Final Frontier* was named Worst Picture. William Shatner was a Razzie double "winner," named both Worst Actor and Worst Director. The picture was also nominated for Worst Picture of the Decade, Worst Supporting Actor (DeForest Kelley), and Worst Screenplay (David Loughery, Shatner, and Harve Bennett). Had Wilson introduced the Razzies a few years earlier, *Star Trek: The Motion Picture* (1979) would have been a serious contender in several categories.

The Hugo Awards

Aside from the Oscars and the Emmys, the awards that are most meaningful for many *Star Trek* fans are the Hugos, presented annually since 1955 by the World Science Fiction Convention. Named for *Amazing Stories* publisher Hugo Gernsback (who coined the term "science fiction"), the Hugos exist primarily to celebrate achievement in SF literature and rank among the genre's highest accolades. In 1960, an award was added for Best Dramatic Presentation, which until 2002 was a catchall category that encompassed film, television, and other media. During its first two seasons, *Star Trek* dominated this category like no TV show before or since, winning back-to-back Hugos in 1967 and 1968. In '68, all five nominations in the category were *Trek* episodes, including the Hugo-winning "City on the Edge of Forever." That year, Gene Roddenberry was also granted a special Hugo for *Star Trek.* Since then, however, the Best Dramatic Presentation Hugo has usually gone to a motion picture. Every *Star Trek* feature film, with the exceptions of *Star Trek V: The Final Frontier* and *Star Trek Nemesis,* earned Hugo nominations, but no *Trek* movie has ever won the award. *Star Trek: The Next Generation* broke through with a Hugo win in 1993 (for "The Inner Light"), becoming the first TV episode to win the award since "The City on the Edge of Forever." *Next Gen,* which had earned a nomination for its series premiere "Encounter at Farpoint" in 1988, collected a second Hugo for its series finale, "All Good Things . . . ," in 1995. *Deep Space Nine* and *Enterprise* earned two Hugo nominations apiece, but neither show won the award.

The Saturn Awards

Since 1972, the Academy of Science Fiction, Fantasy and Horror Films has presented annual Saturn Awards for excellence in genre productions for film, television, and other media. While not as well known as the Oscars, Emmys, and Hugos, the Saturn Awards remain prestigious, especially within the SF community. Over the decades, the *Star Trek* franchise has raked in eighteen Saturn Awards and such a whopping number of nominations (more than a hundred and counting) that a detailed accounting is space prohibitive. However, every *Trek* feature film from *Star Trek: The Motion Picture* through *Star Trek IV: The Voyage Home* was nominated as Best Science Fiction Film, as were *Star Trek VI: The Undiscovered Country*, *Star Trek: First Contact*, and *Star Trek* (2009). *The Undiscovered Country* won the category in 1993. *The Next Generation* was nominated six times as Best Television Series and won the award in 1990 and 1991. In 2005, the committee honored *Next Gen*, *DS9*, *Voyager*, and *Enterprise* with a Special Recognition Award for the excellence of all *Star Trek* series from 1987 through 2005. And in 2008, Leonard Nimoy and producer Jeffrey Katzenberg received Lifetime Achievement Awards for their work with the franchise.

Technical Commendations

If voters in prestigious categories like Best Picture, Best Drama, and Best Actor have ignored *Star Trek* over the decades, members of the various film and television technical unions and guilds—industry insiders who know good craftsmanship when they see it—have recognized the franchise repeatedly. Although these awards are little-known outside Hollywood, they are cherished by the technicians and artisans who receive them because they represent their peers' highest accolades.

- By far, the organization that has honored *Star Trek* most frequently is the American Society of Composers, Authors and Publishers, which bestows its ASCAP Film and Television Music Awards each year. ASCAP named *The Next Generation* Top TV Series in 1995. *Deep Space Nine* won the same award in 1996, 1997, and 1998. Then *Voyager* won it in 1999, 2000, and 2001. *Enterprise* continued *Star Trek*'s dominance by winning the award in 2002. In addition, *Star Trek Generations* was named the ASC's Top Box Office Film in 1995.
- The Art Directors Guild has also decorated *Star Trek* several times. *Deep Space Nine* won its award for Best Television Series in 1996. *Voyager* earned nominations in the same category four years in a row, from 1997 to 2000. And Abrams's *Star Trek* was nominated as Best Fantasy Film in 2009. Guild members appreciate the tremendous effort and skill it takes to conjure "new life and new civilizations" on a weekly basis.
- The Cinema Audio Society of America also has frequently honored the franchise. *The Next Generation* episode "The Descent" won a CAS Award in 1994 for Outstanding Achievement in Sound Mixing for Television. In 1995, the *Next Gen* adventure "Genesis" was nominated in the same category. So

were installments of *Voyager* in 1998, 2000, and 2001. Abrams's *Star Trek* was nominated for Outstanding Achievement in Sound Mixing for Motion Pictures in 2010.

- The American Society of Cinematographers nominated both *Star Trek IV: The Voyage Home* and the 1998 *DS9* episode "Crossover" for its ASC Awards.
- Despite the lack of Oscar and Emmy recognition for the show's cast, the Screen Actors Guild awarded the franchise, as an entity, a special award in 1995 for "Outstanding Portrayal of the American Scene." In 2009, the Abrams *Star Trek* won an award for the ensemble work of its stunt performers.
- In 1990, Melinda Snodgrass's *Next Generation* teleplay "The Measure of a Man" was nominated as Best Episodic Drama by the Writers Guild of America. In 2010, the Guild nominated Roberto Orci and Alex Kurtzman's *Star Trek* script for Best Adapted Screenplay.

Other Awards

The franchise has claimed a handful of additional awards over the decades. Other notable accomplishments include the following:

- *The Next Generation* episode "The Big Goodbye" won a George Foster Peabody Award for excellence in broadcasting. Although not as widely known, this is the equivalent of an Emmy to television professionals.
- *Star Trek* is widely admired for its depiction of minorities, and its cast members have reaped accolades as a result. Nichelle Nichols won one of the first NAACP Image Awards in 1967. Avery Brooks of *Deep Space Nine* was nominated for an Image Award in 1995. And LeVar Burton has won an astounding five Image Awards—in 1994, 1995, 1999, 2002, and 2003—but none of them were for *Star Trek*. They were all for his acclaimed PBS children's series *Reading Rainbow*. The ALMA Awards, sponsored by the National Council of LaRaza and serving a similar purpose as the NAACP Image Awards for persons of Latino heritage, has honored *Star Trek* twice. In 2000, it gave its Outstanding Achievement in a Television Series award to Robert Beltran and Roxann Dawson of *Voyager*, and in 2010, Clifton Collins Jr. and Zoe Saldana were both nominated for their roles in Abrams's *Star Trek*.
- Abrams's film remains the most-laureled of all *Trek* productions. In addition to the honors already mentioned, the picture earned an Eddie Award nomination from the American Cinema Editors. It was nominated for five different Taurus World Stunt Awards, bestowed annually since 2001 by the Taurus World Stunt Academy for excellence in stunt work. It received two nominations from the British Academy of Film and Television Arts (the British Oscars) for its sound and visual effects. Its soundtrack album was nominated for a Grammy. It was nominated as Favorite Movie at the 2010 People's Choice Awards. And actor Chris Pine was nominated as both "Best Breakout Star" and "Best Badass Star" at the 2010 MTV Movie Awards.

40

Star Trek Lives!

The Continuing Voyages

When *Star Trek: Enterprise* was cancelled in May 2005, there was no TV series standing ready to replace it and no new *Trek* movie in the pipeline. Many assumed that the franchise was finished. Critics eulogized *Star Trek*, and fans poured out their emotions in blogs and on Internet message boards. "As long as there are fans thinking, writing, and doing, *Trek* . . . will never die," someone identified as "Kesvirit," an administrator on the Klingon Imperial Forums website, posted on July 1, 2005. *Star Trek* and its ideals will survive, the fan continued, "so long as they are kept alive in our minds and deeds." At the 2005 Saturn Awards, a Special Achievement Award was bestowed on "the *Star Trek* TV Series (1987–2005)," encompassing *The Next Generation*, *Deep Space Nine*, *Voyager*, and *Enterprise*. The honor was considered posthumous. Once again, however, *Star Trek* refused to stay dead.

False Starts

It wasn't easy to kill *Star Trek* in the first place. Even a low-rated series like *Enterprise*, unpopular even with many die-hard Trekkers, inspired extraordinary rescue efforts. "Superfan" Tim Brazeal founded the TrekUnited campaign, which collected more than $143,000 in cash and more than $3 million in pledges from *Trek* fans willing to help fund a fifth season of *Enterprise*. Finally, John Wentworth, Paramount's vice president of marketing, was forced to issue a statement on March 15, 2005. "Paramount Network Television and the producers of *Star Trek: Enterprise* are very flattered and impressed by the fans' passionate outpouring of attention for the show and their efforts to raise funds to continue the show's production," he wrote. But "the recent decision to conclude the show's run on UPN is final. We cannot and will not be able to accept funds from viewers to produce *Star Trek: Enterprise* or any other series." Nevertheless, the TrekUnited effort proved that, even with its membership diminished, Trekdom remained a powerful market force. Paramount's allied media divisions continued to publish *Star Trek* novels and comic books, and to sell *Trek* merchandise of every conceivable variety. That's why, even as the media was administering *Star Trek*'s last rites, studio executives were searching for ways to resurrect the franchise.

Programming executives at CBS Interactive, the Internet division of CBS Television—which, like Paramount, was then owned by media conglomerate

Viacom—proposed a new *Star Trek* animated series modeled after the popular *Star Wars Clone Wars* series, which had debuted in 2003. The plan was to introduce the series though short "webisodes" released on StarTrek.com. In late 2005, CBS hired Zero Room Productions to produce five six-minute shorts, but development never continued past the script phase. Titled *Star Trek: Final Frontier*, the proposed series was extremely dark in tone. It was set in the twenty-sixth century, following a devastating war between the Federation and the Romulan Empire that left much of the galaxy impassable to warp-drive starships. In the wake of this carnage, according to a plot synopsis posted on the Zero Room website, "starships once responsible for exploring the galaxy and maintaining diplomatic relations with non-Federation worlds were recalled to patrol the borders, and the scientific mandate of Starfleet was abandoned in favor of isolation and protectionism." But Captain Alexander Chase of the USS *Enterprise* defies orders and strikes out to explore strange new worlds and new civilizations, regardless of the consequences. The five completed teleplays, as well as character designs, storyboards, and other illustrations, are available at the website http://zeroroom.squarespace.com.

Around the same time CBS hired Zero Room to create *Final Frontier*, Paramount entered into discussions with writer-producer-director Bryan Singer—who had enjoyed success in both motion pictures (including the first two installments of the *X-Men* series) and television (as producer of the hit medical drama *House*)—about a proposed new TV show titled *Star Trek: Federation*. The concept, developed by Singer along with writer Christopher McQuarrie and producer Meyer Burnett, was similar in some respects to the animated *Final Frontier*. *Federation* would have been set in the year 3000, in an era when the United Federation of Planets, having achieved its utopian goals, has grown complacent and corrupt. Vulcan (now reunified with Romulus), Bajor, and Betazed have left the alliance, and the Ferengi have emerged as a powerful force. When a mysterious new threat known as the Scourge appears, Captain Alexander Kirk (a descendent of James T.) and the latest starship *Enterprise* are assigned to investigate. Work on both *Final Frontier* and *Federation* was abandoned in spring of 2006, when Paramount announced that *Star Trek*'s return would happen not on TV or the Internet, but on movie screens.

From the outset, Paramount executives' preferred vehicle for the revival of *Star Trek* was a feature film, which involved a smaller up-front investment and fewer risks than creating a new TV show, and promised greater financial returns than an Internet cartoon series. Savvy fans knew this and, on *Star Trek* websites, lobbied for a new *Next Generation* movie, or a *Trek* superfilm that would involve the combined *Next Gen*, *Deep Space Nine*, and *Voyager* casts. Executive producer Rick Berman and writer Erik Jendresen wrote a screenplay called *Star Trek: The Beginning*, which was set during the era between *Enterprise*, which had concluded with the founding of the United Federation of Planets, and the classic series. But none of these ideas were seriously considered by studio executives, who believed that whatever course the franchise took next, it needed to be radically different than anything in recent memory. Like many fans, they also felt that the franchise needed new leadership. Paramount announced in April 2006 that Berman was no longer associated with *Star Trek* and had moved on to other projects. By then, the studio was wooing his successor.

New Directions

After tentative discussions with Sam Raimi, maker of the *Evil Dead* and *Spider-Man* films, fizzled out, Paramount began pursuing writer-producer-director J. J. Abrams, the creative force behind the smash TV shows *Lost* and *Alias*. Initial reports linked Abrams with *Star Trek* as early as spring of 2006, but Abrams didn't officially announce that he had agreed to produce and direct the eleventh *Star Trek* picture until February 2007. The studio granted full creative control to Abrams and his Bad Robot Productions team, including writers Roberto Orci and Alex Kurtzman, both of whom were avid Trekkers. Abrams, Orci, Kurtzman, and producers Damon Lindelof and Bryan Burk were tasked with "rebooting" the franchise—rebranding *Star Trek* to widen its appeal without alienating its core fans. After much brainstorming, Abrams and company arrived at the same conclusion producer Harve Bennett had reached fifteen years earlier—that the best way to invite new audiences into *Star Trek* was to recast the classic roles and start over, from the beginning. The Bad Robot team immediately began work on a prequel that would reveal the origins of the Kirk-Spock team during Kirk's tenure at Starfleet Academy. The concept bore many similarities to Bennett's proposed *Star Trek: The Academy Years* movie, which Paramount scuttled in 1990. (For the full story behind this project, see Chapter 19, "The Trek Not Taken.")

For the prequel concept to have dramatic credibility, Abrams and his collaborators believed, the franchise's vacuum-sealed, force-field-protected continuity had to be broken. After all, if audiences already knew every detail about the characters' future lives, what's the point? To open the scenario to new possibilities, Orci and Kurtzman suggested a time-travel story involving an alternate timeline in which the events of *Star Trek* "history" could unfold differently. This tactic allowed the writers to cherry-pick those elements of *Trek* mythology that interested them while disregarding anything they didn't like. The resulting screenplay offered a more belligerent Captain Kirk and a more emotional Commander Spock and featured the destruction of the planet Vulcan, radical changes that incensed some fans. However, Abrams was quick to point out that his movie's alternate timeline did not invalidate events in the separate, already established "primary" *Star Trek* timeline. Orci cited the *Next Generation* episode "Parallels" as canonical evidence of other, alternate *Trek* universes like the one in which the movie takes place. The classic, Roddenberrian *Trek*-verse still exists and (at least theoretically) could return as the setting for other movies or TV shows.

To shore up support for this idea, Abrams enlisted the help of a franchise heavyweight. "We knew that changing the timeline was going to be an extremely controversial decision and that's why we knew the only person who could technically be responsible for that would be Mr. Spock himself, Leonard Nimoy," said Kurtzman in a DVD interview. Abrams figured (correctly) that most fans would go along with the concept if it had Nimoy's blessing. Nimoy was impressed with the draft screenplay and eagerly agreed to participate. Abrams also reached out to other original cast members, including William Shatner, Nichelle Nichols, George Takei, and Walter Koenig, all of whom were invited to the set to meet the actors playing their youthful counterparts. Shatner elected not to participate because he was disappointed that he (unlike Nimoy) would have no role in Abrams's film. This was because the incident that hurls Spock back in time and alters history occurs *after* Kirk's death in *Star Trek Generations*.

In one of many decisions aimed at attracting new viewers, Abrams's film was titled simply *Star Trek*, with no roman numerals, colons, or subtitles. Paramount assigned the picture a budget of $140 million, the most of any *Star Trek* feature to date but modest by the contemporary standards of a science fiction blockbuster (James Cameron's *Avatar*, also released in 2009, cost $425 million). Soon Abrams and his Bad Robot team were consumed with polishing the script, hiring a cast, and redesigning the entire *Trek* universe.

New Recruits

Orci and Kurtzman's 128-page screenplay was completed on October 8, 2007, after four drafts. Early versions of the script included Captain Garrovick (Kirk's former commanding officer, mentioned in the classic episode "Obsession"), Carol Marcus (from *Star Trek II*, mother of Kirk's son, David), and other characters later eliminated to tighten the story's focus on Kirk and Spock. The basic plot remained the same throughout all four drafts: Nero, a revenge-crazed Romulan, is drawn into the past along with Ambassador Spock by an astronomical disaster that destroys Romulus. Nero kills Jim Kirk's father, George, and hundreds of other Starfleet officers, sending the entire galaxy down a new path. Twenty years later, cadet Kirk and instructor Spock, heretofore adversaries, unite to stop Nero, who intends to use a superweapon from the future to destroy every Federation planet, beginning with Vulcan. Along the way, Kirk and Spock cross paths with the elder "Spock Prime" (Nimoy), who survived his journey into the past and encounter with Nero. To engage hardcore fans, Orci and Kurtzman laced the screenplay with offhand references to places and characters from classic *Trek* episodes. To appeal to general audiences, they followed Abrams's dictum that the story feature the same sort of frenetic pace and thrilling action sequences as George Lucas's original *Star Wars* trilogy.

Abrams and his collaborators tried to strike a balance, honoring the tradition of the franchise while offering a fresh approach to many aspects of the production. Concept artist Ryan Church, for instance, created an elegant *Enterprise* that closely resembled Matt Jefferies's classic starship. Costume designer Michael Kaplan's Starfleet uniforms were stylish updates of William Ware Theiss's iconic costumes, complete with gold, blue, and red tunics. Makeup artists Joel Harlow and Barney Burman devised modern equivalents of many of Fred Phillips's famous *Star Trek* aliens, and invented several new ones as well. Production designer Scott Chambliss lent the *Enterprise* bridge and other sets a sleek yet functional look strikingly different from any previous version.

April Webster and Alyssa Weisberg, who had served as casting directors on *Lost*, helped Abrams with the most daunting aspect of the production: finding replacements for *Star Trek*'s legendary original cast. Englishman Simon Pegg, who gained stardom in the title role of *Shaun of the Dead* (2004), was invited by Abrams to play Scotty. Most of the rest of the cast had to endure an exhausting audition process. Pittsburgh native Zachary Quinto, who had worked primarily in television, won the coveted role of Spock, while New Zealander Karl Urban, who had played supporting roles in several movies and TV series, was picked to play Dr. McCoy. Three relative unknowns—Korean American John Cho, Russian American Anton Yelchin, and African American Zoe Saldana—were hired to play Sulu, Chekov, and Uhura. The toughest role to cast was James T. Kirk. Eventually, Los Angeles–born Chris Pine, who had also worked mainly on TV, was selected for the role. Canadian Bruce Greenwood and Aussie Eric Bana, both Hollywood veterans, were hired to play important supporting roles as Captain Christopher Pike and the villainous Nero, respectively. Numerous other big-name performers, including Matt Damon, Ben Affleck, Philip Seymour Hoffman, Russell Crowe, and Gary Sinise, were rumored to be in the running for various parts, but most of these reports were erroneous. Majel Barrett-Roddenberry supplied the voice of the *Enterprise* computer, completing her work shortly before her death on December 18, 2008. In postproduction, Wil Wheaton dubbed the voices of several secondary Romulan characters.

Production, which ran from November 7, 2007, through March 27, 2008, proceeded without incident, even though the shoot was complicated by a Writers Guild strike for the first three months. During the strike, no changes could be made to the shooting script, although Abrams could make suggestions and cast members were allowed to improvise. The picture was shot mostly on Paramount soundstages, some of which—including stages eight and nine—had been used by *Star Trek* for decades. Abrams hired Industrial Light & Magic and Digital Domain, which had worked on *Star Trek Nemesis,* to supply visual effects and composer Michael Giacchino to write the score. Giacchino would win an Oscar for his other 2009 film score, for Disney/Pixar's animated feature *Up. Star Trek* was originally slated for release Christmas Day 2008, but when postproduction ran long (the film wasn't finished until December 23), Paramount announced that it would delay the picture's debut until February 13, 2009. A few weeks later, the studio rethought that decision and pushed *Star Trek*'s release back to May to maximize its box-office potential during the summer blockbuster season. Based on the enthusiastic response of test audiences, the studio knew it had a hit and wanted to make the most of it.

Reception

Abrams's *Star Trek* opened May 8, 2009, and promptly shattered all previous box-office records for the franchise. It earned nearly $258 million in the U.S. and $386 million worldwide, making it easily the most profitable entry in the series, even when factoring in its higher production and marketing costs. The next-best-performing picture was *Star Trek IV: The Voyage Home*, which made $133 million worldwide ($278 million in inflation-adjusted dollars). *Star Trek*'s critical reception was also overwhelmingly positive. The Metacritic website, which compiles critiques from media outlets all over the country, lists thirty-five positive reviews for *Star Trek*, two mixed reviews, and no negative ones. Nearly every important movie critic in the country raved about the picture. The *Washington Post*'s Joe Morgenstern wrote that "*Star Trek* goes back to the legend's roots with a boldness that brings a fatigued franchise back to life." *Slate* critic Dana Stevens ventured that the film "retains the original *Star Trek*'s spirit of optimism, curiosity and humor." Not all Trekkers agreed, however. Metacritic's fan-written User Reviews (as of this writing) include 58 negatives and 41 mixed, against 383 positives. A user identified only as John J. spoke for many naysayers when he wrote, "I can't believe that any *Star Trek* fan enjoyed this movie. It failed, in every aspect, to capture the spirit of what made *Star Trek* great." While it's safe to say that most *Star Trek* fans liked the 2009

During the run-up to the release of *Star Trek into Darkness* in 2013, Paramount issued the landmark *Next Generation* two-parter "The Best of Both Worlds" (remastered and spliced together into a single feature film) to select movie theaters. This one-day-only event was timed to build interest in the upcoming Blu-ray debut of *Next Gen* Season Three and to keep Trekkers happy as they awaited the second J.J. Abrams picture movie, not all of them were as enthusiastic as general audiences. However, this was precisely the result that Abrams—and Paramount—was hoping for: A movie with mass appeal that would remain acceptable to most hardcore devotees. Abrams's movie also garnered more awards than any previous *Trek* feature, including the franchise's first Oscar, for makeup (its sound design, sound editing, and visual effects also earned Academy Award nominations). *Star Trek* was nominated for a Hugo but lost to *Avatar.* For a complete rundown of the picture's many honors, see Chapter 39, "Starfleet Commendations Revisited."

Assessing *Star Trek* (2009)

Abrams's *Star Trek* is an impressive achievement on many levels. Despite the slings and arrows hurled at it by traditionalist fans, it's a credible, twenty-first-century update of Roddenberry's creation. It's faster paced, darker, and sexier than the original, but holds fast to the same guiding optimism and progressive ideals. It's also the very model of a modern sci-fi blockbuster—breathlessly paced and stylishly performed, with a fistful of showstopping action sequences.

The picture hums along at warp six, establishing its altered-timeline setting with an operatic precredit sequence in which Nero destroys the USS *Kelvin* on the day of Jim Kirk's birth (and his father's death). Then the movie immediately introduces the young Kirk and Spock, who remain the focus of the story thereafter as the film zips from one spectacular visual effects sequence to the next, including the gut-wrenching scene in which Nero obliterates Vulcan. In this altered *Trek*-verse, both Kirk and Spock are troubled loners who lash out at bullies and rebel against authority figures. Also, both are younger and more impulsive than the seasoned Kirk and Spock seen on the classic TV series. Pine and Quinto bring surprising emotional depth to their roles. Pine emphasizes Kirk's impulsive, unpredictable side but also radiates enough charisma and self-assurance to make the crew's allegiance to him believable. Quinto's subtle work underscores Spock's emotional wounds without descending into bathos. During Spock's meeting with the Vulcan Science Council, Quinto's acidic delivery of the line "Live long and prosper" makes it sound like code for "Go screw yourself." Pine, Quinto, and the rest of the cast, to their credit, refuse to simply mimic their famous predecessors. All are effective, especially Urban as McCoy, Yelchin as Chekov, and Pegg as Scotty, whose take on the character could not be more different than James Doohan's. Greenwell contributes an outstanding supporting performance as Captain Pike.

However, the picture's frantic pace masks serious flaws in story logic. To cite only the two most egregious examples: The plot hinges, in part, on Uhura intercepting a secret Klingon communiqué and sharing the information with her Orion roommate (and Kirk), but not with her superior officers. It also includes a preposterous coincidence—that Kirk, stuffed in a life pod and jettisoned from the *Enterprise,* crashes on the same planet where Nero has conveniently exiled "Spock Prime" (Nimoy). Scotty is also stationed there, improbably. Sometimes

Abrams's desire to make his *Star Trek* more *Star Wars*–like gets the better of him. Kirk's adventures on the ice planet Delta Vega seem uncomfortably similar to the early Hoth scenes from *The Empire Strikes Back* (1980), and Scotty's diminutive alien friend Keenser (played by Deep Roy) plays like a cross between a Jawa and an Ewok. Some of the reimagined characters are more likeable than others. This Dr. McCoy seems unusually bitter and cynical, although the recentness of his heartbreaking divorce (which is part of *Trek* lore but was seldom discussed in previous episodes and movies) may account for this. The film works best if viewers simply accept that this is an alternate universe populated by different versions of the familiar characters.

Despite these flaws, *Star Trek* succeeds because it's a work of unbridled energy, imagination, and ambition. Although fans may disagree with some of the choices made by Abrams, Orci, and Kurtzman, the reality is that after *Nemesis* and *Enterprise*, the franchise had been written into a corner. Abrams and his compatriots simply did what was necessary to break out of that trap, while crafting a livelier, more sensational, and more emotional *Star Trek* with wide appeal beyond the Trekker faithful. The film may or may not mark the passing of the previous, statelier version of the franchise, but its success has assured that *Trek* will continue, in some form or another, for years to come.

The Continuing Voyages

As of this writing (in the fall of 2012), Abrams's sequel *Star Trek into Darkness* was slated for release in May of 2013—just a couple of weeks prior to the projected publication date for this book. As with every other *Trek* film, details of the plot have been closely guarded. No trailers have yet been released. Many media outlets have reported that the film will feature Englishman Benedict Cumberbatch, best known as Sherlock Holmes on the BBC series *Sherlock*, as Khan Noonien Singh, although Urban, in an interview published on the TrekMovie.com website, said Cumberbatch would play Gary Mitchell, the villain from the second *Star Trek* pilot, "Where No Man Has Gone Before." Whatever the content of the film, however, Abrams's sophomore effort represents a potential turning point for the franchise. Another smash on the scale of the 2009 picture would all but guarantee *Star Trek*'s continuance for the foreseeable future; a flop would threaten the franchise's momentum, at the very least. Rarely has *Star Trek* managed back-to-back critical and popular successes. Further, for the franchise to reclaim the glory of its late 1980s heyday, Paramount will have to continue the film series for at least another couple of entries and eventually invest in another TV series. Some fans have even speculated about the possibility of recasting and rebooting *The Next Generation*. No such projects are currently in development, but in the world of *Star Trek*, as Spock once said, there are always possibilities.

Bibliography

Books

Alexander, David. *Star Trek Creator: The Authorized Biography of Gene Roddenberry.*
New York: Penguin, 1994.

Block, Paula M., with Terry J. Erdman. *Star Trek: The Original Series 365.* New
York: Abrams, 2010.

Block, Paula M., with Terry J. Erdman. *Star Trek: The Next Generation 365.* New
York: Abrams, 2012.

Bond, Jeff. *The Music of Star Trek.* Hollywood, CA: Lone Eagle, 1999.

Brooks, Tim, and Earle Marsh. *The Complete Directory to Prime Time Network and
Cable TV Shows 1946–Present* (7th ed.). New York: Ballantine, 1999.

Doohan, James, with Peter David. *Beam Me Up, Scotty: Star Trek's "Scotty" in His
Own Words.* New York: Pocket Books, 1996.

Engel, Joel. *Gene Roddenberry: The Myth and the Man Behind Star Trek.* New York:
Hyperion, 1994.

Erdmann, Terry J. *The Secrets of Star Trek: Insurrection.* New York: Pocket Books,
1998.

Fern, Yvonne. *Gene Roddenberry: The Last Conversation.* New York: Pocket Books,
1994.

Gerrold, David. *The World of Star Trek.* New York: Ballantine, 1973.

Gross, Edward. *Trek: The Lost Years.* Las Vegas, NV: Pioneer, 1989.

Gross, Edward, and Mark Altman. *Captains' Logs: The Unauthorized Complete Trek
Voyages.* New York: Little, Brown, 1995.

Gross, Edward, and Mark Altman. *Great Birds of the Galaxy: Gene Roddenberry and
the Creators of Star Trek.* New York: Image, 1992.

Kelley, Steve. *Star Trek: The Collectibles.* Iola, WI: Krause, 2008.

Koenig, Walter. *Warped Factors: A Neurotic's Guide to the Universe.* Dallas: Taylor,
1997.

Meyer, Nicholas. *The View from the Bridge: Memories of Star Trek and a Life in
Hollywood.* New York: Viking, 2009.

McNeil, Alex. *Total Television: The Complete Guide to Programming from 1948 to the
Present* (4th Ed.) New York: Penguin, 1996.

Nichols, Nichelle. *Beyond Uhura: Star Trek and Other Memories.* New York:
Boulevard, 1994.

Nimoy, Leonard. *I Am Not Spock.* Cutchogue, NY: Buccaneer, 1976.

Nimoy, Leonard. *I Am Spock.* New York: Hyperion, 1995.

Phillips, Mark, and Frank Garcia. *Science Fiction Television Series: Episode Guides, Histories, and Casts and Credits for 62 Prime-Time Shows, 1959–1989.* Jefferson, NC: McFarland, 2006.

Rioux, Terry Lee. *From Sawdust to Stardust: The Biography of DeForest Kelley, Star Trek's Dr. McCoy.* New York: Pocket Books, 2005.

Sackett, Susan. *Inside Trek: My Secret Life with Star Trek Creator Gene Roddenberry.* Tulsa, OK: Hawk, 2002.

Sackett, Susan, and Gene Roddenberry. *The Making of Star Trek: The Motion Picture.* New York: Pocket Books, 1980.

Schuster, Hal. *The Trekker's Guide to The Next Generation: Complete, Unauthorized and Uncensored.* Rocklin, CA: Prima, 1997.

Shatner, Lisabeth. *Captain's Log: William Shatner's Personal Account of the Making of Star Trek V: The Final Frontier.* New York: Pocket Books, 1989.

Shatner, William, and Chris Kreski. *Star Trek Movie Memories.* New York: HarperCollins, 1994.

Shatner, William, with David Fisher. *Up Till Now.* New York: St. Martin's, 2008.

Shrager, Adam. *The Finest Crew in the Fleet: The Next Generation Cast on Screen and Off.* New York: Wolf Valley, 1997.

Smith, Christine. *DeForest Kelley—A Harvest of Memories: My Life and Times with a Remarkable Gentleman Actor.* Self-Published, 2001.

Solow, Herbert F., and Robert Justman. *Inside Star Trek: The Real Story.* New York: Pocket Books, 1996.

Stevens Jr., George (ed.). *Conversations with the Great Moviemakers of Hollywood's Golden Age at the American Film Institute.* New York: Knopf, 2006.

Takei, George. *To the Stars: The Autobiography of George Takei, Star Trek's Mr. Sulu.* New York: Pocket Books, 1995.

Van Hise, James. *The Unauthorized Trekker's Guide to The Next Generation and Deep Space Nine.* New York: HarperPrism, 1995.

Wheaton, Wil. *Just a Geek: Unflinchingly Honest Tales of the Search for Life, Love and Fulfillment Beyond the Starship Enterprise.* Sebastopol, CA: O'Reilly, 2004.

Wheaton, Wil. *Memories of the Future, Volume 1.* Arcadia, CA: Monolith, 2011.

Whitney, Grace Lee, with Jim Denney. *The Longest Trek: My Tour of the Galaxy* (2nd Ed.). Sanger, CA: Quill Driver, 2007.

Periodicals

"The End of a Golden Era: The Final Year of the Most Successful Science Fiction Series Ever on Television," Dale Kutzera. *Cinefantastique*, Vol. 25 No. 6/Vol. 26 No. 1 (double issue), December 1994.

"Patrick Stewart Lets Down His Hair," David Rensin. *TV Guide*, July 31, 1993.

DVDs

I, Claudius. Image Entertainment, 2000.
Mind Meld: Secrets Behind the Voyage of a Lifetime. Goldhill Home Media, 2001.
Night Court: Complete Seasons 1–3. Warner Home Video, 2010.
Star Trek: Deep Space Nine—The Complete Series. Paramount Pictures, 2004.
Star Trek: Digital Copy Special Edition. Paramount Pictures, 2009.
Star Trek: Enterprise—The Complete Series. Paramount Pictures, 2005.
Star Trek: First Contact—Special Collector's Edition. Paramount Pictures, 2005.
Star Trek Generations—Special Collector's Edition. Paramount Pictures, 2004.
Star Trek II: The Wrath of Khan—The Director's Edition. Paramount Pictures, 2002.
Star Trek III: The Search for Spock—Special Collector's Edition. Paramount Pictures, 2002.
Star Trek: Insurrection—Special Collector's Edition. Paramount Pictures, 2005.
Star Trek IV: The Voyage Home—Special Collector's Edition. Paramount Pictures, 2002.
Star Trek Nemesis. Paramount Pictures, 2002.
Star Trek: The Motion Picture—The Director's Edition. Paramount Pictures, 2001.
Star Trek: The Next Generation—Seasons 1–7. Paramount Pictures, 2002.
Star Trek V: The Search for Spock—Special Collector's Edition. Paramount Pictures, 2003.
Star Trek VI: The Undiscovered Country—Special Collector's Edition. Paramount Pictures, 2004.
Star Trek: Voyager—Seasons 1–7. Paramount Pictures, 2004.

Websites

http://bluray.highdefdigest.com/news/show/Fun_Stuff/Star_Trek_The_Next_Generation/Jonathan_Frakes/Tom_Landy/Star_Trek/Comic-Con/HDD_Attends_Central_Canada_Comic-Cons_QA_with_Jonathan_Frakes/7987
http://www.boxofficemojo.com/movies/?id=startrek2.htm
http://www.brooklineconnection.com/history/Personalities/Sallin.html
http://collider.com/colm-meaney-hell-on-wheels-bel-ami-interview/125101/
http://www.digitalspy.com/tv/news/a334351/star-trek-to-return-to-tv-as-animated-series.html
http://www.emmytvlegends.org/interviews/people/rick-berman
http://furiousfanboys.com/2010/09/the-star-trek-insurrection-that-almost-was/
http://herocomplex.latimes.com/2011/06/10/star-trek-nicholas-meyers-explains-his-roddenberry-regret/
http://holykaw.alltop.com/1987-letter-reveals-star-trek-tng-casting-cho?c=1
http://www.imdb.com/
http://www.mailtribune.com/apps/pbcs.dll/article?AID=/20100802/NEWS/8020309/-1/rss01

http://en.memory-alpha.org/wiki/Portal:Main

http://en.memory-alpha.org/wiki/Memory_Alpha:AOL_chats

http://movies.ign.com/articles/444/444306p11.html

http://www.nielsen.com/us/en.html

http://nmeyer.pxl.net/biography.html

http://www.startrek.com/

http://startrekdom.blogspot.com/2007/06/saving-star-trek-from-gene-roddenberry.html

http://www.startrek.com/article/david-warner-recounts-his-trek-adventures

http://www.the-numbers.com/movies/1982/0STK2.php

http://trekmovie.com/2012/03/23/exclusive-brent-spiner-interviewpart-2-talks-bad-tng-episodes-why-nemesis-bombed-jj-trek-franchise-future/

http://trekmovie.com/2007/07/14/interview-with-nicholas-meyer/

http://trekmovie.com/2006/08/01/sirtis-burton-want-trek-xi-to-be-a-tng-filmsay-nemesis-sucked-video/

http://www.trektoday.com/interviews/harve_bennett_2006.shtml

http://www.trektoday.com/interviews/nick_sagan_part_one.shtml

http://trekweb.com/articles/2010/09/22/Michael-Pillers-Unpublished-Book-The-Writing-of-Star-Trek-Insurrection-Available-for-Download-at-TrekCore.shtml

http://tvseriesfinale.com/tv-show/star-trek-cbs-considers-a-new-animated-series/

http://www.usinflationcalculator.com/

http://www.wikipedia.org/

http://www.youtube.com/

Index

"11001001" (episode), 73, 278, 388
1776, 362
2001: A Space Odyssey 4, 8, 124
24,119, 150
48 HRS, 37, 61
7th Heaven, 155
"10", 61
3rd Rock from the Sun, 363, 370

Abatemarco, Frank, 249, 252
ABC Television, 10, 11, 14, 47, 55, 57, 79. 83, 114, 117, 119, 328
Abraham, F. Murray, 164, 314, 315, 318
Abrams, J. J., xv, 119–20, 198, 199, 395–400
Academy Awards, The (Oscars), 6, 8, 13, 17, 19, 33, 42, 91, 93, 94, 99, 125, 148, 159, 164, 179, 186, 187, 188, 194, 206, 213, 301, 307, 308, 314, 315, 320, 323, 324, 326, 364, 385, 389–90, 397, 399
Academy of Science Fiction, Fantasy and Horror Films, 391
Academy of Television Arts and Sciences, 118, 152, 387
"Academy Years, The" (screenplay), 195–99, 395
Adler, Alan, 173
Adventures of Robin Hood, The, 179
Affleck, Ben, 397
*After M*A*S*H*, 185
Agony Booth (website), 102
Agutter, Jenny, 53
Alaimo, Marc,175
Alexander, David, 45, 123
Ali, 364
Alias, 120, 395
Alien, 52, 78, 87, 109, 306, 389
Alien Nation, 181, 340
Alien Resurrection, 305
Aliens 26, 42, 50
"All Good Things . . . " (episode), 83, 94, 118, 132, 160, 230, 239, 242, 244, 251, 278, 292–95, 299, 301, 304, 333–34, 356, 358, 366, 389, 390
All in the Family, 148
"All Our Yesterdays" (episode), 265
All That Jazz, 389
All the President's Men 155
"Allegiance" (episode), 140–41, 334, 388
Allen, Chad, 170
Allen, Corey, 86
Allen, Woody, 56, 192

Alley, Kirstie, 20, 25, 31, 35, 57, 147, 157, 165, 203, 205
Alliance for Creative Theater Education and Research (ACTER), 55
Altered States, 124
Altman, Mark, 45, 65, 140, 177, 196, 281, 301, 302
Amadeus, 164, 315
Amazing Stories, 392
American Cinema Editors, 393
American Playhouse, 56
American Society of Cinematographers, 42, 392
American Society of Composers, Authors and Publishers, 391
American Werewolf in London, An, 53
Amnesty International, 253, 329
"Amok Time" (episode), 67, 70, 264
"And the Children Shall Lead" (episode), 262, 264
Anderson, Erich, 219
Anderson, Harry, 56
Anderson, John, 131, 156–57
Anderson, Judith, 31, 35
Anderson, Lindsay, 158
Andrews, Dana, 254
"Angel One" (episode), 64, 72–73, 268
Anna and the King, 185
Apocalypse Now 174, 312
Apollo, 13 93
"Apple, The" (episode), 69
"Aquiel" (episode), 254
Archive of American Television, 52, 114, 327
"Arena" (episode), 67, 132, 238
Arenberg, Lee, 291
Armageddon, 120
Armstrong, Vaughn, 52, 343
Armus, Burton, 99, 103, 104, 228
Arness, James, 365
Around the World in 80 Days, 12
"Arsenal of Freedom, The", (episode) 64, 76, 82, 271
Art Directors Guild, 391
Asimov, Isaac, 116, 123, 262, 371
Assassins, 16
Associates and Ferren, 124, 125, 128
Astar, Shay, 223
A-Team, The, 153
"Attached" (episode), 285, 291, 356
Auberjonois, Rene, 208, 373, 374
Austin, Karen, 363

Austin Chronicle, 316
Avatar, 390, 396, 399
Aviator, The, 326

Babe, 148, 307
Babylon 5, 87, 308, 370, 374
Bader, Hilary, 173, 218, 284
Bailey, Dennis, 141
Baird, Stuart, 322–23, 324, 326
Bakula, Scott, 51, 376, 377, 386
"Balance of Terror" (episode), 79, 174, 372
Baldwin, Alec, 366
Bana, Eric, 397
Banderas, Antonio, 16
Barbary Coast, 148
Bare Essence, 57
Barnes, Clive, 359
Barrett-Roddenberry, Majel, 31, 41, 70,
    143–144, 150, 180, 184, 191, 218, 222,
    237, 243, 284, 348, 353, 365, 379, 397
Baryshnikov, Mikhail, 14
Bateman, Justine,185
Batman (movie), 126
Batman (TV series), 10
Batman: The Animated Series, 164
Bats, 322
"Battle, The" (episode), 69, 229, 270, 291
Battlestar Galactica, 83, 90
Battlestar Galactica ("Reimagined") 31, 150,
    370, 374
Bay, Michael, 120
Beacham, Stephanie, 254
Beagle, Peter S., 143
Beam Me Up, Scotty, (memoir) 6
Beatles, The, 225
Beatty, Bruce, 289
Beaumont, Gabrielle, 85
Beauty and the Beast (TV series), 322, 370
Beauty and the Beast (Disney movie), 192
Becker, 364
Behr, Ira Steven, 119, 129, 141, 166, 179, 313
Beimler, Hans, 103, 130, 132, 140, 166
Belanoff, Adam, 219
Bell Telephone Hour, The, 83
Beltran, Robert, 29, 376, 392
Belushi, Jim, 120, 366
Ben-10, 367
Bennett, Harve, 10–12, 13, 15, 16, 18, 19,
    20–26, 27–33, 34, 36–41, 46, 122–26,
    195–99, 200, 306, 390, 395
Bennett-Katleman Productions, 11
Bergman, Ingrid, 11
Berman, Eddie, 114
Berman, Elizabeth, 114
Berman, Molly, 114
Berman, Rick, 50, 52–53, 81, 94, 95, 98, 105,
    108, 109, 113–16, 117, 118, 119, 129,
    130, 133, 138, 140, 158, 160, 166–67,
    169, 170, 173, 176, 210, 213, 217, 219,
    221, 222, 223, 232, 234, 235, 247, 256,
    280, 281, 295, 296–97, 298, 299, 300,

    301, 303, 304, 306, 307, 308, 312,
    313, 314, 315, 320, 322, 323, 326, 327,
    328, 330, 339, 355, 372, 374, 375, 385,
    394–95
Berman, Tom, 114
Bernard, Alan, 93
Bernsen, Corbin, 136, 188, 231
Berry, Halle, 362
Besch, Bibi, 21, 25
"Best of Both Worlds, The" (episode), 82, 93,
    94, 95, 130, 142, 144–45, 154, 181, 224,
    232, 239, 293, 304, 330–331, 350
"Best of Both Worlds, Part II, The" (episode),
    82, 93, 94, 95, 154, 167–69, 224, 270,
    304, 330–31, 305, 388
Beverly Hills Cop, 37, 147
Bewitched, 11
Beyond Belief: Fact or Fiction, 363
Beyond Reality, 166
Big Bang Theory, The, 362, 364, 367
Big Blue Marble, The, 114
"Big Goodbye, The" (episode), 64, 70–72, 90,
    102, 111, 267, 386, 388, 392
Big Trouble in Little China, 157
Bikel, Theodore, 169
Biller, Kenneth, 118, 119
Bionic Woman, The, 11
Birkin, David Tristan, 251
"Birthright, Part I" (episode), 148, 228, 256,
    277, 284, 307, 348
"Birthright, Part II" (episode), 93, 148, 161, 228,
    256, 307, 348
Bischoff, David, 141
Black Narcissus, 163
Black, John D. F., 66, 69
Blackman, Robert, 90–91, 129
Blade Runner, 24, 26
Blank Check, 185
Blind Date, 58
Blizzard, 87
Block, Paula M., 63, 144, 247
"Blood and Fire" (fan episode), 380
"Bloodlines" (episode), 242, 281, 291–92
Bludhorn, Charles, 11
Blue Angels, 365
Blue Sky Studios, 315, 323
Bole, Cliff, 81, 82–83, 85, 131, 235, 290, 292
"Bonding, The" (episode), 132, 243, 268
Bonsall, Brian, 172, 185, 218, 220, 222, 291, 341
"Booby Trap" (episode), 85, 132, 177, 193, 351
Borg Invasion 4-D, 307
Born Free, 152
Bowman, Chuck, 83
Bowman, Rob, 81, 83
Bradbury, Ray, 16, 205
Braga, Brannon, 118–19, 120, 159, 162, 167–68,
    178, 194, 210, 216, 221, 223, 248, 250,
    252, 254, 256, 257, 260, 280, 282, 284,
    286, 288, 290, 292, 293, 295, 297–98,
    300, 301, 303, 304–6, 309, 312, 372, 375
Bram Stoker's Dracula, 292

Brand, Judith, 245
Brazeal, Tim, 393
Bridge on the River Kwai, The, 256
British Academy of Film and Television Arts
    (BAFTA Awards), 159, 392
Brocksmith, Roy, 111
"Broken Bow" (episode), 148, 307
Bronson, Charles, 58
Bronson, Fred, 143, 216
Bronx Zoo, 119
Brooks, Avery, 53, 373, 392
Brooks, James E., 259
Brooks, Mel, 360
Brooks, Richard, 59
Brophy, Brian, 105
Brothers, 192
"Brothers" (episode), 169–70, 241, 282, 338–39,
    340–41, 388
Broughton, John, 382, 383
Brown, Caitlyn, 284
Brown, Georgia, 169
Bry, Ellen, 252
Buffy the Vampire Slayer, 188, 370
Burger, Robin, 134
Burk, Bryan, 120, 395
Burman, Barney, 397
Burnett, Meyer, 394
Burt, George, 166, 327
Burton, LeVar, 51, 53, 58–60, 61, 67, 86–87,
    101, 103, 129, 132, 177, 178, 211, 219,
    224, 228, 254, 259, 283, 306, 318, 321,
    323–24, 325, 351–53, 356, 363, 364–65,
    387
Burton, Michaela, 365
Burton, Tim, 17
Butrick, Merritt, 21, 25, 31, 35, 77
Buttons, Red, 215
"By Any Other Name" (episode), 73, 250, 266,
    267

"Cage, The" (episode), 7, 18, 19, 184, 266
Cagney & Lacy, 116
Caine Mutiny, The, 84, 179
California Fever, 117
Caligula, 158
Calk, Ethan H., 382
Cameron, James, 42, 307, 396
Campbell, William O., 52, 102–3
Canary Trainer, The, 14
Candy, John, 14
Cantor, Johanna, 263
Captain Planet and the Planeteers, 364
"Captain's Holiday" (episode), 140, 141, 142,
    179, 188, 229, 273, 275, 334, 361
*Captain's Log: William Shatner's Personal
    Account of the Making of Star Trek V:
    The Final Frontier*, 122
*Captains' Logs: The Unauthorized Complete
    Trek Voyages*, 45, 65, 68, 73, 112, 140,
    177, 281, 292
Carradine, David, 57

Carren, David Bennett, 173
Carrigan-Fauci, Jeanne 282
Carroll, J. Larry, 173
Carson, David, 85, 137, 298, 299, 306
Cartwright, Veronica, 87
Cash, Johnny, 57
Castle, 83, 365
Cattrall, Kim, 157, 203, 204, 208
"Cause and Effect" (episode), 85, 221, 260
Caves, Bob, 383
Cawley, James, 378, 379, 380, 381
CBS Interactive, 393–94
CBS Television, 10, 13, 47, 79, 88, 93, 116, 119,
    370, 393
"Cease Fire" (episode), 111, 190
"Chain of Command, Part I" (episode), 95, 147,
    163, 164, 233, 252–53
"Chain of Command, Part II" (episode), 82,
    93, 95, 163, 164, 233, 252–53, 329–30,
    331, 334
Challenger space shuttle, 41
Chalmers, Chip, 327
Chambliss, Scott, 397
"Changeling, The" (episode), 3, 8, 77
Chao, Rosalind, 53, 174, 185–86, 251, 281
Chariots of Fire, 158
"Charlie X" (episode), 264, 292, 382
Charlie's Angels, 82
Charmed, 154, 364
Charno, Sara 218, 220
Charno, Stuart, 218, 220
*Charting the Undiscovered Country: The
    Making of Star Trek VI*, 196
"Chase, The" (episode), 241, 257, 258
Chattaway, Jay, 94–95, 225
Cheers, 16, 25, 49, 56, 89,114, 147, 189, 205,
    221, 386
Cherished Home, The, 364
Chicago Sun-Times, 10, 126, 301, 316, 324
Chicago Tribune, 6, 301, 316
"Child, The" (episode), 94, 97, 100, 175, 239,
    242, 354, 388
Child's Play, 366
China Beach, 386
CHiPs, 60, 189, 342
Cho, John, 397
Christian, Spencer, 328
Christmas Carol, A (one-man production), 86,
    289, 331, 359
Christmas Carol, A (play), 255, 361
Church, Ryan, 396
Cinema Audio Society, 93, 391–92
Citizen Kane, 320
"City on the Edge of Forever, The" (episode),
    37, 67, 225, 304, 380, 390
Clark, Dennis, 3
Clockstoppers, 364
Clockwork Orange, A, 158, 299
Close Encounters of the Third Kind, 4, 5
Close, Glenn, 361
Closer, The, 154, 186, 364

"Clues" (episode), 72, 175–176
Code Name: Emerald, 55
"Code of Honor" (episode), 64, 66, 67, 70, 82
Coe, George, 177
Collins, Christopher, 104
Collins, Clifton Jr., 392
Collins, Robert, 3
Collins, Stephen, 7, 8, 155, 187
Color Purple, The, 99, 187
Columbia Pictures, 192
Columbia Pictures Television, 11
Combs, Jeffrey, 52
"Come What May" (fan episode), 379
Comedy Relief, 348
"Coming of Age" (episode), 74, 75, 78, 235,
    268, 357, 388
Commitments, The, 150
Company Business, 14
Compton, Richard, 87
Confessions of a Homing Pigeon, 13
Conjuring (screenplay), 13
Conley, Lawrence V., 215
Connaught Theatre, 57
Connery, Sean, 124–25, 128, 332
Conrad, Charles, 60
Conrad, Joseph, 174, 312
"Conspiracy" (episode), 64, 75, 78–79, 82, 235,
    275, 276, 388
"Contagion" (episode), 106, 279
"Conundrum" (episode), 93, 217, 219, 388
Conversations with the Great Moviemakers of
    Hollywood's Golden Age, 336
Conway, James L., 258
Conway, Kevin, 259
Cook, Nick, 384
Cool Hand Luke, 316
Cooper, Charles, 172
Cooper, Gary, 336
Copperfield, David, 93
Coppola, Francis Ford, 174, 292, 312
Corbett, Glenn, 148, 307
Corman, Roger, 87
Correll, Charles, 31
Cosby, Bill, 61
Cosby Show, The, 283, 386
"Cost of Living" (episode), 91, 222, 247, 276,
    348, 388
Costello, Ward, 75, 276
Coto, Manny, 118, 119, 372, 375
"Counter-Clock Incident, The" (episode), 73, 251
"Court Martial" (episode), 75
Cow and Chicken, 365
Cox, Nikki, 107
Cox, Ronny, 147, 252–53, 271
Cozart, Stephanie, 365
Crash, 364
Craven, Wes, 362
Crazy from the Heart, 362
Crichton, Michael, 252
Criminal Minds, 263, 367
Cromwell, James, 135, 147–48, 256, 269, 307,
    309

Crosby, Bing, 61
Crosby, Denise, 51, 52, 61, 66, 78, 99, 136, 137,
    138, 172, 185, 187, 212, 217, 293, 322,
    342, 357–58, 366, 379
Crosby, Dennis, 61
Crossing Jordan, 193
Crowe, Russell, 397
Crucier of Blood, The, 153
Culea, Melinda, 220, 221, 273
Cumberbatch, Benedict, 400
Curry, Dan, 49, 93
Curse of the Pink Panther, 61
Curtis, Robin, 31, 35, 147, 157, 165, 205, 283
Curtiz, Michael, 197
Cusack, John, 197
CW Television, 369

Da Vinci's Inquest, 161
Daily Variety, 311
Dallas, 157
Dalton, Timothy, 14
Damon, Gabriel, 132
Damon, Matt, 397
Daniels, Marc, 81, 128
Danny Kaye Show, The, 83
Danson, Ted, 43, 147
Danus, Richard, 135
Dark Crystal, The, 61
"Dark Page" (episode), 222, 284–85
"Darmok" (episode), 192, 213, 214, 216, 236,
    334
"Data's Day" (episode), 174–75, 278, 338
"Datalore" (episode), 64, 72, 83, 236, 279, 341
"Dauphin, The" (episode), 105, 357
David, Peter, 161
Davies, Robinson, 13
Davis, Daniel, 102, 157, 254
Davis, Deborah Dean, 78
Davis, Martin, 198
Day After, The, 14, 17, 25
Day the Earth Stood Still, The, 1, 176
Days of Our Lives, 60, 61, 89
De Lancie, John, 65, 70, 117, 136, 146, 159–61,
    179, 230, 250, 251, 255, 293
De Lancie, Keegan, 161
Dead Walking, 365
Dead Zone, The, 117
"Deadly Years, The" (episode), 104, 380
"Death Wish" (episode), 161, 231
Death Wish 3, 58
"Defector, The" (episode), 84, 134, 186, 190, 271
DeHaas, Timothy, 178
Dehanny, Elizabeth, 144
"Deja Q" (episode), 82, 93, 135–36, 159, 231,
    232, 235, 239, 269, 279, 388
Deliverance, 147
Demon Seed, 60
Dennehy, Brian, 154
Dennehy, Elizabeth, 154
Depp, Johnny, 186
"Descent" (episode), 86, 232, 260–61, 341, 391

"Descent, Part II" (episode), 86, 186, 232, 282, 341, 356
Desperate Housewives, 193
"Devil and Daniel Webster, The", 175
"Devil in the Dark, The" (episode), 75
"Devil's Due" (episode), 164, 175, 244, 388
Dexter, 366
Diagnosis Murder, 364
Die Another Day, 324
Die Hard, 256, 306, 332
Dieghan, Drew, 139
Diff'rent Strokes, 185
Digital Domain, 323, 324, 397
Diller, Barry, 11
Diones, Bruce, 316
"Disaster" (episode), 85, 185, 215, 242, 248, 276, 354
Doctor and the Devils, The, 55
Doctor Who, 164, 361
Doctors, The, 57
Dolly Dearest, 366
Donner, Richard, 16
Doohan, James, 6, 10, 36, 39, 50, 64, 86, 128, 148, 197, 249, 250, 299, 301, 353, 399
"Doomsday Machine, The" (episode), 3, 76, 87, 215, 380
Dorn, Michael, 51, 53, 60, 76, 83, 92, 111, 133, 138, 139, 140, 150, 151, 169, 172, 179, 181, 189, 204, 205, 208, 211, 213, 218, 222, 252, 259, 262, 286, 289, 292, 321, 324, 341, 342–48, 358, 363, 365, 368, 373, 387
Dornish, William, 21
Dot Records, 15
Douglas, Pamela, 177
Down, Lesley-Anne, 57
Doyle, Sir Arthur Conan, 13, 101, 102, 134, 153, 253
Dozier, Robert, 153
Dr. Quinn, Medicine Woman, 189
Drama Desk Award, 187, 359, 361
Dream On, 366
Drescher, Fran, 158
Drive, He Said, 191
"Drumhead, The" (episode), 84, 138, 163, 179, 244, 253, 271, 275, 306, 331–32, 334
Duane, Diane, 68
Dubois, Marta, 164, 175
Dukes of Hazzard, The, 116
Dummy, 59
Dune, 55
Dunn, Cindy, 114
Dunst, Kirsten, 285
Dynasty 158

Earth: Final Conflict, 364, 370
Eastwood, Clint, 164
Eaves, John 89, 307–8
Ebert, Roger, 43, 126, 158, 301, 308, 309, 316, 324

Echevarria, Rene, 138, 144, 181, 210, 223, 228, 232, 251, 254, 256, 259, 282, 284, 286, 288, 290, 291, 292
Edward Scissorhands, 186
Edwards, Blake, 61
Edwards, Geoffrey, 61, 366
Edwards, Paddi, 105
Eidelman, Cliff, 203
Eisner, Michael, 9, 11, 27–28
"Elaan of Troyius" (episode), 249
"Elementary, Dear Data" (episode), 83, 90, 101, 102, 112, 157, 253, 254, 341, 388
"Emergence" (episode), 292
Emergency Room, 53, 60
"Emissary, The" (episode), 111, 112, 172, 189, 227, 268, 344, 346, 347, 389
"Emissary" (episode), 93, 253, 299
Emmy Award, 11, 14, 49, 53, 58, 68, 70, 71, 72, 73, 75, 79, 88, 89, 90, 91, 93, 94, 95, 99, 100, 102, 104, 109, 114, 116, 138, 140, 141, 142, 144, 147, 149, 152, 159, 162, 163, 164, 169, 170, 175, 178, 180, 186, 192, 193, 194, 213, 217, 219, 222, 224, 225, 248, 252, 253, 289, 290, 291, 295, 307, 318, 320, 329, 330, 334, 361, 362, 376, 385, 386, 387–89
"Empath, The" (episode), 140
Empire Strikes Back, The (Star Wars Episode V), 26, 34, 400
Enberg, Alexander, 118, 248, 288, 289
Enberg, Dick, 117
"Encounter at Farpoint" (episode), 49, 65–66, 80, 86, 100, 160, 230, 235, 244, 271, 272, 276, 279, 293, 299, 390
"Endgame" (episode), 95, 158
"Enemy, The" (episode), 85, 133–34, 229, 344–45
"Enemy: Starfleet" (fan episode), 380
"Enemy Within, The" (episode), 72, 219
Engel, Joel, 12
Ensemble Studio Theater of Los Angeles, 366
Ensign, Michael, 177
"Ensign Ro" (episode), 82, 213–214, 234, 274
"Ensigns of Command, The" (episode), 131, 275, 277
Entertainment Weekly, 138, 140, 169, 177, 222, 225, 253, 255, 295
Erdmann, Terry J. 63, 144, 247, 312
Erwin, Bill, 170
Eschbacher, Roger, 282
"Ethics" (episode), 220
Ethics of Star Trek, The, 245
Eureka, 367
Everton, Deborah, 308
Every Good Boy Deserves Favour, 86, 211, 359
Evil Dead, The, 395
"Evolution" (episode), 130, 131
Executive Decision, 322
"Eye of the Beholder" (episode), 290

"Face of the Enemy" (episode), 254–55, 271, 354

Fade-In: The Writing of Star Trek: Insurrection, 313
Fairchild, Morgan, 57
Falcon Crest, 52, 57, 185
Falconer, Sheila, 55, 188, 361
Fall of Eagles, The, 55
"False Profits" (episode), 133
Fame, 119
"Family" (episode), 169, 170, 251, 266, 285, 330–31, 339, 388
Family Guy, 94, 348
Family Ties, 16, 62, 185
Fandom, The (website), 118, 162
Fantasy Island, 22, 23, 60, 82, 189
"Far Beyond the Stars" (episode), 177
Farrell, J. P., 247
Farrell, Terry, 223, 373
Farrelly Brothers, 155
Fast Times at Ridgemont High, 192
Fatal Attraction, 14
Felicity, 120
Ferguson, Jay, 190
Ferguson, Jessie Lawrence, 67
Ferren, Bran, 124
Fields, Peter Allan, 180, 210, 222, 224, 329
Fifth Business, 13
Fill, Shannon, 148, 288
"Final Mission" (episode), 86, 173, 334
Finn, Denny Martin, 201–2, 203, 205, 208
Finney, Albert, 16
"First Contact" (episode), 82, 176–77, 379
"First Duty, The" (episode), 148, 212, 221–22, 244, 245, 252, 288, 289, 334, 357
"Firstborn" (episode), 161, 190, 291, 348, 389
"Fistful of Datas, A" (episode), 86, 242, 251–52, 340–41, 348, 388
Flanagan, Fionnula, 286
FlashForward, 119
Fleetwood, Mick, 110, 111
Fleetwood Mac, 110, 111
Fly II, The, 17
Flynn, Errol, 197
Fontana, Dorothy ("D.C."), 47, 65, 68, 73, 97, 379, 380
"For the World Is Hollow and I Have Touched the Sky" (episode), 74, 75, 287
Forbes, Michelle, 149–50, 180, 212, 213–14, 224, 234, 251, 281, 292, 358
"Force of Nature" (episode), 281, 285, 286
Ford, Harrison, 120
Forester, C. S. 14
Forman, Milos, 166, 367
Fosse, Bob, 389
Foster, Jodie, 14
Fox, Michael J., 185
Fox Network, 47, 119, 370
Frakes, Jonathan, 51, 52, 56–57, 67, 72, 81, 83, 84–85, 86, 87, 90, 104, 105, 107, 112, 129, 136, 138, 144, 147, 158, 162, 166, 172, 173, 178, 179, 192, 194, 211, 218, 220, 221, 241, 252, 257, 258, 259, 281, 285, 287, 288, 306, 307, 308, 309, 310–11, 312, 315, 316, 318, 321, 322, 323, 325, 335, 337, 347, 349–51, 360, 363–64, 369, 387
"Frame of Mind" (episode), 257–58, 351
Frankenheimer, John, 78, 181, 353
Frankenstein, 289
Franklin & Bash, 159
Frasier, 177, 221, 362
Frears, Stephen, 150
Fresh Hell, 363
Frewer, Matt, 217
Friedman, Jan Michael, 249, 250
Frontier Guard, 384
Fugitive, The, 11, 86, 322
Funny About Love, 44
"Future Imperfect" (episode), 173, 241, 242

Galanter, Dave, 380
"Galaxy's Child" (episode), 177, 193, 236, 351, 352
Gallo, Jeanna F., 288
Ganino, Trent Christopher, 137
"Gambit, Part I" (episode), 87, 165, 236, 283–84, 341
"Gambit, Part II" (episode), 165, 266, 283–84, 341
"Game, The" (episode), 86, 215–16, 276, 357
Ganis, Sid, 197, 198
Gargoyles, 363
Gauthier, Dan, 288
Geer, Ellen, 215
Gendel, Morgan, 224, 225, 256, 329
"Genesis" (episode), 87, 290, 389, 391
Genesis II, 2
Genie Francis, 57, 364
George Dickel Distillery, 267
George Foster Peabody Award for Excellence in Television Broadcasting, 72, 386, 392
Gere, Richard, 14
Gernsback, Hugo, 390
Gerrold, David, 47, 48, 97, 379, 380
Ghost, 17, 188
Ghost Story, 158, 307
Ghostbusters II, 124, 126
Giacchino, Michael, 397
Gibney, Susan, 177, 193
Gibson, Charlie, 328
Gibson, Mel, 120
Giger, H. R., 109
Gladiator, 320
God Thing, The (screenplay), 3, 122
Goldberg, Whoopi, 99, 100, 102, 105, 132, 137, 138, 144, 146, 152, 153, 184, 186–88, 224, 225, 248, 259, 281, 307, 337, 348, 358, 387
Golden Child, The, 38, 42
Golden Globe Awards, 126, 150, 187, 194
Golden Raspberry Awards, 99, 389, 390
Goldsmith, Jerry, 8, 26, 94, 125, 203, 308, 315
Goldwyn, John, 202

Gone with the Wind, 91
Good Morning America, 328
Good Mother, The, 123
GoodFellas, 287
Goodhartz, Shari, 178, 340
Gorbachev, Mikhail, 201
Grammer, Kelsey, 221
Gray, Mike, 99, 104
Gray, Pamela, 218
Great Expectations, 163, 179
Greene, Vanessa, 173
Greenspon, Joq, 282
Greenwood, Bruce, 397
Grey's Anatomy, 364
Griffith, Andy, 117
Grodenchik, Max, 141, 316
Grodin, Charles, 120
Groener, Harry, 141
Gross, Edward, 45, 65, 140, 177, 196, 281
Guiding Light, 149, 154
Guild, The, 367
Gussaw, Mel, 359
Guttenberg, Steve, 43
Guyana Tragedy, 283

Hackman, Gene, 14
Hagen, Uta, 187
Haire, Chris, 94
"Half a Life" (episode), 82, 94, 149, 180, 184,
    190–91, 222, 241, 248, 272, 388
Half of Two Lives, A, 14
Hamlet, 23, 58, 163, 179, 361
Hammett, Dashiell, 70
Hancock, Herbie, 389
Haney, Anne, 131, 156
Hanks, Tom, 14, 307
Happy Days, 17
Hard Time on Planet Earth, 116
Hardin, Jerry, 225, 248, 269
Hardy, Tom, 322
Harlow, Joel, 387
Harrison, George, 225
Harrison, Harry, 262
Harry Potter and the Chamber of Secrets, 324
Harry-O, 316
Hatfield, James, 166, 327
Hathaway, Henry, 336
Hatton, Christopher, 283, 289
"Haven" (episode), 70, 87, 111, 184, 388
Hawke, Ethan, 197
Hawking, Stephen, 260, 261
Hawks, Howard, 252, 336
HBO, 320, 348, 362, 366
Heart of Darkness, 174, 312, 313, 314
"Heart of Glory" (episode), 76, 83, 227, 272,
    342–44, 346
Heaven & Hell: North and South, Book III, 383
"Heavy Lies the Crown" (fan episode), 384
Heinlein, Robert A., 197, 262, 371
Henglaar, M.D., 384
Henson, Jim, 61

Hercules: The Legendary Journeys, 370
Here's Lucy, 185
"Hero Worship" (episode), 86, 218, 243, 276,
    341
Herron, Robert, 259
Hertzler, J. G., 382
Hetrick, Jennifer, 140, 141, 179, 188, 334, 361
Hicks, Catherine, 38
"Hide and Q" (episode), 64, 59–70, 230, 268,
    272, 276
"High Ground, The" (episode), 135, 271, 272
Highlander: The Series, 370
Highway to Heaven, 62
Higley, Sarah, 142
Hill, George Roy, 389
Hill Street Blues, 35, 49, 56, 85, 116, 130
Hiller, Arthur, 13
Hitchcock, Alfred, 19, 77, 156, 157
Hizzoner, 152
Hoffman, Philip Seymour, 397
Hoist, 364
Holbrook, Hal, 57
"Hollow Pursuits" (episode), 82, 142, 153, 178,
    388
"Home Soil" (episode), 75, 269
Homefront, 85
"Homeward" (episode), 244, 287, 348
Homicide: Life on the Street, 150, 194
Honey, I Shrunk the Kids, 126
Honeymooners, The, 86
Hook, 217
Hopkins, Anthony, 14
Horner, James, 26, 94
"Host, The" (episode), 180, 221, 356
House, 104, 394
House of Gold, 366
How I Met Your Mother, 190, 364
Howard Anderson Company, The, 4, 9
Howard, Merri, 247
Howe, Desson, 206
Hubbard, Jamie, 105
Hughes, Wendy, 193, 257
Hugo, 93, 326
Hugo Awards, 24, 33, 42, 66, 87, 126, 132, 206,
    210, 225, 295, 301, 308, 316, 324, 379,
    381, 390, 391, 399
Human Stain, The, 14
Hunt for Red October, The, 366
"Hunted, The" (episode), 134–35, 148, 356,
    271, 307
Hunter, 58
Hunter, Stephen, 324
Hunter, The, 59
Hurley, Maurice, 67, 69, 73, 79, 83, 97, 99, 100,
    104, 106, 108, 109, 112, 116, 130, 177,
    232, 296–97, 343
Hurt Locker, The, 390
Hyman, Charles, 344

I, Claudius, 55
I, Q, 161

I Am Not Spock (memoir), 28
I Am Sam, 186
I Am Spock (memoir), 28, 64, 200, 212
I Am Weasel, 365
"I Borg" (episode), 186, 210, 223–24, 232, 241,
    260, 282, 353
I Love Lucy, 86
"Icarus Factor, The" (episode), 107, 244, 275
"Identity Crisis" (episode), 118, 178, 353, 388
If . . . 158
"Imaginary Friend" (episode) 223
Iman 204, 208
Impossible Ragtime Theatre Company, 56
"Immunity Syndrome, The" (episode), 75
"In a Mirror, Darkly" (episode), 148, 307
"In Harm's Way" (fan episode), 379–80
In the Heat of the Night, 117, 386
"In Theory" (episode), 86, 181, 273, 339–40
In Thy Image (screenplay), 2
InAlienable, 364
Independence Day, 309, 311, 362
Indiana Jones and the Last Crusade, 124, 126
Industrial Light & Magic, 21, 31, 49, 124, 203,
    308, 315, 323, 397
Informant, The, 14
Ingalls, Don, 73
"Inheritance" (episode), 286, 287
"Inner Light, The" (episode), 87, 91, 95, 193,
    210, 224–25, 257, 329, 331, 388, 390
Innocents, The, 288
"Interface" (episode) 282–83
International Academy of Television Arts &
    Sciences 387
Introducing Dorothy Dandridge 362
Invaders, The 52, 152
Invasion of the Bee Girls, 13
Invasion of the Body Snatchers, 78, 216
Invasion of the Body Snatchers (1978), 87
"Is There in Truth No Beauty?" (episode), 152, 240
Iscove, Robert, 107

Jaffe, Stanley, 203
Jaffe, Steven-Charles, 17, 202
James, Henry, 288
James, Richard, 90
Janssen, David, 316
Janssen, Famke, 223
Jefferies, Matt, 88, 250, 379, 396
Jeffrey, 360, 361
Jemison, Mae, 259–60
Jendresen, Erik, 394
Jennings, Joe, 22
Jens, Salome, 257
Jeopardy!, 79
Joffe, Roland, 389
Johnson, Jimm, 383
Johnson, Joshua, 383
Johnson, Penny, 287
Jones, James Earl, 193
Jones, Renee, 254
Jones, Ron, 94–95, 144, 169, 294

Jones, Tommy Lee, 322
"Journey to Babel" (episode), 31, 68, 188, 380
"Journey's End" (episode), 86, 233, 238, 240,
    279, 290–91, 292, 318
*Journey's End: The Saga of Star Trek the Next
    Generation*, 293
Joy Luck Club, The, 186
Judd, Ashley, 213, 215–16, 357
Judge Dee and the Monastery Murders, 13
Judgment at Nuremberg, 84, 179
Junior American Red Cross of the Air, 16
Just a Geek (memoir), 211, 327, 367
"Justice" (episode), 69, 244, 269, 271, 272
Justice League, 365
Justman, Robert H., 47, 48, 50, 52, 53, 54, 55,
    60, 63, 98, 115, 116, 342

Kahn, James, 219
Kamel, Stanley, 68
Kaplan, Michael, 13, 396
Katleman, Harris, 11
Katzenberg, Jeffrey, 3, 9, 37, 391
Kava, Caroline, 220
Keane, Kerrie, 135, 271
Kelley, DeForest, 2, 7, 10, 19, 35, 36, 40, 43, 65,
    66, 99, 123, 126, 128, 152, 208, 299, 390
Kelley, John, 381, 382, 383
Kemp, Jeremy, 169
Kemper, David, 111, 133
Kennedy, John F., 19, 30, 40
Khambatta, Persis, 7, 8, 100, 154
Kidman, Nicole, 14
Killing, The, 150
Kimball, Jeffrey, 325
King, Stephen, 53, 62, 117, 282, 366
Kirkpatrick, David, 202
Kiss Meets the Phantom of the Park, 316
Klugman, Jack, 258
Knepper, Rob, 70
Knight Rider, 83
Koenig, Walter, 6, 8, 10, 20, 25, 40, 197, 299,
    364, 379, 380, 382, 396
Koeppel, Dan, 286
Kolbe, Winrich, 81, 82–83, 85, 177, 178, 294,
    299
Kolchak, the Night Stalker, 84
Konner, Lawrence, 201
Kotto, Yaphet, 52
Krige, Alice, 158, 306, 307, 309
Krikes, Peter, 37, 38, 40
Krofft, Sid and Marty, 89
Kubrick, Stanley, 4, 158, 163, 299
Kurosawa, Akira, 136
Kurtzman, Alex, 120, 198, 392, 395–96, 400

L.A. Confidential, 148
L.A. Law, 85, 99, 152, 188, 366, 386
L.A. Story, 360
LA Weekly, 367
La Beauf, Sabrina, 283
Labyrinth, 61

Land of the Lost, 89
Landau, Les, 67, 81–82, 178
Lane, Brian Alan, 102
Lansing, Robert, 11
Lansing, Sherry, 198, 296, 300, 301, 304
Lapine, James, 56, 315
Larroquette, John, 56, 164
"Last Outpost, The" (episode), 67–68, 111, 112, 229, 230, 274
Laura, 254
Lauritson, Peter, 87, 99
Laverne & Shirley, 17
Law & Order, 150, 386
LaZebnik, Philip, 175, 213
Lean, David, 163, 179, 256
Lecoq, Jacques, 61
"Legacy" (episode), 172
Legato, Robert, 49, 93
Legend, 117
Legion of Super-Heroes, 367
Le Guin, Ursula K., 219
Leiber, Jeffrey, 120
Leigh, Janet, 19, 77
Lemmon, Jack, 362
Lenard, Mark, 31, 143, 184, 188, 189, 204, 217, 334
Lennon, John, 114
Leonetti, Matthew, 308, 309
"Lessons" (episode), 193, 257
"Let That Be Your Last Battlefield" (episode), 73, 76, 77, 240
Lethal Weapon II, 126, 322
Leverage, 85, 363
Lewin, Robert, 48, 72, 73, 76, 98
Leydon, Joe, 311
"Liaisons" (episode), 282, 284, 285
Librarian: Curse of the Judas Chalice, The, 364
Librarian: Return to King Solomon's Mines, The, 364
Lifeforce, 55
Lindelof, Damon, 120, 395
Link, William, 116
Linville, Joanne, 254
Lion in Winter, The, 361
Little House on the Prairie, 117, 170
Little Romance, A, 389
Live and Let Die, 52
Livingston, David, 99, 181, 247
Livingston, Harold, 2, 3–4, 7
Lizzie McGuire, 192
Lloyd, Christopher, 31, 34
Lloyd, Norman, 257
Lofton, Cirroc, 373, 382
Logan, John, 320–21, 322, 324, 326
Logan's Run, 53
Lois & Clark: The New Adventures of Superman, 81
"Lonely Among Us" (episode), 68–69, 100, 102, 175, 276
Long Hunt of April Savage, The, 11
Long Way Home, A, 61

Look Who's Talking, 126, 147
Looking for Mr. Goodbar, 59
Lopez, Jennifer, 323
Lord of the Rings: The Two Towers, The, 324
"Loss, The" (episode), 173–74, 354
Lost, 120, 162, 287, 395, 397
Lost in Space, 86, 88
"Loud as a Whisper" (episode) 103, 161
Loughery, David, 122, 123–24, 125, 126, 195–96, 197, 390
Love & War, 190
Love Boat, The, 60, 84
Love Story, 13
Love Story Story, The, 13
Lovelace, Frank, 371
"Lower Decks" (episode), 85, 148, 154, 281, 288–89
Lowry-Johnson, Junie, 50, 54, 95, 158, 307, 315
Luc, Frank, 180
Lucas, John Meredith, 3
Lucas, George, 5, 23, 49, 192, 324, 396
Lucia, Chip, 248
Luckinbill, Larry, 124, 125, 128
Luna, Barbara, 380
Lunden, Joan, 328
Lynch, David, 55
Lyne, Adrian, 14

M*A*S*H, 90, 180, 185, 190, 192
Macbeth, 361
MacGyver, 81, 82, 114, 157, 170, 324
Macon County Line, 87
Mad About You, 190, 366
Mad Men, 366
Magnum, P.I. 83, 117, 170
Maid in Manhattan, 323
Maizlish, Leonard, 123
Major Crimes, 186
Maltese Falcon, The, 70, 141
Maltin, Leonard, 38
Mama's Family, 56
Mamet, David, 153
"Man of the People" (episode), 248–49, 354
Man Who Loved Women, The, 61
Mancuso, Frank, 197, 198, 200, 201, 203
"Manhunt" (episode), 72, 106, 110–11, 184, 243, 270
Manning, Richard, 99, 103, 130, 132, 140, 166
March, Barbara, 161–62, 212, 291
Marshall, Jack, 378–79
Martin, George R. R., 262
Martin, Quinn, 52, 152
Martin, Steve, 360
Marvel Comics, 17, 57, 360
Mary Tyler Moore Show, The, 60, 342
Masada, 164
"Masks" (episode), 289
Maslin, Janet, 23, 206
Mason, John, 99, 104
Massett, Patrick, 172, 346

"Masterpiece Society, The" (episode), 104, 219, 269
Matchmaker, The, 61
Matlock, 386
"Matter of Honor, A" (episode), 91, 104, 112, 227, 235, 239, 265, 266, 350, 388
"Matter of Perspective, A" (episode), 136
"Matter of Time, A" (episode), 93, 217, 219, 388
Matthais, Jean Louise, 250, 257, 288
Matthau, Walter, 362
Max Headroom, 185, 217, 370
Mayberry, Russ, 67, 82
Maybury, 55
McBride, 164
McCarthy, Dennis, 94, 100, 137, 180, 217
McCloud, 152
McCormick, Carolyn, 73
McCoy, Matt, 133
McDonald, Christopher, 137, 154, 358
McDowell, Malcolm, 13, 158–59, 235, 299
McFadden, Gates, 51, 53, 60–61, 82, 86, 87, 98, 99, 129, 135, 144, 152, 170, 173, 174, 180, 211, 220, 241, 242, 257, 258, 282, 285, 288, 290, 302, 317, 318, 324, 338, 354–56, 360, 366, 387
McKellan, Ian, 361
McMillan & Wife, 160
McNeill, Robert Duncan, 222, 376
McQ, 152
McQuarrie, Christopher, 394
McQueen, Steve, 59
McTiernan, John, 306, 307
Meaney, Colm, 86, 100, 107, 150–51, 154, 174, 175, 185, 211, 220, 248, 251, 281, 293, 360, 363, 373
"Measure of a Man, The" (episode), 84, 96, 102, 104–5, 107, 110, 112, 135, 138, 174, 244, 252, 270, 331–32, 337, 338, 392
Medved, Michael, 301
Meerson, Steve, 37, 38, 40
Mees, Jim, 90
Melville, Herman, 215
Memories of the Future, Volume 1, 367
"Ménage a Troi" (episode), 143, 229, 273
"Menagerie, Parts I and II, The" (episodes), 30, 380
Menosky, Joe, 172, 175, 178, 181, 210, 213, 218, 219, 225, 241, 248, 257, 258, 282, 289, 292
Menyuk, Eric 53, 68, 171, 193, 291
"Metamorphosis" (episode), 148, 307
Meyer, Dina, 322
Meyer, Nicholas, 12–14, 15, 16, 17, 18, 19, 20, 21, 22, 23, 24, 25, 26, 27, 28, 34, 38, 40, 41, 43, 94, 122, 128, 157, 158, 162, 164, 200, 201, 202, 203, 204, 205, 206, 207, 208, 299
Miami Vice, 31, 116
Milkis, Edward, 47, 48, 50, 115
Miller, Arthur, 361
"Mind's Eye, The" (episode), 180–81, 353
"Mirror, Mirror" (episode), 380, 382

Misery, 282
Miss Firecracker, 362
Mission, The, 389
Mission: Impossible, 86, 385
Mission: Impossible II, 312
Mission: Impossible III, 120
Mitchum, Robert, 57
Moby Dick, 215, 309
Moby Dick (TV movie), 361
Mod Squad, The, 11
Moessinger, David, 118
Monkees, The, 86
Montalban, Ricardo, 12, 19, 22, 23, 24, 82, 162
Moonlighting, 150
Moore, Karen, 13
Moore, Ronald D., 64, 99, 110, 118, 129, 132, 134, 135, 138, 139, 144, 169, 174, 181, 194, 210, 212, 215, 219, 220, 222, 224, 228, 232, 234, 241, 247, 250, 251, 252, 254, 255–56, 257, 259, 280, 283, 286, 287, 289, 290, 291, 293, 297, 298, 299, 300, 301, 303, 304, 305, 306, 309, 312, 345, 346, 347, 375
Moore, Ronald B., 93
Moran, W. Reed, 139
Morgenstern, Joe, 398
Mork & Mindy, 16, 17
Moses, Christina, 379, 381
Mosiman, Marnie, 161
Moss, Arnold, 23
Moss, George, 366
"Most Toys, The" (episode), 142–43, 164, 245, 340
Motel Hell, 17
Mr. Spock's Music from Outer Space, 15
Mr. Stitch, 367
MTV Movie Awards, 392
Muldaur, Diana, 98, 99, 101, 104, 112, 129, 152, 355, 358, 366
Mulgrew, Kate,161, 376
Muppets Take Manhattan, The, 61
Murder, She Wrote, 148, 190, 192, 386
Murphy Brown, 386
Murphy, Donna, 315, 318
Murphy, Eddie, 37–38, 41, 42, 390
Murphy, Kevin, 126
My Favorite Martian, 222
Mysterious Island, 161, 361
Mystery Science Theater 3000, 126

"Naked Now, The" (episode), 66–67, 90, 270, 277, 357
"Naked Time, The" (episode), 66, 250
Nanny, The, 158
Napoli, Antonio, 290
Nardino, Gary, 16–17, 28
NASA, 8
National Academy of Television Arts and Sciences, 387
NBC Television, 1, 18, 19, 47, 80, 89, 113
NCIS Los Angeles, 363
Near Dark, 17

Nebula Award, 141, 379, 381

Nelson, Mike, 126

Nemecek, Larry, 52, 109, 213, 223, 253

Neuss, Wendy, 361

"Neutral Zone, The" (episode), 79, 97, 144, 175, 228, 245, 269, 277

Neuwirth, Bebe, 176, 177

"New Ground" (episode), 218, 348

New York Post, 359

New York Times, 6, 23, 42, 126, 206, 316, 359

New Yorker, 316

Newsweek, 6, 42, 126

"Next Phase, The" (episode), 85, 224, 353, 388

Nichols, Nichelle, 10, 36, 39, 40, 99, 128, 186, 187, 205, 208, 260, 263, 282, 392, 396

Nicholson, Jack, 192

Nielsen ratings, xvi, xvii, 45, 46, 47, 66, 79, 97, 104, 112, 116, 118, 144, 145, 154, 169, 175, 183, 200, 206, 212, 217, 226, 227, 228, 230, 246, 260, 294, 295, 320, 326, 342, 368–69, 371, 372, 386

Night Beast, 120

Night Court, 53, 56

"Night Terrors" (episode), 177–78, 218

Night That Panicked America, The 13

Nighthawks, 155

Nightmare on Elm Street, A, 164

Nimoy, Adam, 86, 251, 260

Nimoy, Leonard, 2, 4, 7, 10, 11, 12, 15–16, 18, 19, 20, 21, 24, 27–43, 45, 63–64, 82, 84, 86, 121, 122, 123, 128, 146, 154, 157, 160, 197, 200–202, 203, 205, 206, 208, 212, 216–17, 226, 249, 298, 299, 300, 301, 335, 368, 386, 391, 396, 399

North and South (ABC miniseries), 52, 57, 147

North and South (BBC miniseries), 55

North and South, Book II, 52, 57, 147

Northern Exposure, 85, 386

Norway Corporation, 9

"Nth Degree, The" (episode), 178

Numb3rs, 367

Nutty Professor, The, 308, 390

Official Star Trek Cooking Manual, The, 264

"Offspring, The" (episode), 84, 94, 138, 142, 144, 172, 192, 239, 242, 271, 275, 306, 336–37, 338

Oh, Madeline, 190

Okuda, Michael, 48, 90, 178

Ol' Yellow Eyes Is Back, 211, 362

Old Vic Theatre (and School), 54, 359

Olivier, Laurence, 163, 179

Olmos, James Edward, 31

Once a Hero, 119

One Flew over the Cuckoo's Nest, 190

One in a Million: The Ron LaFlore Story, 283

One Last Chance, 364

O'Neill, Tricia, 137, 154

Ono, Yoko, 114

Operation Beta Shield (fan film), 383

O'Quinn, Terry, 162, 286–87

Orci, Roberto, 120, 198, 392, 395–96, 400

O'Reilly, Robert, 172, 189, 212, 346

Orlandt, Ken, 391

Orphans of War (fan film), 383

Other, The, 152

Out to Sea, 362

"Outcast, The" (episode), 84, 220–21, 240, 244, 273, 274

Outer Limits, The, 119, 364, 367, 370

"Outrageous Okona, The" (episode), 52, 102–3

Palance, Jack, 114

Palermo, Brian, 363

Paper Chase, The, 56

Paramount Pictures, xvi, 1–2, 3, 4, 5, 6, 9, 11, 13, 14, 16, 17. 18, 20, 21, 23, 27, 28, 31, 32, 36, 37, 38, 41, 42, 44, 45, 46, 47, 49, 50, 52, 53, 65, 97, 99, 114, 117, 119, 120, 121, 122, 123, 124, 125, 129, 152, 160, 166, 168, 179, 195, 197, 198, 200, 201, 202, 206, 212, 226, 241, 246–47, 250, 253, 261, 266, 293, 295, 296, 297, 298, 299, 300, 301, 304, 305, 306, 307, 308, 310, 312, 313, 314, 315, 315, 317, 320, 322, 323, 325, 335, 355, 369–70, 378, 393–95, 396, 397, 399, 400

Paranormal Borderline, 363

"Parallels" (episode), 281, 286, 348, 395

Passion, 315

Patinkin, Mandy, 56

Patrick Stewart: The Unauthorized Biography, 166, 224, 253, 327, 369

"Peak Performance" (episode), 111, 229, 272

Pecheur, Sierra, 174

Pedraza, Carlos, 380

Peeples, Samuel, 19

"Pegasus, The" (episode), 86, 162, 163, 281, 286–87, 351

Pegg, Simon, 397, 399

Peking Opera, 185

"Pen Pals" (episode), 83, 107, 110, 275, 277, 287, 341

Peoples' Choice Awards, 392

Perception, 365

"Perfect Mate, The" (episode), 223, 273

"Private Little War, A" (episode), 73

Perlman, Ron, 322, 324

Pet Sematary, 366

Peters, Bernadette, 56

Pevney, Joseph, 81, 128

Peyton Place, 11

"Phantasms" (episode), 86, 284

Phantom Menace, The (Star Wars Episode I), 315

Phillips, Ethan, 143, 264, 307, 376, 382

Phillips, Fred, 88, 397

Phillips, Michelle, 78

Phish, 362

Phoenix, River, 61, 62

Picardo, Robert, 102, 254, 307, 375, 376

Picasso Summer, The, 16

Piccard, Mary Ann, 264

Picket Fences, 193, 386

"Piece of the Action, A" (episode), 37, 70, 72

Pike, John, 114
Piller, Brent, 117
Piller, Michael, 83, 96, 105, 116–17, 118, 119,
    130–131, 132, 133, 135, 137, 140, 143,
    144, 160, 166, 167, 168, 169, 170, 174,
    176, 177, 178, 210, 213, 215, 217, 219,
    222, 223, 224, 225, 232, 234, 237, 241,
    247, 248, 251, 253, 256, 280, 281, 285,
    293, 296, 297, 312–14, 318, 319, 331,
    345, 354, 371, 373, 374, 375
Piller, Sandra, 117
Piller, Shawn, 117, 290
Pine, Chris, 199, 392, 397, 398, 399
Piscopo, Joe, 102
Plakson, Suzie, 103, 111, 172, 189–90, 231,
    344, 346
Planet Earth, 72, 116, 152
Planet of the Apes, 17
Platoon, 389
Playboy, 61
Plummer, Christopher, 204–5, 208
Polanski, Roman, 258
Police Academy, 157, 197
Poseidon Adventure, The, 215
Povill, John, 100
Powell, Michael, 163
Power, Tyrone, 157
"Power Play" (episode), 220, 354, 388
Practice, The, 366
Predator, 26
"Preemptive Strike" (episode), 86, 149, 233,
    251, 292
Pressburger, Emeric, 163
Previn, Andre, 211, 359
"Price, The" (episode), 133, 134, 141, 229, 264
Prince, Anne, 367
Probe, 83, 116
Probert, Andrew, 48, 89, 90
Prose and Poetry of England, xv
Pryor, Richard, 38
Psycho, 19, 20, 77, 157
Pulitzer Prize, 56, 187
Pushing Daisies, 91

"Q and the Gray, The" (episode), 111
"Q Who" (episode), 83, 93, 94, 107, 108–9,
    112, 144, 230, 231, 232, 235, 270, 279,
    304, 388
"Qpid" (episode), 141, 166, 179, 188, 273, 334,
    361
"Q2" (episode), 161, 231
Quaid, Dennis, 55
Quaid, Randy, 55
"Quality of Life, The" (episode), 252, 341
Quantum Leap, 51, 376, 386
Queen Elizabeth II, 361
Questor Tapes, The, 49, 335
Quincy M. E., 117, 170, 258
Quinn, Jeffrey, 282, 283
Quinto, Zachary, 199, 397, 398, 399
Quiz Kids, 10

Raimi, Sam, 120, 285, 395
Ramsay, Todd, 5
Rapelye, Mary-Linda, 380
Rappaport, David, 142–43, 164
"Rascals" (episode), 86, 251, 260
Rashomon, 136
Reach for Me, 87
Read, James, 57
Reading Rainbow, 53, 58, 59, 364, 392
Reagan, Ronald, 73, 182, 197
Real Frank Zappa Book, The, 262
"Realm of Fear" (episode), 248
"Redemption" (episode), 91, 161, 181–82, 217,
    228, 229, 245, 275
"Redemption II" (episode), 85, 91, 161, 181,
    212–13, 228, 229, 245, 341, 347
"Redshirt Blues" (fan film), 384
Reeves-Stevens, Garfield and Judith, 68, 143,
    243
Regarding Henry, 120
Reiner, Rob, 53, 61, 93
"Relics" (episode), 86, 95, 148, 177, 249–50,
    267, 277, 278, 351, 352–53
"Remember Me" (episode), 170–71, 355–56
Remington Steele, 150
Rent Control, 56
Repplier, Agnes, 156
Repulsion, 258
Return of Sherlock Holmes, The, 58
Return of the Jedi, The (Star Wars Episode VI),
    23, 26, 33
"Return to Tomorrow" (episode), 152, 257
"Reunion" (episode), 84, 94, 111, 118, 171,172,
    183, 185, 189, 190, 228, 242, 306,
    346–47
Rice, Anne, 288
Rich, Lisa, 282
Richard II, 361
Ride Down Mt. Morgan, The, 361
RiffTrax 126
"Rightful Heir" (episode), 228, 259, 348
Rio Bravo, 252
Ripley's Believe It or Not, 114
Ritchie, Michael 38
RKO, 281, 320
Road Warrior, The, 26
Robert Abel & Associates, 4
Roberts, Ted, 180
Robertson, Ed, 245
Robin Hood: Men in Tights, 360
Robocop, 147
Rockford Files, The, 148
Rocky, 60
Rocky Horror Show, The, 58
Rod Serling's Night Gallery, 27
Roddenberry, Gene, xv, 1, 2, 3, 4, 5, 7, 8, 9, 10,
    11, 12, 14, 15, 16, 19–20, 22, 30, 31–32,
    40, 45–49, 50, 51, 52, 53, 54, 60, 63,
    64, 65, 66–67, 69, 72, 73, 76, 78, 80,
    81–82, 86, 90, 95, 97, 98, 99, 101, 107,
    108, 109, 113, 114, 115, 116, 119, 120,
    122, 123, 126, 128, 129, 142, 143, 150,

152, 156, 166, 167, 169, 176, 187, 197, 203, 204, 205–206, 208, 210, 212, 218, 227, 228, 232, 235, 237–44, 247, 262, 281, 283, 296, 305, 312, 318–19, 335, 342, 353, 355, 357, 358, 366, 370, 371, 372–73, 375, 376, 380, 390
Roddenberry, Rod, 379
Rohner, Clayton, 73
Rolfe, Sam, 134
Roman, Ron, 132
Roots, 53, 58, 59
Rose, Margot, 193, 392
Roseanne, 386
Rosenberg, Grant, 218
Rosenthal, Mark, 201
Roswell, 363
Round Midnight, 389
Roy, Deep, 400
Royal Shakespeare Company, 52, 55, 158, 163, 253, 327, 330, 361
"Royale, The" (episode), 106, 110
Rubinek, Saul, 142–43, 164, 340
Ruck, Alan, 382
Ruginis, Vyto, 76
Rush, Marvin, 85, 137, 180, 221
Russ, Tim, 53, 256, 376, 382
Russell, Kurt, 322

Sabarof, Robert, 75, 78
Sabre, Richard, 91
Sackett, Susan, 3, 20, 143, 216
Sagan, Carl, 285
Sagan, Nick, 281, 285, 291–92
St. Elsewhere, 62
Saldana, Zoe, 392, 397, 398
Sallin, Robert, 12, 16
Saltwater Film Society, 364
Salvage 1, 117
"Samaritan Snare" (episode), 109, 255, 275, 334, 357
San Jose Mercury News, 221
Santa Barbara Studios, 315, 323
Santa Fe Trail, The, 197
"Sarek" (episode), 82, 143, 188, 217, 241, 334
Saturday Night Live, 37, 102
Saturn Awards, 23, 33, 42, 158, 206, 309, 324, 391, 393
"Savage Curtain, The" (episode), 131, 259
"Savage Empire, The" (fan episode), 383
Savlov, Marc, 316
Saxon, John, 72
Scarabelli, Michele, 181, 273, 339–40
Scarfe, Alan, 161
Schafer, Ken, 181
Scheerer, Robert, 83–84, 86, 105, 172
Schenkkan, Robert, 75
"Schisms" (episode), 250
"Schizoid Man, The" (episode), 103, 111, 190, 241, 271, 274
Schkolnick, Barry, 219
Schultz, Dwight, 142, 146, 149, 153–54, 178, 248, 290, 307, 372

Scorsese, Martin, 93, 326
Scott, Marilyn, 61
Scott, Ridley, 24, 109, 306, 320
Screen Actors Guild, 15, 152, 194, 295, 334, 292
Seagal, Steven, 256
Seago, Howie, 103
Seaquest 2032, 81
"Second Chances" (episode), 86, 259–60, 351
Secret Empire, The, 117
Secret of NIMH, The, 61
Secrets of Star Trek: Insurrection, The, 312
Selleck, Tom, 43
Selmon, Karole, 66, 67
Seurat, Georges, 56
Seven Days in May, 78
Seven-Percent Solution, The, 13
Sex and the City, 157
Seymour, Carolyn, 177, 254, 271
"Shades of Gray" (episode), 83, 97, 112, 144, 179, 279
Shane, 252
Shankar, Naren, 222, 252, 254, 258, 281, 283, 285, 287, 292
Shatner, Lisabeth, 122
Shatner, William, 2, 3, 4, 6, 7, 10, 12, 16, 18, 19, 23, 24, 27, 32, 34, 36, 39, 40, 43, 52, 64, 72, 82, 121–23, 124, 125, 126, 127, 128, 146, 148, 154, 197, 198, 202, 204, 205, 206, 207–8, 248, 297, 298, 299, 300, 301, 302, 303, 304, 370, 390, 396
Shaun of the Dead, 297
Shearer, Hannah Louise, 74, 78, 98, 107, 133
Sheldon, Lee, 171
Shenandoah, 57
Shepherd, Cybill, 150
Sheppard, W. Morgan, 103, 274
Sherlock, 400
Shimerman, Armin, 68, 111, 229, 230, 291, 316, 373, 374
"Ship in a Bottle" (episode), 86, 157, 253–54
Shocker, 362
"Shore Leave" (episode), 77
Showtime Network, 32, 119
Sidekicks, 116
Sigmund and the Sea Monsters, 89
Silk Stalkings, 148
Simmons, Jean, 57, 163, 179, 332, 334
Simon & Simon, 116, 130
Simpsons, The, 150
Sims, Alan, 265
Sinclair, Madge, 283
Singer, Alexander, 86
Singer, Bryan, 322, 394
Sinise, Gary, 397
"Sins of the Father" (episode), 82, 139–141, 142, 167, 172, 228, 244, 345–346, 347, 388
Sirtis, Marina, 51, 57–58, 72, 78, 100, 112, 133, 144, 173, 178, 211–12, 215, 218, 220, 222, 243, 249, 252, 254, 259, 281, 287, 302, 316, 318, 322–23, 325, 341, 349, 353–54, 356, 363, 364, 387
Siskel, Gene, 43, 301, 308, 316

Sister Act, 188
Six Million Dollar Man, The, 11, 82, 160
"Skin of Evil" (episode), 77–78, 112, 276, 292, 357, 358
Skyfall, 326
Slate, 398
Slater, Christian, 208
Slaughterhouse Five, 293
Sledge Hammer, 56
Sliders, 87, 188, 370
Sloyan, James, 134, 190, 271, 291
Smart House, 364
Snapper, The, 150
Sneak Previews, 301
Snodgrass, Melinda, 96, 105, 107, 110, 130, 131, 135, 392
Sommersby, 14
Sondheim, Stephen, 56, 315
"Sons and Daughters" (episode), 291
Sorvino, Paul, 59, 287
Sounder, 193
Sowards, Jack, 12, 19, 101
Space Cadet, 197
"Space Seed" (episode), 12, 19, 20, 24, 72, 79, 104, 162
Spartacus, 163
"Spectre of the Gun" (episode), 77
Spectres, 354
Spelling, Aaron, 11
Spenser for Hire, 83
Spielberg, Steven, 99, 187, 217
Spiner, Brent, 51, 53, 55–56, 63, 67, 71, 72, 80, 86, 101, 102, 103, 105, 107, 119, 131, 136, 138, 142, 146, 169, 170, 172, 181, 192, 211, 215, 220, 221, 241, 247, 250, 281, 282, 284, 289, 302, 309, 312, 318, 320, 321, 322, 325, 335–41, 347, 349, 351, 360, 362–63, 369, 370, 387
"Spock's Brain" (episode) 74, 75
Spook Show, The, 187
"Squire of Gothos, The" (episode), 66
Stallone, Sylvester, 16, 155
Stand by Me, 53, 61, 62, 356, 367
Stape, William N., 287
Star Trek (2009 movie), xv, 42, 120, 198, 199, 217, 229, 266, 267, 323, 390, 391, 392, 395–400
Star Trek (animated series), 1, 18, 73, 175, 251, 266, 383, 386, 387, 389
Star Trek (classic series), xvi, xvii, 3, 6, 12, 15, 18, 19, 24, 30, 31, 36, 37, 45, 46, 47, 48, 49, 53, 54, 63, 64, 65, 66, 67, 68, 69, 70, 72, 73, 74, 75, 76, 77, 78, 79, 80, 81, 87, 88, 90, 97, 98, 99, 104, 105, 112, 115, 128, 131, 132, 140, 143, 144, 145, 148, 152, 162, 172, 174, 183, 188, 196, 198, 205, 206, 211, 212, 215, 225, 227, 228, 229, 237, 239, 240, 241, 244, 246, 249–50, 254–255, 257, 259, 262, 264, 266, 267, 268, 287, 292, 301, 307, 318, 327, 359, 369, 372, 372, 374, 378, 379, 380, 382, 384, 385, 389, 394, 396, 399

Star Trek Cookbook, The, 264
Star Trek Creator, 123
Star Trek: Deep Space Nine, xvii, 49, 52, 53, 68, 82, 84, 85, 86, 87, 89, 91, 93, 94, 100, 104, 111, 116, 117, 119, 132, 133, 135, 138, 141, 148, 149, 150, 150, 151, 154, 157, 159, 160, 161, 166, 174, 175, 177, 180, 184, 185, 188, 189, 190, 193, 208, 210, 214, 223, 228, 229, 230, 233, 234, 235, 236, 247, 248, 251, 253, 255, 257, 259, 260, 262, 280, 281, 286, 287, 289, 291, 292, 296, 297, 299, 307, 208, 312, 313, 315, 316, 318, 319, 320, 345, 347, 348, 363, 364, 365, 368, 369, 370, 371–72, 373, 374, 375, 382, 388, 389, 390, 391, 392, 393, 394
Star Trek Diplomatic Relations, 384
Star Trek: Enterprise, xv, xvii, 51, 52, 87, 89, 91, 94, 95, 104, 111, 116, 118, 119, 148, 167, 189, 190, 198, 228, 233, 235, 236, 286, 287, 307, 320, 323, 326, 363, 364, 365, 369, 370, 372, 374, 375, 376, 377, 389, 390, 391, 393
Star Trek FAQ: Everything Left to Know About the First Voyages of the Starship Enterprise, xv–xvi, 1, 65–66, 72, 91, 148, 154, 162, 184, 188, 219, 228, 237, 239, 268, 386
Star Trek Generations, 85, 87, 94, 118, 132, 142, 153, 154, 158, 159, 161, 162, 167, 173, 187, 235, 264, 267, 270, 277, 280, 293, 295, 296–303, 304, 306, 307, 307, 308, 309, 312, 317, 329, 369, 374, 382, 391, 396
Star Trek: Federation, 394
Star Trek: Federation One, 384
Star Trek: Final Frontier, 394
Star Trek: First Contact, 72, 84, 85, 87, 91, 118, 132, 135, 148, 154, 158, 160, 167, 173, 194, 233, 238, 256, 266, 267, 271, 277, 290, 304–311, 312, 315, 316, 317, 320, 322, 325, 334, 368, 369, 374, 391
Star Trek: Grissom, 384
Star Trek: Hidden Frontier, 383–84
Star Trek II: The Wrath of Khan, 10, 12, 14, 15, 16, 17, 18–26, 27, 28, 30, 31, 31, 33, 34, 35, 38, 42, 77, 94, 122, 123, 147, 162, 192, 196, 198, 204, 207, 209, 213, 242, 266, 296, 302, 374, 389, 396
Star Trek III: The Search for Spock, 12, 14, 15, 16, 17, 27–35, 37, 42, 77, 121, 147, 165, 188, 200, 203, 283, 389
Star Trek: Insurrection, 84, 85, 87, 89, 96, 117, 131, 160, 164, 237, 238, 273, 278, 287, 312–319, 320, 322, 323, 325, 350, 369, 373, 374, 383
Star Trek into Darkness, 120, 400
Star Trek: Intrepid, 384
Star Trek IV: The Voyage Home, 12, 14, 15, 17, 36–44, 45, 63, 80, 121, 122, 126, 127, 165, 188, 195, 196, 199, 265, 267,

283, 304, 308, 312, 327, 374, 389, 391, 392, 398

Star Trek Movie Memories (memoir), 3, 19, 32, 198, 297, 299

Star Trek Nemesis, xv, 61, 87, 89, 116, 173, 187–88, 229, 236, 266, 273, 274, 286, 291, 307, 320–326, 369, 370, 371, 390, 397, 400

Star Trek: New Voyages/Phase II, 378–82, 383–84

Star Trek: Odyssey, 383

Star Trek: Of Gods and Men, 382

Star Trek: Phase II, 2, 3, 7, 49, 90, 97, 100, 175, 354, 379

Star Trek: The Experience, 158, 233, 307

Star Trek: The Helena Chronicles, 383

Star Trek: The Motion Picture, xvi, 1–8, 9, 11, 18, 22, 23, 24, 29, 49, 94, 100, 113, 124, 125, 127, 154, 155, 162, 187, 188, 202, 237, 301, 308, 315, 389, 390, 391

Star Trek: The Next Generation—The Continuing Mission, 68

Star Trek: The Next Generation Companion, 52, 109, 213, 253

Star Trek: The Next Generation, 365 63, 144, 169, 224

"Star Trek: The Pepsi Generation" (fan film), 384

Star Trek V: The Final Frontier, 6, 12, 14, 17, 89, 121–28, 130, 163, 178, 195, 196, 202, 206, 208, 224, 253, 266, 267, 300, 301, 308, 326, 365, 379, 389, 390

Star Trek VI: The Undiscovered Country, 14, 15, 16, 17, 23, 157, 163, 175, 188, 198, 199, 200–209, 217, 226, 242, 253, 265, 266, 296, 299, 302, 326, 368, 374, 389, 391

Star Trek: Voyager, xvii, 53, 68, 82, 84, 95, 86, 87, 89, 90, 91, 94, 95, 102, 111, 116, 117, 118, 119, 132, 133, 142, 143, 149, 150, 153, 158, 160, 161, 167, 186, 190, 222, 230, 231, 232, 233, 234, 235, 240, 254, 256, 262, 264, 265, 267, 280, 289, 290, 291, 292, 307, 308, 312, 315, 317, 320, 323, 363, 364, 368, 369, 370, 372, 374, 375, 376, 382, 391, 392, 393, 394

Star Trek World Tour, 161

Star Wars, 1, 4, 5, 6, 23, 34, 324, 396

Star Wars: Clone Wars, 394

Stardust Memories, 56

Stargate SG-1, 364, 370

"Starship Down" (episode) 148, 307

Starship Exeter 383

Starship Farragut, 382–83

"Starship Mine" (episode), 256–57, 332

"Steam Trek" (fan film), 384

Steel, Kat, 363

Steele, Dawn, 38

Steenburgen, Mary, 13, 40, 159

Stefano, Joseph, 77

Steingasser, Spike, 287

Stepfather, The, 162

Sternbach, Rick, 48, 89, 90

Steuer, John, 172, 185, 346

Stevens, Dana, 398

Stevens, George, 252

Stevenson, Parker, 147

Stewart, Daniel, 226

Stewart, Patrick, 51, 52, 53, 54–55, 57, 63, 71, 72, 78, 80, 81, 82, 86, 91, 101, 105, 107, 117, 129, 134, 140, 141, 143, 144, 146, 163, 166, 169, 173, 179, 181, 188, 193, 211, 218, 219, 221, 222, 223, 224, 225, 226, 241, 252, 253, 255, 257, 280, 281, 285, 287, 289, 291, 292, 295, 297, 299, 301, 302, 305, 306, 308, 309, 313, 314, 318, 321, 322, 324, 325, 327–34, 335, 337, 347, 349, 357, 359–61, 368, 385–86, 387, 388

Stiers, David Ogden, 180, 190–92

Stillwell, Eric, 95–96, 137, 210

Stoker, Bram, 13

Stone, Oliver, 389

Stoppard, Tom, 211, 359

Strange Days, 17

Strange World, 119

Strangis, Sam and Greg, 45–46

Stratford Shakespeare Festival, 161, 204

Summers, Jaron, 100

"Sub Rosa" (episode), 287–88, 356

"Suddenly Human" (episode), 117, 170, 173, 239

Sunday in the Park with George, 56

Sunspots, The (band), 211

Superman II, 4

Superman III, 38

Superman: The Animated Series, 365

Superman: The Movie, 4, 322

Supernatural, 82

"Survivors, The" (episode), 131, 156, 241

"Suspicions" (episode), 154, 258–59, 356

Swayze, Patrick, 57

Swenson, Inga, 57

SyFy Channel (Sci Fi Channel), 160, 363, 367

Sylk, August William, 366

Sylk, Ken, 366

"Symbiosis" (episode), 366

T. J. Hooker, 27, 32, 82, 121, 154

TableTop, 367

Takei, George, 10, 19, 39, 40, 67, 379, 381, 396

Taking Care of Business, 120, 366

Tales from the Crypt, 367

Tales from the Darkside, 56

Taliesin, 14

Tanen, Ned, 195, 197

"Tapestry" (episode), 109, 160, 230, 236, 239, 251, 255–56, 331

Target Practice, 13

Tartikoff, Brandon, 206, 246

Taurus World Stunt Awards, 392

Taxi, 16, 31

Taylor, Elizabeth, 57

Taylor, Jeri, 117–18, 119, 167, 170, 171, 173, 177, 179, 186, 210, 212, 215, 217, 218, 219, 221, 222, 224, 232, 233, 242, 247, 248, 253, 254, 258, 280, 281, 285, 288, 289, 312, 330, 354, 355, 369, 374, 376
Taylor, Shari, 177
Teen Titans, 367
Tempest, The, 361
Tennant, David, 361
Terminator, The, 26, 172, 305
Terminator 2: Judgment Day, 206, 389
Terra Nova, 119
Texas, 158
That Thing You Do!, 307
That's Impossible, 363
Theiss, William Ware, 47, 49, 90, 91, 379, 396
"Thine Own Self" (episode), 272, 289, 341, 389
Thinnes, Roy, 52
Thirtysomething, 386
"This Side of Paradise" (episode), 318
Thorn Birds, The, 163
Thornton, Noley, 223
Three Men and a Baby, 43, 121
Three Stooges, The, 155
Threshold, 119
Throne, Malachi, 380
Thunderbirds, 364
Thunderbirds (aviation team), 365
Tierney, Gene, 254
Tiger Woods Story, The, 87, 364
Time After Time, 13, 17, 38, 40, 158, 159, 164, 299
Time Bandits, 164
"Time Squared" (episode), 106–7
"Time's Arrow" (episode), 82, 175, 210, 225–26, 341
"Time's Arrow, Part II" (episode), 82, 91, 247–48, 269, 341, 388
"Timescape" (episode), 86, 260
"Tin Man" (episode), 93, 141, 236, 288
"Tin Woodman" 141
Titanic, 323
TNT Network, 85, 154, 159, 186, 263, 365
"To Serve All My Days" (fan episode), 380
To the Stars (memoir), 67
Todd, Hallie 138, 192, 337
Todd, Tony, 139
Tom Jones, 163
"Tomorrow Is Yesterday" (episode), 37, 262
"Too Short a Season" (episode), 73, 241, 368
Tony Award, 56, 57, 153, 158, 186, 315, 326, 361, 362
Tormé, Tracy, 70, 78, 106, 370
Total Recall, 147
Toussaint, Beth, 172
Toy Soldiers, 367
Trail of the Pink Panther, 61
"Transfigurations" (episode), 144
Transformers, 323
Transformers: Rescue Bots, 365
Travolta, John, 147
Trekker Cookbook, The, 263, 265

Trekkies, 366
Trekkies 2, 366
TrekUnited (fund-raising campaign), 393
"Tressaurian Intersection, The" (fan episode), 383
Trevino, Jack, 382
Trois Hommes et un Couffin, 43
Tron, 164
"Trouble with Tribbles, The" (episode), 37, 47, 264
"True Q" (episode), 84, 231, 250–51, 277
Truman Show, The, 316
Trumbull, Douglas, 4
Turn of the Screw, The, 288
"Turnabout Intruder" (episode), 68, 140
TV Guide 7, 22, 32, 70, 79, 117, 127, 138, 207, 300, 316, 328, 371, 379
Twentieth Century-Fox, 1, 23, 305
Twilight Zone, The (classic series), 157, 248, 363, 370
Twilight Zone, The (revival), 56
Twin Peaks, 386

U.S. Marshalls, 322
U.S. Steel Hour, 16
Under Siege, 150, 256
Unforgiven, 164
"Unification I" (episode) 94, 154, 188, 189, 206, 212, 216–17, 226, 229, 240, 249, 251, 254, 265, 298, 334, 388
"Unification II" (episode), 82, 206, 212, 216–17, 226, 229, 240, 249, 251, 254, 277, 298, 388
Universal Pictures Television, 11
"Unnatural Selection" (episode), 103–4, 152, 278, 388
Up the Elephant and Round the Castle, 58
"Up the Long Ladder" (episode), 109–10, 112, 270
UPN Network, 117, 369, 393
Urban, Karl, 397, 399, 400
USA Network, 117

Valmont, 166, 367
Variety, 6, 126, 253, 308, 316, 330
"Vengeance Factor, The" (episode), 134
Vereen, Ben, 283
Verne, Jules, 12, 161, 361
Veronica's Closet, 147
Vickery, James, 152
View, The, 188
View from the Bridge, The, 14, 162, 202
Village Voice, 316
Vincent, 27
"Violations" (episode), 218–19, 354
Visitor, Nana, 117, 150, 214, 373, 374
Volunteers, 14
Von Sydow, Max, 124, 156, 128
Vonnegut, Kurt, 293
Voyages of the USS Los Angeles, 383

Wagner, Michael, 116, 130, 131, 132

Waiting for Godot, 361
Waley, Alison, 14
Walker, Alice, 187
Walker, Robert, Jr., 382
Walker, Texas Ranger, 148
Walsh, Gwynyth, 159, 161–62, 212, 291
Walston, Ray, 222
Walt Disney Pictures, 90, 185, 192, 195, 363, 397
Waltons, The, 49, 57
Wang, Garrett, 376, 382
War of the Worlds (radio broadcast), 13
Warehouse 13, 363
Warner Brothers Pictures, 13, 17, 114, 369
Warner, David, 13, 163–64, 204, 208, 252, 253, 329, 330, 334
Warner, Julie, 132
Warren, Diane, 94, 376
Washington *City Paper*, 379
Washington Post, 6, 23, 42, 126, 206, 324, 398
Water Engine, The, 153
Waterfall Arts Center, 364
Waxwork II: Lost in Time, 364
"Way to Eden, The" (episode), 380
WB Network, 369
WBBM-TV, 116
WBTV-TV, 116
Webster, 348
Webster, April, 397
Weisberg, Alyssa, 397
Welles, Orson, 2, 13, 320
Wellman, William, Jr., 382
"We'll Always Have Paris" (episode), 78
Wells, H. G., xv
Wentworth, John, 393
Werewolf, 370
West, Jonathan, 258
West End Horror, The, 13
Westmore, Michael, 91–92, 234, 290, 308, 317
Westside Medical, 190
Westworld, 252
What Dreams May Come, 186, 323
Wheaton, Wil, 51, 53, 61–62, 67, 105, 109, 130, 146, 166, 173, 211, 212, 216, 222, 242, 281, 291, 327, 334, 355, 356, 367, 387, 397
Wheel of Fortune, 79
Whelpley, John, 170
"When the Bough Breaks" (episode), 73–74, 75, 243, 269
"Where No Man Has Gone Before" (episode), 19, 50, 69, 400
"Where No One Has Gone Before" (episode), 68, 171, 238, 291, 379, 388
"Where Silence Has Lease" (episode), 83, 100–101, 275
White, Lisa Putnam, 141
Whitney, Grace Lee, 208, 379, 382
"Who Mourns for Adonais?" (episode), 132

"Who Watches the Watchers" (episode), 131–32, 272
Wiemer, Robert, 218
Wild Geese II, 55
Wilde, Oscar, 13
Wilder, Billy, 336
Wilder, Gene, 43
Wildfire, 117
Wilkerson, Ron, 250, 257, 288
Williams, Robin, 217
Willis, Bruce, 150
Windom, William 380
Winter, Ralph, 17, 122, 124, 125, 202
Winters, Shelley 215
Wise, Robert, 1, 2, 3, 4, 5, 6, 7, 9, 11
Wistrom, Bill, 93
Witching Hour, The, 288
"Wolf in the Fold" (episode), 249–50
Woman Called Golda, A, 11, 16
Woodard, Alfre, 194, 307, 309, 334
Woods, Barbara Alyn, 103
"World Enough and Time" (fan episode), 279, 381
World of Star Trek, The, 47
World Science Fiction Convention (WorldCon), 24, 42, 390
Worthy, James, 283
"Wounded, The" (episode), 174–75, 233, 264, 275, 312
Wounded Sky, The, 68
Wright, Frank Lloyd, 14
Wright, Herbert, 48, 210
Wright, Patty, 380
Wrong Mountain, 158

X2, 360
Xena: Warrior Princess, 370
X-Files, The, 82, 83, 87, 119, 188, 366, 370
X-Men, 17, 223, 322, 360, 361, 394
X-Men: The Last Stand, 360

Yasutake, Patti, 154, 173, 289, 307
Yelchin, Anton, 397, 399
"Yesterday's Enterprise" (episode), 85, 94, 96, 107, 136–38, 140, 141, 142, 154, 212, 224, 298, 326, 358, 366, 388
Yothers, Tina, 185
"You Are Cordially Invited" (episode), 291
Young, Dick, 114
Young Justice, 362

Zapata, Joy, 91
Zappa, Frank, 262
Zerbe, Anthony, 315, 318
Zero Room Productions, 394
Zicree, Mark Scott, 176, 177, 379
Zimmerman, Herman, 48, 49, 89–90, 307, 308, 309, 315, 322
Zuckerman, Ed, 136